Business Essentials

Business Essentials

Fifth Edition

■ **RONALD J. EBERT**
University of Missouri-Columbia

■ **RICKY W. GRIFFIN**
Texas A&M University

PEARSON

Prentice
Hall

Upper Saddle River, New Jersey 07458

Ebert, Ronald J.
   Business essentials / Ronald J. Ebert, Ricky W. Griffin.— 5th ed.
     p. cm
   Various multi-media instructional tools are available to supplement the text.
   ISBN 0-13-144158-2
     1. Industrial management—United States. 2. Business enterprises—United States.
   I. Griffin, Ricky W. II. Title.

HD70.U5E2 2005
658—dc22

2003066423

Senior Mananging Editor: Jennifer Glennon
VP/Editor-in-Chief: Jeff Shelstad
Assistant Editor: Melanie Olsen
Senior Developmental Editor: Ronald Librach
Marketing Manager: Anke Braun
Marketing Assistant: Patrick Danzuso
Senior Managing Editor (Production): Judy Leale
Production Editor: Theresa Festa
Production Assistant: Joe DeProspero
Permissions Supervisor: Suzanne Grappi
Manufacturing Buyer: Diane Peirano
Design Manager: Maria Lange
Art Director: Janet Slowik
Interior Design: Karen Quigley
Cover Design: Karen Quigley
Cover Illustration: Illustrationworks
Illustrator (Interior): ElectraGraphics, Inc.
Manager, Print Production: Christy Mahon
Composition/Full-Service Project Management: Pre-Press Company, Inc.
Printer/Binder: R.R. Donnelley & Sons/Lehigh Press

Credits and acknowledgments borrowed from other sources and reproduced, with permission, in this textbook appear on appropriate page within text.

Pearson Education LTD.
Pearson Education Singapore, Pte. Ltd
Pearson Education, Canada, Ltd
Pearson Education–Japan

Pearson Education Australia PTY, Limited
Pearson Education North Asia Ltd
Pearson Educación de Mexico, S.A. de C.V.
Pearson Education Malaysia, Pte. Ltd

10 9 8 7 6 5 4 3 2 1
ISBN 0-13-144158-2

Dedicated To

E. Allen Slusher III

A devoted friend, intellectual, colleague, and humanitarian whose presence has elevated the lives of so many people.

— R.J.E.

— R.W.G.

OVERVIEW

CONTENTS

Contents

**CHAPTER 9: MOTIVATING, SATISFYING,
AND LEADING EMPLOYEES 258**

■ PART VI: UNDERSTANDING FINANCIAL ISSUES

CHAPTER 14: UNDERSTANDING MONEY AND BANKING   418

FROM THE AUTHORS
RON EBERT and RICKY GRIFFIN

As we gathered our thoughts for preparing this revision, we were impressed by the vast flow of new developments taking place alongside traditional, long-established business practices. In assessing the landscape of current practices, we often found ourselves returning to the question, "What's really new in business, and what's not?" New investment strategies, for example, are seriously challenging the traditional principle of investing for long-term results in today's fast-paced markets. Commenting on long-term investing in the stock market, Peter L. Bernstein recently remarked, "We've reached a funny position where long run doesn't work. . . . the long-run evidence doesn't fit circumstances as they are today. Forget investing for the long haul. The long run, right now, is irrelevant."

We suspect that Mr. Bernstein isn't advocating that investors forget about long-term strategies altogether but, instead, that they study and understand alternative approaches, so they can adapt to new conditions and goals. The same holds true in all areas of business: Successful practitioners recognize that "new versus old" isn't the crucial issue so much as how to combine the best of both as circumstances change. History tells us that we can expect accelerating changes from dramatic events that will reshape the ways we live, work, and prepare for the future. The foremost business dilemma is how to provide some sort of stability—for employees, owners, suppliers, and consumers—while steering through new uncharted paths. The answer lies in businesses maintaining an adaptive organizational culture, one that expects change as a way of life and builds processes for change into its business strategy. More than ever before, leading businesses have learned how to anticipate new developments and how to respond quickly and creatively.

Therefore, for our introductory business students, there is great value to be gained from understanding how business, government, and citizens, together influence the ways that business is conducted in different societies. Students need to gain a fundamental working knowledge about every aspect of business and the environment in which business prospers. And make no mistake about it, we have prosperity despite occasional, sometimes even violent, disruptions. Through it all, businesses continue to adapt; the rules of the game are constantly changing throughout the business environment and across the range of business practices. Nowadays, companies come together on short notice for collaborative projects and then, just as quickly, return to their original shapes as separate (and often competing) entities. Employees and companies share new ideas about work—about how it gets done, about who determines roles and activities in the workplace. With communications technologies having shattered the barriers of physical distance, tight-knit teams with members positioned around the world share information just as effectively as groups huddled together in the same room.

In nearly every aspect of business today, from relationships with customers and suppliers to employees and stockholders, there are new ways of doing things, and a lot of them are surpassing traditional business practices, with surprising speed and often with better competitive results. Along with new ways come a host of unique ethical and legal issues to challenge the leadership, creativity and judgment of people who do business. For all of these reasons we, as authors and teachers, felt a certain urgency when it became obvious that, in revising *Business Essentials* for its fifth edition, we had to capture the flavor and convey the excitement of business in all of its evolving practices.

ABOUT THE AUTHORS

Ronald J. Ebert is Emeritus Professor at the University of Missouri-Columbia where he lectures in the Management Department and serves as advisor to students and student organizations. Dr. Ebert draws upon more than 30 years of teaching experience at such schools as Sinclair College, University of Washington, University of Missouri, Lucian Blaga University of Sibiu (Romania), and Consortium International University (Italy). His consulting alliances include such firms as Mobay Corporation, Kraft Foods, Oscar Mayer, Atlas Powder, and John Deere. He has designed and conducted management development programs for such diverse clients as the American Public Power Association, the United States Savings and Loan League, and the Central Missouri Manufacturing Training Consortium.

His experience as a practitioner has fostered an advocacy for integrating concepts with best business practices in business education. The five business books he has written include translations in Spanish, Chinese, Malaysian, and Romanian languages. Dr. Ebert has served as the editor of the *Journal of Operations Management*. He is a past-president and fellow of the Decision Sciences Institute. He has served as consultant and external evaluator for *Quantitative Reasoning for Business Studies* an introduction-to-business project sponsored by the National Science Foundation.

Ricky W. Griffin is Distinguished Professor of Management and holds the Blocker Chair in Business in the Mays School of Business at Texas A&M University. He also currently serves as executive associate dean. He previously served as Head of the Department of Management and as director of the Center for Human Resource Management at Texas A&M. His research interests include workplace aggression and violence, executive skills and decision making, and workplace culture. Dr. Griffin's research has been published in such journals as *Academy of Management Review, Academy of Management Journal, Administrative Science Quarterly*, and *Journal of Management*. He has also served as editor of *Journal of Management*. Dr. Griffin has consulted with such organizations as Texas Instruments, Tenneco, Amoco, Compaq Computer, and Continental Airlines.

Dr. Griffin has served the Academy of Management as chair of the organizational behavior division. He has also served as president of the southwest division of the Academy of Management and on the Board of Directors of the Southern Management Association. He is a fellow of both the Academy of Management and the Southern Management Association. He is also the author of several successful textbooks, each of which is a market leader. In addition, they are widely used in dozens of countries and have been translated into numerous foreign languages, including Spanish, Polish, Malaysian, and Russian.

BUSINESS ESSENTIALS

Welcome to the new edition of *Business Essentials!* This revision builds on what you have always loved and what has made this book the number-one brief Introduction to Business text. As instructors across the country have confirmed in reviews and focus groups, current world events are calling for a changed emphasis within the Introduction to Business course and text. The focus on practical skills, knowing the basics and highlighting important developments in business makes for a brief book but a rich experience. Taking your comments seriously, we have added the following features to the fifth edition of *Business Essentials:*

NEW! Entrepreneurship and New Ventures

ENTREPRENEURSHIP and New Ventures

One Businessperson's Trash Is Another's New Venture

Norcal Waste Systems (*www.sunsetscavenger.com*) isn't a small company; it boasts 400,000 residential, industrial, and commercial customers in 50 California communities, including San Francisco. But size and 50 years' success aren't slowing the company's innovative approach to garbage collection and waste management. In fact, its entrepreneurial spirit is propelling this 100-percent employee-owned firm into a new venture in creative recycling: turning food scraps to fine wine.

The transformation is not exactly direct. Norcal jumped at the opportunity to invest in a unique idea for turning organic waste—food trimmings from produce markets and food waste from restaurants—into a useful product. Instead of dumping it in a landfill, Norcal collects organic material to use in a process that converts waste into finished compost. The compost is then bagged and sold as a soil reconditioner, mostly to California vineyards. Always looking for better ways to grow stronger grapevines, vineyard managers in Sonoma–Napa Valley apply Norcal compost between rows of vines because it returns nitrogen and other nutrients to the soil.

"You can't shortchange the soil," says Clarence Jenkins, owner of Madrone Vineyard Management (*www.travelenvoy.com/wine/Napa/Smith-Madrone-Vineyard.htm*). "The Norcal compost is a very good product and is very cost-effective. We get better soil structure, and eventually because of that structure we will get better plants."

Winegrowers and organic farmers prefer compost because, unlike most inorganic fertilizers, it's nontoxic. It also aerates the soil and helps it retain water.

Three Norcal subsidiaries collaborate in the composting process, which features new technologies to separate, collect, and deliver incoming waste to a specially designed production facility. Sunset Scavenger (*www.sunsetscavenger.com/sunset.htm*) and Golden Gate Disposal & Recycling (*www.ysdi.com/goldengate.htm*) collect compostable material from over 1,400 food-related businesses and thousands of households in the San Francisco Bay Area. Every day, more than 300 tons of waste are removed from the standard waste-disposal stream and delivered to Jepson Prairie Organics (*www.jepsonprairieorganics.com*), where finished compost is produced in a three-month conversion cycle.

The various participants in and beneficiaries of the enterprise—customers, waste contributors, and communities—are enthusiastic about Norcal's profitable new twist on recycling. In addition to vineyards, output buyers include wholesalers who sell bagged product to landscapers, nurseries, and garden stores. On the input side, participating businesses benefit because the venture reduces garbage bills. Bay Area officials like it because it reduces the need for landfills. "Innovative programs like Norcal's Composting Program," says Oakland Mayor Jerry Brown, "bring us closer to realizing our waste-reduction goals while providing cost savings for Oakland's businesses."

Whether you are in a large corporation or starting your own business students need to be both entrepreneurial and intrapreneurial.

NEW! "Say What You Mean"

"Say What You Mean" boxes have been added to this edition to sensitize students about cultural differences and teach them to communicate more effectively both orally and in writing.

Say WHAT YOU MEAN

TO BE OR NOT TO BE ON TIME

We all use time to organize our lives, and in the United States, we're particularly avid clock watchers. In some cultures, however, people think a little differently about time, and the differences can have a big impact on the way business is conducted around the world. When we call a friend or business associate in the United States, we expect a quick reply. Not necessarily so in countries where different priorities can mean different time frames for doing things.

If you're supposed to be at an 8:00 A.M. meeting in the United States or northern Europe, you'd better be on time (say, 8:05 at the latest). We expect people to be punctual, whether it's for a board meeting or a family picnic. Time is one of our ways of imposing order on our activities, and we regard regulated activity as something necessary to our workday productivity. But in some countries, thinking about time is, well, less timely. In Latin America, the Mediterranean, and the Middle East, for example, people generally do business according to relaxed timetables. They're likely to schedule a number of things at once, and if this habit means that schedules get ignored and some "scheduled" activities get delayed, it doesn't really matter.

There are, of course, advantages as well as disadvantages. Sometimes a more relaxed attitude toward making productive use of your time means taking time to develop relationships and getting to know someone instead of just achieving a specific goal in a specific time frame. Whatever the case, if you're operating in another country and culture, you need to know how people regard time and timeliness. Not only will you know when to show up at meetings and other events, but you may also have more luck in scheduling production and delivery dates. The most successful companies know their host cultures and are prepared to make allowances for local conditions.

NEW! Self-Check Questions

SELF-CHECK QUESTIONS 1–3

You should now be able to answer Self-Check Questions 1–3.*

1 **True/False** Whereas the term *production* refers primarily to the creation of physical goods, the term *operations* refers to activities for providing services to customers.

2 **Multiple Choice** Which of the following is *not* true regarding *operations processes*? [select one]: **(a)** In high-contact service processes, the customer is a part of the process. **(b)** All goods-manufacturing processes may be classified as either analytic or synthetic. **(c)** A chicken-processing plant (one that prepares chickens for grocery stores) is a good example of an analytic process. **(d)** Foot surgery is a good example of a low-contact operation.

3 **Multiple Choice** Which of the following is **true** regarding *differences between service and manufacturing operations*? [select one]: **(a)** Whereas manufacturing operations focus on the outcome of the production process, service operations focus on both the transformation process and its outcome. **(b)** The products offered by most service operations are intangible and do not involve physical goods. **(c)** Whereas service operations are customized for customers, manufacturing operations focus on mass-production processes. **(d)** Customers generally use the same measures for judging the quality of service products and physical goods products.

Answers to Self-Check Questions 1–3 can be found on pp. 00–00.

To help students review their understanding of the core concepts presented before moving on to study further materials, these special self-check assessment exercises are introduced at three points in the chapter. Answers to these questions in the back of the book reference textbook pages to ensure complete mastery of the concepts.

NEW! Internet Field Trips

These two-part exercises, focused on real world organizations, begin on the back of the AIME edition's tabbed insert and are designed to provide an interactive learning experience that continues online with more detailed questions. Final answers can be checked online at www.prenhall.com/ebert.

MID-CHAPTER

INTERNET FIELD TRIP

Is Quality Manageable?

In the first part of this chapter, we examined basic ideas about *productivity* and *quality*, including the *productivity-quality connection*. We offered some examples of the ways companies increase productivity by improving *internal processes*, introduced the concept of *Six Sigma* quality, and described the activities involved in *quality management*.

■ **Performing** these activities effectively means that managers must maintain up-to-date skills

■ Information on developments relating to quality and productivity.

■ What sources for information are available! How do managers keep abreast of recent developments?

What kinds of resources are available to assist managers in continuing their professional developments as quality professionals? What kinds of resources are available to assist managers in continuing their professional developments?

Let's explore some of these questions by visiting the Web site of a pre-eminent association for quality professionals—the American Society for Quality (ASQ)—at (*www.asq.org*). At the top of the home page, you will find that the Web site is divided into six categories: **Publication, Information, Certification, Training Standards,** and **Networking**. Start by clicking on Information.

1 Are any of the items in the list related to productivity? Which items are not directly related?

After returning to the top of the home page, click on Training. On the Training page, scan down to the section entitled Publing Training Courses and the drop-down menu labeled Select a Course. Scan the various courses in the Select a Course listing and then respond to the following item:

2 Determing if any of ASQ's public training courses might be useful for improving productivity. Explain.

Go back to the top of the home page and click on Networking. From among the new options appearing on the screen, select Divisions, which will give you access to a page intitled Divisions and Groups.

In the drop-down menu [Go Directly to a Division], click on Quality Management Division and then respond to the following item:

3 Who are members of the Quality Management Division of ASQ! What is the mission of the division? How might a quality manager benefit from membership in this division?

Now go to the bottom of the home page. Click on About ASQ and then on What is ASQ? Respond to the following item:

4 Identify and briefly describe any five services that ASQ offers to professional members.

After returning to the top of the home page, click on Certification. Next click on Certifications, read the list of types of certification, and then respond to the following item:

5 From the listing of various types of certifications, choose any three and identify some of ASQ's requirements for each of the types you have chosen.

To continue on your Internet Field Trip, click on (www.prenhall.com).

NEW! Planning for Your Career

PLANNING FOR YOUR CAREER

WHAT CAN YOU MANAGE?

Many people studying business have a general aspiration to be a "manager." Most of them, however, aren't entirely sure just what they want to manage. Remember that, as we saw in Chapter 5, managers are responsible for dealing with various kinds of resources. Moreover, there are several different areas of management. This exercise will give you some more insights into the kinds of activities that managers in different areas actually perform.

Assignment
Start by reviewing the discussion in Chapter 5 of the different areas of management. Next, review Chapter 5 in *Beginning Your Career Search*, 3d ed., by James S. O'Rourke IV, in order to learn more about researching companies that you might want to work for. Finally, make a list of up to ten different large companies in which you have some general interest.

To complete this exercise, do the following:
1 Research each company on your list to find out what kinds of management positions it currently has avail-

able. One way is to access the "careers" option on a company Web site.

2 Try to find two or three examples representing each of the various areas of management that we identified in Chapter 5.

3 Reflect on the various jobs that you've researched and then rank them in terms of the extent to which they seem potentially appealing to you.

4 See if you can identify any common themes among those jobs toward the top of your list. How about those jobs on the bottom and in the middle of your list?

5 If there are common themes, what might they suggest regarding your career interests? Do they suggest ways in which you might better prepare yourself for a future career?

6 If there appear to be *no* common themes, what might this fact suggest about your current career interests. In this case, what can you do to better prepare yourself for a future career?

Directed, detailed career-planning activities help students tie the content of each textbook part to their career-planning efforts.

All the Hallmark features that you've always loved about this text have been maintained

- **Two-Part Case Vignettes** – fully updated

- **Extensive End-of-Chapter Materials** – to help students to review, apply the chapter concepts and build skills.

- **NEW! Key Terms** – with page references

- **Exercising Your Ethics** What could be more timely? The students are presented with an ethical dilemma and are encouraged to answer questions and think critically about how to approach and resolve these ethical challenges.

- **Building Your Business Skills** These popular end-of-chapter exercises consist of activities that allow students to apply their knowledge and critical thinking skills to an extended problem drawn from a wide range of realistic business experiences. Each of these exercises has been specifically designed to satisfy the general criteria laid out in the Secretary of Labor's Commission of Achieving Necessary Skills (SCANS) requirements.

- **Crafting Your Business Plan Exercises** These chapter-ending exercises help the students apply chapter material to the task of developing a business plan. Students examine sample plans from a variety of businesses and personalize their own professional business plan by following the step-by-step instruction of the Windows-based Business Plan Pro software. The educational version of the best-selling Palo Alto Business Plan Pro software can be packaged with the text for a nominal cost.

- **Video Exercises** Tied to our exciting new videos these exercises help students to see how real-life businesses and the people who run them apply fundamental business principles on a daily basis. (See descriptions of these videos in the instructor learning package section.)

MANAGING OPERATIONS AND IMPROVING QUALITY

"The challenge will be to keep an organization intact, not lose momentum through confusion and inexperience, integrate various demands from outside parties, and keep the huge customer set engaged, onboard, and excited."

—Tom Burbage, Lockheed manager, on the Joint Strike Fighter Project

rival Boeing, Lockheed had captured the largest defense contract ever awarded—the $200 billion Joint Strike Fighter (JSF) contract (which could be worth more than $320 billion over the next two or three decades).

Lockheed's design for the next generation of supersonic, radar-evading combat jet was just the beginning. The contract was awarded on the basis of experimental versions of the aircraft. Now the real work—detailed planning for production and then production itself—begins. Many observers think that the next phase—system development and demonstration (SDD)—will be the most difficult. SDD calls for building and demonstrating 22 aircraft (known in the United States as the F-35) to be delivered by 2005. The next phase—gearing up to full production—begins in 2008, with plans calling for the produc-

3

▶ CRAFTING YOUR BUSINESS PLAN

SPORTING A FRIENDLIER ATMOSPHERE

Business PlanPro

The Purpose of the Assignment

1 To acquaint students with production and operations issues that a sample firm addresses in developing its business plan in the framework of the *Business PlanPro (BPP) 2003* software package (Version 6.0).

2 To demonstrate how choices of goods and services, characteristics of the transformation process, facilities and equipment, and product quality considerations can be integrated as components in the *BPP* planning environment.

Assignment

After reading Chapter 7 in the textbook, open the BPP software and look around for information about plans for

operations processes as they apply to a sample firm, a sports bar: Take Five Sports Bar & Grill. *To find Take Five, do the following:*

Open *Business PlanPro*. Go to the toolbar and click on the "Sample Plans" icon. In the **Sample Plan Browser**, do a search using the **search category** *Eating and drinking places, restaurants, cafeterias.* From the resulting list, select the category entitled *Bar—Sports*, which is the location for *Take Five Sports Bar & Grill.* The screen you are looking at is the introduction page for the business plan of *Take Five.* On this page, scroll down until you reach the **Table of Contents** for the *Take Five* business plan.

NOW RESPOND TO THE FOLLOWING ITEMS:

1 What type of product—physical good or service—is *Take Five Sports Bar & Grill* creating in its operations

STUDENT LEARNING PACKAGE

These text-specific student supplements are designed to simplify the task of learning:

- Study Guide
- Exciting new text Companion Website provides a robust, turnkey solution for both instructors and students. Students are encouraged to actively use quizzing, section summaries, learning activities, hot links for Web sites mentioned throughout the text, and student PowerPoints to prepare for class and tests. With an access code card students are able to view additional student tools on the OneKey site such as the E-book, an English/Spanish business terms glossary, *In the News* articles, Research Navigator, and additional quizzes.

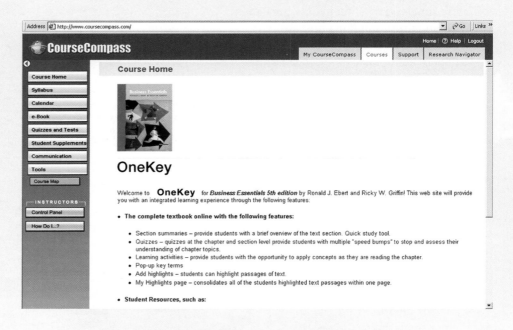

Here is a more in-depth look at some of the OneKey features:

- **E-Book** – the complete textbook online with the following integrated features:
  - ☐ Section summaries – provide students with a brief overview of the text section. Quick study tool.
  - ☐ Quizzes – quizzes at the chapter and section level provide students with multiple "speed bumps" to stop and assess their understanding of chapter topics.
  - ☐ Learning activities – provide students with the opportunity to apply concepts as they are reading the chapter.
  - ☐ Pop-up key terms
  - ☐ Add highlights – students can highlight passages of text.
  - ☐ My Highlights page – consolidates all of the students highlighted text passages within one page. Study tool.

- Student Supplement section will contain:
  - ☐ Student PowerPoints
  - ☐ English-Spanish Business Terms with Audio Glossary
  - ☐ *In the News* Articles

The New Responsibilities of Business Leaders Are as Old as Commerce Itself

LEAD STORY-DATELINE: Directorship, January 2003.

In an op-ed piece, Hank McKinnell, the Chairman and CEO of Pfizer Inc., discusses management's "new" roles, responsibilities and relationships in the post-Enron era that should be shaped by honesty, transparency, and fairness. There is nothing new about these words, and the companies that stuck with them through the fast times and easy money of the 1990s now find themselves celebrated as visionary.

It is heartening to note the response of corporate leaders to the demands of new laws and regulations designed to publicly affirm the value of honesty. Corporate leaders must set a climate of transparency at every level, from the boardroom to the factory floor. Managers have to willingly provide the information and the opportunities for independent board members to act independently. What is true for the board must also be true for the company's employees.

The *In the News* articles highlight current news about companies featured in this text or this text's videos along with questions for the students to explore.

- Additional quizzes that may be assigned as homework
- Free access to **Research Navigator** helps your students make the most of their research time. From finding the right articles and journals, to citing sources, drafting and writing effective papers, and completing research assignments, this site simplifies and streamlines the entire process.

Additional Student Learning Tools That Teach with a Hands-On Approach

- Student discounts for *The New York Times*, *Wall Street Journal*, and *Financial Times* subscriptions
- Mastering Business Essentials CD
- *Building Your Personal Stock Portfolio* by Marian Burk Wood
- *Building a Business Plan featuring Business Plan Pro Software* by David Tooch
- *Building Your Personal Career Portfolio: A Step-by-Step Guide for Building Your Career Portfolio, Third Edition* by James S. O'Rourke
- *Business Ethics in Uncertain Times* by Marian Burk Wood

TEACHING TOOLS FOR INSTRUCTORS...

... EVERYTHING YOU NEED FOR A COURSE THAT GETS STUDENTS EXCITED AND INVOLVED!

The new and most important addition to the instructor support package is the Annotated Instructor's Media Edition (AIME). Thumbnail tabs at the beginning of each chapter put our unparalleled support materials at your fingertips. Easily integrated into your classroom presentation are the following media resources:

- Instructor Resource Center on CD
- OneKey Web site
- 15 video segments tied directly to the video cases in each chapter (See a description of these videos on page xxvii.)
- 16 additional video segments that reenforce fundamental business concepts
- Electronic test generator powered by Test Gen EQ
- Test Item File – including page references and difficulty levels

The following additional support materials are available for *Business Essentials*:

- Instructor's Manual
- Telephone Test Preparation
- Course management content for WebCT, Blackboard, and CourseCompass
- Color overhead transparencies
- Adopters can receive a 15-week discounted subscription to *Financial Times*, the *Wall Street Journal*, or *The New York Times*
- Prentice Hall Personal Response System (see inside back cover)

The following is a detailed description of the Instructor Resource Center CD-ROM and the instructor's side of the OneKey Web site.

Instructor Resource Center CD-ROM – One Stop Shopping!

This Instructor's Resource Center CD-ROM is an interactive library of presentation and classroom resources. By navigating through this CD, adopters can collect the materials including images from the text most relevant to their interests, edit to create powerful class lectures, copy them to their own computer's hard drive and/or upload them to an online course management system. This CD writes custom "index" pages, which assist the user in navigating through and viewing the various assets they have collected. This CD runs on both the Windows and Mac platforms and employs interactive techniques that will be familiar to those who use internet-based search engines.

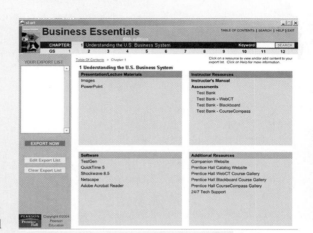

Select a chapter from the table of contents, and you can see a list of resources, such as Instructor's Manual, Test Bank, Exhibits, and PowerPoints. The resources are further broken down into subcategories, so you can find what you need. Or, you can simply search by keyword. All of the resources have been associated with the appropriate text keywords.

After you've found the files you'd like to present or post to a Web site, select them with one click, put them into your export list (like a shopping cart), and export them to your hard drive or disk. The Presentation Manager will organize them for you into folders according to file type, and even provide a simple Web page for easy viewing.

On the Instructor Resource Center CD, you will find the following faculty supplements:

- PowerPoints – Two PowerPoint packages are available with this text. The first is the standard set of instructor's PowerPoints. The second is an enhanced, interactive version of the first with video clips and Web links in each chapter. Both versions contain teaching notes.
- Online courses in WebCT, Blackboard, and CourseCompass
- Electronic test generator powered by Test Gen EQ
- Instructor's Manual
- Test Item File
- All of the art files from the text

OneKey Web site

In addition to the student's side of the OneKey Web site, the instructor has access to the following course management capabilities of this all-in-one media resource:

- Online graded homework with grade book
- Online quizzing capabilities
- Communication tools such as broadcast e-mails, bulletin boards, and chat room
- Ability to customize the online textbook for your students to read

CURRENT, EXCITING, RELEVANT

NEW CUSTOM VIDEOS

All chapters have corresponding videos, which help students see how real businesses and the people who run them apply fundamental business principles on a daily basis. Companies include the following:

U.S. Department of Commerce, 2003, running time: 10:26. Learn how the U.S. economic system works through an interview with Bobby Hines, the international trade specialist, whose job it is to help companies accustomed to the U.S. economic system expand into world markets, and as a result, different economic systems. This video looks at the U.S. economic system, how that system is affected by supply and demand, and the resources the United States has for engaging in business.

American Red Cross, 2003, running time: 10:31. The American Red Cross was founded to aid the victims of war. Since that time, the role of the Red Cross has been increased to aid victims of natural disasters as well as victims of man-made disasters such as nuclear attacks and the terrorist attacks of September 11, 2001. With more than 1,000 local chapters, how does this organization maintain it's high moral ideals? Get the answer to this question in this segment.

Printrak International, 2003, running time: 11:42. Fingerprint tracking originated in America, and companies like Printrak International have helped move this innovative technology into the countries that need it most. Discover how Printrak leveraged capital to expand into foreign markets, how it negotiated trade barriers and accounted for differences in the demands and expectations of various foreign markets.

Boeing Satellite Systems, 2003, running time: 12:11. Many of us would love to have a television in our computer at work. At Boeing Satellite systems, IPTV, is just one of the ways its more than 8,000 employees are kept in communication with other offices around the world. In such a technologically-driven market, Boeing Satellite explains how information systems have changed its business and how Boeing uses information systems to save money in daily processes.

Amy's Ice Creams, 2003, running time: 13:36. Americans consume nearly 1.6 billions gallons of ice cream a year! Learn how a small Texas ice-cream-store chain got its start in this big business and how it came to be successful through planning and differentiating their product.

Creative Age Publications, 2003, running time: 9:49. Learn from the president and CEO of Creative Age, what goes into managing a publishing company that produces seven different magazines ranging on topics from nail care to kidney dialysis. Students will hear what long- and short-term goals have been set for the company, what management skills are looked for in prospective managers, and how corporate culture can stimulate creativity and teamwork.

Nantucket Nectars, 2003, running time: 14:46. In 1989, the Juice Guys started their business with a blender and sold their blended peach nectar drinks off their boats to people visiting Nantucket. See how this company has dramatically changed since it first started, how it keeps lines of communication open within its headquarters, and how it uses technology to keep its remote office in touch.

Body Glove, 2003, running time: 13:52. This well-known maker of wetsuits has expanded to other products ranging from cell phone covers to resort hotels. How did it get there? Interviews with Scott Daley (vice president of marketing) and Russ Lesser (president) explain how the company came up with its products ideas, where it found the materials used in many of its products, and how services (like diving cruises) fit into the whole picture.

Kingston Technology, 2003, running time: 13:30. The owners of the company don't have corner offices; when a new employee starts, the owners stop by to introduce themselves; everyone at the company receives 10 percent cash back on company profits. Sound like a great company to work for? Developing a feeling of family, loyalty, and trust has been the key in creating Kingston Technology's happy family of more than 1,500 employees who are all committed to the success of the company.

Park Place Entertainment, 2003, running time: 13:19. What do Caesar's Palace, Bally's, the Las Vegas Hilton, and Paris have in common? Each of these hotels is owned and operated by Park Place

Entertainment, the world's largest gaming company. With more than 52,000 employees, learn how the Park Place Entertainment human resources department recruits, develops its management team, and evaluates each worker's performance.

Sketchers USA, 2003, running time: 12:19. Sketchers designs cool shoes for cool people. Sketchers makes sure its shoes are seen in cool places, cool magazines, cool television shows. But how did it get there? The success of Sketchers is a culmination of its employees, the branding of its product, addressing the needs of consumers through in-house market research, communicating one-on-one with consumers, and differentiating its product from others.

Clos du Bois Winery, 2003, running time: 11:12. Riding a tidal wave of U.S. consumer interest in California wines, Clos du Bois Winery sells its wines from coast to coast. The company now produces and ships more than one million cases of wine every year, although less than 20 percent is sold in California. In order to keep its distribution organized, Clos du Bois ships its wines from a central warehouse to more than 300 wholesalers' warehouses around the United States.

McDonald's, 2003, running time: 12:27. With billions served in nearly every country in the world, McDonald's explains how accounting information flows through such a large organization, what regional differences it had to manage in unifying financial information, and what tracking methods it uses to collect and process financial reports and projections.

Coast Business Credit, 2003, running time: 9:51. Find out why it's often difficult for upstart business to find venture capital, what Coast Business Credit looks for in a loan prospect, and what type of companies one should avoid when making financial loans.

Understanding Investments: Motley Fool, 2003, running time: 16:53. The chances of winning the lottery are probably about a million to one and unless you come up with the next great idea (the pet rock has already been taken) becoming a millionaire overnight may not be in your future. Chances are you will have a better chance of getting rich if you learn to select investments that are appropriate for your long-term financial goals. Motley Fool educates students about securities and investment strategies in this risky business.

AND FURTHERMORE . . .

A *second set of topically oriented videos are available with this text covering hot business issues!*

Guides for these videos are available on the text Web site.

Education and Earnings: What is the relationship? 2004

Conducting Business Ethically and Responsibly: Patagonia, 2002

Nidek–Responding to the Challenges of Globalization, 2003

EMotion – Beyond Pictures and Video Clips to Virtual Images, 2003. EMotion is one of the first companies to think globally across industries with its pay-per-use system and a completely digital database.

Sytel – A CEO Who Makes Things Happen, 2003. Learn how Jeanette Lee Whitel's cutting-edge approach to leadership has helped her company to make the *Inc.* 500 list several times, and why she has won a national entrepreneur award from *Working Woman* magazine.

Quova: Leading with Integrity and Compassion, 2003. In the crowded field of information technology, leadership can make all the difference. By adopting a "hands-under" leadership style, Quova Inc.'s president and CEO, Marie Alexander, has created a corporate culture that strives to help people not only achieve the company's goals, but to achieve their personal goals as well.

Organizational Change at Student Advantage, 2002.

Beyond Components, 2004. Lou Dinkel's company, Beyond Components, not only strives to be a socially responsible company—it is actually able to accomplish it.

Labor Relations, 2002. Watch as human resources professional, Daryl Hulme, deals with the sensitive situation of putting a young woman just starting out in her career at ease at HotJobs.com

Recruitment and Placement, 2002. Go behind the scenes of Bertelsman, one of the world's top music distributors with its vice president of human resources, Paul Fiolek, where he faces the possibility that the wrong person has been hired for a job.

Starbucks, 2004. Starbucks' strategy is based on four pillars: (1) providing the best coffee, (2) offering the finest products associated with coffee, (3) creating an environment that is inviting, and 4) being socially responsible. The phenomenal growth of this Seattle-based company can be found through the implementation of these pillars by its employees. The result is a company that is passionate about creating a coffeehouse experience.

Snapple, 2004. Snapple is an example of a brand that started as an American success story, lost its way, then refound itself over a period of 20 years. This video chronicles Snapple's successes and failures over this time.

A Walk Down a Store Aisle, 2004. Federated Direct, which owns Bloomingdale's and Macy's, was losing market share due to intense competition from discount stores, online retailers, and specialty shops until Dawn Robertson, president and chief merchandising officer, stepped in. See what Dawn and her group implemented to keep customers happy and keep them coming back.

Exile on 7eventh – Thriving in the Wake of the "Tech Wrek," 2003. In a time when many dot-coms have folded, Exile on 7eventh is alive and well. With clients like Earthlink, Microsoft, and eBay, Exile on 7eventh is striving to find cost-effective online advertising solutions when the climate of the advertising industry is plagued by a lack of confidence. Learn how the company's ability to marry creativity to accountability has lead to its success.

The Federal Reserve System, 2004. What three words appear across the top of the front of a one-dollar bill? The answer is Federal Reserve Note, But what does this mean and what does the Federal Reserve do? Wayne Ayers, a former Federal Reserve economist and Deb Bloomberg, an economic education specialist at the Federal Reserve Bank of Boston provide an overview of the Federal Reserve System and its impact on the economy.

Business Ethics, 2004. Over the past few years it seems we are hearing more and more about companies acting unethically. This video discusses the incentives for firms to engage in fraud and the role regulators play. Reference is made to Enron, Tyco, and Worldcom. The Securities and Exchange Commission (SEC), its goals and its obligation to protect small investors is also discussed.

ACKNOWLEDGMENTS

Although two names appear on the cover of the book, we could never have completed the fifth edition without the assistance of many fine individuals. Everyone who worked on the book was committed to making it the best that it could be. Quality and closeness to the customer are things that we read a lot about today. Both we and the people who worked with us took these concepts to heart in this book and made quality our watchword by listening to our users and trying to provide what they want.

First, we would like to thank all the professionals who took time from their busy schedules to review materials for *Business Essentials:*

Roanne Angiello
Bergen Community College

Michael Baldigo
Sonoma State University

Ed Belvins
DeVry Institute of Technology

Mary Jo Boehms
Jackson State Community College

Harvey Bronstein
Oakland Community

Ronald Cereola
James Madison University

Gary Christiansen
North Iowa Area Community College

Michael Cicero
Highline Community College

Karen Collins
Lehigh University

James Darnell
Ivy Tech-Kokomo

Richard Drury
Northern Virginia Community College

Pat Ellebracht
Truman State University

John Gubbay
Moraine Valley Community College

Dr. Shiv Gupta
University of Findlay

Karen W. Harris
Montgomery College

Jeff Harper
Texas Tech University

Edward M. Henn
Broward Community College

Jim Hess
Ivy Tech-Fort Wayne

Jerry Hufnagel Horry
Georgetown Technical College

Robert W. James
Devry University

Jeffrey Jones
Community College of Southern Nevada

James H. Kennedy
Angelina College

Betty Ann Kirk
Tallahassee Community College

Sofia B. Klopp
Palm Beach Community College

Kenneth J. Lacho
University of New Orleans

Keith Leibham
Columbia Gorge Community College

Robert Markus
Babson College

John F. Mastriani
El Paso Community College

William E. Matthews
William Paterson University

Bronna McNeeley
Midwestern State University

Thomas J. Morrisey
Buffalo State College

William Morrison
San Jose State

David William Murphy
Madisonville Community College

Scott Norwood
San Jose State University

Joseph R. Novak
Blinn College

Mark Nygren
Brigham Young University-Idaho

Glenn Perser
Houston Community College System

Constantine Petrides
Borough of Manhattan Community College

Roy R. Pipitone
Eric Community College

William D. Raffield
University of St. Thomas

Richard Randall
Nassau Community College

Betsy Ray
Indiana Business College

Richard Reed
Washington State University

Christopher Rogers
Miami-Dade Community College

Phyllis Schafer
Brookdale Community College

Lewis Schlossinger
Community College of Aurora

David Sollars
Auburn University-Montgomery

Robert N. Stern
Cornell University

Arlene Strawn
Tallahassee Community College

Peggy Takahashi
University of San Francisco

Jane A. Treptow
Broward Community College

Janna P. Vice
Eastern Kentucky University

Patricia R. Ward
Upper Iowa University

Phillip A Weatherford
Embry-Riddle Aeronautical University

Jerry E. Wheat
Indiana University Southeast

Lynne Spellman White
Trinity Christian College

JoAnn Wiggins
Walla Walla College

Pamela J. Winslow
Berkeley College of Business

Gerrit Wolf
SUNY-Stonybrook

A number of other professionals also made substantive contributions to the text, ranging from draft material on specialized topics to suggested resource materials to proposals for cases and examples. In particular, we are greatly indebted to Elisa Adams, developmental editor, for her inventive and timely contributions as a professional writer and researcher. The supplements package for *Business Essentials, Fifth Edition,* also benefited from the able contributions of several individuals at Prentice Hall. We would like to thank those people for developing the finest set of instructional and learning materials for this field.

Meanwhile, a superb team of professionals at Prentice Hall made this book a pleasure to write. Authors often get the credit when a book is successful, but the success of this book must be shared with an outstanding group of people in New Jersey. Our development editor, Ron Librach, has been a true product champion and has improved both the book and the package in more ways than we can list. Senior managing editor in production Judy Leale and Theresa Festa, the production editor, also made many truly outstanding contributions to the project.

We also want to acknowledge the contributions of the entire team at Prentice Hall Business Publishing, including Senior Managing Editor Jennifer Glennon; Jeff Shelstad, editor in chief; Anke Braun, marketing manager; Annie Todd, director of marketing; Steve Deitmer, director of development; Diane Peirano, manufacturing buyer; Melinda Alexander, photo researcher; and Janet Slowik, art director, who designed this edition of *Business Essentials*.

Our colleagues at the University of Missouri-Columbia and Texas A&M University also deserve recognition. Each of us has the good fortune to be a part of a community of scholars who enrich our lives and challenge our ideas. Without their intellectual stimulation and support, our work would suffer greatly. Phyllis Washburn, Dr. Griffin's staff assistant, deserves special mention of the myriad contributions she has made to this project as well.

Finally, our families. We take pride in the accomplishments of our wives, Mary and Glenda and draw strength from the knowledge that they are there for us to lean on. And we take joy from our children, Matt, Kristen, Ashley, and Dustin. Sometimes in the late hours when we're ready for sleep but have to get one or two more pages written, looking at your pictures keeps us going. Thanks to all of you for making us what we are.

Ronald J. Ebert
Ricky W. Griffin

1

After reading this chapter, you should be able to:

1 Define the nature of U.S. *business* and identify its main goals and functions.

2 Describe the different types of global *economic systems* according to the means by which they control the *factors of production* through *input* and *output markets*.

3 Show how *markets, demand,* and *supply* affect resource distribution in the United States.

4 Identify the elements of *private enterprise* and explain the various degrees of *competition* in the U.S. economic system.

5 Explain the importance of the economic environment to business and identify the factors used to evaluate the performance of an economic system.

MEGAWATT LAUNDERING AND OTHER BRIGHT BUSINESS IDEAS

The final chapters haven't been written yet, but the Enron saga has already become a part of American business lore. As just about everybody knows by now, Enron Corporation is the largest U.S. company ever to fail (also managing to bring down its lead

UNDERSTANDING THE U.S. BUSINESS ENVIRONMENT

"**I**t never occurred to us that something so vital to society would be treated like a casino."

—David Freeman, California energy official, on the tactics of power companies in the state's power shortage

auditor, Arthur Andersen, in the process). Enron is no doubt destined to figure in dozens of case studies on such themes as fraudulent financial practices, corrupt corporate strategy, and lawless leadership.

The Enron story also throws light on some of the basics of the capitalistic free enterprise system— namely, supply, demand, and freedom of choice. As we will see, Enron managers exploited the relationships between supply and demand to an almost unprecedented degree in their quest for riches beyond legitimate profit.

This chapter of the Enron story opens in California. Like most states, California had long regulated public utility companies. A state agency dictated how much energy was produced and the prices at which it was sold. In the process, the profits of utility companies were indirectly controlled as well. Regulation also meant that supply and demand were closely aligned. Utilities produced just as much energy as customers needed. After all, there was no reason to produce more than they could sell, and the state wouldn't let them produce any less. State rules also required each customer to buy energy from a single local provider authorized to conduct business in a specified geographic area.

But in the late 1990s, California adopted a new hands-off policy regarding supply and demand in the utilities business. This shift in thinking resulted from a massive lobbying effort by major utilities interests, as representatives from Enron and other big energy companies persuaded the state to loosen its grip on the production and delivery of electricity. They argued that increased competition among producers and suppliers would make them deliver energy more efficiently while allowing consumers to choose their own providers.

Under the new system, responsibility for matching supply and demand fell to an independent system operator (ISO). This intermediary agent (or wholesaler) bought electricity from unregulated providers such as Enron, Dynergy, and Calpine and then sold it to local energy retailers such as Pacific Gas & Electric. The ISO paid providers to sell excess electricity out of state if supplies grew too large. Consumers, meanwhile, could choose to buy electricity from different retailers, making decisions based on price, service, and so forth.

The integrity of the system required the big companies involved to operate with a sense of social responsibility and fair play. Says David Freeman, top energy adviser to former California governor Gray Davis, "It never occurred to us in our innocence that something so vital to society would be treated like a casino. We thought that somehow the [invisible] hand of Adam Smith would be benign."

Another flaw in the system was the fact that the state hadn't really created a free market for electricity. It had merely laid down a new and more bewildering array of rules and regulations. In some cases, regulations actually masked incentives for companies to misuse the system. With or without such incentives, however, Enron—and other energy providers—seized every opportunity they could to exploit the system by ducking through highly profitable loopholes.

One of Enron's most notorious plans, code-named *Ricochet,* was a scheme known as "megawatt laundering." To protect consumers from price gouging by unregulated suppliers, California had set price caps for electrical power. Those caps, however, applied only to electricity that was bought and transmitted within the state. Enron began buying electricity in California, which it then transmitted across state lines over a regional power grid. It then turned around and transmitted the same electricity back to California. Naturally, it looked as if it were coming from out of state. Because California price caps didn't apply, Enron was free to sell the rerouted power at much higher prices.

Our opening story is continued on page 27.

THE CONCEPT OF BUSINESS AND THE CONCEPT OF PROFIT

business
An organization that provides goods or services to earn profits

profits
The difference between a business's revenues and its expenses

What do you think of when you hear the word *business*? Does it conjure up images of successful corporations, such as General Motors and IBM? Or of less successful operations, such as Enron and Kmart? Are you reminded of smaller firms, such as your local supermarket or car-repair shop? Or do you think of even smaller one-person operations, such as the dry cleaner around the corner or your neighborhood pizzeria?

All of these organizations are **businesses**—organizations that provide goods or services to earn profits. Indeed, the prospect of earning **profits**—the difference between a business's revenues and expenses—is what encourages people to open and expand businesses. After all, profits reward owners for risking their money and time. The legitimate right to pursue profits distinguishes a business from those organizations, such as most universities, hospitals, and government agencies, which run in much the same way but which generally don't seek profits.[1]

Consumer Choice and Demand In a capitalistic system, then, businesses exist in order to earn profits for owners who are free to set them up. But consumers also have freedom of choice. In choosing how to pursue profits, businesses must take into account what consumers want and need. No matter how efficient a business is, it won't survive if there is no demand for its goods or services. Neither a snowblower shop in Florida nor a beach-umbrella store in Alaska is likely to do very well.

Opportunity and Enterprise But if enterprising businesspeople can identify either unmet consumer needs or better ways of satisfying consumer needs, they can be successful. In other words, someone who can spot a promising opportunity and then develop a good plan for capitalizing on it can succeed. The opportunity always involves goods or services that consumers need and/or want—especially if no one else is supplying them or if existing businesses are doing so inefficiently or incompletely.

Quality of Life Businesses produce most of the goods and services we consume and employ most working people. They create most new innovations and provide a vast range of opportunities for new businesses, which serve as their suppliers. A healthy business climate also contributes directly to quality of life and standard of living. New forms of technology, service businesses, and international opportunities promise to keep production, consumption, and employment growing indefinitely. Business profits enhance the personal incomes of millions of owners and stockholders, and business taxes help to support governments at all levels. Many businesses support charities and provide community leadership.

In this chapter, we begin our introduction to business by examining economic systems around the world. Once you understand the differences among them, you will better appreciate the workings of the U.S. system. We also investigate the concepts of markets, demand, and supply and their roles in private enterprise. Next, we explain how you can better understand economic performance. Finally, we examine emerging issues and trends that promise to shape business in the twenty-first century.

"Your Honor, my client pleads guilty to an overzealous but well-intentioned pursuit of the profit motive."

THE U.S. ECONOMIC SYSTEM

economic system
A nation's system for allocating its resources among its citizens

A U.S. business operates differently from a business in, say, France or the People's Republic of China, and businesses in these countries differ from those in Japan or Brazil. A key factor in these differences is the economic system of a firm's *home country*—the nation in which it does most of its business. An **economic system** is a nation's system for allocating its resources among its citizens, both individuals and organizations. In this section, we show how economic systems differ according to the ownership or control of these resources, which are often called *factors of production*. We will also describe the economic systems of a few selected other countries.

Factors of Production

factors of production
Resources used in the production of goods and services—labor, capital, entrepreneurs, physical resources, and information resources

A basic difference among economic systems is the way in which they manage the **factors of production**—the resources that a country's businesses use to produce goods and services.[2] Economists have long focused on four factors of production: labor, capital, entrepreneurs, and physical resources. Newer perspectives, however, broaden the idea of natural resources to include all physical resources. In addition to the classic four, information resources are now often considered as well.[3] (The concept of factors of production can also be applied to the resources that an organization manages in order to produce goods and services.)

labor (or human resources)
The physical and mental capabilities of people as they contribute to economic production

Labor People who work for businesses provide labor. Sometimes called **human resources**, **labor** includes the physical and intellectual contributions people make while engaged in economic production. AOL Time Warner *(www.aoltimewarner.com)*, for example, employs 88,000 people. Such large operations require widely skilled workforces, ranging from software engineers and media experts to financial analysts.

capital
The funds needed to create and operate a business enterprise

Capital Obtaining and using labor and other resources requires **capital**—the financial resources needed to operate an enterprise. You need capital to start a new business and then to keep it running and growing. AOL Time Warner needs millions of dollars in cash (and millions more in equipment and other assets) to run its operations. A major source of capital for small businesses is personal investment by owners. Investments can come from individual entrepreneurs, from partners who start businesses together, and from investors who buy stock. Revenue from the sale of products is a key and ongoing source of capital once a business has opened its doors.

Capital can also include the market value of corporate stock. When America Online acquired Time Warner for $106 billion in 2001, the deal involved very little actual cash. Most of it was handled through transfers of stock. Bank lines of credit and the market value of *liquid assets* (those that can be quickly and easily sold for cash) are also forms of capital.

entrepreneur
An individual who accepts the risks and opportunities involved in creating and operating a new business venture

Entrepreneurs An **entrepreneur** is an individual who accepts the risks and opportunities entailed by creating and operating a new business. AOL was started by James Kimsey, who had the technical skills to understand how the Internet works, the conceptual skills to see its huge future potential, and the risk-taking acumen to bet his own career and capital on the idea of AOL. Both Time Inc. and Warner Brothers Studios, two established companies that later merged into Time Warner, were also started (both in 1922) by entrepreneurs who risked personal fortunes on the success of their new ventures.

Say WHAT YOU MEAN

THE CULTURE OF RISK

Risk taking has been a defining feature of U.S. business culture for a long time. From the early pioneers and prospectors heading west to the would-be dot-com billionaires of the 1990s, Americans are known not only for their readiness to try out new ideas but also for their willingness to risk everything for the chance to make it big. That philosophy persists, although it's more influential in some areas than others. You can still hear Texans talking about how the spirit of nineteenth-century "wildcatters" spurred local traditions in oil drilling. Risk taking has become an important part of California's business culture, especially in the entertainment and high-tech industries, and New York is home to high rollers in the world of finance.

Risk taking in the United States differs by industry and size of company. Small companies are more likely to make risky decisions than large ones, where elaborate vetting processes may slow things down. Likewise, publicly traded companies whose stockholders usually keep a close eye on investments are less likely to take big risks than are privately held firms.

Americans' propensity to take risks is one of the reasons that the so-called "New Economy" took root here more firmly than it did elsewhere (and perhaps helps to explain why the dot-com bubble burst so resoundingly). Fledgling companies were encouraged by rules and regulations designed to bolster a spirit of change. In fact, risk taking can be seen in the attitudes of U.S. lawmakers and regulators as well as in the entrepreneurial spirit of American businesspeople, particularly when it comes to tax policies and the financial-markets system.

Easier access to capital also encourages entrepreneurship, as does the American attitude toward those who fail in business. For people who lose their bets and end up bankrupt, systems are in place to help them get solvent again. It's not uncommon for an American business to start up again under a new name and resume operations right on the heels of a failed venture. Of course, even if failure is an accepted, almost time-honored tradition in this country, that's not to say that bankruptcy is taken lightly. Businesspeople who stumble can pick themselves up again, but they usually have some rehabbing to do, both to strengthen their reputations and to restore the trust once shared with former customers and associates.

In 2001, the entrepreneurial vision of leaders at both AOL and Time Warner saw the potential benefits of merging the two firms. Most economic systems encourage entrepreneurs both to start new businesses and to make the decisions that turn small businesses into larger ones big enough to move into new markets.

Physical Resources **Physical resources** are the tangible things that organizations use to conduct their business. They include natural resources and raw materials, offices, storage, production facilities, parts and supplies, computers and peripherals, and a variety of other equipment. AOL Time Warner, for example, needs land, buildings, and computers. The CDs on which it distributes its software and music and the videotapes and DVDs on which it distributes movies are supplied by other manufacturers; forest products are used for packaging.

physical resources
Tangible things organizations use in the conduct of their business

Information Resources The production of tangible goods once dominated most economic systems, but today **information resources** play a major role. Businesses rely on market forecasts, on the specialized knowledge of people, and on economic data for much of their work. In turn, much of what they do results either in the creation of new information or the repackaging of existing information for new users.

AOL Time Warner produces few tangible products. Instead, America Online provides online services for millions of subscribers who pay monthly access fees. Time

information resources
Data and other information used by business

Some sectors of the economy tend to get a lift even when the overall economy slips. Entrepreneur Jonathan Fields found out that physical and spiritual therapy is one of them when he opened his Sonic Yoga NYC *(http://sonicyoga.com)* in Manhattan one month after 9/11. Within 30 days, he had three times as many clients as he had projected, and the business continues to flourish. "So far, so good," says Fields, a one-time lawyer with the Securities and Exchange Commission.

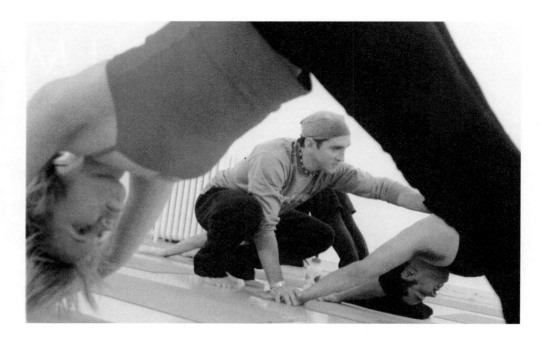

Warner Entertainment produces movies and television programming. A subsidiary, Turner Broadcasting System, gathers information about world events and then transmits it to consumers over its Cable News Network (CNN). Essentially, then, AOL Time Warner is in the information business.[4]

Types of Economic Systems

Different types of economic systems manage these factors of production differently. In some systems, all ownership is private; in others, all factors of production are owned or controlled by the government. Most systems fall between these extremes.

Economic systems also differ in the ways decisions are made about production and allocation. A **planned economy** relies on a centralized government to control all or most factors of production and to make all or most production and allocation decisions. In a **market economy**, individual producers and consumers control production and allocation by creating combinations of supply and demand. We will describe each of these types of economic systems and then discuss mixed market economies.

planned economy
Economy that relies on a centralized government to control all or most factors of production and to make all or most production and allocation decisions

market economy
Economy in which individuals control production and allocation decisions through supply and demand

Planned Economies There are two basic forms of planned economies: *communism* (discussed here) and *socialism* (discussed as a mixed market economy). As envisioned by nineteenth-century German economist Karl Marx, communism is a system in which the government owns and operates all factors of production. Marx proposed an economy in which individuals would contribute according to their abilities and receive benefits according to their needs. He also expected government ownership of production factors to be temporary: Once society had matured, government would wither away and workers would take direct ownership of the factors of production.

The former Soviet Union and many Eastern European countries embraced communism until the end of the twentieth century. In the early 1990s, one country after another renounced communism as both an economic and a political system. Today Cuba, North Korea, Vietnam, and the People's Republic of China are among the few nations with openly communist systems. Even in these countries, however, planned economic systems are making room for features of the free enterprise system.

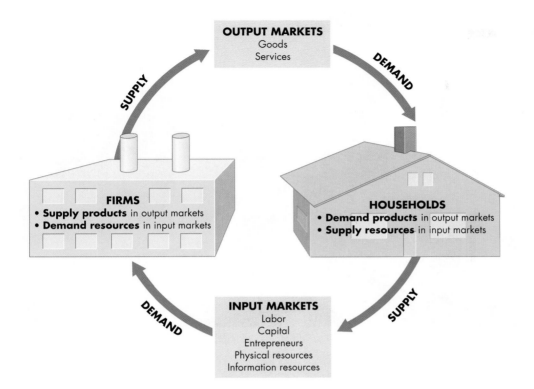

FIGURE 1.1

Circular Flow in a Market Economy

Market Economies A **market** is a mechanism for exchange between the buyers and sellers of a particular good or service. (Like *capital*, the term *market* can have multiple meanings.) Market economies rely on capitalism and free enterprise to create an environment in which producers and consumers are free to sell and buy what they choose (within certain limits). As a result, items produced and prices paid are largely determined by supply and demand.

To understand how a market economy works, consider what happens when you go to a fruit market to buy apples. While one vendor is selling apples for $1 per pound, another is charging $1.50. Both vendors are free to charge what they want, and you are free to buy what you choose. If both vendors' apples are of the same quality, you will buy the cheaper ones. If the $1.50 apples are fresher, you may buy them instead. In short, both buyers and sellers enjoy freedom of choice.

A relatively new kind of market is one that functions electronically. eBay, for instance, functions in just such a market. Virtually anyone can offer goods or services for sale on the eBay Web site, and just about everybody can bid on them. Another less visible electronic market is called "business-to-business," or "B2B." Whereas most early commercial Internet applications were directed toward consumers, B2B is a more recent development. Some experts think that it will be handling trillions of dollars annually in just a few years. As the term suggests, B2B involves electronic transactions between two or more businesses.

Input and Output Markets Figure 1.1 shows a more complete model for better understanding how factors of production work in a pure market economy. According to this view, businesses and households interact in two different market relationships.[5] In the **input market**, firms buy resources from households, which are thus resource suppliers. In the **output market**, firms supply goods and services in response to household demand. (We provide a more detailed discussion of supply and demand later in this chapter.)

market
Mechanism for exchange between buyers and sellers of a particular good or service

input market
Market in which firms buy resources from supplier households

output market
Market in which firms supply goods and services in response to demand on the part of households

According to the model of circular flow in a market economy, this shopper at an Atlanta Target store plays a role in the *output market*. She demands goods that are supplied by a firm in the retailing business. Think of the employees who work for the firms from which Target *(www.target.com)* buys its products as households that supply the *input market* with labor, time, and skills.

As you can see, the activities of these two markets create a circular flow. Ford Motor Company, for example, relies on various kinds of inputs. It buys labor directly from households, which may also supply capital by using their savings to buy Ford stock. Consumer buying patterns furnish information when Ford must decide which models to produce and which to discontinue. In turn, Ford uses inputs to become a supplier to households, designing and building automobiles, trucks, and sports utility vehicles and offering them for sale to consumers.

Capitalism Individuals, meanwhile, are free to work for Ford or anyone else, and they are free to invest in Ford stock or to put their money elsewhere, whether saving it or spending it on products they need or want. Likewise, Ford can create the vehicles it chooses and sell them at the prices it chooses. Consumers, of course, are free to buy their next car from Ford or Toyota or BMW. This process contrasts markedly with that of a planned economy, in which individuals may be told where they can and cannot work, companies may be told what they can and cannot make, and consumers may have little or no choice in what they purchase or how much they pay. The political basis of market processes is called **capitalism**, which sanctions the private ownership of the factors of production and encourages entrepreneurship by offering profits as an incentive. The economic basis of market processes is the operation of demand and supply, which we discuss in the next section.

capitalism
Market economy that provides for private ownership of production and encourages entrepreneurship by offering profits as an incentive

Mixed Market Economies There is no such thing as "pure" planned or "pure" market economies. Most countries rely on some form of **mixed market economy** that features characteristics of both planned and market economies. Even a market economy that strives to be as free and open as possible, such as the U.S. economy, restricts certain activities. Some products can't be sold legally, others can be sold only to people of a certain age, advertising must be truthful, and so forth.

mixed market economy
Economic system featuring characteristics of both planned and market economies

Many former Eastern bloc countries have adopted market mechanisms through **privatization**—the process of converting government enterprises into privately owned companies. In recent years, the practice has spread to many other countries as

privatization
Process of converting government enterprises into privately owned companies

well. For example, the postal system in many countries is government owned and government managed. The Netherlands, however, recently began privatizing its TNT Post Group N.V., already among the world's most efficient postal operations. Canada has privatized its air traffic control system. In each case, the new enterprise reduced its payroll, boosted efficiency and productivity, and quickly became profitable.

Socialism In the partially planned system called **socialism**, the government owns and operates selected major industries. In such mixed market economies, the government may control banking, transportation, or industries producing such basic goods as oil and steel. Smaller businesses, such as clothing stores and restaurants, are privately owned. Many Western European countries, including England and France, allow free market operations in most economic areas but keep government control of others, such as health care.

socialism
Planned economic system in which the government owns and operates only selected major sources of production

SELF-CHECK QUESTIONS 1–3

You should now be able to answer Self-Check Questions 1–3.*

1 **Multiple Choice** Which of the following is **not** considered a basic *factor of production*? [select one] **(a)** labor; **(b)** buildings and equipment; **(c)** capital; **(d)** entrepreneurs; **(e)** physical resources.

2 **Multiple Choice** If you buy stock in Newell Rubbermaid Corp., you have entered which of the following *markets*? [select one] **(a)** over the counter; **(b)** reseller; **(c)** labor; **(d)** output; **(e)** input.

3 **True/False** If 18 percent of its total production and 16 percent of its total employment are created by its government, which also collects 30 percent of its total income in taxes, a nation does not really have a *free market economy*.

***** **Answers to Self-Check Questions 1–3 can be found on p. 507.**

THE ECONOMICS OF A MARKET SYSTEM

Understanding the complex nature of the U.S. economic system is essential to understanding the environment in which U.S. businesses operate. In this section, we describe the workings of the U.S. market economy. Specifically, we examine markets, the nature of demand and supply, private enterprise, and degrees of competition.

Demand and Supply in a Market Economy

A market economy consists of many different markets. We have already described input and output markets, but we need to remember that the inputs used by business and the products created by business have their own markets. In each of these markets, businesses decide what inputs to buy, what to make and in what quantities, and what prices to charge. Likewise, customers decide what to buy and how much they want to pay. Literally billions of such exchanges take place every day between businesses and individuals; between businesses; and among individuals, businesses, and governments. Moreover, exchanges conducted in one area often affect exchanges elsewhere.

Since 2000, for example, several factors have influenced computer purchases. In the late 1990s, for instance, many companies increased computer budgets in anticipation of Y2K problems but then cut them once the scare was over. Some companies began to reallocate outlays for technology, spending less on desktop computers and more on back-office equipment for e-business.

In addition, some firms simply started to slow down their upgrade cycles because brand-new computers were not sufficiently superior to those they had purchased just a few years earlier. Rather than upgrade every two or three years, as they had in the 1990s, many firms now upgrade every three or four years. As U.S. demand dropped, firms like Dell and IBM cut prices to keep sales from slumping too far, and lower prices mean lower profits per unit. At the same time, however, demand in other parts of the world, notably in China and India, has continued to rise, though not enough to offset domestic declines. Finally, lower profit expectations induced investors to pay less for the stocks of some computer firms, causing those prices to fall as well.[6]

The Laws of Demand and Supply On all economic levels, decisions about what to buy and what to sell are determined primarily by the forces of demand and supply.[7] **Demand** is the willingness and ability of buyers to purchase a product (a good or a service). **Supply** is the willingness and ability of producers to offer a good or service for sale. Generally speaking, demand and supply follow basic laws:

- The **law of demand**: Buyers will purchase (*demand*) more of a product as its price drops and less as its price increases.
- The **law of supply**: Producers will offer (*supply*) more of a product for sale as its price rises and less as its price drops.

The Demand and Supply Schedule To appreciate these laws in action, consider the market for pizza in your town (or neighborhood). If everyone is willing to pay $25 for a pizza (a relatively high price), the town's only pizzeria will produce a large supply. But if everyone is willing to pay only $5 (a relatively low price), it will make fewer pizzas. Through careful analysis, we can determine how many pizzas will be sold at different prices. These results, called a **demand and supply schedule**, are obtained from marketing research, historical data, and other studies of the market. Properly applied, they reveal the relationships among different levels of demand and supply at different price levels.

Demand and Supply Curves The demand and supply schedule can be used to construct demand and supply curves for pizza in your town. A **demand curve** shows how many products—in this case, pizzas—will be demanded (bought) at different prices. A **supply curve** shows how many pizzas will be supplied (baked or offered for sale) at different prices.

Figure 1.2 shows demand and supply curves for pizzas. As you can see, demand increases as price decreases; supply increases as price increases. When demand and supply curves are plotted on the same graph, the point at which they intersect is the **market price** or **equilibrium price**—the price at which the quantity of goods demanded and the quantity of goods supplied are equal. In Figure 1.2, the equilibrium price for pizzas in our example is $10. At this point, the quantity of pizzas demanded and the quantity of pizzas supplied are the same: 1,000 pizzas per week.

Surpluses and Shortages What if the pizzeria decides to make some other number of pizzas? For example, what would happen if the owner tried to increase profits by

---

demand
The willingness and ability of buyers to purchase a good or service

supply
The willingness and ability of producers to offer a good or service for sale

law of demand
Principle that buyers will purchase (demand) more of a product as its price drops and less as its price increases

law of supply
Principle that producers will offer (supply) more of a product for sale as its price rises and less as its price drops

demand and supply schedule
Assessment of the relationships between different levels of demand and supply at different price levels

demand curve
Graph showing how many units of a product will be demanded (bought) at different prices

supply curve
Graph showing how many units of a product will be supplied (offered for sale) at different prices

market price (or **equilibrium price**)
Profit-maximizing price at which the quantity of goods demanded and the quantity of goods supplied are equal

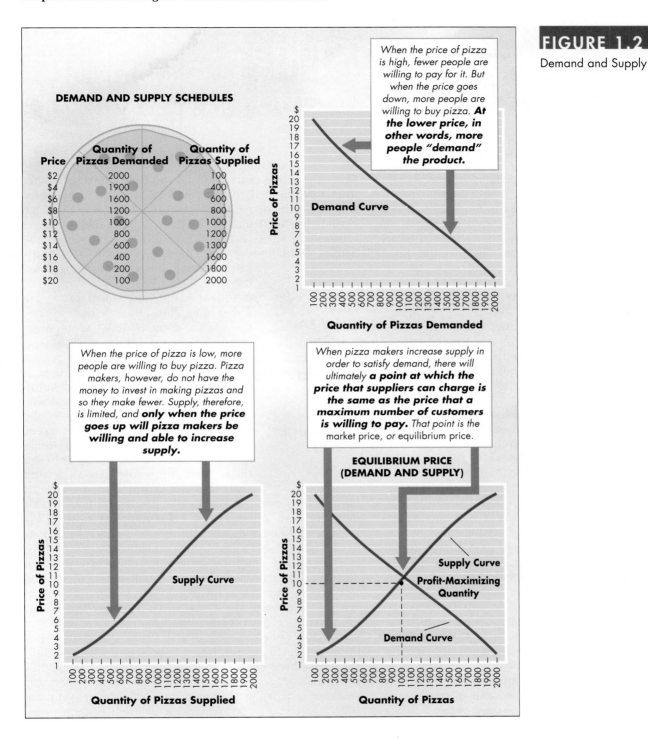

FIGURE 1.2

Demand and Supply

making *more* pizzas to sell? Or what if the owner wanted to lower overhead, cut back on store hours, and *reduce* the number of pizzas offered for sale? In either case, the result would be an inefficient use of resources and lower profits. For instance, if the pizzeria supplies 1,200 pizzas and tries to sell them for $10 each, 200 pizzas will not be bought. Our demand schedule shows that only 1,000 pizzas will be demanded at this price. The pizzeria will therefore have a **surplus**—a situation in which the quantity supplied exceeds the quantity demanded. It will lose the money that it spent making those extra 200 pizzas.

surplus
Situation in which quantity supplied exceeds quantity demanded

ENTREPRENEURSHIP and New Ventures

Grinding Out Competitive Success

Can an increase in supply fuel new demand? It would be an unusual situation, but that appears to be what's happened in the retail-coffee industry—thanks to Starbucks. When Starbucks first opened a new store near It's A Grind, an independent coffeehouse in Long Beach, California, locals feared that the giant chain would put their neighborhood favorite out of business. Likewise, natives of San Diego turned out to protest a Starbucks opening in the vicinity of some of their locally owned coffeehouses. But both California coffee-shop owners and customers were in for a pleasant surprise: Wherever the international chain has established a foothold, sales have increased for all the coffeehouses in the area.

On the surface, customer qualms about the danger to local favorites appear to make sense: Why wouldn't a huge multinational firm such as Starbucks enjoy competitive advantages in pricing, new product development, and other areas? From Standard Oil, Sears, and General Motors to Wal-Mart, throwing their weight around has been a common tactic among big businesses for decades. "A big company like Starbucks," explained the *Indianapolis Star* in an editorial on the passage of a local coffeehouse, "can come in and lose money for two years until they wipe everybody else out. It's the old Wal-Mart thing."

In some cases, fear of Starbucks prompted small businesspeople to take extraordinary measures to reduce the consequences of head-to-head competition. Courtney Bates of Kansas City's City Market Coffee Co. made her landlord put a clause in her lease that prevented rental to any other coffeehouse. Another owner was approached by Starbucks about a possible buyout but was suspicious of commercial espionage. "I don't think they really wanted to buy," claims Jeff Schmidt, owner of LatteLand in Kansas City. "They just wanted a peek inside my business." In Kansas City, 1,000 coffeehouse customers signed a petition asking the city to ban Starbucks. Starbucks, says Katerina Carson, owner of Katerina's in Chicago, "is a corporate monster."

Interestingly, however, the statistics just don't support the assumption that Starbucks is quashing competition and slashing profits in the coffeehouse industry. In fact, while

> "A big company like Starbucks can come in and lose money for two years until they wipe everybody else out. It's the old Wal-Mart thing."
>
> —Editorial in the Indianapolis Star, eulogizing the passage of a locally owned coffeehouse

Starbucks outlets in the United States have grown in number from 1,000 in 1997 to more than 3,000 today, independent stores have increased from 7,000 to 10,000 over the same period. The total number of coffeehouses, therefore, has grown from 8,000 to 13,000 since 1997—an increase of 62 percent. Sales, however, have more than *doubled*. Obviously, sales volume *per store* has increased dramatically.

Indeed, many independent owners are forced to admit that, in spite of their fears, their own sales increased when Starbucks moved into the neighborhood. "Starbucks helped our business," acknowledges Jon Cates, co-owner of the Broadway Cafe in Kansas City, who adds, "I don't want to give them any credit for it." Meanwhile, some owners have actually embraced the idea of Starbucks in their local markets. "Competition is good," reasons Norma Slaman, owner of Newbreak Coffee in San Diego. Slaman saw sales rise 15 percent after Starbucks' arrival. Some local chains have even adopted the strategy of following Starbucks into a neighborhood. Reports Doug Zell, who placed two of his Intelligentsia Coffee Roasters stores near Starbucks locations in Chicago, "It's been double-digit growth every year."

Even though Starbucks is putting competitive pressure on independent coffeehouses, independents are prospering right along with the giant chain. Why? Perhaps because they're so nervous about Starbucks that they implement improvements even before the chain arrives. When a Starbucks opened nearby, It's A Grind fixed up stores, improved customer service, and bolstered staff training. Sales have been up at least 10 percent annually ever since. Other independents have copied Starbucks by banning smoking or roasting their own beans. They can also compete by focusing on local activities and local customer preferences, sponsoring poetry readings, live jazz, the work of local artists, and regional food fairs.

Starbucks, it seems, has not merely increased competition but has also shifted industry dynamics in areas such as customer expectations and new entrants. Although Starbucks and its independent competitors are more profitable than ever, it appears that, for now, the customers are the big winners in this evolving industry.

Economically speaking, surfing's up, but demand for surfware is riding an even higher crest—about 20 percent higher than a year ago. "Surfware" covers a lot of products—from wet suits to bikinis and boardshorts—and the demand comes from free-spending though notoriously fickle teenagers. Suppliers have to work hard not merely to meet demand but also to figure out what's going to be hot from one week to the next. "I hang out at high schools and shopping malls," admits one designer. "I try to be a sponge and see what they want."

Conversely, if the pizzeria supplies only 800 pizzas, a **shortage** will result. The quantity demanded will be greater than the quantity supplied. The pizzeria will "lose" the extra profit that it could have made by producing 200 more pizzas. Even though consumers may pay more for pizzas because of the shortage, the pizzeria will still earn lower total profits than if it had made 1,000 pizzas. It will also risk angering customers who cannot buy pizzas and encourage other entrepreneurs to set up competing pizzerias to satisfy unmet demand. Clearly, then, businesses should seek the ideal combination of price charged and quantity supplied so as to maximize profits, maintain goodwill among customers, and discourage competition. This ideal combination is found at the equilibrium point.

shortage
Situation in which quantity demanded exceeds quantity supplied

Our example involves only one company, one product, and a few buyers. Obviously, the U.S. economy is far more complex. Thousands of companies sell hundreds of thousands of products to millions of buyers every day. In the end, however, the result is much the same: Companies try to supply the quantity and selection of goods that will earn them the largest profits.

SELF-CHECK QUESTIONS 4–6

You should now be able to answer Self-Check Questions 4–6.*

4 **True/False** If the price of pizzas goes up, less beer will probably be sold.

5 **Multiple Choice** Pierre discovered that when he lowered the price of his paintings, more people commissioned portraits from him. Pierre is experiencing which of the following? [select one] **(a)** discounting; **(b)** the law of supply; **(c)** a supply shortage; **(d)** the law of demand; **(e)** economic justice.

6 **Multiple Choice** According to the principle of *demand and supply*, which of the following should happen if the price of eggs goes up? [select one] **(a)** Egg importers will try to persuade egg exporters to produce more eggs. **(b)** Producers will produce fewer eggs. **(c)** Shoppers will buy fewer eggs. **(d)** Shoppers will buy more eggs. **(e)** All of the above.

*Answers to Self-Check Questions 4–6 can be found on p. 507.

Private Enterprise and Competition in a Market Economy

private enterprise
Economic system that allows individuals to pursue their own interests without undue governmental restriction

Market economies rely on a **private enterprise** system—one that allows individuals to pursue their own interests with minimal government restriction. In turn, private enterprise requires the presence of four elements: private property rights, freedom of choice, profits, and competition.

- *Private property.* Ownership of the resources used to create wealth is in the hands of individuals.
- *Freedom of choice.* You can sell your labor to any employer you choose. You can also choose which products to buy, and producers can usually choose whom to hire and what to produce.
- *Profits.* The lure of profits (and freedom) leads some people to abandon the security of working for someone else and to assume the risks of entrepreneurship. Anticipated profits also influence individuals' choices of which goods or services to produce.
- *Competition.* If profits motivate individuals to start businesses, competition motivates them to operate those businesses efficiently. **Competition** occurs when two or more businesses vie for the same resources or customers. To gain an advantage over competitors, a business must produce its goods or services efficiently and be able to sell them at a reasonable profit. To achieve these goals, it must convince customers that its products are either better or less expensive than those of its competitors. Competition, therefore, forces all businesses to make products better or cheaper. A company that produces inferior, expensive products is likely to fail. We discuss competition more fully in the next section.

competition
Vying among businesses for the same resources or customers

Degrees of Competition Even in a free enterprise system, not all industries are equally competitive. Economists have identified four degrees of competition in a private enterprise system: *perfect competition, monopolistic competition, oligopoly*, and *monopoly*. Table 1.1 summarizes the features of these four degrees.

perfect competition
Market or industry characterized by numerous small firms producing an identical product

Perfect Competition For **perfect competition** to exist, two conditions must prevail: (1) All firms in an industry must be small, and (2) the number of firms in the industry must be large. Under these conditions, no single firm is powerful enough to influence the price of its product. Prices are therefore determined by such market forces as supply and demand.

TABLE 1.1

Degrees of Competition

Characteristic	Perfect Competition	Monopolistic Competition	Oligopoly	Monopoly
Example	Local farmer	Stationery store	Steel industry	Public utility
Number of competitors	Many	Many, but fewer than in pure competition	Few	None
Ease of entry into industry	Relatively easy	Fairly easy	Difficult	Regulated by government
Similarity of goods or services offered by competing firms	Identical	Similar	Can be similar or different	No directly competing goods or services
Level of control over price by individual firms	None	Some	Some	Considerable

In addition, these two conditions also reflect four principles:

1 The products of each firm are so similar that buyers view them as identical to those of other firms.
2 Both buyers and sellers know the prices that others are paying and receiving in the marketplace.
3 Because each firm is small, it is easy for firms to enter or leave the market.
4 Going prices are set exclusively by supply and demand and accepted by both sellers and buyers.

U.S. agriculture is a good example of perfect competition. The wheat produced on one farm is the same as that from another. Both producers and buyers are aware of prevailing market prices. It is relatively easy to start producing wheat and relatively easy to stop when it's no longer profitable.

Monopolistic Competition Fewer sellers are involved in **monopolistic competition** than in pure competition, but because there are still many buyers, sellers try to make products at least seem to differ from those of competitors. Differentiating strategies include brand names (Tide and Cheer), design or styling (Polo and Tommy Hilfiger jeans), and advertising (Coke and Pepsi). For example, in an effort to attract health-conscious consumers, the Kraft Foods division of Philip Morris promotes such differentiated products as low-fat Cool Whip, low-calorie Jell-O, and sugar-free Kool-Aid.

> **monopolistic competition**
> Market or industry characterized by numerous buyers and relatively numerous sellers trying to differentiate their products from those of competitors

Monopolistically competitive businesses may be large or small, but they can still enter or leave the market easily. For example, many small clothing stores compete successfully with large apparel retailers such as Liz Claiborne and Limited Brands. bebe stores is a good case in point. The small clothing chain controls its own manufacturing facilities and can respond just as quickly as firms like Gap to changes in fashion tastes.[8] Many single-store clothing businesses in college towns compete by developing their own T-shirt and cap designs with copyrighted slogans and logos.

Product differentiation also gives sellers some control over prices. For instance, even though Sears shirts may have similar styling and other features, Ralph Lauren Polo shirts can be priced with little regard for lower Sears prices. But the large number of buyers relative to sellers applies potential limits to prices: Although Polo might be able to sell shirts for, say, $20 more than a comparable Sears shirt, it could not sell as many shirts if they were priced at $200 more.

Oligopoly When an industry has only a handful of sellers, an **oligopoly** exists. As a general rule, these sellers are quite large. The entry of new competitors is hard because large capital investment is needed. Thus oligopolistic industries (the automobile, airline, and steel industries) tend to stay that way. Only two companies make large commercial aircraft: Boeing (a U.S. company) and Airbus (a European consortium). Furthermore, as the trend toward globalization continues, most experts believe that, as one forecaster puts it, "Global oligopolies are as inevitable as the sunrise."

> **oligopoly**
> Market or industry characterized by a handful of (generally large) sellers with the power to influence the prices of their products

Oligopolists have more control over their strategies than do monopolistically competitive firms, but the actions of one firm can significantly affect the sales of every other firm in the industry. For example, when one firm cuts prices or offers incentives to increase sales, the others usually protect sales by doing the same. Likewise, when one firm raises prices, others generally follow suit. Therefore, the prices of comparable products are usually similar. When an airline announces new fare discounts, others adopt the same strategy almost immediately. Just as quickly, when discounts end for one airline, they usually end for everyone else.

> **"Global oligopolies are as inevitable as the sunrise."**
>
> **—Louis Galambos, business historian**

monopoly
Market or industry in which there is only one producer, which can therefore set the prices of its products

natural monopoly
Industry in which one company can most efficiently supply all needed goods or services

Monopoly A **monopoly** exists when an industry or market has only one producer. Obviously, a sole supplier enjoys complete control over the prices of its products. Its only constraint is a decrease in consumer demand due to increased prices. In the United States, laws such as the Sherman Antitrust Act (1890) and the Clayton Act (1914) forbid many monopolies and regulate prices charged by **natural monopolies**—industries in which one company can most efficiently supply all needed goods or services.[9] Many electric companies are natural monopolies because they can supply all the power needed in a local area. Duplicate facilities—such as two power plants and two sets of power lines—would be wasteful. In addition, the Enron debacle (as chronicled in our chapter-opening story) shows what kinds of things can happen if utilities are carelessly deregulated.

■ UNDERSTANDING ECONOMIC PERFORMANCE

Because economic forces are so volatile and can be affected by so many things, the performance of a country's economic system varies over time. Sometimes it gains strength and brings new prosperity to its members; other times it weakens and damages the fortunes of its members. Given the importance of the economic environment to U.S. business, we will closely examine the two key goals of the U.S. economic system: *economic growth* and *economic stability*. We begin by focusing on the tools with which we measure economic growth, including *aggregate output*, *standard of living*, *gross domestic product*, and *productivity*. We then discuss the main threats to economic stability—namely, *inflation* and *unemployment*. We conclude this section by discussing government attempts to manage the U.S. economy in the interest of meeting national economic goals.

Economic Growth

At one time, about half the population of this country was involved in producing the food that we needed. Today, less than 2.5 percent of the U.S. population works in agriculture. Agricultural efficiency has improved because we devised better ways of producing products and invented better technology for getting the job done. We can therefore say that agricultural production has grown because we have been able to increase total output in the agricultural sector.

business cycle
Pattern of short-term ups and downs (expansions and contractions) in an economy

aggregate output
Total quantity of goods and services produced by an economic system during a given period

Aggregate Output and Standard of Living
We can apply the same concepts to a nation's economic system, but the computations are vastly more complex. A fundamental question, then, is how we know whether or not an economic system is growing. Experts call the pattern of short-term ups and downs (or, better, expansions and contractions) in an economy the **business cycle**. The main measure of *growth* during the business cycle is **aggregate output**: the total quantity of goods and services produced by an economic system during a given period.[10]

To put it simply, an increase in aggregate output is growth (or economic growth). When output grows more quickly than the population, two things usually follow: Output per capita—the quantity of goods and services per person—goes up and the system provides relatively more of the goods and services that people want. And when these two things occur, people living in an economic system benefit from a higher **standard of living**, which refers to the total quantity and quality of goods and services that they can purchase with the currency used in their economic system.

Among other things, then, growth makes possible higher standards of living. Thus, in order to know how much your standard of living is improving, you need to know how much your nation's economic system is growing. Let's start to address this question by considering the data in Table 1.2.

Gross Domestic Product The first number, **GDP**, or **gross domestic product**, refers to the total value of all goods and services produced within a given period by a national economy through domestic factors of production. Obviously, GDP is a measure of aggregate output. Generally speaking, if GDP is going up, aggregate output is going up; if aggregate output is going up, the nation is experiencing *economic growth*.

Real Growth Rate Look at the middle column in Table 1.2. Here we find that the real growth rate of U.S. GDP—the growth rate of GDP *adjusted for inflation and changes in the value of the country's currency*—is 4.1 percent. How good is that rate? Remember that *growth depends on output increasing at a faster rate than population*. The U.S. population is growing at a rate of 0.91 percent. The *real growth rate* of the U.S. economic system, therefore, seems quite healthy, and our standard of living should be improving.

GDP per Capita The number in the third column of Table 1.2 is, in fact, a reflection of standard of living: *GDP per capita* means GDP per person. We get this figure by dividing total GDP ($9.255 trillion) by total population, which happens to be about 275.5 million. In a given period (usually calculated on an annual basis), the United States produces goods and services equal in value to $33,900 for every person in the country. Figure 1.3 shows both GDP and GDP per capita in the United States between 1900 and 2000. GDP per capita is a better measure than GDP itself of the economic well-being of the average person.

Real GDP "Real GDP" means that GDP has been adjusted. To understand why adjustments are necessary, assume that pizza is the only product in a hypothetical economy. In 2002, a pizza cost $10; the next year, a pizza cost $11. In both years, exactly 1,000 pizzas were produced. In 2002, the local GDP was $10,000 ($10 × 1,000); in 2003, the local GDP was $11,000 ($11 × 1,000). Has the economy grown? No. Because 1,000 pizzas were produced in both years, *aggregate output* remained the same. The point is not to be misled into believing that an economy is doing better than it is. If it is not adjusted, local GDP for 2003 is **nominal GDP**: GDP measured in current dollars or with all components valued at current prices.[11] In this example, *current prices* would be 2004 prices. On the other hand, we calculate **real GDP** when we calculate GDP to account for *changes in currency values and price changes*.

---

standard of living
Total quantity and quality of goods and services that a country's citizens can purchase with the currency used in their economic system

gross domestic product (GDP)
Total value of all goods and services produced within a given period by a national economy through domestic factors of production

nominal GDP
GDP measured in current dollars or with all components valued at current prices

real GDP
GDP calculated to account for changes in currency values and price changes

---

Gross Domestic Product (GDP) ($ Billion)	GDP: Real Growth Rate (%)	GDP per Capita: Purchasing Power Parity
9,255.00	4.1	$33,900

TABLE 1.2

U.S. GDP and GDP per Capita

FIGURE 1.3

GDP and GDP per Capita

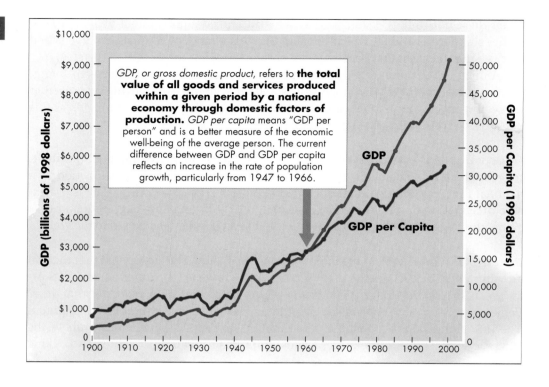

GDP, or gross domestic product, refers to **the total value of all goods and services produced within a given period by a national economy through domestic factors of production.** GDP per capita means "GDP per person" and is a better measure of the economic well-being of the average person. The current difference between GDP and GDP per capita reflects an increase in the rate of population growth, particularly from 1947 to 1966.

productivity
Measure of economic growth that compares how much a system produces with the resources needed to produce it

Productivity A major factor in the growth of an economic system is **productivity**, which is a measure of economic growth that compares how much a system produces with the resources needed to produce it. Let's say, for instance, that it takes 1 U.S. worker and 1 U.S. dollar to make 10 soccer balls in an 8-hour workday. Let's also say that it takes 1.2 Saudi workers and the equivalent of $1.2 (in riyals, the currency of Saudi Arabia) to make 10 soccer balls in the same 8-hour workday. We can say, then, that the U.S. soccer-ball industry is more productive than the Saudi soccer-ball industry. The two factors of production in this extremely simple case are labor and capital.

Now let's look at productivity from a different perspective. If more products are being produced with fewer factors of production, what happens to the prices of these products? They go down. As a consumer, therefore, you would need less of your currency to purchase the same quantity of these products. In short, your standard of living—at least with regard to these products—has improved. If your entire economic system increases its productivity, then your overall standard of living improves. In fact, *standard of living improves only through increases in productivity.*[12] Real growth in GDP reflects growth in productivity.

Productivity in the United States is increasing, and as a result, so are GDP and GDP per capita. Ultimately, increases in these measures of growth mean an improvement in the standard of living. Obviously, however, things don't always proceed so smoothly. What factors can inhibit the growth of an economic system? There are several such factors, but we'll focus on two of them: balance of trade and the national debt.

Balance of Trade Its *balance of trade* is the economic value of all the products that a country exports minus the economic value of its imported products. The principle here is quite simple:

- A *positive* balance of trade results when a country exports (sells to other countries) more than it imports (buys from other countries).
- A *negative* balance of trade results when a country imports more than it exports.

A negative balance of trade is commonly called a *trade deficit*. In 2001, the United States compiled a deficit (as it has every year since the mid-1970s), spending nearly $360 billion more on imports than it received for exports. The United States is thus a *debtor nation* rather than a *creditor nation*.

How does a trade deficit affect economic growth? The deficit exists because the amount of money spent on foreign products has not been paid in full. In effect, therefore, it is borrowed money, and borrowed money costs more money in the form of interest. The money that flows out of the country to pay off the deficit can't be used to invest in productive enterprises, either at home or overseas.

National Debt Its **national debt** is the amount of money that the government owes its creditors. As of this writing, the U.S. national debt is over $6.5 trillion. (You can find out the national debt on any given day by going to any one of several Internet sources, including the U.S. National Debt Clock at *(www.brillig.com/debt_clock).*)

national debt
Amount of money that a government owes its creditors

How does the national debt affect economic growth? While taxes are the most obvious way the government raises money, it also sells *bonds*—securities through which it promises to pay buyers certain amounts of money by specified future dates. The government sells bonds to individuals, households, banks, insurance companies, industrial corporations, nonprofit organizations, and government agencies, both at home and overseas.[13] These bonds are attractive investments because they are extremely safe: The U.S. government is not going to default on them (that is, fail to make payments when due). Even so, they must also offer a decent return on the buyer's investment, and they do this by paying interest at a competitive rate. By selling bonds, therefore, the U.S. government competes with every other potential borrower—individuals, households, businesses, and other organizations—for the available supply of loanable money. The more money the government borrows, the less money is available for the private borrowing and investment that increase productivity.

Economic Stability

We have now learned a great deal about economic systems and the ways in which they allocate resources among their citizens. We know that households, for example, receive capital in return for labor. We know that when households enter consumer markets to purchase goods and services, their decisions (and those of the firms trying to sell them goods and services) are influenced by the laws of demand and supply. We know that the laws of demand and supply result in equilibrium prices when the quantity of goods demanded and the quantity of goods supplied are equal. We know that households enjoy higher standards of living when there is balanced growth in the quantity of goods demanded and the quantity of goods supplied. We know that we can measure growth and productivity in terms of gross domestic product and standard of living in terms of the purchasing power parity of a system's currency: Living standards are stable when purchasing power parity remains stable.[14]

stability
Condition in an economic system in which the amount of money available and the quantity of goods and services produced are growing at about the same rate

We may thus conclude that a chief goal of an economic system is **stability**: a condition in which the amount of money available in an economic system and the quantity of goods and services produced in it are growing at about the same rate.

Now we can focus on certain factors that threaten stability—namely, inflation and unemployment.

inflation
Occurrence of widespread price increases throughout an economic system

Inflation Inflation occurs when there are widespread price increases throughout an economic system. How does it threaten stability? Inflation occurs when the amount of money injected into an economy outstrips the increase in actual output. When this happens, people will have more money to spend, but there will still be the same quantity of products available for them to buy. As they compete with one another to buy available products, prices go up. Before long, high prices will erase the increase in the amount of money injected into the economy. Purchasing power, therefore, declines.

Obviously, then, inflation can also hurt you as a consumer because your primary concern when deciding whether to purchase a product is often price. In other words, you will probably decide to make a purchase if the value of the product justifies the price that you'll have to pay. Now look at Table 1.3, which reduces a hypothetical purchase decision to three bare essentials:

1 Your household income over a three-year period
2 The price of a hamburger over a three-year period
3 The rates of increase for both over a three-year period

In which year did the cost of a hamburger go up? At first glance, you might say in both YR2 and YR3 (to $4 and to $7.50). In YR2, your income kept pace: Although a hamburger cost twice as much, you had twice as much money to spend. In effect, the price to you was actually the same. In YR3, however, your income increased by 250 percent while the price of a hamburger increased by 275 percent. In YR3, therefore, you got hit by inflation (how hard, of course, depends on your fondness for hamburgers). This ratio—the comparison of your increased income to the increased price of a hamburger—is all that counts if you want to consider inflation when you're making a buying decision. Inflation, therefore, can be harmful to you as a consumer because *inflation decreases the purchasing power of your money.*

consumer price index (CPI)
Measure of the prices of typical products purchased by consumers living in urban areas

Measuring Inflation: The CPI How do we measure inflation? Remember our definition of inflation as the occurrence of widespread price increases throughout an economic system. It stands to reason, therefore, that we can measure inflation by measuring price increases. To do this, we can turn to such price indexes as the **consumer price index (CPI)**: a measure of the prices of typical products purchased by consumers living in urban areas.[15]

TABLE 1.3

Hamburger Inflation

YR1 Income	YR2 Income	YR2 % Increase over YR1 Base	YR3 Income	YR3 % Increase over YR1 Base
$5,000	$10,000	100	$17,500	250

YR1 Hamburger Price	YR2 Hamburger Price	YR2 % Increase over YR1 Base	YR3 Hamburger Price	YR3 % Increase over YR1 Base
$2	$4	100	$7.50	275

Here's how the CPI works. First, we need a *base period*—an arbitrarily selected time period against which other time periods are compared. The CPI base period is 1982–84, which has been given an average value of 100. Table 1.4 gives CPI values computed for selected years. The CPI value for 1951, for instance, is 26. This means that 1 dollar's worth of typical purchases in 1982–84 would have cost 26 cents in 1951. Conversely, you would have needed $1.63 to purchase the same 1 dollar's worth of typical goods in 1998. The difference registers the effect of inflation. In fact, that's what an *inflation rate* is—the *percentage change in a price index*.

We can thus calculate the *CPI rate of inflation* by using the data in Table 1.4. To find the inflation rate between 1997 and 1998, you need to know the change from one year to the next. To find this change, simply subtract the value of 1997 from the value of 1998: 163.0 − 160.5 = 2.5.

Now apply the following formula:

$$\text{Inflation rate} = \frac{\text{Change in price index}}{\text{Initial price index}} \times 100$$

or

$$\frac{2.5}{160.5} \times 100 = 1.6\%$$

TABLE 1.4

Selected CPI Values

Year	CPI
1951	26.0
1961	29.9
1971	40.6
1981	90.9
1989	124.0
1990	130.7
1991	136.2
1992	140.3
1993	144.5
1994	148.2
1995	152.4
1996	156.9
1997	160.5
1998	163.0

Unemployment Finally, we need to consider the effect of unemployment on economic stability. **Unemployment** is the level of joblessness among people actively seeking work in an economic system. When unemployment is low, there is a shortage of labor available for businesses to hire. As they compete with one another for the available supply of labor, businesses raise the wages that they are willing to pay. Then because higher labor costs eat into profit margins, they raise the prices of their products. Thus, although consumers have more money to inject into the economy, this increase is soon erased by higher prices. Purchasing power declines.

unemployment
Level of joblessness among people actively seeking work in an economic system

There are at least two related problems. If wage rates get too high, businesses will respond by hiring fewer workers and unemployment will, therefore, go up. Businesses could, of course, raise prices to counter increased labor costs, but if they charge higher prices, they won't be able to sell as much of their products. Because of reduced sales, they will cut back on hiring and, once again, unemployment will go up. What if the government tries to correct this situation by injecting more money into the economic system—say, by cutting taxes or spending more money? Prices in general may go up because of increased consumer demand. Again, purchasing power declines and, indeed, inflation may set in.[16]

Recessions and Depressions Finally, unemployment is sometimes a symptom of a system-wide disorder in the economy. During a downturn in the business cycle, people in numerous different sectors may lose their jobs at the same time. As a result, overall income and spending may drop. Feeling the pinch of reduced revenues, businesses may cut spending on the factors of production—including labor. Yet more people will be put out of work and unemployment will only increase further. Unemployment that results from this vicious cycle is called *cyclical unemployment.*

In examining the relationship between unemployment and economic stability, we are thus reminded that when prices get high enough, consumer demand for goods and services goes down. We are also reminded that when demand for products goes down, producers cut back on hiring and, not surprisingly, eventually start producing less. Consequently, of course, aggregate output decreases. When we go through a period during which aggregate output declines, we have a recession. During a *recession*, producers need fewer employees—less labor—to produce products. Unemployment, therefore, goes up.

How do we know whether or not we're in a recession? Clearly, we must start by measuring aggregate output. Recall that this is the function of real GDP, which we find by making necessary adjustments to the total value of all goods and services produced within a given period by a national economy through domestic factors of production. A **recession**, therefore, is more precisely defined as a period during which aggregate output, as measured by real GDP, declines. A prolonged and deep recession is a **depression**.

recession
Period during which aggregate output, as measured by real GDP, declines

depression
Particularly severe and long-lasting recession

Managing the U.S. Economy

> **"A warning light is flashing on the dashboard of the economy. We just can't drive on and hope for the best."**
>
> **—President George W. Bush, January 2001**

The government acts to manage the U.S. economic system through two sets of policies: fiscal and monetary. It manages the collection and spending of its revenues through **fiscal policies**. Tax increases can function as fiscal policies, not only to increase revenues but to manage the economy as well. Thus, in January 2001, President George W. Bush proposed a tax cut of $1.6 trillion, saying, "A warning light is flashing on the dashboard of the economy. We just can't drive on and hope for the best." Bush was referring to evidence that the economy was slowing—or, more accurately, that its growth rate was decreasing—and was arguing that his tax cut would stimulate renewed economic growth. The administration was calling for government action to bring stability to the economic system.

fiscal policies
Economic policies that determine how the government collects and spends its revenue

monetary policies
Government economic policies that determine the size of a nation's monetary supply

Monetary policies focus on controlling the size of the nation's money supply. Working primarily through the Federal Reserve System (the nation's central bank), the government can influence the ability and willingness of banks throughout the country to lend money. It can also influence the supply of money by prompting interest rates to go up or down.

In the year preceding President Bush's call for a tax cut, the Federal Reserve Bank (the Fed) had cut interest rates six times. Why? Because it saw signs of an economy threatened by both inflation (rising prices) and recession (a slowing growth rate). The power of the Fed to make changes in the supply of money is the centerpiece of the U.S. government's monetary policy. The principle is fairly simple:

■ Higher interest rates make money more expensive to borrow and thereby reduce spending by those who produce goods and services; when the Fed restricts the money supply, we say that it is practicing a *tight monetary policy*.

■ Lower interest rates make money less expensive to borrow and thereby increase spending by those who produce goods and services; when the Fed loosens the money supply—and thus stimulates the economy—we say that it is practicing an *easy monetary policy*. Thus, the Fed cut interest rates several times in late 2001 to help the economy recover from the terrorist attacks in the United States on September 11.

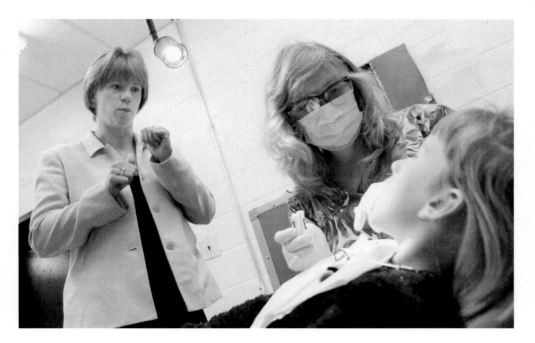

Accountancy, dentistry, and medical technology might not have been the professions of choice during the dot-com boom years of the late 1990s, but they offered steady employment during the recession that followed. Donna Beacham (left) works at Health Promotion Specialists, a South Carolina dentistry company founded in 2000 by Tammi Byrd, a hygienist who responded to the promise of steady employment by opening offices in areas where dental services were scarce. The Department of Commerce predicts that nationwide demand for hygienists will increase 36 percent by 2008.

In short, the Fed can influence the aggregate market for products by influencing the supply of money. Taken together, fiscal policy and monetary policy make up **stabilization policy**: government economic policy whose goal is to smooth out fluctuations in output and unemployment and to stabilize prices.

stabilization policy
Government policy, embracing both fiscal and monetary policies, whose goal is to smooth out fluctuations in output and unemployment and to stabilize prices

The Aftermath of 9/11

At this point, it seems almost trite to say that the events of September 11, 2001, changed things. But there is value in revisiting the tragic events of that day and in examining the ways in which they continue to affect the U.S. economy. In many ways, September 11 demonstrated dramatically that the U.S. business system works. In other ways, the events of that day did indeed change profoundly the way business operates in the United States.[17]

In some ways, the year after September 11, 2001, demonstrated conclusively the resilience of U.S. institutions. The 12 months following the terrorist attacks witnessed a declining stock market, a significant drop in personal wealth, widespread corporate corruption, and as much uncertainty as the nation has faced since the attack on Pearl Harbor in 1941. In the wake of these events, some skeptics—admittedly, those of the gloomiest faction—predicted that the United States was doomed to become a terrorist-racked, depression-ridden nation spiraling out of control.

In reality, the flexibility and strength inherent in the U.S. political and economic systems became just as obvious as their flaws. Most people kept their jobs, and most businesses kept going. Even as some economic sectors declined, others continued to expand. Exports continue to flow into other countries, as did foreign direct investment.

On the other hand, American business now faces major changes. For the last 20 years, the government has maintained a fairly low profile in business-related matters. Since President Ronald Reagan proclaimed in his first inaugural address in 1981 that "government is not the solution to our problems, government is the problem," free markets, deregulation, and private enterprise have carried the day. But history since

Monitoring the capital's major buildings is just one task in safeguarding American lives and property. The federal Office of Homeland Security (*www.whitehouse.gov/ deptofhomeland/*) is responsible for developing programs and standards to protect against and minimize damage from terrorist attacks. Standard & Poor's (*www.standardandpoors.com*) estimates that corporate America spent $70 billion to comply with new security standards in 2002: $35 billion on insurance, $20 billion on work place security upgrades, and $15 billion on information systems backups.

September 11 promises to change all that. Government is already beginning to resume its traditional role as provider of homeland security. In the wake of September 11 and the rash of scandals in corporate governance that dominated the news in 2002, we will probably see more market controls and hear more calls for regulation.

A more specific effect that businesses themselves are already addressing involves workplace security. Gated entrances, restricted access to sensitive areas, and the requirement that visitors sign in and wear badges are longtime practices at many firms. But the events of September 11 have further heightened security concerns in many firms, and many firms have bolstered existing measures. Some are conducting more extensive background checks when hiring new employees. Others have not only beefed up security, both for physical work sites and information networks, but also developed elaborate crisis plans.

The U.S. War with Iraq   In early 2003, the United States led an invasion of Iraq with the stated goal of deposing Saddam Hussein as leader of that country. The war was relatively brief, but the conflict nevertheless resulted in hundreds of civilian causalities and enormous loss of property and damage to infrastructure. The economic implications of the war, meanwhile, are not likely to be fully known for years.

On the one hand, because sanctions imposed after the first Persian Gulf War had made it nearly impossible for Iraq to sell its oil on the world market, the liberation of Iraq will provide a major new energy source for the rest of the world. In addition, businesses from all corners of the world will be called on to help rebuild Iraq, resulting in new jobs and a boost in revenues. President George W. Bush clearly believes that the war will help bring stability to a long-troubled part of the world.

Unfortunately, however, the war created deep divisions among the world's current and emerging economic powerhouses. For example, Great Britain, Spain, and Australia were among those countries that supported the U.S. position, and each provided troops and other support. But France, Germany, and Russia vehemently opposed the war. It remains unclear how quickly disagreements will be overcome and whether opposing views can be resolved in order to reshape global economic patterns.

SELF-CHECK QUESTIONS 7–9

You should now be able to answer Self-Check Questions 7–9.*

7 Multiple Choice Which of the following is **not** generally used as a measure of economic growth? [select one] **(a)** standard of living; **(b)** inflation; **(c)** aggregate output; **(d)** productivity; **(e)** gross domestic product.

8 Multiple Choice Which of the following statements about *gross domestic product* and *gross national product* is **true**? [select one] **(a)** They mean the same thing. **(b)** They mean different things and are usually very different from one another. **(c)** They mean different things but are usually very similar to one another. **(d)** They both lead directly to inflation. **(e)** They are added together to determine purchasing power parity.

9 True or False When the Federal Reserve Board tightens interest rates, the government is exercising fiscal policy.

***Answers to Self-Check Questions 7–9 can be found on p. 507.**

Continued from page 4

BLACKOUTS AND OTHER DARK FORCES

The energy situation in California became dire in late 2000. Weakened by complicated market patterns and the schemes of Enron and other energy providers, the state's ISO could no longer monitor everything, and control of the process was essentially abandoned. An early cold spell in Oregon and Washington forced those states to keep all their surplus energy, thus reducing the supply of power available for sale to California. Meanwhile, Enron and other suppliers had managed to manufacture their own power shortage in California by sending much of their electricity to other markets with higher prices. Blackouts became more common because the electricity supply could not meet consumer demand.

In response, California lifted its price caps, raising the price of a megawatt-hour from $43.80 at the beginning of 2000 to $292.10 at the beginning of 2001. Although the supply of power increased immediately, consumer electric bills shot up by 67 percent, causing a statewide uproar. Price caps were reinstated in June 2001, but only as a temporary measure. Shortly thereafter, Enron began to collapse like a house of cards, and California seems to have been spared future shenanigans. Critics of current measures, however, worry that if price caps are permanently lifted, other companies can step in and do the same sort of things that Enron did.

Although Adam Smith lived in simpler times, it's amazing how well his theories of free enterprise hold up today. But in our complex business world, it is also clear that in the process of amassing profits, businesses that focus exclusively on profits can do a great deal of harm. Although Enron is today's standard for abuse of the free enterprise system, other examples will no doubt emerge in years to come. On the other hand, we shouldn't forget that there are literally thousands of businesses that routinely rely on supply and demand and freedom of choice while applying ethical and socially responsible principles, appropriate corporate strategies, and effective leadership in their pursuit of legitimate goals.

Questions for Discussion

1 What were the basic factors of production used by Enron?

2 Describe the concepts of input and output markets as they apply to Enron's operations.

3 Explain how the concepts of demand and supply affected both Enron's successes and failures.

4 Does the Enron case increase or decrease your confidence in a capitalistic system based on private enterprise?

5 What degree of competition exists in a regulated utility environment? What kind of competition did California attempt to create?

■ SUMMARY OF LEARNING OBJECTIVES

1 Define the nature of U.S. *business* and identify its main goals and functions.

A **business** is an organization that provides goods or services to earn profits. The prospect of earning **profits**—the difference between a business's revenues and expenses—encourages people to open and expand businesses. Businesses produce most of the goods and services that Americans consume and employ most working people. New forms of technology, service businesses, and international opportunities promise to keep production, consumption, and employment growing indefinitely.

2 Describe the different types of *global economic systems* according to the means by which they control the *factors of production* through *input* and *output markets*.

Economic systems differ in the ways in which they manage the five **factors of production** (1) **labor,** or **human resources,** (2) **capital,** (3) **entrepreneurship,** (4) **physical resources,** and (5) **information resources.** A **planned economy** relies on a centralized government to control factors of production and make decisions. Under **communism,** the government owns and operates all sources of production. In a **market economy,** individuals—producers and consumers—control production and allocation decisions through supply and demand. A **market** is a mechanism for exchange between the buyers and sellers of a particular product or service. Sellers can charge what they want, and customers can buy what they choose.

In a market economy, businesses and households interact in two different relationships. In the **input market,** firms buy resources from households, which are thus suppliers. In the **output market,** firms supply goods and services in response to demand on the part of households. The political basis of market processes is **capitalism,** which fosters private ownership of the factors of production and encourages entrepreneurship by offering profits as an incentive. Most countries rely on some form of **mixed market economy**—a system featuring characteristics of both planned and market economies.

3 Show how *markets, demand,* and *supply* affect resource distribution in the United States.

Decisions about what to buy and what to sell are determined by the forces of demand and supply. **Demand** is the willingness and ability of buyers to purchase a product or service. **Supply** is the willingness and ability of producers to offer a product or service for sale. A **demand and supply schedule** reveals the relationships among different levels of demand and supply at different price levels.

4 Identify the elements of *private enterprise* and explain the various degrees of *competition* in the U.S. economic system.

Market economies reflect the operation of a **private enterprise** system—a system that allows individuals to pursue their own interests without government restriction. Private enterprise works according to four principles: (1) private property rights, (2) freedom of choice, (3) profits, and (4) competition. Economists have identified four degrees of **competition** in a private enterprise system: (1) **perfect competition,** (2) **monopolistic competition,** (3) **oligopoly,** and (4) **monopoly.**

5 Explain the importance of the economic environment to business and identify the factors used to evaluate the performance of an economic system.

The overall health of the economic environment—the economic system in which they operate—affects organizations. The two key goals of the U.S. system are economic growth and economic stability. Growth is assessed by **aggregate output.** Among the factors that can inhibit growth, two of the most important are **balance of trade** and the **national debt.** Economic **stability** means that the amount of money available in an economic system and the quantity of goods and services produced in it are growing at about the same rate. There are two key threats to stability: **inflation** and **unemployment.** The government manages the economy through two sets of policies: **fiscal policies** (such as tax increases) and **monetary policies** that focus on controlling the size of the nation's money supply.

■ KEY TERMS

business (p. 4)
profits (p. 4)
economic system (p. 6)
factors of production (p. 6)
labor (or human resources) (p. 6)
capital (p. 6)
entrepreneur (p. 6)
physical resources (p. 7)
information resources (p. 7)
planned economy (p. 8)
market economy (p. 8)
market (p. 9)
input market (p. 9)
output market (p. 9)
capitalism (p. 10)
mixed market economy (p. 10)
privatization (p. 10)
socialism (p. 11)

demand (p. 12)
supply (p. 12)
law of demand (p. 12)
law of supply (p. 12)
demand and supply schedule (p. 12)
demand curve (p. 12)
supply curve (p. 12)
market price (or equilibrium price) (p. 12)
surplus (p. 13)
shortage (p. 15)
private enterprise (p. 16)
competition (p. 16)
perfect competition (p. 16)
monopolistic competition (p. 17)
oligopoly (p. 17)
monopoly (p. 18)
natural monopoly (p. 18)

business cycle (p. 18)
aggregate output (p. 18)
standard of living (p. 19)
gross domestic product (GDP) (p. 19)
nominal GDP (p. 19)
real GDP (p. 19)
productivity (p. 20)
national debt (p. 21)
stability (p. 21)
inflation (p. 22)
consumer price index (p. 22)
unemployment (p. 23)
recession (p. 24)
depression (p. 24)
fiscal policies (p. 24)
monetary policies (p. 24)
stabilization policy (p. 25)

■ QUESTIONS AND EXERCISES

Questions for Review

1 What are the factors of production? Is one factor more important than the others? If so, which one? Why?

2 What is a demand curve? A supply curve? What is the term for the point at which they intersect?

3 What is GDP? Real GDP? What does each measure?

4 Why is inflation both good and bad? How does the government try to control it?

Questions for Analysis

5 In recent years, many countries have moved from planned economies to market economies. Why do you think this has occurred? Can you envision a situation that would cause a resurgence of planned economies?

6 Cite an instance in which a surplus of a product led to decreased prices. Cite an instance in which a shortage led to increased prices. What eventually happened in each case? Why?

7 Explain how current economic indicators such as inflation and unemployment affect you personally. Explain how they will affect you as a manager.

8 At first glance, it might seem as though the goals of economic growth and stability are inconsistent with one another. How can you reconcile this apparent inconsistency?

Application Exercises

9 Visit a local shopping mall or shopping area. List each store that you see and determine what degree of competition it faces in its immediate environment. For example, if there is only one store in the mall that sells shoes, that store represents a monopoly. Note those businesses with direct competitors (two jewelry stores) and show how they compete with one another.

10 Interview a business owner or senior manager. Ask this individual to describe for you the following things: (1) what business functions, if any, he or she outsources; (2) whether or not he or she is focusing more attention on business process management; and (3) how the events of September 11, 2001, have affected his or her work (not so much how it has affected him or her as a human being, but how it has affected the jobs, the organization, and so forth).

BUILDING YOUR BUSINESS SKILLS

PAYING THE PRICE OF DOING E-BUSINESS

This exercise enhances the following SCANS workplace competencies: demonstrating basic skills, demonstrating thinking skills, exhibiting interpersonal skills, and working with information.

Goal
To encourage students to understand how the competitive environment affects a product's price.

The Situation
Assume that you own a local business that provides Internet access to individuals and businesses. Yours is one of four such businesses in the local market. Each one charges the same price: $12 per month for unlimited dial-up service. You also provide e-mail service, as do two of your competitors. Two competitors give users free personal Web pages. One competitor just dropped its price to $10 per month, and the other two have announced that they'll follow suit. Your breakeven price is $7 per customer—that is, you must charge $7 for your service package in order to cover your costs. You are concerned about getting into a price war that may destroy your business.

Method
Divide into groups of four or five people. Each group should develop a general strategy for responding to competitors' price changes. Be sure to consider the following factors:

1 How demand for your product is affected by price changes

2 The number of competitors selling the same or a similar product

3 The methods you can use—other than price—to attract new customers and retain current customers

Analysis
Develop specific pricing strategies based on each of the following situations:

- A month after dropping the price to $10, one of your competitors raises it back to $12.
- Two of your competitors drop their prices even further— to $8 a month. As a result, your business falls off by 25 percent.
- One of the competitors who offers free Web pages announces that the service will become optional for an extra $2 a month.
- Two competitors announce that they will charge individual users $8 a month but will charge a higher price (not yet announced) for businesses.
- All four providers (including you) are charging $8 a month. One goes out of business, and you know that another is in poor financial health.

FOLLOW-UP QUESTIONS
1 Discuss the role that various inducements other than price might play in affecting demand and supply in this market.
2 Is it always in a company's best interest to feature the lowest prices?
3 Eventually, what form of competition is likely to characterize this market?

EXERCISING YOUR ETHICS

PRESCRIBING A DOSE OF COMPETITIVE MEDICINE

The Purpose of the Assignment

Demand and supply are key elements of the U.S. economic system. So, too, is competition. This exercise will challenge you to better understand the ethical dimensions of a system that relies on demand, supply, and competition.

The Situation

You are a businessperson in a small town, where you run one of two local pharmacies. The population and economic base are fairly stable. Each pharmacy controls about 50 percent of the market. Each is reasonably profitable, generating solid if unspectacular revenues.

The Dilemma

You have just been approached by the owner of the other pharmacy. He has indicated an interest either in buying

your pharmacy or in selling his to you. He argues that neither of you can substantially increase your profits and complains that if one pharmacy raises its prices, customers will simply go to the other one. He tells you outright that if you sell to him, he plans to raise prices by 10 percent. He believes that the local market will have to accept the increase for two reasons: (1) The town is too small to attract national competitors, such as Walgreens, and (2) local customers can't go elsewhere to shop because the nearest town with a pharmacy is 40 miles away.

QUESTIONS FOR DISCUSSION

1 What are the roles of supply, demand, and competition in this scenario?
2 What are the underlying ethical issues?
3 What would you do if you were actually faced with this situation?

 ## CRAFTING YOUR BUSINESS PLAN

EXPLORING SOFTWARE FOR A WINNING BUSINESS PLAN

The Purpose of the Assignment

1 To introduce you to the process of navigating the *Business PlanPro (BPP) 2003* software package (Version 6.0).
2 To stimulate your thinking about what's involved in developing a business plan, considering the topics to be included, how to organize the plan, and the format for its effective presentation.

Assignment

Open the Business PlanPro *software. When it asks you to respond, indicate that you want to "create a new business*

plan." Look around BPP's *home page to acquaint yourself with its toolbar including, especially, five icons—Wizard Tasks, Plan Outline, Sample Plans, Plan Review, and Resources—for the current assignment. Then do the following:*

1 Go to the toolbar and click on the "*Wizard Tasks*" icon, which will reveal the list of **EasyPlan Wizard Tasks**. *To do*: (1) Click on each task, from top to bottom in the list, to see the series of tasks, step-by-step, that the *BPP* planning process recommends you consider for developing a business plan. (2) At the far left of the screen is a small box for each task that allows you to expose more detailed subtasks. Click on one of the boxes [+ or −] to see how to reveal and then hide the subtasks.

Are you surprised at the number of tasks? The variety of tasks? Explain.

2 Go to the toolbar and click on the *"Plan Outline"* icon. *To do:* Examine the list of information categories that are included in the *BPP* planning process. Click on an outline topic, such as **1.0 Executive Summary**, and read the *Wizard's Instructions* for writing on that topic in the business plan. Describe how you might use the *"Plan Outline"* information for developing a business plan of your own.

3 Return to the toolbar and click on the *"Sample Plans"* icon. After reading instructions in the **Sample Plan Browser**, do a search using *flower importer* as the key-word. *To do:* Open the sample plan for the flower importer. What is the firm's name? What is its SIC code number? How many pages are listed in the **Table of Contents** for the sample plan?

4 Return to the toolbar and click on the *"Plan Review"* icon. *To do:* Describe how *Plan Review* might be helpful for improving your business plan.

5 Return to the toolbar and click on the *"Resources"* icon. Explore the various kinds of resources for planning. *To do:* Suppose you have a need for *industry data*. How many featured resources are available in *Resources*?

▶ VIDEO EXERCISE

HELPING BUSINESSES DO BUSINESS: U.S. DEPARTMENT OF COMMERCE

Learning Objectives

The purpose of this video is to help you:

1 Understand world economic systems and their effect on competition.
2 Identify the factors of production.
3 Discuss ways in which supply and demand affect a product's price.

Synopsis

The U.S. Department of Commerce (DOC) *(www.commerce.gov)* seeks to support U.S. economic stability and help U.S.-based companies do business in other countries. In contrast to the planned economy of the People's Republic of China, the United States features a market economy in which firms are free to set their own missions and transact business with any other company or individual. They do, however, face some constraints. U.S. firms must comply with governmental regulations that set such standards as minimum safety requirements. When doing business in other countries, they must consider tariffs and other restrictions that govern imports to those markets. In addition, supply and demand affect a company's ability to set prices and generate profits.

DISCUSSION QUESTIONS

1 **For analysis:** If a U.S. company must pay more for factors of production such as human resources, what is the likely effect on its competitiveness in world markets?
2 **For analysis:** Is the equilibrium price for a company's product likely to be the same in every country? Explain your answer.
3 **For application:** To which factors of production might a small U.S. company have the easiest access? How would this access affect the company's competitive position?
4 **For application:** Is a company likely to see more competitors enter a market when supply exceeds demand or when demand exceeds supply?
5 **For debate:** Should the U.S. Department of Commerce, which is funded by tax money, be providing advice and guidance to U.S. companies that want to profit by doing business elsewhere? Support the position you take.

Online Exploration

Visit the U.S. Department of Commerce Web site *(www.commerce.gov)* and follow some of the links from the home page in order to identify some of the agency's resources for business. Also follow the link inviting you to read about the DOC, including its mission and history. What assistance can a U.S. business expect from the DOC? Why would the agency include environmental management on its list of resources for businesses? How do the agency's offerings fulfill its stated mission?

After reading this chapter, you should be able to:

1 Explain how individuals develop their personal *codes of ethics* and why ethics are important in the workplace.

2 Distinguish *social responsibility* from *ethics*, identify *organizational stakeholders*, and characterize social consciousness today.

3 Show how the concept of social responsibility applies both to environmental issues and to a firm's relationships with customers, employees, and investors.

4 Identify four general *approaches to social responsibility* and describe the four steps that a firm must take to implement a social responsibility program.

5 Explain how issues of social responsibility and ethics affect small business.

THE RULES OF TIPPING

Just a few years ago, ImClone *(www.imclone.com)* was a darling of the biotech world. But recent improprieties have caused the firm to crash and burn, and its CEO has been found guilty of numerous criminal charges. The scandal has even rubbed off on popu-

CONDUCTING BUSINESS ETHICALLY AND RESPONSIBLY

"In placing my trade I had no improper information. My transaction was entirely lawful."

—Martha Stewart, on charges of insider trading of ImClone stock

lar lifestyle maven Martha Stewart. Much of the problem, as it turns out, all hinges on who said what, when, and to whom.

Dr. Samuel Waksal spent much of his career as a respected immunologist. But in 1984, he decided to leave the research field and launch a biotech business called ImClone. Its mission was to explore new treatment options for serious illnesses such as cancer. Shortly after launching the company, Waksal hired his brother Harlan, also a physician, to help run it. For the next several years, they struggled to keep the enterprise afloat, dividing their time between seeking investment money and trying to develop drugs that would make them rich.

It seemed that they'd found just the ticket in the early 1990s, when a professional acquaintance, research scientist John Mendelsohn, indicated that he'd made a discovery that might eventually be a major breakthrough in the fight against cancer. Based on

Mendelsohn's preliminary tests, Erbitux, as the new drug was called, seemed to show significant potential for treating certain forms of cancer. With additional funding, Mendelsohn was confident that he could get federal approval to market the drug. The Waksals convinced Mendelsohn to license Erbitux to ImClone.

For the next few years, as the drug was being further developed and refined, Samuel Waksal devoted much of his time to building enthusiasm for Erbitux. After all, a medical breakthrough on the cancer front would have incredible market value. Waksal's marketing efforts paid off. Investors seemed to be lining up at his door, and ImClone became the talk of New York. Mick Jagger came to Waksal's Christmas party, and the Doobie Brothers entertained at the ImClone party at a major cancer-research meeting. Waksal himself partied with Martha Stewart and dated her daughter.

As Erbitux drew closer to becoming a reality, enthusiasm continued to mount. The American Society of Clinical Oncologists predicted that Erbitux would be for the twenty-first century what polio and smallpox vaccines were for the twentieth. Waksal, meanwhile, began dropping hints that the testing process at the Food and Drug Administration (FDA) was going well and that he anticipated full approval just as soon as FDA evaluations were complete.

In the fall of 2001, Bristol-Myers Squibb *(www.bms.com)* announced plans to invest $2 billion in ImClone. In return, the giant drugmaker gained a 20 percent stake in ImClone and a share of the U.S. rights to Erbitux. Fueled in part by the Bristol-Myers investment and in part by Waksal's promotional campaign, ImClone stock, already performing impressively, took off, reaching a high of $75.45 a share in early December 2001. But then a giant shoe dropped.

In early December 2001, rumors began to circulate among key Bristol-Myers and ImClone officials that the Erbitux approval was in trouble. Allegedly, Samuel and Harlan Waksal launched furious lobbying efforts with personal contacts at the FDA in order to get the decision delayed or deferred. On December 6, Harlan sold $50 million of his ImClone stock. On December 26, Samuel learned that the FDA had made up its mind: It had denied the Erbitux application and refused to approve commercial production.

That night and early the next morning, Waksal reportedly relayed this information to certain family members and close friends. On December 27, family members sold more than $9 million in ImClone stock. Waksal tried to unload $5 million in ImClone stock but was refused by his broker, who had already put a hold on all ImClone transactions. On the same day, good friend Martha Stewart sold 3,928 shares of ImClone. Responding to suggestions that she had acted on the basis of inside information, Stewart stated, "In placing my trade I had no improper information. My transaction was entirely lawful. After directing my broker to sell, I called Dr. Waksal's office to inquire about ImClone. I did not reach Dr. Waksal and he did not return my call."

The official FDA announcement came on December 28. On December 31, the first day of trading after the announcement, the volume of ImClone trading increased 179 percent as its value dropped 15 percent. Throughout the spring of 2002, ImClone stock continued to plummet, and by June 2002, it stood at a measly $7.83 a share. The ImClone board persuaded Samuel Waksal to resign because the Securities and Exchange Commission (SEC) investigation into his actions was hurting the firm's performance.

On June 12, 2002, the FBI arrested Samuel Waksal, charging him with insider trading and obstruction of justice. Although no other formal charges were filed at that time, investigators continued to look into Harlan Waksal's stock sale of December 6 and Stewart's sale of December 27. Things remained quiet for several weeks, but so far, only one shoe had dropped.

Our opening story continues on page 62.

ETHICS IN THE WORKPLACE

Just what is ethical behavior? **Ethics** are beliefs about what's right and wrong or good and bad. An individual's values and morals, plus the social context in which his or her behavior occurs, determine whether behavior is regarded as ethical or unethical. In other words, **ethical behavior** conforms to individual beliefs and social norms about what's right and good. **Unethical behavior** is behavior that individual beliefs and social norms define as wrong and bad. **Business ethics** is a term often used to refer to ethical or unethical behaviors by employees of commercial organizations.

> **ethics**
> Beliefs about what is right and wrong or good and bad in actions that affect others

Individual Ethics

Because ethics are based on both individual beliefs and social concepts, they vary from person to person, from situation to situation, and from culture to culture. Social standards are broad enough to support differences in beliefs. Without violating general standards, therefore, people may develop personal codes of ethics reflecting a wide range of attitudes and beliefs.

> **ethical behavior**
> Behavior conforming to generally accepted social norms concerning beneficial and harmful actions

Thus, ethical and unethical behavior is determined partly by the individual and partly by the culture. For instance, virtually everyone would agree that if you see someone drop a $20 bill, it would be ethical to return it to the owner. But there'll be less agreement if you find $20 and don't know who dropped it. Should you turn it in to the lost-and-found department? Or, since the rightful owner isn't likely to claim it, can you just keep it?

> **unethical behavior**
> Behavior that does not conform to generally accepted social norms concerning beneficial and harmful actions

Ambiguity, the Law, and the Real World Societies generally adopt formal laws that reflect prevailing ethical standards or social norms. For example, because most people regard theft as unethical, we have laws against such behavior and ways of punishing those who steal. We try to make unambiguous laws, but interpreting and applying them can still lead to ethical ambiguities. Real-world situations can often be interpreted in different ways, and it isn't always easy to apply statutory standards to real-life behavior. Samuel Waksal has been charged with insider trading for tipping off certain investors, such as Martha Stewart and members of his own family, about the impending fall of ImClone stock.

> **business ethics**
> Ethical or unethical behaviors by a manager or employer of an organization

But what about the behavior of Stewart? She says that she'd already ordered her broker to sell the stock if it slipped below $60. Whether she had or hadn't, she's widely suspected of questionable behavior, and the stock of her own company, Martha Stewart Living Omnimedia, has dropped 60 percent. Meanwhile, Waksal's daughter, who also sold her ImClone stock after getting information from her father, has so far been treated as an "innocent tippee"—someone who got inside information but didn't think that's what it was at the time.[1]

Unfortunately, the epidemic of recent scandals ranging from Enron and Arthur Andersen to Tyco and WorldCom only serves to show how willing people can be to take advantage of potentially ambiguous situations—indeed, to create them. In 1997, a U.S. company named Tyco *(www.tyco.com)* effectively sold itself in a merger with a firm called ADT Ltd. ADT was smaller than Tyco, but because its new parent company was based in the tax haven of Bermuda, Tyco no longer had to pay U.S. taxes on its non-U.S. income. In 2000 and 2001, Tyco's subsidiaries in such tax-friendly nations doubled from 75 to 150, and the company slashed its 2001 U.S. tax bill by $600 million. "Tyco," complained a U.S. congressman, "has raised

> *"Tyco has raised tax avoidance to an art."*
>
> **—Congressman Richard E. Neal**

tax avoidance to an art," but one tax expert replies that Tyco's schemes "are very consistent with the [U.S.] tax code."[2]

Individual Values and Codes How should we deal with business behavior that we regard as unethical—especially when it's legally ambiguous? No doubt we have to start with the individuals in a business—its managers, employees, agents, and other legal representatives. Each of these people's personal code of ethics is determined by a combination of factors. We start to form ethical standards as children in response to our perceptions of the behavior of parents and other adults. Soon we enter school, where we're influenced by peers, and as we grow into adulthood, experience shapes our lives and contributes to our ethical beliefs and our behavior. We also develop values and morals that contribute to ethical standards. If you put financial gain at the top of your priority list, you may develop a code of ethics that supports the pursuit of material comfort. If you set family and friends as a priority, you'll no doubt adopt different standards.

Business and Managerial Ethics

managerial ethics
Standards of behavior that guide individual managers in their work

Managerial ethics are the standards of behavior that guide individual managers in their work. Although your ethics can affect your work in any number of ways, it's helpful to classify them in terms of three broad categories.

Behavior Toward Employees This category covers such matters as hiring and firing, wages and working conditions, and privacy and respect. Ethical and legal guidelines suggest that hiring and firing decisions should be based solely on ability to perform a job. A manager who discriminates against African Americans in hiring exhibits both unethical and illegal behavior. But what about the manager who hires a friend or relative when someone else might be more qualified? Although such decisions may not be illegal, they may be objectionable on ethical grounds.

Wages and working conditions, though regulated by law, are also areas for controversy. Consider a manager who pays a worker less than he deserves because the manager knows that the employee can't afford to quit or risk his job by complaining. While some people will see the behavior as unethical, others will see it as smart business. Cases such as these are hard enough to judge, but consider the behavior of Enron management toward company employees. It encouraged employees to invest retirement funds in company stock and then, when financial problems began to surface, refused to permit them to sell the stock (even though top officials were allowed to sell). Ultimately, the firm's demise cost thousands of jobs.

Behavior Toward the Organization Ethical issues also arise from employee behavior toward employers, especially in such areas as conflict of interest, confidentiality, and honesty. A *conflict of interest* occurs when an activity may benefit the individual to the detriment of his or her employer. Most companies have policies that forbid buyers from accepting gifts from suppliers. Businesses in highly competitive industries—software and fashion apparel, for example—have safeguards against designers selling company secrets to competitors.

Relatively common problems in the general area of honesty include such behavior as stealing supplies, padding expense accounts, and using a business phone to make personal long-distance calls. Most employees are honest, but most organizations are nevertheless vigilant. Again, Enron is a good example of employees' unethical behavior toward an organization. Top managers not only misused corporate assets, but also they often committed the company to risky ventures in order to further personal interests.

In Houston, former employees protest their treatment by Enron (left), which laid off or suspended 7,500 workers in December 2001. In October and November, Enron had barred employees from selling any company stock in their retirement accounts, and as the value of the stock plummeted, many lost 70–90 percent of their retirement assets. In February 2002, former Enron chairman Kenneth L. Lay (right) told Congress that he felt "a profound sadness about what has happened to . . . current and former employees [and] retirees." During the freeze of employee assets, Lay reportedly sold Enron stock worth $101.3 million.

Behavior Toward Other Economic Agents Ethics also comes into play in the relationship between the firm and its employees with so-called *primary agents of interest*—mainly customers, competitors, stockholders, suppliers, dealers, and unions. In dealing with such agents, there is room for ethical ambiguity in just about every activity—advertising, financial disclosure, ordering and purchasing, bargaining and negotiation, and other business relationships.

For example, businesses in the pharmaceuticals industry are under criticism because of the rising prices of drugs. They argue that high prices cover the costs of research and development programs to develop new drugs. The solution to such problems seems obvious: Find the right balance between reasonable pricing and *price gouging* (responding to increased demand with overly steep price increases). But like so many questions involving ethics, there are significant differences of opinion about the proper balance.[3]

Another recent area of concern is financial reporting, especially by high-tech firms like WorldCom. Some of these companies have been very aggressive in presenting their financial positions in a positive light, and in a few cases, they have overstated earnings projections in order to entice more investment.[4] Certainly, Samuel Waksal's aggressive promotion of ImClone stock fits into this category. And, again, there's Enron.

- Senior officials continued to mislead investors into thinking that the firm was solvent long after they knew that it was in serious trouble.
- The company violated numerous state regulations during the California energy crisis, causing thousands of consumers hardships and inconvenience.
- Many of its partnerships with other firms violated terms of full disclosure and honesty, resulting in losses for other firms and their employees.

Another problem is global variation in business practices. In many countries, bribes are a normal part of doing business. U.S. law, however, forbids bribes, even if rivals from other countries are paying them. A U.S. power-generating company recently lost a $320 million contract in the Middle East because it refused to pay bribes that a Japanese firm used to get the job.

Say WHAT YOU MEAN

THE ETHICAL SOFT-SHOE

To bribe or not to bribe? That is the question. Well, actually, it's not really a question at all because the textbook answer is a non-negotiable no. No matter what business environment you're in, whatever culture or country you're in, the answer is always no.

In reality, of course, it's a little more complicated than that. Business dealings that ignore the strict letter of the law happen all the time—more so in some countries than in others. Not just bribes, but offering or accepting incentives to get things done or extracting a personal favor or two. In reality, we do it all the time in the United States—using the power and influence of people we know to get things done the way we want. Granted, American business practices overseas are subject to certain constraints, such as those embodied in the Foreign Corrupt Practices Act.

Elsewhere, however, the answer to the question is not necessarily no. A hallmark of Brazilian business culture, for example, is a creative approach to problem solving known as *jeitinho*. *Jeitinho* means "to find a way." For Brazilians, there's always another way to get something done. If you need some kind of official document, for instance, you might set out on the straight and narrow path, determined to take all the proper bureaucratic steps to get it. Unfortunately, you may soon find yourself in a maze of rules and regulations from which it's impossible to extricate yourself. That's when you're most likely to resort to *jeitinho*—using personal connections, bending the rules, making a "contribution," or simply approaching the problem from a different angle.

The focus of *jeitinho* appears to be on the goal—in this case, on obtaining a document. For Brazilians, however, it's really on the *process of accomplishing it*—on being willing and able to find another way no matter what the obstacle. After all, every obstacle forces you in another direction, and during the process of negotiating the maze, you may even be forced to change your original destination. *Jeitinho* almost never involves butting heads with authority. Rather, it's a complex dance that enables individuals to go around problems instead of having to go through them. It's a philosophy in which ends justify a sometimes complicated web of means.

But of course, even if you're operating in a country (like Brazil) in which sidestepping the rules is business as usual, you don't *have* to do an ethical soft-shoe. In fact, many global companies have strict ethical guidelines for doing business, and the steps generally don't change just because you're dancing with a foreign partner. The key is understanding the culture of the host country—observing the way business is conducted and preparing yourself for any challenges—before you get out on the dance floor.

Assessing Ethical Behavior

What distinguishes ethical from unethical behavior is often subjective and subject to differences of opinion.[5] So how can we decide whether a particular action or decision is ethical? Figure 2.1 presents a simplified three-step model for applying ethical judgments to situations that may arise during the course of business activities:

1 Gather the relevant factual information.
2 Analyze the facts to determine the most appropriate moral values.
3 Make an ethical judgment based on the rightness or wrongness of the proposed activity or policy.

Unfortunately, the process doesn't always work as smoothly as the scheme in Figure 2.1 suggests. What if the facts aren't clear-cut? What if there are no agreed-upon moral values? Nevertheless, a judgment and a decision must be made. Experts point out that, otherwise, trust is impossible. And trust is indispensable in any business transaction.

In order to assess more fully the ethics of specific behavior, we need a more complex perspective. Consider a common dilemma faced by managers with expense

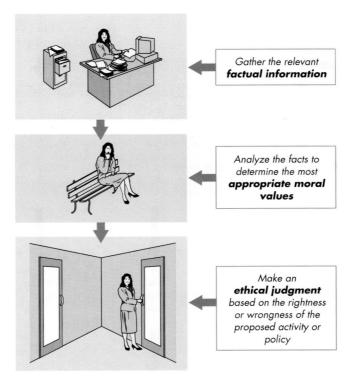

FIGURE 2.1

Steps in Making Ethical
Judgments

Gather the relevant **factual information**

Analyze the facts to determine the most **appropriate moral values**

Make an **ethical judgment** based on the rightness or wrongness of the proposed activity or policy

accounts. Companies routinely provide managers with accounts to cover work-related expenses—hotel bills, meals, rental cars, or taxis—when they're traveling on company business or entertaining clients for business purposes. They expect employees to claim only work-related expenses.

For example, if a manager takes a client to dinner and spends $100, submitting a $100 reimbursement receipt for that dinner is accurate and appropriate. But suppose that our manager has a $100 dinner the next night with a good friend for purely social purposes. Submitting that receipt for reimbursement would be unethical, but some managers rationalize that it's okay to submit a receipt for dinner with a friend. Perhaps they'll tell themselves that they're underpaid and just "recovering" income due to them.

Ethical *norms* also come into play in a case like this. Consider four such norms and the issues they entail:[6]

■ *Utility*: Does a particular act optimize the benefits to those who are affected by it?
■ *Rights*: Does it respect the rights of the individuals involved?
■ *Justice*: Is it consistent with what's fair?
■ *Caring*: Is it consistent with people's responsibilities to each other?

Figure 2.2 is an expanded version of Figure 2.1 that incorporates the consideration of these ethical norms.

Now let's return to our case of the inflated expense account. Although the utility norm acknowledges that the manager benefits from a padded account, others, such as coworkers and owners, don't. Most experts would also agree that the act doesn't respect the rights of others (such as investors, who have to foot the bill). Moreover, it's clearly unfair and compromises the manager's responsibilities to others. This particular act, then, appears to be clearly unethical.

Figure 2.2, however, also provides mechanisms for dealing with unique circumstances—those that apply only in limited situations. Suppose, for example, that our manager loses the receipt for the legitimate dinner but retains the receipt for the social dinner. Some people will now argue that it's okay to submit the illegitimate receipt because the manager is only doing so to get proper reimbursement. Others, however,

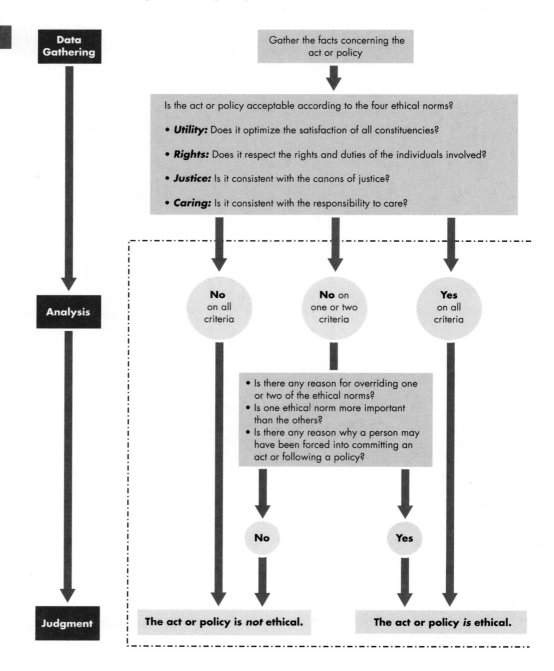

FIGURE 2.2

Expanded Model of Ethical
Judgment Making

will reply that submitting the alternative receipt is wrong under any circumstances. We won't pretend to arbitrate the case, and we will simply make the following point: Changes in most situations can make ethical issues either more or less clear-cut.

Company Practices and Business Ethics

As unethical and even illegal activities by both managers and employees plague more and more companies, many firms have taken additional steps to encourage ethical behavior in the workplace. Many set up codes of conduct and develop clear ethical positions on how the firm and its employees will conduct business. An increasingly controversial area regarding business ethics and company practices involves the privacy of e-mail and other communications that take place inside an organization.

Perhaps the single most effective step that a company can take is to demonstrate top management support of ethical standards. This policy contributes to a corporate culture that values ethical standards and announces that the firm is as concerned with good citizenship as with profits. When United Technologies (UT) *(www.utc.com)*, a Connecticut-based industrial conglomerate, published its 21-page code of ethics, it also named a vice president for business practices to see that UT conducted business ethically and responsibly. With a detailed code of ethics and a senior official to enforce it, the firm sends a signal that it expects ethical conduct from its employees. Two of the most common approaches to formalizing top management commitment to ethical business practices are adopting written codes and instituting ethics programs.

Adopting Written Codes Many companies have written codes that formally announce their intent to do business in an ethical manner. The number of such companies has risen dramatically in the last three decades, and today almost all major corporations have written codes of ethics. Even Enron had a code of ethics, but managers must follow the code if it's going to work. On one occasion, Enron's board of directors voted to set aside the code in order to complete a deal that would have violated it.

Figure 2.3 illustrates the role that corporate ethics and values should play in corporate policy. You can use it to see how a good ethics statement might be structured. Basically, the figure suggests that although strategies and practices can change frequently and objectives can change occasionally, an organization's core principles and values should remain steadfast. Hewlett-Packard *(www.hp.com)*, for example, has had the same written code of ethics, called *The HP Way*, since 1957. Its essential elements are as follows:

- We have trust and respect for individuals.
- We focus on a high level of achievement and contribution.
- We conduct our business with uncompromising integrity.
- We achieve our common objectives through teamwork.
- We encourage flexibility and innovation.

Instituting Ethics Programs Many examples suggest that ethical responses can be learned through experience. For instance, in a classic case some years ago, a corporate saboteur poisoned Tylenol capsules, resulting in the deaths of several consumers. Employees at Johnson & Johnson *(www.jnj.com)*, maker of Tylenol, all knew that without waiting for instructions or a company directive, they should get to retailers' shelves and pull the product as quickly as possible. In retrospect, they reported simply

FIGURE 2.3

Core Principles and Organizational Values

ENTREPRENEURSHIP and *New Ventures*

The Electronic Equivalent of Paper Shredding

In virtually every major corporate scandal of the last few years, the best-laid plans of managerial miscreants have come unraveled, at least in part, when supposedly private e-mail surfaced as a key piece of evidence. At Citigroup *(www.citigroup.com)*, for example, analyst Jack Grubman changed stock recommendations in exchange for favors from CEO Sandy Weill and then sent an e-mail to confirm the arrangement. Investigators found that David Duncan, Arthur Andersen's head Enron auditor, had deleted incriminating e-mails shortly after the start of the Justice Department's investigation. After Tim Newington, an analyst for Credit Suisse First Boston *(www.csfb.com)*, refused to give in to pressure to change a client's credit rating, an e-mail circulated on the problem of Newington's troublesome integrity: "Bigger issue," warned an upper manager, "is what to do about Newington in general. I'm not sure he's salvageable at this point."

Not surprisingly, many corporations are nervous about the potential liability that employee e-mail may incur, but some entrepreneurs detect an opportunity in this same concern. A few software-development houses are busily designing programs to meet the needs of cautious corporate customers.

Products from Tumbleweed Communications *(www.tumbleweed.com)* encrypt e-mail messages so that only intended recipients can view them. Tumbleweed software is sophisticated enough to analyze messages and can ensure, for example, that the word *breast* is acceptable only if it occurs in the vicinity of the word *chicken*. It also searches for banned words, especially those related to dubious activities. Questionable messages are blocked and rerouted to supervisors for review.

Software from Authentica *(www.authentica.com)* controls e-mail routing. Rebecca Burr of chipmaker Xilinx relies on it to secure confidential information. "It would be my worst nightmare," she explains, "if the competition knew our product strategy or had our pricing books." Start-up Omniva Policy Systems—whose Web site appears at *(www.disappearing.com)*—uses ultra-secure 128-bit encryption. Senders specify an expiration date after which garbled messages can no longer be decrypted—the electronic equivalent of paper shredding. In addition, Omniva software can also prevent resending or printing, and users cannot unilaterally delete their own e-mail on their own initiative. In the event of a lawsuit or investigation, administrators can hit a "red button" that prevents all deletions.

"Our goal," says Omniva CEO Kumar Sreekanti, "is to keep the honest people honest. . . . We help organizations comply with regulations automatically so they don't have to rely on people to do it." Removing responsibility (and temptation) has become an increasingly popular strategy among executives who, like those at Metropolitan Life, the CIA, drugmaker Eli Lilly, and many other organizations, are looking to e-mail–security systems to help them avoid the kind of exposure encountered by Citigroup, Arthur Andersen, and Credit Suisse.

> *"We help organizations comply with regulations automatically so they don't have to rely on people to do it."*
>
> **—CEO Kumar Sreekanti of Omniva Policy Systems, on keeping e-mailers honest**

knowing that this was what the company would want to do. But can business ethics be taught, either in the workplace or in schools? Not surprisingly, business schools have become important players in the debate about ethics education. Most analysts agree that even though business schools must address the issue of ethics in the workplace, companies must take the chief responsibility for educating employees. In fact, more and more firms are doing so.

For example, both ExxonMobil *(www.exxonmobil.com/overview)* and Boeing *(www.boeing.com/companyoffices/aboutus/ethics)* have major ethics programs. All managers must go through periodic ethics training to remind them of the importance of ethical decision making and to update them on the most current laws and regulations that might be particularly relevant to their firms. Others, such as Texas Instruments *(www.ti.com)*, have ethical hot lines—numbers that an employee can call, either to discuss the ethics of a particular problem or situation or to report unethical behavior or activities by others.

"From a purely business viewpoint, taking what doesn't belong to you is usually the cheapest way to go."

SELF-CHECK QUESTIONS 1–3

You should now be able to answer Self-Check Questions 1–3.*

1 **Multiple Choice** Suppose a manager cheats on an expense account. Into which of the following areas of managerial *ethics* does this behavior fall? [select one] **(a)** organizational behavior toward other economic agents; **(b)** employee behavior toward the organization; **(c)** organizational behavior toward the employee; **(d)** individual behavior toward other economic agents; **(e)** behavior of other economic agents toward the organization.

2 **Multiple Choice** Which of the following is **not** one of the norms for assessing *ethical behavior* discussed in this section? [select one] **(a)** utility; **(b)** rights; **(c)** justice; **(d)** caring; **(e)** regulation.

3 **True/False** Every business is legally required to develop and publish a corporate *code of ethics*.

***Answers to Self-Check Questions 1–3 can be found on p. 507.**

■ SOCIAL RESPONSIBILITY

Ethics affect individual behavior in the workplace. **Social responsibility** is a related concept, but it refers to the overall way in which a business itself tries to balance its commitments to relevant groups and individuals in its social environment.[7] These groups and individuals are often called **organizational stakeholders**—those groups, individuals, and organizations that are directly affected by the practices of an organization and, therefore, have a stake in its performance.[8] Major corporate stakeholders are identified in Figure 2.4.

social responsibility
The attempt of a bussiness to balance its commitments to groups and individuals in its environment, including customers, other businesses, employees, investors, and local communities.

organizational stakeholders
Those groups, individuals, and organizations that are directly affected by the practices of an organization and who therefore have a stake in its performance

The Stakeholder Model of Responsibility

Most companies that strive to be responsible to their stakeholders concentrate first and foremost on five main groups: *customers, employees, investors, suppliers,* and the

FIGURE 2.4

Major Corporate Stakeholders

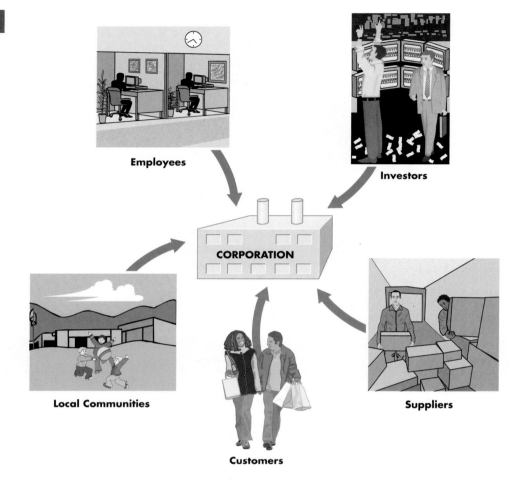

local communities where they do business. They may then select other stakeholders that are particularly relevant or important to the organization and try to address their needs and expectations as well.

Customers Businesses that are responsible to their customers strive to treat them fairly and honestly. They also seek to charge fair prices, honor warranties, meet delivery commitments, and stand behind the quality of the products they sell. L.L. Bean *(www.llbean.com)*, Lands' End *(www.landsend.com)*, Dell Computer *(www.dell.com)*, and Johnson & Johnson *(www.jnj.com)* are among those companies with excellent reputations in this area. In recent years, many small banks have increased their profits by offering much stronger customer service than the large national banks (such as Wells Fargo and Bank of America). For instance, some offer their customers free Starbucks coffee and child care while they are in the bank conducting business. According to Gordon Goetzmann, a leading financial services executive, "Big banks just don't get it" when it comes to understanding what customers want. As a result, small bank profits have been growing at a rate of 11.8 percent annually, while profits for the larger chain banks have remained around 8.5 percent.[9]

> **"Big banks just don't get it."**
>
> **—Gordon Geotzmann, financial services expert on why service-oriented small banks are growing faster**

Employees Businesses that are socially responsible in their dealings with employees treat workers fairly, make them a part of the team, and respect their dignity and basic human needs. Organizations such as MBNA *(www.mbna.com/about_careers)*,

In August 2000, Bridgestone/Firestone Inc. *(www.firestone.com)* announced a consumer-protection recall of 6.5 million light-truck tires that blew or lost tread and that may have contributed to dozens of fatal accidents. The cost to the tire manufacturer was $350 million. The cost to Ford Motor Co. *(www.ford.com)*, which had installed—and issued warranties for—most of those 6.5 million tires on its sport-utility vehicles, ran to $500 million. The next year, following further consumer-protection measures, Ford took an after-tax charge of $2.1 billion to replace another 13 million Firestone tires.

Continental Airlines *(www.continental.com)*, 3M Corporation *(www.3m.com)*, Hoechst Celanese *(www.hoechst.com)*, and Southwest Airlines *(www.southwest.com)* have all established strong reputations in this area. In addition, many of the same firms also go to great lengths to find, hire, train, and promote qualified minorities. Each year, *Fortune* magazine publishes lists of the best companies to work for in America and the best companies for minorities. These lists, in turn, attract more individuals who are anxious to work for such highly regarded employers.

Investors To maintain a socially responsible stance toward investors, managers should follow proper accounting procedures, provide appropriate information to shareholders about financial performance, and manage the organization to protect shareholder rights and investments. These managers should be accurate and candid in assessing future growth and profitability, and they should avoid even the appearance of impropriety in such sensitive areas as insider trading, stock price manipulation, and the withholding of financial data.

In 2002, for example, WorldCom, a giant telecommunications business and owner of MCI, announced that it had overstated previous years' earnings by as much as $6 billion. The SEC also announced that it was investigating the firm's accounting practices, and investors learned that the firm had lent CEO Bernard Ebbers $366 million that he might not be able to repay. On the heels of these problems, WorldCom's stock price dropped by over 43 percent, and the company eventually had to seek bankruptcy protection as it attempted to dig out of the hole it had created for itself.[10]

Suppliers Relations with suppliers should also be managed with care. For example, it might be easy for a large corporation to take advantage of suppliers by imposing unrealistic delivery schedules and reducing profit margins by constantly pushing for lower and lower prices. Many firms now recognize the importance of mutually beneficial partnership arrangements with suppliers. Thus, they keep them informed about future plans, negotiate delivery schedules and prices that are acceptable to both firms, and so forth. Ford *(www.ford.com)* and Wal-Mart *(www.walmart.com)* are among the firms acknowledged to have excellent relationships with their suppliers.

Local Communities Finally, most businesses try to be socially responsible to their local communities. They may contribute to local programs like Little League baseball,

Abigail Martínez used to make 55 cents an hour sewing clothes for 18 hours a day in an El Salvador factory that had neither ventilation nor drinkable water. Then Gap *(www.gap.com)*, one of the factory's biggest customers, stepped in to demand improved conditions. The factory is now cooled by breezes, there's an out-door cafeteria, and managers don't lock the restrooms. Unfortunately for laborers in El Salvador, the only alternative to subsistence-level work is no work. Besides, the name of the game is still holding down costs, especially labor costs, so Martínez now makes just 60 cents an hour.

get actively involved in charitable programs like the United Way, and strive to simply be good corporate citizens by minimizing their negative impact on the community. Target stores *(www.targetcorp.com)*, for example, donate a percentage of sales to the local communities where they do business.

The stakeholder model can also provide some helpful insights on the conduct of managers in international business. In particular, to the extent that an organization acknowledges its commitments to its stakeholders, it should also recognize that it has multiple sets of stakeholders in each country where it does business. DaimlerChrysler *(www.daimlerchrysler.com)*, for example, has investors not only in Germany but also in the United States, Japan, and other countries where its shares are publicly traded. It also has suppliers, employees, and customers in multiple countries, and its actions affect many different communities in dozens of different countries. Similarly, international businesses must also address their responsibilities in areas such as wages, working conditions, and environmental protection across different countries that have varying laws and norms regulating such responsibilities.

Contemporary Social Consciousness

Social consciousness and views toward social responsibility continue to evolve. The business practices of such entrepreneurs as John D. Rockefeller, J. P. Morgan, and Cornelius Vanderbilt raised concerns about abuses of power and led to the nation's first laws regulating basic business practices. In the 1930s, many people blamed the Great Depression on a climate of business greed and lack of restraint. Out of this economic turmoil emerged new laws that dictated an expanded role for business in protecting and enhancing the general welfare of society.

In the 1960s and 1970s, business was again characterized as a negative social force. Some critics even charged that defense contractors had helped to promote the Vietnam War to spur their own profits. Eventually, increased social activism prompted increased government regulation in a variety of areas. Health warnings were placed on cigarettes, for instance, and stricter environmental protection laws were enacted.

During the 1980s and 1990s, the general economic prosperity enjoyed in most sectors of the economy led to another period of laissez-faire attitudes toward business. Although there was the occasional scandal or major business failure, people for the most part seemed to view business as a positive force in society and one that was generally able to police itself through self-control and free market forces. And many businesses continue to operate in enlightened and socially responsible ways. For example, retailers such as Sears *(www.sears.com)* and Target have policies against selling handguns and other weapons. Likewise, national toy retailers KayBee and Toys "R" Us *(www.toysrus.com)* refuse to sell toy guns that look too realistic. And Anheuser Busch promotes the concept of responsible drinking in some of its advertising.

Firms in numerous other industries have also integrated socially conscious thinking into their production plans and marketing efforts. The production of environmentally safe products has become a potential boom area as many companies introduce products designed to be environmentally friendly. Electrolux, a Swedish appliance maker *(www.electrolux.com)*, has developed a line of water-efficient washing machines, a solar-powered lawn mower, and ozone-free refrigerators. Ford *(www.ford.com)* has set up an independent brand called Think to develop and market low-pollution, electric-powered vehicles.[11]

Unfortunately, the spate of corporate scandals and incredible revelations in the last few years may revive negative attitudes and skepticism toward business. As just a single illustration, there was widespread moral outrage when some of the perquisites provided to former Tyco International CEO Dennis Kozlowski were made public in 2002. These perks included such extravagances as a $50 million mansion in Florida and an $18 million apartment in New York, along with $11 million for antiques and furnishings (including a $6,000 shower curtain). The firm even paid for a $2.1 million birthday party for Kozlowski's wife in Italy. It's not as though Kozlowski was a pauper—he earned almost $300 million between 1998 and 2001 in salary, bonuses, and stock proceeds. (Kozlowski is now under investigation for tax evasion.)[12]

In Washington, critics and government officials alike are already calling for tighter standards for business practices and increased control on accounting procedures. And to the extent that society begins to see economic problems as stemming from irresponsible business activities and unethical executive conduct, there may indeed be a return to the mind-set of the 1930s. Such a shift could result in business being seen as less capable of controlling itself and thus requiring increased control and constraint by the government.[13]

SELF-CHECK QUESTIONS 4–6

You should now be able to answer Self-Check Questions 4–6.*

4 **True/False** Though closely related, *ethics* and *social responsibility* do not mean the same thing.

5 **Multiple Choice** The *stakeholder model of social responsibility* generally includes which of the following? [select one] **(a)** customers; **(b)** employees; **(c)** suppliers; **(d)** investors; **(e)** all of these.

6 **Multiple Choice** Contemporary social consciousness toward business currently reflects which of the following? [select one] **(a)** universal admiration; **(b)** calls for higher taxes; **(c)** universal condemnation; **(d)** growing skepticism and concern regarding responsible corporate governance; **(e)** a laissez-faire philosophy.

*Answers to Self-Check Questions 4–6 can be found on p. 507.

■ AREAS OF SOCIAL RESPONSIBILITY

When defining its sense of social responsibility, a firm typically confronts four areas of concern: responsibilities toward the *environment*, its *customers*, its *employees*, and its *investors*.

Responsibility Toward the Environment

During the first several months of his administration, the harshest criticism directed at President George W. Bush was leveled at his environmental policies. For example, he openly championed proposals for oil exploration in protected areas of Alaska, and he has steadfastly rejected the proposals of the 1997 Kyoto Protocol dealing with global warming. Most of the world's major countries endorsed that agreement, designed to slow global warming, but the United States has been condemned for its refusal to participate. "We know the surface temperature of the earth is rising," admits Bush, but he argues that his policies reflect a sound combination of free market expansion and exploration balanced against environmental protection and conservation.

Figure 2.5, however, tells a troubling story. The chart shows atmospheric carbon dioxide (CO_2) levels for the period between 1750 and 2000, and it offers three possible scenarios for future levels under different sets of conditions. The three projections—lowest, middle, highest—were developed by the Intergovernmental Panel on Climate Change *(www.ipcc.ch)*, which calculated likely changes in the atmosphere during this century if no efforts were made to reduce so-called greenhouse emissions—waste industrial gases that trap heat in the atmosphere. The criteria for estimating changes are population, economic growth, energy supplies, and technologies: The less pressure exerted by these conditions, the less the increase in CO_2 levels. Energy supplies are measured in *exajoules*—roughly the annual energy consumption of the New York metropolitan area.

Under the lowest, or best-case, scenario, by 2100 the population would only grow to 6.4 billion people, economic growth would be no more than 1.2 to 2.0 percent a

When President George W. Bush met with leaders of the European Union in Goteborg, Sweden, protestors gathered to pillory his papier-mâché image. The main bone of contention—between Bush and European leaders as well as Bush and European protestors—was what to do about global warming. Although no EU government ever ratified the agreement, the Europeans support the so-called Kyoto Protocol, which calls for industrialized nations to reduce greenhouse gas emissions below 1990 levels. Bush argues that we can cut global warming and do less damage to the economy by developing new technologies.

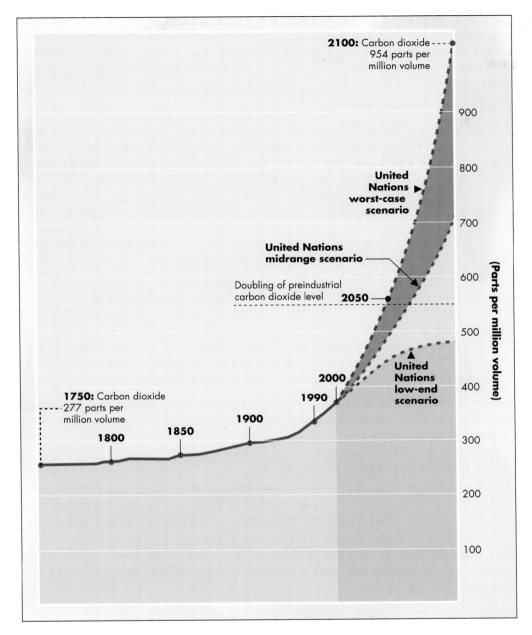

FIGURE 2.5
CO$_2$ Emissions, Past and Future

year, and energy supplies would require only 8,000 exajoules of conventional oil. However, under the highest, or worst-case, scenario, the population would increase to 11.3 billion people, annual economic growth would be between 3.0 and 3.5 percent, and energy supplies would require as much as 18,400 exajoules of conventional oil.

The resulting changes in climate would be relatively mild; we would hardly experience any day-to-day changes in the weather. We would, however, increase the likelihood of having trouble-some weather around the globe: droughts, hurricanes, winter sieges, and so forth. The charges leveled against greenhouse emissions are disputed, but as one researcher puts it, "The only way to prove them for sure is hang around 10, 20, or 30 more years, when the evidence would be overwhelming. But in the meantime, we're conducting a global experiment. And we're all in the test tube."[14]

"In the meantime, we're conducting a global experiment. And we're all in the test tube."

—Researcher on greenhouse emissions

Controlling *pollution*—the injection of harmful substances into the environment—is a significant challenge for contemporary business. Although noise pollution is now attracting increased concern, air, water, and land pollution remains the greatest problem in need of solutions from governments and businesses alike. In the following sections, we focus on the nature of the problems in these areas and on some of the current efforts to address them.

Air Pollution   Air pollution results when several factors combine to lower air quality. Carbon monoxide emitted by automobiles contributes to air pollution, as do smoke and other chemicals from manufacturing plants. Air quality is usually worst in certain geographic locations, such as the Denver area and the Los Angeles basin, where pollutants tend to get trapped in the atmosphere. For this very reason, the air around Mexico City is generally considered to be the most polluted in the entire world.

Legislation has gone a long way toward controlling air pollution. Under new laws, many companies must now install special devices to limit the pollutants they expel into the air. But such efforts are costly. Air pollution is compounded by such problems as acid rain, which occurs when sulfur is pumped into the atmosphere, mixes with natural moisture, and falls to the ground as rain. Much of the damage to forests and streams in the eastern United States and Canada has been attributed to acid rain originating in sulfur from manufacturing and power plants in the midwestern United States. NAFTA also includes provisions that call for increased controls on air pollution, especially targeting areas that affect more than one member nation.

Water Pollution   Water becomes polluted primarily from chemical and waste dumping. For years, businesses and cities dumped waste into rivers, streams, and lakes with little regard for the consequences. Cleveland's Cuyahoga River was once so polluted that it literally burst into flames one hot summer day. After an oil spill in 1994, a Houston ship channel burned for days.

Thanks to new legislation and increased awareness, water quality in many areas of the United States is improving. The Cuyahoga River now boasts fish and is even used for recreation. Laws forbidding phosphates (an ingredient found in many detergents) in New York and Florida have helped to make Lake Erie and other major waters safe for fishing and swimming again. Both the Passaic River in New Jersey and the Hudson River in New York are much cleaner now than they were just a few years ago.

Land Pollution   There are two key issues in land pollution. The first is how to restore the quality of land that has already been damaged. Land and water damaged by toxic waste, for example, must be cleaned up for the simple reason that people still need to use them. The second problem, of course, is the prevention of future contamination. New forms of solid-waste disposal constitute one response to these problems. Combustible wastes can be separated and used as fuels in industrial boilers, and decomposition can be accelerated by exposing waste matter to certain microorganisms.

Toxic Waste Disposal   An especially controversial problem in land pollution is toxic waste disposal. Toxic wastes are dangerous chemical or radioactive by-products of manufacturing processes. U.S. manufacturers produce between 40 and 60 million tons of such material each year. As a rule, toxic waste must be stored; it cannot be destroyed or processed into harmless material. Few people, however, want toxic waste storage sites in their backyards. American Airlines *(www.im.aa.com)* recently pled guilty—and became the first major airline to gain a criminal record—to a felony charge that it had mishandled some hazardous materials packed as cargo in passenger airplanes.[15] While fully acknowledging the firm's guilt, Anne McNamara, American's general counsel, argued that "this is an incredibly complicated area with many layers of regulation. It's very easy to inadvertently step over the line."

Recycling Recycling is another controversial area in land pollution. Recycling—the reconversion of waste materials into useful products—has become an issue not only for municipal and state governments but also for many companies engaged in high-waste activities. Certain products, such as aluminum beverage cans and glass, can be very efficiently recycled. Others, such as plastics, are more troublesome. For example, brightly colored plastics like detergent and juice bottles must be recycled separately from clear plastics like milk jugs. Most plastic bottle caps, meanwhile, contain a vinyl lining that can spoil a normal recycling batch. Amber plastic beer containers, currently being test-marketed by Philip Morris's Miller Brewing Co. *(www.millerbrewing.com)*, cannot be mixed for recycling with clear soda bottles. Nevertheless, many local communities actively support various recycling programs, including curbside pickup of aluminum, plastics, glass, and pulp paper. Unfortunately, consumer awareness and interest in this area—and, thus, the policy priorities of business—are more acute at some times than at others.

Responsibility Toward Customers

A company that does not act responsibly toward its customers will ultimately lose their trust—and thus their business. Moreover, the government controls or regulates many aspects of what businesses can and cannot do regarding consumers. The Federal Trade Commission (FTC) *(www.ftc.gov)* regulates advertising and pricing practices. The Food and Drug Administration (FDA) *(www.fda.gov)* enforces guidelines for labeling food products.

Unethical and irresponsible business practices toward customers can result in government-imposed penalties and expensive civil litigation. For example, a few years ago, Abbott Laboratories *(www.abbott.com)* agreed to pay $100 million to settle accusations that the firm failed to meet federal quality standards when it made hundreds of different medical test kits. The FDA indicated that at the time it was the largest fine the agency had ever levied.

Social responsibility toward customers generally falls into two categories: providing quality products and pricing products fairly. Naturally, firms differ as much in their level of concern about their responsibility toward customers as in their approaches to environmental responsibility. Yet unlike environmental problems, many customer problems do not require expensive solutions. In fact, most problems can be avoided if companies simply adhere to regulated practices and heed laws regarding consumer rights.

Consumer Rights Much of the current interest in business responsibility toward customers can be traced to the rise of **consumerism**: social activism dedicated to protecting the rights of consumers in their dealings with businesses. The first formal declaration of consumer rights protection came in the early 1960s when President John F. Kennedy identified four basic consumer rights. Since that time, general agreement on two additional rights has also emerged; these rights are also backed by numerous federal and state laws:

consumerism
Form of social activism dedicated to protecting the rights of consumers in their dealings with businesses

1 **Consumers have a right to safe products.** Businesses can't knowingly sell products that they suspect are defective. For example, a central legal argument in the recent problems involving Firestone tires was whether or not company officials knew in advance that the firm was selling defective tires.

2 **Consumers have a right to be informed about all relevant aspects of a product.** For example, apparel manufacturers are now required to provide full

disclosure on all fabrics used (cotton, silk, polyester, and so forth) and instructions for care (dry clean, machine wash, hand wash).

3   **Consumers have a right to be heard.**   Labels on most products sold today have either a telephone number or address through which customers can file complaints or make inquiries.

4   **Consumers have a right to choose what they buy.**   Customers getting auto repair service are allowed to know and make choices about pricing and warranties on new versus used parts. Similarly, with the consent of their doctors, people have the right to choose between name-brand medications versus generic products that might be cheaper.

5   **Consumers have a right to be educated about purchases.**   All prescription drugs now come with detailed information regarding dosage, possible side effects, and potential interactions with other medications.

6   **Consumers have a right to courteous service.**   This right, of course, is hard to legislate. But as consumers become increasingly knowledgeable, they're more willing to complain about bad service. Consumer hot lines can also be used to voice service-related issues.

American Home Products *(www.ahp.com)* provides an instructive example of what can happen to a firm that violates one or more of these consumer rights. Throughout the early 1990s, the firm aggressively marketed a drug called Pondimin, its brand name for a diet pill containing fenfluramine. In 1996, doctors wrote 18 million prescriptions for Pondimin and other medications containing fenfluramine. In 1997, however, the FDA reported a linkage between the pills and heart-valve disease. A class-action lawsuit against the firm charged that the drug was unsafe and that users had not been provided with complete information about possible side effects. American Home Products eventually agreed to pay $3.75 billion to individuals who had used the drug.[16]

collusion
Illegal agreement between two or more companies to commit a wrongful act

Unfair Pricing   Interfering with competition can take the form of illegal pricing practices. **Collusion** occurs when two or more firms agree to collaborate on such wrongful acts as *price fixing.* The U.S. Justice Department *(www.usdoj.gov)* recently charged three international pharmaceutical firms with illegally controlling worldwide supplies and prices of vitamins. France's Rhone-Poulenc *(www.aventis.com)* cooperated with the investigation, helped break the case several months earlier than expected, and was not fined. Switzerland's F. Hoffmann-LaRoche *(www.larochesa/fr)* was fined $500 million and one of its senior executives was sentenced to four months in a U.S. prison. Germany's BASF *(www.basf.com)* was fined $225 million.[17]

Under some circumstances, firms can also come under attack for *price gouging*—responding to increased demand with overly steep (and often unwarranted) price increases. For example, when DaimlerChrysler launched its PT Cruiser in 2000, demand for the vehicles was so strong that some dealers sold them only to customers willing to pay thousands of dollars over sticker prices. A similar practice was adopted by some Ford dealers when the new Thunderbird was launched in 2002. There were even widespread reports of gasoline retailers doubling or even tripling prices immediately after the events of September 11, 2001. They were apparently counting on consumer panic in response to fear and uncertainty.

Ethics in Advertising   In recent years, increased attention has been given to ethics in advertising and product information. Because of controversies surrounding the potential misinterpretation of words and phrases such as *light, reduced calorie, diet,* and *low fat,* food producers are now required to use a standardized format for listing ingredients on product packages. Similarly, controversy arose in 2001 when it was discovered that Sony had literally created a movie critic who happened to be particularly

Up until about 1993, London-based Sotheby's *(www.sothebys.com)* and New York–based Christie's *(www.christies.com)* competed for 90 percent of the world's art auctions. Then, however, Sotheby CEO A. Alfred Taubman and Christie CEO Sir Anthony Tenant secretly agreed to charge the same rates for all sales. Within a few years, they had collected an extra half billion dollars in commissions paid by sellers. The U.S. Justice Dept. *(www.usdoj.gov)* began investigating in 1999, and in 2002 the two auction houses agreed to split a $537 million settlement with former customers. Sotheby's has to pay an additional fine of $45 million, and Taubman is looking at three years in prison.

fond of movies released by Sony's Columbia Pictures *(www.spe.sony.com)* unit. The studio had been routinely using glowing quotes from a fictitious critic in advertising its newest theatrical releases. After *Newsweek* magazine reported what was going on, Sony hastily stopped the practice and apologized.

Another issue concerns advertising that some consumers consider morally objectionable. Examples include advertising for products such as underwear, condoms, alcohol, tobacco products, and firearms. Laws regulate some of this advertising (for instance, tobacco can no longer be promoted in television commercials but can be featured in print ads in magazines), and many advertisers use common sense and discretion in their promotions. But some companies, such as Calvin Klein and Victoria's Secret, have come under fire for being overly explicit in their advertising.

Responsibility Toward Employees

In Chapter 8, we will see how a number of human resource management activities are essential to a smoothly functioning business. These activities—recruiting, hiring, training, promoting, and compensating—are also the basis for social responsibility toward employees.

Legal and Social Commitments Socially responsible behavior toward employees has both legal and social components. By law, businesses cannot practice numerous forms of illegal discrimination against people in any facet of the employment relationship. For example, a company cannot refuse to hire someone because of ethnicity or pay someone a lower salary than someone else on the basis of gender. Such actions must be taken for job-related purposes only. A company that provides its employees with equal opportunities for rewards and advancement without regard to race, sex, or other irrelevant factors is meeting both its legal and its social responsibilities. Firms that ignore these responsibilities run the risk of losing productive, highly motivated employees. They also leave themselves open to lawsuits.

In the opinion of many people, however, social responsibility toward employees goes beyond equal opportunity. According to popular opinion, an organization should

Even before the company collapsed in November 2001, Enron had a so-called "forced ranking" policy by which all employees were periodically rated. Those in the bottom 20 percent were shortly out of jobs. Of those who survived, 4,200 were fired in December 2001. Many expressed complete shock at the sudden demise of a company that, less than a year earlier, had been valued at about $60 billion.

strive to ensure that the workplace is physically and socially safe. It should also recognize its obligations to help protect the health of its employees by providing opportunities to balance work and life pressures and preferences. From this point of view, social responsibility toward workers would also include helping them maintain proper job skills and, when terminations or layoffs are necessary, treating them with respect and compassion.

Ethical Commitments: The Special Case of Whistle-Blowers Respecting employees as people also means respecting their behavior as ethically responsible individuals. Suppose, for instance, an employee discovers that a business has been engaging in practices that are illegal, unethical, or socially irresponsible. Ideally, this employee should be able to report the problem to higher-level management, confident that managers will stop the questionable practices. Enron's Sherron Watkins reported concerns about the company's accounting practices well before the company's problems were made public, warning top management that Enron would "implode in a wave of accounting scandals." CEO Kenneth Lay commissioned a legal review of the firm's finances but told his investigators not to "second-guess" decisions by Enron's auditor, accounting firm Arthur Andersen.

Too often, people who try to act ethically on the job find themselves in trouble with their employers. If no one in the organization will take action, the employee might elect to drop the matter. Occasionally, however, the individual will inform a regulatory agency or perhaps the media. At this point, he or she becomes a **whistle-blower**—an employee who discovers and tries to put an end to a company's unethical, illegal, or socially irresponsible actions by publicizing them. The 1999 movie *The Insider*, with Al Pacino and Russell Crowe, told the true story of a tobacco-industry whistle-blower named Jeffrey Wigand.

Unfortunately, whistle-blowers are sometimes demoted—and even fired—when they take their accusations public. Jeffrey Wigand was fired. "I went from making $300,000 a year," he reports, "plus stock options, plus, plus, plus—to making $30,000. Yes, there is a price I've paid."[18] Even if they retain their jobs, they may still be treated as outsiders and suffer resentment or hostility from coworkers. Many coworkers see whistle-blowers as people who simply can't be trusted. One recent study suggests that about half of all whistle-blowers eventually get fired, and about

whistle-blower
Employee who detects and tries to put an end to a company's unethical, illegal, or socially irresponsible actions by publicizing them

half of those who get fired subsequently lose their homes and/or families.[19]

The law does offer some recourse to employees who take action. The current whistle-blower law stems from the False Claims Act of 1863, which was designed to prevent contractors from selling defective supplies to the Union Army during the Civil War. With 1986 revisions to the law, the government can recover triple damages from fraudulent contractors. If the Justice Department does not intervene, a whistle-blower can proceed with a civil suit. In that case, the whistle-blower receives 25 to 30 percent of any money recovered.[20]

When Phillip Adams worked in the computer industry, he discovered a flaw in the chip-making process that, under certain circumstances, could lead to data being randomly deleted or altered. He reported the flaw to manufacturers, but several years later, he found that one company, Toshiba *(www.toshiba.com)*, had ignored the problem and continued to make flawed chips for 12 years. He went on to report the problem and became actively involved in a class-action lawsuit based heavily on his research. Toshiba eventually agreed to a $2.1 billion settlement. Adams's share was kept confidential, but he did receive a substantial reward for his efforts.[21] Unfortunately, the prospect of large cash rewards has also generated a spate of false or questionable accusations.

> **"I went from making $300,000 a year plus stock options, plus, plus, plus—to making $30,000."**
>
> **—Jeffrey Wigand, tobacco industry whistle-blower**

Responsibility Toward Investors

Because shareholders are the owners of a company, it may sound odd to say that a firm can act irresponsibly toward its investors. Managers can abuse their responsibilities to investors in several ways. As a rule, irresponsible behavior toward shareholders means abuse of a firm's financial resources. In such cases, the ultimate losers are indeed the shareholder-owners who do not receive their due earnings or dividends. Companies can also act irresponsibly toward shareholder-owners by misrepresenting company resources.

Improper Financial Management Occasionally, organizations or their officers are guilty of blatant financial mismanagement—offenses that are unethical but not necessarily illegal. Some firms, for example, have been accused of paying excessive salaries to senior managers, of sending them on extravagant "retreats" to exotic and expensive resorts, and of providing frivolous perks, including ready access to corporate jets, lavish expense accounts, and memberships at plush country clubs.

In such situations, creditors can often do little, and stockholders have few options. Trying to force a management changeover is a difficult process that can drive down stock prices—a penalty that shareholders are usually unwilling to impose on themselves.

Check Kiting Certain unethical practices are also illegal. **Check kiting**, for instance, involves writing a check against money that has not yet arrived at the bank on which it is drawn. In a typical scheme, managers deposit customer checks totaling, say, $1 million into the company account. Knowing that the bank will not collect all of the total deposit for several days, they proceed to write checks against the total amount deposited, knowing that their account is so important to the bank that the checks will be covered until the full deposits have been collected.

Insider Trading When someone uses confidential information to gain from the purchase or sale of stocks, that person is practicing **insider trading**. Suppose, for example, that a small firm's stock is currently trading at $50 a share. If a larger firm is going

check kiting
Illegal practice of writing checks against money that has not yet been credited at the bank on which the checks are drawn

insider trading
Illegal practice of using special knowledge about a firm for profit or gain

to buy the smaller one, it might have to pay as much as $75 a share for a controlling interest. Individuals who are aware of the impending acquisition before it is publicly announced might, therefore, be able to gain by buying the stock at $50 in anticipation of selling it for $75 after the proposed acquisition is announced. Individuals in a position to take advantage of such a situation generally include managers of the two firms and key individuals at banking firms working on the financial arrangements.

At the other extreme, informed executives can avoid financial loss by selling stock that's about to drop in value. Selling stock, of course, is not illegal, but, legally, you can sell only on the basis of public information that's available to all investors. Potential violations of this regulation are at the heart of investigations into ImClone, Samuel Waksal, and Martha Stewart. Did Waksal warn Stewart that her stock was going to drop in value before the FDA rejected Erbitux? Was prior knowledge the basis of her decision to sell? If the answer is yes, both could be guilty of insider trading. But if Stewart didn't know about the impending news and the timing of her stock sale was purely coincidental, then she did nothing wrong.

Misrepresentation of Finances Certain behaviors regarding financial representation are also illegal. In maintaining and reporting its financial status, every corporation must conform to generally accepted accounting principles (GAAP) (see Chapter 13). Sometimes, however, unethical managers project profits far in excess of what they actually expect to earn; others go so far as to hide losses and/or expenses in order to boost paper profits. When the truth comes out, however, the damage is often substantial.

Various issues involving the misrepresentation of finances were central in the Enron case. One review, for example, called Enron's accounting practices "creative and aggressive." It seems that CFO Andrew Fastow had set up a complex network of partnerships that were often used to hide losses. Enron, for instance, could report all of the earnings from a partnership as its own while transferring all or most of the costs and losses to the partnership. Inflated profits would then support increased stock prices.

IMPLEMENTING SOCIAL RESPONSIBILITY PROGRAMS

Thus far, we have discussed social responsibility as if there were some agreement on how organizations should behave. In fact, there are dramatic differences of opinion concerning the role of social responsibility as a business goal. Some people oppose any business activity that threatens profits. Others argue that social responsibility must take precedence over profits.

Even businesspeople who agree on the importance of social responsibility will cite different reasons for their views. Some skeptics of business-sponsored social projects fear that if businesses become too active, they will gain too much control over the ways in which those projects are addressed by society as a whole. These critics point to the influence that many businesses have been able to exert on the government agencies that are supposed to regulate their industries. Other critics claim that business organizations lack the expertise needed to address social issues. They argue, for instance, that technical experts, not businesses, should decide how to clean up polluted rivers.

Proponents of socially responsible business believe that corporations are citizens and should, therefore, help to improve the lives of fellow citizens. Still others point to the vast resources controlled by businesses and note that they help to create many of the problems social programs are designed to alleviate.

Approaches to Social Responsibility

Given these differences of opinion, it is little wonder that corporations have adopted a variety of approaches to social responsibility. Not surprisingly, organizations themselves adopt a wide range of positions on social responsibility.[22] As Figure 2.6 illustrates, the four stances that an organization can take concerning its obligations to society fall along a continuum ranging from the lowest to the highest degree of socially responsible practices.

Obstructionist Stance The few organizations that take what might be called an **obstructionist stance** to social responsibility usually do as little as possible to solve social or environmental problems. When they cross the ethical or legal line that separates acceptable from unacceptable practices, their typical response is to deny or cover up their actions. Firms that adopt this position have little regard for ethical conduct and will generally go to great lengths to hide wrongdoing. IBP, a leading meat-processing firm, has a long (and undistinguished) record of breaking environmental protection, labor, and food processing laws and then trying to cover up its offenses.

obstructionist stance
Approach to social responsibility that involves doing as little as possible and may involve attempts to deny or cover up violations

Defensive Stance One step removed from the obstructionist stance is the **defensive stance**, whereby the organization will do everything that is required of it legally but nothing more. This approach is most consistent with arguments against corporate social responsibility. Managers who take a defensive stance insist that their job is to generate profits. Such a firm, for example, would install pollution-control equipment dictated by law but would not install higher-quality equipment even though it might further limit pollution.

Tobacco companies generally take this position in their marketing efforts. In the United States, they are legally required to include warnings to smokers on their products and to limit advertising to prescribed media. Domestically, they follow these rules to the letter of the law but use more aggressive marketing methods in countries that have no such rules. In many Asian and African countries, cigarettes are heavily promoted, contain higher levels of tar and nicotine than those sold in the United States, and carry few or no health warning labels. Firms that take this position are also unlikely to cover up wrongdoing, will generally admit to mistakes, and will take appropriate corrective actions.

defensive stance
Approach to social responsibility by which a company meets only minimum legal requirements in its commitments to groups and individuals in its social environment

Accommodative Stance A firm that adopts an **accommodative stance** meets its legal and ethical requirements but will also go further in certain cases. Such firms voluntarily agree to participate in social programs, but solicitors must convince them that given programs are worthy of their support. Both Shell and IBM, for example, will match contributions made by their employees to selected charitable causes. Many organizations respond to requests for donations to Little League, Girl Scouts, youth soccer programs, and so forth. The point, however, is that someone has to knock on

accommodative stance
Approach to social responsibility by which a company, if specifically asked to do so, exceeds legal minimums in its commitments to groups and individuals in its social environment

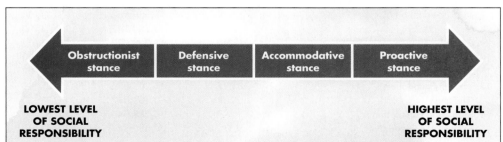

FIGURE 2.6

Spectrum of Approaches to Corporate Social Responsibility

the door and ask. Accommodative organizations do not necessarily or proactively seek avenues for contributing.

proactive stance
Approach to social responsibility by which a company actively seeks opportunities to contribute to the well-being of groups and individuals in its social environment

Proactive Stance The highest degree of social responsibility that a firm can exhibit is the **proactive stance**. Firms that adopt this approach take to heart the arguments in favor of social responsibility. They view themselves as citizens in a society and proactively seek opportunities to contribute. The most common—and direct—way to implement this stance is by setting up a foundation through which to provide direct financial support for various social programs. Table 2.1 lists the top 15 largest corporate foundations based on total giving to social programs.

Unfortunately, recent economic difficulties and the decline of stock prices have caused donors to reduce philanthropic giving or to earmark funds over longer periods of time. Ted Turner, former vice chairman of AOL Time Warner, has pledged $250 million to an organization dedicated to reducing the threat of nuclear war. But because of a drop in the value of his stock holdings, he has been forced to fund his commitment over a period of seven years rather than the five that he'd originally intended.[23]

An excellent example of a different kind of proactive stance is the Ronald McDonald House *(www.mcdonalds.com)* program undertaken by McDonald's Corp. These houses, located close to major medical centers, can be used by families for minimal cost while sick children are receiving medical treatment nearby. Similarly, some firms, such as UPS *(www.ups.com)*, Home Depot *(www.homedepot.com)*, and US West *(www.uswest.com)*, employ individuals who hope to compete in the Olympics and support them in various ways. UPS, for instance, underwrites the training and travel costs of four employees competing for Olympic berths and allows them to maintain flexible work schedules. These and related programs exceed the accommodative stance—they indicate a sincere commitment to improving the general social welfare and thus represent a proactive stance to social responsibility.

Remember, however, that these categories are not sharply distinct: They merely label stages along a continuum of approaches. Organizations do not always fit neatly into one category or another. The Ronald McDonald House program has been widely applauded, but McDonald's has also come under fire for allegedly misleading consumers about the nutritional value of its food products. Likewise, although UPS has sincere motives for helping Olympic athletes, the company will also benefit by featuring the athletes' photos on its envelopes and otherwise promoting its own benevolence. And even though Enron may have taken an obstructionist stance in the past,

TABLE 2.1

Top 15 Corporate Foundations

Foundation	State	Total Giving	Fiscal Date
1. Ford Motor Company Fund	MI	$169,100,475	12/31/00
2. Bank of America Foundation	NC	85,755,841	12/31/00
3. SBC Foundation	TX	68,678,574	12/31/00
4. Wal-Mart Foundation	AR	62,617,641	1/31/00
5. J. P. Morgan Chase Foundation	NY	44,656,806	12/31/00
6. Lucent Technologies Foundation	NJ	43,932,312	9/30/00
7. AT&T Foundation	NY	43,539,963	12/31/00
8. General Motors Foundation	MI	43,280,242	12/31/00
9. Citigroup Foundation	NY	43,068,029	12/31/00
10. ExxonMobil Foundation	TX	42,188,567	12/31/00
11. Aventis Pharmaceuticals Health Care Foundation	NJ	41,558,325	12/31/00
12. Verizon Foundation	NY	41,205,556	12/30/00
13. GE Fund	CT	40,701,047	12/31/00
14. Prudential Foundation	NJ	36,219,045	12/31/00
15. Fannie Mae Foundation	DC	34,835,347	12/31/00

many individual employees and managers at the firm no doubt made substantial contributions to society in a number of different ways.

Managing Social Responsibility Programs

Making a company socially responsible in the full sense of the social response approach takes a carefully organized and managed program. In particular, managers must take steps to foster a companywide sense of social responsibility. Figure 2.7 summarizes those steps.[24]

1 **Social responsibility must start at the top and be considered as a factor in strategic planning.** Without the support of top management, no program can succeed. Thus, top management must embrace a strong stand on social responsibility and develop a policy statement outlining that commitment.

2 **A committee of top managers must develop a plan detailing the level of management support.** Some companies set aside percentages of profits for social programs. Levi Strauss, for example, earmarks 2.4 percent of pretax earnings for worthy projects. Managers must also set specific priorities. For instance, should the firm train the hard-core unemployed or support the arts?

3 **One executive must be put in charge of the firm's agenda.** Whether the role is created as a separate job or added to an existing one, the selected individual must monitor the program and ensure that its implementation is consistent with the firm's policy statement and strategic plan.

4 **The organization must conduct occasional social audits: systematic analyses of its success in using funds earmarked for its social responsibility goals.**[25] Consider the case of a company whose strategic plan calls for spending $100,000 to train 200 hard-core unemployed people and to place 180 of them in jobs. If at the end of a year, the firm has spent $98,000, trained 210 people, and filled 175 jobs, a social audit will confirm the program's success. But if the program has cost $150,000, trained only 90 people, and placed only 10 of them, the audit will reveal the program's failure. Such failure should prompt a rethinking of the program's implementation and its priorities.

social audit
Systematic analysis of a firm's success in using funds earmarked for meeting its social responsibility goals

Social Responsibility and the Small Business

As the owner of a garden supply store, how would you respond to a building inspector's suggestion that a cash payment will speed your application for a building permit? As the

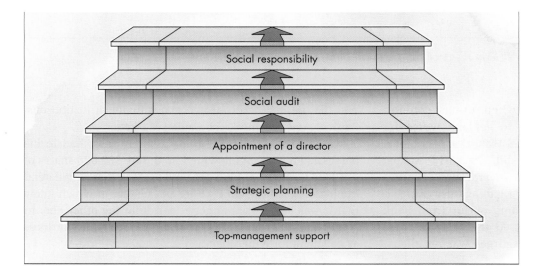

Social responsibility

Social audit

Appointment of a director

Strategic planning

Top-management support

FIGURE 2.7

Establishing a Social Responsibility Program

manager of a liquor store, would you call the police, refuse to sell, or sell to a customer whose identification card looks forged? As the owner of a small laboratory, would you call the state board of health to make sure that it has licensed the company with which you want to contract to dispose of medical waste? Who will really be harmed if a small firm pads its income statement to help it get a much-needed bank loan?

Many of the examples in this chapter illustrate big-business responses to ethical and social responsibility issues. Such examples, however, show quite clearly that small businesses must answer many of the same questions. Differences are primarily differences of scale.

At the same time, these are largely questions of *individual* ethics. What about questions of *social* responsibility? Can a small business, for example, afford a social agenda? Should it sponsor Little League baseball teams, make donations to the United Way, and buy lightbulbs from the Lion's Club? Do joining the chamber of commerce and supporting the Better Business Bureau cost too much? Clearly, ethics and social responsibility are decisions faced by all managers in all organizations, regardless of rank or size. One key to business success is to decide in advance how to respond to the issues that underlie all questions of ethical and social responsibility.

SELF-CHECK QUESTIONS 7–9

You should now be able to answer Self-Check Questions 7–9.*

7 **Multiple Choice** Which of the following is **not** an area of *social responsibility*? [select one] **(a)** responsibility toward the board of directors; **(b)** responsibility toward the environment; **(c)** responsibility toward customers; **(d)** responsibility toward employees; **(e)** responsibility toward investors.

8 **Multiple Choice** General *approaches to social responsibility* include which of the following?

[select one] **(a)** obstructionist; **(b)** defensive; **(c)** accommodative; **(d)** proactive; **(e)** all of these.

9 **True/False** Because of their size and limited financial resources, small businesses should not be concerned about *social responsibility*.

***Answers to Self-Check Questions 7–9 can be found on p. 507.**

Continued from page 36

WHEN DOES A STOCK WARRANT WARRANT A WARRANT FOR ARREST?

Just when things couldn't seem to get any worse for Samuel Waksal and ImClone, they did. In early August 2002, several new charges were filed against Waksal, including perjury and bank fraud. At the heart of these new charges was an allega-tion that he had deceived two major financial institutions, Bank of America and Refco Capital Markets.

Authorities claim that in late 1999, Waksal had in his possession a warrant allowing him to buy 350,000 shares of ImClone for $5.50 a share. He used that warrant as collateral in obtaining loans from each lender, neither of which knew that it was being used to get a loan from the other one. In 2000, Waksal cashed in the warrant, rendering it worthless as collateral for either loan.

Later that year, Bank of America requested confirmation from Waksal that he still held the warrant. According to indictments handed down in August 2002, Waksal forged the signature of ImClone's general counsel on a letter dated November 10, 2000, verifying that the warrant was still valid as collateral.

This news, of course, only fueled suspicions about Waksal's other activities. The prospect of additional charges loomed large, and family members and friends came under growing scrutiny. The two major lenders wrote off their loans to Waksal as worthless, and ImClone's stock value plummeted. The pressure also began to build on Martha Stewart. Waksal's trial was concluded in summer 2003. He pled guilty to eight counts of fraud and was sentenced to more than seven years in prison. He was also fined $3 million. Martha Stewart, meanwhile, was indicted in June 2003 on charges of conspiracy, obstruction of justice, lying to investigators, and securities fraud. Her trial was tentatively

set for January 2004. Investors in both ImClone and Stewart's home decorating empire can only hope that there are no more shoes waiting to fall.

Questions for Discussion

1 What are the major legal issues in this case? What are the major ethical issues?

2 Aside from personal greed, what factors might lead a drug company like ImClone to aggressively promote potential new products before they have been approved?

3 Some observers argue that the FDA should be more open in sharing news of pending product reviews with the public. What are the pros and cons of such an argument?

4 Distinguish between ethical issues and social responsibility issues as they apply to the ImClone case.

■ SUMMARY OF LEARNING OBJECTIVES

1 Explain how individuals develop their personal *codes of ethics* and why ethics are important in the workplace.

Ethics are beliefs about what's right and wrong or good and bad. **Ethical behavior** conforms to individual beliefs and social norms about what's right and good. **Unethical behavior** is behavior that individual beliefs and social norms define as wrong and bad. Managerial ethics are standards of behavior that guide managers. There are three broad categories of ways in which managerial ethics can affect people's work: (1) *behavior toward employees*; (2) *behavior toward the organization*; and (3) *behavior toward other economic agents*.

One model for applying ethical judgments to business situations recommends the following three steps: (1) *Gather relevant factual information*; (2) *analyze the facts to determine the most appropriate moral values*; and (3) *make an ethical judgment based on the rightness or wrongness of the proposed activity or policy*. Four other principles may affect any situation: (1) *utility*; (2) *rights*; (3) *justice*; and (4) *caring*. Perhaps the single most effective step that a company can take is to demonstrate top management support. In addition to promoting attitudes of honesty and openness, firms can also take specific steps to formalize their commitment: (1) *adopting written codes* and (2) *instituting ethics programs*.

2 Distinguish *social responsibility* from ethics, identify *organizational stakeholders*, and characterize social consciousness today.

Ethics affect individuals. **Social responsibility** refers to the way a firm attempts to balance its commitments to **organizational stakeholders**—those groups, individuals, and organizations that are directly affected by the practices of an organization and, therefore, have a stake in its performance. Many companies concentrate on five main groups: (1) *customers*; (2) *employees*; (3) *investors*; (4) *suppliers*; and (5) *local communities*. Attitudes toward social responsibility have changed. In the late nineteenth century concern about unbridled business activity was soon translated into laws regulating business practices. Out of the economic turmoil of the 1930s, when greed was blamed for business failures and the loss of jobs, came new laws protecting and enhancing social well-being. During the 1960s and 1970s, activism prompted increased government regulation in many areas of business. Today's attitudes stress a greater social role for business. Perhaps globalization and environmentalism have made businesses more sensitive to their social responsibilities. This view, combined with the economic prosperity of the 1980s and 1990s, marked a return to the *laissez-faire* philosophy, but the recent epidemic of corporate scandals threatens to revive the 1930s' call for more regulation and oversight.

3 **Show how the concept of social responsibility applies both to environmental issues and to a firm's relationships with customers, employees, and investors.**

A firm confronts four areas of concern: (1) *responsibility toward the environment*; (2) *responsibility toward customers*; (3) *responsibility toward employees*; and (4) *responsibility toward investors*. Organizations and managers may be guilty of *financial mismanagement*—offenses that are unethical but not necessarily illegal. In such situations, creditors can often do little, and stockholders have few options. But certain unethical practices are illegal. **Check kiting** involves writing a check against money that has not yet arrived at the bank on which it is drawn. Using confidential information to gain from a stock transaction is **insider trading**. Certain behavior regarding financial representation is also unlawful.

4 **Identify four general *approaches to social responsibility* and describe the four steps that a firm must take to implement a social responsibility program.**

A business can take one of four stances concerning its social obligations to society: (1) **obstructionist stance**; (2) **defen-** sive stance; (3) **accommodative stance**; or (4) **proactive stance**. One model suggests a four-step approach to fostering a companywide sense of social responsibility: (1) Social responsibility must start at the top and be included in strategic planning. (2) Top managers must develop a plan detailing the level of management support. (3) One executive must be put in charge of the agenda. (4) The organization must conduct occasional **social audits**—analyses of its success in using funds earmarked for social responsibility goals.

5 **Explain how issues of social responsibility and ethics affect small business.**

For small businesspeople, ethical issues are questions of *individual* ethics. But in questions of *social* responsibility, they must ask themselves if they can afford a social agenda—sponsoring Little League baseball teams or making donations to the United Way, for example. They should also realize that managers in all organizations face issues of ethics and social responsibility.

■ KEY TERMS

ethics (p. 37)
ethical behavior (p. 37)
unethical behavior (p. 37)
business ethics (p. 37)
managerial ethics (p. 38)
social responsibility (p. 45)

organizational stakeholders (p. 45)
consumerism (p. 53)
collusion (p. 54)
whistle-blower (p. 56)
check kiting (p. 57)
insider trading (p. 57)

obstructionist stance (p. 59)
defensive stance (p. 59)
accommodative stance (p. 59)
proactive stance (p. 60)
social audit (p. 61)

■ QUESTIONS AND EXERCISES

Questions for Review

1 What basic factors should be considered in any ethical decision?

2 Who are an organization's stakeholders? Who are the major stakeholders with whom most businesses must be concerned?

3 What are the major areas of social responsibility with which businesses should be concerned?

4 What are the four basic approaches to social responsibility?

5 In what ways do you think your personal code of ethics might clash with the operations of some companies? How might you try to resolve these differences?

Questions for Analysis

6 What kind of wrongdoing would most likely prompt you to be a whistle-blower? What kind of wrongdoing would be least likely? Why?

7 In your opinion, which area of social responsibility is most important? Why? Are there areas other than those noted in the chapter that you consider important?

8 Identify some specific ethical or social responsibility issues that might be faced by small-business managers and employees in each of the following areas: environment, customers, employees, and investors.

Application Exercises

9 Develop a list of the major stakeholders of your college or university. As a class, discuss the ways in which you think the school prioritizes these stakeholders. Do you agree or disagree with this prioritization?

10 Using newspapers, magazines, and other business references, identify and describe at least three companies that take a defensive stance to social responsibility, three that take an accommodative stance, and three that take a proactive stance.

 ## BUILDING YOUR BUSINESS SKILLS

TO LIE OR NOT TO LIE: THAT IS THE QUESTION

This exercise enhances the following SCANS workplace competencies: demonstrating basic skills, demonstrating thinking skills, exhibiting interpersonal skills, and working with information.

Goal
To encourage students to apply general concepts of business ethics to specific situations.

Background
Workplace lying, it seems, has become business as usual. According to one survey, one-quarter of working American adults said that they had been asked to do something illegal or unethical on the job. Four in 10 did what they were told. Another survey of more than 2,000 secretaries showed that many employees face ethical dilemmas in their day-to-day work.

Method

Step 1
Working with four other students, discuss ways in which you would respond to the following ethical dilemmas. When there is a difference of opinion among group members, try to determine the specific factors that influence different responses.

■ Would you lie about your supervisor's whereabouts to someone on the phone?

■ Would you lie about who was responsible for a business decision that cost your company thousands of dollars to protect your own or your supervisor's job?

■ Would you inflate sales and revenue data on official company accounting statements to increase stock value?

■ Would you say that you witnessed a signature when you did not if you were acting in the role of a notary?

■ Would you keep silent if you knew that the official minutes of a corporate meeting had been changed?

■ Would you destroy or remove information that could hurt your company if it fell into the wrong hands?

Step 2
Research the commitment to business ethics at Johnson & Johnson *(www.jnj.com)* and Texas Instruments *(www.ti.com/corp/docs/ethics/home.htm)* by clicking on their respective Web sites. As a group, discuss ways in which these statements are likely to affect the specific behaviors mentioned in Step 1.

Step 3
Working with group members, draft a corporate code of ethics that would discourage the specific behaviors mentioned in Step 1. Limit your code to a single typewritten page, but make it sufficiently broad to cover different ethical dilemmas.

FOLLOW-UP QUESTIONS

1 What personal, social, and cultural factors do you think contribute to lying in the workplace?

2 Do you agree or disagree with the following statement? "The term *business ethics* is an oxymoron." Support your answer with examples from your own work experience or that of a family member.

3 If you were your company's director of human resources, how would you make your code of ethics a "living document"?

4 If you were faced with any of the ethical dilemmas described in Step 1, how would you handle them? How far would you go to maintain your personal ethical standards?

EXERCISING YOUR ETHICS

TAKING A STANCE

The Situation

A perpetual debate revolves around the roles and activities of business owners in contributing to the greater social good. Promoting the so-called *proactive stance*, some people argue that businesses should be socially responsible by seeking opportunities to benefit the society in which they are permitted to conduct their affairs. Others maintain that because businesses exist to make profits for owners, they have no further obligation to society than that (the *defensive stance*).

The Dilemma

Pair up with one of your classmates. Using a coin toss, each of you should select or be assigned one side of this debate. You and your partner should then enter into a dialogue to formulate the three most convincing arguments possible to support each side. Then select the single strongest argument in support of each position. Each team of two partners should then present to the class its strongest arguments for and against social responsibility on the part of business.

QUESTIONS FOR DISCUSSION

1 Which side of the debate is easier to defend? Why?
2 What is your personal opinion about the appropriate stance that a business should take regarding social responsibility?
3 To what extent is the concept of social responsibility relevant to nonbusiness organizations such as universities, government units, health care organizations, and so forth?

CRAFTING YOUR BUSINESS PLAN

GOING IN THE ETHICAL DIRECTION

The Purpose of the Assignment

1 To familiarize students with some of the ethical and social responsibility considerations faced by a sample firm in developing its business plan in the planning framework of the *Business PlanPro (BPP) 2003* software package (Version 6.0).
2 To show where ethical and social responsibility considerations can be found in various sections of the *BPP* planning environment.

Assignment

After reading Chapter 2 in the textbook, open the BPP *software and look around for information about the types of ethical considerations and social responsibility factors that would be of concern to the sample firm:* Southeast Health Plans Inc. *To find* Southeast Health Plans, *do the following:*

Open *Business PlanPro*. Go to the toolbar and click on the "*Sample Plans*" icon. In the **Sample Plan Browser**, do a search using the **search category** *Insurance agents, brokers, and service*. From the resulting list, select the category entitled *Plan administration—health*, which is the location for *Southeast Health Plans Inc*. The screen you are looking at is the introduction page for *Southeast's* business plan. On this page, scroll down until you reach the **Table of Contents** for the company's business plan.

NOW RESPOND TO THE FOLLOWING QUESTIONS:

1 Do you think a company in *Southeast's* line of business should have a code of ethics? Call up *Southeast's* Table of Contents page. In which sections of the company's business plan would you expect to find its code of ethics? Go into those sections and identify information pertaining to the firm's code of ethics. What did you find?
2 The textbook states that a firm's social responsibility includes providing quality products for its customers. Explore *Southeast's* business plan and describe its position on providing quality products. [Sites to see in *BPP* for this item: On the Table of Contents page, click on **1.0 Executive Summary**. Then click on and read each of the following in turn: **1.1 Objectives**, **1.2 Mission**, and **1.3 Keys to Success**.]
3 Another dimension of social responsibility is pricing products fairly. Search through *Southeast's* plan for

information about its policies for pricing services. Does *Southeast*'s planned gross margin reflect "fair pricing"? Why or why not? [Sites to see in *BPP*: From the Table of Contents page, click on **3.1 Competitive Comparison** and then on **3.3 Fulfillment**. After returning to the Table of Contents page, click on **5.1.1 Pricing Strategy** and then **1.0 Executive Summary**.]

 VIDEO EXERCISE

DOING THE RIGHT THING: AMERICAN RED CROSS

Learning Objectives

The purpose of this video is to help you:

1 Identify some of the social responsibility and ethics challenges faced by a nonprofit organization.
2 Discuss the purpose of an organizational code of ethics.
3 Understand the potential conflicts that can emerge between an organization and its stakeholders.

Synopsis

Founded in 1881 by Clara Barton, the American Red Cross is a nonprofit organization dedicated to helping victims of war, natural disasters, and other catastrophes. The organization's 1,000 chapters are governed by volunteer boards of directors who oversee local activities and enforce ethical standards in line with community norms and the Red Cross's own code of ethics. Over the years, the Red Cross has been guided in its use of donations by honoring donor intent. This policy helped the organization deal with a major ethical challenge after the terrorist attacks of September 11, 2001. The Red Cross received more than $1 billion in donations and initially diverted some money to ancillary operations, such as creating a strategic blood reserve. After donors objected, however, the organization reversed its decision and—honoring donor intent—used the contributions to directly benefit people who were affected by the tragedy.

DISCUSSION QUESTIONS

1 **For analysis:** What are the social responsibility implications of the decision to avoid accepting donations of goods for many local relief efforts?

2 **For analysis:** What kinds of ethical conflicts might arise because the American Red Cross relies so heavily on volunteers?
3 **For application:** What can the American Red Cross do to ensure that local chapters are properly applying its code of ethics?
4 **For application:** How might a nonprofit such as the American Red Cross gain a better understanding of its stakeholders' needs and preferences?
5 **For debate:** Should the American Red Cross have reversed its initial decision to divert some of the money donated for September 11 relief efforts to pressing but ancillary operations? Support your chosen position.

Online Exploration

Visit the American Red Cross site *(www.redcross.org)* and scan the headlines referring to the organization's response to recent disasters. Also look at the educational information available through links to news stories, feature articles, and other material. Next, carefully examine the variety of links addressing the needs and involvement of different stakeholder groups. What kinds of stakeholders does the American Red Cross expect to visit its Web site? Why are these stakeholders important to the organization? Do you think the organization should post its code of ethics prominently on this site? Explain your answer.

1 Define *small business*, discuss its importance to the U.S. economy, and explain which *types of small business* are most likely to succeed.

2 Explain *entrepreneurship* and describe some key characteristics of entrepreneurial personalities and activities.

3 Describe the *business plan* and the *start-up decisions* made by small businesses and identify sources of *financial aid*.

4 Explain the main reasons why new business start-ups are increasing and identify the reasons for success and failure in small businesses.

5 Explain *sole proprietorships* and *partnerships* and discuss the advantages and disadvantages of each.

6 Describe the different kinds of *corporations* and the advantages and disadvantages of each, explain the basic issues in creating and managing, and identify recent trends in corporate ownership.

THE COMPETITOR FROM OUT OF THE BLUE

For years now, Southwest Airlines *(www.iflyswa.com)* has been flying high in the short-haul, low-fare market. Its emphasis on reliability and customer service, combined with a dedication to cost control and a corporate culture that attracts only the best employees,

UNDERSTANDING ENTREPRENEURSHIP AND BUSINESS OWNERSHIP

"**J**etBlue is not merely a clone of Southwest Airlines; it is the new gold standard among low-cost carriers."

—James Craun, airline industry consultant

has allowed Southwest to remain virtually unchallenged. Literally dozens of upstarts and spin-offs from existing airlines have attempted to achieve Southwest's level of success, but none of them has ever managed to get off the ground.

Why has it been so hard for start-up airlines to emulate the operational success of competitor Southwest? For one thing, the airline industry is challenging for managers. An airline needs people skilled in scheduling, purchasing, customer service, and mechanical maintenance. Teams of individuals performing a wide variety of jobs, from piloting planes to handling baggage, must be coordinated. In addition, fixed costs for planes and equipment are high and revenues uncertain. And last but not least, competition is intense. In this hostile environment, few companies survive—both United and

US Airways declared bankruptcy recently. Of the 27 carriers that have gone public since 1980, only eight are still in the air.

Then along came Blue—JetBlue *(www.jetblue.com)*. Since its founding in 1999, the new airline has become one of the most profitable start-up carriers in the United States, and it has done so in large part by learning and applying many of the lessons professed by Southwest. How has JetBlue managed to do what no other carrier has managed to do? First and foremost, credit CEO David Neeleman's creativity as a manager and marketer. In 1984, Neeleman founded Morris Air, a discount carrier based in Salt Lake City, which he sold to Southwest in 1993 for $128 million. When he was fired after a brief stint at Southwest, Neeleman set out to play his own hand in his former employer's own game. He consulted—and in some cases, hired—experienced managers from competitors. He copied elements of Southwest's discount strategy, such as point-to-point scheduling, reliance on a single type of aircraft, and use of nonunion employees. Then he added some extras: reserved seats, upscale snacks, leather chairs, and seat-back televisions with 24 channels of DirecTV. "JetBlue," reports one industry consultant, "is not merely a clone of Southwest Airlines; it is the new gold standard among low-cost carriers."

Relying on his extensive industry experience, Neeleman focused most of his energy on a few key factors that he felt would make or break his company. By hiring younger, more productive workers and giving them stock options in lieu of high wages, JetBlue kept labor expenses down to 25 percent of revenues (compared to Southwest's 33 percent and Delta's 44 percent). JetBlue fills planes to capacity, gets more flying hours out of each aircraft, and saves on maintenance costs because its fleet is brand new. Even the luxurious leather seats are cost-effective—they're easier to clean. Because Neeleman regards on-time arrival as a critical element in customer service, his pager (which he wears to bed) beeps whenever a JetBlue flight touches down more than one minute late.

Our opening story continues on page 93.

WHAT IS A "SMALL" BUSINESS?

The term *small business* defies easy definition. Locally owned and operated restaurants and hair salons are small businesses, and giant corporations such as Sony, Caterpillar, and Eastman Kodak are big businesses. Between these two extremes fall thousands of companies that cannot be easily categorized.

Small Business Administration (SBA)
Federal agency charged with assisting small businesses

The U.S. Department of Commerce *(www.osec.doc.gov)* considers a business small if it has fewer than 500 employees. The U.S. **Small Business Administration (SBA)** *(www.sba.gov)*, a government assistance agency, regards some companies with 1,500 employees as small. The SBA relies on two different factors: (1) *number of employees* and (2) *total annual sales*. Manufacturers may be small according to the first criterion, and grocery stores may be small according to the second. Although an independent grocery store with $13 million in sales may sound large, the SBA sees it as small when comparing its revenues to those of truly large food retailers.

small business
Independently owned and managed business that does not dominate its market

Because it's sometimes hard to deal in strictly numerical terms, we define a **small business** as one that is independently owned and managed and does not dominate its market. A small business, then, can't be part of another business and must have relatively little influence in its market. Dell Computer *(www.dell.com)* was a small business when founded by Michael Dell in 1984, but today it's number one in the personal computer market and is not small in any sense of the term.

The Importance of Small Business in the U.S. Economy

As Figure 3.1 shows, most U.S. businesses employ fewer than 100 people, and most U.S. workers are employed by small firms. Figure 3.1(a) shows that 86.09 percent of all businesses employ 20 or fewer people and another 11 percent between 20 and 99 people. Only about one-tenth of 1 percent employ 1,000 or more. Figure 3.1(b) shows that 25.60 percent of all workers are employed by firms with fewer than 20 people; another 29.10 percent work in firms that employ between 20 and 99. The vast majority of these companies are owner operated.[1] Figure 3.1(b) also shows that only 12.70 percent of workers are employed by firms with 1,000 or more employees.

We can measure the contribution of small business in terms of its impact on key aspects of the U.S. economic system, including *job creation, innovation*, and *importance to big business*.

Job Creation Relative job growth among businesses of different sizes is hard to determine. For one thing, when a successful small business starts adding employees at a rapid clip, it may quickly cease being small. Dell Computer had one employee in 1984 (Michael Dell himself). But the payroll grew to 100 employees in 1986, to 2,000 in 1992, and to 40,000 in 2001. Although there was no precise point at which Dell turned from "small" into "large," some of the jobs it created should be counted in the small business sector and some in the large.

Small businesses—especially in certain industries—are an important source of new (and often high-earning) jobs. In recent years, small businesses have accounted for 38 percent of all new jobs in high-technology sectors of the economy.[2] Jobs, of

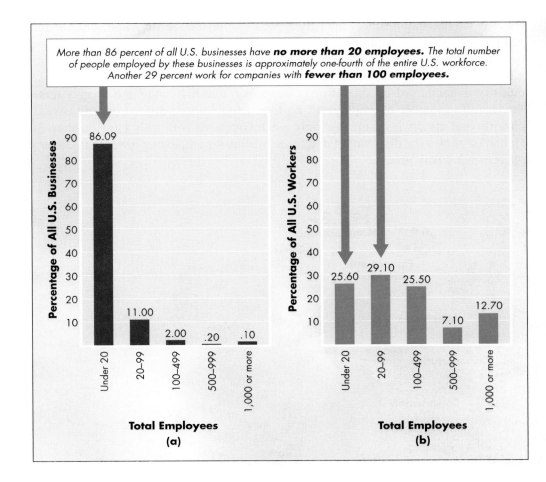

FIGURE 3.1

The Importance of Small Business in the United States

course, are created by companies of all sizes, all of which hire and lay off workers. Although small firms often hire at a faster rate, they are likely to cut jobs at a far higher rate. They are the first to hire in times of economic recovery, but big firms are the last to lay off workers during downswings.

Innovation History reminds us that major innovations are as likely to come from small businesses (or individuals) as from big ones. Small firms and individuals invented the PC and the stainless-steel razor blade, the transistor radio and the photocopier, the jet engine and the self-developing photograph. The device used to repair Vice President Dick Cheney's ailing heart was developed by a small business, as was the new battery-powered one-person vehicle called the Segway Human Transporter.[3]

In addition, innovations are not always new *products*. Michael Dell didn't invent the PC, but he developed an innovative way to build it (buy finished components and then assemble them) and an innovative way to sell it (directly to consumers, first by telephone and now via the Internet). Today, says the SBA, small business supplies 55 percent of all innovations that reach the U.S. marketplace.

Importance to Big Business Most of the products made by big businesses are sold to consumers by small ones. Most dealerships that sell Fords, Toyotas, and Volvos are independently operated. Moreover, small businesses provide big ones with many of their services and raw materials. Microsoft *(www.microsoft.com)*, for instance, relies on hundreds of small firms for most of its routine code-writing functions.

Popular Areas of Small-Business Enterprise

Not surprisingly, small businesses are more common in some industries than in others. The major small-business industry groups are *services, construction, finance and insurance, wholesaling*, and *transportation and manufacturing*. Each industry differs in its needs for employees, money, materials, and machines, but as a general rule, the more resources required, the harder it is to start a business and the less likely an industry is dominated by small firms. Remember, too, that *small* is a relative term. The criteria (number of employees and total annual sales) differ from industry to industry and are often meaningful only when compared with truly large businesses. Figure 3.2 shows the distribution of all U.S. businesses employing fewer than 20 people across industry groups.

FIGURE 3.2

Small Business by Industry

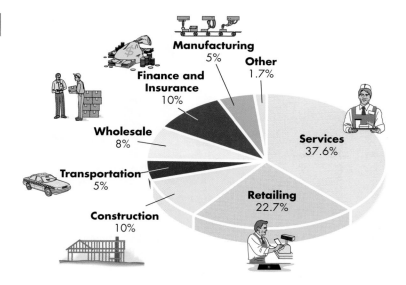

Manufacturing
5%

Other
1.7%

Finance and
Insurance
10%

Wholesale
8%

Transportation
5%

Construction
10%

Services
37.6%

Retailing
22.7%

Services Small-business services range from marriage counseling to computer software, from management consulting to professional dog walking. Partly because they require few resources, service providers are the fastest-growing segment of small business. A retailer, for example, sells products made by other firms directly to consumers. Usually, people who start small retail businesses favor specialty shops—say, big men's clothing or gourmet coffees—that let them focus limited resources on narrow market segments.

Construction About 10 percent of businesses with fewer than 20 employees are involved in construction. Because many construction jobs are small local projects, local firms are often ideal contractors.

Finance and Insurance Financial and insurance firms also account for about 10 percent of all firms with fewer than 20 employees. Most of these businesses are affiliates of or agents for larger national firms.

Wholesaling Small-business owners often do well in wholesaling; about 8 percent of businesses with fewer than 20 employees are wholesalers. Wholesalers buy products from manufacturers or other producers and sell them to retailers. They usually purchase goods in bulk and store them in quantities at locations convenient for retailers. For a given volume of business, therefore, they need fewer employees than manufacturers, retailers, or service providers.

Transportation and Manufacturing Some small firms—about 5 percent of all companies with fewer than 20 employees—do well in transportation and related businesses. These include taxi and limousine companies, charter airplane services, and tour operators. More than any other industry, manufacturing lends itself to big business, but this doesn't mean that there are no small businesses that do well in manufacturing; about 5 percent of firms with fewer than 20 employees are involved in manufacturing. Indeed, small manufacturers sometimes outperform big ones in such innovation-driven industries as electronics, toys, and computer software.

Peter and Christina Ruprecht operate a small business in the service sector. Located in Fairfield, New Jersey, Drive-Master Co. Inc. (www.drivemaster.net) makes driving systems for persons with physical challenges and adapts vans so that they can be driven from wheelchairs. The company was started by Ruprecht's father, who lost the use of both legs to polio in 1952, and today it distributes through 400 dealerships nationwide.

■ ENTREPRENEURSHIP

We noted earlier that Dell Computer started as a one-person operation and grew into a giant corporation. Dell's growth was spurred by the imagination and skill of Michael Dell, the entrepreneur who founded the company. Although the concepts of *entrepreneurship* and *small business* are closely related, we begin by discussing some important, though often subtle, differences between them. Then we describe some key characteristics of entrepreneurial personalities and activities.

Distinctions Between Entrepreneurship and Small Business

entrepreneur
Businessperson who accepts both the risks and the opportunities involved in creating and operating a new business venture

Entrepreneurs are people who assume the risk of business ownership with a primary goal of growth and expansion.[4] Many small business owners characterize themselves as entrepreneurs, but a lot of them don't really aspire to expand their business the way the true entrepreneur does. Indeed, a person may be a small-business owner only, an entrepreneur only, or both. Consider Jack Matz, a former corporate executive in Houston who lost his job when his firm was merged. Rather than look for another management position, Matz opened a photocopying business near a local university. His goal is to earn enough money to lead a comfortable life until he retires in 10 years. Matz is a small-business owner, but with no plans to grow and expand, he's not really an entrepreneur.

Conversely, an entrepreneur would open one copy center with the idea of creating a national chain to rival Kinko's. Although this person may begin as a small-business owner, the firm's growth depends on entrepreneurial vision and astute business planning. Thus, the key distinctions between small-business ownership and entrepreneurship are vision, aspiration, and strategy. Whereas the small business owner has no plans for dramatic growth, seeking only a secure and comfortable income, the entrepreneur is motivated to grow, expand, and build—that is, to risk.

Entrepreneurial Characteristics

Many successful entrepreneurs share characteristics that set them apart from most other business owners—for example, resourcefulness and a concern for good, often personal, customer relations. Most of them also have a strong desire to be their own bosses. Many express a need to "gain control over my life" or "build for the family" and believe that building successful businesses will help them do it. They can also deal with uncertainty and risk.

Yesterday's entrepreneur was often stereotyped as "the boss"—self-reliant, male, and able to make quick, firm decisions. Today's entrepreneur is seen more often as an open-minded leader who relies on networks, business plans, and consensus. Although today's entrepreneur may be male, she is just as likely to be female. Past and present entrepreneurs also have different views on such topics as how to succeed, how to automate business, and when to rely on experience in the trade or basic business acumen.[5]

Consider Patrick Byrne. Byrne runs Overstock.com, an e-commerce firm that buys excess inventory from makers of clothing, electronics, and other products, and then offers the merchandise for resale on the Internet at deeply discounted prices. Byrne started out by creating a personal-investment fund called High Plains. After amassing a $100 million portfolio, he bought Overstock.com. Along the way, he earned a Ph.D. in philosophy from Stanford and a black belt in tae kwon do. He bicycled across the United States three times, studied more philosophy at Cambridge, and learned five languages. He discovered Overstock.com when its owners came to High Plains seeking capital. "The financials," admits Byrne, "were a joke. But buried in all that was this billion-dollar idea." And so instead of investing in the business, Byrne bought it. Unlike many Internet ventures, Overstock.com has prospered.[6]

Among other things, Byrne's story illustrates the role of risk in entrepreneurship. Risk is almost always a key element in entrepreneurship. Interestingly, most successful entrepreneurs seldom see what they do as risky. Whereas others may focus on possibilities for failure and balk at gambling everything on a new venture, most entrepreneurs are so passionate about their ideas and plans that they see little or no likelihood of failure. Byrne, for example, detected major problems in Overstock.com's financial outlook but believed so strongly in its promise that he took an enormous gamble on the company's prospects for success.

> "The financials were a joke. But buried in all that was this billion-dollar idea."
>
> **—Entrepreneur Patrick Byrne, on why he bought a struggling Internet venture**

SELF-CHECK QUESTIONS 1–3

You should now be able to answer Self-Check Questions 1–3.*

1 **Multiple Choice** Which of the following is the **best** definition of a *small business*? [select one] **(a)** one that employs fewer than 25 people; **(b)** one that operates out of a single location; **(c)** one with annual revenues of less than $100,000; **(d)** one that does business in a single country; **(e)** one that is independently owned and managed and does not dominate its market.

2 **Multiple Choice** Which area of small business is likely to be the most difficult to enter? [select one] **(a)** services; **(b)** manufacturing; **(c)** construction; **(d)** wholesaling; **(e)** transportation.

3 **True/False** Small-business owners and entrepreneurs have extremely similar profiles.

*Answers to Self-Check Questions 1–3 can be found on p. 507.

■ STARTING AND OPERATING THE SMALL BUSINESS

The Internet has changed the rules for starting and operating a small business. Setting up is easier and faster than ever before, there are more potential opportunities than at any time in history, and the ability to gather and assess information is at an all-time high. Today, for example, many one-person retailers do most of their business—both buying and selling—on Internet auction sites such as eBay.

Even so, would-be entrepreneurs must make the right start-up decisions. They must decide how to get into business—should they buy an existing business or build from the ground up? They must know when to seek expert advice and where to find sources of financing. If, for example, a new firm needs financial backing from investors or a line of credit from vendors or distributors, the entrepreneur should have in place a comprehensive, well-crafted business plan.

Crafting a Business Plan

The starting point for virtually every new business is a **business plan** in which the entrepreneur summarizes business strategy for the new venture and shows how it will be implemented.[7] A real benefit of a business plan is the fact that in the act of preparing

business plan
Document in which the entrepreneur summarizes her or his business strategy for the proposed new venture and how that strategy will be implemented

it, the would-be entrepreneur must develop the business idea on paper and firm up his or her thinking about how to launch it before investing time and money in it. The idea of the business plan isn't new. What is new is the use of specialized business plans, mostly because creditors and investors demand them as tools for deciding whether to finance or invest.

Setting Goals and Objectives A business plan describes the match between the entrepreneur's abilities and experiences and the requirements for producing and/or marketing a particular product. It also defines strategies for production and marketing, legal elements and organization, and accounting and finance. In particular, a business plan should answer three questions: (1) What are the entrepreneur's goals and objectives? (2) What strategies will be used to obtain them? (3) How will these strategies be implemented?

Revenue Forecasting Business plans should also account for the sequential nature of strategic decision making in new ventures. Entrepreneurs, for example, can't forecast revenue or sales without first researching markets. Simply asserting that the new venture will sell 100,000 units per month is not credible. Instead, the entrepreneur must demonstrate an understanding of the current market, of the strengths and weaknesses of existing firms, and of the means by which the new venture will compete. In fact, the *revenue forecast* is among the most important elements in the business plan. Without it, no one can estimate the required size of a plant, store, or office or decide how much inventory to carry and how many employees to hire.

Financial Planning Financial planning refers to the entrepreneur's plan for turning all other activities into dollars. It generally includes a cash budget, an income statement, balance sheets, and a breakeven chart. Most important is the cash budget, which shows how much money you need before you open for business and how much you need to keep the business going before it starts earning a profit.[8]

Starting the Small Business

An old Chinese proverb says that a journey of 1,000 miles begins with a single step. This is also true of a new business. The first step, of course, is the individual's commitment to becoming a business owner. In preparing a business plan, the entrepreneur must choose the industry and market in which he or she plans to compete. This choice means assessing not only industry conditions and trends but also one's own abilities and interests. Like big-business managers, small-business owners must understand the nature of the enterprises in which they are engaged.

Buying an Existing Business Next, the entrepreneur must decide whether to buy an existing business or start from scratch. Many experts recommend the first approach because, quite simply, the odds are better: If it's successful, an existing business has already proven its ability to attract customers and generate profit. It has also established relationships with lenders, suppliers, and other stakeholders. Moreover, an existing track record gives potential buyers a much clearer picture of what to expect than any estimate of a new business's prospects.

Ray Kroc bought McDonald's as an existing business, added entrepreneurial vision and business acumen, and produced a multinational giant. Both Southwest Airlines and Starbucks were small struggling operations when entrepreneurs took over and made them successful. About 35 percent of all new businesses that were started in the past decade were bought from someone else.

Starting from Scratch Despite the odds, some people seek the satisfaction that comes from planting an idea and growing it into a healthy business. There are also practical reasons to start from scratch. A new business doesn't suffer the ill effects of a prior owner's errors, and the start-up owner is free to choose lenders, equipment, inventories, locations, suppliers, and workers. Of all new businesses begun in the past decade, 64 percent were started from scratch.

But as we have already noted, the risks of starting a business from scratch are greater than those of buying an existing firm. New-business founders can only make projections about their prospects. Success or failure depends on identifying a genuine opportunity, such as a product for which many customers will pay well but which is currently unavailable. To find openings, entrepreneurs must study markets and answer the following questions:

- Who are my customers?
- Where are they?
- At what price will they buy my product?
- In what quantities will they buy?
- Who are my competitors?
- How will my product differ from those of my competitors?

Financing the Small Business

Although the choice of how to start is obviously important, it's meaningless unless you can get the money. Among the more common sources for funding are family and friends, personal savings, lending institutions, investors, and governmental agencies. Lending institutions are more likely to help finance the purchase of an existing business because the risks are better understood. Individuals starting new businesses will probably have to rely on personal resources.

According to the National Federation of Independent Business *(www.nfibonline.com)*, personal resources, not loans, are the most important source of money. Including money borrowed from friends and relatives, personal resources account for over two-thirds of all money invested in new small businesses and one-half of that is used to purchase existing businesses. Getting money from banks, independent investors, and government loans requires extra effort. At a minimum, banks and private investors will want to review business plans, and government loans have strict eligibility guidelines.

Other Sources of Investment **Venture capital companies** are groups of small investors seeking to make profits on companies with rapid growth potential. Most of these firms do not lend money. They invest it, supplying capital in return for partial ownership. They may also demand representation on boards of directors. In some cases, managers need approval from the venture capital company before making major decisions. Of all venture capital currently committed in the United States, 29 percent comes from true venture capital firms. The economic downturn that plagued U.S. business in mid-2002, however, sharply reduced new investment by venture capitalists.[9]

venture capital company
Group of small investors who invest money in companies with rapid growth potential

Small-business investment companies (SBICs) also invest in companies with potential for rapid growth. They are federally licensed to borrow money from the SBA and to invest it in or lend it to small businesses, and they are themselves investments for their shareholders. Past beneficiaries of SBIC capital include Apple Computer, Intel, and FedEx. The government also sponsors minority enterprise *small-business investment companies (MESBICs)*. As the name suggests, MESBICs target minority-owned businesses.

small-business investment company (SBIC)
Government-regulated investment company that borrows money from the SBA to invest in or lend to a small business

"The lust for entrepreneurship has not changed," says Hans Severiens (left). "And now there are great bargains to be had." Why are there so many "bargains"—so many good new companies to invest in? For one thing, venture-capital investment is down more than 50 percent. Severiens is a managing director of Band of Angels (*www.bandangels.com*), a club of about 150 private investors, or "angels," who get together once a month to hear pitches from companies looking for seed money. If they like what they hear, interested members may write personal checks (up to about $100,000) for small stakes in bankrolled firms.

SBA Financial Programs Since its founding in 1953, the SBA has sponsored financing programs for small businesses that meet standards in size and independence. Eligible firms must be unable to get private financing at reasonable terms. Under the SBA's *guaranteed loans program*, for example, small businesses can borrow from commercial lenders. The SBA guarantees to repay 75 to 85 percent of the loan up to $750,000. Through the *immediate participation loans program*, the SBA and a bank each put up shares of a loan. Under the *local development companies (LDCs)* program, the SBA works with a local corporation devoted to boosting the local economy. Spurred in large part by the boom in Internet businesses, both venture capital and loans are becoming easier to get. Most small businesses report that it has generally gotten easier to obtain loans over the last 10 years.

Other SBA Programs Even more important than its financing role is the SBA's role in helping small-business owners improve their management skills. It's easy for entrepreneurs to spend money; SBA programs show them how to spend it wisely. The SBA offers management counseling programs at virtually no cost. For example, a small-business owner who needs help in starting a new business can get it free through the *Service Corps of Retired Executives (SCORE) (www.score.org)*. All SCORE members are retired executives, and all are volunteers.

The newest of the SBA's management counseling projects is its **Small Business Development Center (SBDC)** program *(www.sba.gov/sbdc)*. Begun in 1976, SBDCs are designed to consolidate information from various disciplines and institutions, including technical and professional schools. Then they make this knowledge available to new and existing small businesses.

Small Business Development Center (SBDC)
SBA program designed to consolidate information from various disciplines and make it available to small businesses

■ FRANCHISING

McDonald's, Subway, 7-Eleven, RE/Max, Ramada, and Blockbuster are all franchises operating under licenses issued by parent companies to local owners. A

"Eventually I'd like to have a business where the money rolls in and I wouldn't have to be there much."

franchise permits the *franchisee* (buyer) to sell the product of the *franchiser* (seller, or parent company) and is a well-traveled road to entrepreneurship.

Franchisees benefit from the parent corporation's experience and expertise, and the franchiser may even supply financing. It may pick the store location, negotiate the lease, design the store, and purchase equipment. It may train the first set of employees and managers and issue standard policies and procedures. Once the business is open, the franchiser may offer savings by allowing the franchisee to purchase from a central location. Marketing strategy (especially advertising) may also be handled by the franchiser. In short, franchisees receive—that is, invest in—not only their own ready-made businesses but also expert help in running them.

franchise
Arrangement in which a buyer (*franchisee*) purchases the right to sell the good or service of the seller (*franchiser*)

Advantages and Disadvantages of Franchising

Franchises have advantages for both sellers and buyers. Franchisers can grow rapidly by using the investment money provided by franchisees. The franchisee gets to own a business and has access to big-business management skills. The franchisee does not have to build a business step by step, and because each franchise outlet is probably a carbon copy of every other outlet, failure is less likely.

Perhaps the most significant disadvantage in owning a franchise is the start-up cost. Franchise prices vary widely. The fee for a Fantastic Sam's *(www.fantasticsams.com)* hair salon is $30,000, but a McDonald's franchise costs $650,000 to $750,000, and a professional sports team can cost several hundred million dollars. Franchisees may also be obligated to contribute percentages of sales to parent corporations.

An unhappy General Nutrition Companies *(www.gnc.com)* franchisee in West Lafayette, Indiana, Ed Bishop is one of 300 GNC franchise owners who are suing their franchiser. The plaintriffs' main complaint is that the parent company is opening too many stores of its own and, what's worse, supplying them with multi-vitamins, muscle-building supplements, and herbal remedies. The result, they claim, is a dual pricing structure that works against franchise outlets. "Our worst competition," says a franchisee in Washington state, "is the company."

■ SUCCESS AND FAILURE IN SMALL BUSINESS

For every Henry Ford, Walt Disney, Mary Kay Ash, or Bill Gates—people who transformed small businesses into big ones—there are many small-business owners who fail. Figure 3.3 illustrates recent trends in new business start-ups and failures. As you can see, over a recent 10-year period, new business start-ups have numbered between 150,000 and 190,000 per year. Failures have run between 50,000 and 100,000, with a high of 97,000. In this section, we look first at a few key trends in small-business start-ups. Then we examine some of the reasons for success and failure in small-business undertakings.

Trends in Small-Business Start-Ups

Thousands of new businesses are started in the United States every year. Several factors account for this trend, and in this section, we focus on five of them.

Emergence of E-Commerce The most significant recent trend is the rapid emergence of electronic commerce. Because the Internet provides fundamentally new ways of doing business, savvy entrepreneurs have created and expanded new businesses faster and easier than ever before.10 Such leading-edge firms as America Online, Amazon.com, E*Trade™, and eBay owe their very existence to the Internet. Figure 3.4 underscores this point by summarizing the growth in online commerce from 1997 through 2001.

Crossovers from Big Business More businesses are being started by people who have opted to leave big corporations and put their experience to work for themselves. In some cases, they see great new ideas that they want to develop. Others get burned out in the corporate world. Some have lost their jobs, only to discover that working for themselves was a better idea anyway. John Chambers, the CEO of Cisco Systems *(www.cisco.com)*, is acknowledged as one of the best entrepreneurs around. But he spent several years working at IBM and Wang Laboratories *(www.wang.com/GLOBAL)*

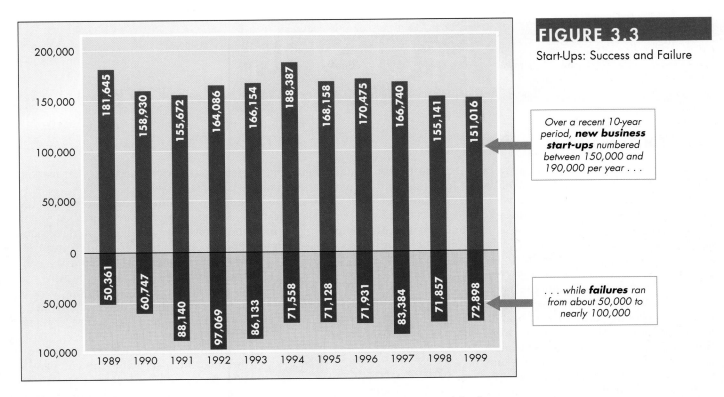

FIGURE 3.3
Start-Ups: Success and Failure

*Over a recent 10-year period, **new business start-ups** numbered between 150,000 and 190,000 per year . . .*

*. . . while **failures** ran from about 50,000 to nearly 100,000*

before he set out on his own. Under his leadership, Cisco has become one of the largest and most important technology companies in the world.

Opportunities for Minorities and Women More small businesses are also being started by minorities and women.[11] The number of businesses owned by African Americans increased by 46 percent during the most recent five-year period for which data are available and now totals about 620,000. Hispanic-owned businesses have grown at an even faster rate of 76 percent and now number about 862,000.

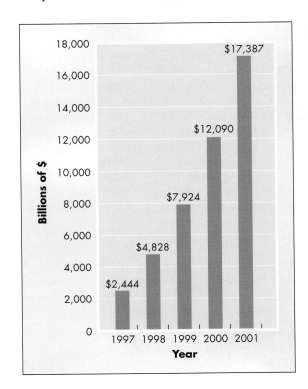

FIGURE 3.4
Growth of Online Commerce

ENTREPRENEURSHIP and New Ventures

Food for Thought

Once upon a time, dot-com start-ups were all the rage. One of the highest profiles belonged to WebVan, a firm that sold food on the Internet for home delivery. In 2001, however, WebVan went spectacularly bankrupt—to the tune of $1 billion. Many similar businesses also failed, but a new firm called FreshDirect *(www.freshdirect.com)* is building a successful online grocery business by downplaying *online* and emphasizing *grocery*. The firm's motto: "It's all about the food."

A few online food sellers have achieved modest success by partnering with traditional groceries. Most of them work through "personal shoppers" who push carts around the store and select purchases to be delivered to customers. The method, unfortunately, is not very efficient and requires the store to charge a 35-percent markup. FreshDirect uses a unique, low-cost business model. For starters, CEO Joe Fedele is a grocery expert who has already founded one thriving traditional store. Fedele likes to say, "This is a company based on food people, not dot-com people."

At FreshDirect, most of the inventory is purchased directly from suppliers rather than from intermediaries. This strategy not only cuts costs by 25 percent but also increases freshness. (FreshDirect is capitalizing on changing consumer tastes: In 1970, 30 percent of food dollars were spent on fresh—not packaged—food; now it's 70 percent.) The firm doesn't own a store. Instead, it's located in a state-of-the-art 300,000-square-foot warehouse on Long Island, near Manhattan. FreshDirect offers baked goods, prepared meals, fresh pasta, deli salads, and more, all prepared by chefs trained at top restaurants. The company delivers to 22 zip codes, all in Manhattan, Queens, and Long Island, and to "depots" set up at large corporations, where employees can get groceries delivered at the end of the day. The delivery charge is a flat $3.95, the minimum order is $40, and there is no tipping. Deliveries are scheduled only for evening and weekend hours, when Manhattan traffic is lighter. All of these policies allow FreshDirect to offer unique and tempting goods for a lower price than the corner market, plus the convenience of home delivery.

Information technology is integrated throughout the Long Island warehouse, with nine climate-controlled rooms providing optimal conditions for everything from avocados to smoked salmon. Equipment is linked to controls in a central room, where alarms sound if a conveyer belt stops or a freezer warms up. To ensure food safety, the entire plant is automatically hosed down nightly with antiseptic foam and then sprayed with an antibacterial coating.

> *"I'm not a corporate CEO. I'm not a dot-commer. I'm just a %#&@ lunatic who knows about food."*
>
> —Joe Fedele, CEO of online grocer FreshDirect

Although Fedele focuses mostly on the food, he also wants the company's Web pages to be simple and appealing. The site is attractive, uncluttered, and easy to navigate. You can change your view—with or without pictures, with large pictures or thumbnails—and sign-up takes just minutes. Categories, subcategories, and a search feature make it easy to find products. You can sort items by brand or price, and there are expert recommendations and lists of top sellers.

In its most ambitious move yet, FreshDirect has asked each of its chefs to develop recipes to be programmed by artificial intelligence software. If, during the preparation process, an ingredient's barcode readout, electronic-scale reading, or computer-controlled oven setting is not correct, the equipment shuts down. Because this practice ensures that hourly workers follow recipes exactly, FreshDirect controls quality while using less-expensive labor.

Some users have reported problems—overripe grapes, mixed-up deliveries. Some people worry about the lack of direct contact, especially those who want to sniff the melons or squeeze the bread. A few cite online commerce in general when bemoaning the impersonal nature of contemporary society. Most shoppers, however, seem to find online grocery shopping a liberating experience. Fedele likes to remind customers that "I'm not a corporate CEO. I'm not a dot-commer. I'm just a %#&@ lunatic who knows about food."

Ownership among Asians and Pacific Islanders has increased 56 percent, to over 600,000. Although ownership among Native Americans and Alaskan natives is still modest, at slightly over 100,000, the total represents a five-year increase of 93 percent.

Finally, there are now 9.1 million businesses owned by women—38 percent of all businesses in the United States. Combined, they generate nearly $4 trillion in revenue a year—an increase of 132 percent since 1992. Since 1992, the number of people that they employ has grown to around 27.5 million—an increase of 108 percent.[12]

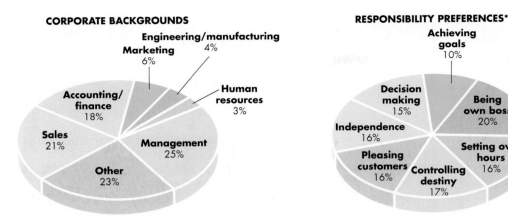

FIGURE 3.5

Profiles of Women Entrepreneurs

*The total is more than 100% because multiple responses were allowed.

Figure 3.5 summarizes the corporate backgrounds of women entrepreneurs and provides some insight into what they like about running their own businesses. Corporate positions in general management (25 percent), sales (21 percent), and accounting and finance (18 percent) account for almost two-thirds of the women who start their own businesses. Once in charge of their own businesses, women also report that they like being their own bosses, setting their own hours, controlling their own destinies, relating to customers, making decisions, and achieving goals. "Women-owned businesses," says Teresa Cavanaugh, director of the Women Entrepreneur's Connection at BankBoston, "are the largest emerging segment of the small-business market. Women-owned businesses are an economic force that no bank can afford to overlook."

> "Women-owned businesses are an economic force that no bank can afford to overlook."
>
> —Teresa Cavanaugh, Women Entrepreneur's Connection, BankBoston

Global Opportunities Many entrepreneurs are also finding new opportunities in foreign markets. Doug Mellinger is founder and CEO of PRT Group Inc., a software development company. One of Mellinger's biggest problems was finding trained programmers. There aren't enough American programmers to go around, and foreign-born programmers face strict immigration quotas. So Mellinger set up shop on Barbados, a Caribbean island where the government helps him attract foreign programmers and does everything it can to make things easier. Today, PRT, which is a part of enherent Corp. *(www.enherent.com)*, has customers and suppliers from dozens of nations.

Better Survival Rates Finally, more people are encouraged to test their skills as entrepreneurs because the small-business failure rate has declined. During the 1960s and 1970s, less than half of all new start-ups survived more than 18 months; only one in five lasted 10 years. Now, however, new businesses have a better chance. Of all those started in the 1980s, over 77 percent remained in operation for at least three years. The SBA now estimates that 40 percent can expect to survive for six years.

Reasons for Failure

Unfortunately, 63 percent of all new businesses will not celebrate a sixth anniversary. Why do some succeed and others fail? Although no set pattern has been established, four general factors contribute to failure:

1 **Managerial incompetence or inexperience.** Some entrepreneurs put their faith in common sense, overestimate their own managerial skills, or believe that

Say WHAT YOU MEAN

THE WIDE WORLD OF RISK

One reason why globalization has become such a factor in everyday business life is the expanded reach and power of multinational companies. Many large corporations have actually become engines for innovation as well as growth, adapting to new markets and new economic circumstances. In a highly interconnected world, however, it's often hard to figure out the complex ownership and organizational structures of many global corporations. Sometimes, for example, their branding practices and management structures lead people to think that they're local companies when, in fact, the real source of corporate power may lie thousands of miles away on another continent.

One thing's for sure: If you're going to be dealing with a company overseas, you'd better have a good idea of where and how decisions are made and, of course, who has the real power to make them.

Remember, too, that different cultures have different attitudes when it comes to entrepreneurship.

In some countries and cultures, like that of the United States, there's a lively entrepreneurial spirit. Businesspeople are open to taking risks, and if they fail, they tend to pick themselves up and move on to something else. In Japan, however, the entrepreneurial spirit is often tempered by the need for consensus and getting everyone on board. This approach requires a lot of patience and the ability to compromise. Moreover, when it comes to failure, it's not so easy for Japanese businesspeople to brush off past mistakes. Knowing the cultural forces that shape both a business organization and people's attitudes toward risk, success, and failure is an elementary but important component of international business.

In any case, global companies are major players in today's business world, and a lot of people are demanding that they also be good global citizens by respecting human rights covenants and cultural diversity, being sensitive to local environments, and giving back to the communities in which they operate.

hard work alone ensures success. If managers don't know how to make basic business decisions or don't understand basic management principles, they aren't likely to succeed in the long run.

2 **Neglect.** Some entrepreneurs try to launch ventures in their spare time, and others devote only limited time to new businesses. But starting a small business demands an overwhelming time commitment. If you aren't willing to put in the time and effort that a business requires, you aren't likely to survive.

3 **Weak control systems.** Effective control systems keep a business on track and alert managers to potential trouble. If your control systems don't signal impending problems, you may be in serious trouble before you spot more obvious difficulties.

4 **Insufficient capital.** Some entrepreneurs are overly optimistic about how soon they'll start earning profits. In most cases, it takes months or even years. Amazon.com didn't earn a profit for 10 years but obviously still required capital to pay employees and to cover other expenses. Experts say you need enough capital to operate at least six months without earning a profit; some recommend enough to last a year.[13]

Reasons for Success

Four basic factors are also typically cited to explain small-business success:

1 **Hard work, drive, and dedication.** Small-business owners must be committed to succeeding and willing to spend the time and effort to make it happen. Gladys

Edmunds, a single mother in Pittsburgh, washed laundry, made chicken dinners to sell to cab drivers, and sold fire extinguishers door to door to earn start-up money. Today, Edmunds Travel Consultants employs eight people and earns about $6 million a year.[14]

2 Market demand for the products or services being provided. Careful analysis of market conditions can help small-business owners assess the probable reception of their products. Attempts to expand restaurants specializing in baked potatoes, muffins, and gelato have largely failed, but hamburger and pizza chains continue to expand.

3 Managerial competence. Successful owners may acquire competence through training or experience or by drawing on the expertise of others. Few, however, succeed alone or straight out of college. Most spend time in successful companies or partner with others in order to bring expertise to a new business.

4 Luck. After Alan McKim started Clean Harbors *(www.cleanharbors.com)*, an environmental cleanup firm in New England, he struggled to keep his business afloat. Then the U.S. government committed $1.6 billion to toxic waste cleanup—McKim's specialty. He landed several large government contracts and put his business on solid financial footing. Had the government fund not been created at just the right time, McKim may well have failed.

SELF-CHECK QUESTIONS 4–6

You should now be able to answer Self-Check Questions 4–6.*

4 True/False Preparing a *business plan* is usually an optional step for a would-be entrepreneur.

5 Multiple Choice Which of the following is usually the most important source of financing for a new business? [select one] **(a)** banks; **(b)** investors; **(c)** government agencies such as the SBA; **(d)** personal resources; **(e)** lottery winnings.

6 Multiple Choice Which of the following is **not a** common cause of business failure? [select one] **(a)** managerial incompetence and inexperience; **(b)** neglect; **(c)** weak controls; **(d)** employee theft or sabotage; **(e)** insufficient capital.

***Answers to Self-Check Questions 4–6 can be found on p. 507.**

■ NONCORPORATE BUSINESS OWNERSHIP

Whether they intend to run small farms, large factories, or online e-tailers, all business operators must decide which form of legal ownership best suits their goals: *sole proprietorship, partnership,* or *corporation.* Because this choice affects a host of managerial and financial issues, few decisions are more critical. Entrepreneurs must consider their own preferences, their immediate and long-range needs, and the advantages and disadvantages of each form. Table 3.1 compares the most important differences among the three major ownership forms.

TABLE 3.1

Comparative Summary: Three Forms of Business

Business Form	Liability	Continuity	Management	Sources of Investment
Proprietorship	Personal, unlimited	Ends with death or decision of owner	Personal, unrestricted	Personal
General Partnership	Personal, unlimited	Ends with death or decision of any partner	Unrestricted or depends on partnership agreement	Personal by partner(s)
Corporation	Capital invested	As stated in charter, perpetual or for specified period of years	Under control of board of directors, which is selected by stockholders	Purchase of stock

Sole Proprietorships

sole proprietorship
Business owned and usually operated by one person who is responsible for all of its debts

The **sole proprietorship** is owned and usually operated by one person. About 73 percent of all U.S. businesses are sole proprietorships; however, they account for only about 5 percent of total business revenues.[15] Though usually small, they may be as large as steel mills or department stores.

Advantages of Sole Proprietorships Freedom may be the most important benefit of sole proprietorships. Because they own their businesses, sole proprietors answer to no one but themselves. Sole proprietorships are also easy to form. Sometimes you can go into business simply by putting a sign on the door. The simplicity of legal setup procedures makes this form appealing to self-starters and independent spirits, as do low start-up costs.

Another attractive feature is the tax benefits extended to businesses that are likely to suffer losses in their early stages. Tax laws permit owners to treat sales revenues and operating expenses as part of their personal finances. They can thus cut taxes by deducting business losses from income earned from personal sources other than the business.

unlimited liability
Legal principle holding owners responsible for paying off all debts of a business

Disadvantages of Sole Proprietorships A major drawback is **unlimited liability**: A sole proprietor is personally liable for all debts incurred by the business. If it fails to generate enough cash, bills must be paid out of the owner's pocket. Another disadvantage is lack of continuity: A sole proprietorship legally dissolves when the owner dies. Although the business can be reorganized by a successor, executors or heirs must otherwise sell its assets.

Finally, a sole proprietorship depends on the resources of one person whose managerial and financial limitations may constrain the business. Sole proprietors often find it hard to borrow money to start up or expand. Many bankers fear that they won't be able to recover loans if owners become disabled or insolvent.

Partnerships

general partnership
Business with two or more owners who share in both the operation of the firm and the financial responsibility for its debts

The partnership is frequently used by professionals. The most common type, the **general partnership**, is a sole proprietorship multiplied by the number of partner-owners. There is no legal limit to the number of parties, but the average is slightly under 10. Partners may invest equal or unequal sums of money and may earn profits that bear no relation to their investments. Thus, a partner with no financial investment in a two-person partnership could receive 50 percent or more of the profits if he or she has made some other contribution—say, a well-known name or special expertise.

Advantages of Partnerships The most striking advantage of general partnerships is the ability to grow by adding new talent and money. Because banks prefer to make loans to enterprises that are not dependent on single individuals, partnerships find it easier to borrow than sole proprietorships. They can also invite new partners to join by investing money.

Like a sole proprietorship, a partnership can be organized by meeting only a few legal requirements. Even so, all partnerships must begin with an agreement of some kind. In all but two states, the Revised Uniform Limited Partnership Act requires the filing of specific information about the business and its partners. Partners may also agree to bind themselves in ways not specified by law. In any case, an agreement should answer questions such as the following:

- Who invested what sums?
- Who will receive what share of the profits?
- Who does what and who reports to whom?
- How may the partnership be dissolved? In the event of dissolution, how will assets be distributed?
- How will surviving partners be protected from claims made by a deceased partner's heirs?

The partnership agreement is strictly a private document. No laws require partners to file agreements with any government agency. Nor are partnerships regarded as legal entities. In the eyes of the law, a partnership is just two or more people working together. Because partnerships have no independent legal standing, the Internal Revenue Service (IRS) taxes partners as individuals.

Disadvantages of Partnerships For general partnerships as for sole proprietorships, unlimited liability is the greatest drawback. Each partner may be liable for all debts incurred by the partnership. If any partner incurs a business debt (with or without the knowledge of the others), all partners may be liable.

Partnerships also share with sole proprietorships the potential lack of continuity. When one partner dies or leaves, the original partnership dissolves, even if one or more of the other partners want it to continue. But dissolution need not mean a loss of sales revenues. Survivors may form a new partnership to retain the old firm's business. A related disadvantage is difficulty in transferring ownership. No partner may sell out without the consent of the others. A partner who wants to retire or to transfer interest to a son or daughter must have the other partners' consent.

limited partnership
Type of partnership consisting of limited partners and an active or managing partner

Alternatives to General Partnerships Because of these disadvantages, general partnerships are among the least popular forms of business. Roughly 1.86 million U.S. partnerships generate only about 6 percent of total sales revenues. To resolve some of the problems inherent in general partnerships, especially unlimited liability, some partners have tried alternative agreements. The **limited partnership** allows for **limited partners** who invest money and also are liable for debts only to the extent of their investments. They cannot, however, take active roles in business operations. A limited partnership must have at least one **general** (or **active**) **partner**, mostly for liability purposes. This is usually the person who runs the business and is responsible for its survival and growth.

limited partner
Partner who does not share in a firm's management and is liable for its debts only to the limits of said partner's investment

general (or **active**) **partner**
Partner who actively manages a firm and who has unlimited liability for its debts

■ CORPORATIONS

There are about 4.85 million corporations in the United States. As you can see from Figure 3.6, they account for about 20 percent of all U.S. businesses but generate about 89 percent of all sales revenues.[16] Almost all large businesses use this form, and corporations dominate global business. According to the most recent data, Wal-Mart Stores *(www.walmartstores.com)*, the world's largest retailer, posted annual revenue of over $246 billion, with total profits of $8 billion. Even "smaller" large corporations post huge sales figures. Another retailer, Neiman Marcus *(www.neimanmarcus.com)*, though 500th among U.S. corporations, posted a profit of $99 million on annual sales of $2.9 billion. Given the size and influence of this form of ownership, we will devote a great deal of attention to various aspects of corporations.[17]

The Corporate Entity

When you think of corporations, you probably think of giant operations such as General Motors and IBM. The very word *corporation* inspires images of size and power. In reality, however, your corner newsstand has as much right to incorporate as a giant automaker. Moreover, the newsstand and GM would share the characteristics of all **corporations**: legal status as separate entities, property rights and obligations, and indefinite life spans.

In 1819, the U.S. Supreme Court defined a corporation as "an artificial being, invisible, intangible, and existing only in contemplation of the law." The Court, thus, defined the corporation as a legal person. Corporations may, therefore, perform the following activities:

■ Sue and be sued
■ Buy, hold, and sell property
■ Make and sell products
■ Commit crimes and be tried and punished for them

corporation
Business that is legally considered an entity separate from its owners and is liable for its own debts; owners' liability extends to the limits of their investments

Advantages of Incorporation The biggest advantage of corporations is **limited liability**: Investor liability is limited to personal investment in the corporation. In the event of failure, the courts may seize and sell a corporation's assets but cannot touch

limited liability
Legal principle holding investors liable for a firm's debts only to the limits of their personal investments in it

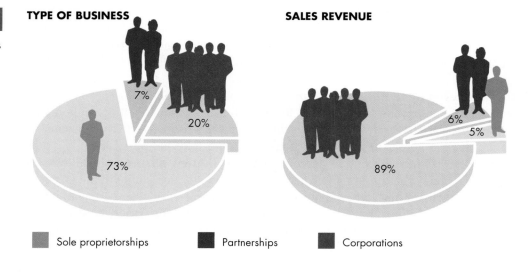

FIGURE 3.6

Proportions of U.S. Firms in Terms of Organization Type and Sales Revenue

TYPE OF BUSINESS

7%
20%
73%

SALES REVENUE

6%
5%
89%

■ Sole proprietorships   ■ Partnerships   ■ Corporations

the investors' personal possessions. If, for example, you invest $1,000 in a corporation that goes bankrupt, you may lose your $1,000, but no more. In other words, $1,000 is the extent of your liability.

Another advantage is continuity. Because it has a legal life independent of founders and owners, a corporation can, at least in theory, continue forever. Shares of stock may be sold or passed on to heirs, and most corporations also benefit from the continuity provided by professional management. Finally, corporations have advantages in raising money. By selling stock, they expand the number of investors and the amount of available funds. Continuity and legal status tend to make lenders more willing to grant loans.

Disadvantages of Incorporation Although a chief attraction is ease of transferring ownership, this same feature can create complications. For example, using a legal process called a **tender offer**—an offer to buy shares made by a prospective buyer directly to a corporation's shareholders—a corporation can be taken over against the will of its managers. Another disadvantage is start-up cost. Corporations are heavily regulated, and incorporation entails meeting the complex legal requirements of the state in which the firm is chartered.

Double Taxation The biggest disadvantage of incorporation is **double taxation**. First, a corporation pays income taxes on company profits. In addition, stockholders pay taxes on income returned by their investments in the corporation. Thus, the profits earned by corporations are taxed twice—once at the corporate level and again at the ownership level. Because profits are treated as owners' personal income, sole proprietorships and partnerships are taxed only once.

The advantages and disadvantages of corporate ownership have inspired laws establishing different kinds of corporations. Most are intended to help businesses take advantage of the benefits of the corporate model without assuming all of the disadvantages. We discuss these corporate forms next.

Types of Corporations

We can classify corporations as either *public* or *private*. But within these broad categories, we can identify several specific types of corporations, some of which are summarized in Table 3.2.

- The most common form of U.S. corporation is the **closely held corporation** (or simply **private corporation**). Stock is held by only a few people and is not available for sale to the public. The controlling group of stockholders may be a family, a management group, or even the firm's employees. When shares are publicly issued, the firm becomes a **publicly held** (or **public**) **corporation**. Stock is widely held and available for sale to the public.
- The **S corporation** is a hybrid of a closely held corporation and partnership. It is organized and operates like a corporation, but it is treated like a partnership for tax purposes. To qualify, firms must meet stringent legal conditions.
- Another hybrid is the **limited liability corporation**, or **LLC**. Owners are taxed like partners, each paying personal taxes only. However, they also enjoy the benefits of limited liability accorded to publicly held corporations. LLCs have grown in popularity in recent years, partially because of IRS rulings that allow corporations, partnerships, and foreign investors to be partial owners.
- **Professional corporations** are most likely comprised of doctors, lawyers, accountants, or other professionals. They are not immune from unlimited liability.

tender offer
Offer to buy shares made by a prospective buyer directly to a target corporation's shareholders, who then make individual decisions about whether to sell

double taxation
Situation in which taxes may be payable both by a corporation on its profits and by shareholders on dividend incomes

closely held (or **private**) **corporation**
Corporation whose stock is held by only a few people and is not available for sale to the general public

publicly held (or **public**) **corporation**
Corporation whose stock is widely held and available for sale to the general public

S corporation
Hybrid of a closely held corporation and a partnership, organized and operated like a corporation but treated as a partnership for tax purposes

limited liability corporation (LLC)
Hybrid of a publicly held corporation and a partnership in which owners are taxed as partners but enjoy the benefits of limited liability

professional corporation
Form of ownership allowing professionals to take advantage of corporate benefits while granting them limited business liability and unlimited professional liability

TABLE 3.2

Types of Corporations

Type	Distinguishing Features	Examples
Closely Held	Stock held by only a few people	Blue Cross/Blue Shield
	Subject to corporate taxation	MasterCard
		Primestar
Publicly Held	Stock widely held among many investors	Dell Computer
	Subject to corporate taxation	Starbucks
		Texas Instruments
Subchapter S	Organized much like a closely held corporation	Minglewood Associates
	Subject to additional regulation	Entech Pest Systems
	Subject to partnership taxation	Frontier Bank
Limited Liability	Organized much like a publicly held corporation	Pacific Northwest Associates
	Subject to additional regulation	Global Ground Support
	Subject to partnership taxation	Ritz Carlton
Professional	Organized like a partnership	Norman Hui, DDS & Associates
	Subject to partnership taxation	B & H Engineering
	Limited business liability	Anderson, McCoy & Orta
	Unlimited professional liability	
Multinational	Spans national boundaries	Toyota
	Subject to regulation in multiple countries	Nestlé
		General Electric

Professional negligence by a member entails personal liability on the individual's part.

■ As the term implies, the **multinational** or **transnational corporation** spans national boundaries. Stock may be traded on the exchanges of several countries, and managers are likely to be of different nationalities.

multinational or **transnational corporation**
Form of corporation spanning national boundaries

Managing a Corporation

Creating any type of corporation can be complicated. In addition, once the corporate entity comes into existence, it must be managed by people who understand the principles of **corporate governance**—the roles of shareholders, directors, and other managers in corporate decision making. In this section, we discuss the principles of *stock ownership* and *stockholders' rights* and describe the role of *boards of directors*. We then examine some important trends in corporate ownership.

corporate governance
Roles of shareholders, directors, and other managers in corporate decision making

Corporate Governance Corporate governance is established by the firm's bylaws and usually involves three distinct bodies. **Stockholders** (or **shareholders**) are the owners of a corporation—investors who buy ownership shares in the form of stock. The *board of directors* is a group elected by stockholders to oversee corporate management. Corporate *officers* are top managers hired by the board to run the corporation on a day-to-day basis.

stockholder (or **shareholder**)
Owner of shares of stock in a corporation

stock
Share of ownership in a corporation

Stock Ownership and Stockholders' Rights Corporations sell shares, called **stock**, to investors who then become stockholders, or shareholders. Profits are distributed among stockholders in the form of dividends, and corporate managers serve at stockholders' discretion. In a closely held corporation, only a few people own stock. Shares of publicly held corporations are widely held.

preferred stock
Stock that offers its holders fixed dividends and priority claims over assets but no corporate voting rights

   Preferred stock pays fixed dividends, much like the interest on savings accounts. Preferred stockholders are so called because they have preference, or priority, over common stockholders when dividends are distributed and, if a business

"I had no idea the company was in anything but excellent shape," pleads former Enron CEO Jeffrey K. Skilling. Skilling, who quit Enron in August 2001, five months before the company filed for the nation's largest-ever bankruptcy, was CEO for only six months but had been chief operating officer since 1996. He has implied that his gravest sin as chief executive was losing touch with subordinates who turned out to be corrupt.

liquidates, when the value of assets is distributed. Preferred stockholders do not vote. **Common stock** usually pays dividends only if the company makes a profit, and common stockholders have the last claims to any of a bankrupt company's assets. They do, however, enjoy voting rights, with each share worth one vote. Dividends on all stock are paid on a per-share basis.

common stock
Stock that pays dividends and guarantees corporate voting rights but offers last claims over assets

Boards of Directors The governing body of a corporation is its **board of directors**. Boards communicate with stockholders and other stakeholders through such channels as the annual report—a summary of the firm's financial health. They also set policy on dividends, major spending, and executive compensation. They are legally responsible for corporate actions and are increasingly being held liable for them.

board of directors
Governing body of a corporation that reports to its shareholders and delegates power to run its day-to-day operations while remaining responsible for sustaining its assets

Officers Although board members oversee operations, most do not participate in day-to-day management. Rather, they hire a team of managers to run the firm. This team, called *officers*, is usually headed by the firm's **chief executive officer**, or **CEO**, who is responsible for overall performance. Other officers typically include a *president*, who is responsible for internal management, and *vice presidents*, who oversee various functional areas such as marketing and operations.

chief executive officer (CEO)
Top manager hired by the board of directors to run a corporation

One of the outgrowths of the Enron debacle is heightened criticism of corporate governance in the United States.[18] Many Enron-related lawsuits target the firm's officers and directors. In a classic example of how governing bodies can fail shareholders, Enron's board of directors formally voted in at least one instance to set aside the company's code of ethics because its members wanted to approve an action that violated it. Similar charges have been leveled at the board of WorldCom. Other corporations whose boards have come under ethical scrutiny include Bank of America, Eastman Kodak, Lucent, Xerox, and ICN Pharmaceuticals.[19] Of course, many other boards continue to function very effectively, including those at Texas Instruments, Intel, Pfizer, Target, and Coca-Cola.

Special Issues in Corporate Ownership

In recent years, several issues have grown in importance in the area of corporate ownership, including *joint ventures* and *strategic alliances*, *employee stock ownership plans*, and *institutional ownership*. Other important issues in contemporary corporate ownership involve *mergers, acquisitions, divestitures*, and *spin-offs*.

strategic alliance
Strategy in which two or more organizations collaborate on a project for mutual gain

Joint Ventures and Strategic Alliances In a **strategic alliance**, two or more organizations collaborate on a project for mutual gain. When partners share ownership of what is essentially a new enterprise, it is called a **joint venture**. The number of strategic alliances has increased rapidly in recent years on both domestic and international fronts.

joint venture
Strategic alliance in which the collaboration involves joint ownership of the new venture

Employee Stock Ownership Plans An **employee stock ownership plan (ESOP)** allows employees to own a significant share of the corporation through trusts established on their behalf. Current estimates count almost 10,000 ESOPs in the United States. The growth rate in new ESOPs has slowed a bit in recent years, but they still are an important part of corporate ownership patterns in the United States.[20]

employee stock ownership plan (ESOP)
Arrangement in which a corporation holds its own stock in trust for its employees, who gradually receive ownership of the stock and control its voting rights

institutional investor
Large investor, such as a mutual fund or a pension fund, that purchases large blocks of corporate stock

Institutional Ownership Most individual investors don't own enough stock to exert influence on corporate managers. In recent years, however, more stock has been purchased by **institutional investors**. Because they control enormous resources, these investors—especially mutual and pension funds—can buy huge blocks of stock. The national teachers' retirement system (TIAA-CREF) *(www.tiaa-cref.org)* has assets of over $255 billion, much of it invested in stocks. Institutional investors own almost 40 percent of all the stock issued in the United States.

Mergers, Acquisitions, Divestitures, and Spin-Offs Another important set of issues includes mergers, acquisitions, divestitures, and spin-offs. Mergers and acquisitions involve the legal joining of two or more corporations. A divestiture occurs when a corporation sells a business operation to another corporation; with a spin-off, it creates a new operation.

merger
The union of two corporations to form a new corporation

Mergers and Acquisitions (M&As) A **merger** occurs when two firms combine to create a new company. In an **acquisition**, one firm buys another outright. Many deals that are loosely called mergers are really acquisitions. Why? Because one of the two firms will usually control the newly combined ownership. In general, when the two firms are roughly the same size, the combination is usually called a merger even if one firm is taking control of the other. When the acquiring firm is substantially larger than the acquired firm, the deal is really an acquisition. So-called *M&As* are an important form of corporate strategy. They let firms increase product lines, expand operations, go international, and create new enterprises.

acquisition
The purchase of one company by another

Divestitures and Spin-Offs Sometimes a corporation decides to sell a part of its existing business operations or set it up as a new and independent corporation. There may be several reasons for such a step. A firm might decide, for example, that it should focus more specifically on its core businesses; thus, it will sell off unrelated and/or underperforming businesses. Such a sale is called a **divestiture**.

divestiture
Strategy whereby a firm sells one or more of its business units

When a firm sells part of itself to raise capital, the strategy is known as a **spin-off**. A spin-off may also mean that a firm deems a business unit more valuable as a separate company. The Limited *(www.limited.com)*, for example, spun off three of its subsidiaries—Victoria's Secret, Bath & Body Works, and White Barn Candle Co.— to create a new firm called Intimate Brands, Inc. *(www.intimatebrands.com)*, which it then offered through an IPO. The Limited retained 84-percent ownership of Intimate Brands while getting an infusion of new capital.

spin-off
Strategy of setting up one or more corporate units as new, independent corporations

SELF-CHECK QUESTIONS 7-9

You should now be able to answer Self-Check Questions 7-9.*

7 Multiple Choice The *sole proprietorship* enjoys which of the following advantages? [select one] **(a)** freedom; **(b)** simplicity; **(c)** tax benefits; **(d)** all of the above; **(e)** none of the above.

8 True/False Because of their numerous advantages, *general partnerships* are among the most popular forms of business ownership.

9 Multiple Choice Which of the following is **not** a kind of *corporation*? [select one] **(a)** public corporation; **(b)** private corporation; **(c)** master limited corporation; **(d)** limited liability corporation; **(e)** professional corporation.

*Answers to Self-Check Questions 7-9 can be found on p. 507.

Continued from page 70

HOW HIGH CAN AN AIRLINE FLY?

David Neeleman's dedication to monitoring JetBlue's performance is matched by his passion for feedback. He jumps on a plane once a week or so, and not just to ride: He loads baggage and serves drinks. Along the way, he smiles politely when passengers tell him how well he's doing but prefers to hear more about their complaints. No concern is too small or too large, whether a desire for better biscotti or a request for more flights to Chicago. Customers' suggestions are taken seriously. In response to customer input, for example, Neeleman instituted a frequent-flyer program in July 2002. He also gives employees the authority to make immediate customer-service decisions. "Employees at other airlines," he explains, "get so caught up in procedure—rules, rules, rules—that they often forget there is a paying customer there." JetBlue passengers get discount coupons and free accommodations if their flight is diverted, compensation that rival airlines don't always provide.

JetBlue is clearly a successful enterprise. But the question still remains: Can success be sustained? Expansion, for example, is the trap that ensnared many now-failed airline ventures, and Neeleman intends to expand. "I can't believe how quickly we got out of the gate and how profitable we became," he says. "Now I don't think there's a limit to how big JetBlue can get." Many observers, however, think that successful expansion will be a big challenge for the company: "It's easy for JetBlue to be golden with 30 airplanes," observes one industry expert, "but it doesn't mean it can manage 100." As increasing size leads to increasing complexity, Neeleman will have to guard against inefficiencies and too much bureaucracy. In addition, costs will undoubtedly rise, as planes age and skilled workers demand raises, and unionization (which will also increase labor costs) is probably on the horizon.

There is, of course, some room for growth. "In a lot of places now," says Neeleman, "there's no low-fare nonstop service. That creates some opportunities for us." In the future, however, JetBlue will have a harder and harder time finding opportunities to foster growth. At present, funds for expansion are cheap because JetBlue raised start-up capital from outside investors. But to buy more planes, the firm will have borrow money, and that will increase debt expense.

> **E**mployees at other airlines get so caught up in procedure—rules, rules, rules—that they often forget there is a paying customer there."
>
> **—JetBlue CEO David Neeleman**

Questions for Discussion

1 Why do you think JetBlue has succeeded where so many other start-up airlines have failed?

2 Is David Neeleman an entrepreneur? Why or why not?

3 Could JetBlue's success be emulated in the same way that JetBlue has emulated Southwest? Why or why not?

4 Is JetBlue a small business? Why or why not?

■ SUMMARY OF LEARNING OBJECTIVES

1 Define *small business,* discuss its importance to the U.S. economy, and explain which *types of small business* are most likely to succeed.

A **small business** is independently owned and managed and does not dominate its market. The contribution of small business can be measured by its effects on three aspects of the economic system: (1) *job creation*; (2) *innovation*; and (3) *importance to big business*. The major small-business industry groups are (1) *services*; (2) *construction*; (3) *finance and insurance*; (4) *wholesaling*; and (5) *transportation and manufacturing*. The more resources an industry requires, the harder it is to start a business in it and the less likely it is to be dominated by small firms.

2 Explain *entrepreneurship* and describe some key characteristics of entrepreneurial personalities and activities.

Entrepreneurs assume the risk of business ownership with a primary goal of growth and expansion. Many small-business owners like to think of themselves as entrepreneurs, but a person may be a small-business owner only, an entrepreneur only, or both. The basic distinction between small-business ownership and entrepreneurship is aspiration—the entrepreneur's desire to start a business and make it grow. Most successful entrepreneurs are resourceful and concerned with customer relations. They have a strong desire to be their own bosses and can handle ambiguity and surprises. Today's entrepreneur is often an open-minded leader who relies on networks, business plans, and consensus and is just as likely to be female as male. Finally, although successful entrepreneurs understand the role of risk, they do not necessarily regard what they do as risky. Whereas others may see possibilities for failure and balk at gambling on a new venture, most entrepreneurs feel so strongly about their ideas and plans that they see little or no likelihood of failure.

3 Describe the *business plan* and the *start-up decisions* made by small businesses and identify sources of *financial aid*.

The starting point for virtually every new business is a **business plan**, in which the entrepreneur summarizes business strategy for the new venture and shows how it will be implemented. Business plans are increasingly important because creditors and investors demand them as tools for deciding whether to finance or invest. Then entrepreneurs must decide whether to buy an existing business or to start from scratch. Common funding sources include family and friends, savings, lenders, investors, and government agencies.

Banks and private investors usually want to see formal business plans—detailed outlines of proposed businesses and markets, owners' backgrounds, and other sources of funding. Government loans have strict eligibility guidelines. Other sources include **venture capital companies**—groups of small investors seeking to make profits on companies with rapid growth potential. Federally licensed to borrow money from the **Small Business Administration (SBA)** and to invest in or lend to small businesses, **small-business investment companies (SBICs)** also seek profits in companies with potential for rapid growth. Minority enterprise small-business investment companies (MESBICs) specialize in financing minority-owned and -operated businesses.

4 Explain the main reasons why new business start-ups are increasing and identify the reasons for success and failure in small businesses.

Five factors account for the fact that thousands of new businesses are started in the United States every year: (1) *the emergence of e-commerce*; (2) *entrepreneurs who cross over from big business*; (3) *increased opportunities for minorities and women*; (4) *new opportunities in global enterprise*; and (5) *improved rates of survival*. Four factors contribute to small-business failure: (1) *managerial incompetence or inexperience*; (2) *neglect*; (3) *weak control systems*; and (4) *insufficient capital*. Similarly, four basic factors explain most small-business success: (1) *hard work, drive, and dedication*; (2) *market demand for the goods or services being provided*; (3) *managerial competence*; and (4) *luck*.

5 Explain *sole proprietorships* and *partnerships* and discuss the advantages and disadvantages of each.

The **sole proprietorship** is owned and usually operated by one person. There are tax benefits for new businesses that are likely to suffer losses in early stages: Because sole proprietors may treat revenues and expenses as part of their personal finances, they can cut their taxes by deducting business losses from income earned elsewhere. A major drawback is **unlimited liability**. Another disadvantage is lack of continuity: A sole proprietorship dissolves when the owner dies. Finally, a sole proprietorship depends on the resources of a single individual.

The **general partnership** is a sole proprietorship multiplied by the number of partner-owners. The biggest advantage is its ability to grow by adding new talent and money. Partners are taxed as individuals, and unlimited liability is a drawback. Partnerships may lack continuity, and transferring ownership may be hard. No partner may sell out without the consent of the others. To resolve some of these problems, other types of agreements, such as the **limited partnership**, have been developed.

6 **Describe the different kinds of *corporations* and the advantages and disadvantages of each, explain the basic issues in creating and managing, and identify recent trends in corporate ownership.**

All **corporations** share certain characteristics: legal status as separate entities, property rights and obligations, and indefinite life spans. They may sue and be sued; buy, hold, and sell property; make and sell products; commit crimes and be tried and punished for them. The biggest advantage of incorporation is **limited liability**. Another advantage is continuity. Finally, corporations have advantages in raising money. By selling **stock**, they expand the number of investors and the amount of available funds. Legal protections tend to make lenders more willing to grant loans.

One disadvantage is that by means of a **tender offer**, a corporation can be taken over against the will of its managers. Another disadvantage is start-up cost. Corporations are heavily regulated and must meet complex legal requirements in the states in which they're chartered. The greatest potential drawback to incorporation is **double taxation**.

The corporate entity is managed by people who understand the principles of **corporate governance**—the roles of **shareholders**, directors, and other managers in corporate decision making. The governing body of a corporation is its **board of directors**.

In a **strategic alliance**, two or more organizations collaborate on a project for mutual gain. The **employee stock ownership plan (ESOP)** allows employees to own a significant share of the corporation through trusts established on their behalf. A **merger** occurs when two firms combine to create a new company. In an **acquisition**, one firm buys another outright. A **divestiture** occurs when a corporation sells a part of its existing business operations or sets it up as a new and independent corporation. When a firm sells part of itself to raise capital, the strategy is known as a **spin-off**.

■ KEY TERMS

Small Business Administration (SBA) (p. 70)

small business (p. 70)

entrepreneur (p. 74)

business plan (p. 75)

venture capital company (p. 77)

small-business investment company (SBIC) (p. 77)

Small Business Development Center (SBDC) (p. 78)

franchise (p. 79)

sole proprietorship (p. 86)

unlimited liability (p. 86)

general partnership (p. 86)

limited partnership (p. 87)

limited partner (p. 87)

general (or active) partner (p. 87)

corporation (p. 88)

limited liability (p. 88)

tender offer (p. 89)

double taxation (p. 89)

closely held (or private) corporation (p. 89)

publicly held (or public) corporation (p. 89)

S corporation (p. 89)

limited liability corporation (LLC) (p. 89)

professional corporation (p. 89)

multinational or transnational corporation (p. 90)

corporate governance (p. 90)

stockholder (or shareholder) (p. 90)

stock (p. 90)

preferred stock (p. 90)

common stock (p. 91)

board of directors (p. 91)

chief executive officer (CEO) (p. 91)

strategic alliance (p. 92)

joint venture (p. 92)

employee stock ownership plan (ESOP) (p. 92)

institutional investor (p. 92)

merger (p. 92)

acquisition (p. 92)

divestiture (p. 92)

spin-off (p. 92)

■ QUESTIONS AND EXERCISES

Questions for Review

1 Why are small businesses important to the U.S. economy?

2 What is the basic difference between a small-business owner and an entrepreneur?

3 From the standpoint of the franchisee, what are the primary advantages and disadvantages of most franchise arrangements?

4 Which industries are easiest for start-ups to enter? Which are hardest? Why?

Questions for Analysis

5 Why might a closely held corporation choose to remain private? Why might it choose to be publicly traded?

6 If you were going to open a small business, what type would it be? Why?

7 Would you prefer to buy an existing business or start from scratch? Why?

8 Under what circumstances might it be wise for an entrepreneur to reject venture capital? Under what circumstances might it be advisable to take more venture capital than an entrepreneur actually needs?

Application Exercises

9 Interview the owner-manager of a sole proprietorship or a general partnership. What characteristics of that business form led the owner to choose it? Does he or she ever contemplate changing the form of the business?

10 Identify two or three of the fastest-growing businesses in the United States during the last year. What role has entrepreneurship played in the growth of these firms?

BUILDING YOUR BUSINESS SKILLS

WORKING THE INTERNET

This exercise enhances the following SCANS workplace competencies: demonstrating basic skills, demonstrating thinking skills, exhibiting interpersonal skills, and working with information.

Goal
To encourage students to define the opportunities and problems for small companies doing business on the Internet.

The Situation
Let's say that you and two partners own a company that specializes in special-occasion gift baskets for individual and corporate clients. You're doing well, but you think there may be opportunity for growth through a virtual storefront on the Internet.

Method

Step 1
Join with two other students and assume the role of business partners. Start by researching Internet businesses. Look at books and articles at the library, and contact the following Web sites for help:

■ Small Business Administration *(www.sba.gov)*
■ IBM Small Business Center
  (www.business center.ibm.com)
■ Apple Small Business Home Page
  (www.smallbusiness.apple.com)
  These sites may lead you to others, so keep an open mind.

Step 2
Based on your research, determine the importance of the following small-business issues:

■ Analyzing changing company finances as a result of expansion onto the Internet
■ Analyzing your new competitive marketplace (the world) and how it affects your current marketing approach, which focuses on your local community
■ Identifying sources of management advice as expansion proceeds
■ Specifying the role of technology consultants in launching and maintaining a Web site
■ Establishing customer-service policies in a virtual environment

FOLLOW-UP QUESTIONS

1 Do you think your business would be successful on the Internet? Why or why not?

2 Based on your analysis, how will Internet expansion affect your current business practices? What specific changes are you likely to make?

3 Do you think that operating a virtual storefront will be harder or easier than doing business in your local community? Explain your answer.

 # EXERCISING YOUR ETHICS

BREAKING UP IS HARD TO DO

The Situation

Connie and Mark began a 25-year friendship after finishing college and discovering their mutual interest in owning a business. Established as a general partnership, their home-furnishings center is a successful business sustained for 20 years by a share-and-share-alike relationship. Start-up cash, daily responsibilities, and profits have all been shared equally. The partners both work four days each week except when busy seasons require both of them to be in the store. Shared goals and compatible personalities have led to a solid give-and-take relationship that helps them overcome business problems while maintaining a happy interpersonal relationship.

The division of work is a natural match and successful combination because of the partners' different but complementary interests. Mark buys the merchandise and maintains up-to-date contacts with suppliers; he also handles personnel matters (hiring and training employees). Connie manages the inventory, buys shipping supplies, keeps the books, and manages the finances. Mark does more selling, with Connie helping out only during busy seasons. Both partners share in decisions about advertising and promotions.

The Dilemma

Things began changing two years ago, when Connie became less interested in the business and got more involved in other activities. Whereas Mark's enthusiasm remained high, Connie's time was increasingly consumed by travel, recreation, and community-service activities. At first, she reduced her work commitment from four to three days a week. Then she indicated that she wanted to cut back further, to just two days. "In that case," Mark replied, "we'll have to make some changes."

Mark insisted that profit sharing be adjusted to reflect his larger role in running the business. He proposed that Connie's monthly salary be cut in half (from $4,000 to $2,000). Connie agreed. He recommended that the $2,000 savings be shifted to his salary because of his increased workload, but this time Connie balked, arguing that Mark's current $4,000 salary already compensated him for his contributions. She proposed to split the difference, with Mark getting a $1,000 increase and the other $1,000 going into the firm's cash account. Mark said no and insisted on a full $2,000 raise. To avoid a complete falling out, Connie finally gave in, even though she thought it unfair for Mark's salary to jump from $4,000 per month to $6,000. At that point, she made a promise to herself: "To even things out, I'll find a way to get $2,000 worth of inventory for personal use each month."

QUESTIONS FOR DISCUSSION

1 Identify the ethical issues, if any, regarding Mark's and Connie's respective positions on Mark's proposed $2,000 salary increase.

2 What kind of salary adjustments do you think would be fair in this situation? Explain why.

3 There is, of course, another way for Mark and Connie to solve their differences: Because the terms of participation have changed, it might make sense to dissolve the existing partnership. What do you recommend in this regard?

CRAFTING YOUR BUSINESS PLAN

FITTING THE ENTREPRENEURIAL MOLD

The Purpose of the Assignment

1 To familiarize students with the ways in which entrepreneurship and small business considerations enter into the business planning framework of the *Business PlanPro (BPP) 2003* software package (Version 6.0).

2 To encourage students to think about how to apply their textbook information on entrepreneurship to the preparation of a small business plan using the *BPP* planning environment.

Assignment

After reading Chapter 3 in the textbook, open the BPP *software and look around for information about the types of small business and entrepreneurship considerations that would be of concern to a sample firm:* Corporate Fitness. *To find* Corporate Fitness, *do the following:*

Open *Business PlanPro.* Go to the toolbar and click on the "*Sample Plans*" icon. In the **Sample Plan Browser**, do a **keyword search** using the phrase *corporate fitness.* From the resulting list, select the category entitled **Health Fitness Program**, which is the location for *Corporate Fitness.* The screen you are looking at is the introduction page for the *Corporate Fitness* business plan. On this page, scroll down until you reach the **Table of Contents** for the company's business plan.

NOW RESPOND TO THE FOLLOWING ITEMS:

1 In the Table of Contents page, click on **1.0 Executive Summary** to familiarize yourself with an overview of

this firm. Which industry category for small business—construction, wholesaling, services, transportation, or manufacturing—best describes the *Corporate Fitness* line of business?

2 The textbook identifies several characteristics of successful entrepreneurs. Judging by its business plan, do you think the management team of *Corporate Fitness* has an entrepreneurial orientation? Explain why or why not. [Sites to see in *BPP* for this item: On the Table of Contents page, click on each of the following in turn: **6.0 Management Summary, 6.2 Management Team,** and **6.3 Management Team Gaps.**]

3 The textbook identifies several sources of advice and assistance for starting and running small businesses. Judging from its business plan, do you think that *Corporate Fitness* is planning to seek advice from any of those sources in getting started? Do you think it is a good idea to discuss the planned uses of such sources in the business plan? Explain why or why not. [Sites to see in *BPP*: From the Table of Contents page, explore the *Corporate Fitness* business plan using your judgment as to where you would expect to find information on start-up advice.]

4 What sources of advice and assistance do you recommend for getting *Corporate Fitness* off to a sound start? In which areas of the business and for which of its business activities will it benefit the most from outside advice and assistance? Where in its business plan do you recommend reporting its planned use of such assistance?

VIDEO EXERCISE

DOING BUSINESS PRIVATELY: AMY'S ICE CREAM

Learning Objectives

The purpose of this video is to help you:

1 Distinguish among types of corporations.

2 Consider the advantages and disadvantages of incorporation.

3 Understand the role that shareholders play in a privately held corporation.

Synopsis

Amy's Ice Cream, based in Austin, Texas, is a privately held corporation formed in 1984 by Amy Miller and owned by Miller and a small group of family members and friends. At the outset, one of the most important decisions Miller faced was choosing an appropriate legal ownership structure for the new business. Fueled by the founder's dedication to creating happy ice cream memories for customers, Amy's has continued to evolve and grow. The company now operates nine stores and rings up close to $3.5 million in annual sales. Applying for a job is an adventure in creativity, and Miller welcomes employees' suggestions for new flavors and new promotions.

DISCUSSION QUESTIONS

1 **For analysis:** How does Amy's Ice Cream differ from a publicly held corporation?
2 **For analysis:** What are some of the particular advantages of corporate ownership for a firm such as Amy's Ice Cream?
3 **For application:** How well do you think Amy's is working to ensure its continued survival and success?

Looking ahead to future growth, what marketing, financial, or other suggestions would you make?
4 **For application:** What are some of the issues that Amy Miller may have to confront because her 22 investors are family members and friends?
5 **For debate:** Should Amy's Ice Cream become a publicly held corporation? Support your chosen position.

Online Exploration

Find out what's required to incorporate a business in your state. You might begin by searching the CCH Business Owner's Toolkit site at *(www.toolkit.cch.com)*. If you were going to start a small business, would you choose incorporation or a different form of legal organization? List the pros and cons that incorporation presents for the type of business that you would consider.

4

After reading this chapter, you should be able to:

1 Discuss the rise of international business and describe the *major world marketplaces*.

2 Explain how differences in *competitive advantage, import-export balances, exchange rates*, and *foreign competition* determine the ways in which countries and businesses respond to the international environment.

3 Discuss the factors involved in deciding to do business internationally and in selecting the appropriate *levels of international involvement* and *international organizational structure*.

4 Describe some of the ways in which *social, cultural, economic, legal*, and *political differences* among nations affect international business.

WHERE DOES MANAGEMENT STAND ON BEER BREAKS?

What's there left to be said about an enormous retailer that has become the most profitable corporation on earth? Wal-Mart *(www.walmartstores.com)* is gigantic, by any measure. It has 1.3 million workers in 4,300 worldwide stores that are visited by more than 100 million customers every week. Total sales in 2001 exceeded $210 billion, and in

UNDERSTANDING THE GLOBAL CONTEXT OF BUSINESS

" **G**ermans don't want to be paying the salary of that guy at the door."

—Local banker on the German attitude toward Wal-Mart greeters

2002, Wal-Mart topped the *Fortune* 500—the first time that a nonmanufacturing firm has ever occupied that position.

But with U.S. sales flat and the domestic discount market approaching saturation, Wal-Mart has set its sights on aggressive expansion in this country. It is already invading the markets of specialty retailers, such as PETsMART, Albertson's, Toys "R" Us, and Best Buy, and it continues to introduce new products into existing stores. "Wal-Mart's aggressive rollout of retail gas stations," speculates one retail consultant, "could be followed closely with the company selling used cars, financial services, home improvement, and food service." But even with all this domestic activity, Wal-Mart still finds expansion into international markets its most appealing option.

Wal-Mart's international expansion began in 1991, when a Sam's Club opened near Mexico City. Today, the firm's International Division operates 1,100 overseas outlets, with stores in Argentina, Brazil, Canada, China, Germany, Korea, Mexico, Puerto Rico, and the United Kingdom. Interestingly, in each of these markets, acquisitions have played as important a role as expansion from within. In Canada, for example, Wal-Mart entered the market by buying up 122 Woolco stores. German operations began with the acquisition of 21 Wertkauf hypermarkets and 74 Interspar stores. Most ambitious to date, however, have been the company's activities in Britain, where it bought 230 ASDA stores in 1999. The process for integrating acquired stores into Wal-Mart operations involves changing names, renovating facilities, bringing in American store managers, and altering product mixes.

Wal-Mart is still learning how to deal effectively with international differences in culture and business practices. An initial problem was the relatively small size of the acquired stores, most of which had only one-third the floor space of a typical Wal-Mart. Wal-Mart's "one-stop" strategy depends, in part, on size—having everything under one roof—but European customers don't like the impersonal feel of very large stores. In addition, because they typically shop more frequently than Americans and buy less at each visit, they see no reason to be pushing large carts around. Thus the dilemma for Wal-Mart management: Although smaller carts would allow it to cram more products into limited store space, small carts don't encourage large purchases. Finally, Europeans don't care for greeters. "Germans are skeptical," explains an analyst at Deutsche Bank. "They don't want to be paying the salary of that guy at the door."

Regulation creates yet another set of hurdles. In England and Germany 24-hour stores are banned. A German court upheld employees' rights to wear earrings and sport facial hair, and when the company tried to forbid English employees from drinking beer during lunch breaks, English labor unions threatened to go to court. European laws are also quite strict about the sale of "loss leaders"—popular products that are sold below cost in order to bring customers into the store. Negotiations with suppliers are also heavily regulated. In Mexico, Wal-Mart ran afoul of local authorities when it demanded deep discounts from many suppliers.

Our opening story continues on page 157.

THE RISE OF INTERNATIONAL BUSINESS

globalization
Process by which the world economy is becoming a single interdependent system

import
Product made or grown abroad but sold domestically

export
Product made or grown domestically but shipped and sold abroad

The total volume of world trade is immense—over $8 trillion in merchandise trade each year. Foreign investment in the United States and U.S. investment abroad have each passed the $1 trillion mark.[1] As more firms engage in international business, the world economy is fast becoming an interdependent system—a process called **globalization**.[2] We often take for granted the diversity of products we can buy as a result of international trade. Your TV set, your shoes, and even your morning coffee are probably **imports**—products made or grown abroad and sold domestically in the United States. At the same time, the success of many U.S. firms depends on **exports**—products made or grown here and shipped for sale abroad.

The Contemporary Global Economy

International trade is becoming increasingly important to most nations and their largest businesses. Many countries that once followed strict policies to protect domestic business now encourage trade just as aggressively. They are opening borders to for-

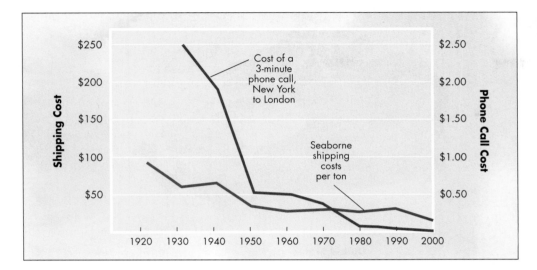

FIGURE 4.1
The Price of Global Communication

eign business, offering incentives for domestic businesses to expand internationally, and making it easier for foreign firms to partner with local firms. Likewise, as more industries and markets become global, so, too, are the firms that compete in them.

Several forces have combined to spark and sustain globalization. For one thing, governments and businesses are more aware of the benefits of globalization to businesses and shareholders. For another, new technologies have made international travel, communication, and commerce much faster and cheaper than ever before. Figure 4.1, for example, shows the decrease in the costs of two international business activities over the last several decades: the cost of a 3-minute phone call from New York to London and the cost of transatlantic shipping per ton. Today, too, travelers can easily fly between most major cities in the United States and Europe in less than a day. Finally, there are competitive pressures. Sometimes a firm must expand into foreign markets simply to keep up with competitors.

Trade Agreements Various legal agreements have also sparked international trade. Indeed, virtually every nation has formal trade treaties with other nations. Among the most significant multilateral agreements are the General Agreement on Tariffs and Trade and the North American Free Trade Agreement. The European Union and the World Trade Organization, both governed by treaties, are also instrumental in promoting international business activity.

General Agreement on Tariffs and Trade The **General Agreement on Tariffs and Trade (GATT)** was signed after World War II. Its purpose is to reduce or eliminate trade barriers, such as tariffs and quotas. It does so by encouraging nations to protect domestic industries within agreed-upon limits and to engage in multilateral negotiations.

A revision of GATT went into effect in 1994, but many issues remain unresolved—for example, the opening of foreign markets to most financial services. Governments may still subsidize builders of civil aircraft, and there is no agreement to limit the distribution of American cultural exports—movies, music, and the like—in Europe. Thanks to those agreements that are in place, however, world commerce increased another $270 billion by 2002.

North American Free Trade Agreement The **North American Free Trade Agreement (NAFTA)** removes tariffs and other trade barriers among the United States, Canada, and Mexico (Figure 4.2) and includes agreements on environmental issues and labor abuses. Some barriers came down on January 1, 1994, and others

General Agreement on Tariffs and Trade (GATT) International trade agreement to encourage the multilateral reduction or elimination of trade barriers

North American Free Trade Agreement (NAFTA) Agreement to gradually eliminate tariffs and other trade barriers among the United States, Canada and Mexico

FIGURE 4.2

The North American Marketplace
and the Nations of NAFTA

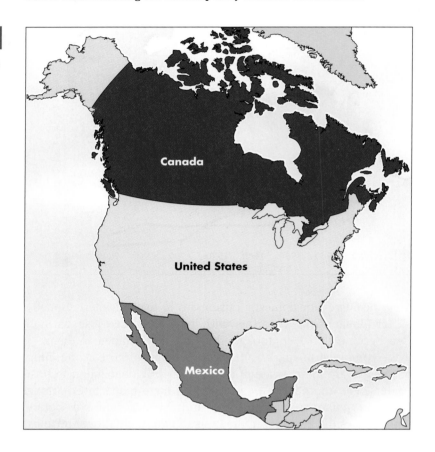

will follow at 5-, 10-, or 15-year intervals. In its first year, observers agreed that NAFTA had achieved its basic purpose—to create a more active North American market. The following were among its first-year results:

- Direct foreign investment increased. With $2.4 billion, U.S. and Canadian firms accounted for 55 percent of all foreign investment in Mexico. Companies from other nations—for instance, Japan's Toyota—also made new investments to take advantage of the freer movement of goods.
- U.S. exports to Mexico increased by about 20 percent. Procter & Gamble, for example, enjoyed an increase of nearly 75 percent, and the giant agribusiness firm Archer Daniels Midland tripled exports to Mexico. Mexico passed Japan as the second-largest buyer of U.S. goods, and trade with Canada rose 10 percent (twice the gain in Europe and Asia).
- U.S. imports from Mexico and Canada rose even faster than rates in the opposite direction, setting records of $48 billion and $120 billion, respectively. In particular, electronics, computers, and communications products came into the United States twice as fast as they went out. "We pointed out," says one NAFTA opponent, "that there was a fairly sophisticated manufacturing base in Mexico that pays peanuts, and the numbers bear that out."
- NAFTA created fewer jobs than proponents had hoped. Although the U.S. economy added 1.7 million new jobs in 1994, perhaps only 100,000 were NAFTA related. At the same time, however, the flood of U.S. jobs lost to Mexico predicted by NAFTA critics, especially labor unions, did not occur. In fact, Ford Motor Co.'s Mexican division claims that it has created jobs in both countries. Ford's exports of Mexican-made vehicles to the United States went up 30 percent, but 80 percent

Fisherman Ratish Karthikeyan can sometimes double the revenue from a day's take by phoning around to compare prices at markets within reach of his boat. That's one reason why companies like AT&T (United States) and Hutchison Telecom (Hong Kong) are finding India a thriving export market for cellular phones. For another, about half of India's 600,000 rural communities aren't even wired for fixed-line phone service. Between now and 2005, the number of mobile-phone users should jump from 3 million to 30 million.

of all components in those cars are American-made. Ford also reports that its exports of American-made cars to Mexico rose from 1,200 to 30,000.

European Union Originally called the Common Market, the **European Union (EU)** includes the principal Western European nations, which have eliminated most quotas and set uniform tariff levels on products imported and exported within their group. In 1992, virtually all internal trade barriers went down, making the EU the largest free marketplace in the world. We discuss the EU more fully later in the chapter.

European Union (EU)
Agreement among major Western European nations to eliminate or make uniform most trade barriers affecting group members

World Trade Organization To further globalization, most of the world's countries joined to create the **World Trade Organization (WTO)** *(www.wto.org)*, which was begun on January 1, 1995. The 140 member countries are required to open markets to international trade, and the WTO is empowered to pursue three goals:

World Trade Organization (WTO)
Organization through which member nations negotiate trading agreements and resolve disputes about trade policies and practices

1 Promote trade by encouraging members to adopt fair trade practices.
2 Reduce trade barriers by promoting multilateral negotiations.
3 Establish fair procedures for resolving disputes among members.

In the remainder of this section, we examine some other key factors that shaped—and are still shaping—today's global business environment. First, we identify the major world marketplaces. Then we discuss some important factors that determine the ways in which both nations and businesses respond to the international environment: the roles of different forms of *competitive advantage, import-export balances*, and *exchange rates*.

The Major World Marketplaces

The world economy revolves around three major marketplaces: North America, Europe, and Asia. These three geographic regions are home to most of the world's largest economies, biggest multinational corporations, most influential financial markets, and highest-income consumers.

The World Bank, an agency of the United Nations *(www.worldbank.org)*, uses per capita income—average income per person—as a measure to divide countries into one of three groups:[3]

- **High-income countries:** those with per capita income greater than $9,386. These include the United States, Canada, most of the countries in Europe, Australia, New Zealand, Japan, South Korea, Kuwait, the United Arab Emirates, Israel, Singapore, and Taiwan. Hong Kong, though technically no longer an independent nation, also falls into this category.
- **Middle-income countries:** those with per capita income of less than $9,386 but more than $765. This group includes, among others, the Czech Republic, Greece, Hungary, Poland, most of the countries of the former Soviet bloc, Turkey, Mexico, Argentina, and Uruguay. Some of these nations, most notably Poland, Argentina, and Uruguay, are developing economically and will soon move into the high-income category.
- **Low-income countries, also called *developing countries*:** those with per capita income of less than $765. Some of these countries, such as China and India, have huge populations and are seen as potentially attractive markets. Due to low literacy rates, weak infrastructures, and unstable governments, other countries in this group are less attractive. For example, the East African nation of Somalia, plagued by drought, starvation, and internal strife and civil war, plays virtually no role in the world economy.

North America As the world's largest national marketplace and most stable economy, the United States dominates the North American market. Canada also plays a major role in the international economy, and the United States and Canada are each other's largest trading partner. Many U.S. firms, such as General Motors *(www.gmcanada.com)* and Procter & Gamble *(www.pg.com/canada)*, have maintained successful Canadian operations for years, and many Canadian firms, such as Northern Telecom *(www.nt.com)* and Alcan Aluminum *(www.alcan.com)*, are also major international competitors.

Mexico has become a major manufacturing center, especially along the U.S. border, where cheap labor and low transportation costs have encouraged many firms from

This boy's home country, the arid landlocked African nation of Burkina Faso, is a "low-income" country. That's why he's working on a cocoa plantation in the Ivory Coast, one of the continent's more prosperous nations, for about 50 cents a day. Even at that rate, he's far from the bottom rung on Africa's economic ladder. As for the cocoa farmer who pays him, he's finally been able to buy a tractor after farming 48 acres for 33 years. The cocoa is sold to local buyers and then to exporters who sell it to companies such as Nestlé and Hershey.

the United States and other countries to build factories. The auto industry has been especially active, with DaimlerChrysler *(www.daimlerchrysler.com)*, General Motors *(www.gm.com)*, Volkswagen *(www.vw.com)*, Nissan *(www.nissandriven.com)*, and Ford *(www.ford.com)* all running large assembly plants in the region. Several major suppliers have also built facilities in the area. From 1993 to 2001, exports of cars and automobile parts from Mexico increased from $7.2 billion to $23.6 billion, and the Mexican auto industry now employs over 400,000 workers. The industry grew by 10 percent in 2003.[4]

Europe Europe is often regarded as two regions—Western and Eastern. Western Europe, which is dominated by Germany, the United Kingdom, France, and Italy, has long been a mature but fragmented marketplace. But the transformation of the EU into a unified marketplace in 1992 further increased the region's importance (see Figure 4.3). Major international firms such as Unilever *(www.unilver.com)*, Renault *(www.renault.com)*, Royal Dutch/Shell *(www.shell.com)*, Michelin *(www.michelin.com)*, Siemens *(www.siemens.de)*, and Nestlé *(www.nestle.com)* are all headquartered in Western Europe.

E-commerce and technology have also become increasingly important in this region. There has been a surge in Internet start-ups in southeastern England, the Netherlands, and the Scandinavian countries; and Ireland is now the world's number-two exporter of software (after the United States). Strasbourg, France, is a major center for biotech start-ups. Barcelona, Spain, has many flourishing software and Internet companies, and the Frankfurt region of Germany is dotted with both software and biotech start-ups.

FIGURE 4.3

Europe and the Nations of the European Union

Eastern Europe, once primarily communist, has also gained in importance, both as a marketplace and as a producer. Such multinational corporations as Daewoo *(www.daewoo.com)*, Nestlé, General Motors, and ABB Asea Brown Boveri *(www.abb.com)* have all set up operations in Poland. Ford, General Motors, Suzuki *(www.suzuki.com)*, and Volkswagen have all built new factories in Hungary. On the other hand, governmental instability has hampered development in Russia, Bulgaria, Albania, Romania, and other countries.

Pacific Asia Pacific Asia consists of Japan, China, Thailand, Malaysia, Singapore, Indonesia, South Korea, Taiwan, the Philippines, and Australia. Some experts still distinguish Hong Kong, though now part of China, as a part of the region, and others include Vietnam. Fueled by strong entries in the automobile, electronics, and banking industries, the economies of these countries grew rapidly in the 1970s and 1980s. Unfortunately, a currency crisis in the late 1990s slowed growth in virtually every country of the region.

The currency crisis aside, however, Pacific Asia is an important force in the world economy and a major source of competition for North American firms. Led by firms such as Toyota, Toshiba *(www.toshiba.com)*, and Nippon Steel *(www.nsc.co.jp/english)*, Japan dominates the region. South Korea, home to such firms as Samsung *(www.samsung.com)* and Hyundai *(www.hyundai.com)*; Taiwan, owner of Chinese Petroleum *(www.cpc.com.tw/english)* and manufacturing home of many foreign firms; and Hong Kong (a major financial center) are also successful players in the international economy. China, the world's most densely populated country, has emerged as an important market and now boasts the world's third-largest economy behind that of the United States and only slightly behind that of Japan.

As in North America and Western Europe, technology promises to play an increasingly important role in the future of this region. In Asia, however, the emergence of technology firms has been hampered by a poorly developed electronic infrastructure, slower adoption of computers and information technology, and a higher percentage of lower-income consumers. Thus, although the future looks promising, technology companies are facing several obstacles as they work to keep pace with foreign competitors.[5]

Figure 4.4 is a map of the Association of Southeast Asian Nations (ASEAN) *(www.aseansec.org)* countries of Pacific Asia. ASEAN (pronounced OZZIE-on) was

FIGURE 4.4

The Nations of ASEAN

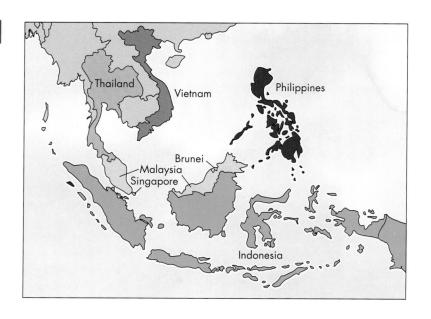

TABLE 4.1

The Major Trading Partners of the United States

Top 25 U.S. Supplier Countries Rank/Country	2000 Imports ($ bil.)	Top 25 U.S. Export Markets Rank/Country	2000 Exports ($ bil.)
1 Canada	230.8	1 Canada	178.9
2 Japan	146.5	2 Mexico	111.3
3 Mexico	135.9	3 Japan	64.9
4 China	100.0	4 United Kingdom	41.6
5 Germany	58.5	5 Germany	29.4
6 United Kingdom	43.3	6 Korea	27.8
7 Taiwan	40.5	7 Taiwan	24.4
8 Korea, South	40.3	8 Netherlands	21.8
9 France	29.8	9 France	20.4
10 Malaysia	25.6	10 Singapore	17.8
11 Italy	25.0	11 China	16.2
12 Singapore	19.2	12 Brazil	15.3
13 Venezuela	18.6	13 Hong Kong	14.6
14 Ireland	16.5	14 Belgium + Luxembourg	14.3
15 Thailand	16.4	15 Australia	12.5
16 Saudi Arabia	14.4	16 Italy	11.1
17 Philippines	13.9	17 Malaysia	10.9
18 Brazil	13.9	18 Switzerland	10.0
19 Israel	13.0	19 Philippines	8.8
20 Hong Kong	11.4	20 Israel	7.7
21 India	10.7	21 Ireland	7.7
22 Nigeria	10.5	22 Thailand	6.6
23 Indonesia	10.4	23 Spain	6.3
24 Belgium + Luxembourg	10.3	24 Saudi Arabia	6.2
25 Switzerland	10.2	25 Venezuela	5.6

founded in 1967 as an organization for economic, political, social, and cultural cooperation. In 1995, Vietnam became the group's first communist member. Today, the ASEAN group has a population of over 500 million and a GDP of approximately $800 billion.[6]

Table 4.1 lists the major trading partners of the United States. As we noted earlier, these partners are located all over the world and include high-, middle-, and low-income countries. The left side of the table identifies the 25 countries from which the United States buys the most products. Germany, for example, is our fifth-biggest supplier, Malaysia tenth, and Thailand fifteenth. The right side identifies the 25 largest export markets for U.S. businesses. Germany is our fifth-biggest customer, Singapore tenth, and Australia fifteenth. Note that many countries are on both lists (indeed, Canada is at the top of both).

Forms of Competitive Advantage

Why is there so much international business activity? Because no country can produce everything that it needs, countries tend to export what they can produce better or less expensively than other countries and use the proceeds to import what they can't produce as effectively.

Of course, this principle doesn't fully explain why nations export and import what they do. Such decisions hinge partly on the advantages that a particular country enjoys regarding its abilities to create and/or sell certain products and resources.[7] Traditionally, economists focused on absolute and comparative advantage to explain international trade. But because this approach focuses narrowly on such factors as natural resources and labor costs, the more complex view of national competitive advantage has emerged.

absolute advantage
The ability to produce something more efficiently than any other country can

Absolute Advantage An **absolute advantage** exists when a country can produce something more cheaply and/or of higher quality than any other country. Saudi oil, Brazilian coffee beans, and Canadian timber come close, but examples of true absolute advantage are rare. In reality, "absolute" advantages are always relative. For example, most experts say that the vineyards of France produce the world's finest wines. But the burgeoning wine business in California demonstrates that producers there can also make very good wine—wines that rival those from France but come in more varieties and at lower prices.

comparative advantage
The ability to produce some products more efficiently than others

Comparative Advantage A country has a **comparative advantage** in goods that it can produce more efficiently or better than other goods. If businesses in a given country can make computers more efficiently than they can make automobiles, then that nation has a comparative advantage in computer manufacturing. The United States has comparative advantages in the computer industry (because of technological sophistication) and in farming (because of fertile land and a temperate climate). South Korea has a comparative advantage in electronics manufacturing because of efficient operations and cheap labor. As a result, U.S. firms export computers and grain to South Korea and import VCRs and stereos from South Korea. South Korea, of course, can produce food, and the United States can build VCRs, but each nation imports certain products because the other holds a comparative advantage in the relevant industry.

national competitive advantage
International competitive advantage stemming from a combination of factor conditions, demand conditions, related and supporting industries, and firm strategies, structures, and rivalries

National Competitive Advantage In recent years, a theory of national competitive advantage has become a widely accepted model of why nations engage in international trade.[8] **National competitive advantage** derives from four conditions:

1 *Factor conditions* are the factors of production that we identified in Chapter 1.
2 *Demand conditions* reflect a large domestic consumer base that promotes strong demand for innovative products.
3 *Related and supporting industries* include strong local or regional suppliers and/or industrial customers.
4 *Strategies, structures, and rivalries* refer to firms and industries that stress cost reduction, product quality, higher productivity, and innovative products.

Figure 4.5 shows why these four attributes are referred to as a national diamond: The interaction of the four elements determines the environment in which a nation's firms compete. When all attributes exist, a nation is likely to do international business. Japan, for instance, has an abundance of natural resources and strong domestic demand for automobiles. Its carmakers have well-oiled supplier networks, and domestic firms have competed intensely with each other for decades. These circumstances explain why Japanese car companies like Toyota *(www.toyota.com)*, Honda *(www.hondacorporate.com)*, Nissan *(www.nissandriven.com)*, and Mazda *(www.mazda.com)* are successful in foreign markets.

Import-Export Balances

Although international trade has many advantages, it can pose problems if a country's imports and exports don't strike an acceptable balance. In deciding whether an

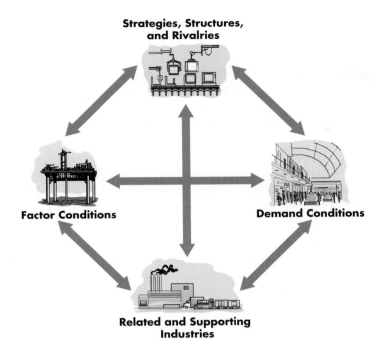

FIGURE 4.5

Attributes of National
Competitive Advantage

overall balance exists, economists use two measures: *balance of trade* and *balance of payments*.

Balance of Trade A nation's **balance of trade** is the total economic value of all products that it exports minus the total value of everything it imports. Relatively small trade imbalances are common and are unimportant. Large imbalances, however, are another matter. In 2000, for example, the United States had a negative balance in merchandise trade of $466.8 billion and a positive balance in service trade of $76.5 billion. The result was an overall negative balance of $390.3 billion—large enough to be a concern for U.S. business and political leaders.[9]

balance of trade
Economic value of all products a country exports minus the economic value of all products it imports

Trade Deficits and Surpluses When a country's imports exceed its exports—that is, when it has a negative balance of trade—it suffers a **trade deficit**. In short, more money is flowing out than flowing in. A positive balance occurs when exports exceed imports, and then the nation enjoys a **trade surplus**: More money is flowing in than flowing out. Trade deficits and surpluses are influenced by several factors, such as absolute, comparative, or national competitive advantages, general economic conditions, and the effect of trade agreements. For example, higher domestic costs, greater international competition, and continuing economic problems among some of its regional trading partners have slowed the tremendous growth in exports that Japan once enjoyed. But rising prosperity in China and India has led to strong increases in both exports from and imports to those countries.

trade deficit
Situation in which a country's imports exceed its exports, creating a negative balance of trade

In general, the United States suffers from large deficits with Japan ($81.6 billion), China ($83.8 billion), Germany ($29.1 billion), Canada ($51.9 billion), Mexico ($24.6 billion), and Taiwan ($16.1 billion). In any given year, the United States may also have smaller deficits with other countries. Our present deficit with Singapore is only $1.4 billion.

trade surplus
Situation in which a country's exports exceed its imports, creating a positive balance of trade

On the other hand, we enjoy healthy surpluses with many countries. The most current figures report a $10.6 billion surplus with the Netherlands, $7.5 billion with

Australia, $4 billion with Belgium-Luxembourg, and $2.8 billion with Egypt. More modest surpluses with Jordan and Haiti are about $250 million each.[10]

balance of payments
Flow of all money into or out of a country

Balance of Payments The **balance of payments** refers to the flow of money into or out of a country. The money that a nation pays for imports and receives for exports—its balance of trade—comprises much of its balance of payments. Other financial exchanges are also factors. Money spent by tourists, money spent on foreign-aid programs, and money exchanged by buying and selling currency on international money markets all affect the balance of payments.

For many years, the United States enjoyed a positive balance of payments (more inflows than outflows). Recently, the balance has been negative, but the trend is gradually reversing itself, and many economists soon expect a positive balance. Some U.S. industries have positive balances, and others have negative balances. Such firms as Dow Chemical *(www.dow.com)* and Monsanto *(www.pharmacia.com)* are among world leaders in chemical exports. The cigarette, truck, and industrial-equipment industries also have positive balances. Conversely, the metalworking-machinery, airplane-parts, and auto industries suffer negative balances because we import more than we export.

Exchange Rates

exchange rate
Rate at which the currency of one nation can be exchanged for the currency of another country

The balance of imports and exports between two countries is affected by the rate of exchange between their currencies. An **exchange rate** is the rate at which the currency of one nation can be exchanged for that of another.[11] The exchange rate between U.S. dollars and British pounds is about 1.5 dollars to 1 pound. This means that it costs 1 pound to "buy" 1.5 dollars or 1 dollar to "buy" 0.67 pounds. It also means that 1 pound and 1.5 dollars have the same purchasing power.

At the end of World War II, the major nations agreed to set *fixed exchange rates.* The value of any country's currency relative to that of another would remain constant. Today, however, *floating exchange rates* are the norm, and the value of one country's currency relative to that of another varies with market conditions. For example, when many British citizens want to spend pounds to buy U.S. dollars (or goods), the value of the dollar relative to the pound increases. Demand for the dollar is high, and a currency is strong when demand for it is high. It's also strong when there's high demand for the goods manufactured at the expense of that currency. Thus, the value of the dollar rises with the demand for U.S. goods. On a daily basis, exchange rates fluctuate very little. Significant variations usually occur over greater time spans.

Exchange rate fluctuation can have an important impact on the balance of trade. Suppose you want to buy some English tea for 10 pounds per box. At an exchange rate of 1.5 dollars to the pound, a box will cost you $15 (10 pounds × 1.5 = 15). But what if the pound is weaker? At an exchange rate of, say, 1.25 dollars to the pound, the same box would cost you only $12.50 (10 pounds × 1.25 = 12.50).

If the dollar is strong in relation to the pound, the prices of all American-made products will rise in England and the prices of all English-made products will fall in the United States. The English would buy fewer American-made products, and Americans would be prompted to spend more on English-made products. The result will probably be a U.S. trade deficit with England.

euro
A common currency shared among most of the members of the European Union (excluding Denmark, Sweden, and the United Kingdom)

One of the most significant developments in foreign exchange has been the introduction of the **euro**—a common currency among most of the members of the

European Union (Denmark, Sweden, and the United Kingdom do not participate). The euro was officially introduced in 2002 and is replacing existing currencies such as the German deutsche mark and the French franc. The EU anticipates that the euro will become as important as the dollar and the yen in international commerce. Though subject to fluctuation, of course, the euro is currently equal to about one dollar.

Exchange Rates and Competition Companies with international operations must watch exchange rate fluctuations closely because changes affect overseas demand for their products and can be a major factor in competition. In general, when the value of a country's currency rises—becomes stronger—companies based there find it harder to export products to foreign markets and easier for foreign companies to enter local markets. It also makes it more cost-efficient for domestic companies to move operations to lower-cost foreign sites. When the value of a currency declines—becomes weaker—the opposite occurs. As the value of a country's currency falls, its balance of trade should improve because domestic companies should experience a boost in exports. There should also be less reason for foreign companies to ship products into the domestic market.

A good case in point is the recent decline of the Canadian dollar relative to the U.S. dollar. In the mid-1990s, because the Canadian dollar was relatively strong compared to the U.S. dollar, Canadian consumers shopped for bargains in the United States. But a global currency crisis in 1997 had longer-lasting effects in Canada than in the United States, weakening the Canadian dollar relative to the U.S. dollar. It's now cheaper for U.S. consumers to do what their Canadian counterparts used to do— drive across the border to shop. Table 4.2 illustrates the effects of this trend. The same hamburger costing $2.39 in Niagara Falls, New York, sells for $2.18 (in U.S. currency) just across the border in Ontario, Canada. A café latte in Seattle costs $2.70 but only $2.29 (again, in U.S. currency) in Vancouver.[12]

The U.S. Economy and Foreign Trade Figures 4.6 and 4.7 highlight two series of events: (1) recent trends in U.S. exports and imports and (2) the resulting trade deficit. As Figure 4.6 shows, both imports into the United States and U.S. exports to other countries have increased steadily for 10 years—a trend that's projected to continue.

TABLE 4.2

Canadian vs. U.S. Prices

Common Product	Niagara Falls, New York	Niagara Falls, Ontario
Saturday stay at Days Inn, with jacuzzi	$260	$165
Whopper with cheese at Burger King	$2.39	$2.18

	Seattle	Vancouver, British Columbia
Lauryn Hill CD	$17.99	$12.60
Nintendo 64 game system	$130	$119
Grande latte at Starbucks	$2.70	$2.29
Levi's 501 jeans at the Original Levi's Store	$50	$45

FIGURE 4.6

U.S. Imports and Exports

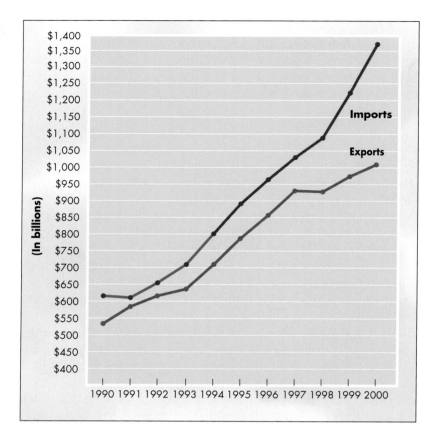

In 2001, the United States exported $1,068 billion in goods and services. In the same year, the United States imported $1,438 billion in goods and services. Because imports exceeded exports, the United States had a trade deficit of $369 billion (the difference between imports and exports). Trade deficits between 1991 and 2001 are shown in Figure 4.7: There was a deficit in each of these years because more money flowed out to pay for foreign imports than flowed in to pay for U.S. exports. Had exports exceeded imports, we would have had a surplus.

FIGURE 4.7

U.S. Trade Deficit

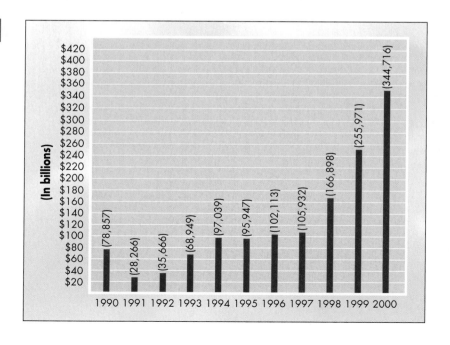

You should now be able to answer Self-Check Questions 1–3.*

1 **Multiple Choice** In general, which of the following has the **least** impact on U.S. business? [select one]: **(a)** General Agreement on Tariffs and Trade; **(b)** World Trade Organization; **(c)** Association of South American Agricultural Producers; **(d)** North American Free Trade Association; **(e)** European Union.

2 **True/False** The World Bank places countries into five categories based on *per capita income* levels— high income, moderately high income, middle income, moderately low income, and low income.

3 **Multiple Choice** The United States has a *comparative advantage* in which of the following? [select one]: **(a)** consumer electronics products; **(b)** coffee growing; **(c)** athletic shoe production; **(d)** movies and other filmed entertainment; **(e)** fine watches.

***Answers to Self-Check Questions 1–3 can be found on p. 507.**

■ INTERNATIONAL BUSINESS MANAGEMENT

Wherever a firm is located, its success depends largely on how well it's managed. International business is so challenging because basic management tasks—planning, organizing, directing, and controlling—are much more difficult when a firm operates in markets scattered around the globe.

Managing means making decisions. In this section, we examine the three basic decisions that a company must make when considering globalization. The first decision is whether to go international at all. Once that decision has been made, managers must decide on the level of international involvement and on the organizational structure that will best meet the firm's global needs.

"Grab some lederhosen, Sutfin. We're about to climb aboard the globalization bandwagon."

Going International

As the world economy becomes globalized, more firms are conducting international operations. Wal-Mart, for example, was described in our opening story. Other U.S. firms aggressively expanding abroad today include Starbucks, Dell Computer, and United Parcel Service (UPS). At the same time, foreign companies such as BP and Nestlé continue to expand into foreign markets as well, including the U.S. market.

This route, however, isn't appropriate for every company. If you buy and sell fresh fish, you'll find it more profitable to confine your activities to limited geographic areas because storage and transport costs may be too high to make international operations worthwhile. As Figure 4.8 shows, several factors affect the decision to go international. One key factor is the business climate in other nations. Even experienced firms have met cultural, legal, and economic roadblocks (problems that we discuss in more detail later in this chapter).

Gauging International Demand In considering international expansion, a company should also consider at least two other questions:

1 Is there a demand for its products abroad?
2 If so, must the company adapt those products for international consumption?

Products that are successful in one country may be useless in another. Snowmobiles are popular for transportation and recreation in Canada and actually revolutionized reindeer herding in Lapland, but there's no demand for them in Central America. Although this is an extreme example, the point is basic: Foreign demand for a company's product may be greater than, the same as, or weaker than domestic demand. Market research and/or the prior market entry of competitors may indicate whether there's an international demand for a firm's products.

One large category of U.S. products that travels well is American popular culture. Many U.S. movies, for example, earn as much or more abroad than they do in domestic release. In its opening weekend of May 2–4, 2003, in the United States *X2: X-Men United* racked up ticket sales of $85.6 million; during the same period, it grossed another $70 million in foreign markets. Billions of dollars are also involved in popular music, TV shows, books, and even street fashions. Super Mario Brothers is advertised

FIGURE 4.8

Going International

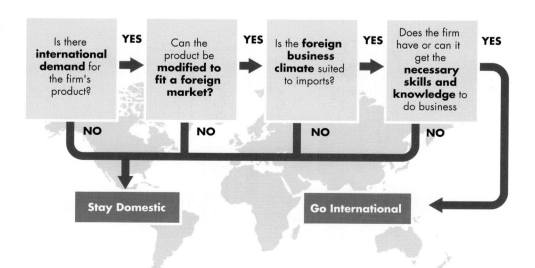

ENTREPRENEURSHIP and *New Ventures*

Rolling in the Worldwide Dough

Is any business more confined to a local market than a bakery? Breads and pastries get stale quickly, and even the largest operations, such as those that make buns for McDonald's, only move products over short distances. But a baker in Paris has refused to accept geographic limitations and is now selling his famous bread in global markets.

When Lionel Poilane took over the family business about 30 years ago, he was determined to return breadmaking to its roots. As a result of studying the craft of breadmaking, Poilane built clay ovens based on sixteenth-century plans and technology. Then he trained his breadmakers in ancient techniques and soon began selling old-style dark bread known for a thick, chewy, fire-tinged flavor. It quickly became a favorite in Parisian bistros, and demand soared.

To help meet demand, Poilane built two more bakeries in Paris, and today he sells 15,000 loaves of bread a day— about 2.5 percent of all the bread sold in Paris. Poilane has opened a bakery in London, but his efforts to expand to

"I'm not eager to have a business card that says 'Paris, London, New York' on it."

—French baker Lionel Poilane on why he used the Internet to globalize

Japan were stymied: Local ordinances prohibited wood-burning ovens, and Poilane refused to compromise. During this negotiation process, however, he realized that he didn't really *want* to build new bakeries all over the world. "I'm not eager to have a business card that says 'Paris, London, New York' on it," he explains.

Instead, he turned to modern technology to expand his old-fashioned business. The key was the big FedEx hub at Roissy-Charles-de-Gaulle airport near Poilane's largest Paris bakery. After launching a Web site with minimal marketing support, Poilane started taking international orders. New orders are packaged as the bread cools and then picked up by FedEx. At about 4 pounds, the basic loaf travels well, and a quick warm-up in the customer's oven gives it the same taste as it had when it came out of Poilane's oven. Today, a loaf of bread baked in Paris in the morning can easily be reheated for tomorrow night's dinner in more than 20 countries.

on billboards in Bangkok, Thailand, and Bart Simpson piñatas are sold at Mexico City bazaars. Teenagers in Rome and Beirut sport American baseball caps, and vintage Levi's from the 1950s and 1960s sell for $3,000 in Finland and Australia.

Adapting to Customer Needs If there is demand for its product, a firm must decide whether and how to adapt it to meet the special demands of foreign customers. To satisfy local tastes, McDonald's sells wine in France, beer in Germany, and meatless sandwiches in India. Ford cars must have steering wheels mounted on the right if they're to be sold in England and Japan. When Toyota launches upscale cars at home, it keeps the Toyota nameplate. The same cars, however, sell under the Lexus nameplate *(www.lexus.com)* in the United States because the firm has concluded that Americans won't pay a premium price for a Toyota.

Levels of Involvement

After deciding to go international, a firm must determine the level of its involvement. Several levels are possible: A firm may act as an exporter or importer, organize as an international firm, or (like most of the world's largest industrial firms) operate as a multinational firm.

exporter
Firm that distributes and sells products to one or more foreign countries

importer
Firm that buys products in foreign markets and then imports them for resale in its home country

international firm
Firm that conducts a significant portion of its business in foreign countries

multinational firm
Firm that designs, produces, and markets products in many nations

independent agent
Foreign individual or organization that agrees to represent an exporter's interests

Exporters and Importers An **exporter** makes products in one country to distribute and sell in others. An **importer** buys products in foreign markets and imports them for resale at home. Both conduct most of their business in their home nations. Both kinds of doing business entail the lowest level of involvement in international operations, and both are good ways to learn the fine points of global business. Many large firms entered international business as exporters. IBM *(www.ibm/planetwide/europe)* and Coca-Cola *(www.thecocacolacompany.com/world)*, among others, exported to Europe for several years before producing there.

Exporting and importing have steadily increased over the last several decades. U.S. exports totaled $344 billion in 1980 and $708 billion in 1990, and they exceeded $1.3 trillion in 2000. Imports into the United States have risen from $335 billion in 1980 to $1 trillion in 1990 and $1.4 trillion in 2000.[13] Although big business was responsible for much of this growth, many smaller firms are successful exporters. San Antonio's Pace Foods *(www.pacefoods.com)*, a maker of Tex-Mex products, began exporting to Mexico after discovering that Mexican consumers enjoyed its picante sauce as much as U.S. consumers.

International Firms As exporters and importers gain experience and grow, many move to the next level of involvement. **International firms** conduct a good deal of their business abroad and may even maintain overseas manufacturing facilities. Starbucks, for instance, is an international firm: Although most of its stores are in the United States, the company is rapidly expanding into foreign markets.

An international firm may be large, but it's still basically a domestic company with international operations. Its main concern is its domestic market, and marketing decisions typically reflect this concern. Burlington Industries *(www.burlington.com)*, Toys "R" Us *(www.toysrus.com)*, and BMW *(www.bmw.com)* are also international firms.

Multinational Firms Most **multinational firms**, such as ExxonMobil, Nestlé, IBM, and Ford, don't think of themselves as having domestic and international divisions. Headquarters locations are almost irrelevant, and planning and decision making are geared to international markets.

We can't underestimate the economic importance of multinationals. Consider just the impact of the 500 largest multinationals. In 2001, these 500 firms generated $14 trillion in revenues and $306 billion in owner profits. They employed almost 48 million people, bought materials and equipment from literally thousands of other firms, and paid billions in taxes. Moreover, their products affected the lives of hundreds of millions of consumers, competitors, investors, and even protestors.[14]

International Organizational Structures

Different levels of international involvement entail different kinds of organizational structure. A structure that would help coordinate an exporter's activities would be inadequate for those of a multinational. In this section, we consider the spectrum of organizational strategies, including *independent agents, licensing arrangements, branch offices, strategic alliances,* and *foreign direct investment.*

Independent Agents An **independent agent** is a foreign individual or organization that represents an exporter in foreign markets. Independent agents often act as sales representatives: They sell the exporter's products, collect payment, and make sure that customers are satisfied. They often represent several firms at once and usually don't specialize in a particular product or market. Levi Strauss *(www.levi.com)* uses agents to market products in many small countries in Africa, Asia, and South America.

Licensing Arrangements Companies seeking more substantial involvement may opt for **licensing arrangements**. Firms give foreign individuals or companies exclusive rights to manufacture or market their products in that market. In return, the exporter receives a fee plus ongoing payments called royalties that are calculated as a percentage of the license holder's sales. Franchising is an increasingly popular form of licensing. McDonald's *(www.mcdonalds.com/corporate/franchise/outside)* and Pizza Hut *(www.pizzahut.com)* franchise around the world. Accor SA *(www.accor.com/sf)*, a French hotel chain, franchises Ibis, Sofitel, and Novotel hotels in the United States.

licensing arrangement
Arrangement in which firms choose foreign individuals or organizations to manufacture or market their products in another country

Branch Offices Instead of developing relationships with foreign agents or companies, a firm may send its own managers to overseas **branch offices**, where it has more direct control than it does over agents or license holders. Branch offices also furnish a more visible public presence in foreign countries, and foreign customers tend to feel more secure when there's a local branch office.

branch office
Foreign office set up by an international or multinational firm

Strategic Alliances In a **strategic alliance**, a company finds a partner in the country in which it wants to do business. Each party agrees to invest resources and capital into a new business or else to cooperate in some mutually beneficial way. This new business—the alliance—is owned by the partners, who divide its profits. Although such alliances are sometimes called *joint ventures*, the term *strategic alliance* has arisen because such partnerships are playing increasingly important roles in the strategies of major companies.

strategic alliance
Arrangement (also called *joint venture*) in which a company finds a foreign partner to contribute approximately half of the resources needed to establish and operate a new business in the partner's country

The number of strategic alliances among major companies has increased significantly over the last decade and is likely to grow even more. The new Disney theme park near Hong Kong is a joint venture with local partners, and in many countries, such as Mexico, India, and China, laws make alliances virtually the only way to do international business. Mexico, for example, requires that all foreign firms investing there have local partners.

In addition to easing the way into new markets, alliances give firms greater control over foreign activities than agents and licensees. (Even so, all partners retain some say in an alliance's decisions.) Perhaps most important, alliances allow firms to benefit from the knowledge and expertise of foreign partners. Microsoft, for example, relies heavily on alliances as it expands into international markets. This approach has helped the firm learn the intricacies of doing business in China and India, two of the hardest emerging markets to crack.

foreign direct investment (FDI)
Arrangement in which a firm buys or establishes tangible assets in another country

Foreign Direct Investment Foreign direct investment (FDI) involves buying or establishing tangible assets in another country.[15] Dell Computer, for example, has built assembly plants in Europe and China. Disney is building a theme park in Hong Kong, and Volkswagen is building a factory in Brazil. Each of these activities represents FDI by a firm in another country. Ford's purchase of Land Rover from the German firm BMW is

"There can be no doubt that foreign direct investment has joined international trade as a primary motor of globalization."

—Renato-Ruggerio, director-general, World Trade Organization

an instance of FDI, as is the acquisition of both Ben & Jerry's and Slim-Fast by the Dutch company Unilever.[16] FDI in the United States by foreign firms in 1999 totaled $294 billion. U.S. firms invested $980 billion in other countries.[17] "There can be no doubt," says the director-general of the World Trade Organization, "that foreign direct investment has joined international trade as a primary motor of globalization."[18]

SELF-CHECK QUESTIONS 4–6

You should now be able to answer Self-Check Questions 4–6.*

4 **Multiple Choice** Which of the following is **not** an immediate consideration when making the decision to "go international"? [select one]: **(a)** international demand; **(b)** exchange rates; **(c)** foreign business climate; **(d)** ease of product modification; **(e)** availability of knowledge and expertise.

5 **True/False** As relatively low levels of *international involvement*, importing and exporting are excellent

entry strategies for firms just launching international activities.

6 **Multiple Choice** The most complex form of *international organizational structure* involves which of the following? [select one]: **(a)** foreign direct investment; **(b)** independent agents; **(c)** licensing arrangements; **(d)** branch offices; **(e)** an international division.

***Answers to Self-Check Questions 4–6 can be found on p. 507.**

■ BARRIERS TO INTERNATIONAL TRADE

Whether a business is truly multinational or sells to only a few foreign markets, several factors will affect its international operations. Success in foreign markets will largely depend on the ways it responds to *social, economic, legal*, and *political barriers* to international trade.

Social and Cultural Differences

Any firm planning to conduct business abroad must understand the social and cultural differences between host country and home country. Some differences are obvious. You must, for example, consider language factors when adjusting packaging, signs, and logos. Pepsi *(www.pepsico.com)* is the same product in Seattle and Moscow—except for the lettering on the bottle. Less universal products, however, face several conditions that force them to make adjustments. When Bob's Big Boy *(www.bobs.net)* launched new restaurants in Thailand, it had to add deep-fried shrimp to the menu. Kentucky Fried Chicken *(www.kfc.com)* has altered menus, ingredients, and hours of operation to suit Thai culture.

A wide range of subtle value differences can also affect operations. For example, many Europeans shop daily for groceries. To U.S. consumers accustomed to weekly

Say WHAT YOU MEAN

PLAYING BY THE RULES OF ENGAGEMENT

Venturing into the wide world of global business requires not only knowledge about local people and cultures but also sensitivity to their ways of doing things. The sights and sounds of another country will, of course, be new, and more importantly, so will the rules of engagement—the policies that govern business activities, the ways in which your competition operates, and so forth. When it comes to doing global business, there's a good deal that's going to be beyond your control, but cultivating a little cultural understanding and personal flexibility will take you a long way toward business success.

Despite the effects of globalization, local conditions have a big impact on the way business is conducted around the world. Even the largest multinationals adapt their ways of doing things to the cultural conditions that prevail in host countries. It's a basic fact of business life that local culture is far too important, and far too powerful, to be ignored. If you're going to be a member of the global business community, you're going to need good adaptation skills, and the more readily you accept the

need to adapt, the more likely you'll be to thrive in a multicultural world.

We've all been raised with a certain set of cultural values that tells us how to interact with other people—how to work, to think, to negotiate, to learn, to relax. That's how we know the "right" way to act in most situations. In order to adapt to cultural differences, we have to make a conscious effort to remember that our values are not necessarily the ones that should govern our behavior in someone else's culture.

Here are a few key things to bear in mind if you're thinking about doing business on a multicultural scale:

- Despite the impact of globalization, local culture is extremely important when it comes to the way business is conducted in different places.
- We're all raised with a set of cultural values that determines the way we view the world and that we may have to adapt to do business with people who have different values.
- The international businessperson must understand cultural differences and see them not as a challenge but as an opportunity to improve interactions of all kinds, not just business transactions.

supermarket trips, the European pattern may seem like a waste of time. For many Europeans, however, shopping is not just a matter of buying food; it's also an outlet for meeting friends and exchanging political views. Consider the implications of this difference for U.S. firms selling food and food-related products in Europe where large American supermarkets are not the norm in many parts of Europe.

Economic Differences

Although cultural differences are often subtle, economic differences can be fairly pronounced. In dealing with mixed economies like those of France and Sweden, firms must know when—and to what extent—the government is involved in a given industry. The French government, for instance, is heavily involved in all aspects of airplane design and manufacturing. The impact of economic differences can be even greater in planned economies like those of China and Vietnam.

Legal and Political Differences

Governments can affect international business in many ways. They can set conditions for doing business within their borders and even prohibit doing business altogether.

On the first Muslim holy day after American warplanes went into Afghanistan, this crowd in Karachi, Pakistan, set fire to a (locally owned) KFC outlet. The immediate problem was a political one: Pakistanis objected to their government's support of the U.S. assault on the Muslim government of neighboring Afghanistan. A deeper problem, however, reflects social and cultural conflict: Muslim societies resent the invasion of foreign influences that often rip holes in the fabric of traditional social life. The red, white, and blue logo of KFC *(www.kfc.com)*, which runs 6,000 restaurants abroad, is a conspicuous symbol of those influences.

They can control the flow of capital and use tax legislation to discourage or encourage activity in a given industry. They can even confiscate the property of foreign-owned companies. In this section, we discuss some of the more common legal and political issues in international business: *quotas, tariffs,* and *subsidies*; *local content laws*; and *business practice laws.*

Quotas, Tariffs, and Subsidies Even free market economies have some quotas and/or tariffs, both of which affect prices and quantities of foreign-made products. A **quota** restricts the number of products of a certain type that can be imported and, by reducing supply, raises the prices of those imports. That's why Belgian ice-cream makers can't ship any more than 922,315 kilograms to the United States each year. Canada can ship no more than 14.7 billion board feet of softwood timber per year. Quotas are often determined by treaties. Better terms are often given to friendly trading partners, and quotas are typically adjusted to protect domestic producers.

The ultimate quota is an **embargo**: a government order forbidding exportation and/or importation of a particular product—or even all products—from a specific country. Many nations control bacteria and disease by banning certain agricultural products. Because the United States has embargoes against Cuba, Iraq, Libya, and Iran, American firms can't invest in these countries, and their products can't legally be sold on American markets.

Tariffs are taxes on imported products. They raise the prices of imports by making consumers pay not only for the products but also for tariff fees. Tariffs take two forms. Revenue tariffs are imposed to raise money for governments, but most tariffs, called protectionist tariffs, are meant to discourage particular imports. Did you know that firms that import ironing-board covers into the United States pay a 7-percent tariff on the price of the product? Firms that import women's athletic shoes pay a flat rate of 90 cents per pair plus 20 percent of the product price. Such figures are determined through a complicated process designed to put foreign and domestic firms on competitive footing.

A **subsidy** is a government payment to help a domestic business compete with foreign firms. They're actually indirect tariffs that lower the prices of domestic goods rather than raise the prices of foreign goods. Many European governments subsidize farmers to help them compete against U.S. grain imports.

quota
Restriction on the number of products of a certain type that can be imported into a country

embargo
Government order banning exportation and/or importation of a particular product or all products from a particular country

tariff
Tax levied on imported products

subsidy
Government payment to help a domestic business compete with foreign firms

Quotas and tariffs are imposed for numerous reasons. The U.S. government aids domestic automakers by restricting the number of Japanese cars imported into this country. Because of national security concerns, we limit the export of technology (for example, computer and nuclear technology to China). The United States, of course, isn't the only country that uses tariffs and quotas. To protect domestic firms, Italy imposes high tariffs on electronic goods. As a result, a Sony Walkman costs $150 there, and CD players are prohibitively expensive.

The Protectionism Debate In the United States, **protectionism**—the practice of protecting domestic business at the expense of free market competition—is controversial. Supporters argue that tariffs and quotas protect domestic firms and jobs as well as shelter new industries until they're able to compete internationally. They contend that we need such measures to counter steps taken by other nations. Other advocates justify protectionism in the name of national security. A nation, they argue, must be able to produce efficiently the goods needed for survival in case of war. Thus, the U.S. government requires the Air Force to buy planes only from U.S. manufacturers.

protectionism
Practice of protecting domestic business against foreign competition

Critics cite protectionism as a source of friction between nations. They also charge that it drives up prices by reducing competition. They maintain that although jobs in some industries would be lost as a result of free trade, jobs in other industries (for example, electronics and automobiles) would be created if all nations abandoned protectionist tactics.

Protectionism sometimes takes on almost comic proportions. Neither Europe nor the United States grows bananas, but both European and U.S. firms buy and sell bananas in foreign markets. Problems arose when the EU put a quota on bananas imported from Latin America—a market dominated by two U.S. firms, Chiquita *(www.chiquita.com)* and Dole *(www.dole.com)*—in order to help firms based in current and former European colonies in the Caribbean. To retaliate, the United States imposed a 100-percent tariff on certain luxury products imported from Europe, including Louis Vuitton handbags *(www.vuitton.com)*, Scottish cashmere sweaters, and Parma ham.[19]

local content law
Law requiring that products sold in a particular country be at least partly made there

Local Content Laws Many countries, including the United States, have **local content laws**—requirements that products sold in a country be at least partly made there.

At a rally in Washington, D.C., steelworkers urge the government to protect the U.S. steel industry from low-priced imports. Three months later, the Bush administration announced tariffs of 8 percent to 30 percent on certain foreign steel products. In the last few years, 25 old-line U.S. steel companies have filed for bankruptcy, and in two decades, employment in the industry has fallen from 450,000 to 150,000. But even in the United States, so-called mini-mills, which run high-tech, low-cost operations, oppose the protectionist measure as corporate welfare for inefficient competitors.

Firms seeking to do business in a country must either invest there directly or take on a domestic partner. In this way, some of the profits from doing business in a foreign country stay there rather than flowing out to another nation. In some cases, the partnership arrangement is optional but wise. In Mexico, for instance, Radio Shack de Mexico is a joint venture owned by Tandy Corp. *(www.radioshackunlimited.com)* (49 percent) and Mexico's Grupo Gigante *(www.gigante.com.mx)* (51 percent). Both China and India currently require that when a foreign firm enters into a joint venture with a local firm, the local partner must have controlling ownership stake.

Business Practice Laws Many businesses entering new markets encounter problems in complying with stringent regulations and bureaucratic obstacles. Such practices are affected by the **business practice laws** by which host countries govern business practices within their jurisdictions. As part of its entry strategy in Germany, Wal-Mart has had to buy existing retailers rather than open brand-new stores. Why? Because the German government is not currently issuing new licenses to sell food products. Wal-Mart also had to stop refunding price differences on items sold for less by other stores because the practice is illegal in Germany. Finally, Wal-Mart must comply with business-hour restrictions: Stores can't open before 7 A.M., must close by 8 P.M. on weeknights and 4 P.M. on Saturday, and must remain closed on Sunday.

business practice law
Law or regulation governing business practices in given countries

Cartels and Dumping Sometimes a legal—even an accepted—practice in one country is illegal in another. In some South American countries, for example, it is sometimes legal to bribe business and government officials. The existence of **cartels**—associations of producers that control supply and prices—gives tremendous power to some nations, such as those belonging to the Organization of Petroleum Exporting Countries (OPEC). U.S. law forbids both bribery and cartels.

cartel
Association of producers whose purpose is to control supply and prices

Finally, many (but not all) countries forbid **dumping**—selling a product abroad for less than the cost of production at home. U.S. antidumping legislation sets two conditions for determining whether dumping is being practiced:

dumping
Practice of selling a product abroad for less than the cost of production

1 Products are being priced at "less than fair value."
2 The result unfairly harms domestic industry.

In 1999, the United States charged Japan and Brazil with dumping steel at prices 70 percent below normal value. In order to protect local manufacturers, the government imposed a significant tariff on steel imported from those countries.

SELF-CHECK QUESTIONS 7–9

You should now be able to answer Self-Check Questions 7–9.*

7 **Multiple Choice** Which of the following does **not** serve as a *barrier to international trade*? [select one]: **(a)** social differences; **(b)** cultural differences; **(c)** economic differences; **(d)** political differences; **(e)** transportation differences.

8 **Multiple Choice** Which of the following is **not** a *legal barrier to international trade*? [select one]: **(a)** quotas and tariffs; **(b)** exchange rate parameters; **(c)** local content laws; **(d)** business practice laws; **(e)** subsidies.

9 **True/False** *Protectionism* refers to the practice of hiring local mobsters to protect a foreign company from local competitors.

***Answers to Self-Check Questions 7–9 can be found on p. 507.**

Continued from page 102

MARIACHI BANDS AND OTHER WEAPONS OF THE RETAIL WARS

Wal-Mart's entry into a new market "is a nightmare for a lot of retailers," says retail consultant Michael P. Godliman. To fight back, local retailers have imitated Wal-Mart strategy—namely, by cutting costs and increasing variety—and many have also added products and services geared to local tastes. Soriana supermarkets of Mexico, for example, wages war with in-store mariachi concerts. "Wal-Mart is formidable, but we aren't afraid of the challenge," says Soriana CEO Ricardo Martín. Hoping to forestall Wal-Mart's entry into France, the second-largest retail market in Europe, domestic retailer Carrefour has added amenities such as travel agents and shoe fitters and banned fluorescent lighting. More importantly, a recently announced merger with France's number-two retailer, Promodes, boosts Carrefour's market power. Carrefour, testifies one French retail executive, is "just relentless. The toughest competitor I've ever seen anywhere." Other European retailers, such as Dutch grocer Ahold, are also considering preemptive mergers.

In 2002, Wal-Mart's results from international operations were mixed. The firm had a modest increase in sales, though far less than the increases enjoyed in previous years.

Its gross margin on international sales was just 4.1 percent, compared to 7.1 percent for domestic stores. But the company is flush with the profits from its thousands of domestic stores and does not intend to be deterred. The international retailing industry will undoubtedly consolidate until just a

" **W**al-Mart's entry into a new market is a nightmare for a lot of retailers."

—Retail consultant Michael P. Godliman

few very large, cross-border retailers remain. Wal-Mart will obviously be one of them.

Questions for Discussion

1 What are some of the advantages that Wal-Mart hopes to gain by globalization? What are some of the challenges that it faces in its efforts to globalize?

2 What methods has Wal-Mart used to globalize? Are they the most appropriate methods for the firm? Why or why not?

■ SUMMARY OF LEARNING OBJECTIVES

1 Discuss the rise of international business and describe the *major world marketplaces.*

The world economy is becoming a complex interdependent system—a process called **globalization**. Several forces combined to spark and sustain globalization: (1) Governments and businesses are more aware of the benefits of globalization; (2) new technologies make international travel, communication, and commerce faster and cheaper; (3) competitive pressures sometimes force firms to expand into foreign markets just to keep up with competitors; (4) treaties and trade agreements also play a major role. The four most important influences are (1) General Agreement on Tariffs and Trade (GATT); (2) North American Free Trade Agreement (NAFTA); (3) European Union (EU); and (4) World Trade Organization (WTO). The contemporary world economy revolves around three major marketplaces: North America, Europe, and Pacific Asia.

2 Explain how differences in *competitive advantage, import-export balances, exchange rates,* and *foreign competition* determine the ways in which countries and businesses respond to the international environment.

Countries export what they can produce better or less expensively than other countries and use the proceeds to import what they can't produce as effectively. Economists once focused on two forms of advantage to explain international trade: **absolute advantage** and **comparative advantage**. The new theory of **national competitive advantage** is a widely accepted model of why nations engage in international trade.

A nation's **balance of trade** is the total economic value of all products that it imports minus the total economic value of all products that it exports. When a country's imports exceed its exports—when it has a negative balance of trade—it suffers a **trade deficit**; a positive balance occurs when exports exceed imports, resulting in a **trade surplus**. The **balance of payments** refers to the flow of money into or out of a country.

An **exchange rate** is the rate at which one nation's currency can be exchanged for that of another. A significant development in foreign exchange is the introduction of the **euro**—a common currency among most members of the

European Union. Under *floating exchange rates*, the value of one currency relative to that of another varies with market conditions.

3 Discuss the factors involved in deciding to do business internationally and in selecting the appropriate *levels of international involvement* and *international organizational structure.*

Several factors enter into the decision to go international. One overriding factor is the business climate in other nations. Even experienced firms have encountered cultural, legal, and economic roadblocks. A company should also consider at least two other issues: (1) Is there a demand for its products abroad? (2) If so, must it adapt those products for international consumption?

After deciding to go international, a firm must decide on its level of involvement. Several levels are possible: (1) exporters and importers; (2) international firms; and (3) multinational firms. Different levels of involvement require different kinds of organizational structure. The spectrum of international organizational strategies includes the following: (1) **independent agents**; (2) **licensing arrangements**; (3) **branch offices**; (4) **strategic alliances** (or *joint ventures*); and (5) **foreign direct investment (FDI)**.

4 Describe some of the ways in which *social, cultural, economic, legal,* and *political differences* among nations affect international business.

Some social and cultural differences, like language, are obvious, but a wide range of subtle value differences can also affect operations. Economic differences can be fairly pronounced. In dealing with mixed economies, firms must be aware of when—and to what extent—the government is involved in a given industry. The impact of economic differences can be even greater in planned economies. Governments can set conditions for doing business and even prohibit it altogether. They can control the flow of capital and use taxes to influence activity in a given industry. They can even confiscate foreign-owned property. Common legal and political issues in international business include **quotas, tariffs, subsidies, local content laws**, and **business practice laws**.

■ KEY TERMS

globalization (p. 102)
import (p. 102)
export (p. 102)
General Agreement on Tariffs and
   Trade (GATT) (p. 103)
North American Free Trade
   Agreement (NAFTA) (p. 103)
European Union (EU) (p. 105)
World Trade Organization (WTO)
   (p. 105)
absolute advantage (p. 110)
comparative advantage (p. 110)
national competitive advantage
   (p. 110)

balance of trade (p. 111)
trade deficit (p. 111)
trade surplus (p. 111)
balance of payments (p. 112)
exchange rate (p. 112)
euro (p. 112)
exporter (p. 118)
importer (p. 118)
international firm (p. 118)
multinational firm (p. 118)
independent agent (p. 118)
licensing arrangement (p. 119)
branch office (p. 119)

strategic alliances (p. 119)
foreign direct investment (FDI)
   (p. 119)
quota (p. 122)
embargo (p. 122)
tariff (p. 122)
subsidy (p. 122)
protectionism (p. 123)
local content law (p. 123)
business practice law (p. 124)
cartel (p. 124)
dumping (p. 124)

■ QUESTIONS AND EXERCISES

Questions for Review

1 How does the balance of trade differ from the balance of payments?
2 What are the three possible levels of involvement in international business? Give examples of each.
3 How does a country's economic system affect the decisions of foreign firms interested in doing business there?
4 What aspects of the culture in your state or region would be of particular interest to a foreign firm thinking about locating there?

Questions for Analysis

5 List all the major items in your bedroom, including furnishings. Try to identify the country in which each item was made. Offer possible reasons why a given nation might have a comparative advantage in producing a given good.
6 Suppose that you're the manager of a small firm seeking to enter the international arena. What basic information would you need about the market that you're thinking of entering?
7 Do you support protectionist tariffs for the United States? If so, in what instances and for what reasons? If not, why not?
8 Do you think that a firm operating internationally is better advised to adopt a single standard of ethical conduct or to adapt to local conditions? Under what kinds of conditions might each approach be preferable?

Application Exercises

9 Interview the manager of a local firm that does at least some business internationally. Why did the company decide to go international? Describe the level of the firm's international involvement and the organizational structure(s) it uses for international operations.
10 Select a product familiar to you. Using library reference works to gain some insight into the culture of India, identify the problems that might arise in trying to market this product to Indian consumers.

BUILDING YOUR BUSINESS SKILLS

FINDING YOUR PLACE

This exercise enhances the following SCANS workplace competencies: demonstrating basic skills, demonstrating thinking skills, exhibiting interpersonal skills, and working with information.

Goal

To encourage students to apply global business strategies to a small-business situation.

Background

Some people might say that Yolanda Lang is a bit too confident. Others might say that she needs confidence—and more—to succeed in the business she's chosen. But one thing is certain: Lang is determined to grow INDE, her handbag design company, into a global enterprise. At only 28 years of age, she has time on her side—if she makes the right business moves now.

These days, Lang spends most of her time in Milan, Italy. Backed by $50,000 of her parents' personal savings, she is trying to compete with Gucci, Fendi, and other high-end handbag makers. Her target market is American women willing to spend $200 on a purse. Ironically, Lang was forced to set up shop in Italy because of the snobbishness of these customers, who buy high-end bags only if they're European-made. "Strangely enough," she muses, "I need to be in Europe to sell in America."

To succeed, she must first find ways to keep production costs down—a tough task for a woman in a male-dominated business culture. Her fluent Italian is an advantage, but she's often forced to turn down inappropriate dinner invitations. She also has to figure out how to get her 22-bag collection into stores worldwide. Retailers are showing her bags in Italy and Japan, but she's had little luck in the United States. "I intend to be a global company," says Lang. The question is how to succeed first as a small business.

Method

Step 1

Join together with three or four other students to discuss the steps that Lang has taken so far to break into the U.S. retail market. These steps include:

- Buying a mailing list of 5,000 shoppers from high-end department store Neiman Marcus and selling directly to these customers.

- Linking with a manufacturer's representative to sell her line in major U.S. cities while she herself concentrates on Europe.

Step 2

Based on what you learned in this chapter, suggest other strategies that might help Lang grow her business. Working with group members, consider whether the following options would help or hurt Lang's business. Explain why a strategy is likely to work or likely to fail.

- Lang could relocate to the United States and sell abroad through an independent agent.
- Lang could relocate to the United States and set up a branch office in Italy.
- Lang could find a partner in Italy and form a strategic alliance that would allow her to build her business on both continents.

Step 3

Working alone, create a written marketing plan for INDE. What steps would you recommend that Lang take to reach her goal of becoming a global company? Compare your written response with those of other group members.

FOLLOW-UP QUESTIONS

1 What are the most promising steps that Lang can take to grow her business? What are the least promising?

2 Lang thinks that her trouble breaking into the U.S. retail market stems from the fact that her company is unknown. How would this circumstance affect the strategies suggested in Steps 1 and 2?

3 When Lang deals with Italian manufacturers, she is a young, attractive woman in a man's world. Often she must convince men that her purpose is business and nothing else. How should Lang handle personal invitations that get in the way of business? How can she say no while still maintaining business relationships? Why is it often difficult for American women to do business in male-dominated cultures?

4 The American consulate has given Lang little business help because her products are made in Italy. Do you think the consulate's treatment of an American businessperson is fair or unfair? Explain your answer.

5 Do you think Lang's relocation to Italy will pay off? Why or why not?

6 With Lang's goals of creating a global company, can INDE continue to be a one-person operation?

EXERCISING YOUR ETHICS

PAYING HEED TO FOREIGN PRACTICES

The Purpose of the Assignment

Managers conducting business in other countries must often contend with differences in legal systems, customs, mores, and business practices. This exercise will help you better understand how such differences can affect the success of managers and companies trying to conduct business in foreign markets.

The Situation

Assume that you're an up-and-coming manager in a regional U.S. distribution company. Firms in your industry are just beginning to enter foreign markets, and you've been assigned to head up your company's new operations in a Latin American country. Because at least two of your competitors are also trying to enter this same market, your boss wants you to move as quickly as possible. You also sense that your success in this assignment will likely determine your future with the company.

You have just completed meetings with local government officials, and you're pessimistic about your ability to get things moving quickly. You've learned, for example, that it will take 10 months to get a building permit for a needed facility. Moreover, once the building's up, it will take another six months to get utilities. Finally, the phone company says that it may take up to two years to install the phone lines that you need for high-speed Internet access.

The Dilemma

Various officials have indicated that time frames could be considerably shortened if you were willing to pay special "expediting" fees. You realize, of course, that these "fees" are bribes, and you're well aware that the practice of paying such "fees" is both unethical and illegal in the United States. In this foreign country, however, it's not illegal and not even considered unethical. Moreover, if you don't pay and one of your competitors does, you'll be at a major competitive disadvantage. In any case, your boss isn't likely to understand the long lead times necessary to get the operation running. Fortunately, you have access to a source of funds that you could spend without the knowledge of anyone in the home office.

QUESTIONS FOR DISCUSSION

1 What are the key ethical issues in this situation?
2 What do you think most managers would do in this situation?
3 What would you do?

 CRAFTING YOUR BUSINESS PLAN

CONSIDERING THE WORLD

The Purpose of the Assignment

1 To familiarize students with issues faced by a firm that has decided to go global.
2 To determine where, in the framework of the *BPP* business plan, global issues might appropriately be presented.

Assignment

After reading Chapter 4 in the textbook, open the Business PlanPro (BPP) 2003 *software (Version 6.0) and examine the information dealing with the types of global business considerations that would be of concern to the sample firm of* Acme Consulting. *To find* Acme Consulting, *do the following:*

Open *Business PlanPro.* Go to the toolbar and click on the "*Sample Plans*" icon. In the **Sample Plan Browser,** do a **keyword search** using the word *consulting.* From the resulting list, select the category entitled **Consulting—High-Tech Mar. . . ,** which is the location for *Acme Consulting.* The screen you are looking at is the introduction page for the *Acme Consulting* business plan. On this page, scroll down until you reach the **Table of Contents** for the company's business plan.

NOW RESPOND TO THE FOLLOWING ITEMS:

1 What products does *Acme* plan to offer and in which international markets will they be competing? [Sites to see in *BPP* (for this assignment): On the Table of Contents page, click on **1.0 Executive Summary;** then

click on **1.2 Mission** and then **4.0 Market Analysis Summary** and **4.1 Market Segmentation**. Next, click on **2.0 Company Summary**.]

2 In *Acme*'s business plan, see if you can find any discussion of the international organizational structures used by *Acme*'s competitors. Do you think this information is adequate or inadequate? [Sites to see in *BPP* for this item: On the Table of Contents page, click on **4.3.2 Distribution Service** and **4.3.4 Main Competitors**.]

3 Chapter 4 states that going international requires "necessary skills and knowledge." Does *Acme*'s business plan indicate that the company possesses the skills and knowledge to succeed internationally? [Sites to see in *BPP* for this item: On the Table of Contents page, click on **6.0 Management Summary** and then on **6.2 Management Team**. Next, click on **3.1 Service Description**, and then click on **3.2 Competitive Comparison**.]

 VIDEO EXERCISE

GLOBALIZING THE LONG ARM OF THE LAW: PRINTRAK

Learning Objectives

The purpose of this video is to help you:

1 Understand how and why a company adapts to the needs of foreign customers.
2 Identify the levels of international involvement that are available to companies.
3 Discuss the differences that can affect a company's international operations.

Synopsis

Scotland Yard and the Canadian Mounties are only two of the many organizations around the world that use security technology from Printrak *(www.printrakinternational.com)*, a Motorola company. Starting with a computerized fingerprint-management system, Printrak has added a number of security and criminal information products as it has expanded from its California headquarters to serve customers around the globe. General manager Darren Reilly and his management team study each country's legal, political, economic, and cultural differences and analyze local demand and customer needs. Rather than invest in local plants and equipment, Printrak works through local sales agents to ensure that products are marketed in a culturally savvy way. Despite country-by-country differences in business customs and ethics, the decisions and actions of Printrak employees are guided by Motorola's code of conduct.

DISCUSSION QUESTIONS

1 **For analysis:** What are some of the barriers that affect Printrak's ability to do business in foreign markets?

2 **For analysis:** From Printrak's perspective, what are the advantages and disadvantages of hiring and training local sales agents to work with customers in each foreign market?
3 **For application:** In addition to establishing user committees, what else should Printrak do to track changing customer needs in other countries?
4 **For application:** How would you suggest that Printrak build on its relations with "beachhead customers" to expand in particular regions?
5 **For debate:** Printrak employees and managers must comply with Motorola's global ethics policy. Should local sales agents be allowed to take any actions they deem necessary to make sales in local markets, regardless of Motorola's policy? Support your chosen position.

Online Exploration

Browse Printrak's home page at *(www.printrakinternational.com)*, see where the company has customers, and read some of the news releases about international operations. Also look at the resource links that Printrak has posted for customers and site visitors. Why would Printrak publicize its customer list in this way? Why would it include a glossary of security-related terms and acronyms on its Web site? Finally, do you think the company should translate some or all of its Web site to accommodate foreign customers? Explain your response.

PLANNING FOR YOUR CAREER

KNOWING WHAT YOU WANT

What kind of job do you want when you finish school? A glamorous position with a global firm that routinely flies you from New York, to London, Tokyo, and Rio? To start your own business and perhaps become the next Bill Gates? Or maybe just the "perfect job"—the one that will fulfill all your needs while providing adequate security and satisfying rewards? In a perfect world, of course, you can take your pick. But in the world we live in, of course, none of these options is likely to be available—at least not right away and not without any hitches.

Even global giants such as Nestlé and Toyota assign entry-level managers to domestic tasks. New businesses are also difficult to start with no experience, capital, or business plan. Many people change jobs at least a few times until they find one they truly want. So, what can you do *now* to better prepare for a future career? This exercise gives you an opportunity to take a closer look at yourself in order to get a better idea of where you might be headed.

Assignment

Begin by reading Chapter 1 in *Beginning Your Career Search*, 3d ed., by James S. O'Rourke IV. Use this chapter as a frame of reference in doing the following activities:

1 Develop a list of your major personal strengths. Examples might include such things as (1) excellent communications skills, (2) strong math background, (3) fluency in multiple languages, and so forth.

2 Develop a list of your major personal weaknesses, such as (1) fear of speaking in front of a group, (2) limited knowledge of foreign cultures, (3) weak science background, and so forth.

3 Develop a list of the qualities or characteristics that you think best reflect who and what you are. Are you (1) a risk-taker, (2) a person who prefers to work

alone, (3) a person who prefers to follow others, and so forth? (Note that none of these qualities is necessarily good or bad.)

4 Develop a list of the things that are most likely to be important to you in a career, at least initially. Examples might be (1) a job that will provide strong training and development opportunities, (2) a job in a certain geographic area, (3) a job with a certain kind of company, and so forth.

5 Develop a list of the things you hope to avoid in your career, if possible—(1) stress and long hours, (2) a lot of travel, (3) working with overly aggressive and competitive people, and so forth.

Now, draft an action plan that you can follow—some guidelines that might help you to better prepare for a job or career in relation to each of your five lists. Your plan should address ways to capitalize on your strengths, overcome your weaknesses, fit a job to your personal characteristics, meet many of your preferences, and avoid most of the things you dislike. For instance, if you have a fear of speaking in front of a group, you might plan to take a speech communications course. If you are indeed a risk-taker, you might begin by exploring career options that include some opportunity to take risks (such as working in a new venture or start-up operation) as opposed to options that involve less risk (such as working for a national retail chain that has a variety of standard operating procedures).

Remember, of course, that this action plan is indeed simply a draft. Even if you try to apply it to your educational choices, you'll need to revise and update it constantly. Jobs will change, the world will change, and you will change. But that's part of the fun of thinking about your future, isn't it? After all, it's a blank screen for you to write on, to edit, to erase, and then to write on some more.

5

After reading this chapter, you should be able to:

1 Explain the importance of setting *goals* and formulating *strategies* as the starting points of effective management.

2 Describe the four activities that constitute the *management process.*

3 Identify *types of managers* by level and area.

4 Describe the five basic *management skills.*

5 Describe the development and explain the importance of *corporate culture.*

YELLOW DELIVERS THE GOODS

Since its founding in 1923, Yellow Corp. *(www.yellowcorp.com)* has been among the leaders in the transportation industry by using its trucks to haul large and heavy shipments between cities and major distribution centers in the United States, Canada, and Mexico. For decades the firm achieved considerable success by concentrating virtually all of its attention on ruthlessly increasing efficiency at every turn.

MANAGING
THE BUSINESS
ENTERPRISE

> "**W**e were a defensive company. We were yearning for leadership."
>
> —James Welch, Yellow Corp. COO

For instance, Yellow has been a master at ensuring that all of its trucks were full before they left a warehouse or other shipping center. Similarly, the firm also developed and religiously adhered to precisely timed delivery schedules. This precision, however, proved to be a double-edged sword—shippers could count on getting their shipments on time, but Yellow also had difficulty responding to last-minute changes or special requests by customers.

Yellow eventually fell victim to its own success. For example, as operational efficiency increased, customer service was given less and less attention. This lack of attention, in turn, allowed newer and more responsive companies to lure away some of the firm's customers. Compounding this problem was that the customers most likely to seek a different and more service-oriented transportation provider were also the very ones who were willing to pay premium prices for the extra service. As a result, Yellow's financial performance began to decline, slowly at first but then more dramatically. This decline, in turn, also led to poorer across-the-board service.

To help turn Yellow around, the firm's board of directors offered to Bill Zollars the position of chief executive officer (CEO) in 1996. Already a highly respected manager, Zollars was intrigued by the opportunity to revitalize the carrier. James Welch, president and chief operating officer, recollects, "We were a defensive company—a follower, not a leader. We were yearning for leadership. This company was ready for change."

Zollars quickly learned that a successful organizational transformation at Yellow would need to be profound. Over a sustained period that spanned decades many people throughout the company had come to accept mediocrity and were often willing only to do the minimal amount necessary to get their jobs done. Hence, Zollars knew that he had to alter the attitudes, behaviors, and performance of each of the firm's 30,000 employees.

Communication was one of the first keys to Zollars's attempt to turn things around at Yellow. The CEO spent 18 months traveling to the company's several hundred locations and at each site talked face-to-face with customers and with employees at all levels in the organization. He asked for opinions and comments from everyone he met and consistently provided his own message that enhanced customer service was to become the firm's calling card. But unlike the hollow claims that executives sometimes make, his meetings consisted of more than just empty promises and motivational speeches.

For example, the firm's previous leaders often glossed over problems and refused to divulge information about the firm's performance. Zollars, however, openly acknowledged the company's true defect rate—the percentage of shipments that were late, wrong, or damaged. Indeed, Yellow employees were stunned to find that the company's defect rate was a whopping 40 percent. But that knowledge was necessary to enhance motivation and provide a benchmark for improvement. Zollars also instituted the company's first ongoing program for surveying customer satisfaction. The reports of these surveys were then reported openly throughout the company.

Zollars's leadership created a sense of motivation and pride among employees that, in turn, led to continuing high levels of productivity and performance. He made a real effort to listen to employees, seriously consider their suggestions, and give them increased authority to make decisions. He also developed an enviable reputation for honesty and commitment, attempting to "walk the walk," as well as "talk the talk." Zollars asserts, "If people doing the work don't believe what's coming from the leadership, it doesn't get implemented. Period."

Our opening story continues on page 157.

All corporations depend on effective management. Regardless of whether managers run a major international shipping business like Yellow or a small local or regional delivery company, they perform many of the same functions, are responsible for many of the same tasks, and have many of the same responsibilities. The work of all managers involves developing strategic and tactical plans. Along with numerous other things, they must analyze their competitive environments and plan, organize, direct, and control day-to-day operations.

By focusing on the learning objectives of this chapter, you will better understand the nature of managing and the range of skills that managers like Bill Zollars need if they are to compete effectively and the importance of corporate culture.

Although our focus is on managers in business settings, remember that the principles of management apply to all kinds of organizations. Managers work in charities, churches, social organizations, educational institutions, and government agencies. The prime minister of Canada, the curator at the Museum of Modern Art, the dean of your college, and the chief administrator of your local hospital are all managers. Remember, too, that managers bring to small organizations much the same kinds of skills—the ability to make decisions and respond to a variety of challenges—as they bring to large ones.

Regardless of the nature and size of an organization, managers are among its most important resources. Consider the profiles of the following three managers:

■ Texas native Marjorie Scardino runs Pearson PLC *(www.pearson.com)*, a huge British media company. When she was named CEO, Pearson was considered a stodgy old-line company that had diversified into too many different areas. Scardino set about systematically pruning unrelated businesses and sharpening the firm's focus into three basic business groups. One group is heavily involved in educational publishing; the second operates the *Financial Times*, a leading business newspaper; and the third consists of the Penguin publishing group. The current economic climate has limited her ability to focus on additional growth and look for new acquisitions. Instead, Scardino is currently looking for ways to increase efficiency and lower costs. If she is successful, Pearson will be well positioned for new growth when economic conditions improve.[1]

■ Kenneth Chenault is considered one of the best young senior managers around. He joined American Express *(www.americanexpress.com)* in 1981 as a marketing specialist and then systematically worked his way up the corporate ladder until he became president in 1997. During the next two years, Chenault presided over a major overhaul at AmEx as the firm sought to undo an ill-fated diversification strategy undertaken by a previous CEO. So impressive was Chenault's performance that in April 2001 he was named chairman and CEO of the company. Having reorganized a huge number of services into four core businesses—Global Financial Services, U.S. Consumer and Small Business Services, Global Corporate Services, and Global Establishment Services and Travelers Cheque Group—Chenault now has to show that AmEx can profitably service 52 million cardholders and 2.3 million financial services customers.[2]

■ Twenty years ago, when he was running PepsiCo *(wwwpepsico.com)*, Andrall Pearson was identified as one of the 10 toughest bosses in America. Much of that reputation was based on his tendency to humiliate employees and to lead through fear and intimidation. Although he was credited with increasing the firm's revenues from less than $1 billion to over $8 billion, he was also vilified by almost everyone who worked for him. Today, however, Pearson runs Tricon Global Restaurants *(wwwtriconglobal.com)* (owners of KFC, Pizza Hut, and Taco Bell) with a much different approach. He remains demanding and results oriented, but he has become much more concerned about the personal and professional welfare of his employees. Indeed, colleagues describe his current leadership style in terms of his warmth, energy, and charisma.[3]

Although Marjorie Scardino, Kenneth Chenault, and Andrall Pearson are clearly different people who work in different kinds of organizations and have different approaches to what they do, they also share one fundamental commonality with other high-level managers: responsibility for the performance and effectiveness of business enterprises. Thus, they are accountable to shareholders, employees, customers, and other key constituents. In this chapter, we describe the management process and the skills that managers must develop to perform their functions in organizations. Perhaps you will then have a better feel for the reasons why organizations value good managers so highly.

■ SETTING GOALS AND FORMULATING STRATEGY

goal
Objective that a business hopes and plans to achieve

strategy
Broad set of organizational plans for implementing the decisions made for achieving organizational goals

corporate strategy
Strategy for determining the firm's overall attitude toward growth and the way it will manage its businesses or product lines

business (or **competitive**) **strategy**
Strategy, at the business-unit or product-line level, focusing on a firm's competitive position

The starting point in effective management is setting **goals**—objectives that a business hopes and plans to achieve. Every business needs goals. We begin, therefore, by discussing the basic aspects of organizational goal setting. Remember, however, that deciding what it *intends* to do is only the first step for an organization. Managers must also make decisions about *actions* that will and will not achieve company goals. Decisions cannot be made on a problem-by-problem basis or merely to meet needs as they arise. In most companies, a broad program underlies those decisions. That program is called a **strategy**, which is a broad set of organizational plans for implementing the decisions made for achieving organizational goals.

Types of Strategy Figure 5.1 shows the relationship among the three types of strategy that are usually considered by a company:[4]

■ The purpose of **corporate strategy** is to determine the firm's overall attitude toward growth and the way it will manage its businesses or product lines. A company may decide to grow by increasing its activities or investment or to *retrench* by reducing them. Under Kenneth Chenault, AmEx corporate strategy calls for strengthening operations through a principle of growth called e-partnering—buying shares of small companies that can provide technology that AmEx itself does not have.

■ **Business** (or **competitive**) **strategy**, which takes place at the level of the business unit or product line, focuses on improving the company's competitive position. At this level, AmEx makes decisions about how best to compete in an industry that includes Visa, MasterCard, and other credit card companies. In this respect, the company has committed heavily to expanding its product offerings and serving customers through new technology.

FIGURE 5.1

Hierarchy of Strategy

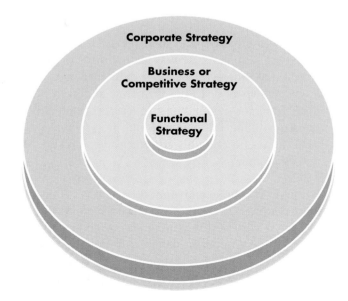

■ At the level of **functional strategy**, managers in specific areas decide how best to achieve corporate goals by being as productive as possible. At AmEx, each business unit has considerable autonomy in deciding how to use the single Web site at which the company has located its entire range of services.

functional strategy
Strategy by which managers in specific areas decide how best to achieve corporate goals through productivity

Of course, the real challenges—and opportunities—lie in successfully creating these strategies. Therefore, we now turn our attention to the basic steps in strategy formulation.

Setting Business Goals

Goals are performance targets—the means by which organizations and their managers measure success or failure at every level. For example, Marjorie Scardino's current goals at Pearson are tied to cost reductions and improved profitability; in the future she will likely focus more on growth. At AmEx, however, Kenneth Chenault is focusing more on revenue growth and the firm's stock price. Andrall Pearson's goals, meanwhile, focus generally on motivating lower-wage workers in a highly competitive business environment while simultaneously leading a major global expansion.

Purposes of Goal Setting An organization functions systematically because it sets goals and plans accordingly. An organization commits its resources on all levels to achieving its goals. Specifically, we can identify four main purposes in organizational goal setting:

1 **Goal setting provides direction and guidance for managers at all levels.** If managers know precisely where the company is headed, there is less potential for error in the different units of the company. Starbucks, for example, has a goal of increasing capital spending by 15 percent, with all additional expenditures devoted to opening new stores. This goal clearly informs everyone in the firm that expansion into new territories is a high priority for the firm.

2 **Goal setting helps firms allocate resources.** Areas that are expected to grow will get first priority. The company allocates more resources to new projects with large sales potential than it allocates to mature products with established but stagnant sales potential. Thus, Starbucks is primarily emphasizing new store expansion, while its e-commerce initiatives are currently given a lower priority. "Our management team," says CEO Howard Schultz, "is 100% focused on growing our core business without distraction . . . from any other initiative."

3 **Goal setting helps to define corporate culture.** For years, the goal at General Electric has been to push each of its divisions to first or second in its industry. The result is a competitive (and often stressful) environment and a culture that rewards success and has little tolerance for failure. At the same time, however, GE's appliance business, television network (NBC), aircraft engine unit, and financial services businesses are each among the very best in their respective industries. Eventually, legendary former CEO Jack Welch set an even higher companywide standard—to make the firm the most valuable in the world.

4 **Goal setting helps managers assess performance.** If a unit sets a goal of increasing sales by 10 percent in a given year, managers in that unit who attain or exceed the goal can be rewarded. Units failing to reach the goal will also be compensated accordingly. GE has a long-standing reputation for stringently evaluating managerial performance, richly rewarding those who excel, and getting rid of those who do not. Each year the lower 10 percent of GE's managerial force

> "Our management team is 100% focused on growing our core business without distraction from any other initiative."
>
> —Howard Schultz, CEO of Starbucks

mission statement
Organization's statement of how it will achieve its purpose in the environment in which it conducts its business

is informed either to make dramatic improvements in performance or consider alternative career directions.

Kinds of Goals Goals differ from company to company, depending on the firm's purpose and mission. Every enterprise has a *purpose* or a reason for being. Businesses seek profits, universities seek to discover and transmit new knowledge, and government agencies seek to set and enforce public policy. Many enterprises also have missions and **mission statements**—statements of how they will achieve their purposes in the environments in which they conduct their business.

A company's mission is usually easy to identify, at least at a basic level. Dell Computer *(www.dell.com)*, for example, set out to make a profit by selling personal computers directly to consumers. In San Francisco, Platinum Concepts Inc. *(www.mousedriver.com)* intends to become profitable by developing "unique and innovative products." So far, the company's only product is the MouseDriver, a computer mouse shaped like the head of a golf club, but it expects to sell $1 million worth of MouseDrivers this year.[5]

Businesses often have to rethink their missions as the competitive environment changes. In 1999, for example, Starbucks announced that Internet marketing and sales were going to become core business initiatives. Managers subsequently realized, however, that this initiative did not fit the firm as well as they first thought. As a result, they scaled back this effort and, as we noted, made a clear recommitment to their existing retail business. The demands of change force many companies to rethink their missions and, thus, revise their statements of what they are and what they do. (We discuss more fully the problems in managing change—as well as some solutions—later in this chapter.)

At many companies, top management drafts and circulates detailed mission statements. Because such a statement reflects a company's understanding of its activities as a marketer, it is not easily described. Consider the similarities and differences between Timex and Rolex. Although both firms share a common purpose of selling watches at a profit, they have very different missions. Timex *(www.timex.com)* sells low-cost, reliable watches in outlets ranging from department stores to corner drugstores. Rolex sells high-quality, high-priced watches through selected jewelry stores.

Regardless of a company's purpose and mission, however, every firm has long-term, intermediate, and short-term goals:

long-term goal
Goal set for an extended time, typically five years or more into the future

- **Long-term goals** relate to extended periods of time, typically five years or more. For example, American Express might set a long-term goal of doubling the number of participating merchants during the next 10 years. Kodak might adopt a long-term goal of increasing its share of the digital camera market by 10 percent during the next eight years.

intermediate goal
Goal set for a period of one to five years into the future

- **Intermediate goals** are set for a period of one to five years. Companies usually set intermediate goals in several areas. For example, the marketing department's goal might be to increase sales by 3 percent in two years. The production department might want to reduce expenses by 6 percent in four years. Human resources might seek to cut turnover by 10 percent in two years. Finance might aim for a 3-percent increase in return on investment in three years.

short-term goal
Goal set for the very near future, typically less than one year

- **Short-term goals** are set for perhaps one year and are developed for several different areas. Increasing sales by 2 percent this year, cutting costs by 1 percent next quarter, and reducing turnover by 4 percent over the next six months are examples of short-term goals.

Formulating Strategy

Planning is often concerned with the nuts and bolts of setting goals, choosing tactics, and establishing schedules. In contrast, strategy tends to have a wider scope. It is by definition a "broad program" that describes an organization's intentions. A business strategy outlines how the business intends to meet its goals and includes the organization's responsiveness to new challenges and new needs. Because a well-formulated strategy is so vital to a business's success, most top managers devote substantial attention and creativity to this process. **Strategy formulation** involves three basic steps summarized in Figure 5.2.[6]

It is interesting to note at least one change in contemporary thinking about the role of strategy. Once the responsibility of top management, strategy made its way into the everyday world of setting and implementing goals (planning) by means of a fairly rigid top-down process. Today, however, in many organizations strategy formulation is often a much more inclusive process involving people throughout the organization.

strategy formulation
Creation of a broad program for defining and meeting an organization's goals

Setting Strategic Goals Described as long-term goals, **strategic goals** are derived directly from a firm's mission statement. For example, Ferdinand Piëch, CEO of Volkswagen *(www.vw.com)*, has clear strategic goals for the European carmaker. When he took over 10 years ago, Volkswagen was only marginally profitable, regarded as an also-ran in the industry, and thinking about pulling out of the U.S. market altogether because its sales were so poor. Over the next few years, however, Piëch totally revamped the firm and has it making big profits. Volkswagen is now a much more formidable force in the global automobile industry. It competes with Toyota for the number-three spot in the industry (behind only General Motors and Ford), but Piëch is clearly not finished. "For the moment," he reports, "we are happy with the bronze medal. But we want to step up the stairway."[7]

strategic goal
Long-term goal derived directly from a firm's mission statement

After strategic goals have been established, organizations usually go through a process called a **SWOT analysis** as they continue to formulate their strategy. This process involves assessing organizational strengths and weaknesses (the **S** and **W**) and environmental opportunities and threats (the **O** and **T**). In formulating strategy they then attempt to capitalize on organizational strengths and take advantage of environmental opportunities. During this same process they may seek ways to overcome or offset organizational weaknesses and avoid or counter environmental threats.[8]

SWOT analysis
Identification and analysis of organizational strengths and weaknesses and environmental opportunities and threats as part of strategy formulation

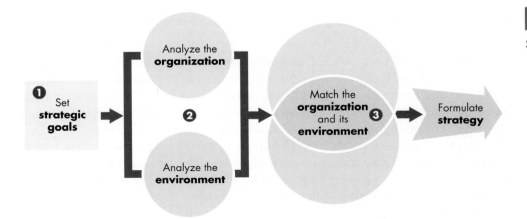

FIGURE 5.2

Strategy Formulation

Analyzing the Organization and Its Environment Scanning the environment for threats and opportunities is often called environmental analysis. Changing consumer tastes and hostile takeover offers are *threats*, as are new government regulations that will limit a firm's opportunities. Even more important threats come from new products and new competitors. *Opportunities*, meanwhile, are areas in which the firm can potentially expand, grow, or take advantage of existing strengths.

Consider the case of British entrepreneur Sir Richard Branson and his company, Virgin Group Ltd. *(www.virgin.com)*. Branson started the firm in 1968, when he was 17, naming it in acknowledgment of his own lack of experience in the business world. Over the years, he has built Virgin into one of the world's best-known brands, comprising a conglomeration of over 200 entertainment, media, and travel companies worldwide. Among the best known of his enterprises are Virgin Atlantic (an international airline), Virgin Megastores (retailing), and V2 Music (record labels). Branson sees potential threats in the form of other competitors such as British Airways (airlines), Tower Records (retailing), and the EMI Group (recorded music).

He also sees significant opportunities because of his firm's strong brand name (especially in Europe). One of his most recent ventures is a new e-commerce firm. The business is called Virgin Mobile *(www.virginmobile.com)* and operates like a cellular telephone company. But in addition to providing conventional cellular service, the Virgin telephone permits the user to press a red button to go directly to a Virgin operator who can sell products, make airline and hotel reservations, and provide numerous other services. A companion Web site also complements the cellular service and its related programs. Virgin Mobile signed up more than a million new customers during its first year of operation and is now one of the market leaders in Great Britain.[9]

environmental analysis
Process of scanning the business environment for threats and opportunities

In addition to performing an **environmental analysis**, which is an analysis of external factors, managers must also examine internal factors. The purpose of **organizational analysis** is to better understand a company's strengths and weaknesses. Strengths might include surplus cash, a dedicated workforce, an ample supply of managerial talent, technical expertise, or little competition. A cash shortage, aging factories, a heavily unionized workforce, and a poor public image can all be important weaknesses.

organizational analysis
Process of analyzing a firm's strengths and weaknesses

Branson, for example, started Virgin Mobile in part because he saw so many of his current operations as old-line, traditional businesses that might be at future risk from new forms of business and competition. One strength he employs is the widespread name recognition his businesses enjoy. Another relates to finances. He sold 49 percent of Virgin Atlantic to Singapore Airlines for almost $1 billion in cash, retaining ownership control but raising funds he needed to launch his new venture. On the other hand, he also admits that neither he nor many of his senior managers have much experience in or knowledge about e-commerce, which may be a significant weakness.

Matching the Organization and Its Environment The final step in strategy formulation is matching environmental threats and opportunities against corporate strengths and weaknesses. This matching process is the heart of strategy formulation. More than any other facet of strategy, matching companies with their environments lays the foundation for successfully planning and conducting business.

Over the long term, this process may also determine whether a firm typically takes risks or behaves more conservatively. Either strategy can be successful. Blue Bell *(www.bluebell.com)*, for example, is one of the most profitable ice-cream makers in the world, even though it sells its products in only about a dozen states. Based in rural Brenham, Texas, Blue Bell controls more than 50 percent of the market in each state where it does business. The firm, however, has resisted the temptation to expand

ENTREPRENEURSHIP and New Ventures

Sam Adams Makes Headway

In the mid-1980s, James Koch was a high-flying management consultant pulling in over $250,000 a year. To the surprise of his family and friends, however, he quit this job and invested his life's savings to start a business from scratch and go head-to-head with international competitors in a market that had not had a truly successful specialty product in decades. To everyone's even greater surprise, he succeeded.

Koch's company is Boston Beer *(www.samadams.com)*, and its flagship product is a premium beer called Samuel Adams. The Koch family had actually been brewing beer for generations, and James started with a recipe developed by his great-great-grandfather, who had sold the beer in St. Louis in the 1870s under the name Louis Koch Lager. To fund his start-up, James Koch put up $100,000 in personal savings and another $300,000 invested by his friends.

He set up shop in an old warehouse in Boston, bought some surplus equipment from a large brewery, and started operations. Because he used only the highest-quality ingredients, Koch had to price his product at about $1 more per case than such premium imports as Heineken. Boston-area distributors, meanwhile, doubted that consumers would pay $6 per six-pack for an American beer, and most refused to carry it. So Koch began selling his beer directly to retailers and bars.

His big break came when he entered Samuel Adams Lager in the Great American Beer Festival, where it won the consumer preference poll—the industry's equivalent of an Oscar. Koch quickly turned this victory into an advertising mantra, proclaiming Samuel Adams "The Best Beer in America." As sales took off, national distributors came calling, and in order to meet surging demand, Koch contracted part of his brewing operations to a nearly defunct Stroh's facility in Pittsburgh.

During the early 1990s, sales of Sam Adams products grew at an annual rate of over 50 percent and today exceed $250 million per year. Boston Beer even exports Samuel Adams to Germany, where it's become quite popular among finicky beer drinkers. Koch, who retains controlling interests in the business, still oversees day-to-day brewing operations. Indeed, he claims that he has sampled at least one of the firm's products every day, primarily as a way of monitoring quality.

Koch's success has not gone unnoticed, especially by industry giant Anheuser-Busch (AB) *(www.anheuser-busch.com)*. AB and other national brewers have seen their sales take a hit from so-called *microbreweries* like Sam Adams—small regional or local companies that sell esoteric brews made in small quantities and deriving cachet from their scarcity. The Boston Beer Co. was the first microbrewery to make it big, and most of the others are trying to follow in Koch's footsteps. Obviously, AB wants to keep small start-ups from gaining too much market share, most of which would come at its own expense.

Recently, for example, Koch learned that AB had made inquiries about buying his entire crop from a German hops farmer who has an exclusive arrangement with Boston Beer. Had AB succeeded, Koch admits, he would have been out of business. AB has also complained that Sam Adams labeling is misleading because it neglects the fact that its Pittsburgh-made beer is actually produced under contract by Stroh's. The industry giant has even tried to convince wholesalers, who are highly dependent on such AB products as Budweiser, to stop selling specialty beers. Koch, meanwhile, simply sees all this attention as a clear sign that he's made an impact on the market.

too quickly. Its success is based on product freshness and frequent deliveries—strengths that may suffer if the company grows too large.

A Hierarchy of Plans Plans can be viewed on three levels: strategic, tactical, and operational. Managerial responsibilities are defined at each level. The levels constitute a hierarchy because implementing plans is practical only when there is a logical flow from one level to the next.

- **Strategic plans** reflect decisions about resource allocations, company priorities, and the steps needed to meet strategic goals. They are usually created by the firm's top management team but, as noted earlier, often rely on input from others

strategic plan
Plan reflecting decisions about resource allocations, company priorities, and steps needed to meet strategic goals

tactical plan
Generally short-range plan concerned with implementing specific aspects of a company's strategic plans

operational plan
Plan setting short-term targets for daily, weekly, or monthly performance

in the organization. General Electric's decision that viable businesses must rank first or second within their respective markets is a matter of strategic planning.

■ **Tactical plans** are shorter-range plans for implementing specific aspects of the company's strategic plans. They typically involve upper and middle management. Coca-Cola's recent decision to increase sales in India by upgrading its distribution network in that country is an example of tactical planning.

■ **Operational plans**, which are developed by midlevel and lower-level managers, set short-term targets for daily, weekly, or monthly performance. McDonald's, for example, establishes operational plans when it explains to franchisees precisely how Big Macs are to be cooked, warmed, and served.

Contingency Planning and Crisis Management

Because business environments are often difficult to predict, and because the unexpected can create major problems, most managers recognize that even the best-laid plans sometimes simply do not work out. For instance, when the Walt Disney Co. *(www.disney.go.com)* announced plans to launch a cruise line replete with familiar Disney characters and themes, managers also began aggressively developing and marketing packages linking three- and four-day cruises with visits to Disney World in Florida. Indeed, the inaugural sailing was sold out more than a year in advance, and the first year was booked solid six months before the ship was launched. Three months before the first sailing, however, the shipyard constructing Disney's first ship (the *Disney Magic*) notified the company that it was behind schedule and that delivery would be several weeks late. When similar problems befall other cruise lines, they can offer to rebook passengers on alternative itineraries. But because Disney had no other ship, it had no choice but to refund the money it had collected as prebooking deposits for its first 15 cruises.

The 20,000 displaced customers were offered big discounts if they rebooked on a later cruise. Many of them, however, could not rearrange their schedules and requested full refunds. Moreover, quite a few blamed Disney, and a few expressed outrage at what they saw as poor planning by the entertainment giant. Fortunately for Disney, however, the *Disney Magic* was eventually launched and has now become very popular and very profitable.[10]

Because managers know such things can happen, they often develop alternative plans in case things go awry. Two common methods of dealing with the unknown and unforeseen are *contingency planning* and *crisis management*.

contingency planning
Identifying aspects of a business or its environment that might entail changes in strategy

Contingency Planning Contingency planning recognizes the need to find solutions to specific aspects of a problem. By its very nature, a contingency plan is a hedge against changes that might occur. **Contingency planning**, then, is planning for change: It seeks to identify in advance important aspects of a business or its market that might change. It also identifies the ways in which a company will respond to changes. Today, many companies use computer programs for contingency planning.

Suppose, for example, that a company develops a plan to create a new division. It expects sales to increase at an annual rate of 10 percent for the next five years and develops a marketing strategy for maintaining that level. But suppose that sales have increased by only 5 percent by the end of the first year. Does the firm abandon the venture, invest more in advertising, or wait to see what happens in the second year? Any of these alternatives is possible. Regardless of the firm's choice, however, its efforts will be more efficient if managers decide in advance what to do in case sales fall below planned levels. Contingency planning helps them do exactly that. Disney learned from its mistake with its first ship, and when the second (the *Disney Wonder*) was launched a year later, managers did several things differently. For one thing, they allowed for an extra two weeks between when the ship was supposed to be ready for sailing and its first scheduled cruise. They also held open a few cabins on the *Disney Magic* as a backup for any especially disgruntled customers who might need accommodations if there were unexpected delays launching the *Disney Wonder*.

Crisis Management A crisis is an unexpected emergency requiring immediate response. **Crisis management** involves an organization's methods for dealing with emergencies. The tragic events of September 11, 2001, clearly served to underscore the importance of crisis management. In addition to the horrific loss of human life, virtually every business in the United States experienced direct or indirect financial costs. For example, because all U.S. airlines were shut down for several days and air traffic was slow to return, they lost billions of dollars. The ripple effects lasted for months, resulting in, among other things, the bankruptcy of U.S. Airways and major cutbacks at American Airlines in mid-2002.

crisis management
Organization's methods for dealing with emergencies

But other businesses were also affected. Tourist destinations like Disney World and resort hotels lost customers. Because fewer people traveled in the months after September 11, profits also declined at restaurants, car rental agencies, and gasoline retailers. Broadway shows in New York sold fewer tickets and shaken consumers across the country delayed major purchases and withdrew funds from their bank. Shipping companies like FedEx and UPS found it necessary to subject cargo to more intense (and costly) security screenings. And many people simply stayed home for a few days after that tragic day, resulting in lost work time and a drop in productivity.

As a result of September 11, more firms than ever before have developed crisis management plans. For example, both Reliant Energy *(www.reliantenergy.com)* and Duke Energy *(www.duke-energy.com)* rely on computer trading centers where trading managers actively buy and sell energy-related commodities. If a terrorist attack or natural disaster such as a hurricane were to strike their trading centers, they would essentially be out of business. Prior to September 11, each firm had relatively vague and superficial crisis plans. But now they and most other companies have much more detailed and comprehensive plans in the event of another crisis. Both Reliant and Duke, for example, have created secondary trading centers at other locations. In the

SELF-CHECK QUESTIONS 1–3

You should now be able to answer Self-Check Questions 1–3.*

1 **Multiple Choice** Which of the following is **not** a basic purpose served by *goal setting*? [select one]: **(a)** Goals show the government what the firm hopes to achieve. **(b)** Goals set direction and guidance. **(c)** Goals help direct resource allocation. **(d)** Goals help define corporate culture. **(e)** Goals help managers assess performance.

2 **True/False** Although organizations need to set *long-term, intermediate,* and *short-term goals,* there is little relationship among these three kinds of goals.

3 **Multiple Choice** Which of these is a *contingency plan*? [select one]: **(a)** setting guidelines for when supplies will be ordered; **(b)** placing an ad to hire new employees; **(c)** creating a new advertising campaign; **(d)** deciding which division to sell if a firm runs short of cash; **(e)** all of these are contingency plans.

*Answers to Self-Check Questions 1–3 can be found on p. 508.

It's a problem that neither Filterfresh (www.filterfresh.com), a national coffee distributor, nor delivery man Rusty Pasquale (left) could have predicted. Since 9/11, Pasquale can no longer simply enter clients' buildings and do his job. Security measures have added an hour to his route and that of every company driver. Nationwide, reports Filterfresh, the slowdown adds up to 1,250 hours per week that have to be filled by an additional 24 delivery people. "That's a 10-percent increase in our labor costs, just so we can hold our ground," says a company manager.

event of a shutdown at their main trading center, these firms can quickly transfer virtually all their core trading activities to their secondary centers within 30 minutes or less. Unfortunately, however, because it is impossible to forecast the future precisely, no organization can ever be perfectly prepared for every eventuality.

■ THE MANAGEMENT PROCESS

management
Process of planning, organizing, directing, and controlling an organization's resources to achieve its goals

Management is the process of planning, organizing, directing, and controlling an organization's financial, physical, human, and information resources to achieve its goals. Managers oversee the use of all these resources in their respective firms. All aspects of a manager's job are interrelated. In fact, any given manager is likely to be engaged in each of these activities during the course of any given day.

Planning

planning
Management process of determining what an organization needs to do and how best to get it done

Determining what the organization needs to do and how best to get it done requires **planning**. Planning has three main components. As we have seen, it begins when managers determine the firm's goals. Next, they develop a comprehensive strategy for achieving those goals. After a strategy is developed, they design tactical and operational plans for implementing the strategy.

When Yahoo! (www.yahoo.com) was created, for example, the firm's top managers set a strategic goal of becoming a top firm in the then-emerging market for Internet search engines. But then came the hard part—figuring out how to do it. They started by assessing the ways in which people actually use the Web and concluded that users wanted to be able to satisfy a wide array of needs, preferences, and priorities by going to as few sites as possible to find what they were looking for.

Thus, one key component of Yahoo!'s strategy was to foster partnerships and relationships with other companies so that potential Web surfers could draw on several sources through a single portal—which would be Yahoo!. Thus, the goal of partnering emerged as one set of tactical plans for moving forward. Yahoo! managers then began fashioning alliances with such diverse partners as Reuters *(www.reuters.com)*, Standard & Poor's *(www.standardpoor.com)*, and the Associated Press *(www.ap.org)* (for news coverage), RE/Max *(www.remax.com)* (for real estate information), and a wide array of information providers specializing in sports, weather, entertainment, shopping, and travel. The creation of individual partnership agreements with each of these partners represents a form of operational planning.

Organizing

Once one of the leading-edge high-technology firms in the world, Hewlett-Packard (HP) *(www.hewlett-packard.com)* began to lose some of its luster a few years ago. Ironically, one of the major reasons for its slide could be traced back to what had once been a major strength. Specifically, HP had long prided itself on being little more than a corporate confederation of individual businesses. Sometimes these businesses even ended up competing among themselves. This approach had been beneficial for much of the firm's history: It was easier for each business to make its own decisions quickly and efficiently, and the competition kept each unit on its toes. By the late 1990s, however, problems had become apparent, and no one could quite figure out what was going on.

Enter Ann Livermore, then head of the firm's software and services business. Livermore realized that the structure that had served so well in the past was now holding the firm back. To regain its competitive edge, HP needed an integrated, organization-wide Internet strategy. Unfortunately, the company's highly decentralized organization made that impossible. Livermore led the charge to create one organization to drive a single Internet plan. "I felt we could be the most powerful company in the industry," she said, "if we could get our hardware, software, and services aligned." Eventually, a new team of top managers was handed control of the company, and every major component of the firm's structure was reorganized. Today, under the leadership of new CEO Carly Fiorina and with its acquisition of Compaq Computer, HP is showing signs of recreating the magic from its early years.[11]

This process of determining the best way to arrange a business's resources and activities into a coherent structure is called **organizing**. (We explore this topic further in Chapter 6.)

organizing
Management process of determining how best to arrange an organization's resources and activities into a coherent structure

Directing

Managers have the power to give orders and demand results. Directing, however, involves more complex activities. When **directing**, a manager works to guide and motivate employees to meet the firm's objectives. Andrall Pearson, for example, has clearly changed his entire approach to directing employees. Gordon Bethune, CEO of Continental Airlines *(www.continental.com)*, is an excellent example of a manager who excels at motivating his employees. When he took the helm of the troubled carrier in 1994, morale was dismal, most employees hated their jobs, and the company's performance was among the worst in the industry.

directing
Management process of guiding and motivating employees to meet an organization's objectives

Almost immediately, Bethune started listening to his employees to learn about their problems and hear how they thought the company could be improved. He also

As field boss of the New York Yankees *(www.yankees.com)*, Joe Torre (center) has managed (since 1996) to hold on to a slippery job (the team has had 21 managers in 25 years). Of course, he's won 4 World Series in a 7-year stretch, and by most accounts, Torre's success stems from his ability as a motivator. He prefers one-on-one dealings with "subordinates" (multimillion-dollar baseball players), and he sees no reason to punish failure (which is a routine pitfall of a baseball player's job). Many observers—including Torre's boss, George Steinbrenner—think that his approach would be effective in a business setting.

began to reward everyone when things went well and continued communicating with all Continental employees on a regular basis. Today, the firm is ranked among the best in the industry and is regularly identified as one of the best places to work in the United States. In both 2000 and 2001, Continental was named the highest-quality airline in the United States, based on the J.D. Powers Survey of Customer Satisfaction.[12]

Controlling

controlling
Management process of monitoring an organization's performance to ensure that it is meeting its goals

Controlling is the process of monitoring a firm's performance to make sure that the firm is meeting its goals. All CEOs must pay close attention to costs and performance. Indeed, skillful controlling, like innovative directing, is one reason that Gordon Bethune has been so successful at Continental. For example, the firm focuses almost relentlessly on numerous indicators of performance that can be constantly measured and adjusted. Everything from on-time arrivals to baggage-handling errors to the number of empty seats on an airplane to surveys of employee and customer satisfaction are regularly and routinely monitored. If on-time arrivals start to slip, Bethune focuses on the problem and gets it fixed. If a manager's subordinates provide less than glowing reviews, that manager loses part of his or her bonus. As a result, no single element of the firm's performance can slip too far before it's noticed and fixed.

Figure 5.3 illustrates the control process that begins when management establishes standards, often for financial performance. If, for example, a company wants to increase sales by 20 percent over the next 10 years, then an appropriate standard might be an increase of about 2 percent a year.

Managers then measure actual performance against standards. If the two amounts agree, the organization continues along its present course. If they vary significantly, however, one or the other needs adjustment. If sales have increased 2.1 percent by the end of the first year, things are probably fine. If sales have dropped 1 percent, some revision in plans may be needed. Perhaps the original goal should be lowered or more money should be spent on advertising.

Control can also show where performance is running better than expected and, thus, serve as a basis for providing rewards or reducing costs. For example, when Ford

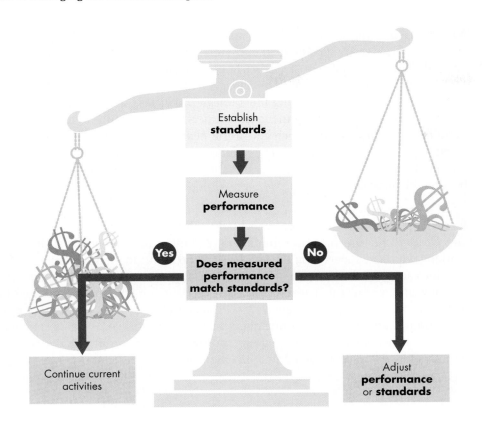

FIGURE 5.3
The Control Process

recently introduced the Explorer SportsTrac (an SUV with a pickup bed), initial sales were so strong the firm was able to delay a major advertising campaign for three months because it was selling all of the vehicles it could make anyway.

TYPES OF MANAGERS

Although all managers plan, organize, direct, and control, not all managers have the same degree of responsibility for these activities. Thus, it is helpful to classify managers according to levels and areas of responsibility.

Levels of Management

The three basic levels of management are *top, middle,* and *first-line management.* Most firms have more middle managers than top managers and more first-line managers than middle managers. Both the power of managers and the complexity of their duties increase as they move up the ladder.

Top Managers Like Marjorie Scardino, Kenneth Chenault, and Andrall Pearson, the fairly small number of executives who get the chance to guide the fortunes of most companies are top managers. Common titles for top managers include *president, vice president, treasurer, chief executive officer (CEO),* and *chief financial officer (CFO).* **Top managers** are responsible for the overall performance and effectiveness of the firm. They set general policies, formulate strategies, approve all significant decisions, and represent the company in dealings with other firms and with government bodies.

top manager
Manager responsible to the board of directors and stockholders for a firm's overall performance and effectiveness

Middle Managers Just below the ranks of top managers is another group of managers who also occupy positions of considerable autonomy and importance and who are called middle managers. Titles such as *plant manager, operations manager*, and *division manager* designate middle-management slots. In general, **middle managers** are responsible for implementing the strategies, policies, and decisions made by top managers. For example, if top management decides to introduce a new product in 12 months or to cut costs by 5 percent in the next quarter, middle management must decide how to meet these goals. The manager of an American Express service center, a Pearson distribution center, or a regional collection of Tricon restaurants will likely be a middle manager.

middle manager
Manager responsible for implementing the strategies, policies, and decisions made by top managers

First-Line Managers Those who hold such titles as *supervisor, office manager*, and *group leader* are **first-line managers**. Although they spend most of their time working with and supervising the employees who report to them, first-line managers' activities are not limited to that arena. At a building site, for example, the project manager not only ensures that workers are carrying out construction as specified by the architect but also interacts extensively with materials suppliers, community officials, and middle- and upper-level managers at the home office. A sales manager for Pearson's educational publishing group and the manager for an individual Taco Bell outlet would also be considered first-line managers.

first-line manager
Manager responsible for supervising the work of employees

Areas of Management

In any large company, top, middle, and first-line managers work in a variety of areas including human resources, operations, marketing, information, and finance. For the most part, these areas correspond to the types of managerial skills described later in this chapter and to the wide range of business principles and activities discussed in the rest of this book.

Human Resource Managers Most companies have *human resource managers* who hire and train employees, evaluate performance, and determine compensation. At large firms, separate departments deal with recruiting and hiring, wage and salary levels, and labor relations. A smaller firm may have a single department—or a single person—responsible for all human resource activities. (We discuss some key issues in human resource management in Chapter 9.)

Operations Managers As we will see in Chapter 7, the term *operations* refers to the systems by which a firm produces goods and services. Among other duties, operations managers are responsible for production, inventory, and quality control. Manufacturing companies such as Texas Instruments, Ford, and Caterpillar have a strong need for operations managers at many levels. Such firms typically have a *vice president for operations* (top), *plant managers* (middle), and *production supervisors* (first-line managers). In recent years, sound operations management practices have become increasingly important to a variety of service organizations.

Marketing Managers As we will see in Chapter 10, marketing encompasses the development, pricing, promotion, and distribution of goods and services. Marketing managers are responsible for getting products from producers to consumers. Marketing is especially important for firms that manufacture consumer products, such as Procter & Gamble, Coca-Cola, and Levi Strauss. Such firms often have large numbers of marketing managers at several levels. For example, a large consumer products firm is likely to have a *vice president for marketing* (top), several *regional marketing managers* (middle), and several *district sales managers* (first-line managers). (The different areas of marketing are discussed in Part 4.)

Information Managers Occupying a fairly new managerial position in many firms, information managers design and implement systems to gather, organize, and distribute information. Huge increases in both the sheer volume of information and the ability to manage it have led to the emergence of this important function.

Although relatively few in number, the ranks of *information managers* are growing at all levels. Some firms have a top management position called a *chief information officer (CIO)*. Middle managers help design information systems for divisions or plants. Computer systems managers within smaller businesses are usually first-line managers. (Information management is discussed in more detail in Chapter 12.)

Financial Managers Nearly every company has financial managers to plan and oversee its accounting functions and financial resources. Levels of financial management may include *chief financial officer (CFO)* or *vice president for finance* (top), a *division controller* (middle), and an *accounting supervisor* (first-line manager). Some institutions—NationsBank *(www.nationsbank.com)* and Prudential *(www.prudential.com)*, for example—have even made effective financial management the company's reason for being. (Financial management is treated in more detail in Part 6.)

Other Managers Some firms also employ other specialized managers. Many companies, for example, have public relations managers. Chemical and pharmaceutical companies such as Monsanto *(www.pharmacia.com)* and Merck *(www.merck.com)* have research and development managers. The range of possibilities is wide, and the areas of management are limited only by the needs and imagination of the firm.

At *Business Week*'s annual CFO Forum, the chief financial officers of such companies as GE Capital, Toysrus.com, and Oracle Corp. stressed the fact that the CFO is no longer just a high-ranking numbers cruncher. In a world that's constantly being changed by technology, today's CFO plays a key role in so-called "e-transformation," especially in evaluating new technologies as investment opportunities and figuring out how to finance new business models.

SELF-CHECK QUESTIONS 4–6

You should now be able to answer Self-Check Questions 4–6.*

4 Multiple Choice Which of these activities is **not** part of the *management process*? [select one]: **(a)** planning; **(b)** organizing; **(c)** coordinating; **(d)** directing; **(e)** controlling.

5 True/False In general, there are three basic *levels of management* in most organizations.

6 Multiple Choice Which of the following is a basic *area of management*? [select one:] **(a)** human resources; **(b)** operations; **(c)** marketing; **(d)** finance; **(e)** all of these are areas of management.

*Answers to Self-Check Questions 4–6 can be found on p. 508.

■ BASIC MANAGEMENT SKILLS

Although the range of managerial positions is almost limitless, the success that people enjoy in those positions is often limited by their skills and abilities. Effective managers must develop *technical, human relations, conceptual, decision-making*, and *time management skills*. Unfortunately, these skills are quite complex, and it is the rare manager who excels in every area.

technical skills
Skills needed to perform specialized tasks

Technical Skills The skills needed to perform specialized tasks are called **technical skills**. A programmer's ability to write code, an animator's ability to draw, and an accountant's ability to audit a company's records are all examples of technical skills. People develop technical skills through a combination of education and experience. Technical skills are especially important for first-line managers. Many of these managers spend considerable time helping employees solve work-related problems, training them in more efficient procedures, and monitoring performance.

human relations skills
Skills in understanding and getting along with people

Human Relations Skills Effective managers also generally have good **human relations skills**—specifically, skills in understanding and getting along with other people. A manager with poor human relations skills may have trouble getting along with subordinates, cause valuable employees to quit or transfer, and contribute to poor morale. Today, Andrall Pearson works well with people, has fun when he works, and makes everyone feel excited about the work. He also genuinely cares about the welfare of his employees. So, too, does Gordon Bethune, who routinely visits his employees throughout the company. Reports one baggage manager at Continental's Newark, New Jersey, hub: "Anybody who's worked here longer than two months can recognize Gordon."

"Anybody who's worked here longer than two months can recognize Gordon."

—Baggage manager at Continental's Newark, New Jersey, hub, on the airline's CEO, Gordon Bethune

Although human relations skills are important at all levels, they are probably most important for middle managers, who must often act as bridges between top managers, first-line managers, and managers from other areas of the organization. Managers should possess good communication skills. Many managers have found that being able to understand others, and to get others to understand them, can go a long way toward maintaining good relations in an organization.[13]

"I like to think of myself as a nice guy. Naturally, sometimes you have to step on a few faces."

Conceptual Skills **Conceptual skills** refer to a person's ability to think in the abstract, to diagnose and analyze different situations, and to see beyond the present situation. Conceptual skills help managers recognize new market opportunities and threats. They can also help managers analyze the probable outcomes of their decisions. The need for conceptual skills differs at various management levels: Top managers depend most on conceptual skills, first-line managers least. Although the purposes and everyday needs of various jobs differ, conceptual skills are needed in almost any job-related activity.

In many ways, conceptual skills may be the most important ingredient in the success of executives in e-commerce businesses. For example, the ability to foresee how a particular business application will be affected by or can be translated to the Internet is clearly conceptual in nature.

conceptual skills
Abilities to think in the abstract, diagnose and analyze different situations, and see beyond the present situation

Decision-Making Skills **Decision-making skills** include the ability to define problems and select the best course of action. Figure 5.4 illustrates the following basic steps in decision making:

decision-making skills
Skills in defining problems and selecting the best courses of action

1 **Define the problem, gather facts, and identify alternative solutions.** Managers at Porsche *(www.porsche.com)* recently determined that their firm had become so small relative to other automobile companies that if something wasn't done they might become the target of a hostile takeover. Thus, they defined their problem as how to best prevent a hostile takeover. They subsequently determined that there were two alternatives: seeking a larger company of their own choice to sell to or else growing their business larger as a way to ensure their continued independence.

2 **Evaluate each alternative and select the best one.** Porsche managers decided that although there were two automobile companies that they might potentially be comfortable in joining, the preferred option was to grow instead. Of course, this required additional decisions as they looked at different ways to grow.

3 **Implement the chosen alternative, periodically following up and evaluating the effectiveness of that choice.** Porsche managers decided that the best

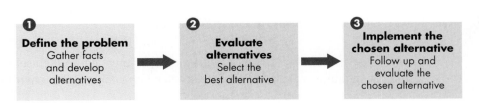

❶ Define the problem
Gather facts and develop alternatives

❷ Evaluate alternatives
Select the best alternative

❸ Implement the chosen alternative
Follow up and evaluate the chosen alternative

FIGURE 5.4

The Decision-Making Process

route to growth was to introduce new products into high-growth markets. Thus, they recently launched the Cayenne, a sports utility vehicle projected to almost double the firm's unit sales. If the Cayenne is indeed successful, Porsche intends to begin introducing other new models. If not, they may revisit the option of being acquired by another firm.[14] In the words of Porsche CEO Wendelin Wiedeking, "Porsche wants to grow and we want to have only exclusive products. We want to stay independent."

time management skills
Skills associated with the productive use of time

Time Management Skills **Time management skills** refer to the productive use that managers make of their time. In 2002, for example, ExxonMobil CEO Lee Raymond was paid $500,000 in salary. Assuming that he worked 50 hours a week and took 2 weeks' vacation, Raymond earned $2,000 an hour—about $33 per minute. Any amount of time that Raymond wastes clearly represents a large cost to ExxonMobil and its stockholders. Most managers, of course, receive much smaller salaries than Raymond. Their time, however, is valuable, and poor use of it still translates into costs and wasted productivity. (Actually, this example underestimates Raymond's earnings; he also received additional deferred compensation such as stock options and retirement benefits.)

To manage time effectively, managers must address four leading causes of wasted time:

1 **Paperwork.** Some managers spend too much time deciding what to do with letters and reports. Most documents of this sort are routine and can be handled quickly. Managers must learn to recognize those documents that require more attention.

2 **Telephone.** Experts estimate that managers get interrupted by the telephone every five minutes. To manage this time more effectively, they suggest having an assistant screen all calls and setting aside a certain block of time each day to return the important ones. Unfortunately, the explosive use of cell phones seems to be making this problem even worse for many managers.

3 **Meetings.** Many managers spend as much as four hours a day in meetings. To help keep this time productive, the person handling the meeting should specify a clear agenda, start on time, keep everyone focused on the agenda, and end on time.

4 **E-mail.** Increasingly, more and more managers are also relying heavily on e-mail and other forms of electronic communication. Like memos and telephone calls, many e-mail messages are not particularly important—some are even trivial. As a result, time is wasted when managers have to sort through a variety of electronic folders, in-baskets, and archives. As the average number of electronic messages grows, the potential time wasted also increases.[15]

Management Skills for the Twenty-First Century

Although the skills discussed in this chapter have long been an important part of every successful manager's career, new skill requirements continue to emerge. At the beginning of the twenty-first century, most experts point to the growing importance of skills involving *global management* and *technology*.

Global Management Skills Tomorrow's managers must equip themselves with the special tools, techniques, and skills necessary to compete in a global environment.

They will need to understand foreign markets, cultural differences, and the motives and practices of foreign rivals.

On a more practical level, businesses will need managers who are capable of understanding international operations. In the past, most U.S. businesses hired local managers to run their operations in the various countries in which they operated. More recently, however, the trend has been to transfer U.S. managers to foreign locations. This practice helps firms better transfer their corporate cultures to foreign operations. In addition, foreign assignments help managers become better prepared for international competition as they advance within the organization. General Motors *(www.gm.com)* now has almost 500 U.S. managers in foreign posts.

Management and Technology Skills Another significant issue facing tomorrow's managers is technology, especially as it relates to communication. Managers have always had to deal with information. In today's world, however, the amount of information has reached staggering proportions. In the United States alone, people exchange hundreds of millions of e-mail messages every day. New forms of technology have added to a manager's ability to process information while simultaneously making it even more important to organize and interpret an ever-increasing wealth of input.

Technology has also begun to change the way the interaction of managers shapes corporate structures. Computer networking, for example, exists because it is no longer too expensive to put a computer on virtually every desk in the company. In turn, this elaborate network controls the flow of the firm's lifeblood—information. This information no longer flows strictly up and down through hierarchies. It now flows to everyone simultaneously. As a result, decisions are made more quickly, and more people are directly involved. With e-mail, teleconferencing, and other forms of communication, neither time nor distance—nor such corporate "boundaries" as departments and divisions—can prevent people from working more closely together. More than ever, bureaucracies are breaking down, while planning, decision making, and other activities are beginning to benefit from group building and teamwork.

To run its operations in China, MTV *(www.mtv.com)* needed someone who understood both conservative Chinese television regulators and China's young urban elite. The company chose 37-year-old Li Yifei, a former Baylor University political science student, U.N. intern, public relations consultant, and tai chi champion. Li has already brought the Chinese equivalent of the MTV awards to state-owned television, and although the show got only a 7.9-percent rating, she's quick to point out that in China, that's 150 million people (about half the U.S. population).

■ MANAGEMENT AND THE CORPORATE CULTURE

corporate culture
The shared experiences, stories, beliefs, and norms that characterize an organization

Every organization—big or small, more successful or less successful—has an unmistakable "feel" to it. Just as every individual has a unique personality, so every company has a unique identity, called **corporate culture**: the shared experiences, stories, beliefs, and norms that characterize an organization. This culture helps define the work and business climate that exists in an organization.

A strong corporate culture serves several purposes. For one thing, it directs employees' efforts and helps everyone work toward the same goals. Some cultures, for example, stress financial success to the extreme, whereas others focus more on quality of life. In addition, corporate culture helps newcomers learn accepted behaviors. If financial success is the key to a culture, newcomers quickly learn that they are expected to work long, hard hours and that the "winner" is the one who brings in the most revenue. But if quality of life is more fundamental, newcomers learn that it's more acceptable to spend less time at work and that balancing work and nonwork is encouraged.

Where does a business's culture come from? In some cases it emanates from the days of an organization's founder. Firms such as the Walt Disney Co., Hewlett-Packard, Wal-Mart *(www.walmart.com)*, and JCPenney, for example, still bear the imprint of their founders. In other cases, an organization's culture is forged over a long period of time by a constant and focused business strategy. PepsiCo *(www.pepsico.com)*, for example, has an achievement-oriented culture tied to its long-standing goal of catching its biggest competitor, Coca-Cola *(www.cokecce.com)*. Similarly, Apple Computer *(www.apple.com)* has a sort of "counterculture" culture stemming from its self-styled image as the alternative to the staid IBM *(www.ibm.com)* corporate model for computer makers.

Communicating the Culture and Managing Change

Corporate culture influences management philosophy, style, and behavior. Managers, therefore, must carefully consider the kind of culture they want for their organization, then work to nourish that culture by communicating with everyone who works there. Wal-Mart, for example, is acutely conscious of the need to spread the message of its culture as it opens new stores in new areas. One of the company's methods is to regularly assign veteran managers to lead employees in new territories. Gordon Bethune delivers weekly messages for all Continental employees to update them on what's going on in the firm; the employees can either listen to the messages on a closed-circuit broadcast or call an 800 telephone number and hear a recorded version at their own convenience.

Communicating the Culture   To use a firm's culture to its advantage, managers must accomplish several tasks, all of which hinge on effective communication. First, managers themselves must have a clear understanding of the culture. Second, they must transmit the culture to others in the organization. Thus, communication is one aim in training and orienting newcomers. A clear and meaningful statement of the organization's mission is also a valuable communication tool. Finally, managers can maintain the culture by rewarding and promoting those who understand it and work toward maintaining it.

Back when the company was worth $60 billion (or a lot of people thought it was), Enron paid little attention to the cost of trotting elephants into employee meetings. Secretary's Day called for gifts of Waterford Crystal, and on the day Enron stock topped $50, employees found $100 bills on their desks. The company furnished state-of-the-art laptops and ergonomic chairs, and just about everybody traveled first class and stayed in five-star hotels. Enron had a risk-taking, full-speed-ahead culture, and experts agree that one of the reasons for its failure was the absence of controls on overly aggressive behavior among managers at all levels.

Managing Change Organizations must sometimes change their cultures. In such cases, they must also communicate the nature of the change to both employees and customers. According to the CEOs of several companies that have undergone radical change in the last decade or so, the process usually goes through three stages:

1 **At the highest level, analysis of the company's environment highlights extensive change as the most effective response to its problems.** This period is typically characterized by conflict and resistance.
2 **Top management begins to formulate a vision of a new company.** Whatever that vision may be, it must include renewed focus on the activities of competitors and the needs of customers.
3 **The firm sets up new systems for appraising and compensating employees who enforce the firm's new values.** The purpose is to give the new culture solid shape from within the firm.

Although some firms like to build on their legacies, others know better. When Gordon Bethune announced his rebuilding plans at Continental, he dubbed it the "Go Forward" program. He stressed that the firm had little to look back on with pride and he wanted everyone to look only to the future. Likewise, Procter & Gamble *(www.pg.com)* is in the midst of a major overhaul designed to remake its corporate culture into one more suited to today's competitive global business environment. Because its brands have been dominant for such a long time, managers at P&G have been criticized for having tunnel vision—focusing only on the ways they've done things in the past and then trying to repeat them. Procter & Gamble's popular Tide laundry detergent, for example, has been through more than 60 formula upgrades since it was first introduced. A new top management team, however, is working to shake things up by advocating new approaches, new ways of thinking, and new models of product development.[16]

Say WHAT YOU MEAN

COMMUNICATING THE CORPORATE MESSAGE

The business environment is in a constant state of change, sometimes providing a company with major opportunities, sometimes presenting it with serious challenges, sometimes both at once. The most successful companies take change for granted, continually adapting to ensure the best possible business outcomes. Being adaptable means communicating effectively, not only with stakeholders but also with the public at large.

Corporate communications—the means by which a company communicates to its stakeholders—is an increasingly important business activity. In fact, many major companies now maintain corporate communications teams whose members are skilled in the art of public relations, who understand the media, and who can communicate a company's mission. They're also responsible for dealing with problems that may affect the relationship between the company and the larger environment in which it operates.

In recent years, the pace of corporate change has been unprecedented: mergers, acquisitions, corporate failures, and the emergence of new names and brands—all have caused profound shifts in the business landscape. In addition, one of the biggest ongoing challenges to any company is effectively communicating what it does and where it stands on the major issues in the public mind, including social responsibility, the environment, human rights, and diversity, to name just a few.

The most successful companies control their communications activities by making clear mission statements, remaining open about both internal policies and external relationships, and making sure that the public knows that they are ready to respond to environmental change. The process, of course, varies from company to company. In some instances, top managers become spokespeople, attracting media attention and providing the organization with a face. In other cases, groups of people interact on a daily basis with the media, interest groups, politicians, and the general public to project a company's image and respond to concerns.

One thing is certain: The ever-increasing pace of change makes it harder for companies to stay ahead of the curve. They can't afford to be perceived as outdated and unresponsive and must project images of dynamic, up-to-date organizations that know how to get engaged with the larger community.

SELF-CHECK QUESTIONS 7–9

You should now be able to answer Self-Check Questions 7–9.*

7 **Multiple Choice** The ability to think in the abstract reflects which of the following *managerial skills*? [select one]: **(a)** technical skills; **(b)** human relations skills; **(c)** conceptual skills; **(d)** decision-making skills; **(e)** time management skills.

8 **Multiple Choice** Which of the following identifies two emerging new skill sets that managers need to master in the twenty-first century? [select one]: **(a)** interpersonal and global; **(b)** global and technology; **(c)** time management and conceptual; **(d)** conceptual and technology; **(e)** technical and human relations.

9 **True/False** Although every corporate organization has a unique culture, it is for the most part not particularly important.

*Answers to Self-Check Questions 7–9 can be found on p. 508.

Continued from page 134

"OUR BUSINESS ISN'T REALLY ABOUT MOVING FREIGHT"

Of course, leadership alone is seldom enough to turn around a major company, especially one as complex as Yellow. Indeed, technology has also played an important role in Yellow's success. For instance, the firm implemented a variety of automated systems to improve customer service and satisfaction. The systems provide up-to-the-minute information about a shipment's progress via the Internet, maintain a customer database that enables faster scheduling, and develop the truck loading procedures and routes that will ensure on-time delivery. However, the real technology success story at Yellow isn't merely the innovative and efficient use of technology but also the savvy application of those systems in support of the employees and customers.

Beyond leadership and technology, however, perhaps the most challenging and yet the most important change at Yellow was the revisioning of the company's mission, transforming it from the delivery of freight to a strong and consistent focus on customer service. For instance, when the firm's employees saw their primary goal as the efficient movement of cargo, the firm focused on one set of processes.

But now, thanks to the efforts of Zollars and other managers, employees realize that supporting customers by meeting their delivery needs is their paramount task. This shift in perspective enables the firm to provide better ser-

 "**O**ur business is about earning the trust of the consumers of our services."

—Bill Zollars, CEO of Yellow Freight

vice to its customers, to develop innovative new products and service, to improve its performance, and ultimately, to successfully compete in an increasingly tough industry. As Bill Zollars says in the firm's 2000 annual report, "Our business really isn't about moving freight. It's about earning the trust of the consumers of our services."

Questions for Discussion

1 Describe the role of goals and strategy at Yellow.
2 What kind of crisis or contingency plans does a firm like Yellow need?
3 Identify examples to illustrate each of the various parts of the management process at Yellow.
4 Identify and briefly describe management titles that Yellow most likely has that reflect both the different levels and the different areas of management.
5 Discuss how Bill Zollars has used various management skills in his turnaround of Yellow.

■ SUMMARY OF LEARNING OBJECTIVES

1 **Explain the importance of setting goals and formulating *strategies* as the starting points of effective management.**

The starting point in effective management is setting **goals**—objectives that a business hopes and plans to achieve. There are four main purposes in organizational

goal setting: (1) providing direction and guidance for managers at all levels; (2) helping to allocate resources; (3) helping to define corporate culture; and (4) helping managers assess performance. Firms set long-term goals, intermediate goals, and short-term goals.

Planning is often concerned with the nuts and bolts of setting goals, choosing tactics, and establishing schedules.

In contrast, **strategy** outlines how the business intends to meet its goals and includes the organization's responsiveness to new challenges and new needs. Three types of strategy usually considered by a company are **corporate, business** (or **competitive**), and **functional strategy. Strategy formulation** involves setting strategic goals, analyzing the organization and its environment, and matching the organization and its environment. The heart of strategy formulation is matching environmental threats and opportunities against corporate strengths and weaknesses.

Plans can be viewed on three levels that constitute a hierarchy because implementing plans is practical only when there is a logical flow from one level to the next. **Strategic plans** reflect decisions about resource allocations, company priorities, and the steps needed to meet strategic goals. **Tactical plans**, which typically involve upper and middle management, are shorter-range plans for implementing specific aspects of the company's strategic plans. **Operational plans**, which are developed by mid-level and lower-level managers, set short-term targets for daily, weekly, or monthly performance.

Finally, companies often develop alternative plans for dealing with the unknown and unforeseen. A **contingency plan** is a hedge against changes that might occur. It seeks to identify in advance important aspects of a business or its market that might change. It also identifies the ways in which a company will respond to changes. **Crisis management** involves an organization's methods for dealing with emergencies.

2 Describe the four activities that constitute the management process.

Management is the process of planning, organizing, leading, and controlling an organization's financial, physical, human, and information resources to achieve its goals. **Planning** is determining what the organization needs to do and how best to get it done. The process of determining the best way to arrange a business's resources and activities into a coherent structure is called **organizing**. When **directing**, a manager works to guide and motivate employees to meet the firm's objectives. **Controlling** is the process of monitoring a firm's performance to make sure that the firm is meeting its goals.

3 Identify types of managers by level and area.

There are three basic levels of management. The fairly small number of executives who get the chance to guide the fortunes of most companies are **top managers**. Just below the ranks of top managers is another group of managers who also occupy positions of considerable autonomy and importance and who are called **middle managers**.

In any large company, most top, middle, and **first-line managers** work in one of five areas. *Human resource managers* hire and train employees, evaluate performance, and determine compensation. *Operations managers* are responsible for the systems by which a firm produces goods and services; among other duties, operations managers are responsible for production, inventory, and quality control. Because marketing encompasses the development, pricing, promotion, and distribution of goods and services, *marketing managers* are responsible for getting products from producers to consumers. Occupying a fairly new managerial position in many firms, *information managers* design and implement systems to gather, organize, and distribute information. Nearly every company has *financial managers* to plan and oversee its accounting functions and financial resources.

4 Describe the five basic management skills.

Effective managers must develop skills in five areas. The skills needed to perform specialized tasks are called **technical skills** (such as a programmer's ability to write code or an accountant's ability to audit company records). Effective managers also generally have good **human relations skills**—specifically, skills in understanding and getting along with other people. **Conceptual skills** refer to a person's ability to think in the abstract, to diagnose and analyze different situations, and to see beyond the present situation. **Decision-making skills** include the ability to define problems and select the best course of action. **Time management skills** refer to the productive use that managers make of their time. At the beginning of the twenty-first century, most experts point to the growing importance of skills in two other areas: *global management skills* and *technology management skills*.

5 Describe the development and explain the importance of corporate culture.

Just as every individual has a unique personality, so every company has a unique identity, called **corporate culture**: the shared experiences, stories, beliefs, and norms that characterize an organization. This culture helps define the work and business climate that exists in an organization. A strong corporate culture directs employees' efforts and helps everyone work toward the same goals. Organizations must sometimes change their cultures. In such cases, they must also communicate the nature of the change to both employees and customers.

■ KEY TERMS

goal (p. 136)
strategy (p. 136)
corporate strategy (p. 136)
business (or competitive) strategy (p. 136)
functional strategy (p. 137)
mission statement (p. 138)
long-term goal (p. 138)
intermediate goal (p. 138)
short-term goal (p. 138)
strategy formulation (p. 139)
strategic goal (p. 139)

SWOT analysis (p. 139)
environmental analysis (p. 140)
organizational analysis (p. 140)
strategic plan (p. 141)
tactical plan (p. 142)
operational plan (p. 142)
contingency planning (p. 142)
crisis management (p. 143)
management (p. 144)
planning (p. 144)
organizing (p. 145)
directing (p. 145)

controlling (p. 146)
top manager (p. 147)
middle manager (p. 148)
first-line manager (p. 148)
technical skills (p. 150)
human relations skills (p. 150)
conceptual skills (p. 151)
decision-making skills (p. 151)
time management skills (p. 152)
corporate culture (p. 154)

■ QUESTIONS AND EXERCISES

Questions for Review

1 What are the four main purposes of setting goals in an organization?

2 Identify and explain the three basic steps in strategy formulation.

3 Relate the five basic management skills to the four activities in the management process. For example, which skills are most important in directing?

4 What is corporate culture? How is it formed? How is it sustained?

Questions for Analysis

5 Select any group of which you are a member (your company, your family, or a club or organization, for example). Explain how planning, organizing, directing, and controlling are practiced in that group.

6 Identify managers by level and area at your school, college, or university.

7 In what kind of company would the technical skills of top managers be more important than human relations or conceptual skills? Are there organizations in which conceptual skills are not important?

8 What differences might you expect to find in the corporate cultures of a 100-year-old manufacturing firm based in the Northeast and a 1-year-old e-commerce firm set in Silicon Valley?

Application Exercises

9 Interview the manager at any level of a local company. Identify that manager's job according to level and area. Show how planning, organizing, directing, and controlling are part of this person's job. Inquire about the manager's education and work experience. Which management skills are most important for this manager's job?

10 Compare and contrast the corporate cultures of two companies that do business in most communities. Be sure to choose two companies in the same industry—for example, a Sears department store and a Wal-Mart discount store.

BUILDING YOUR BUSINESS SKILLS

SPEAKING WITH POWER

This exercise enhances the following SCANS workplace competencies: demonstrating basic skills, demonstrating thinking skills, exhibiting interpersonal skills, and working with information.

Goal

To encourage students to appreciate effective speaking as a critical human relations skill.

Background

A manager's ability to understand and get along with supervisors, peers, and subordinates is a critical human relations skill. At the heart of this skill, says Harvard University professor of education Sarah McGinty, is the ability to speak with power and control. McGinty defines "powerful speech" in terms of the following characteristics:
- The ability to speak at length and in complete sentences
- The ability to set a conversational agenda
- The ability to deter interruptions
- The ability to argue openly and to express strong opinions about ideas, not people
- The ability to make statements that offer solutions rather than pose questions
- The ability to express humor

Taken together, says McGinty, "all this creates a sense of confidence in listeners."

Method

Step 1

Working alone, compare your own personal speaking style with McGinty's description of powerful speech by taping yourself as you speak during a meeting with classmates or during a phone conversation. (Tape both sides of the conversation only if the person to whom you are speaking gives permission.) Listen for the following problems:
- Unfinished sentences
- An absence of solutions
- Too many disclaimers ("I'm not sure I have enough information to say this, but. . .")

- The habit of seeking support from others instead of making definitive statements of personal conviction (saying, "I recommend consolidating the medical and fitness functions," instead of, "As Emily stated in her report, I recommend consolidating the medical and fitness functions")
- Language fillers (saying, "you know," "like," and "um" when you are unsure of your facts or uneasy about expressing your opinion)

Step 2

Join with three or four other classmates to evaluate each other's speaking styles. Finally:
- Have a 10-minute group discussion on the importance of human relations skills in business.
- Listen to other group members and take notes on the "power" content of what you hear.
- Offer constructive criticism by focusing on what speakers say rather than on personal characteristics (say, "Bob, you sympathized with Paul's position, but I still don't know what you think," instead of, "Bob, you sounded like a weakling").

FOLLOW-UP QUESTIONS

1 How do you think the power content of speech affects a manager's ability to communicate? Evaluate some of the ways in which effects may differ among supervisors, peers, and subordinates.

2 How do you evaluate yourself and group members in terms of powerful and powerless speech? List the strengths and weaknesses of the group.

3 Do you agree or disagree with McGinty that business success depends on gaining insight into your own language habits? Explain your answer.

4 In our age of computers and e-mail, why do you think personal presentation continues to be important in management?

5 McGinty believes that power language differs from company to company and that it is linked to the corporate culture. Do you agree, or do you believe that people express themselves in similar ways no matter where they are?

EXERCISING YOUR ETHICS

MAKING ROOM FOR ALTERNATIVE ACTIONS

The Situation

Assume that you are the manager of a large hotel adjacent to a medical center in a major city. The medical center itself consists of 10 major hospitals and research institutes. Two of the hospitals are affiliated with large universities and two with churches. Three are public and three are private. The center has an international reputation and attracts patients from around the world.

Because so many patients and their families travel great distances to visit the medical center and often stay for days or weeks, there are also eight large hotels in the area, including three new ones. The hotel that you manage is one of the older ones and, frankly, is looking a bit shabby. Corporate headquarters has told you that the hotel will either be closed or undergo a major remodeling in about two years. In the meantime, you are expected to wring every last cent of profit out of the hotel.

The Dilemma

A tropical storm has just struck the area and brought with it major flooding and power outages. Three of the medical center hospitals have been shut down indefinitely, as have six of the nearby hotels. Fortunately, your hotel sustained only minor damage and is fully functional. You have just called a meeting with your two assistant managers to discuss what actions, if any, you should take.

One assistant manager has urged you to cut room rates immediately for humanitarian purposes. This manager also wants you to open the hotel kitchens 24 hours a day to prepare free food for rescue workers and meals to donate to the hospitals, whose own food service operations have been disrupted. The other assistant manager, meanwhile, has urged just the opposite approach: raise room rates by at least 20 percent and sell food to rescue workers and hospitals at a premium price. Of course, you can also choose to follow the advice of neither and continue doing business as usual.

QUESTIONS FOR DISCUSSION

1 What are the ethical issues in this situation?
2 What do you think most managers would do in this situation?
3 What would you do?

 ## CRAFTING YOUR BUSINESS PLAN

FURNISHING YOURSELF WITH MANAGEMENT SKILLS

The Purpose of the Assignment

1 To familiarize students with management-related issues that a sample firm may address in developing its business plan, in the planning framework of the *Business PlanPro (BPP) 2003* software package (Version 6.0).

2 To demonstrate how three chapter topics—business goals, business strategies, and management skills—

can be integrated as components in the *BPP* planning environment.

Assignment

After reading Chapter 5 in the textbook, open the BPP *software and search for information about business goals, business strategies, and management skills as they apply to a sample firm:* Willamette Furniture. *To find* Willamette Furniture, *follow the steps on the next page:*

Open *Business PlanPro*. Go to the toolbar and click on the "*Sample Plans*" icon. In the **Sample Plan Browser**, do a search using the **search category**, *Furniture and fixtures*. From the resulting list, select the category entitled, **Furniture Mfr.—office**, which is the location for *Willamette Furniture*. The screen you are looking at is the introduction page for *Willamette*'s business plan. Scroll down this page until you reach the **Table of Contents** for the company's business plan.

NOW RESPOND TO THE FOLLOWING ITEMS:

1 Evaluate *Willamette Furniture*'s business objectives. Are they clearly stated? Are they measurable? [Sites to see in *BPP* (for this item): On the Table of Contents page, click on **1.1 Objectives**.]

2 Evaluate *Willamette*'s mission and strategy statements. Do they clearly state how Willamette Furniture intends to achieve its purposes? [Sites to see in *BPP*: On the

Table of Contents page, click on **1.0 Executive Summary**. Then click on **1.2 Mission**. Next, click on each of the following in turn: **5.0 Strategy and Implementation Summary** and **5.1 Strategy Pyramids**.]

3 In what areas of the business does each of *Willamette*'s top managers work? [Sites to see in *BPP*: From the Table of Contents page, click on **6.0 Management Summary**. Now click on each of the following: **6.1 Organizational Structure** and **6.2 Management Team**.]

4 What management skills areas are lacking in *Willamette Furniture*'s management team? Would you classify the missing skills as technical, human resources, conceptual, or decision-making skills? [Sites to see in *BPP*: On the Table of Contents page, click on **6.3 Management Team Gaps**.]

 VIDEO EXERCISE

IMAGINATIVE MANAGEMENT: CREATIVE AGE PUBLICATIONS

Learning Objectives

The purpose of this video is to help you:

1 Understand how and why managers set organizational goals.
2 Identify the basic skills that managers need to be effective.
3 Discuss ways in which corporate culture can affect an organization.

Synopsis

Creative Age Publications uses creativity in managing its beauty-industry publications. With offices or franchised operations in Europe, Japan, Russia, and other areas of the world, the company has expanded rapidly—thanks to sound management practices. In fact, one of the company's goals is to avoid overtaxing its management team by growing more slowly in the near future. The CEO is working toward

delegating most or all decisions to her management team, and as Creative Age managers move up through the ranks, they hone both their technical skills and their skill in working with others. "Having heart" is a major part of the company's culture—an important element that, in the CEO's opinion, many companies lack.

DISCUSSION QUESTIONS

1 **For analysis:** How does global growth affect Creative Age's emphasis on the management skill of interacting well with other people?
2 **For analysis:** How does moving Creative Age's managers up through the ranks help them develop conceptual skills?
3 **For application:** How would you suggest that the CEO spread the Creative Age culture throughout its global offices?
4 **For application:** How might the CEO manage growth through the process of controlling?

5 **For debate:** Do you agree with the CEO's policy of allowing managers and employees to work on any company magazine they choose? Support your position.

Online Exploration

Visit the Creative Age Web site *(www.creativeage.com)* and follow the link to *Day Spa* magazine. Scan the magazine's home page and then click on the **About Us** link to read more about the magazine and its parent company. Why would Creative Age call attention to each magazine's goals and market rather than focusing on the parent company? How might Creative Age use a corporate Web site to communicate with other people and organizations that affect its ability to achieve its goals?

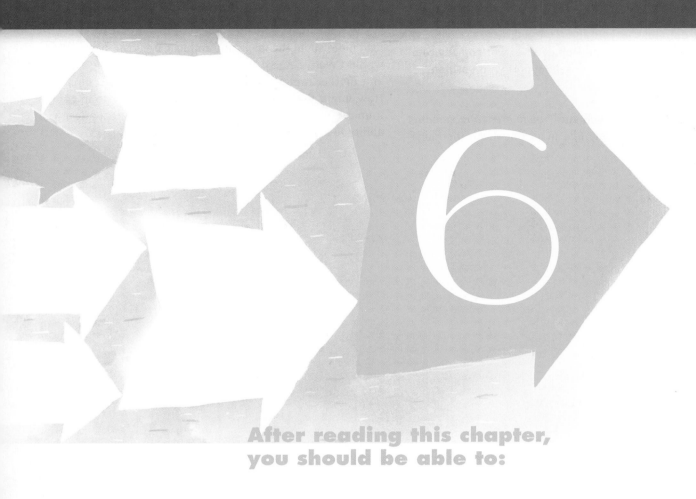

6

After reading this chapter,
you should be able to:

1   Discuss the elements that influence a firm's *organizational structure*.

2   Explain *specialization* and *departmentalization* as the building blocks of organizational structure.

3   Distinguish among *responsibility, authority, delegation*, and *accountability* and explain the differences between decision making in *centralized* and *decentralized organizations*.

4   Explain the differences among *functional, divisional, matrix*, and *international organizational structures* and describe the most popular new forms of organizational design.

5   Describe the *informal organization* and discuss *intrapreneuring*.

COOKING UP A NEW STRUCTURE

A few years ago, Sara Lee CEO John H. Bryan realized that he had a problem. During the 25 years of his tenure, the firm had grown beyond its foundation in food products to encompass dozens of lines of business—everything from cake mixes to insecticide to lingerie. The new businesses were acquisitions, and the original managers controlled each

ORGANIZING THE BUSINESS ENTERPRISE

one as if it were a separate company. Calculating the cost of all this duplication, Bryan reached the conclusion that the company could not afford high costs at a time when price competition was heating up.

In an effort to fix things, starting in 1997, Bryan sold or eliminated about one-quarter of the firm's 200 products. He cut redundant factories and the workforce, reduced the number of products, and standardized companywide processes. He called his extensive restructuring program "deverticalization," and his goal was to remove Sara Lee from manufacturing while strengthening its focus and effectiveness as a marketer. In the meantime, however, he continued to acquire rival firms in order to sustain the company's growth. Eventually, despite Bryan's efforts, Sara Lee suffered from high costs and remained unfocused and inefficient. Said one industry analyst about Bryan's strategy: "Sometimes, the more chairs you move around, the more dust you see behind the chairs."

In 2000, C. Steven McMillan took over from Bryan at Sara Lee, and in the immortal words of Yogi Berra, "It was *déjà vu* all over again." McMillan quickly realized that Bryan's moves had had little impact on the firm's performance and that he himself would need to start making some big changes. Borrowing a page from rival Kraft Foods, he began by merging the sales forces that specialized in various brands to create smaller, customer-focused teams. In meats alone, for instance, Sara Lee had 10 different brands, including Ball Park, Hillshire Farms, Bryan, and Jimmy Dean. "So if you're . . . a Kroger or a Safeway," explained McMillan, "you've got to deal with 10 different organizations and multiple invoices." Teams reduced duplication and were more convenient for buyers—a win-win situation. National retailers like Wal-Mart responded by increasing their orders for Sara Lee products.

McMillan also centralized decision making at the firm by shutting down 50 weaker regional brands and reorganizing the firm into three broad product categories: Food and Beverage, Intimates and Underwear, and Household Products. He abolished several layers of corporate hierarchy, including many of the middle managers whom the firm had inherited from its acquisitions. He created category managers to oversee related lines of business, and the flattened organizational structure led to improved accountability and more centralized control over Sara Lee's far-flung operations.

McMillan also borrowed some tactics from his predecessor, divesting 15 businesses, including Coach leather goods, and laying off 10 percent of his workers. In another move that was widely questioned by industry observers, he paid $2.8 billion for breadmaker Earthgrains. The move increased Sara Lee's market share in baked goods, but many observers felt that McMillan paid too much for a small potential return.

Our opening story continues on page 187.

■ WHAT IS ORGANIZATIONAL STRUCTURE?

What do we mean by the term *organizational structure*? Consider a simple analogy. In some ways, a business is like an automobile. All cars have engines, four wheels, fenders, and other structural components. They all have passenger compartments, storage areas, and various operating systems (fuel, braking, climate control). Although each component has a distinct purpose, it must also work in accord with the others. In addition, although the ways they look and fit may vary widely, all automobiles have the same basic components.

Similarly, all businesses have common structural and operating components, each composed of a series of *jobs to be done* and each with a *specific overall purpose*. From company to company, these components look different and fit together differently, but in every organization, components have the same fundamental purpose—each must perform its own function while working in concert with the others.

Although all organizations feature the same basic elements, each must develop the structure that is most appropriate for it. What works for Texas Instruments will not work for Shell Oil, Amazon.com, or the U.S. Department of Justice. The structure of the American Red Cross will probably not work for Union Carbide or the University of Minnesota. We define **organizational structure** as the specification of the jobs to be done within an organization and the ways in which those jobs relate to one another.

organizational structure
Specification of the jobs to be done within an organization and the ways in which they relate to one another

Determinants of Organization

How is an organization's structure determined? Does it happen by chance, or is there some logic that managers use to create structure? Does it develop by some combination of circumstance and strategy? Ideally, managers carefully assess a variety of important factors as they plan for and then create a structure that will allow their organization to function efficiently.

Many elements work together to determine an organization's structure. Chief among them are the organization's *purpose, mission,* and *strategy*. A dynamic and rapidly growing enterprise, for example, achieved that position because of its purpose and successful strategies for achieving it. Such a firm will need a structure that contributes to flexibility and growth. A stable organization with only modest growth will function best with a different structure.

Size, technology, and changes in the organization's environment also affect structure. As we saw in Chapter 5, organizing is a function of managerial planning. As such, it is conducted with an equal awareness of both a firm's external and internal environments. A large manufacturer operating in a strongly competitive environment—say, Boeing or Hewlett-Packard—requires a different structure than a local barbershop or video store. Moreover, even after a structure has been created, it is rarely free from tinkering—or even outright re-creation. Most organizations change their structures on an almost continuing basis.

Since it was first incorporated in 1903, Ford Motor Co. *(www.ford.com)* has undergone literally dozens of major structural changes, hundreds of moderate changes, and thousands of minor changes. In the last 10 years alone, Ford has initiated several major structural changes. In 1994, for instance, the firm announced a major restructuring plan called Ford 2000, which was intended to integrate all of Ford's vast international operations into a single, unified structure by the year 2000.

By 1998, however, midway through implementation of the grand plan, top Ford executives announced major modifications, indicating that (1) additional changes would be made, (2) some previously planned changes would not be made, and (3) some recently realigned operations would be changed again. In early 1999, managers announced another set of changes intended to eliminate corporate bureaucracy, speed decision making, and improve communication and working relationships among people at different levels of the organization.[1] Early in 2001, Ford announced yet more sweeping changes intended to boost the firm's flagging bottom line and stem a decline in product quality.[2] More changes followed in 2003.

Chain of Command

Most businesses prepare **organization charts** to clarify structure and to show employees where they fit into a firm's operations. Figure 6.1 is an organization chart for Contemporary Landscape Services Inc., a small but thriving business in Bryan, Texas. Each box in the chart represents a job. The solid lines define the **chain of command**, or *reporting relationships*, within the company. For example, the retail shop, nursery, and landscape operations managers all report to the owner and president, Mark Ferguson. Within the landscape operation is one manager for residential accounts and another for commercial accounts. Similarly, there are other managers in the retail shop and the nursery.

The organization charts of large firms are far more complex and include individuals at many more levels than those shown in Figure 6.1. Size prevents many large firms from even having charts that include all their managers. Typically, they create one organization chart showing overall corporate structure and separate charts for each division.

organization chart
Diagram depicting a company's structure and showing employees where they fit into its operations

chain of command
Reporting relationships within a company

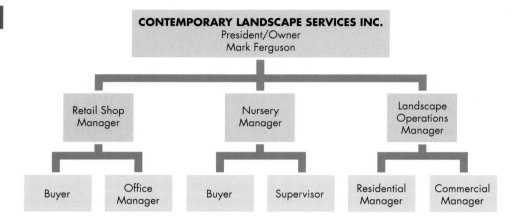

FIGURE 6.1
The Organization Chart

THE BUILDING BLOCKS OF ORGANIZATIONAL STRUCTURE

The first step in developing the structure of any business, large or small, involves two activities:

- **Specialization:** determining who will do what
- **Departmentalization:** determining how people performing certain tasks can best be grouped together

These two activities are the building blocks of all business organizations.[3]

Specialization

job specialization
The process of identifying the specific jobs that need to be done and designating the people who will perform them

The process of identifying the specific jobs that need to be done and designating the people who will perform them leads to **job specialization**. In a sense, all organizations have only one major job, such as making cars (Ford), selling finished goods to consumers (Wal-Mart), or providing telecommunications services (AT&T). Usually, the job is more complex in nature. For example, the job of Chaparral Steel *(www.txi.com/steel)* is converting scrap steel (such as wrecked automobiles) into finished steel products (such as beams and reinforcement bars).

To perform this one overall job, managers actually break it down, or specialize it, into several smaller jobs. Thus, some workers transport the scrap steel to the company's mill in Midlothian, Texas. Others operate shredding equipment before turning raw materials over to the workers who then melt them into liquid form. Other specialists oversee the flow of the liquid into molding equipment in which it is transformed into new products. Finally, other workers are responsible for moving finished products to a holding area before they are shipped out to customers. When the overall job of the organization is thus broken down, workers can develop real expertise in their jobs, and employees can better coordinate their work with that done by others.

Specialization and Growth In a very small organization, the owner may perform every job. As the firm grows, however, so does the need to specialize jobs so that others can perform them. To see how specialization can evolve in an organization, consider the case of the Walt Disney Company *(www.disney.go.com)*. When Walt Disney first opened his studio, he and his brother Roy did everything. For example, when they created the very first animated feature, *Steamboat Willy*, they wrote the story, drew the pictures, transferred the pictures to film, provided the voices, and then went out and sold the cartoon to theater operators.

Today, in sharp contrast, a Disney animated feature is made possible only through the efforts of hundreds of creators. The job of one cartoonist may be to draw the face of a single character throughout an entire feature. Another artist may be charged with erasing stray pencil marks inadvertently made by other illustrators. People other than artists are responsible for the subsequent operations that turn individual animated cells into a moving picture or for the marketing of the finished product.

Job specialization is a natural part of organizational growth. It also has certain advantages. For example, specialized jobs are learned more easily and can be performed more efficiently than nonspecialized jobs, and it is also easier to replace people who leave an organization. However, jobs at lower levels of the organization are especially susceptible to overspecialization. If such jobs become too narrowly defined, employees may become bored and careless, derive less satisfaction from their jobs, and lose sight of their roles in the organization.[4]

Departmentalization

After jobs are specialized, they must be grouped into logical units, which is the process of **departmentalization**. Departmentalized companies benefit from the division of activities. Control and coordination are narrowed and made easier, and top managers can see more easily how various units are performing.

departmentalization
Process of grouping jobs into logical units

Departmentalization allows the firm to treat a department as a **profit center**—a separate company unit responsible for its own costs and profits. Thus, Sears *(www.sears.com)* can calculate the profits it generates from men's clothing, appliances, home furnishings, and every other department within a given store. Managers can then use this information in making decisions about advertising and promotional events, space allocation, and so forth.

profit center
Separate company unit responsible for its own costs and profits

Obviously, managers do not departmentalize jobs randomly. They group them logically, according to some common thread or purpose. In general, departmentalization may occur along *customer*, *product*, *process*, *geographic*, or *functional* lines (or any combination of these).

Customer Departmentalization Stores such as Sears and Macy's *(www.macys.com)* are divided into departments—a men's department, a women's

SMILE WHEN YOU SAY THAT
ABOUT MY DEPARTMENT, J.B.

YOU PEOPLE ARE
BANKRUPTING
THE COMPANY.

customer departmentalization
Departmentalization according to types of customers likely to buy a given product

department, a luggage department, and so on. Each department targets a specific customer category (men, women, people who want to buy luggage). **Customer departmentalization** makes shopping easier by providing identifiable store segments. Thus, a Sears customer shopping for a baby's playpen can bypass Lawn and Garden Supplies and head straight for Children's Furniture. Stores can also group products in locations designated for deliveries, special sales, and other service-oriented purposes. In general, the store is more efficient, and customers get better service because salespeople tend to specialize and gain expertise in their departments.

Product Departmentalization Manufacturers and service providers often opt for **product departmentalization**—dividing an organization according to the specific product or service being created. This approach is used at Lucent Technologies. For example, the wireless communications department focuses on cellular telephones and services, while the optical networking department focuses on fiber optical and other cable and communications technologies. Because each of them represents a defined group of products or services, Lucent managers are able—in theory—to focus on specific product lines in a clear and defined way.

product departmentalization
Departmentalization according to specific products being created

process departmentalization
Departmentalization according to production processes used to create a good or service

Process Departmentalization Other manufacturers favor **process departmentalization**, in which the organization is divided according to production processes. This principle is logical for the pickle maker Vlasic *(www.vlasic.com)*, which has separate departments to transform cucumbers into fresh-packed pickles, pickles cured in brine, and relishes. Cucumbers destined to become fresh-packed pickles must be packed into jars immediately, covered with a solution of water and vinegar, and prepared for sale. Those slated to be brined pickles must be aged in brine solution before packing. Relish cucumbers must be minced and combined with a host of other ingredients. Each process requires different equipment and worker skills.

geographic departmentalization
Departmentalization according to areas served by a business

Geographic Departmentalization Some firms are divided according to the areas of the country or the world that they serve. Levi Strauss, for instance, has one division for the United States *(www.levi.com)*, one for Europe *(www.eu.levi.com)*, one for the Asia Pacific region *(www.levi.co.kr)*, and one for Latin America *(www.levi.com/lar)*. Within the United States, **geographic departmentalization** is

This "financial exploratorium" in New York is one of five opened by E*Trade (www.etrade.com)to accommodate customers in need of any one of the company's growing line of service products. Started in 1982 as a software service for brokers, E*Trade has grown by adding product departments to its core services and is now the No. 3 online brokerage, No. 3 ATM network, and No. 12 savings bank. Its goal is to become a financial services supermarket: In addition to its brokerage business, E*Trade offers checking accounts and mortgages and will soon be in the credit card and insurance businesses.

This truck-frame plant in Stockton, California, represents the commitment of Toyota Motor Co. (www.global.toyota.com) to geography as a factor in the division of its activities. Operating in North America requires Toyota to forge relationships with such U.S. suppliers as Dana Corp. (www.dana.com), an Ohio-based firm that furnishes Toyota with frame assemblies from its Parish Structural Products facility (which is also located in Stockton). At the same time, Toyota combines product with geographic departmentalization: At Stockton, it makes frames for its Tacoma-model trucks, not for its Tundra-model trucks.

common among utilities. Pacific Power and Light is organized as four geographic departments—Southwestern, Columbia Basin, Mid-Oregon, and Wyoming.

Functional Departmentalization Many service and manufacturing companies, especially smaller ones, develop departments according to a group's functions or activities—a form of organization known as **functional departmentalization**. Such firms typically have production, marketing and sales, human resources, and accounting and finance departments. Departments may be further subdivided. For example, the marketing department might be divided geographically or into separate staffs for market research and advertising.

> **functional departmentalization** Departmentalization according to groups' functions or activities

Because different forms of departmentalization have different advantages, larger companies tend to adopt different types of departmentalization for various levels. The company illustrated in Figure 6.2 uses functional departmentalization at the top level.

FIGURE 6.2

Multiple Forms of Departmentalization

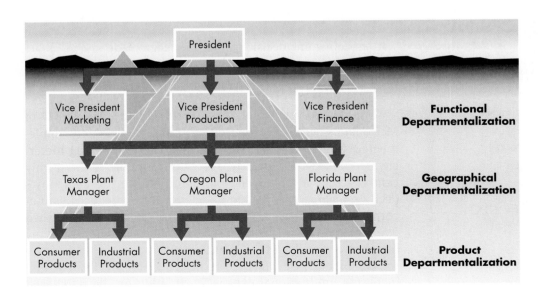

At the middle level, production is divided along geographic lines. At a lower level, marketing is departmentalized by product group.

SELF-CHECK QUESTIONS 1–3

You should now be able to answer Self-Check Questions 1–3.*

1 **True/False** Organizations create a stable *structure* for themselves and then seldom have to change it.
2 **Multiple Choice** Which of the following jobs is likely to reflect the highest degree of *specialization*? [select one]: **(a)** chief executive officer; **(b)** sales representative; **(c)** assembly line worker;

(d) human resource manager; **(e)** public relations spokesperson.
3 **Multiple Choice** Which of the following is **not** a common basis for *departmentalization*? [select one]: **(a)** sequence; **(b)** function; **(c)** process; **(d)** product; **(e)** customer.

***Answers to Self-Check Questions 1–3 can be found on p. 508.**

◾ ESTABLISHING THE DECISION-MAKING HIERARCHY

After jobs have been appropriately specialized and grouped into manageable departments, the next step in organizing is to establish the decision-making hierarchy. That is, managers must explicitly define *reporting relationships* among positions so that everyone will know who has responsibility for various decisions and operations. The goal is to figure out how to structure and stabilize the organizational framework so that everyone works together to achieve common goals. Companies vary greatly in the ways in which they handle the delegation of tasks, responsibility, and authority.

A major question that must be asked about any organization is this one: *Who makes which decisions?* The answer almost never focuses on an individual or even on a small group. The more accurate answer usually refers to the decision-making hierarchy. Generally speaking, the development of this hierarchy results from a three-step process:

1 **Assigning tasks:** determining who can make decisions and specifying how they should be made
2 **Performing tasks:** implementing decisions that have been made
3 **Distributing authority:** determining whether the organization is to be centralized or decentralized

> **"For 40 years, all we did was open restaurants. That's not enough anymore."**
>
> **—Jack Greenberg, former CEO of McDonald's**

For example, when Jack Greenberg took over as CEO of McDonald's *(www.mcdonalds.com)*, he immediately implemented several changes in the firm's decision-making hierarchy. McDonald's has always been—and continues to be—highly centralized. But Greenberg restructured both the company's decision-making process and its operations. He reduced staff at corporate headquarters in Oak Brook, Illinois, and established five regional offices throughout the United States. Now, many decisions are made at the regional level.

Greenberg also clamped a lid on domestic growth and increased international expansion. In addition, he purchased stakes in three new restaurant chains with an eye on expansion: Donatos Pizza *(www.donatos.com)*, Chipotle Mexican Grill *(www.chipotle.com)*, and Aroma, a British coffee chain. Greenberg then installed four new managers, one to head up international operations and the others to oversee the three new restaurant partner groups. All four of these executives reported directly to Greenberg. Why the changes? "Maybe it was arrogance," said Greenberg. "For 40 years, all we did was open restaurants. That's not enough anymore."[5]

Assigning Tasks: Responsibility and Authority

The question of who is supposed to do what and who is entitled to do what in an organization is complex. In any company with more than one person, individuals must work out agreements about responsibilities and authority. **Responsibility** is the duty to perform an assigned task. **Authority** is the power to make the decisions necessary to complete the task.

> **responsibility**
> Duty to perform an assigned task

For example, imagine a midlevel buyer for Macy's department store who encounters an unexpected opportunity to make a large purchase at an extremely good price. Assume that an immediate decision is absolutely necessary—a decision that this buyer has no authority to make without confirmation from above. The company's policies on delegation and authority are inconsistent because the buyer is responsible for purchasing the clothes that will be sold in the upcoming season, but he or she lacks the authority to make the needed purchases.

> **authority**
> Power to make the decisions necessary to complete a task

Performing Tasks: Delegation and Accountability

Trouble occurs when appropriate levels of responsibility and authority are not clearly delineated in the working relationships between managers and subordinates. Here, the issues become delegation and accountability. **Delegation** begins when a manager assigns a task to a subordinate. **Accountability** falls to the subordinate, who must then complete the task. If tasks are effectively delegated and performed, the organization will function smoothly. But if the subordinate does not perform the task as assigned—perhaps doing a poor job or not getting the work done on time—problems can arise. The work unit may suffer, and the employee's performance abilities or motivation may be called into question.

> **delegation**
> Assignment of a task, responsibility, or authority by a manager to a subordinate

> **accountability**
> Liability of subordinates for accomplishing tasks assigned by managers

Fear of Delegating Unfortunately, many managers actually have trouble delegating tasks to others.[6] This is especially true in small businesses in which the owner-manager started out doing everything. Experts pinpoint certain reasons why some small-business managers may have trouble delegating effectively:

- The feeling that employees can never do anything as well as the manager can
- The fear that something will go wrong if someone else takes over a job
- The lack of time for long-range planning because the manager is bogged down in day-to-day operations
- The sense of being in the dark about industry trends and competitive products because of the time the manager devotes to day-to-day operations

To overcome these tendencies, small-business owners must begin by admitting that they can never go back to running the entire show and that they can in fact prosper—with the help of their employees—if they learn to let go. This problem, however, isn't always confined to small businesses. Some managers in big companies also don't delegate as much or as well as they should. There are also several reasons for this problem:

■ The fear that subordinates don't really know how to do the job
■ The fear that a subordinate might "show the manager up" in front of others by doing a superb job
■ The desire to keep as much control as possible over how things are done
■ A simple lack of ability as to how to effectively delegate to others

The remedies in these instances are a bit different. First, all managers should recognize that they can't do everything themselves. Second, if subordinates can't do a job, they should be trained so that they can assume more responsibility in the future. Third, managers should actually recognize that if a subordinate performs well, it also reflects favorably on the manager. Finally, a manager who simply doesn't know how to delegate might need specialized training in how to divide up and assign tasks to others.

Distributing Authority: Centralization and Decentralization

Delegation involves a specific relationship between managers and subordinates. Most businesses must also make decisions about general patterns of authority throughout the company. This pattern may be largely centralized or decentralized (or, usually, somewhere in between).

centralized organization
Organization in which most decision-making authority is held by upper-level management

Centralized Organizations In a **centralized organization**, most decision-making authority is held by upper-level managers. Most lower-level decisions must be approved by upper management before they can be implemented.[7] As we noted earlier, McDonald's practices centralization as a way to maintain standardization. All restaurants must follow precise steps in buying products and making and packaging burgers and other menu items. Most advertising is handled at the corporate level, and any local advertising must be approved by a regional manager. Restaurants even have to follow prescribed schedules for facilities' maintenance and upgrades like floor polishing and parking lot cleaning. Similarly, the CEO of JC Penney, Allen Questrom, has been systematically centralizing decision making as part of his efforts to revive the venerable retailer.[8] Centralized authority is also typical of small businesses.

decentralized organization
Organization in which a great deal of decision-making authority is delegated to levels of management at points below the top

Decentralized Organizations As a company gets larger, increasingly more decisions must be made; thus, the company tends to adopt a more decentralized pattern. In a **decentralized organization**, much decision-making authority is delegated to levels of management at various points below the top. The purpose of decentralization is to make a company more responsive to its environment by breaking the company into more manageable units, ranging from product lines to independent businesses. Reducing top-heavy bureaucracies is also a common goal. Jack Welch, former CEO of General Electric *(www.ge.com/businesses)*, is a longtime proponent of decentralized management. As he put it, "If you don't let managers make their own decisions, you're never going to be anything more than a one-person business." This logic also explains why cereal maker Kellogg has been decentralizing its organization. Top managers realize that in order to keep pace with today's eat-on-the-run lifestyles, lower level managers need more autonomy to make decisions and rush new products to market.[9]

The oil industry giant Exxon-Mobil *(www.exxon.mobil.com)* owns vast reserves of natural gas, like this field in the former Soviet republic of Turkmenistan. It does not, however, have much experience in the business of natural gas, which is becoming increasingly valuable as an alternative to coal and oil. In most respects, ExxonMobil is a highly centralized company, but in this less stable market, which tends to evolve and innovate rapidly, many experts are skeptical about the company's ability to decentralize the control that management exercises over corporate operations.

Tall and Flat Organizations Related to the concept of centralized or decentralized authority are the concepts of tall and flat organizational structures. With relatively fewer layers of management, decentralized firms tend to reflect a **flat organizational structure** like that of the hypothetical law firm described in Figure 6.3(a). In contrast, companies with centralized authority systems typically require multiple layers of management and thus **tall organizational structures**. As you can see from Figure 6.3(b), the United States Army is a good example. Because information, whether moving upward or downward, must pass through so many organizational layers, tall structures are prone to delays in information flow.

As organizations grow in size, it is both normal and necessary that they become at least somewhat taller. For instance, a small firm with only an owner-manager and a few employees is likely to have two layers—the owner-manager and the employees who report to that person. But as the firm grows, more layers will be needed. Born Information Services *(www.born.com)*, for instance, is a small consulting firm created and run by Rick Born. At first, all his employees reported to him. But when the size of his firm grew to more than 20 people, Born knew that he needed help in supervising and coordinating projects. As a result, he added a layer of management consisting of what he called staff managers to serve as project coordinators. This move freed up time for Born to seek new business clients. Like other managers, however, Born must ensure that he has only the number of layers his firm needs. Too few layers can create chaos and inefficiency, whereas too many layers can create rigidity and bureaucracy.

Span of Control As you can see from Figure 6.3, the distribution of authority in an organization also affects the number of people who work for any individual manager. In a flat organizational structure, the number of people managed by one supervisor—the manager's **span of control**—is usually wide. In tall organizations, span of control tends to be relatively narrower. Span of control, however, depends on many factors. Employees' abilities and the supervisor's managerial skills help determine whether span of control is wide or narrow, as do the similarity and simplicity of

"If you don't let managers make their own decisions, you're never going to be anything more than a one-person business."

—Jack Welch, Former CEO of General Electric

flat organizational structure
Characteristic of decentralized companies with relatively few layers of management and relatively wide spans of control

tall organizational structure
Characteristic of centralized companies with multiple layers of management and relatively narrow spans of control

span of control
Number of people supervised by one manager

FIGURE 6.3

Organizational Structure and Span of Control

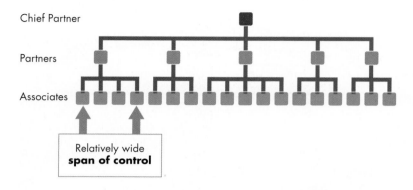

(a) FLAT ORGANIZATION: Typical Law Firm

Chief Partner

Partners

Associates

Relatively wide **span of control**

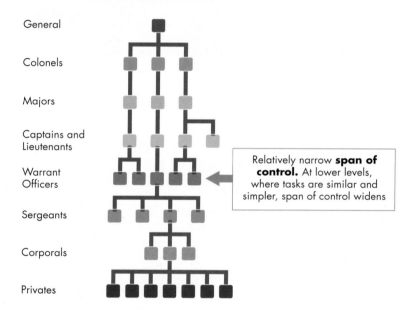

(b) TALL ORGANIZATION: United States Army

General

Colonels

Majors

Captains and Lieutenants

Warrant Officers

Sergeants

Corporals

Privates

Relatively narrow **span of control.** At lower levels, where tasks are similar and simpler, span of control widens

those tasks performed under the manager's supervision and the extent to which they are interrelated.

If lower-level managers are given more decision-making authority, their supervisors will thus have less work to do because some of the decisions they previously made will be transferred to their subordinates. By the same token, these managers may then be able to oversee and coordinate the work of more subordinates, resulting in an increased span of control. We have already seen that at McDonald's the creation of five regional offices freed up time for CEO Jack Greenberg. In turn, reorganization allowed him to then create four new executive positions, one to oversee international expansion and the others to work with new restaurant partners.

Similarly, when several employees perform either the same simple task or a group of interrelated tasks, a wide span of control is possible and often desirable. For instance, because all the jobs are routine, one supervisor may well control an entire assembly line. Moreover, each task depends on another. If one station stops, everyone stops. Having one supervisor ensures that all stations receive equal attention and function equally well.

In contrast, when jobs are more diversified or prone to change, a narrow span of control is preferable. In Racine, Wisconsin, for example, the Case Corp. *(www.casecorp.com)* factory makes farm tractors exclusively to order in five to six

ENTREPRENEURSHIP and New Ventures

The Dragon Lady Comes to the Rescue

When subordinates referred to her as the "Dragon Lady," Pamela Forbes Lieberman didn't get mad. She hung up a painting of a dragon in her office. Lieberman recently became the first woman in the top spot at TruServ (*www.truserv.com*), a hardware cooperative. Not surprisingly, her no-nonsense style helped her overcome the "ole-boy" attitude ingrained at TruServ. So did the fact that the ole boys needed a fresh perspective: The firm was on the verge of bankruptcy, with spiraling debt, top-heavy and outdated management, poorly performing locations, and too much inventory. "In a turnaround situation," observed Lieberman, "it doesn't matter what the gender of the person is, as long as they can be successful."

Lieberman first joined TruServ as chief financial officer in February 2001. Prior to that, she had earned an M.B.A. from Northwestern, worked for Price Waterhouse for 13 years, and held management positions in a number of distribution and manufacturing firms. TruServ board members quickly realized the depth of her experience and ability, and she was promoted to chief operating officer in July 2001 and then to CEO four months later.

> *"If [employees] succeed, then they will be rewarded. But if they don't, then we're going to have to look for new people sitting in their chairs."*
>
> **—Pamela Forbes Lieberman, CEO of TruServ Corp.**

In addition to its fiscal problems, TruServ was under investigation by the Securities and Exchange Commission for sloppy record keeping. Her predecessor had assured Lieberman that the firm could cover its debt obligations, but only after taking the job did she learn that management had already missed scheduled payments. She began by selling off the company's unprofitable Canadian stores and then proceeded to slash operating expenses, all the while earning a reputation as a stern taskmaster and a manager willing to make changes. "If [employees] succeed," she announced, "then they will be rewarded. But if they don't, then we're going to have to look for new people sitting in their chairs." Lieberman's frankness and willingness to take necessary steps were crucial factors in restoring TruServ's reputation.

So far, the restructuring is working. Debt and inventory are down, as is payroll, and TruServ met SEC filing requirements in August 2002. Unfortunately, the co-op's membership has fallen from more than 8,000 in 1998 to 6,700 today, and Lieberman expects more stores to leave. Currently, she's visiting owners to persuade them to be patient, assuring them that "there's nothing so broken here it can't be fixed."

weeks. Farmers can select from among a wide array of options, including engines, tires, power trains, and even a CD player. A wide assortment of machines and processes is used to construct each tractor. Although workers are highly skilled operators of their assigned machines, each machine is different. In this kind of setup, the complexities of each machine and the advanced skills needed by each operator mean that one supervisor can oversee only a small number of employees.[10]

Three Forms of Authority

Whatever type of structure a company develops, it must decide who will have authority over whom. As individuals are delegated responsibility and authority in a firm, a complex web of interactions develops. These interactions may take one of three forms of authority: line, staff, or committee and team. Like departmentalization, all three forms may be found in a given company, especially a large one.

Line Authority The type of authority that flows up and down the chain of command is **line authority**. Most companies rely heavily on **line departments**—those directly linked to the production and sales of specific products. For example, Clark

line authority
Organizational structure in which authority flows in a direct chain of command from the top of the company to the bottom

line department
Department directly linked to the production and sales of a specific product

Equipment Corp. has a division that produces forklifts and small earthmovers. In this division, line departments include purchasing, materials handling, fabrication, painting, and assembly (all of which are directly linked to production) along with sales and distribution (both of which are directly linked to sales).

Each line department is essential to an organization's success. Line employees are the doers and producers in a company. If any line department fails to complete its task, the company cannot sell and deliver finished goods. Thus, the authority delegated to line departments is important. A bad decision by the manager in one department can hold up production for an entire plant. Say, for example, that the painting department manager at Clark Equipment changes a paint application on a batch of forklifts, which then show signs of peeling paint. The batch will have to be repainted (and perhaps partially reassembled) before the machines can be shipped.

staff authority
Authority based on expertise that usually involves advising line managers

Staff Authority Most companies also rely on **staff authority**, which is based on special expertise and usually involves counseling and advising line managers. Common staff members include specialists in areas such as law, accounting, and human resource management. A corporate attorney, for example, may be asked to advise the marketing department as it prepares a new contract with the firm's advertising agency. Legal staff members, however, do not actually make decisions that affect how the marketing department does its job. **Staff members**, therefore, aid line departments in making decisions but do not have the authority to make final decisions.

staff members
Advisers and counselors who aid line departments in making decisions but do not have the authority to make final decisions

Typically, the separation between line authority and staff responsibility is clearly delineated. As Figure 6.4 shows, this separation is usually indicated in organization charts by solid lines (line authority) and dotted lines (staff responsibility). It may help to understand this separation by remembering that whereas staff members generally provide services to management, line managers are directly involved in producing the firm's products.

committee and team authority
Authority granted to committees or work teams involved in a firm's daily operations

Committee and Team Authority Recently, more and more organizations have started to use **committee and team authority**—authority granted to committees or work teams that play central roles in the firm's daily operations. A committee, for example, may consist of top managers from several major areas. If the work of the committee is especially important and if the committee members will be working together for an extended time, the organization may even grant it special authority as a decision-making body that goes beyond the individual authority possessed by each of its members.

At the operating level, many firms today are also using work teams—groups of operating employees who are empowered to plan and organize their own work and to perform that work with a minimum of supervision. As with permanent committees,

FIGURE 6.4

Line and Staff Organization

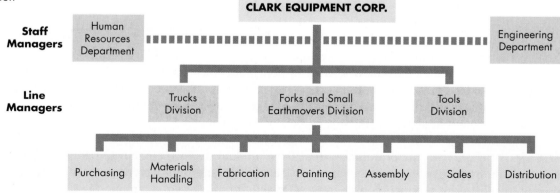

the organization will usually find it beneficial to grant special authority to work teams so that they may function more effectively.

BASIC FORMS OF ORGANIZATIONAL STRUCTURE

Organizations can structure themselves in an almost infinite number of ways—according to specialization, for example, or departmentalization or the decision-making hierarchy. Nevertheless, it is possible to identify four basic forms of organizational structure that reflect the general trends followed by most firms: *functional, divisional, matrix*, and *international*.

Functional Organization

Functional organization is the approach to organizational structure used by most small to medium-size firms. Such organizations are usually structured around basic business functions (marketing, operations, finance). Thus, within the company, there is a marketing department, an operations department, and a finance department. The benefits of this approach include specialization within functional areas and smoother coordination among them. Experts with specialized training, for example, are hired to work in the marketing department, which handles all marketing for the firm.

In large firms, coordination across functional departments becomes more complicated. Functional organization also fosters centralization (which may possibly be desirable) and makes accountability more difficult. As organizations grow, therefore, they tend to shed this form and move toward one of the other three structures.

functional organization
Form of business organization in which authority is determined by the relationships between group functions and activities

Divisional Organization

A **divisional organization** relies on product departmentalization. The firm creates product-based divisions, each of which may then be managed as a separate enterprise.

divisional organization
Organizational structure in which corporate divisions operate as autonomous businesses under the larger corporate umbrella

division
Department that resembles a
separate business in producing and
marketing its own products

Organizations using this approach are typically structured around several **divisions**—departments that resemble separate businesses in that they produce and market their own products. The head of each division may be a corporate vice president or, if the organization is large, a divisional president. In addition, each division usually has its own identity and operates as a relatively autonomous business under the larger corporate umbrella.

H. J. Heinz *(www.heinz.com)*, for example, is one of the world's largest food-processing companies. Heinz makes literally thousands of different products and markets them around the world. The firm is organized into seven basic divisions: food service (selling small packaged products such as mustard and relish to restaurants), infant foods, condiments (Heinz ketchup, steak sauce, and tomato sauce), Star-Kist tuna, pet foods, frozen foods, and one division that handles miscellaneous products, including new lines being test marketed and soups, beans, and pasta products. Because of its divisional structure, Heinz can evaluate the performance of each division independently. Until recently, Heinz also had a division for its Weight Watchers business, but because this business was performing poorly, the company sold the Weight Watchers classroom program and folded its line of frozen foods into its existing frozen-foods division.[11] Because divisions are relatively autonomous, a firm can take such action with minimal disruption to its remaining business operations.

Like Heinz, other divisionalized companies are free to buy, sell, create, and disband divisions without disrupting the rest of their operations. Divisions can maintain healthy competition among themselves by sponsoring separate advertising campaigns, fostering different corporate identities, and so forth. They can also share certain corporate-level resources (such as market research data). Of course, if too much control is delegated to divisional managers, corporate managers may lose touch with daily operations. Competition between divisions can also become disruptive, and efforts in one division may be duplicated by those of another.

Matrix Organization

matrix structure
Organizational structure in which
teams are formed and team members
report to two or more managers

In a **matrix structure**, teams are formed in which individuals report to two or more managers. One manager usually has functional expertise, whereas the other has more of a product or project orientation. This structure was pioneered by the National Aeronautics and Space Administration (NASA) *(www.nasa.gov)* for use in developing specific programs. It is a highly flexible form that is readily adaptable to changing circumstances. Matrix structures rely heavily on committee and team authority.

In some companies, the matrix organization is a temporary measure, installed to complete a specific project and affecting only one part of the firm. In these firms, the end of the project usually means the end of the matrix—either a breakup of the team or a restructuring to fit it into the company's existing line-and-staff structure. Ford, for example, uses a matrix organization to design new models. Design teams comprised of people from engineering, marketing, operations, and finance are created to design new cars and trucks. After its work is done, the team members move back to their permanent functional jobs.

In other settings, the matrix organization is a semipermanent fixture. Figure 6.5 shows how Martha Stewart Living Omnimedia Inc. *(www.marthastewart.com)* has created a permanent matrix organization for its burgeoning lifestyle business. Given her current problems with the U.S. Department of Justice, Stewart is no longer CEO, but regardless of the outcome of the case, the company itself isn't likely to alter its basic structure. As you can see, the company is organized broadly into media and merchandising groups, each of which has specific products and product groups.

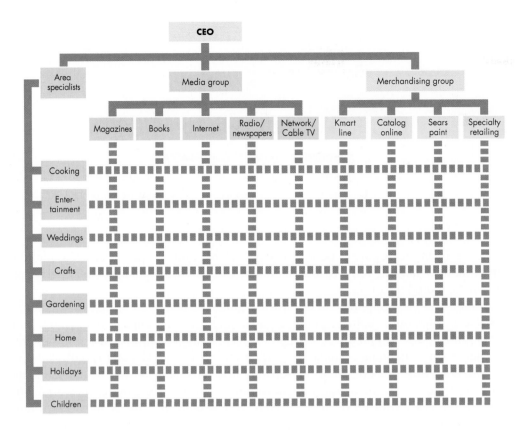

FIGURE 6.5

Matrix Organization at Martha Stewart

Layered on top of this structure are teams of lifestyle experts organized into groups such as cooking, crafts, weddings, and so forth. Although each group targets specific customer needs, they all work, as necessary, across all product groups. A wedding expert, for example, might contribute to an article on wedding planning for a Martha Stewart magazine, contribute a story idea for a Martha Stewart cable television program, and supply content for a Martha Stewart Web site. This same individual might also help select fabrics suitable for wedding gowns that are to be retailed.[12]

International Organization

As we saw in Chapter 4, many businesses today manufacture, purchase, and sell in the world market. Thus, several different **international organizational structures** have emerged. Moreover, as competition on a global scale becomes more complex, companies often find that they must experiment with the ways in which they respond.[13]

For example, when Wal-Mart *(www.walmartstores.com)* opened its first store outside the United States in 1992, it set up a special projects team to handle the logistics. As more stores were opened abroad in the mid-1990s, the firm created a small international department to handle overseas expansion. By 1999, however, international sales and expansion had become such a major part of Wal-Mart's operations that the firm created a separate international division headed up by a senior vice president. By 2002, international operations had become so important to Wal-Mart that the international division was further divided into geographic areas where the firm does business, such as Mexico and Europe.[14]

Organizations with important international operations often begin with the form of organization outlined in Figure 6.6. Other firms have also developed a wide range of approaches to international organizational structure. The French food giant Danone Group *(www.danonegroup.com)*, for instance, has three major product groups: dairy

international organizational structures
Approaches to organizational structure developed in response to the need to manufacture, purchase, and sell in global markets

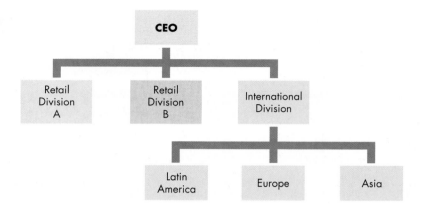

FIGURE 6.6

International Division Structure

products (Danone yogurts), bottled water (Evian), and cookies (Pim's). Danone's structure does not differentiate internationally but rather integrates global operations within each product group.[15]

Finally, some companies adopt a truly global structure in which they acquire resources (including capital), produce goods and services, engage in research and development, and sell products in whatever local market is appropriate, without any consideration of national boundaries. Until a few years ago, General Electric kept its international business operations as separate divisions. Now, however, the company functions as one integrated global organization. GE businesses around the world connect and interact with each other constantly, and managers freely move back and forth among them. This integration is also reflected in the top management team. The head of GE's audit team is French, the head of quality control is Dutch, and a German runs one of GE's core business groups.[16]

Organizational Design for the Twenty-First Century

As the world grows increasingly complex and fast-paced, organizations also continue to seek new forms of organization that permit them to compete effectively. Among the most popular of these new forms are the *boundaryless organization*, the *team organization*, the *virtual organization*, and the *learning organization*.

Boundaryless Organization The *boundaryless organization* is one in which traditional boundaries and structures are minimized or eliminated altogether. For example, General Electric's fluid organization structure, in which people, ideas, and information flow freely between businesses and business groups, approximates this concept. Similarly, as firms partner with their suppliers in more efficient ways, external boundaries disappear. Some of Wal-Mart's key suppliers are tied directly into the retailer's vaunted information system. As a result, when Wal-Mart distribution centers start running low on Wrangler blue jeans, the manufacturer gets the information as soon as the retailer. Wrangler proceeds to manufacture new inventory and to restock the distribution center without Wal-Mart's having to place a new order.

Team Organization *Team organization* relies almost exclusively on project-type teams, with little or no underlying functional hierarchy. People float from project to project as dictated by their skills and the demands of those projects. At Cypress Semiconductor *(www.cypress.com)*, T. J. Rodgers refuses to allow the organization to grow so large that it can't function this way. Whenever a unit or group starts getting

Say WHAT YOU MEAN

WHAT TO CALL THE BOSS

One of the big reasons why global companies are organized in different ways is the culture of their home countries. Consequently, not only organization but also culture influences the way decisions are made and communicated. In some companies, there's a big gap between senior management and those on the lower rungs, and communication across the gap is often quite formal. In other companies, because the vertical structure is less rigid, people tend to communicate in more familiar terms.

German companies, for example, tend to have fairly rigid structures, with jobs, authority, and responsibility clearly defined. Likewise, people in German organizations tend to respect status and titles. They're usually respectful of superiors and continue to use last names even where they're communicating with people they've known for years. Surprisingly, when it comes to decision making, German companies like to keep everyone in the loop and be sure that people at all levels know what's going on.

In contrast, U.S. companies tend to have formal organizational structures while fostering communication—even between senior managers and lower-level workers—that's often casual and easygoing, right down to the use of first names. Bosses command respect, but once they're outside the workplace, people from different levels interact easily.

In many Latin and South American cultures, bosses have a great deal of power and authority, and workers give them a corresponding degree of respect. Mexican workers sometimes call the boss *patrón*, and as the title suggests, the *patrón* is expected to provide employees with more than orders in the workplace: He's supposed to be a source of moral support and even material assistance and is a regular guest at weddings, funerals, and christenings (where he's often called on to serve as godfather).

Sensitivity to local workplace behavior and attitudes—to the ways in which information is communicated and authority exercised and accepted—is one of the most important qualities that a global company can bring to its relationships with foreign organizations.

---

too large, he simply splits it into smaller units. Therefore, the organization is composed entirely of small units. This strategy allows each unit to change direction, explore new ideas, and try new methods without having to deal with a rigid bureaucratic superstructure. Although few large organizations have actually reached this level of adaptability, Apple Computer *(www.apple.com)* and Xerox *(www.xerox.com)* are among those moving toward it.

Virtual Organization   Closely related to the team organization is the *virtual organization*. A *virtual organization* has little or no formal structure. Typically, it has only a handful of permanent employees, a very small staff, and a modest administrative facility. As the needs of the organization change, its managers bring in temporary workers, lease facilities, and outsource basic support services to meet the demands of each unique situation. As the situation changes, the temporary workforce changes in parallel, with some people leaving the organization and others entering. Facilities and the subcontracted services also change. In other words, the virtual organization exists only in response to its own needs.[17]

Global Research Consortium (GRC) *(www.worldvest.com)* is a virtual organization. GRC offers research and consulting services to firms doing business in Asia. As clients request various services, GRC's staff of three permanent employees subcontracts the work to an appropriate set of several dozen independent consultants and researchers with whom it has relationships. At any given time, therefore, GRC may

As the name suggests, the boundaryless organization has erased certain boundaries. GE Power Systems (*www.gepower.com/en_us*), which sells electricity-generating turbines, uses the Internet to eliminate a boundary that once separated its traditional functions from those of its customers. Using the Web to connect with GE's turbine optimizer, any operator of a GE turbine can compare its performance with other turbines of the same model. GE will also calculate the long-term savings of a given improvement—another task that, in the pre–e-business era, would have been performed by the buyer-operator.

have several projects under way with 20 or 30 people working on various projects. As the projects change, so too does the composition of the organization. Figure 6.7 illustrates a hypothetical virtual organization.

Learning Organization The so-called *learning organization* works to integrate continuous improvement with continuous employee learning and development. Specifically, a learning organization works to facilitate the lifelong learning and personal development of all of its employees while continually transforming itself to respond to changing demands and needs.

Whereas managers might approach the concept of a learning organization from a variety of perspectives, the most frequent goals are improved quality, continuous

FIGURE 6.7

The Virtual Organization

improvement, and performance measurement. The idea is that the most consistent and logical strategy for achieving continuous improvement is to constantly upgrade employee talent, skill, and knowledge. For example, if each employee in an organization learns one new thing each day and can translate that knowledge into work-related practice, continuous improvement will logically follow. Indeed, organizations that wholeheartedly embrace this approach believe that only through constant employee learning can continuous improvement really occur.

In recent years, many different organizations have implemented this approach on various levels. Shell Oil Co. (*www.countonshell.com*), for example, recently purchased an executive conference center north of its headquarters in Houston. Called the Shell Learning Center, the facility boasts state-of-the-art classrooms and instructional technology, lodging facilities, a restaurant, and recreational amenities, such as a golf course, swimming pool, and tennis courts. Line managers at the firm rotate through the center and serve as teaching faculty. Teaching assignments last anywhere from a few days to several months. At the same time, all Shell employees routinely attend training programs, seminars, and related activities, all the while gathering the latest information they need to have in order to contribute more effectively to the firm. Recent seminar topics have included time management, implications of the Americans with Disabilities Act, balancing work and family demands, and international trade theory.[18]

INFORMAL ORGANIZATION

Much of our discussion has focused on the organization's *formal structure*—its official arrangement of jobs and job relationships. In reality, however, all organizations also have another dimension—an *informal organization* within which people do their jobs in different ways and interact with other people in ways that do not follow formal lines of communication.

Formal Versus Informal Organizational Systems

The formal organization of a business is the part that can be seen and represented in chart form. The structure of a company, however, is by no means limited to the organization chart and the formal assignment of authority. Frequently, the **informal organization**—everyday social interactions among employees that transcend formal jobs and job interrelationships—effectively alters a company's formal structure. Indeed, this level of organization is sometimes just as powerful—if not more powerful—than the formal structure.

On the negative side, the informal organization can reinforce office politics that put the interests of individuals ahead of those of the firm. Likewise, a great deal of harm can be caused by distorted or inaccurate information communicated without management input or review. For example, if the informal organization is highlighting false information about impending layoffs, valuable employees may act quickly (and unnecessarily) to seek other employment. Among the more important elements of the informal organization are informal groups and the organizational grapevine.

informal organization
Network, unrelated to the firm's formal authority structure, of everyday social interactions among company employees

Informal Groups *Informal groups* are simply groups of people who decide to interact among themselves. They may be people who work together in a formal sense or who just get together for lunch, during breaks, or after work. They may talk about business, the boss, or nonwork-related topics like families, movies, and sports. Their impact on the organization may be positive (if they work together to support the organization), negative (if they work together in ways that run counter to the organization's interests), or irrelevant (if what they do is unrelated to the organization).

grapevine
Informal communication network
that runs through an organization

Organizational Grapevine The **grapevine** is an informal communication network that can run through an entire organization.[19] Grapevines are found in all organizations except the very smallest, but they do not always follow the same patterns as formal channels of authority and communication, nor do they necessarily coincide with them. Moreover, because the grapevine typically passes information orally, such information often becomes distorted in the process.

Attempts to eliminate the grapevine are fruitless, but, fortunately, managers do have some control over it. By maintaining open channels of communication and responding vigorously to inaccurate information, they can minimize the damage the grapevine can cause. In fact, the grapevine can actually be an asset. By getting to know the key people in the grapevine, for example, the manager can partially control the information they receive and use the grapevine to sound out employee reactions to new ideas (for example, a change in human resource policies or benefit packages). The manager can also get valuable information from the grapevine and use it to improve decision making.

Intrapreneuring

Sometimes organizations actually take steps to encourage the informal organization. They do so for a variety of reasons, two of which we have already discussed. First, most experienced managers recognize that the informal organization exists whether they want it or not. Second, many managers know how to use the informal organization to reinforce the formal organization. Perhaps more important, however, the energy of the informal organization can be harnessed to improve productivity.

intrapreneuring
Process of creating and maintaining
the innovation and flexibility of a
small-business environment within
the confines of a large organization

Many firms, including Rubbermaid, 3M, and Xerox, support a process called **intrapreneuring**: creating and maintaining the innovation and flexibility of a small-business environment within the confines of a large bureaucratic structure. The concept is basically sound. Historically, most innovations have come from individuals in small businesses (see Chapter 3). As businesses increase in size, however, innovation and creativity tend to become casualties in the battle for more sales and profits. In some large companies, new ideas are even discouraged, and champions of innovation have been stalled in midcareer.

Compaq *(www.compaq.com)*, which is now part of Hewlett-Packard, is an excellent example of how intrapreneuring works to counteract this trend. The firm has one major division, which is called the New Business Group. When a manager or engineer has an idea for a new product or product application, the individual takes it to the New Business Group and "sells" it. The managers in the group itself are then encouraged to help the innovator develop the idea for field-testing. If the product takes off and does well, it is then spun off into its own new business group or division. If it doesn't do as well as hoped, it may still be maintained as part of the New Business Group, or it may be phased out.

SELF-CHECK QUESTIONS 7–9

You should now be able to answer Self-Check Questions 7–9.*

7 Multiple Choice Which of the following is **not** a basic form of *organizational design?* [select one]: **(a)** functional organization; **(b)** process organization; **(c)** divisional organization; **(d)** matrix organization; **(e)** international organization.

8 Multiple Choice *Organizational designs for the twenty-first century* include which of the following?

[select one]: **(a)** boundaryless organization; **(b)** team organization; **(c)** virtual organization; **(d)** learning organization; **(e)** all of these.

9 True/False Few large businesses have informal organizations because of their formal and rigid organization charts.

***Answers to Self-Check Questions 7–9 can be found on p. 508.**

Continued from page 166

IS THERE SYNERGY AMONG BAKED GOODS, SHOE POLISH, AND UNDERWEAR?

C. Steven McMillan still has a few tricks up his sleeves. One bold move was developing a chain of retail stores called Inner Self. Each store features a spa-like atmosphere in which to sell Sara Lee's Hanes, Playtex, Bali, and Wonderbra products. Susan Nedved, head of development for Inner Self, thinks that the company-owned stores provide a more realistic and comforting environment for making underwear purchases than do some specialty outlets. "There seems to be an open void for another specialty concept that complements Victoria's Secret," says Nedved. "There was a need for shopping alternatives that really cater to the aging population."

McMillan remains confident that his strategy—more centralization, coordination, and focus—will do the trick at Sara Lee. "I do believe the things we're doing will enhance the growth rate of our company," he says. But many observers are less optimistic. As for Inner Self and under-wear, one analyst points out that "even if you fix that business, it's still apparel, and it's not really viewed as a high-value-added business."

And even if McMillan's strategy does manage to cut costs and increase market share, skeptics point out that there is no logic behind the idea of housing baked goods, meats, coffee, underwear, shoe polish, and household cleaners under one corporate roof. Unless McMillan can find some as yet undiscovered synergy among such disparate units, Sara Lee is probably headed for a breakup into several smaller, more focused, more profitable companies.

Questions for Discussion

1 Describe the basic structural components at Sara Lee.
2 What role does specialization play at Sara Lee?
3 What kinds of authority are reflected in this case?
4 What kind of organizational structure does Sara Lee seem to have?
5 What role has the informal organization played in Sara Lee's various acquisitions and divestitures?

■ SUMMARY OF LEARNING OBJECTIVES

1 Discuss the elements that influence a firm's *organizational structure*.

Common structural and operating components in all businesses include a series of *jobs to be done* and a *specific overall purpose*. Each organization must develop the most appropriate **organizational structure**—the specification of the jobs to be done and the ways in which they relate to one another.

Firms prepare **organization charts** to clarify structure and to show employees where they fit into a firm's operations. Each box represents a job, and solid lines define the **chain of command**, or *reporting relationships*. The charts of large firms are complex and include individuals at many levels. Because size prevents them from charting every manager, they may create single organization charts for overall corporate structure and separate charts for divisions.

2 Explain *specialization* and *departmentalization* as the building blocks of organizational structure.

Two activities constitute the building blocks of all organizations. The process of identifying specific jobs and designating people to perform them leads to **job specialization**. After they're specialized, jobs are grouped into logical units—the process of **departmentalization**. Departmentalization follows one (or any combination) of five forms: (1) **customer departmentalization**; (2) **product departmentalization**; (3) **process departmentalization**; (4) **geographic departmentalization**; or (5) **functional departmentalization**. Larger companies take advantage of different types of departmentalization for various levels.

3 Distinguish among *responsibility, authority, delegation,* and *accountability* and explain the differences between decision making in *centralized* and *decentralized organizations*.

After jobs have been specialized and departmentalized, firms establish decision-making hierarchies. They define reporting relationships so everyone will know who has responsibility for various decisions and operations. The development of this hierarchy results from a three-step process: (1) *assigning tasks*: determining who can make decisions and specifying how they're to be made; (2) *performing tasks*: implementing decisions that have been made; and (3) *distributing authority*: deciding whether the organization is to be centralized or decentralized. With fewer management layers, decentralized firms reflect a flat organizational structure.

4 Explain the differences among *functional, divisional, matrix,* and *international organizational structures* and describe the most popular new forms of organizational design.

Most firms rely on one of four basic forms of organizational structure: (1) **functional organization**; (2) **divisional organization**; (3) **matrix structure**; or (4) **international structure**. As global competition becomes more complex, companies may experiment with ways to respond. Some adopt truly global structures, acquiring resources and producing and selling products in local markets without consideration of national boundaries. Organizations continue to seek new forms of organization that permit them to compete effectively. Four of the most popular new forms are (1) the *boundaryless organization*; (2) the *team organization*; (3) the *virtual organization*; and (4) the *learning organization*.

5 Describe the *informal organization* and discuss *intrapreneuring*.

The formal organization is the part that can be represented in chart form. The **informal organization**—everyday social interactions among employees that transcend formal jobs and job interrelationships—may alter formal structure. There are two important elements in most informal organizations: (1) *informal groups* and (2) the **grapevine**. Many firms support **intrapreneuring**—creating and maintaining the innovation and flexibility of a small business within the confines of a large bureaucratic one.

■ KEY TERMS

organizational structure (p. 166)
organization chart (p. 167)
chain of command (p. 167)
job specialization (p. 168)
departmentalization (p. 169)

profit center (p. 169)
customer departmentalization
    (p. 170)
product departmentalization (p. 170)
process departmentalization (p. 170)

geographic departmentalization
    (p. 170)
functional departmentalization (p. 171)
responsibility (p. 173)
authority (p. 173)

delegation (p. 173)
accountability (p. 173)
centralized organization (p. 174)
decentralized organization (p. 174)
flat organizational structure (p. 175)
tall organizational structure (p. 175)
span of control (p. 175)

line authority (p. 177)
line department (p. 177)
staff authority (p. 178)
staff members (p. 178)
committee and team authority (p. 178)
functional organization (p. 179)
divisional organization (p. 179)

division (p. 180)
matrix structure (p. 180)
international organizational structures (p. 181)
informal organization (p. 185)
grapevine (p. 186)
intrapreneuring (p. 186)

■ QUESTIONS AND EXERCISES

Questions for Review

1 What is an organization chart? What purpose does it serve?

2 Explain the significance of size as it relates to organizational structure. Describe the changes that are likely to occur as an organization grows.

3 What is the difference between responsibility and authority?

4 Why do some managers have difficulties in delegating authority? Why does this problem tend to plague smaller businesses?

5 Why is a company's informal organization important?

Questions for Analysis

6 Draw up an organization chart for your college or university.

7 Describe a hypothetical organizational structure for a small printing firm. Describe changes that might be necessary as the business grows.

8 Compare and contrast the matrix and divisional approaches to organizational structure. How would you feel personally about working in a matrix organization in which you were assigned simultaneously to multiple units or groups?

Application Exercises

9 Interview the manager of a local service business—a fast-food restaurant. What types of tasks does this manager typically delegate? Is the appropriate authority also delegated in each case?

10 Using books, magazines, or personal interviews, identify a person who has succeeded as an intrapreneur. In what ways did the structure of the intrapreneur's company help this individual succeed? In what ways did the structure pose problems?

▶ BUILDING YOUR BUSINESS SKILLS

GETTING WITH THE PROGRAM

This exercise enhances the following SCANS workplace competencies: demonstrating basic skills, demonstrating thinking skills, exhibiting interpersonal skills, and working with information.

Goal

To encourage students to understand the relationship between organizational structure and a company's ability to attract and keep valued employees.

Situation

You are the founder of a small but growing high-technology company that develops new computer software. With your current workload and new contracts in the pipeline, your business is thriving except for one problem: You cannot find computer programmers for product development. Worse yet, current staff members are being lured away by other high-tech firms. After suffering a particularly discouraging personnel raid in which competitors captured three of your most valued employees, you schedule a meeting with your director of human resources to plan organizational changes designed to encourage worker loyalty. You already pay top dollar, but the continuing exodus tells you that programmers are looking for something more.

Method

Working with three or four classmates, identify some ways in which specific organizational changes might improve the working environment and encourage employee loyalty. As you analyze the following factors, ask yourself the obvious question: If I were a programmer, what organizational changes would encourage me to stay?

■ **Level of job specialization.** With many programmers describing their jobs as tedious because of the focus on detail in a narrow work area, what changes, if any, would you make in job specialization? Right now, for instance, few of your programmers have any say in product design.

■ **Decision-making hierarchy.** What decision-making authority would encourage people to stay? Is expanding employee authority likely to work better in a centralized or decentralized organization?

■ **Team authority.** Can team empowerment make a difference? Taking the point of view of the worker, describe the ideal team.

■ **Intrapreneuring.** What can your company do to encourage and reward innovation?

FOLLOW-UP QUESTIONS

1 With the average computer programmer earning nearly $70,000, and with all competitive firms paying top dollar, why might organizational issues be critical in determining employee loyalty?

2 If you were a programmer, what organizational factors would make a difference to you? Why?

3 As the company founder, how willing would you be to make major organizational changes in light of the shortage of qualified programmers?

 ## EXERCISING YOUR ETHICS

MINDING YOUR OWN BUSINESS

The Situation
Assume that you have recently gone to work for a large high-tech company. You have discovered an interesting arrangement in which one of your coworkers is engaging. Specifically, he blocks his schedule for the hour between 11:00 A.M. and 12:00 noon each day and does not take a lunch break. During this one-hour interval, he is actually running his own real estate business.

The Dilemma
You recently asked him how he manages to pull this off. "Well," he responded, "the boss and I never talked about it,

but she knows what's going on. They know they can't replace me, and I always get my work done. I don't use any company resources. So, what's the harm?" Interestingly, you also have a business opportunity that could be pursued in the same way.

QUESTIONS FOR DISCUSSION
1 What are the ethical issues in this situation?
2 What do you think most people would do in this situation?
3 What would you do in this situation?

 ## CRAFTING YOUR BUSINESS PLAN

DOCTORING THE ORGANIZATION

The Purpose of the Assignment
1 To provide an example that illustrates ways in which organizational options can be presented in a business plan in the framework of the *Business PlanPro (BPP) 2003* software package (Version 6.0).

2 To demonstrate how three chapter topics—organization structure, departmentalization, and authority and

responsibility—can be integrated as components in the *BPP* planning environment.

Assignment
After reading Chapter 6 in the textbook, open the BPP software and look around for information about organizational structure, departmentalization, and authority and responsibility as they apply to a sample firm: Medquip, Inc. *To find* Medquip, Inc., *do the following:*

Open *Business PlanPro*. Go to the toolbar and click on the "*Sample Plans*" icon. In the **Sample Plan Browser**, do a search using the **search category** *Instruments and related products*. From the resulting list, select the category entitled **Medical Equipment Develo. . .**, which is the location for *Medquip, Inc.* The screen you are looking at is the introduction page for *Medquip*'s business plan. Next, scroll down until you reach the **Table of Contents** for the *Medquip* business plan.

NOW RESPOND TO THE FOLLOWING QUESTIONS:

1 Construct an organization chart for *Medquip, Inc.* [Sites to see in *BPP* for this item: On the Table of Contents page, click on each of the following in turn:

6.0 Management Summary, 6.1 Organizational Structure, 6.2 Management Team, and **6.4 Personnel Plan**, including **Table: Personnel.**]

2 Explain how *Medquip*'s organizational structure is set up to take advantage of its competitor's weakness in product innovation. [Sites to see in *BPP*: On the Table of Contents page, click on **4.2.4 Main Competitors.**]

3 Which type of departmentalization—*customer, product, functional, or process*—does *Medquip* use? Give examples from *Medquip*'s business plan to support your answer.

4 For each job position at *Medquip*, how clearly are authority and responsibility delineated in the business plan?

 VIDEO EXERCISE

JUICING UP THE ORGANIZATION: NANTUCKET NECTARS

Learning Objectives
The purpose of this video is to help you:
1 Recognize how growth affects an organization's structure.
2 Discuss the reasons why businesses departmentalize.
3 Understand how flat organizations operate.

Synopsis
Tom Scott and Tom First founded Nantucket Nectars in 1989 with an idea for a peach drink. In the early days, the two ran the entire operation from their boat. These days, Nantucket Nectars has more than 130 employees split between headquarters in Cambridge, Massachusetts, and several field offices. As a result, management has developed a more formal structure. The company relies on cross-functional teams to handle special projects, such as the implementation of new accounting software. This and other strategies have helped Nantucket Nectars successfully manage rapid growth.

DISCUSSION QUESTIONS
1 **For analysis:** What type of organization is in place at Nantucket Nectars?
2 **For analysis:** How would you describe the top-level span of management at Nantucket Nectars?

3 **For application:** Nantucket Nectars may need to change its organization structure as it expands into new products and new markets. Under what circumstances might some form of divisional departmentalization be appropriate?

4 **For application:** Assume that Nantucket Nectars is purchasing a well-established beverage company with a tall structure stressing top-down control. What are some of the problems that management might face in integrating the acquired firm into the existing organization structure of Nantucket Nectars?

5 **For debate:** Assume that someone who is newly promoted into a management position at Nantucket Nectars cannot adjust to delegating work to lower-level employees. Should this new manager be demoted? Support your chosen position.

Online Exploration
Visit the Nantucket Nectars site at *(www.juiceguys.com)* and follow the links to read about the company and its products. Then use Hoover's Online at *(www.hoovers.com)* to search for the latest news about the company, which is formally known as Nantucket Allserve. Has it been acquired by a larger company, or has it acquired one or more smaller firms? What are the implications for the chain of command and decision making and the organizational structure of Nantucket Nectars?

After reading this chapter,
you should be able to:

1 Explain the meaning of the term *production* or *operations* and describe the four kinds of *utility* that operations processes provide.

2 Identify the characteristics that distinguish *service operations* from *goods production* and explain the main differences in the *service focus*.

3 Describe the factors involved in *operations planning*.

4 Identify some of the key tools for *total quality management*, including strategies for getting closer to the customer.

5 Explain how a *supply chain strategy* differs from traditional strategies for coordinating operations among firms.

A SUPERSONIC PROJECT GETS OFF THE GROUND

When the battle ended on October 26, 2001, Lockheed Martin Aeronautics Co. *(www.lockheedmartin.com)* had been given the green light to launch one of the biggest production projects in U.S. history. Capping a five-year, winner-take-all competition with rival Boeing, Lockheed had captured the largest defense contract ever awarded—the $200

MANAGING OPERATIONS AND IMPROVING QUALITY

> " The challenge will be to keep an organization intact, not lose momentum through confusion and inexperience, integrate various demands from outside parties, and keep the huge customer set engaged, onboard, and excited."
>
> —Tom Burbage, Lockheed manager, on the Joint Strike Fighter Project

billion Joint Strike Fighter (JSF) contract (which could be worth more than $320 billion over the next two or three decades).

Lockheed's design for the next generation of supersonic, radar-evading combat jet was just the beginning. The contract was awarded on the basis of experimental versions of the aircraft. Now the real work—detailed planning for production and then production itself—begins. Many observers think that the next phase—system development and demonstration (SDD)—will be the most difficult. SDD calls for building and demonstrating 22 aircraft (known in the United States as the F-35) to be delivered by 2005. The next phase—gearing up to full production—begins in 2008, with plans calling for the production of 3,000 planes—each worth from $28 million to $38 million—by 2040. During each phase, the U.S. Defense Department *(www.defenselink.mil)* will insist that aircraft perform reliably, that deliveries be on time, and that costs be met.

To get started, Lockheed's JSF team needs about 4,500 additional personnel (up from 500) during the first 18 months. But organizing the project goes far beyond Lockheed's walls because Lockheed, as prime contractor, is collaborating with Northrop Grumman Corp. *(www.northgrum.com)* and Britain's BAE Systems PLC *(www.baesystems.com)*. More than 70 U.S. and 18 international subcontractors at some 187 locations are involved, and, all told, more than 1,500 firms will supply everything from radar systems to bolts. Teamwork and technology will be key elements in tracking hundreds of thousands of components, and by 2005, specialists sitting at some 40,000 remote computers will be collaborating on the project.

Of course, the JSF aircraft is more than just hardware. Computers provide onboard brainpower for the advanced-performance capabilities of this electronic weapons platform. Combining huge arrays of electronic and software systems is the name of the game for JSF. Lockheed Martin is responsible for final integration, and although the technical hurdles are enormous, managerial logistics is also an area of concern. Reflecting on the number of people that his team must hire, Lockheed program manager Tom Burbage admits, "We've got a big scaling up to do. The challenge will be trying to keep an organization intact, not lose momentum through confusion and inexperience, integrate various demands from outside parties, and keep the huge customer set engaged, onboard, and excited about the airplane."

Satisfying multiple customers won't be easy. The three U.S. armed services want different versions of the fighter, as do military customers from Britain, Italy, Canada, Denmark, and Norway—all of whom want their own defense industries to share in the program. About 80 percent of all parts will be common to each model, but the rest will vary. The JSF production system, therefore, will have to be flexible enough to produce multiple models on schedule and within budget. Such requirements call for suppliers who can provide reliable components and subsystems—and the right ones for each model—to ensure a final assembly that meets delivery commitments.

Our opening story is continued on page 219.

■ GOODS AND SERVICE OPERATIONS

service operations
Activities producing intangible and tangible products, such as entertainment, transportation, and education

goods production
Activities producing tangible products, such as radios, newspapers, buses, and textbooks

You're always involved in business activities that provide goods and services to customers. You wake up to the sound of your favorite radio station and pick up a newspaper on your way to the bus stop, where you catch your ride to work or school. Your instructors, the bus driver, the clerk at the 7-Eleven store, and the morning radio announcer all work in **service operations**. They provide intangible and tangible service products, such as entertainment, transportation, education, and food preparation. Firms that make tangible products—radios, newspapers, buses, textbooks—are engaged in **goods production**.

Growth in the Service and Goods Sectors

Although the term *production* has historically referred to companies engaged in goods production, the concept as we now use it also means services. Many of the things that we need or want, from health care to fast food, are produced by service operations. As a rule, service-sector managers focus less on equipment and technology and more on the human element in operations. Why? Because success or failure may depend on provider–customer contact. Employees who deal directly with customers affect customer feelings about the service, and as we will see, a key difference between production and service operations is the customer's involvement in the latter.

Following the terrorist attacks of September 11, 2001, employment in the U.S. manufacturing sector fell to about 19 percent of all private-sector jobs. Even so, the number has remained steady, hovering around 20 percent for four decades, and the economic significance of manufacturing is going up. For example, real income from manufacturing has increased by over 30 percent in the past 10 years. So effective are new manufacturing methods—and so committed are U.S. manufacturers to using them—that in 2001, the United States remained ahead of Germany and Japan in manufactured exports, retaining the number-one spot for the eighth straight year.

Of course, both goods and service industries are important, but employment has risen significantly in the service sector while remaining stagnant in goods production. By 2002, service employment accounted for 81 percent of the U.S. private-sector workforce—107 million jobs. Much of this growth comes from e-commerce and from business services, health care, amusement and recreation, and education. Employment projections indicate that services will remain the faster-growing job source in the immediate future.[1] The gap in average wages between the two sectors has closed to just $19 per week more for goods-producing workers. More important, the distribution of high-paying and low-paying jobs in each sector is now equal.

By 2001, the service sector also provided 52 percent of national income, as opposed to about 50 percent in 1947. The service sector's greater percentage of gross domestic product (GDP)—the value of all the goods and services produced by the economy, excluding foreign income—has climbed since 1984 until it is now 33 percent more than goods-producing GDP. At the same time, the 19 percent of the workforce in manufacturing produces nearly 40 percent of the nation's GDP.[2] In China, by contrast, manufacturing employs 70 percent of the urban labor force but produces only 30 percent of the national income.

Although companies are typically classified as either goods producers or service providers, the distinction is often blurred. For one thing, all businesses are service operations to some extent. Consider General Electric *(www.ge.com)*, which inspires thoughts of appliances (and jet engines). But GE is not just a goods producer. According to its own annual report, "The General Electric Company is the world's largest diversified services company as well as a provider of high-quality, high-technology industrial and consumer products." GE service operations include broadcasting (NBC), finance, insurance, investment, and real estate.

The Growth of Global Operations

Global competition has made production a faster-paced, more complex activity. Although the factory remains the centerpiece in manufacturing, it bears little resemblance to its counterpart of a decade ago. Smoke and grease and the clang of steel on steel have been replaced by computers and other high-tech machines in contaminant-free, climate-controlled "clean rooms."

Today's firm may no longer face the pressures of continuous mass production, but it does face constant change. New technologies make machines that run cleaner, faster, and safer and that operate on a global scale. For online manufacturing, machines can log on to the Internet, adjust their own settings, and make minor decisions without human help. They can communicate with other machines in the company (via an

Quanta Computer Inc. *(www.quantata.com)* of Taiwan supplies Dallas-based Dell Computer *(www.dell.com)* with 55 percent of its notebook PCs. The world's number-one notebook maker does just about everything for Dell's notebook unit and pretty much does it by matching Dell's renowned skill at just-in-time manufacturing: Quanta can assemble the hardware, install the software, test the final product, and ship to Dell in 48 hours. The key is the Internet, which allows Dell and other customers much greater freedom in placing customized orders around the clock.

intranet) and with other companies' machines (via the Internet). With the Internet, producers of both services and goods can integrate their production activities with those of far-off suppliers and customers.

■ CREATING VALUE THROUGH OPERATIONS

utility
A product's ability to satisfy a human want

To understand a firm's production processes, we need to know what kinds of benefits its production provides, both for itself and for its customers. Production, of course, provides businesses with economic results: profits, wages, and goods purchased from other companies. At the same time, it provides consumers with **utility**—the ability of a product to satisfy a want or need.

Production helps to provide four kinds of utility:

■ When a company turns out ornaments in time for Christmas, it creates *time utility*; that is, it makes products available when consumers want them.

■ When a department store opens its annual Trim-a-Tree department, it creates *place utility*: It makes products available where they are convenient for consumers.

■ By making a product available for consumers to own and use, production creates *ownership* or *possession utility*, which customers enjoy when they buy boxes of ornaments and decorate their trees.

■ Production makes products available in the first place: By turning raw materials into finished goods, production creates *form utility*, as when an ornament maker combines glass, plastic, and other materials to create tree decorations.

Although production can contribute to all four kinds of utility, its role in two areas is most obvious. It provides *time utility* by making products available when consumers want them and *form utility* by converting raw materials and human skills into finished goods and services.

Because the term *production* has long been associated with manufacturing, writers have recently replaced it with *operations*, a term reflecting both service and goods production. **Operations** (or **production**) **management** is the systematic direction and control of the processes that transform resources into finished services and goods that create value for and provide benefits to customers. In overseeing production, inventory, and quality control, **operations** (or **production**) **managers** are responsible for ensuring that operations processes create value and provide benefits.

As Figure 7.1 shows, operations managers draw up plans to transform resources into products. First, they bring together basic resources: knowledge, physical materials, equipment, and labor. Then they put them to effective use in the production facility. As demand for a product increases, they schedule and control work to produce the required amount. Finally, they control costs, quality levels, inventory, and facilities and equipment.

Some operations managers work in factories; others work in offices and stores. Farmers are operations managers who create utility by transforming soil, seeds, fuel, and other inputs into soybeans, milk, and other outputs. They may hire crews of workers to plant and harvest, opt instead for automated machinery, or prefer some combination of workers and machinery. These decisions affect costs, the role of buildings and equipment in operations, and the quality and quantity of goods produced.

operations (or **production**) **management**
Systematic direction and control of the processes that transform resources into finished products that create value and provide benefits to customers

operations (or **production**) **managers**
Managers responsible for production, inventory, and quality control

Operations Processes

An **operations process** is a set of methods and technologies used to produce a good or a service. We classify types of production according to differences in operations processes. We can classify goods by asking whether an operations process combines resources or breaks them into component parts. We can classify services according to the extent of customer contact required.

operations process
Set of methods used in the production of a good or service

analytic process
Production process in which resources are broken down into components to create finished products

Goods-Manufacturing Processes: Analytic Versus Synthetic Processes

All goods-manufacturing processes can be classified by the *analytic* or *synthetic* nature of the transformation process. An **analytic process** breaks down resources into

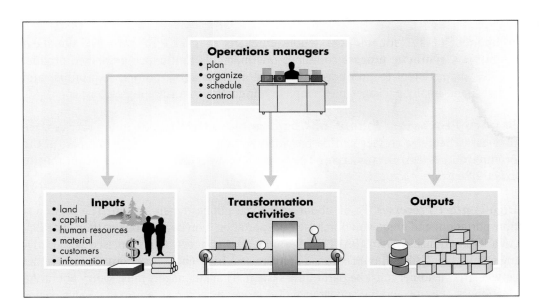

FIGURE 7.1

Resource Transformation Process

ENTREPRENEURSHIP and *New Ventures*

One Businessperson's Trash Is Another's New Venture

Norcal Waste Systems *(www.sunsetscavenger.com)* isn't a small company; it boasts 400,000 residential, industrial, and commercial customers in 50 California communities, including San Francisco. But size and 50 years' success aren't slowing the company's innovative approach to garbage collection and waste management. In fact, its entrepreneurial spirit is propelling this 100-percent employee-owned firm into a new venture in creative recycling: turning food scraps to fine wine.

The transformation is not exactly direct. Norcal jumped at the opportunity to invest in a unique idea for turning organic waste—food trimmings from produce markets and food waste from restaurants—into a useful product. Instead of dumping it in a landfill, Norcal collects organic material to use in a process that converts waste into finished compost. The compost is then bagged and sold as a soil reconditioner, mostly to California vineyards. Always looking for better ways to grow stronger grapevines, vineyard managers in Sonoma–Napa Valley apply Norcal compost between rows of vines because it returns nitrogen and other nutrients to the soil.

"You can't shortchange the soil," says Clarence Jenkins, owner of Madrone Vineyard Management *(www. travelenvoy.com/wine/Napa/ Smith-Madrone-Vineyard.htm)*. "The Norcal compost is a very good product and is very cost-effective. We get better soil structure, and eventually because of that structure we will get better plants."

Winegrowers and organic farmers prefer compost because, unlike most inorganic fertilizers, it's nontoxic. It also aerates the soil and helps it retain water.

Three Norcal subsidiaries collaborate in the composting process, which features new technologies to separate, collect, and deliver incoming waste to a specially designed production facility. Sunset Scavenger *(www.sunsetscavenger. com/sunset.htm)* and Golden Gate Disposal & Recycling *(www.ysdi.com/goldengate.htm)* collect compostable material from over 1,400 food-related businesses and thousands of households in the San Francisco Bay Area. Every day, more than 300 tons of waste are removed from the standard waste-disposal stream and delivered to Jepson Prairie Organics *(www.jepsonprairieorganics.com)*, where finished compost is produced in a three-month conversion cycle.

The various participants in and beneficiaries of the enterprise—customers, waste contributors, and communities—are enthusiastic about Norcal's profitable new twist on recycling. In addition to vineyards, output buyers include wholesalers who sell bagged product to landscapers, nurseries, and garden stores. On the input side, participating businesses benefit because the venture reduces garbage bills. Bay Area officials like it because it reduces the need for landfills. "Innovative programs like Norcal's Composting Program," says Oakland Mayor Jerry Brown, "bring us closer to realizing our waste-reduction goals while providing cost savings for Oakland's businesses."

---

synthetic process
Production process in which resources are combined to create finished products

components (as Tyson reduces whole chickens to packaged parts for the meat counter). A **synthetic process** combines raw materials to produce a finished product (as GE shapes steel to produce a refrigerator; then adds motors, lightbulbs, and shelves; and finally packages the complete refrigerator in a shipping carton).

Service Processes: Extent of Customer Contact In classifying services, we may ask whether a service can be provided without the customers being part of the production system. In answering this question, we classify services according to *extent of customer contact*.[3]

High-Contact Processes Think about your local public transit system. The service is transportation, and when you purchase transportation, you board a bus or train. The Bay Area Rapid Transit System (BART) *(www.bart.gov)* connects San Francisco with outlying suburbs and, like all public transit systems, is a **high-contact system**: To receive the service, the customer must be part of the system. Thus, managers must worry about the cleanliness of trains and the appearance of stations. By contrast, a firm that ships coal is not concerned with the appearance of its trains. It is a low-contact system.

high-contact system
Level of customer contact in which the customer is part of the system during service delivery

Low-Contact Processes Now consider the check-processing operations at your bank. Workers sort checks that have been cashed that day and send them to the banks on which they were drawn. This operation is a **low-contact system**: Customers are not in contact with the bank while the service is performed. They receive the service—funds are transferred to cover checks—without setting foot in the processing center. Utilities, auto repair shops, and lawn-care services are also low-contact systems.

low-contact system
Level of customer contact in which the customer need not be a part of the system to receive the service

Differences Between Service and Manufacturing Operations

Both service and manufacturing operations transform raw materials into finished products. In service operations, however, the raw materials, or inputs, are not glass or steel. Rather, they are people who have either unsatisfied needs or possessions needing care or alteration. In service operations, then, finished products or outputs are people with needs met and possessions serviced.

Focus on Performance Thus, there is at least one obvious difference between service and manufacturing operations. Whereas goods are *produced*, services are *performed*. Therefore, customer-oriented performance is a key factor in measuring the effectiveness of a service company. The reputation of Wal-Mart *(www.walmart.com)* stems in part from a policy of speedy product delivery that measures efficiency not in days but in minutes and seconds. A strong customer-focus strategy means getting fast supplier responses, streamlining transactions, and keeping the right merchandise on store shelves. To implement this strategy, Wal-Mart has made technology—namely, its vaunted computer and telecommunications system—a core competency.

There are four areas of service operations that often make them more complex than goods production: *focus on process and outcome, focus on service characteristics, focus on the customer-service link*, and *focus on service quality considerations*.

Focus on Process and Outcome Manufacturing operations focus on the outcome of the production process—for example, on the finished refrigerator. But the products of most service operations are really combinations of goods and services. Services, therefore, must focus on the transformation process as well as on its outcome—both on making a pizza and on delivering it. Service workers thus need different skills. Gas company employees may need interpersonal skills to calm frightened customers who have reported gas leaks. The job, therefore, can mean more than just repairing pipes. Factory workers who install gas pipes in mobile homes don't need such skills.

Focus on Service Characteristics Service transactions reflect the fact that service products are characterized by three qualities: *intangibility, customization*, and *unstorability*.

1 **Intangibility.** Often services can't be touched, tasted, smelled, or seen. An important value, therefore, is the *intangible* value that the customer receives in the form of pleasure, satisfaction, or a feeling of safety. When you hire an attorney, you purchase not only the intangible quality of legal expertise but also the equally intangible reassurance that help is at hand. Some services also provide tangible elements. Your attorney, for instance, can draw up a will that you can keep in your safe-deposit box.

2 **Customization.** When you visit a doctor, you expect to be treated for your symptoms, not someone else's. Likewise, when you buy insurance or get your

hair cut, you expect these services to meet your needs. They must, in other words, be *customized*.

3 **Unstorability.** Many services—trash collection, transportation, child care, and house cleaning—can't be produced ahead of time and then stored. If a service isn't used when available, it's usually wasted. Services, then, are typically characterized by a high degree of *unstorability*.

Focus on the Customer-Service Link Because they transform customers or their possessions, service operations often treat the customer as part of the operations process itself. To get a haircut, for example, most of us have to go to the barbershop or beauty salon.

As physical participants in the operations process, consumers can affect it. As a customer, you expect the salon to be conveniently located, to be open for business at convenient times, and to offer needed services at reasonable prices. Accordingly, the manager sets hours of operation, available services, and an appropriate number of employees to meet customer requirements.

E-Commerce: The "Virtual Presence" of the Customer E-commerce introduces a "virtual," as opposed to the physical, presence of customers. Consumers interact with sellers electronically and in real time, collecting information about product features, delivery schedules, and postsale service. You enjoy 24-hour access to information via automated call centers, and if you want human interaction, you can talk with live respondents or log on to chat rooms. Many companies invite virtual customers into the system by building customer-communications relationships. The online travel agency Expedia.com responds to your personalized profile with an e-mail greeting, presents you with a tailor-made Web page the next time you sign on, maintains chat rooms where you can compare notes with other customers, and notifies you of upcoming special opportunities.[4]

Focus on Service Quality Considerations Consumers use different measures to judge services and goods. Most service managers know that quality of work and quality of service are not necessarily the same thing. Your car, for example, may have

Studies have shown that acupuncture can help relieve nausea, pain, and headaches, and hospitals looking for a competitive edge through a wider array of services now offer alternative forms of medicine, including chiropractic, homeopathy, and herbal medicine. There's also a treatment called "remote healing," in which therapeutic prayers are sent to distant patients, but most alternative treatments, like most traditional treatments, are customized, high-contact services: They're tailored to meet the needs of a specific patient who must schedule a visit to a specialized service center.

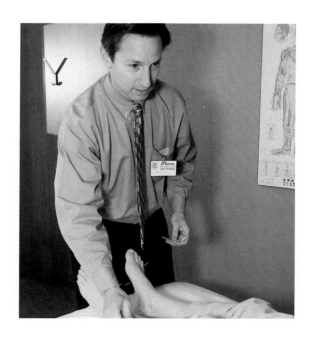

been flawlessly repaired, but you'll probably be unhappy with the service if you're forced to pick it up a day later than promised.

SELF-CHECK QUESTIONS 1–3

You should now be able to answer Self-Check Questions 1–3.*

1 **True/False** Whereas the term *production* refers primarily to the creation of physical goods, the term *operations* refers to activities for providing services to customers.

2 **Multiple Choice** Which of the following is **not** true regarding *operations processes*? [select one]: **(a)** In high-contact service processes, the customer is a part of the process. **(b)** All goods-manufacturing processes may be classified as either analytic or synthetic. **(c)** A chicken-processing plant (one that prepares chickens for grocery stores) is a good example of an analytic process. **(d)** Foot surgery is a good example of a low-contact operation.

3 **Multiple Choice** Which of the following is **true** regarding *differences between service and manufacturing operations*? [select one]: **(a)** Whereas manufacturing operations focus on the outcome of the production process, service operations focus on both the transformation process and its outcome. **(b)** The products offered by most service operations are intangible and do not involve physical goods. **(c)** Whereas service operations are customized for customers, manufacturing operations focus on mass-production processes. **(d)** Customers generally use the same measures for judging the quality of service products and physical goods products.

***Answers to Self-Check Questions 1–3 can be found on p. 508.**

■ OPERATIONS PLANNING

Now that we've contrasted goods and services, let's turn to a general discussion of production as an activity that results in both goods and services. Like all good managers, we start with planning. Managers from many departments contribute to decisions about operations. As Figure 7.2 shows, however, no matter how many decision makers are involved, the process is a series of logical steps. Success depends on the final result of this logical sequence of decisions.

The business plan and forecasts developed by top managers guide operations planning. The business plan outlines goals and objectives, including the specific goods and services that the firm will offer. In this section, we survey the main elements of operations planning, discussing the planning activities that fall into one of five categories: *capacity, location, layout, quality*, and *methods planning*.

Capacity Planning

The amount of a product that a company can produce under normal conditions is its **capacity**. A firm's capacity depends on how many people it employs and the number and size of its facilities. Long-range planning considers both current and future capacity.[5]

capacity
Amount of a product that a company can produce under normal working conditions

FIGURE 7.2

Operations Planning and Control

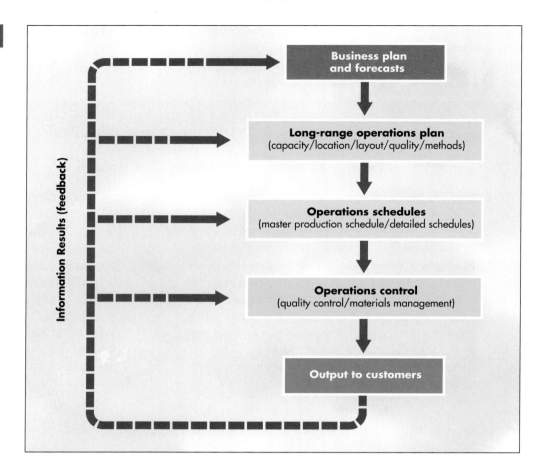

Capacity Planning for Producing Goods   Capacity planning for producing goods means ensuring that a firm's capacity slightly exceeds normal demand for its product. To see why this is the best policy, consider the alternatives. If capacity is too small for demand, the company must turn away customers—a situation that cuts into profits and alienates both customers and salespeople. If capacity greatly exceeds demand, the firm is wasting money by maintaining a plant that's too large, by keeping excess machinery online, or by employing too many workers.

The stakes are high in capacity decisions: While expanding fast enough to meet future demand and to protect market share from competitors, firms must also weigh the increased costs of expanding. In part, Intel Corp. *(www.intel.com)* enjoys more than 70-percent market share in the semiconductor business because of the $11 billion invested in capacity expansion between 1991 and 1995 and the $625 million spent to buy Digital Equipment's Massachusetts factory in 1998.[6]

Capacity Planning for Producing Services   In low-contact processes, maintaining inventory lets managers set capacity at the level of average demand. The JCPenney *(www.jcpenney.com)* catalog warehouse may hire enough order fillers to handle 1,000 orders daily. When orders exceed this average, some are placed in inventory—set aside in a "to be done" file—and then processed on a day when fewer than 1,000 orders come in. In high-contact processes, managers must plan capacity to meet peak demand. A supermarket, for instance, has far more cash registers than it needs on an average day, but on Saturday morning or during the three days before Thanksgiving, they'll all be running at full capacity.

Location Planning

Because location affects its production costs and flexibility, sound location planning is crucial for factories, offices, and stores. Depending on its site, a company may be able to produce low-cost products or find itself at a cost disadvantage relative to its competitors.

Location Planning for Producing Goods In goods-producing operations, location decisions are influenced by proximity to raw materials and markets, availability of labor, energy and transportation costs, local and state regulations and taxes, and community living conditions. At General Motors in Brazil, for example, GM and its suppliers operate a highly efficient assembly plant that relies on outside producers to supply large components such as fully assembled dashboards. Operations are more efficient because each supplier specializes in one component, and to resupply parts and reduce transportation costs, the factories of 16 suppliers share on-site floor space. They reduce needless inventory by delivering customized modules in just-in-time sequence to the nearby final assembly line.[7]

Location Planning for Producing Services Low-contact services can be located either near to or far from resource supplies, labor, or transportation outlets. At Wal-Mart, for example, distribution managers regard Wal-Mart outlets as their customers. In order to ensure that truckloads of merchandise flow quickly to stores, distribution centers are located near the hundreds of Wal-Mart stores that they supply, not near the companies that supply them.

High-contact services must locate near the customers who participate in the system. Thus, fast-food restaurants such as Taco Bell and McDonald's now locate in nontraditional locations with high traffic—dormitories, hospital cafeterias, and shopping malls. They can also be found in Wal-Mart outlets and Meijer Supermarkets that draw large crowds. Some McDonald's outlets are located at highway rest stops, and Domino's Pizza and KFC can be found on military bases.

Layout Planning

Layout of machinery, equipment, and supplies determines whether a company can respond efficiently to demand for more and different products or whether it finds itself unable to match competitors' speed and convenience.

Layout Planning for Producing Goods In facilities that produce goods, layout must be planned for three types of space:

1 **Productive facilities:** workstations and equipment for transforming raw materials, for example
2 **Nonproductive facilities:** storage and maintenance areas
3 **Support facilities:** offices, restrooms, parking lots, cafeterias, and so forth

In this section, we focus on productive facilities. Alternatives include *process, cellular,* and *product layouts*.

Process Layouts In a **process layout**, which is well suited to *job shops* specializing in custom work, equipment and people are grouped according to function. In a custom bakery, machines blend batter in an area devoted to mixing, baking occurs in the oven

process layout
Spatial arrangement of production activities that groups equipment and people according to function

area, and cakes are decorated on tables in a finishing area. Machine, woodworking, and dry cleaning shops often use process layouts.

cellular layout
Spatial arrangement of production facilities designed to move families of products through similar flow paths

Cellular Layouts **Cellular layouts** work well when a family (or similar group) of products follows a fixed flow path. A clothing manufacturer may dedicate a cell, or designated area, to making pockets—pockets for shirts, coats, blouses, trousers, and slacks. Although each type of pocket is unique in shape, size, and style, all go through the same steps. Within the cell, various types of equipment (for cutting, trimming, and sewing) are arranged close together in the appropriate sequence. All pockets pass stage by stage through the cell from beginning to end in a nearly continuous flow.

Cellular layouts have several advantages. Because similar products require less machine adjustment, equipment setup time is less than that entailed by process layouts. Because flow distances are usually shorter, there is less material handling and transit time. Inventories of goods in progress are lower and paperwork is simpler because material flows are more orderly.

product layout
Spatial arrangement of production activities designed to move resources through a smooth, fixed sequence of steps

assembly line
Product layout in which a product moves step-by-step through a plant on conveyor belts or other equipment until it is completed

Product Layouts A **product layout** is set up to make one type of product in a fixed sequence and is arranged according to its production requirements. It is efficient for producing large volumes of product quickly and often uses an **assembly line**: A partially finished product moves step-by-step through the plant on conveyor belts or other equipment, often in a straight line, until the product is completed. Automobile, food-processing, and television-assembly plants use product layouts.

They are efficient because the work skill is built into the equipment, allowing unskilled labor to perform simple tasks. But they are often inflexible, especially if they require specialized equipment that's hard to rearrange for new applications. Workers can also get bored, and when someone is absent or overworked, those farther down the line can't help out.

Layout Planning for Producing Services Service firms use some of the same layouts as goods producers. In a low-contact system, the facility should be arranged to enhance the performing of the service. A mail-processing facility at UPS or FedEx, therefore, looks very much like a factory product layout. Machines and people are arranged in the order in which they help to mass-process mail. In contrast, Kinko's Copy Centers *(www.kinkos.com)* use process layouts for custom jobs. Specific functions such as photocopying, computing, binding, photography, and laminating are performed in specialized areas of the store.

High-contact systems should be arranged to meet customer needs. Piccadilly Cafeterias *(www.piccadilly.com)* focuses both layout and services on the groups that eat there most: families and elderly people. As you can see in Figure 7.3, customers enter to find high chairs and rolling baby beds for wheeling children through the line. Servers carry trays for the elderly and those pushing strollers. Note that customers must pass by the whole serving line before making selections. Not only does this layout help them make up their minds; it also tempts them to select more.

Quality Planning

Every operations plan must ensure that products meet the firm's quality standards. The American Society for Quality *(www.asq.org)* defines *quality* as the combination of "characteristics of a product or service that bear on its ability to satisfy stated or implied needs."[8] Such features may include a reasonable price and consistent performance in delivering the benefits it promises. Quality planning prepares employees for continuously improving the firm's products and production methods.

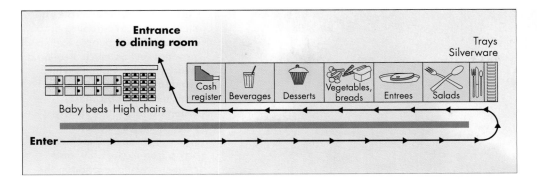

FIGURE 7.3

Layout of a Typical Piccadilly Cafeteria

Methods Planning

In designing operations systems, managers must identify each production step and the specific methods for performing it. They can then reduce waste and inefficiency by examining procedures on a step-by-step basis—an approach sometimes called *methods improvement*.

Methods Improvement in Goods To improve goods production, a manager begins by documenting current methods. A detailed description, often using a diagram called the process flowchart, is helpful in organizing and recording information. The flowchart identifies the sequence of production activities, movements of materials, and work performed at each stage of the process. It can then be analyzed to isolate wasteful activities, sources of delay, and other inefficiencies. The final step is implementing improvements.

At Mercury Marine *(www.mercurymarine.com)*, a study of the process flow from raw materials to assembly (the final production step) revealed inefficiencies in the production of stern-drive units for power boats. Each product passed through 122 steps, traveled nearly 21,000 feet (almost 4 miles), and was handled by 106 people. Analysis revealed that only 27 steps added value to the product (for example, drilling, painting). Work methods were revised to eliminate nonproductive activities. Mercury ultimately saved money in labor, inventory, paperwork, and space requirements. Customer orders were also filled much faster.

Methods Improvement in Services In a low-contact process, methods improvements can speed up services ranging from mowing lawns to drawing up legal documents. At Dell Computer *(www.dell.com)*, for example, methods analysis eliminates unnecessary steps so that orders for computers, whether received online or by phone, are processed quickly. Committed to efficient selling by means of electronic technology, Dell can boast extremely fast delivery as a specific value of its products.

Design for Customer Contact in Services In high-contact services, managers must develop procedures that clearly spell out the ways in which workers interact with customers. Procedures must cover such activities as exchanging information or money, delivering and receiving materials, and even making physical contact. The next time you visit your dentist's office, notice how dental hygienists scrub and wear disposable gloves. They also scrub after patient contact and rescrub before working on the next patient. This high-contact system depends on strict procedures for avoiding contact that can transmit disease.

This control room operates a steel mill in Luxembourg that employs 1,000 people to produce just as much steel as a nearby traditional mill which needed 5,000 people (and which is out of business). Minimills like those run by Luxembourg's Arcelor *(www.arcelor.com)* melt down scrap iron exclusively, and almost every operation in the facility is automated. From the control room, for example, computers move raw materials through electric-arc furnaces, pour liquid steel into copper molds, and cut strips of molded steel into desired lengths. The workforce is really a skeleton crew of technicians.

SELF-CHECK QUESTIONS 4–6

You should now be able to answer Self-Check Questions 4–6.*

4 True/False *Capacity planning* for low-contact service operations differs from capacity planning for high-contact services because of the inventory of waiting jobs in a low-contact facility.

5 Multiple Choice Which of the following is **true** about *layout planning*? [select one]: **(a)** Most high-contact services have facilities with product layouts. **(b)** Process layouts, also called assembly lines, are well suited for high-volume, continuous-flow operations. **(c)** Cellular layouts are useful for making a family of similar (though not identical) products that follow a fixed flow path. **(d)** Process layouts are appropriate for manufacturing operations but not for service operations.

6 Multiple Choice Which of the following is **not** **true** about *operations planning*? [select one]: **(a)** Location planning for goods-producing facilities and for services producers is influenced by proximity to suppliers and customers. **(b)** Methods improvements are feasible in goods-producing operations but are often impossible in service operations because of the unpredictability of customer behavior. **(c)** Operations planning should ensure that customers are satisfied by ensuring that products meet the firm's quality standards. **(d)** The firm's overall business plan, along with forecasts of future demand for current and existing products, should be the driving force for operations planning.

Answers to Self-Check Questions 4–6 can be found on p. 508.

◼ OPERATIONS SCHEDULING

Once they have determined the needed production resources, managers must develop timetables for acquiring and using them. This aspect of operations is called *scheduling*.

Scheduling Goods Operations

Scheduling of goods production occurs at different levels. First, a top-level **master production schedule** shows which products will be produced, when production will take place, and what resources will be used during specified time periods. Logan Aluminum Inc., for example, makes coils of aluminum that its main customers, Atlantic Richfield and Alcan Aluminum, use to make aluminum cans. Logan's master schedule covers 60 weeks and shows how many coils will be made each week. For various types of coils, it specifies how many of each will be produced. "We need this planning and scheduling system," says materials manager Candy McKenzie, "to determine how much of what product we can produce each and every month."

This information, however, is not complete. Manufacturing personnel must also know the location of all coils on the plant floor and their various stages of production. Start-up and stop times must be assigned, and employees need scheduled work assignments. Detailed short-term schedules fill in these blanks; they allow managers to use customer orders and information about equipment status to update sizes and variety of coils to be made each day.

master production schedule
Schedule showing which products will be produced, when production will take place, and what resources will be used

Scheduling Service Operations

Service scheduling may involve both work and workers. In a low-contact service, work scheduling may be based either on desired completion dates or on the time of order arrivals. Let's say, for example, that several cars are scheduled for repairs at your local garage. If your car is not scheduled until 3:30, it may sit idle for several hours even if it was the first to be dropped off. In such businesses, reservations and appointments smooth ups and downs in demand.

In scheduling workers, managers must also consider efficiency and costs. McDonald's guarantees workers that they will be scheduled for at least four hours at a time. To accomplish this goal, McDonald's uses overlapping shifts. The ending hours for some employees overlap the beginning hours for others. The overlap provides maximum coverage during peak periods.

Tools for Scheduling Special projects, such as plant renovations or relocations, often require close coordination and precise timing. In these cases, scheduling is facilitated by special tools, such as *Gantt* and *PERT charts*.

Gantt Charts A **Gantt chart** diagrams steps to be performed and specifies the time required to complete each step. The manager lists all activities needed to complete the work, estimates the time required for each, and checks the progress of the project against the chart. If it's ahead of schedule, some workers may be shifted to another project. If it's behind schedule, workers may be added or completion delayed.[9]

Figure 7.4 shows a Gantt chart for the renovation of a college classroom. It shows progress to date and schedules remaining work. The current date is 5/11. Note that workers are about one-half week behind in removing old floor tiles and reworking tables and chairs.

Gantt chart
Production schedule diagramming the steps in a project and specifying the time required for each

PERT Charts PERT—short for *Program Evaluation and Review Technique*—is useful for customized projects in which numerous activities must be coordinated. Like Gantt charts, **PERT charts** break down a large project into steps and specify the time required to perform each one. Unlike Gantt charts, however, PERT not only shows the necessary *sequence* of activities but also identifies the *critical path* for meeting project goals.[10]

PERT chart
Production schedule specifying the sequence and critical path for performing the steps in a project

FIGURE 7.4

Gantt Chart

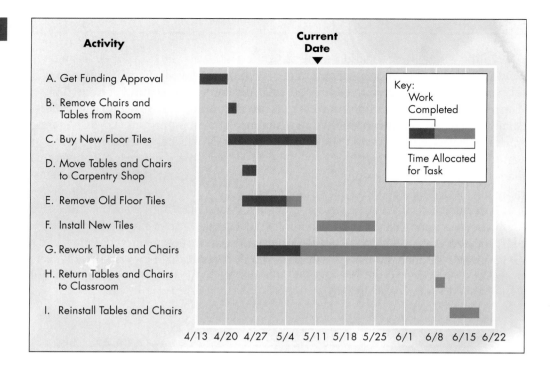

Figure 7.5 shows a PERT chart for the classroom renovation that we visited earlier. The critical path consists of activities *A, B, D, G, H,* and *I.* It's "critical" because any delay in completing any activity will cause workers to miss the completion deadline (9½ weeks after start-up). First, no activity can be started until all preceding activities are done. Chairs and tables can't be returned to the classroom (*H*) until after they've been reworked (*G*) and after new tiles are installed (*F*). Second, the chart identifies activities that will cause delays unless special action is taken at the right time. By reassigning workers and equipment, managers can speed up potentially late activities and keep on schedule.

FIGURE 7.5

PERT Chart

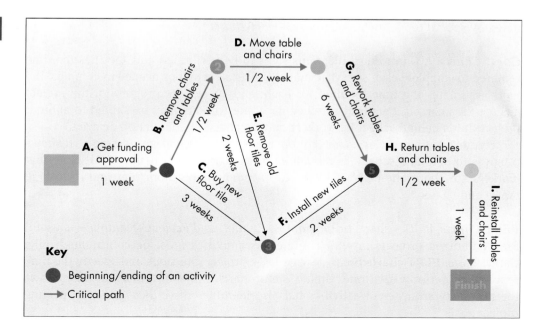

Say WHAT YOU MEAN

TO BE OR NOT TO BE ON TIME

We all use time to organize our lives, and in the United States, we're particularly avid clock watchers. In some cultures, however, people think a little differently about time, and the differences can have a big impact on the way business is conducted around the world. When we call a friend or business associate in the United States, we expect a quick reply. Not necessarily so in countries where different priorities can mean different time frames for doing things.

If you're supposed to be at an 8:00 A.M. meeting in the United States or northern Europe, you'd better be on time (say, 8:05 at the latest). We expect people to be punctual, whether it's for a board meeting or a family picnic. Time is one of our ways of imposing order on our activities, and we regard regulated activity as something necessary to our workday productivity. But in some countries, thinking about time is, well, less timely. In Latin America, the Mediterranean, and the Middle East, for example, people generally do business according to relaxed timetables. They're likely to schedule a number of things at once, and if this habit means that schedules get ignored and some "scheduled" activities get delayed, it doesn't really matter.

There are, of course, advantages as well as disadvantages. Sometimes a more relaxed attitude toward making productive use of your time means taking time to develop relationships and getting to know someone instead of just achieving a specific goal in a specific time frame. Whatever the case, if you're operating in another country and culture, you need to know how people regard time and timeliness. Not only will you know when to show up at meetings and other events, but you may also have more luck in scheduling production and delivery dates. The most successful companies know their host cultures and are prepared to make allowances for local conditions.

■ OPERATIONS CONTROL

Once long-range plans have been put into action and schedules drawn up, **operations control** requires managers to monitor performance by comparing results with detailed plans and schedules. If schedules or quality standards aren't met, managers must take corrective action. **Follow-up**—checking to ensure that production decisions are being implemented—is a key and ongoing facet of operations control.

Operations control includes *materials management* and *operations process control*. Both activities ensure that schedules are met and production goals fulfilled, both in quantity and in quality. In this section, we consider the nature of materials management and look at some important methods of process control.

operations control
Process of monitoring production performance by comparing results with plans

follow-up
Production control activity for ensuring that production decisions are being implemented

Materials Management

All companies use materials. For many manufacturing firms, materials costs make up 50 to 75 percent of total product costs. For goods whose production uses little labor, such as petroleum refining, this percentage is even higher. Thus, companies have good reasons for emphasizing materials management.

The process of **materials management** allows managers not only to control but also to plan and organize materials flow. Even before production starts, materials management focuses on product design by emphasizing **standardization**—the use of standard and uniform components rather than new or different ones for related products. Law firms keep standardized forms and data files for estate wills, trust agreements, and various contracts that can be adjusted easily to meet individual needs.

materials management
Planning, organizing, and controlling the flow of materials from design through distribution of finished goods

standardization
Use of standard and uniform components in the production process

Ford's engine plant in Romeo, Michigan, uses common parts for several different kinds of engines. Standardization also simplifies paperwork, reduces storage requirements, and eliminates unnecessary material flows.

Once a product has been designed, materials managers purchase the necessary materials and monitor the production process through the distribution of finished goods. Thus, there are five major areas in materials management:

■ **Transportation** includes the means of transporting resources to the producer and finished goods to buyers.
■ **Warehousing** is the storage of both incoming materials for production and finished goods for distribution to customers.
■ **Purchasing** is the acquisition of all the raw materials and services that a company needs to produce its products; most large firms have purchasing departments to buy proper materials in the amounts needed.
■ **Supplier selection** means finding and choosing suppliers of services and materials to buy from. It includes evaluating potential suppliers, negotiating terms of service, and maintaining positive buyer–seller relationships.
■ **Inventory control** includes the receiving, storing, handling, and counting of all raw materials, partly finished goods, and finished goods. It ensures that enough materials inventories are available to meet production schedules.[11]

purchasing
Acquisition of the raw materials and services that a firm needs to produce its products

supplier selection
Process of finding and selecting suppliers from whom to buy

inventory control
In materials management, receiving, storing, handling, and counting of all raw materials, partly finished goods, and finished goods

Tools for Operations Process Control

Numerous tools assist managers in controlling operations. Chief among these are *worker training, lean production systems* (including *just-in-time operations*), *material requirements planning*, and *quality control*.

Worker Training Customer satisfaction depends largely on the employees who provide the service. In service-product design, employees are often both the providers of the product and the salespeople. Naturally, good customer relationships don't happen by accident: Service workers can be trained in customer-oriented attitudes. Says Kip Tindell, chief operating officer at the Container Store *(www.containerstore.com)*, a Dallas-based retailer of storage products, "We are just wild-eyed fanatics when it comes to human resources and training." While admitting that human resources and training are "the most difficult . . . part of the retail business," Tindell attributes the Container Store's success to its employees.[12] Like Tindell, human resource experts now realize that without employees trained in customer-relationship skills, businesses such as airlines and hotels can lose customers to better-prepared competitors.

lean system
Production system designed for smooth production flows that avoid inefficiencies, eliminate unnecessary inventories, and continuously improve production processes

just-in-time (JIT) production
Production method that brings together all materials and parts needed at each production stage at the precise moment they are required

"We are just wild-eyed fanatics when it comes to human resources and training."

—Kip Tindell, chief operating officer, Container Store

Lean Production Systems: Just-in-Time Operations **Lean systems** are designed for smooth production flows that avoid inefficiencies, eliminate unnecessary inventories, and continuously improve production processes. **Just-in-time (JIT) production**, a type of lean system, brings together all needed materials at the precise moment they are required for each production stage, not before, thus creating fast and efficient responses to customer orders. All resources flow continuously—from arrival as raw materials to final assembly and shipment of finished products.

JIT reduces to practically nothing the number of goods in process (goods not yet finished). It thus minimizes inventory costs and saves money by replacing stop-and-go production with smooth movement. Once smooth flow is the norm, disruptions are

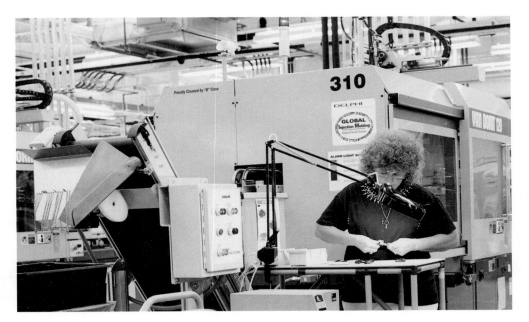

At this Delphi Automotive Systems *(www.delphi.com)* plant in Courtland, Ohio, which makes plastic housings for electrical connectors in cars and telecom equipment, quality checkers are among the members of an increasingly small human workforce. Since 1999, Delphi has spent $30 million for new production equipment, computers, software, and an e-manufacturing network that's so efficient that the plant superintendent can work at home from his own PC. As for these quality checkers, their work is made easier by a defect rate of about 14 parts per million.

more visible and thus get resolved more quickly. Finding and eliminating disruptions by the continuous improvement of production is a major objective of JIT.

Material Requirements Planning Like JIT, **material requirements planning (MRP)** seeks to deliver the right amounts of materials at the right place and the right time. MRP uses a **bill of materials** as a "recipe" for the finished product. It specifies necessary ingredients (raw materials and components), the order for combining them, and the quantity of each for making one batch (say, 2,000 finished telephones). The recipe is fed into a computer that controls inventory and scheduling at each stage of production. The result is fewer stock shortages and lower storage costs. MRP is most valuable when products require complicated assembly, such as the production of cars, appliances, and furniture.

material requirements planning (MRP)
Production method in which a bill of materials is used to ensure that the right amounts of materials are delivered to the right place at the right time

bill of materials
Production control tool that specifies the necessary ingredients of a product, the order in which they should be combined, and how many of each are needed to make one batch

Quality Control **Quality control** means managing the operations process in order to produce goods or supply services that meet specific quality standards. United Parcel Service Inc. (UPS) *(www.ups.com)* delivers 13 million packages every day (mostly to business clients) and promises that all of them will arrive on schedule. It keeps this promise by tracking the locations, schedules, and on-time performance of 500 aircraft and 150,000 vehicles as they carry packages through the delivery system. Quality control is essential because delivery reliability—namely, avoiding late deliveries—is critical for customer satisfaction.

quality control
Management of the production process designed to manufacture goods or supply services that meet specific quality standards

■ QUALITY IMPROVEMENT

It is not enough to measure productivity in terms of numbers of items produced. We must also consider quality; and, in fact, the "quality revolution" ranks among the most profound business developments in the history of modern commerce. In order to compete on a global scale, U.S. companies have adopted a new quality orientation. They are, for example, increasingly customer driven. Producing **quality** means creating fitness for use—offering features that customers want. All employees, not just managers, participate in quality efforts, and firms have embraced new methods to measure

quality
A product's fitness for use; its success in offering features that consumers want

progress objectively and to identify areas for improvement. In many organizations, quality improvement has become a way of life.

Managing for Quality

total quality management (TMQ) (or quality assurance)
The sum of all activities involved in getting high-quality products into the marketplace

Total quality management (TQM) (sometimes called **quality assurance**) includes all of the activities necessary for getting high-quality goods and services into the marketplace. It must consider all aspects of a business, including customers, suppliers, and employees. Says John Kay, director of Oxford University's School of Management, "You can't run a successful company if you don't care about customers and employees, or if you are systematically unpleasant to suppliers." To marshal the interests of all these stakeholders, TQM involves planning, organizing, directing, and controlling.

Planning for Quality To achieve high quality, managers must plan for production processes (including equipment, methods, worker skills, and materials). Planning for quality, however, begins before products are designed or redesigned. Early in the process, managers must set goals for both performance quality and quality reliability. **Performance quality** refers to the *performance features* of a product. For loyal buyers of Godiva premium chocolates *(www.godiva.com)*, performance quality includes such sensory delights such as aroma, flavor, and texture. "Truly fine chocolates," observes Master Chocolatier Thiery Muret, "are always fresh, contain high-quality ingredients like cocoa beans and butter . . . and feature unusual textures and natural flavors." Superior performance quality helps Godiva remain one of the world's top brands.[13]

performance quality
The performance features offered by a product

Performance quality is usually related to **quality reliability**—the consistency of product quality from unit to unit. Cars from Toyota *(www.toyota.com)*, for example, enjoy high-quality reliability. Consistency is achieved by controlling the quality of raw materials, encouraging conscientious work, and maintaining equipment. Naturally, some products offer both high-quality reliability and high-performance quality. Kellogg's *(www.kelloggs.com)*, for example, has a reputation for consistently producing cereals made of high-quality ingredients.

quality reliability
Consistency of a product's quality from unit to unit

"You can't run a successful company if you don't care about customers and employees, or if you are systematically unpleasant to suppliers."

—John Kay, director, Oxford University's School of Management

Organizing for Quality Producing high-quality goods and services requires an effort from all parts of an organization. A separate quality control department is no longer enough. Everyone—purchasers, engineers, janitors, marketers, machinists, and other personnel—must focus on quality. At Merrill Lynch Credit Corp. *(www.ml.com)*, for example, all employees are responsible for taking the initiative in responding to customers' credit needs. The overall goal is to reduce problems to a minimum by providing credit selectively and skillfully from the beginning of the process. The result: Both number of loans and market share are increasing while loan delinquencies are decreasing.

At the same time, many firms assign responsibility for specific aspects of TQM to specific departments or positions. Many companies have *quality assurance* or *quality control* departments staffed by quality experts. They may be called in to solve quality-related problems in any department, and they keep everyone informed about the latest developments in quality-related equipment and methods. They also monitor quality control activities to identify areas for improvement.

Directing for Quality Managers must motivate employees throughout the company to achieve quality goals. They must continually find ways to foster a quality focus by training employees, encouraging involvement, and tying compensation to work quality. If managers succeed, employees will ultimately accept **quality ownership**: the idea that quality belongs to each person who creates it while performing a job. At ITT Industries Inc. *(www.itt.com)*, for example, CEO Louis J. Giuliano implemented a quality program called Value-Based Six Sigma (VBSS) by organizing quality improvement teams and retraining employees to use quality-related equipment. The payoffs have been enormous: Between 1998 and 2001, earnings per share went up from $1.25 to $3.09—an annual growth rate of 35 percent despite a recession and repercussions from the attacks of September 11, 2001.[14]

quality ownership
Principle of total quality management that holds that quality belongs to each person who creates it while performing a job

Controlling for Quality By monitoring products and services, a company can detect mistakes and make corrections. First, however, managers must establish specific standards and measurements. At a bank, for example, the control system for teller services might require supervisors to observe employees periodically and evaluate their work according to a checklist. The results would then be reviewed with employees and either confirm proper performance or indicate changes for bringing performance up to standards.

Tools for Total Quality Management

Many companies rely on proven tools to manage quality. Ideas for improving both products and production processes often come from **competitive product analysis**. Toshiba, for example, might take apart a Xerox copier and test each component. The results would help managers decide which Toshiba product features are satisfactory, which features should be upgraded, and which operations processes need improvement.

competitive product analysis
Process by which a company analyzes a competitor's products to identify desirable improvements

In this section, we will survey six of the most commonly used tools for TQM: *statistical process control, quality/cost studies, getting closer to the customer, ISO 9000, business process reengineering* and *outsourcing.*

Statistical Process Control Although every company would like complete uniformity in its output, all firms experience unit-to-unit variations in products. Companies

statistical process control (SPC)
Methods for gathering data to analyze variations in production activities to see when adjustments are needed

can, however, control product quality by understanding sources of variation. **Statistical process control (SPC)** refers to methods by which employees can gather data and analyze variations in production activities to determine needed adjustments. At EZ Acres, a 500-cow dairy farm near Homer, New York, personnel use SPC to control the dryness and chemical composition of cattle feed, thereby reducing the costs of milk production. Steelcase *(www.steelcase.com)*, an office furniture manufacturer, uses SPC to control the thickness of paint on furniture cabinets. Excessive thickness increases costs and provides no added value for customers. Using SPC, Steelcase improved consistency from painting machines and cut the cost of paint by 15 percent.[15]

Control Charts One of the most common SPC methods is the use of control charts. The charts are helpful for monitoring production processes to keep them from going astray. To detect the onset of departures from normal conditions, employees can check production and plot the results on a **control chart**.[16] Three or four times a day, for example, a Honey Nuggets machine operator might weigh several boxes of cereal to determine the average weight. That average is then plotted on the control chart.

control chart
Process control method that plots test sample results on a diagram to determine when a process is beginning to depart from normal operating conditions

Figure 7.6 shows the control chart for Machine A at the Honey Nuggets plant. As you can see, the first five points are randomly scattered around the center line, indicating that the machine was operating well from 8 A.M. until noon. However, the points for samples 5 through 9 are all above the center line, indicating that something caused boxes to overfill. The last point falls outside the upper control limit, confirming that the process is out of control. At this point, the machine must be shut down so that someone can investigate the cause of the problem: Is it the equipment, people, materials, or work methods? Control is completed when the process is restored to normal.

Quality/Cost Studies SPC helps maintain existing capabilities, but in today's competitive environment, firms must consistently raise quality capabilities. Unfortunately, any improvement in products or processes means additional costs, whether for new facilities, equipment, training, or other changes. Managers must, therefore, identify the improvements that offer the greatest promise. **Quality/cost studies** not only identify a firm's current costs but also reveal areas with the largest cost-savings potential.[17]

quality/cost study
Method of improving quality by identifying current costs and areas with the greatest cost-saving potential

Quality costs are associated with finding, repairing, or preventing defective products. All of these costs should be analyzed in a quality/cost study. Honey Nuggets, for exam-

FIGURE 7.6

Process Control Chart at Honey Nuggets Cereal

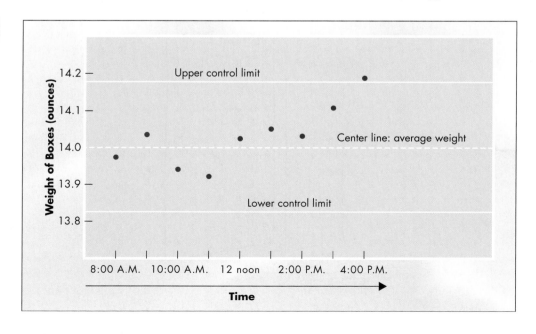

ple, must determine the costs of **internal failures**. These expenses include the costs of overfilling boxes and the costs of sorting out bad boxes incurred during production and before bad products leave the plant. For many U.S. manufacturers, internal-failures costs account for 50 percent of total costs.

Unfortunately, some bad boxes may escape the factory, reach the customer, and generate complaints. These **external failures** are discovered outside the factory. The costs of correcting them (refunds to customers, shipping costs to return bad boxes to the factory, possible lawsuits, and factory recalls) should also be tabulated in the quality/cost study.

internal failures
Reducible costs incurred during production and before bad products leave a plant

external failures
Reducible costs incurred after defective products have left a plant

Getting Closer to the Customer Says one advocate of quality improvement, "Customers are an economic asset. They're not on the balance sheet, but they should be." Struggling companies have often lost sight of customers as the driving force behind all business activity. Perhaps such companies waste resources designing products that customers do not want. Sometimes they ignore customer reactions to existing products or fail to keep up with changing tastes. Meanwhile, successful businesses know what their customers want in the products they consume.

Los Alamos National Bank (LANB) of New Mexico *(www. lanb.com)* gathers public and industry data into 13 measures of customer needs and satisfaction. Employees are trained in listening and learning techniques, enabling them to pick up clues about what customers want, how they think services can be improved, and what the competition is doing. LANB boasts satisfaction ratings of "excellent" from 87 percent of its customers. Not only is its customer satisfaction higher than that of both its competitors and the national average, but there are also bottom-line results: Net income and market share for deposits and loans have grown, and earnings per share have gone up 80 percent in just five years.[18]

> **"Customers are an economic asset. They're not on the balance sheet, but they should be."**
>
> **—Claess Fornell, quality improvement advocate**

ISO 9000 Following September 11, 2001, the AAR-500 of the U.S. Transportation Security Administration (TSA) *(www.its.tc.faa.gov/aar500)* was given responsibility for bolstering security at American airports. To train and certify 28,000 new personnel in a revamped screening system, AAR-500 turned to international quality standards that had been applied successfully in private service businesses. To instill public confidence in the new screening system, AAR-500 also adopted the principle of independent third-party certification of the system.[19] Both the training and certification systems were based on the world-class standards of **ISO 9000** (pronounced *ICE-o nine thousand*)—a certification program attesting to the fact that a factory, a laboratory, or an office has met the rigorous quality management requirements set by the International Organization for Standardization *(www.iso.ch)*. Today, more than 140 countries have adopted ISO 9000 as a national standard.

ISO 9000
Program certifying that a factory, laboratory, or office has met the quality management standards of the International Organization for Standardization

The revised standards of *ISO 9000: 2000* allow firms to show that they follow documented procedures for testing products, training workers, keeping records, and fixing defects. To become certified, companies must document the procedures followed by workers during every stage of production. The purpose, according to the International Division of the U.S. Chamber of Commerce *(www.uschamber.com)*, is to ensure that a manufacturer's product is exactly the same today as it was yesterday and as it will be tomorrow. Ideally, standardized processes would ensure that goods are produced at the same level of quality even if all employees were replaced by a new set of workers.

Process Reengineering Every business consists of processes—activities that it performs regularly and routinely in conducting business. Examples abound: receiving and storing materials from suppliers, billing patients for medical treatment, filing insurance claims for auto accidents, inspecting property for termites, opening checking accounts for new customers, filling customer orders from Internet sales. Any business process can add value and customer satisfaction by performing processes well. By the same token, any business can disappoint customers and irritate business partners by managing them poorly.

business process reengineering
Redesigning of business processes to improve quality, performance, and customer service

Business process reengineering focuses on improving both the productivity and quality of business processes—rethinking each step of an organization's operations by starting from scratch. *Reengineering* is the fundamental rethinking and radical redesign of business processes to achieve dramatic improvements in measures of performance, such as cost, quality, service, and speed.[20] The calling-services company GTE *(www.gte.com)*, for example, found that its over-the-phone service was not user friendly for customers wanting to correct service or billing problems. To provide fast, accurate one-stop service, GTE reengineered the whole service process by improving equipment, retraining employees, and connecting software to formerly inaccessible corporate databases.

As you can see, reengineering is a broad undertaking that requires know-how in technical matters and calls on knowledge about customer needs and how well they are being met. The bottom line in every reengineering process is adopting a companywide customer-first philosophy. Redesign is guided by a desire to improve operations so that goods and services are produced at the lowest possible cost and at the highest value for the customer.

outsourcing
Strategy of paying suppliers and distributors to perform certain business processes or to provide needed materials or resources

Outsourcing **Outsourcing** is the strategy of paying suppliers and distributors to perform certain business processes or to provide needed materials or services. It is an increasingly popular strategy because it helps firms focus on their core activities and avoid getting sidetracked onto secondary activities. In many cases, outsourcing often saves time and money, increases effectiveness in a firm's core business, and results in more value for customers and owners.[21]

The cafeteria at a large bank may be important to employees and some customers, but running it is not the bank's main line of business and expertise. Bankers need to focus on money management and financial services, not food-service operations. That's why most banks outsource cafeteria operations to food-service management companies whose main line of business includes cafeterias. The result, ideally, is more attention to banking by bankers, better food service for cafeteria customers, and formation of a new supplier–client relationship (food-service company/bank). Firms today outsource numerous activities, including payroll, employee training, and research and development.

■ ADDING VALUE THROUGH SUPPLY CHAINS

Managers sometimes forget that a company belongs to a network of firms that must coordinate their activities. The term *supply chain* refers to the group of companies and stream of activities that work together to create a product. A **supply chain** for any product is the flow of information, materials, and services that starts with raw-materials suppliers and continues through other stages in the operations process until the product reaches the end customer.[22]

supply chain
Flow of information, materials, and services that starts with raw-materials suppliers and continues through other stages in the operations process until the product reaches the end customer

Figure 7.7 shows the supply chain activities involved in supplying baked goods to consumers. Each stage adds value for the final customer. Although a typical beginning stage is product design, our bakery example begins with raw materials (grain har-

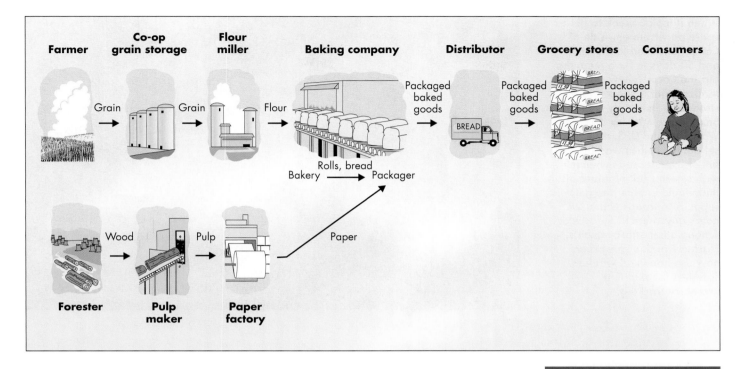

Farmer | **Co-op grain storage** | **Flour miller** | **Baking company** | **Distributor** | **Grocery stores** | **Consumers**

Grain → Grain → Flour → Packaged baked goods → Packaged baked goods → Packaged baked goods →

Bakery → Rolls, bread → Packager

Forester | **Pulp maker** | **Paper factory**

Wood → Pulp → Paper

FIGURE 7.7
Supply Chain for Baked Goods

vested from the farm). It also includes additional storage and transportation activities, factory operations for baking and wrapping, and distribution to retailers. Each stage depends on the others for success in getting fresh-baked goods to consumers.

Supply Chain Strategy

Traditional strategies assume that companies are managed as individual firms rather than as members of a coordinated supply system. Supply chain strategy is based on the idea that members of the chain, working as a coordinated unit, will gain competitive advantage. Although each company looks out for its own interests, it works closely with suppliers and customers throughout the chain. Everyone focuses on the entire chain of relationships rather than on the next stage in the chain.

A traditionally managed bakery, for example, would focus simply on getting production inputs from flour millers and paper suppliers and supplying baked goods to distributors. Unfortunately, this approach limits the chain's performance and doesn't allow for possible improvements when activities are more carefully coordinated. Supply chain management can improve performance and, as a result, provide higher quality at lower prices.

Supply Chain Management Supply chain management (SCM) looks at the chain as a whole in order to improve the overall flow through a system composed of companies working together. Because customers ultimately get better value, SCM gains competitive advantage for each supply chain member.

Dell Computer's supply chain, for example, improves performance by allowing people to share information. Dell shares long-term production plans and up-to-the-minute sales data with suppliers via the Internet. The process starts when customer orders are automatically translated into updated production schedules on the factory floor. These schedules are used not only by operations managers at Dell but also by such parts suppliers as Sony, which adjust their own production and shipping activities

supply chain management (SCM)
Principle of looking at the supply chain as a whole in order to improve the overall flow through the system

When it took a week to get a spare part from one side of Camp Pendleton to the other and 50 days to fix a jeep, the Marine Corps *(www.usmc.mil)* realized that it needed to streamline its supply chain. Studying companies such as Wal-Mart and UPS, the Corps set out to replace warehouses full of overstocked inventory with systems full of information that would enable it to get supplies to troops within 24 hours anywhere in the world. Among other improvements, Marine warehouse workers now use handheld wireless scanners for real-time inventory tracking.

to better meet Dell's production needs. In turn, parts suppliers' updated schedules are transmitted to their materials suppliers, and so on. As Dell's requirements change, suppliers synchronize their schedules to produce the right materials and parts efficiently.

Because the smooth flow of accurate information along the chain reduces unwanted inventories, avoids delays, and cuts supply times, materials move faster to business customers and individual consumers. For both, the efficiency of SCM means faster deliveries and lower costs than customers could get if each member acted only according to its own operations requirements.

SELF-CHECK QUESTIONS 7–9

You should now be able to answer Self-Check Questions 7–9.*

7 Multiple Choice Which of the following is **true** regarding *quality management*? [select one]: **(a)** Total quality management (TQM) focuses on production activities to ensure that products are produced according to specifications. **(b)** In controlling for quality, managers should establish specific standards and measurements. **(c)** Because it sets the tone for everything that follows, planning for quality is the most important stage in quality management. **(d)** Total quality management is sometimes called quality insurance.

8 True/False *Statistical process control* cannot be used to analyze and adjust business processes unless data are gathered and analyzed.

9 Multiple Choice Which of the following is **not** true regarding *supply chains* and *supply chain management*? [select one]: **(a)** Supply chains involve the flow of information as well as materials and services. **(b)** A company using supply chain strategy always focuses on the next stage (either incoming or outgoing) in the chain. **(c)** Efficiency in supply chains means faster on-time deliveries and lower costs. **(d)** Reengineering is used to improve supply chains by cutting costs and better coordinating flows of materials and information.

*Answers to Self-Check Questions 7–9 can be found on p. 508.

Continued from page 194.

"WE'RE USING A LOT OF NEAT STUFF"

Linking all of JSF's companies, customers, and suppliers in real time would be impossible without Web-design and project-management tools. Keeping projects on schedule and holding down costs depend on both. Located all around the globe, thousands of design engineers, equipment engineers, logistics specialists, production planners, suppliers, and customers must move hundreds of thousands of components and share product designs, production schedules, and work flows.

With so many participants, information exchanges are essential in order to avoid lost time and duplicated effort. To save both time and money, Lockheed hosts a Web *collaboration network* or *product data-management system*. For instance, because all engineers working on a particular component are automatically notified when anyone makes a change, no one wastes time working on an outdated design. The system is also accessible by the Department of Defense for tracking progress in real time.

As the cornerstone of this project, Lockheed's Internet-based system does more than help to design the aircraft. It also makes it simple for Lockheed and its suppliers to link inventory and production systems. Project managers can quickly check on inventory status and production schedules as well as determine whether suppliers will have trouble meeting delivery deadlines. In addition to keeping materials flowing throughout the supply chain, the system features shop-floor–management tools to help identify delays, quality problems, and areas for process improvement.

The system also supports the 3D-solid–modeling program that underlies both design and production. Digital definition of the aircraft provides instantaneous information needed for making production tools and for assembling parts and components. Initial plans call for building one airplane every five months, but that time span will be reduced as the team gains experience with new materials and processes.

"We're using a lot of neat stuff," says Martin McLaughlin, Northrop Grumman's chief executive for the JSF product team. "Our use of 3D-solid modeling has revolutionized the machining of parts: [L]asers in the factory ceiling can read the 3D-solid–model data and project directly onto a machine tool an outline of exactly where the mechanic should place the next ply of composite material." Laser imaging cuts production time in half, guarantees precise control over composite materials, and trims inspection time by a whopping 90 percent. Laser technology also rigs assembly fixtures digitally (rather than manually), reduces the number of required parts by 50 percent, and eliminates 90 percent of the tools that would once have been needed to build the JSF. The team expects that manufacturing flow time will eventually be reduced by half.

Finally, the task of coordinating members and activities also falls on the project's Internet-collaboration systems. Although separated by oceans, partners must communicate as if they were in the same room, and this intensive level of communication must be maintained for years to come. The sharing of real-time data is essential for more than just cost control. As the project progresses, the collaboration system will build stronger customer relationships and promote deeper political ties among members.

Questions for Discussion

1 How would you describe the time utility and form utility that customers will receive from the Joint Strike Fighter? List examples of each kind of utility.

2 How might operations control procedures be useful for the JSF project? Using examples from the JSF case description, show how material requirements planning might be used.

3 Suppose you are responsible for planning a full-scale production process slated to begin in 2008. You are concerned about the number of parts and systems suppliers scattered around the globe. What are some major production-planning problems posed by your supply chain and its geographic dispersion?

4 How would you describe the kinds of production or operations that will take place in the next phase of the JSF project, which will be system development and demonstration? Are the main products mostly services or mostly physical goods? Explain.

5 Because Lockheed Martin is responsible for overall project coordination, it must maintain sufficient capacity to fulfill its contract with the Defense Department. How would you describe the kinds of production capacity that will be needed for SDD, the next phase of the project? What kinds of capacity will be needed for the full-scale production phase?

■ SUMMARY OF LEARNING OBJECTIVES

1 **Explain the meaning of the term *production* or *operations* and describe the four kinds of *utility* that operations processes provide.**

Service operations provide intangible and tangible services products, such as entertainment, transportation, education, and food preparation. Firms that make tangible products—radios, newspapers, buses, textbooks—are engaged in **goods production**. Because the term *production* is associated just with manufacturing, we now use *operations* to refer to both service and goods production. **Operations** (or **production**) **management** is the systematic direction and control of the processes that transform resources into finished services and goods that create value for and provide benefits to customers. Resources include knowledge, physical materials, equipment, and labor that are systematically combined in a production facility to create four kinds of **utility** for customers: *time utility* (which makes products available when customers want them), *place utility* (which makes products available where they are convenient for customers), *possession or ownership utility* (by which customers benefit from possessing and using the product), and *form utility* (which results from the creation of the product).

2 **Identify the characteristics that distinguish service operations from *goods production* and explain the main differences in the *service focus*.**

Both service and manufacturing operations transform raw materials into finished products. In service production, the raw materials are people who have either unsatisfied needs or possessions needing some form of care or alteration. "Finished products" are thus people with needs met and possessions serviced. The focus of service operations differs from that of goods production in four ways: (1) *Focus on performance*: Because goods are produced and services performed, customer-oriented performance is crucial to a service company. (2) *Focus on process and outcome*: Because most service products are combinations of goods and services, services focus on both the transformation process and its outcome. (3) *Focus on service characteristics*: Service transactions reflect the three key qualities of service products: (i) *Intangibility*: Because services usually can't be touched, tasted, smelled, or seen, they provide intangible value experienced as pleasure, satisfaction, or a feeling of safety. (ii) *Customization*: Each customer expects a service to be designed (customized) for his or her specific needs.

(iii) *Unstorability*: Because many services can't be produced ahead of time and then stored, they have a high degree of unstorability. (4) *Focus on service quality considerations*: Service providers know that quality of work and quality of service are not necessarily the same thing (a properly repaired car is one thing, but getting it back when you need it is another).

3 **Describe the factors involved in *operations planning*.**

Operations planning involves the analysis of five key factors. In *capacity planning*, the firm analyzes how much of a product it must be able to produce. In **high-contact services**, managers must plan **capacity** to meet peak demand. Capacity planning for goods means ensuring that manufacturing capacity slightly exceeds the normal demand for its product. *Location planning* for goods and for **low-contact services** involves analyzing proposed facility sites in terms of proximity to raw materials and markets, availability of labor, and energy and transportation costs. Location planning for high-contact services involves locating the service near customers, who are part of the system. *Layout planning* involves designing a facility so that customer needs are supplied for high-contact services and to enhance production efficiency. Alternatives include **product, process, and cellular layouts**. In *quality planning*, systems are developed to ensure that products meet a firm's quality standards. Finally, in *methods planning*, specific production steps and methods for performing them are identified. In methods planning, process flowcharts are helpful for identifying all operations activities and eliminating wasteful steps from production.

4 **Identify some of the key tools for *total quality management*, including strategies for getting closer to the customer.**

Total quality management (TQM) includes any activity for getting quality products to the marketplace. TQM tools include **statistical process control (SPC)**—methods whereby employees gather data and analyze variations in production activities. The purpose of SPC is to identify needed adjustments. One SPC tool is the **control chart**, which plots the results of sample measurements from operations to identify when a process is beginning to depart from normal conditions, so that corrections can be made. **Quality/cost studies** are useful because improvements in products or production processes always entail additional costs. This method helps identify areas in which quality can be maintained with the greatest cost savings from making, finding, repairing, or preventing defective goods and services. Getting closer to the customer involves maintaining contact so that the company knows what customers want in the products they consume. It involves communicating with customers so that products are designed to meet their needs. **Business process reengineering** focuses on improving both the productivity and quality of business practices. It involves the fundamental rethinking and radical redesign of business processes to gain dramatic performance improvement. **Outsourcing**—paying suppliers and distributors to perform certain business processes or to provide needed materials or services—often saves time and money, increases effectiveness in a firm's core business, and results in more value for customers and owners.

5 Explain how a *supply chain strategy* differs from traditional strategies for coordinating operations among firms.

The supply chain strategy is based on the idea that members of the **supply chain**—the stream of all activities and companies that creates a product—can gain competitive advantage by working together as a coordinated system of units. In contrast, traditional strategies assume that companies are managed as individual firms, each acting in its own interest. By managing the chain as a whole—using **supply chain management**—companies can more closely coordinate activities in the chain. By sharing information, overall costs and inventories can be reduced, and deliveries to customers can be faster. Provided with better service and at lower prices, the supply chain's products are preferred, with supply chain members gaining an advantage over competitors whose operations are less effective.

■ KEY TERMS

service operations (p. 194)
goods production (p. 194)
utility (p. 196)
operations (or production) management (p. 197)
operations (or production) managers (p. 197)
operations process (p. 197)
analytic process (p. 197)
synthetic process (p. 198)
high-contact system (p. 198)
low-contact system (p. 199)
capacity (p. 201)
process layout (p. 203)
cellular layout (p. 204)
product layout (p. 204)
assembly line (p. 204)
master production schedule (p. 207)

Gantt chart (p. 207)
PERT chart (p. 207)
operations control (p. 209)
follow-up (p. 209)
materials management (p. 209)
standardization (p. 209)
purchasing (p. 210)
supplier selection (p. 210)
inventory control (p. 210)
lean system (p. 210)
just-in-time (JIT) production (p. 210)
material requirements planning (MRP) (p. 211)
bill of materials (p. 211)
quality control (p. 211)
quality (p. 211)
total quality management (TQM) (or quality assurance) (p. 212)

performance quality (p. 212)
quality reliability (p. 212)
quality ownership (p. 213)
competitive product analysis (p. 213)
statistical process control (SPC) (p. 214)
control chart (p. 214)
quality/cost study (p. 214)
internal failures (p. 215)
external failures (p. 215)
ISO 9000 (p. 215)
business process reengineering (p. 216)
outsourcing (p. 216)
supply chain (p. 216)
supply chain management (SCM) (p. 217)

■ QUESTIONS AND EXERCISES

Questions for Review

1 What are the four different kinds of production-based utility?

2 What are the major differences between goods-production operations and service operations?

3 What are the five major categories of operations planning?

4 What activities are involved in total quality management?

5 What is supply chain management?

Questions for Analysis

6 What are the resources and finished products in the following services?
- Real estate firm
- Child-care facility
- Bank
- City water and electric department
- Hotel

7 Analyze the layout of a local firm with which you do business (perhaps a restaurant, a supermarket, or a manufacturing firm). What problems do you see with this layout? What recommendations would you make to management?

8 Select one of your favorite products and identify the supply chain that provides it. How many different firms contribute to the development and delivery of the product from beginning to end?

Application Exercises

9 Interview the manager of a local service business, such as a laundry or dry-cleaning shop. Identify the major decisions involved in planning its service operations. Prepare a class report suggesting areas for improvement.

10 Using a local company as an example, show how you would conduct a quality/cost study. Identify the cost categories and give some examples of the costs in each category. Which categories do you expect to have the highest and lowest costs? Why?

BUILDING YOUR BUSINESS SKILLS

THE ONE-ON-ONE ENTREPRENEUR

This exercise enhances the following SCANS workplace competencies: demonstrating basic skills, demonstrating thinking skills, exhibiting interpersonal skills, and working with information.

Goal

To encourage students to apply the concept of customization to an entrepreneurial idea.

Situation

You are an entrepreneur who wants to start your own service business. You are intrigued with the idea of creating some kind of customized one-on-one service that would appeal to baby boomers, who traditionally have been pampered, and working women, who have little time to get things done.

Method

Step 1

Get together with three or four other students to brainstorm ideas for services that would appeal to harried working people. Here are just a few:
- A concierge service in office buildings that would handle such personal and business services as arranging children's birthday parties and booking guest speakers for business luncheons.

- A personal-image consultation service aimed at helping clients improve appearance, etiquette, and presentation style.
- A mobile pet-care network through which vets and groomers make house calls.

Step 2

Choose one of these ideas or one that your team thinks of. Then write a memo explaining why you think your idea will succeed. Research may be necessary as you target any of the following:
- A specific demographic group or groups (Who are your customers, and why would they buy your service?)
- Features that make your service attractive to this group
- The social factors in your local community that would contribute to success

FOLLOW-UP QUESTIONS

1 Why is the customization of and easy access to personal services so desirable in the twenty-first century?

2 As services are personalized, do you think quality will become more or less important? Why?

3 Why does the trend toward personalized, one-on-one service present unique opportunities for entrepreneurs?

4 In a personal one-on-one business, how important are the human relations skills of those delivering the service? Can you make an argument that they are more important than the service itself?

EXERCISING YOUR ETHICS

CALCULATING THE COST OF CONSCIENCE

The Situation
Product quality and cost affect every firm's reputation and profitability as well as the satisfaction of customers. This exercise will expose you to some ethical considerations that pertain to certain cost and service decisions that must be made by operations managers.

The Dilemma
As director of quality for a major appliance manufacturer, Ruth was reporting to the executive committee on the results of a recent program for correcting problems with a newly redesigned rotary compressor that the company had recently begun putting in its refrigerators. After receiving several customer complaints, the quality lab and the engineering department had determined that some of the new compressor units ran more loudly than expected. Some remedial action was needed. One option was simply waiting until customers complained and responding to each complaint if and when it occurred. Ruth, however, had decided that this approach was inconsistent with the company's policy of offering the highest quality in the industry. Deciding that the firm's reputation called for a proactive, "pro-quality" approach, Ruth had initiated a program for contacting all customers who had purchased refrigerators containing the new compressor. Unfortunately, her "quality-and-customers-first" policy was expensive. Local service representatives had to phone every customer in each area of the country, make appointments for home visits, and replace original compressors with a newer model. But because replacement time was only one-half hour, customers were hardly inconvenienced, and food stayed refrigerated without interruption. Customer response to the replacement program was overwhelmingly favorable.

Near the end of Ruth's report, an executive vice president was overheard to comment, "Ruth's program has cost this company $400 million in service expenses." Two weeks later, Ruth was fired.

QUESTIONS FOR DISCUSSION
1 What are the underlying ethical issues in this situation?
2 What are the respective roles of profits, obligations to customers, and employee considerations for the firm in this situation?
3 Suppose you were an employee who realized that your company was selling defective appliances. Suppose that the cost of correction might put the firm out of business. What would you do?

CRAFTING YOUR BUSINESS PLAN

SPORTING A FRIENDLIER ATMOSPHERE

The Purpose of the Assignment
1 To acquaint students with production and operations issues that a sample firm addresses in developing its business plan in the framework of the *Business PlanPro (BPP) 2003* software package (Version 6.0).
2 To demonstrate how choices of goods and services, characteristics of the transformation process, facilities and equipment, and product quality considerations can be integrated as components in the *BPP* planning environment.

Assignment
After reading Chapter 7 in the textbook, open the BPP *software and look around for information about plans for operations processes as they apply to a sample firm, a sports bar:* Take Five Sports Bar & Grill. *To find* Take Five, *do the following:*

Open *Business PlanPro.* Go to the toolbar and click on the "Sample Plans" icon. In the **Sample Plan Browser,** do a search using the **search category** *Eating and drinking places, restaurants, cafeterias.* From the resulting list, select the category entitled *Bar—Sports,* which is the location for *Take Five Sports Bar & Grill.* The screen you are looking at is the introduction page for the business plan of *Take Five.* On this page, scroll down until you reach the **Table of Contents** for the *Take Five* business plan.

NOW RESPOND TO THE FOLLOWING ITEMS:
1 What type of product—physical good or service—is *Take Five Sports Bar & Grill* creating in its operations

process? Explain. [Sites to see in *BPP* for this item: On the Table of Contents page, click on **1.0 Executive Summary**. Then click on each of the following in turn: **1.2 Mission, 2.3 Company Locations and Facilities**.]

2 Describe the characteristics of the transformation (operations) process that results in this company's products. Be sure to include in your description some comments on the level of customer contact and its implications for the transformation process. [Sites to see in *BPP*: On the Table of Contents page, click on **4.0 Strategy and Implementation Summary**. After returning to the Table of Contents page, click on each of the following in turn: **4.1.2 Promotion Strategy** and **5.1 Organizational Structure**.]

3 Describe the equipment and facilities needed by a typical *Take Five* unit. [Sites to see in *BPP*: From the Table of Contents page, scan any headings that you expect will contain information on equipment and facilities specifications.]

4 How many *Take Five* stores are planned for the future? What steps can be taken in the interest of quality—that is, to ensure that the same consistent services are provided regardless of store location? [Sites to see in *BPP*: On the Table of Contents page, click on **1.1 Objectives**. After returning to the Table of Contents page, click on each of the following in turn: **2.3 Company Locations and Facilities, 4.3 Milestones**, and **5.3 Management Team Gaps**.]

 # VIDEO EXERCISE

MANAGING GLOBAL PRODUCTION: BODY GLOVE

Learning Objectives

The purpose of this video is to help you

1 Recognize some of the operations challenges faced by a growing company.
2 Understand the importance of quality in operations processes.
3 Discuss how and why a company may shift production operations to other countries and other companies.

Synopsis

Riding the wave of public interest in water sports, Body Glove began manufacturing wetsuits in the 1950s. The founders, dedicated surfers and divers, came up with the idea of making the wetsuits from neoprene, which offered more comfortable insulation than the rubber wetsuits of the time. The high costs of both neoprene and labor were major considerations in Body Glove's eventual decision to do its manufacturing in Thailand. The company's constant drive for higher quality was also a factor. Now company management can focus on building Body Glove's image as a California-lifestyle brand without worrying about inventory and other production issues. In licensing its brand for a wide range of goods and services—from cell-phone cases and footwear to flotation devices and vacation resorts—Body Glove has also created a network of partners around the world.

DISCUSSION QUESTIONS

1 **For analysis:** Even though Body Glove makes its products in Thailand, why must managers continually research the ways in which American customers use them?
2 **For analysis:** With which aspects of product quality are wetsuit buyers most likely to be concerned?
3 **For application:** When deciding whether to license its name for a new product, what production issues might Body Glove managers research in advance?
4 **For application:** How might Body Glove's Thailand facility use forecasts of seasonal demand to plan production?
5 **For debate:** Should the products that Body Glove does not manufacture be labeled to alert buyers that they are produced under license? Support your position.

Online Exploration

Visit the Body Glove Web site at *(www.bodyglove.com)*, read the Body Glove story, and look over the variety of products, including electronics products, sold under the Body Glove brand. Then browse the contacts listing to find out which U.S. and international companies have licensed the Body Glove brand. How do various licensed products fit with the Body Glove brand image? What challenges might Body Glove face in coordinating its operations with so many different companies and licensed products?

PLANNING FOR YOUR CAREER

WHAT CAN YOU MANAGE?

Many people studying business have a general aspiration to be a "manager." Most of them, however, aren't entirely sure just what they want to manage. Remember that, as we saw in Chapter 5, managers are responsible for dealing with various kinds of resources. Moreover, there are several different areas of management. This exercise will give you some more insights into the kinds of activities that managers in different areas actually perform.

Assignment

Start by reviewing the discussion in Chapter 5 of the different areas of management. Next, review Chapter 5 in *Beginning Your Career Search*, 3d ed., by James S. O'Rourke IV, in order to learn more about researching companies that you might want to work for. Finally, make a list of up to ten different large companies in which you have some general interest.

To complete this exercise, do the following:

1 Research each company on your list to find out what kinds of management positions it currently has avail-

able. One way is to access the "careers" option on a company Web site.

2 Try to find two or three examples representing each of the various areas of management that we identified in Chapter 5.

3 Reflect on the various jobs that you've researched and then rank them in terms of the extent to which they seem potentially appealing to you.

4 See if you can identify any common themes among those jobs toward the top of your list. How about those jobs on the bottom and in the middle of your list?

5 If there are common themes, what might they suggest regarding your career interests? Do they suggest ways in which you might better prepare yourself for a future career?

6 If there appear to be *no* common themes, what might this fact suggest about your current career interests. In this case, what can you do to better prepare yourself for a future career?

8

After reading this chapter, you should be able to:

1 Define *human resource management* and explain how managers plan for their organization's human resource needs.

2 Identify the tasks in *staffing* a company and discuss ways in which managers *select, develop,* and *appraise* employee performance.

3 Describe the main components of a *compensation system* and explain some of the key legal issues involved in hiring, compensating, and managing workers in today's workplace.

4 Discuss *workforce diversity*, the management of *knowledge workers*, and the use of a *contingent workforce* as important changes in the contemporary workplace.

5 Explain why workers organize into *labor unions* and describe the *collective bargaining process.*

FROM HARD BARGAINS TO HARD TIMES

During the economic boom times of just a few years ago, workers had the advantage in the employment equation. A general labor shortage combined with an acute shortage of knowledge and other skilled workers to make the labor market a seller's market. Top

MANAGING HUMAN RESOURCES AND LABOR RELATIONS

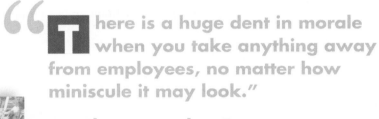

"There is a huge dent in morale when you take anything away from employees, no matter how miniscule it may look."

—Sharon Jordan-Evans, workplace consultant

college graduates had multiple offers, and skilled technical workers could take their pick of jobs. Moreover, businesses began rolling out new benefits, perquisites, and incentives to attract and retain the best and the brightest.

SAS Institute *(www. sas.com)*, a North Carolina software firm, offered employees unlimited sick days, on-site child care, flexible work schedules, and free beverages. In Houston, BMC Software *(www.bmc.com)* greeted employees each morning with a pianist in the lobby and provided fresh vegetables for lunch from the firm's own garden. Other employers offered concierges, laundry pickup and delivery, and even on-site pet care. Some companies offered cash or new cars as signing bonuses.

But as the economy slowed in 2002 and into 2003, the advantage shifted to employers. Throughout the 1990s, as it turns out, companies had relied on technological advances ranging from robotics to the Internet to reduce costs in areas as diverse as advertising, production, and purchasing. When the economy turned sour, they realized that they had cut as many costs as possible from most areas of their operations, and not surprisingly, many turned to their labor forces for the next round of cuts.

Many firms have reduced or stopped hiring, and the hardest hit have even started layoffs. (Many of the dot-coms, among the most aggressive employers in terms of new and innovative benefits, have disappeared altogether.) This trend stems in part from the realization that workers have fewer options, either in finding or leaving jobs. One of the first areas hit was perquisites, or "perks." Among the lost amenities: the employee bowling alley at an Austin-based high-tech firm and Xerox's "Plant Caretaker" (employees must now water their own plants). But don't be fooled into thinking that these are trivial issues. "There is a huge dent in morale when you take anything away from employees, no matter how miniscule it may look," says workplace consultant Sharon Jordan-Evans.

Next in line have been more traditional benefits. Many firms have either reduced contributions to benefits programs or eliminated them altogether. Ford Motor and Lucent Technologies are just two of the many organizations that now pay less for health insurance or retirement plans. Bonuses, sick leave, and vacation time are also being squeezed. As a last resort, some firms are even asking workers to accept pay cuts. Pay at Agilent Technology has dropped 10 percent, and Disney has cut some pay rates by 30 percent.

Our opening story is continued on page 252.

■ THE FOUNDATIONS OF HUMAN RESOURCE MANAGEMENT

human resource management (HRM)
Set of organizational activities directed at attracting, developing, and maintaining an effective workforce

Human resource management (HRM) is the set of organizational activities directed at attracting, developing, and maintaining an effective workforce. Human resource management takes place within a complex and ever-changing environmental context and is increasingly being recognized for its strategic importance.[1]

The Strategic Importance of HRM

Human resources are critical for effective organizational functioning. HRM (or *personnel*, as it is sometimes called) was once relegated to second-class status in many organizations, but its importance has grown dramatically in the last several years. This new importance stems from increased legal complexities, the recognition that human resources are a valuable means for improving productivity, and the awareness today of the costs associated with poor human resource management.

Indeed, managers now realize that the effectiveness of their HR function has a substantial impact on a firm's bottom-line performance. Poor human resource planning can result in spurts of hiring followed by layoffs—costly in terms of unemployment compensation payments, training expenses, and morale. Haphazard compensation systems do not attract, keep, and motivate good employees, and outmoded recruitment practices can expose the firm to expensive and embarrassing legal action. Consequently, the chief human resource executive of most large businesses is a vice president directly accountable to the CEO, and many firms are developing strategic HR plans that are integrated with other strategic planning activities.

Human Resource Planning

As you can see in Figure 8.1, the starting point in attracting qualified human resources is planning. In turn, HR planning involves job analysis and forecasting the demand for and supply of labor.

Job Analysis **Job analysis** is a systematic analysis of jobs within an organization.[2] A job analysis results in two things:

- The **job description** lists the duties and responsibilities of a job; its working conditions; and the tools, materials, equipment, and information used to perform it.
- The **job specification** lists the skills, abilities, and other credentials and qualifications needed to perform the job effectively.

Job analysis information is used in many HR activities. For instance, knowing about job content and job requirements is necessary to develop appropriate selection methods and job-relevant performance appraisal systems and to set equitable compensation rates. Job analysis also determines the most descriptive title for a given job.

Forecasting HR Demand and Supply After managers fully understand the jobs to be performed within an organization, they can start planning for the organization's future HR needs. The manager starts by assessing trends in past HR usage, future

job analysis
Systematic analysis of jobs within an organization

job description
Outline of the duties of a job, working conditions, and the tools, materials, and equipment used to perform it

job specification
Description of the skills, abilities, and other credentials required by a job

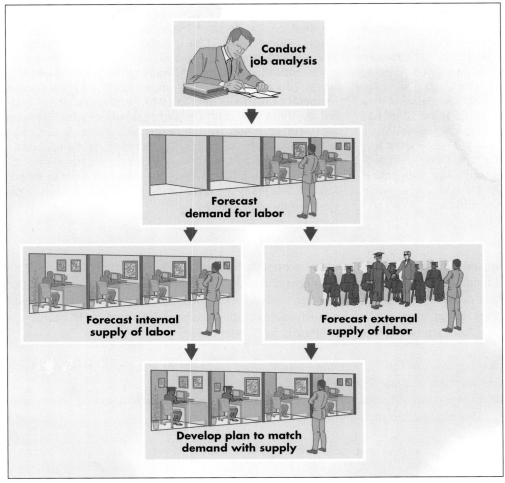

Human Resource Planning Process

ENTREPRENEURSHIP and *New Ventures*

The Guru for Fun Takes a Meeting With the V.P. of Buzz

Rather than dictating standard job titles, some new ventures and entrepreneurial firms now allow incumbents to name their own jobs. Others even let employees *create* their own jobs. Not surprisingly, some interesting twists have emerged.

It started with the Internet bubble. For example, Amy Berkus, a marketing coordinator at a small dot-com, changed her job title to "marketing mechanic." "Everyone was creating new titles in Internet-speak," recalls Berkus. "We wanted titles that conveyed team spirit and a fun atmosphere. . . . It just fit the time." Other catchy designations included "V.P. of Buzz," "Chief People Officer," "Guru of Fun," "Gladiator," and "Chief Evangelist." Under the right circumstances, such titles encouraged creativity and got employees to think differently about their jobs. They also let everyone know that the company was hip. "It was a matter of doing away with everything that seemed to reek of the old," explains business professor Donna Hoffman. "The feeling was, 'We're going to make new rules. We need new titles.'"

But the times, of course, have changed. Executive recruiter Marc Lewis observes that "as the market has cooled, the interest in creative and unusual job titles has diminished." Smaller companies (as well as some larger ones) are now trying to create images of legitimacy, respectability, and honesty. Burkus admits that "the traditional titles [like 'customer care manager' and 'production supervisor'] lend themselves more to the image of a stable company that is driving toward profitability."

> *"The feeling was, 'We're going to make new rules. We need new titles.'"*
>
> *—Business professor Donna Hoffman on the tendency of dot-coms to embrace creative job titles*

Does a return to confidence-inspiring, snooze-inducing job titles mean that companies have abandoned the effort to encourage employee creativity? By no means. Innovation is just as important during tough times as during boom times. The method, however, has changed. Today, entrepreneurial firms that want to encourage and reward creativity aren't willing to settle for window dressing. They're changing the jobs themselves.

Employers are finding, for instance, that basing positions on employee interests can be more effective than trying to fit unique individuals into predetermined job slots. Often a customized job is a reward for high performance. Steve Gluckman, a bicycle designer for REI (*www.rei.com*), a small supplier of outdoor gear, worked his way up from service manager to designer over 13 years. An avid cyclist, he says, "Some people sing. Some people paint. I ride my bike. Like a ballet dancer, like a gymnast, like a skateboarder, I express myself in my job." Starbucks' coffee education manager, Aileen Carrell, travels around the world educating employees about coffee. "I was hired as temporary Christmas help in 1990," explains Carrell, "and I fell madly in love with the fact that coffees came from the most amazing places, like Sulawesi." After working as a store manager for several years, Carrell herself proposed the creation of her new position. Of course, organizations will always have to define most of the jobs that have to be performed, but many are discovering that a little flexibility can lead to a lot of productivity.

---

organizational plans, and general economic trends. A good sales forecast is often the foundation, especially for smaller organizations. Historical ratios can then be used to predict demand for types of employees, such as operating employees and sales representatives. Large organizations use much more complicated models to predict HR needs.

Forecasting the supply of labor is really two tasks:

- Forecasting *internal supply*—the number and type of employees who will be in the firm at some future date.
- Forecasting *external supply*—the number and type of people who will be available for hiring from the labor market at large.

The simplest approach merely adjusts present staffing levels for anticipated turnover and promotions. Again, however, large organizations use extremely sophisticated models to make these forecasts.

Replacement Charts At higher levels of the organization, managers plan for specific people and positions. The technique most commonly used is the **replacement chart**, which lists each important managerial position, who occupies it, how long that person will probably stay in it before moving on, and who (by name) is now qualified or soon will be qualified to move into it. This technique allows ample time to plan developmental experiences for people identified as potential successors to critical managerial jobs. In early times replacement charts were actual charts—paper documents or posters that were displayed on walls or bulletin boards. Now, however, they are much more likely to be electronic.

replacement chart
List of each management position, who occupies it, how long that person will likely stay in the job, and who is qualified as a replacement

Skills Inventories To facilitate both planning and identifying people for transfer or promotion, some organizations also have **employee information systems**, or **skills inventories**. These systems are again electronic and contain information on each employee's education, skills, work experience, and career aspirations. Such a system can quickly locate every employee who is qualified to fill a position requiring, for example, a degree in chemical engineering, three years of experience in an oil refinery, and fluency in Spanish.

employee information system (skills inventory)
Computerized system containing information on each employee's education, skills, work experiences, and career aspirations

Forecasting the external supply of labor is a different problem altogether. How does a manager, for example, predict how many electrical engineers will be seeking work in California or Florida three years from now? To get an idea of the future availability of labor, planners must rely on information from outside sources, such as state employment commissions, government reports, and figures supplied by colleges on the number of students in major fields.

Matching HR Supply and Demand After comparing future demand and internal supply, managers can make plans to manage predicted shortfalls or overstaffing. If a shortfall is predicted, new employees can be hired, present employees can be retrained and transferred into understaffed areas, individuals approaching retirement can be convinced to stay on, or labor-saving or productivity-enhancing systems can be installed.

If the organization needs to hire, the external labor-supply forecast helps managers plan on how to recruit according to whether the type of employee needed is readily available or scarce in the labor market. The use of temporary workers also helps managers in staffing by giving them extra flexibility. If overstaffing is expected to be a problem, the main options are transferring the extra employees, not replacing individuals who quit, encouraging early retirement, and laying people off.[3]

■ STAFFING THE ORGANIZATION

When managers have determined that new employees are needed, they must then turn their attention to recruiting and hiring the right mix of people. Staffing the organization is one of the most complex and important tasks of good HR management. In this section, we will describe both the process of acquiring staff from outside the company (*external staffing*) and the process of promoting staff from within (*internal staffing*). Both external staffing and internal staffing, however, start with effective recruiting.

Recruiting Human Resources Once an organization has an idea of its future HR needs, the next phase is usually recruiting new employees. **Recruiting** is the process of attracting qualified persons to apply for the jobs that are open. Where do recruits

recruiting
Process of attracting qualified persons to apply for jobs an organization is seeking to fill

come from? Some recruits are found internally, whereas others come from outside of the organization.

internal recruiting
Considering present employees as candidates for openings

Internal Recruiting **Internal recruiting** means considering present employees as candidates for openings. Promotion from within can help build morale and keep high-quality employees from leaving. In unionized firms, the procedures for notifying employees of internal job-change opportunities are usually spelled out in the union contract. For higher-level positions, a skills inventory system may be used to identify internal candidates, or managers may be asked to recommend individuals who should be considered.

external recruiting
Attracting persons outside the organization to apply for jobs

External Recruiting **External recruiting** involves attracting people outside of the organization to apply for jobs. External recruiting methods include advertising, campus interviews, employment agencies or executive search firms, union hiring halls, referrals by present employees, and hiring "walk-ins" or "gate-hires" (people who show up without being solicited). A manager must select the most appropriate method for each job. The manager might, for instance, use the state employment service to find a maintenance worker but not a nuclear physicist. Private employment agencies can be a good source of clerical and technical employees, and executive search firms specialize in locating top-management talent. Newspaper ads are often used because they reach a wide audience and thus allow minorities equal opportunity to find out about and apply for job openings.

During the late 1990s, recruiters faced a difficult job as unemployment plummeted. By early 1998, for example, unemployment had dropped to a 23-year low of 4.6 percent. As a result, recruiters at firms such as Sprint, PeopleSoft, and Cognex had to stress how much "fun" it was to work for them, reinforcing this message with ice cream socials, karaoke contests, softball leagues, and free-movie nights. By 2001, however, the situation had begun to change. Unemployment began to creep back up, many larger employers (such as AT&T and Hewlett-Packard) announced major job cutbacks, and recruiters were again able to attract highly qualified employees without having to offer signing bonuses or other extravagant incentives. Although most companies have tried to maintain reasonable benefits programs, many have also been forced to cut back, especially in the area of health care. Companies can also afford to be more selective in the employees they choose to hire.[4]

Selecting Human Resources

Once the recruiting process has attracted a pool of applicants, the next step is to select someone to hire. The intent of the selection process is to gather from applicants information that will predict their job success and then to hire the candidates likely to be most successful. Of course, the organization can only gather information about factors that can be used to predict future performance. The process of determining the predictive value of information is called **validation**.

validation
Process of determining the predictive value of a selection technique

Application Forms The first step in selection is usually asking the candidate to fill out an application. An application form is an efficient method of gathering information about the applicant's previous work history, educational background, and other job-related demographic data. It should not contain questions about areas unrelated to the job such as gender, religion, or national origin. Application form data are generally used informally to decide whether a candidate merits further evaluation, and

Employees of Cingular Wireless (*www.cingular.com*), a specialist in mobile voice and data communications, gather at the hometown Atlanta Zoo. Cingular markets itself as a company that "enhances the customer experience," and it wants to send a comparable message when communicating to employees and potential employees. "We want customers to use the wireless device as a tool to express themselves," says a vice president for human resources, "and we want to give our employees the opportunity to be just as expressive." The point, of course, is to foster productivity and loyalty in an era of impermanence in employer–employee relations.

interviewers use application forms to familiarize themselves with candidates before interviewing them.

Tests Tests of ability, skill, aptitude, or knowledge that is relevant to a particular job are usually the best predictors of job success, although tests of general intelligence or personality are occasionally useful as well. In addition to being validated, tests should be administered and scored consistently. All candidates should be given the same directions, allowed the same amount of time, and offered the same testing environment (temperature, lighting, resources, and so forth).

Interviews Although a popular selection device, the interview is sometimes a poor predictor of job success. For example, biases inherent in the way people perceive and judge others on first meeting affect subsequent evaluations. Interview validity can be improved by training interviewers to be aware of potential biases and by tightening the structure of the interview. In a structured interview, questions are written in advance and all interviewers follow the same question list with each candidate. Such structure introduces consistency into the interview procedure and allows the organization to validate the content of the questions.

For interviewing managerial or professional candidates, a somewhat less structured approach can be used. Although question areas and information-gathering objectives are still planned in advance, specific questions vary with the candidates' backgrounds.

Other Techniques Organizations also use other selection techniques that vary with circumstances. Polygraph tests, once popular, are declining in popularity. On the other hand, organizations occasionally require applicants to take physical exams (being careful that their practices are consistent with the Americans with Disabilities Act). More organizations are using drug tests, especially in situations in which drug-related performance problems could create serious safety hazards. Applicants at a nuclear power plant, for example, will probably be tested for drugs. Some organizations also run credit checks on prospective employees.

DEVELOPING THE WORKFORCE

After a company has hired new employees, it must acquaint them with the firm and their new jobs. Managers also take steps to train employees and to further develop necessary job skills. In addition, every firm has some system for performance appraisal and feedback. Unfortunately, the results of these assessments sometimes require procedures for demoting or terminating employees.

Training

on-the-job training
Training, sometimes informal, conducted while an employee is at work

off-the-job training
Training conducted in a controlled environment away from the work site

vestibule training
Off-the-job training conducted in a simulated environment

As its name suggests, **on-the-job training** occurs while the employee is at work. Much of this training is informal, as when one employee shows another how to use the photocopier. In other cases, it is quite formal. For example, a trainer may teach secretaries how to operate a new e-mail system from their workstations.

Off-the-job training takes place at locations away from the work site. This approach offers a controlled environment and allows focused study without interruptions. For example, the petroleum equipment manufacturer Baker-Hughes uses classroom-based programs to teach new methods of quality control. Chaparral Steel's training program includes four hours a week of general education classroom training in areas such as basic math and grammar.

Other firms use **vestibule training** in simulated work environments to make off-the-job training more realistic. American Airlines, for example, trains flight attendants through vestibule training and uses flight simulators to train pilots; AT&T uses simulations to train telephone operators. Finally, many organizations today are increasingly using computerized and/or Web-based training.[5]

Performance Appraisal

performance appraisal
Evaluation of an employee's job performance in order to determine the degree to which the employee is performing effectively

In some small companies, **performance appraisal** takes place when the owner tells an employee, "You're doing a good job." In larger firms, performance appraisals are designed to show more precisely how well workers are doing their jobs. Typically, the

FIGURE 8.2

Performance Rating Scale

V/M Variety Manufacturing

Employee Name: _____

Supervisor's Name: _____

Part I. *Circle the most descriptive point on each scale.*

Initiative

1   2   3   4   5

Never does anything without being told.   Handles simple matters alone.   Handles all functions without help.

Punctuality

1   2   3   4   5

Is almost always late.   Is seldom late.   Is never late.

Cleanliness

1   2   3   4   5

Work area is always dirty and messy.   Work area is generally clean and orderly.   Work area is always clean and orderly.

Please complete the separate evaluation form on page two.

appraisal process involves a written assessment issued on a regular basis. As a rule, however, the written evaluation is only one part of a multistep process.

The appraisal process begins when a manager defines performance standards for an employee. The manager then observes the employee's performance. If the standards are clear, the manager should have little difficulty comparing expectations with performance. For some jobs, a rating scale like the abbreviated one in Figure 8.2 is useful in providing a basis for comparisons. In addition to scales for initiative, punctuality, and cleanliness, a complete form will include several other scales directly related to performance. Comparisons drawn from such scales form the basis for written appraisals and for decisions about raises, promotions, demotions, and firings. The process is completed when the manager and employee meet to discuss the appraisal.[6]

COMPENSATION AND BENEFITS

Most workers today also expect certain benefits from their employers. Indeed, a major factor in retaining skilled workers is a company's **compensation system**—the total package of rewards that it offers employees in return for their labor.[7]

Although wages and salaries are key parts of all compensation systems, most also include *incentives* and *employee benefits programs*. We discuss these and other types

compensation system
Set of rewards that organizations provide to individuals in return for their willingness to perform various jobs and tasks within the organization

of employee benefits in this section. Remember, however, that finding the right combination of compensation elements is always complicated by the need to make employees feel valued while holding down company costs. Thus, compensation systems differ widely, depending on the nature of the industry, the company, and the types of workers involved.

Wages and Salaries

wages
Compensation in the form of money paid for time worked

salary
Compensation in the form of money paid for discharging the responsibilities of a job

Wages and salaries are the dollar amounts paid to employees for their labor. **Wages** are paid for time worked. For example, workers who are paid by the hour receive wages. A **salary** is paid for discharging the responsibilities of a job. A salaried executive earning $100,000 per year is paid to achieve results even if that means working 5 hours one day and 15 the next. Salaries are usually expressed as an amount paid per year or per month.

In setting wage and salary levels, a company may start by looking at its competitors' levels. A firm that pays less than its rivals knows that it runs the risk of losing valuable personnel. Conversely, to attract top employees, some companies pay more than their rivals. M&M/Mars, for example, pays managerial salaries about 10 percent above the average in the candy and snack food industry. Wal-Mart, meanwhile, starts hourly workers at a rate only slightly above the minimum wage.

A firm must also decide how its internal wage and salary levels will compare for different jobs. For example, Sears must determine the relative salaries of store managers, buyers, and advertising managers. In turn, managers must decide how much to pay individual workers within the company's wage and salary structure. Although two employees may do exactly the same job, the employee with more experience may earn more. Moreover, some union contracts specify differential wages based on experience.

Incentive Programs

incentive program
Special compensation program designed to motivate high performance

Naturally, employees feel better about their companies when they believe that they are being fairly compensated; however, studies and experience have shown that beyond a certain point, more money will not produce better performance. Indeed, neither across-the-board nor cost-of-living wage increases cause people to work harder. Money motivates employees only if it is tied directly to performance. The most common method of establishing this link is the use of **incentive programs**—special pay programs designed to motivate high performance. Some programs are available to individuals, whereas others are distributed on a companywide basis.

bonus
Individual performance incentive in the form of a special payment made over and above the employee's salary

Individual Incentives A sales bonus is a typical incentive. Employees receive **bonuses**—special payments above their salaries—when they sell a certain number or certain dollar amount of goods for the year. Employees who fail to reach this goal earn no bonuses. **Merit salary systems** link raises to performance levels in nonsales jobs.[8] For example, many baseball players have contract clauses that pay them bonuses for hitting over .300, making the All-Star team, or being named Most Valuable Player.

merit salary system
Individual incentive linking compensation to performance in nonsales jobs

Executives commonly receive stock options as incentives. Disney CEO Michael Eisner, for example, can buy several thousand shares of company stock each year at a predetermined price. If his managerial talent leads to higher profits and stock prices, he can buy the stock at a price lower than the market value for which, in theory, he is largely responsible. He is then free to sell the stocks at market price, keeping the prof-

Discovery Communications Inc. *(www.discovery.com)* faced a morale problem because its fixed-pay system meant that people doing a job in one division did not receive raises even when the pay scale for the same job description went up in another division. Employees saw the system as unfair, and so Discovery, which runs 33 cable networks out of its headquarters in Bethesda, Maryland, switched to a pay-for-performance compensation system that allows for healthy bonuses based on supervisors' evaluations and overall corporate performance.

its for himself. Executive stock options have, unfortunately, been at the center of some of the recent accounting scandals plaguing some businesses today. In a nutshell, firms have chosen not to treat them as expenses at the time they were granted, contrary to what accountants suggest. In response to growing criticism, some companies, such as Coca-Cola, have announced plans to change how they account for stock options.

A newer incentive plan is called **pay for performance**, or **variable pay**. In essence, middle managers are rewarded for especially productive output—for producing earnings that significantly exceed the cost of bonuses. Such incentives have long been common among top-level executives and factory workers, but variable pay goes to middle managers on the basis of companywide performance, business unit performance, personal record, or all three factors.

The number of variable pay programs in the United States has been growing consistently for the last decade, and most experts predict that they will continue to grow in popularity. Eligible managers must often forgo merit or entitlement raises (increases for staying on and reporting to work every day), but many firms say that variable pay is a better motivator because the range between generous and mediocre merit raises is usually quite small anyway. Merit raises also increase fixed costs: They are added to base pay and increase the base pay used to determine the retirement benefits that the company must pay out.

Companywide Incentives Some incentive programs apply to all the employees in a firm. Under **profit-sharing plans**, for example, profits earned above a certain level are distributed to employees. Conversely, **gainsharing plans** distribute bonuses to employees when a company's costs are reduced through greater work efficiency. **Pay-for-knowledge plans** encourage workers to learn new skills and to become proficient at different jobs. They receive additional pay for each new skill or job that they master.

Benefits Programs

An important part of nearly every firm's compensation system is its benefits program. **Benefits**—compensation other than wages and salaries offered by a firm to its workers—comprise a large percentage of most compensation budgets. Most companies are

pay for performance (or **variable pay**)
Individual incentive that rewards a manager for especially productive output

profit-sharing plan
Incentive plan for distributing bonuses to employees when company profits rise above a certain level

gainsharing plan
Incentive plan that rewards groups for productivity improvements

pay-for-knowledge plan
Incentive plan to encourage employees to learn new skills or become proficient at different jobs

benefits
Compensation other than wages and salaries

workers' compensation insurance
Legally required insurance for compensating workers injured on the job

required by law to provide social security retirement benefits and **workers' compensation insurance** (insurance for compensating workers injured on the job).

Most businesses also voluntarily provide health, life, and disability insurance (although employees are being asked to pay an increasingly high percentage of the premiums). Some also allow employees to use payroll deductions to buy stock at discounted prices. Another fairly common benefit is paid time-off for vacations and holidays. Counseling services for employees with alcohol, drug, or emotional problems are also common, as are on-site child care centers.[9]

Retirement Plans Retirement plans are also an important—and sometimes controversial—benefit that is available to many employees. Most company-sponsored retirement plans are set up to pay pensions to workers when they retire. In some cases, the company contributes all the money to the pension fund. In others, contributions are made by both the company and employees. Currently, about 60 percent of U.S. workers are covered by pension plans of some kind.

Containing the Costs of Benefits As the range and costs of benefits have grown, so has concern about keeping these costs in check. Many companies are experimenting with cost-cutting plans under which they can still attract and retain valuable employees. One approach is the **cafeteria benefit plan**. A certain dollar amount of benefits per employee is set aside so that each employee can choose from a variety of alternatives.

cafeteria benefit plan
Benefit plan that sets limits on benefits per employee, each of whom may choose from a variety of alternative benefits

Another area of increasing concern is health care costs. Medical procedures that once cost several hundred dollars now cost several thousand dollars. Medical expenses have increased insurance premiums, which in turn have increased the cost to employers of maintaining benefits plans.

Many employers are looking for new ways to cut those costs. One increasingly popular approach is for organizations to create their own networks of health care providers. These providers agree to charge lower fees for services rendered to employees of member organizations. In return, they enjoy established relationships with large employers and thus more clients and patients. Because they must make lower reimbursement payments, insurers also charge less to cover the employees of network members.

■ THE LEGAL CONTEXT OF HR MANAGEMENT

As much or more than any area of business, HR management is heavily influenced by federal law and judicial review. In this section, we summarize some of the most important and far-reaching areas of HR regulation.

Equal Employment Opportunity

equal employment opportunity
Legally mandated nondiscrimination in employment on the basis of race, creed, sex, or national origin

The basic goal of all **equal employment opportunity** regulation is to protect people from unfair or inappropriate discrimination in the workplace.[10] Let's begin by noting that discrimination in itself is not illegal. Whenever one person is given a pay raise and another is not, for example, the organization has made a decision to distinguish one person from another. As long as the basis for this discrimination is purely job related (made, for instance, on the basis of performance or seniority) and is applied objectively and consistently, the action is legal and appropriate.

Problems arise when distinctions among people are not job related. In such cases, the resulting discrimination is illegal. Various court decisions, coupled with interpretations of the language of various laws, suggest that illegal discrimination actions by an organization or its managers cause members of a "protected class" to be unfairly differentiated from other members of the organization.

Protected Classes in the Workplace Illegal discrimination is based on a stereotype, belief, or prejudice about classes of individuals. At one time, for example, common stereotypes regarded black employees as less dependable than white employees, women as less suited to certain types of work than men, and disabled individuals as unproductive employees.

Based on these stereotypes, some organizations routinely discriminated against blacks, women, and the disabled. To combat discrimination, laws have been passed to protect various classes of individuals. A **protected class** consists of all individuals who share one or more common characteristics as indicated by a given law. The most common criteria for defining protected classes include race, color, religion, gender, age, national origin, disability status, and status as a military veteran.[11]

protected class
Set of individuals who by nature of one or more common characteristics are protected under the law from discrimination on the basis of that characteristic

Enforcing Equal Employment Opportunity The enforcement of equal opportunity legislation is handled by two agencies. The **Equal Employment Opportunity Commission**, or **EEOC** *(www.eeoc.gov)*, is a division of the Department of Justice. It was created by Title VII of the 1964 Civil Rights Act and today has specific responsibility for enforcing Title VII, the Equal Pay Act, and the Americans with Disabilities Act.

The other agency charged with monitoring equal employment opportunity legislation is the Office of Federal Contract Compliance Programs, or OFCCP *(www.dol.gov/dol/esa/public/of_org.htm)*. The OFCCP is responsible for enforcing executive orders that apply to companies doing business with the federal government. A business with government contracts must have on file a written **affirmative action plan**—that is, a written statement of how the organization intends to actively recruit, hire, and develop members of relevant protected classes.

Equal Employment Opportunity Commission (EEOC)
Federal agency enforcing several discrimination-related laws

affirmative action plan
Practice of recruiting qualified employees belonging to racial, gender, or ethnic groups who are underrepresented in an organization

In recent years some critics have called into question the continued usefulness of affirmative action. Among their other arguments are that (1) illegal discrimination has become so rare that affirmative action is no longer needed and (2) affirmative action often has the effect of reverse discrimination—discrimination against those not in protected classes. In June 2003, however, a U.S. Supreme Court decision upheld the concept of affirmative action as an appropriate and valid method for continuing to promote equal opportunity.

Legal Issues in Compensation As we noted earlier, most employment regulations are designed to provide equal employment opportunity. Some legislation, however, goes beyond equal employment opportunity and really deals more substantively with other issues. One such area is legislation covering compensation.

Contemporary Legal Issues in HR Management

In addition to these established areas of HR legal regulation, there are several emerging legal issues that will likely become more and more important with the passage of time. These include employee safety and health, various emerging areas of discrimination law, employee rights, and employment-at-will.

"I see by your résumé that you're a woman."

Shanahan

Occupational Safety and Health Act of 1970 (OSHA)
Federal law setting and enforcing guidelines for protecting workers from unsafe conditions and potential health hazards in the workplace

Employee Safety and Health The **Occupational Safety and Health Act of 1970**, or **OSHA** *(www.osha.gov)*, is the single most comprehensive piece of legislation ever passed regarding worker safety and health. OSHA holds that every employer has an obligation to furnish each employee with a place of employment that is free from hazards that cause or are likely to cause death or physical harm. It is generally enforced through inspections of the workplace by OSHA inspectors. If an OSHA compliance officer believes that a violation has occurred, a citation is issued. Nonserious violations may result in fines of up to $1,000 for each incident. Serious or willful and repeated violations may incur fines of up to $10,000 per incident.

Emerging Areas of Discrimination Law There are also several emerging areas of discrimination law that managers must also be familiar with. In this section, we will discuss some of the most important.

AIDS in the Workplace Although AIDS is considered a disability under the Americans with Disabilities Act of 1990, the AIDS situation itself is sufficiently severe enough that it warrants special attention. Employers cannot legally require an AIDS or any other medical examination as a condition for making an offer of employment. Organizations must treat AIDS like any other disease covered by law. They must maintain the confidentiality of all medical records. They cannot discriminate against a person with AIDS, and they should try to educate coworkers about AIDS. They cannot discriminate against AIDS victims in training or in consideration for promotion, and they must accommodate or make a good-faith effort to accommodate AIDS victims.

sexual harassment
Practice or instance of making unwelcome sexual advances in the workplace

Sexual Harassment Sexual harassment has been a problem in organizations for a long time and is a violation of Title VII of the Civil Rights Act of 1964. **Sexual harassment** is defined by the EEOC as unwelcome sexual advances in the work environment. If the conduct is indeed unwelcome and occurs with sufficient frequency to create an abusive work environment, the employer is responsible for changing the environment by warning, reprimanding, or perhaps firing the harasser.[12]

The courts have ruled and defined that there are two types of sexual harassment:

quid pro quo harassment
Form of sexual harassment in which sexual favors are requested in return for job-related benefits

■ In cases of **quid pro quo harassment**, the harasser offers to exchange something of value for sexual favors. A male supervisor, for example, might tell or suggest to a female subordinate that he will recommend her for promotion or give her a raise in exchange for sexual favors.

■ The creation of a **hostile work environment** is a subtler form of sexual harassment. A group of male employees who continually make off-color jokes and lewd comments and perhaps decorate the work environment with inappropriate photographs may create a hostile work environment for a female colleague, who becomes uncomfortable working in that environment. As we noted earlier, it is the organization's responsibility for dealing with this sort of problem.

hostile work environment
Form of sexual harassment deriving from off-color jokes, lewd comments, and so forth

Regardless of the pattern, the same bottom-line rules apply: Sexual harassment is illegal, and the organization is responsible for controlling it.

Employment-at-Will The concept of **employment-at-will** holds that both employer and employee have the mutual right to terminate an employment relationship anytime for any reason and with or without advance notice to the other. Specifically, it holds that an organization employs an individual at its own will and can, therefore, terminate that employee at any time for any reason. Over the last two decades, however, terminated employees have challenged the employment-at-will doctrine by filing lawsuits against former employers on the grounds of wrongful discharge.

employment-at-will
Principle, increasingly modified by legislation and judicial decision, that organizations should be able to retain or dismiss employees at their discretion

In the last several years, such suits have put limits on employment-at-will provisions in certain circumstances. In the past, for example, organizations were guilty of firing employees who filed workers' compensation claims or took excessive time off to serve on jury duty. More recently, however, the courts have ruled that employees may not be fired for exercising rights protected by law.

SELF-CHECK QUESTIONS 4–6

You should now be able to answer Self-Check Questions 4–6.*

4 **Multiple Choice** Which of the following is a common training method today? [select one]: **(a)** on-the-job training; **(b)** off-the-job training; **(c)** vestibule training; **(d)** Web-based training; **(e)** all of these.

5 **Multiple Choice** Both Jason Giambi of the New York Yankees and Sheryl Swoopes of the Houston Comets have contract clauses that pay them extra if they are voted Most Valuable Player of their respective leagues. This clause is an example of which of the following? [select one]: **(a)** individual incentive; **(b)** profit-sharing plan; **(c)** gainsharing plan; **(d)** pay-for-knowledge plan; **(e)** cafeteria benefit plan.

6 **True/False** As long as hiring rules are applied uniformly, an employer can choose not to hire members of a protected class.

*Answers to Self-Check Questions 4–6 can be found on p. 508.

■ NEW CHALLENGES IN THE CHANGING WORKPLACE

As we have seen throughout this chapter, human resource managers face several ongoing challenges in their efforts to keep their organizations staffed with effective workforces. To complicate matters, new challenges arise as the economic and social environments of business change. In the following sections, we take a look at several of the most important human resource management issues facing business today.

Say WHAT YOU MEAN

TOP-DOWN SENSITIVITY

By definition, global companies must communicate with employees in many different countries and cultures, and a firm's success in communicating with local workers can mean success or failure in an overseas operation. The most successful global companies know how to talk to the people who work for them.

In some countries, the gap between managers and workers is quite wide, and managers are used to bridging it with orders that are simply to be followed. In many Asian cultures, for example, you simply don't question the boss's decisions or the policies of the company. In the United States, by contrast, people are often encouraged to provide feedback and to say what they think. The gap is relatively narrow, and communication channels tend to be informal and wide open.

The same arrangements usually apply when it comes to dealing with workplace disputes. In some countries, such as Germany and Sweden, there's a formal system for ensuring that everyone involved gets a say in resolving workplace disputes. In these countries, although communication channels are always open, they're also highly structured.

But being culturally sensitive to local employees means much more than just knowing how to settle workplace disputes. As a rule, companies also need to convey a sense of good "citizenship" in the host country. This means respecting the social and cultural values of employees and communicating to them the fact that it cares about these things.

Managing Workforce Diversity

workforce diversity
Range of workers' attitudes, values, and behaviors that differ by gender, race, and ethnicity

One extremely important set of human resource challenges centers on **workforce diversity**—the range of workers' attitudes, values, beliefs, and behaviors that differ by gender, race, age, ethnicity, physical ability, and other relevant characteristics. In the past, organizations tended to work toward homogenizing their workforces, getting everyone to think and behave in similar ways. Partly as a result of affirmative action efforts, however, many U.S. organizations are now creating more diverse workforces, embracing more women, ethnic minorities, and foreign-born employees than ever before.

Figure 8.3 helps put the changing U.S. workforce into perspective by illustrating changes in the percentages of different groups of workers—males and females, whites, African Americans, Hispanics, Asians, and others—in the total workforce in the years 1986, 1996, and (as projected) 2006. The picture is clearly one of increasing diversity. By 2006, say experts, almost half of all workers in the labor force will be women and almost one-third will be blacks, Hispanics, Asian Americans, and others.

Today, organizations are recognizing not only that they should treat everyone equitably but also that they should acknowledge the individuality of each person they employ. They are also recognizing that diversity can be a competitive advantage.[13] For example, by hiring the best people available from every single group rather than hiring from just one or a few groups, a firm can develop a higher-quality labor force. Similarly, a diverse workforce can bring a wider array of information to bear on problems and can provide insights on marketing products to a wider range of consumers. Says the head of workforce diversity at IBM, "We think it is important for our customers to

> "We think it is important for our customers to look inside and see people like them. If they can't, the prospect of them becoming or staying our customers declines."
>
> —Head of workforce diversity at IBM

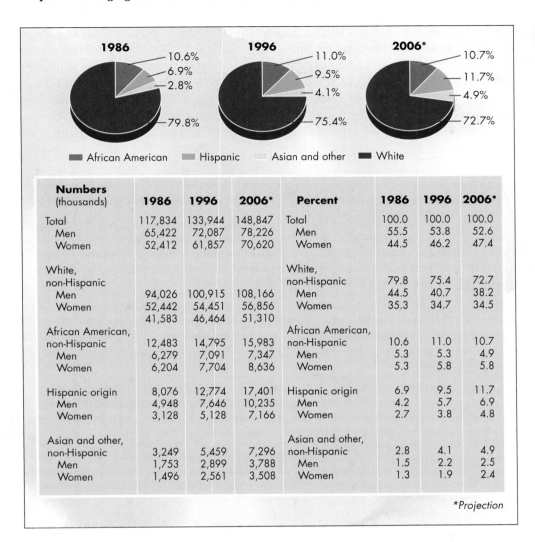

FIGURE 8.3

Changing Composition of the
U.S. Workforce

Numbers (thousands)	1986	1996	2006*	Percent	1986	1996	2006*
Total	117,834	133,944	148,847	Total	100.0	100.0	100.0
Men	65,422	72,087	78,226	Men	55.5	53.8	52.6
Women	52,412	61,857	70,620	Women	44.5	46.2	47.4
White, non-Hispanic				White, non-Hispanic	79.8	75.4	72.7
Men	94,026	100,915	108,166	Men	44.5	40.7	38.2
Women	52,442	54,451	56,856	Women	35.3	34.7	34.5
	41,583	46,464	51,310				
African American, non-Hispanic	12,483	14,795	15,983	African American, non-Hispanic	10.6	11.0	10.7
Men	6,279	7,091	7,347	Men	5.3	5.3	4.9
Women	6,204	7,704	8,636	Women	5.3	5.8	5.8
Hispanic origin	8,076	12,774	17,401	Hispanic origin	6.9	9.5	11.7
Men	4,948	7,646	10,235	Men	4.2	5.7	6.9
Women	3,128	5,128	7,166	Women	2.7	3.8	4.8
Asian and other, non-Hispanic	3,249	5,459	7,296	Asian and other, non-Hispanic	2.8	4.1	4.9
Men	1,753	2,899	3,788	Men	1.5	2.2	2.5
Women	1,496	2,561	3,508	Women	1.3	1.9	2.4

*Projection

look inside and see people like them. If they can't . . . the prospect of them becoming or staying our customers declines."

Managing Knowledge Workers

Traditionally, employees added value to organizations because of what they did or because of their experience. In the information age, however, many employees add value because of what they know.

The Nature of Knowledge Work These employees are usually called **knowledge workers**, and the skill with which they are managed is a major factor in determining which firms will be successful in the future. Knowledge workers, including computer scientists, engineers, and physical scientists, provide special challenges for the HR manager. They tend to work in high-technology firms and are usually experts in some abstract knowledge base. They often like to work independently and tend to identify more strongly with their professions than with any organization—even to the extent of defining performance in terms recognized by other members of their professions.

As the importance of information-driven jobs grows, the need for knowledge workers continues to grow as well. But these employees require extensive and highly

knowledge workers
Employees who are of value because of the knowledge they possess

specialized training, and not every organization is willing to make the human capital investments necessary to take advantage of these jobs. In fact, even after knowledge workers are on the job, retraining and training updates are critical to prevent their skills from becoming obsolete. It has been suggested, for example, that the half-life of a technical education in engineering is about three years. The failure to update such skills will not only result in the loss of competitive advantage but will also increase the likelihood that the knowledge worker will go to another firm that is more committed to updating the worker's skills.

Knowledge Worker Management and Labor Markets In recent years, the demand for knowledge workers has grown at a dramatic rate. Even the economic downturn in 2000 only slowed the demand for highly skilled knowledge workers. As a result, organizations that need these workers must introduce regular market adjustments (upward) in order to pay them enough to keep them. This is especially critical in areas in which demand is still growing, since even entry-level salaries for these employees are continuing to escalate. Once an employee accepts a job with a firm, the employer faces yet another dilemma. Once hired, workers are more subject to the company's internal labor market, which is not likely to be growing as quickly as the external market for knowledge workers as a whole. Consequently, the longer employees remain with a firm, the further behind the market their pay falls—unless it is regularly adjusted upward.

The continuing demand for these workers has inspired some fairly extreme measures for attracting them in the first place. High starting salaries and sign-on bonuses are common. British Petroleum Exploration *(www.bpamoco.com)* was recently paying starting petroleum engineers with undersea platform-drilling knowledge—not experience, just knowledge—salaries in the six figures, plus sign-on bonuses of over $50,000 and immediate profit sharing. Even with these incentives, HR managers complain that in the Gulf Coast region, they cannot retain specialists because young engineers soon leave to accept even more attractive jobs with competitors. Laments one HR executive, "We wind up six months after we hire an engineer having to fight off offers for that same engineer for more money."[14]

> **"We wind up six months after we hire an engineer having to fight off offers for that same engineer for more money."**
>
> **—Eric Campbell, HR executive at Docent Inc.**

Contingent and Temporary Workers

A final contemporary HR issue of note involves the use of contingent and temporary workers. Indeed, recent years have seen an explosion in the use of such workers by organizations.

Trends in Contingent and Temporary Employment In recent years, the number of contingent workers in the workforce has increased dramatically. A **contingent worker** is a person who works for an organization on something other than a permanent or full-time basis. Categories of contingent workers include independent contractors, on-call workers, temporary employees (usually hired through outside agencies), and contract and leased employees. Another category is part-time workers. The financial services giant Citigroup *(www.citigroup.com)*, for example, makes extensive use of part-time sales agents to pursue new clients. About 10 percent of the U.S. workforce currently uses one of these alternative forms of employment relationships. Experts suggest, however, that this percentage is increasing at a consistent pace.

contingent worker
Employee hired on something other than a full-time basis to supplement an organization's permanent workforce

Managing Contingent and Temporary Workers Given the widespread use of contingent and temporary workers, HR managers must understand how to use such employees most effectively. That is, they need to understand how to manage contingent and temporary workers.

One key is careful planning. Even though one of the presumed benefits of using contingent workers is flexibility, it still is important to integrate such workers in a coordinated fashion. Rather than having to call in workers sporadically and with no prior notice, organizations try to bring in specified numbers of workers for well-defined periods of time. The ability to do so comes from careful planning.

A second key is understanding contingent workers and acknowledging their advantages and disadvantages. That is, the organization must recognize what it can and can't achieve from the use of contingent and temporary workers. Expecting too much from such workers, for example, is a mistake that managers should avoid.

Third, managers must carefully assess the real cost of using contingent workers. We noted previously that many firms adopt this course of action to save labor costs. The organization should be able to document precisely its labor-cost savings. How much would it be paying people in wages and benefits if they were on permanent staff? How does this cost compare with the amount spent on contingent workers? This difference, however, could be misleading. We also noted, for instance, that contingent workers might be less effective performers than permanent and full-time employees. Comparing employee for employee on a direct-cost basis, therefore, is not necessarily valid. Organizations must learn to adjust the direct differences in labor costs to account for differences in productivity and performance.

Finally, managers must fully understand their own strategies and decide in advance how they intend to manage temporary workers, specifically focusing on how to integrate them into the organization. On a very simplistic level, for example, an organization with a large contingent workforce must make some decisions about the treatment of contingent workers relative to the treatment of permanent full-time workers. Should contingent workers be invited to the company holiday party? Should they have the same access to such employee benefits as counseling services and child care? There are no right or wrong answers to such questions. Managers must understand that they need to develop a strategy for integrating contingent workers according to some sound logic and then follow that strategy consistently over time.

■ DEALING WITH ORGANIZED LABOR

A **labor union** is a group of individuals working together to achieve shared job-related goals, such as higher pay, shorter working hours, more job security, greater benefits, or better working conditions.[15] **Labor relations** describes the process of dealing with employees who are represented by a union.

Labor unions grew in popularity in the United States in the nineteenth and early twentieth centuries. The labor movement was born with the Industrial Revolution, which also gave birth to a factory-based production system that carried with it enormous economic benefits. Job specialization and mass production allowed businesses to create ever greater quantities of goods at ever lower costs.

But there was also a dark side to this era. Workers became more dependent on their factory jobs. Eager for greater profits, some owners treated their workers like other raw materials: resources to be deployed with little or no regard for the individual worker's well-being. Many businesses forced employees to work long hours—60-hour weeks were common, and some workers were routinely forced to work 12 to

labor union
Group of individuals working together to achieve shared job-related goals, such as higher pay, shorter working hours, more job security, greater benefits, or better working conditions

labor relations
Process of dealing with employees who are represented by a union

16 hours a day. With no minimum-wage laws or other controls, pay was also minimal and safety standards virtually nonexistent. Workers enjoyed no job security and received few benefits. Many companies, especially textile mills, employed large numbers of children at poverty wages. If people complained, nothing prevented employers from firing and replacing them at will.

Unions appeared and ultimately prospered because they constituted a solution to the worker's most serious problem: They forced management to listen to the complaints of all their workers rather than to just the few who were brave (or foolish) enough to speak out. The power of unions, then, comes from collective action. **Collective bargaining** (which we discuss more fully later in this chapter) is the process by which union leaders and managers negotiate common terms and conditions of employment for the workers represented by unions. Although collective bargaining does not often occur in small businesses, many midsize and larger businesses must engage in the process.

collective bargaining
Process by which labor and management negotiate conditions of employment for union-represented workers

Unionism Today

Although understanding the historical context of labor unions is important, so too is appreciating the role of unionism today, especially trends in union membership, union–management relations, and bargaining perspectives. We discuss these topics in the sections that follow.

Trends in Union Membership Since the mid-1950s, U.S. labor unions have experienced increasing difficulties in attracting new members. As a result, although millions of workers still belong to labor unions, union membership as a percentage of the total workforce has continued to decline at a very steady rate. In 1980, for example, nearly 25 percent of U.S. wage and salary employees belonged to labor unions. Today, that figure is about 14 percent. Figure 8.4(a) traces the decades-long decline in union membership. Moreover, if public employees are excluded from consideration, then only around 11 percent of all private industry wage and salary employees currently belong to labor unions. Figure 8.4(b) illustrates the different trends in membership for public employees versus private nonfarm employees.

FIGURE 8.4

Trends in Union Membership

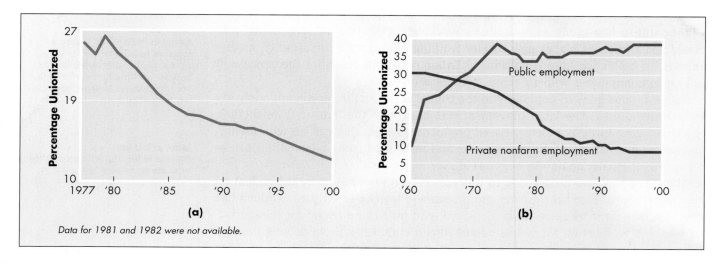

(a)

Data for 1981 and 1982 were not available.

(b)

Furthermore, just as union membership has continued to decline, so has the percentage of successful union-organizing campaigns. In the years immediately following World War II and continuing through the mid-1960s, most unions routinely won certification elections. In recent years, however, labor unions have been winning certification fewer than 50 percent of the time in which workers are called on to vote.

By the same token, of course, unions still do win. Meat cutters at a Florida Wal-Mart store recently voted to unionize—the first-ever successful organizing campaign against the retailing giant. "You'll see a lot more attention to Wal-Mart now," exulted one AFL-CIO official. "It's not like Wal-Mart stands out as some unattainable goal."[16]

From most indications, however, the power and significance of U.S. labor unions, although still quite formidable, are also measurably lower than they were just a few decades ago.

Trends in Union–Management Relations The gradual decline in unionization in the United States has been accompanied by some significant trends in union–management relations. In some sectors of the economy, perhaps most notably the automobile and steel industries, labor unions still remain quite strong. In these areas, unions have large memberships and considerable power in negotiating with management. The United Auto Workers (UAW), for example, is still one of the strongest unions in the United States.

In most sectors, however, unions are clearly in a weakened position, and as a result, many have taken much more conciliatory stances in their relations with management. This situation contrasts sharply with the more adversarial relationship that once dominated labor relations in this country. Increasingly, for instance, unions recognize that they don't have as much power as they once held and that it is in their own best interests, as well as in those of the workers that they represent, to work with management instead of working against it. Ironically, then, union–management relations are in many ways better today than they have been in many years. Admittedly, the improvement is attributable in large part to the weakened power of unions. Even so, however, most experts agree that improved union–management relations have benefited both sides.

Members of the Hotel Employees and Restaurant Employees union (HERE) at a rally in California. What's the issue? As is often the case, it's saving jobs, but this time the problem is unusually severe for both hotel owners and hotel employees. Since 9/11, no less than 40 percent of the union's 175,000 North American members have been laid off, and another 20 percent are working short weeks. Because laid-off workers don't pay dues, HERE is strapped for cash, and union president John Wilhelm has cut his own salary by 20 percent.

Trends in Bargaining Perspectives Given the trends described in the two previous sections, we should not be surprised to find changes in bargaining perspectives as well. In the past, most union–management bargaining situations were characterized by union demands for dramatic increases in wages and salaries. A secondary issue was usually increased benefits for members. Now, however, unions often bargain for different benefits, such as job security. Of particular interest in this area is the trend toward relocating jobs to take advantage of lower labor costs in other countries. Unions, of course, want to restrict job movement, whereas companies want to save money by moving facilities—and jobs—to other countries.

As a result of organizational downsizing and several years of relatively low inflation in this country, many unions today find themselves fighting against wage cuts rather than striving for wage increases. Similarly, as organizations are more likely to seek lower health care and other benefits, a common goal of union strategy is to preserve what's already been won. Unions also place greater emphasis on improved job security. A trend that has become especially important in recent years is the effort to improve pension programs for employees.

Unions have also begun increasingly to set their sights on preserving jobs for workers in the United States in the face of business efforts to relocate production in some sectors to countries where labor costs are lower. For example, the AFL-CIO has been an outspoken opponent of efforts to normalize trade relations with China, fearing that more businesses might be tempted to move jobs there. General Electric *(www.ge.com)* has been targeted for union protests recently because of its strategy to move many of its own jobs—and those of key suppliers—to Mexico.

The Future of Unions Despite declining membership and some loss of power, labor unions remain a major factor in the U.S. business world. The 86 labor organizations in the AFL-CIO, as well as independent major unions such as the Teamsters and the National Education Association (NEA), still play a major role in U.S. business. Moreover, some unions still wield considerable power, especially in the traditional strongholds of goods-producing industries. Labor and management in some industries, notably airlines and steel, are beginning to favor contracts that establish formal mechanisms for greater worker input into management decisions. Inland Steel *(www.inland.com)*, for instance, recently granted its major union the right to name a member to the board of directors. Union officers can also attend executive meetings.

COLLECTIVE BARGAINING

When a union has been legally certified, it assumes the role of official bargaining agent for the workers whom it represents. Collective bargaining is an ongoing process involving both the drafting and the administering of the terms of a labor contract.[17]

Reaching Agreement on Contract Terms

The collective bargaining process begins when the union is recognized as the exclusive negotiator for its members. The bargaining cycle itself begins when union leaders meet with management representatives to agree on a contract. By law, both parties must sit down at the bargaining table and negotiate in good faith.

When each side has presented its demands, sessions focus on identifying the *bargaining zone*. The process is shown in Figure 8.5. For example, although an

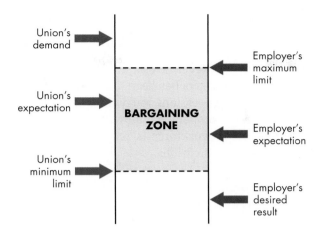

FIGURE 8.5

The Bargaining Zone

employer may initially offer no pay raise, it may expect to grant a raise of up to 6 percent. Likewise, the union may initially demand a 10-percent pay raise while expecting to accept a raise as low as 4 percent. The bargaining zone, then, is a raise between 4 and 6 percent. Ideally, some compromise is reached between these levels, and then the new agreement is submitted for a ratification vote by union membership.

Sometimes this process goes quite smoothly. At other times, however, the two sides cannot—or will not—agree. The speed and ease with which such an impasse is resolved depend in part on the nature of the contract issues, the willingness of each side to use certain tactics, and the prospects for mediation or arbitration.[18]

Contract Issues

The labor contract itself can address an array of different issues. Most of these concern demands that unions make on behalf of their members. In this section, we will survey the categories of issues that are typically most important to union negotiators: compensation, benefits, and job security. Although few issues covered in a labor contract are company sponsored, we will also describe the kinds of management rights that are negotiated in most bargaining agreements.

Compensation The most common issue is compensation. One aspect of compensation is current wages. Obviously, unions want their employees to earn higher wages and try to convince management to raise hourly wages for all or some employees.

Of equal concern to unions is future compensation: wage rates to be paid during subsequent years of the contract. One common tool for securing wage increases is a **cost-of-living adjustment (COLA)**. Most COLA clauses tie future raises to the *consumer price index* (CPI), a government statistic that reflects changes in consumer purchasing power. The premise is that as the CPI increases by a specified amount during a given period of time, wages will automatically be increased. Almost half of all labor contracts today include COLA clauses.

cost-of-living adjustment (COLA)
Labor contract clause tying future raises to changes in consumer purchasing power

Wage reopener clauses are now included in almost 10 percent of all labor contracts. Such a clause allows wage rates to be renegotiated at preset times during the life of the contract. For example, a union might be uncomfortable with a long-term contract based solely on COLA wage increases. A long-term agreement might be more acceptable, however, if management agrees to renegotiate wages every two years.

wage reopener clause
Clause allowing wage rates to be renegotiated during the life of a labor contract

Benefits Employee benefits are also an important component in most labor contracts. Unions typically want employers to pay all or most of the costs of insurance for employees. Other benefits commonly addressed during negotiations include retirement benefits, paid holidays, and working conditions.

Job Security Nevertheless, the UAW's top priority in its most recent negotiations with U.S. automakers has been job security, an increasingly important agenda item in many bargaining sessions today. In some cases, demands for job security entail the promise that a company not move to another location. In others, the contract may dictate that if the workforce is reduced, seniority will be used to determine which employees keep their jobs.

Other Union Issues Other possible issues might include such things as working hours, overtime policies, rest period arrangements, differential pay plans for shift employees, the use of temporary workers, grievance procedures, and allowable union activities (dues collection, union bulletin boards, and so forth).

Management Rights Management wants as much control as possible over hiring policies, work assignments, and so forth. Unions, meanwhile, often try to limit management rights by specifying hiring, assignment, and other policies. At a DaimlerChrysler plant in Detroit, for example, the contract stipulates that three workers are needed to change fuses in robots: a machinist to open the robot, an electrician to change the fuse, and a supervisor to oversee the process. As in this case, contracts often bar workers in one job category from performing work that falls in the domain of another. Unions try to secure jobs by defining as many different categories as possible (the DaimlerChrysler plant has over 100). Of course, management resists the practice, which limits flexibility and makes it difficult to reassign workers.

When Bargaining Fails

An impasse occurs when, after a series of bargaining sessions, management and labor have failed to agree on a new contract or a contract to replace an agreement that is about to expire. Although it is generally agreed that both parties suffer when an impasse is reached and some action by one part against the other is taken, each side can use several tactics to support its cause until the impasse is resolved.[19]

Union Tactics When their demands are not met, unions may bring a variety of tactics to the bargaining table. Chief among these are the strike, which may be supported by pickets and boycotts, and the slowdown.

strike
Labor action in which employees temporarily walk off the job and refuse to work

economic strike
Strike usually triggered by stalemate over one or more mandatory bargaining items

The Strike A **strike** occurs when employees temporarily walk off the job and refuse to work. Most strikes in the United States are **economic strikes**, triggered by stalemates over mandatory bargaining items, including such noneconomic issues as working hours. For example, the Teamsters union struck United Parcel Service (UPS) a few years ago over several noneconomic issues. Specifically, the union wanted the firm to transform many of its temporary and part-time jobs into permanent and full-time jobs. Strikers returned to work only when UPS agreed to create 10,000 new jobs. More recently, the same union struck Union Pacific Corp. *(www.up.com)* in January 2000 over wages and new jobs. In April 2000, machinists at a Lockheed-Martin *(www.lmco.com)* plant in Fort Worth, Texas, staged a two-week strike. Reflected the president of the union local, "I think our people gained a lot of respect for taking a stand. We had a good strike."

Still, there are far fewer strikes today than there were in previous years. For example, there were 222 strikes in the United States in 1960 involving a total of 896,000 workers. In 1970, 2,468,000 workers took part in 381 strikes. But in 1990, there were only 44 strikes involving 185,000 workers. Since 1990, the annual number of strikes has ranged from a high of 45 (in 1994) to a low of 29 (in 1997).[20]

Not all strikes are legal. **Sympathy strikes** (also called **secondary strikes**), which occur when one union strikes in sympathy with action initiated by another, may violate the sympathetic union's contract. **Wildcat strikes**—strikes unauthorized by the union that occur during the life of a contract—deprive strikers of their status as employees and thus of the protection of national labor law.

Other Labor Actions To support a strike, a union faced with an impasse has recourse to additional legal activities:

- In **picketing**, workers march at the entrance to the employer's facility with signs explaining their reasons for striking.
- A **boycott** occurs when union members agree not to buy the products of a targeted employer. Workers may also urge consumers to boycott the firm's products.
- Another alternative to striking is a work **slowdown**. Instead of striking, workers perform their jobs at a much slower pace than normal. A variation is the *sickout*, during which large numbers of workers call in sick. Pilots at American Airlines engaged in a massive sickout in early 1999, causing the airline to cancel thousands of flights before a judge ordered the pilots back into the cockpit.

Management Tactics Like workers, management can respond forcefully to an impasse:

- **Lockouts** occur when employers deny employees access to the workplace. Lockouts are illegal if they are used as offensive weapons to give management a bargaining advantage. However, they are legal if management has a legitimate business need (for instance, avoiding a buildup of perishable inventory). Although rare today, ABC *(www.abc.go.com)* locked out its off-camera employees a few years ago because they staged an unannounced one-day strike during a critical broadcasting period. Likewise, almost half of the 1998–1999 NBA season was lost when team owners *(www.nba.com)* locked out their players over contract issues.
- A firm can also hire temporary or permanent replacements called **strikebreakers**. However, the law forbids the permanent replacement of workers who strike because of unfair practices. In some cases, an employer can also obtain legal injunctions that either prohibit workers from striking or prohibit a union from interfering with its efforts to use replacement workers.

Mediation and Arbitration Rather than wield these often unpleasant weapons against one another, labor and management can agree to call in a third party to help resolve the dispute:

- In **mediation**, the neutral third party (the mediator) can suggest but cannot impose a settlement on the other parties.
- In **voluntary arbitration**, the neutral third party (the arbitrator) dictates a settlement between the two sides, which have agreed to submit to outside judgment.
- In some cases, arbitration is legally required to settle bargaining disputes. **Compulsory arbitration** is used to settle disputes between the government and public employees such as firefighters and police officers.

sympathy strike (or secondary strike)
Strike in which one union strikes to support action initiated by another

wildcat strike
Strike that is unauthorized by the strikers' union

picketing
Labor action in which workers publicize their grievances at the entrance to an employer's facility

boycott
Labor action in which workers refuse to buy the products of a targeted employer

slowdown
Labor action in which workers perform jobs at a slower than normal pace

lockout
Management tactic whereby workers are denied access to the employer's workplace

strikebreaker
Worker hired as permanent or temporary replacement for a striking employee

mediation
Method of resolving a labor dispute in which a third party suggests, but does not impose, a settlement

voluntary arbitration
Method of resolving a labor dispute in which both parties agree to submit to the judgment of a neutral party

compulsory arbitration
Method of resolving a labor dispute in which both parties are legally required to accept the judgment of a neutral party

SELF-CHECK QUESTIONS 7–9

You should now be able to answer Self-Check Questions 7–9*

7 Multiple Choice In general, which of the following is *true* about *workforce diversity*? [select one]: **(a)** It is decreasing. **(b)** It is increasing. **(c)** It remains constant. **(d)** It is becoming less important to business. **(e)** None of these.

8 True/False In recent years, the number of *contingent workers* has sharply increased.

9 Multiple Choice Which of the following is *true* about *union membership* in recent years? [select one]: **(a)** It has generally remained constant. **(b)** It has generally become more diverse. **(c)** Generally, it has steadily increased. **(d)** Generally, it has steadily declined. **(e)** It has generally changed in unknown ways because of new privacy laws.

***Answers to Self-Check Questions 7–9 can be found on p. 508.**

Continued from page 228

TIME OUT ON THE LABOR FRONT

As we explained at the beginning of this chapter, many firms have reduced or frozen hiring, and some are reducing or eliminating benefits and perquisites. These firms are seeking ways to lower costs, and they've found that current economic conditions give them more flexibility than they had just a few years ago. But although these actions may lower costs and protect profits in the short term, firms that follow this path may face problems when the economy rebounds. In particular, they may find that they've tarnished their reputations as employers and find it more difficult to attract workers when they need them again.

The repercussions may include low morale, reduced productivity, or worse. When the Indiana Social Services Administration left job vacancies unfilled in 1990, the state soon led the country in welfare fraud cases. And the effects can be long-lasting. Says one executive whose company instituted pay cuts, "People are lying low, but when the economy improves, they'll be out of here." Workers complain that they shouldn't bear a disproportionate share of the cost-cutting burden, and studies verify that median CEO compensation rose 6 percent in 2002 and worker pay just 3 percent. Company profits, meanwhile, fell 20 percent.

The good news for struggling firms is that there are still effective incentives. The most powerful, and least expensive, perk can be time off. Experts suggest, for example, that up to 20 percent of workers would be willing to work fewer hours for lower pay. Siemens, a German electronics firm, is offering workers a year-long "time-out," with reduced pay and a

> "It's a possibility for us not to lose good workers despite bad times."
>
> —Siemens executive on the company's policy of offering employees a year-long "time-out"

guaranteed job when they return. "It's a possibility for us not to lose good workers despite bad times," says Siemens spokesperson Axel Heim. Firms are also finding that technology workers and professionals, who need to stay on the leading edge of their fields, want more training and increased job responsibilities. Many people, warns Patti Wilson, founder of a high-tech career-management firm, "will jump jobs to learn more or stay if they feel that they're being challenged."

Questions for Discussion

1 What are the basic human resource issues reflected in labor force reductions and other HR cutbacks?

2 What benefits seem to be the most valuable to employees, and what benefits seem trivial or extravagant?

3 Aside from laying off workers, what other costs might be cut in managing an organization's labor force?

4 What other incentives besides benefits might a company be able to offer its best workers in order to retain them?

5 How might current employment trends affect unionization? Why?

■ SUMMARY OF LEARNING OBJECTIVES

1 Define *human resource management* and explain how managers plan for their organization's human resource needs.

Human resource management (HRM) is the set of organizational activities directed at attracting, developing, and maintaining an effective workforce. HR planning involves two tasks. **Job analysis** is a systematic analysis of jobs within an organization. It results in the creation of the **job description** and the **job specification**. Managers must plan for future HR needs by assessing past trends, future plans, and general economic trends. Forecasting labor supply is really two tasks— forecasting *internal supply* and forecasting *external supply*. The next step in HR planning is matching HR supply and demand—dealing with predicted shortfalls or overstaffing. If a shortfall is predicted, new employees can be hired. The external labor forecast helps managers recruit on the basis of which type of workers are available or scarce.

2 Identify the tasks in *staffing* a company and discuss ways in which managers *select, develop,* and *appraise* employee performance.

Staffing an organization means recruiting and hiring the right mix of people. **Recruiting** is the process of attracting qualified persons to apply for open jobs. **Internal recruiting** means considering present employees as candidates—a policy that helps build morale and keep high-quality employees. **External recruiting** involves attracting people from outside the organization. Methods include advertising, campus interviews, employment agencies or executive search firms, union hiring halls, and referrals by present employees. The next step is the selection process—gathering information that will predict applicants' job success and then hiring the most promising candidates. Common selection techniques include application blanks, tests, and interviews. Some organizations also use such selection techniques as polygraphs and drug tests.

New employees must be trained and allowed to develop job skills. **On-the-job training** occurs while the employee is at work. **Off-the-job training** takes place at off-site locations where controlled environments allow focused study. In larger firms, **performance appraisals** show how well workers are doing their jobs. Typically, appraisal involves a regular written assessment as part of a multistep process that begins when a manager defines performance standards for an employee. The manager then observes the employee, and the process ends when manager and employee meet to discuss the appraisal.

3 Describe the main components of a *compensation system* and explain some of the key legal issues involved in hiring, compensating, and managing workers in today's workplace.

A **compensation system** is the total package that a firm offers employees in return for their labor. The right combination of compensation elements will make employees feel valued while holding down company costs. **Wages** are paid for time worked (for example, by the hour). A **salary** is paid for discharging the responsibilities of a job. Beyond a certain point, money motivates employees only when tied directly to performance. One way to establish this link is the use of **incentive programs**—special pay programs designed to motivate high performance. **Benefits**—compensation other than wages and salaries—comprise a large percentage of most compensation budgets. The law requires most companies to provide social security retirement benefits and **workers' compensation insurance** (insurance for compensating workers injured on the job). Most companies provide health, life, and disability insurance; retirement plans pay pensions to workers when they retire. Many companies are experimenting with cost-cutting plans, such as the **cafeteria benefit plan**, in which a certain dollar amount of benefits per employee is set aside so that each employee can choose from a variety of alternatives.

HR management is heavily influenced by the law. One area of HR regulation is **equal employment opportunity**— regulation to protect people from unfair or inappropriate discrimination in the workplace. Because illegal discrimination is based on a prejudice about classes of individuals, laws protect various classes. Enforcement of equal opportunity legislation is handled by the **Equal Employment Opportunity Commission**, or **EEOC**, which is responsible for federal regulations, and the Office of Federal Contract Compliance Programs, or OFCCP, which is responsible for executive orders applying to companies doing business with the government. Other legislation deals with emerging legal issues, including employee safety and health.

4 Discuss *workforce diversity,* the management of *knowledge workers,* and the use of a *contingent workforce* as important changes in the contemporary workplace.

Workforce diversity refers to the range of workers' attitudes, values, beliefs, and behaviors that differ by gender, race, ethnicity, age, and physical ability. Today, many U.S. businesses are working to create workforces that reflect the growing diversity of the population as it enters the labor pool. Although many firms see the diverse workforce as a competitive advantage, not all are equally successful in or eager about implementing diversity programs.

Many firms today also face challenges in managing **knowledge workers**. The recent boom in high-technology companies has led to rapidly increasing salaries and high turnover among the workers who are best prepared to work in those companies. **Contingent workers** are temporary and part-time employees hired to supplement an organization's permanent workforce. Their numbers have grown significantly since the early 1980s and are expected to rise further. The practice of hiring contingent workers is gaining in popularity because it gives managers more flexibility and because temps are usually not covered by employers' benefit programs.

5 **Explain why workers organize into** *labor unions* **and describe the** *collective bargaining process.*

A **labor union** is a group of individuals working together to achieve shared job-related goals. **Labor relations** describes the process of dealing with employees represented by a union. Their power comes from collective action, such as collective bargaining—the process by which union leaders and company managers negotiate conditions of employment for unionized workers. Although millions of workers still belong to unions, membership as a percentage of the total workforce has declined at a steady rate since the mid-1950s.

The **collective bargaining process** begins when the union is recognized as the negotiator for its members. Among issues that are important to union negotiators are (1) compensation, (2) benefits, and (3) job security. An impasse occurs when management and labor fail to agree on a contract. Each side can use several tactics to support its cause until the impasse is resolved. The most important union tactic is the **strike**, which occurs when employees temporarily walk off the job and refuse to work. Unions may also use **picketing, boycotts**, and work **slowdowns**. Management may resort to **lockouts**—denying employees access to the workplace. A firm can also hire temporary or permanent replacements called **strikebreakers**. Rather than use these tactics, labor and management can call in a third party to help resolve the dispute.

■ KEY TERMS

human resource management (HRM) (p. 228)
job analysis (p. 229)
job description (p. 229)
job specification (p. 229)
replacement chart (p. 231)
employee information system (skills inventory) (p. 231)
recruiting (p. 231)
internal recruiting (p. 232)
external recruiting (p. 232)
validation (p. 232)
on-the-job training (p. 234)
off-the-job training (p. 234)
vestibule training (p. 234)
performance appraisal (p. 234)
compensation system (p. 235)
wages (p. 236)
salary (p. 236)
incentive program (p. 236)
bonus (p. 236)
merit salary system (p. 236)

pay for performance (or variable pay) (p. 237)
profit-sharing plan (p. 237)
gainsharing plan (p. 237)
pay-for-knowledge plan (p. 237)
benefits (p. 237)
workers' compensation insurance (p. 238)
cafeteria benefit plan (p. 238)
equal employment opportunity (p. 238)
protected class (p. 239)
Equal Employment Opportunity Commission (EEOC) (p. 239)
affirmative action plan (p. 239)
Occupational Safety and Health Act of 1970 (OSHA) (p. 240)
sexual harassment (p. 240)
quid pro quo harassment (p. 240)
hostile work environment (p. 241)
employment-at-will (p. 241)
workforce diversity (p. 242)

knowledge workers (p. 243)
contingent worker (p. 244)
labor union (p. 245)
labor relations (p. 245)
collective bargaining (p. 246)
cost-of-living adjustment (COLA) (p. 249)
wage reopener clause (p. 249)
strike (p. 250)
economic strike (p. 250)
sympathy strike (or secondary strike) (p. 251)
wildcat strike (p. 251)
picketing (p. 251)
boycott (p. 251)
slowdown (p. 251)
lockout (p. 251)
strikebreaker (p. 251)
mediation (p. 251)
voluntary arbitration (p. 251)
compulsory arbitration (p. 251)

■ QUESTIONS AND EXERCISES

Questions for Review

1 What are the advantages and disadvantages of internal and external recruiting? Under what circumstances is each more appropriate?

2 Why is the formal training of workers so important to most employers? Why don't employers simply let people learn about their jobs as they perform them?

3 What different forms of compensation do firms typically use to attract and keep productive workers?

4 Why do workers in some companies unionize whereas workers in others do not?

Questions for Analysis

5 What are your views on drug testing in the workplace? What would you do if your employer asked you to submit to a drug test?

6 Workers at Ford, GM, and DaimlerChrysler are represented by the UAW. However, the UAW has been unsuccessful in its attempts to unionize U.S. workers employed at Toyota, Nissan, and Honda plants in the United States. Why do you think this is so?

7 What training do you think you are most likely to need when you finish school and start your career?

8 How much will benefit considerations affect your choice of an employer after graduation?

Application Exercises

9 Interview an HR manager at a local company. Focus on a position for which the firm is currently recruiting applicants, and identify the steps in the selection process.

10 Interview the managers of two local companies, one unionized and one nonunionized. Compare the wage and salary levels, benefits, and working conditions of employees at the two firms.

BUILDING YOUR BUSINESS SKILLS

A LITTLE COLLECTIVE BRAINSTORMING

This exercise enhances the following SCANS workplace competencies: demonstrating basic skills, demonstrating thinking skills, exhibiting interpersonal skills, and working with information.

Goal

To encourage students to understand why some companies unionize and others do not.

The Situation

You've been working for the same nonunion company for five years. Although there are problems in the company, you like your job and have confidence in your ability to get ahead. Recently, you've heard rumblings that a large group of workers wants to call for a union election. You're not sure how you feel about this because none of your friends or family are union members.

Method

Step 1

Come together with three other "coworkers" who have the same questions as you. Each person should target four companies to learn about their union status. Avoid small businesses—choose large corporations such as General Motors, Intel, and Sears. As you investigate, answer the following questions:

■ Is the company unionized?

■ Is every worker in the company unionized or just selected groups of workers? Describe the groups.

■ If a company is unionized, what is the union's history in that company?

■ If a company is unionized, what are the main labor–management issues?

■ If a company is unionized, how would you describe the current status of labor–management relations? For example, are they cordial or strained?

■ If a company is not unionized, what factors are responsible for its nonunion status?

To learn the answers to these questions, contact the company, read corporate annual reports, search the company's Web site, contact union representatives, or do research on a computerized database.

Step 2

Go to the Web site of the AFL-CIO *(www.aflcio.org)* to learn more about the current status of the union movement. Then with your coworkers write a short report about the advantages of union membership.

Step 3

Research the disadvantages of unionization. A key issue to address is whether unions make it harder for companies to compete in the global marketplace.

FOLLOW-UP QUESTIONS

1 Based on everything you learned, are you sympathetic to the union movement? Would you want to be a union member?

2 Are the union members you spoke with satisfied or dissatisfied with their union's efforts to achieve better working conditions, higher wages, and improved benefits?

3 What is the union's role when layoffs occur?

4 Based on what you learned, do you think the union movement will stumble or thrive in the years ahead?

 # EXERCISING YOUR ETHICS

OPERATING TACTICALLY

The Situation

Assume that you work as a manager for a medium-size nonunion company that is facing its most serious union organizing campaign in years. Your boss, who is determined to keep the union out, has just given you a list of things to do in order to thwart the efforts of the organizers. For example, he has suggested each of the following tactics:

■ Whenever you learn about a scheduled union meeting, you should schedule a "worker appreciation" event at the same time. He wants you to offer free pizza and barbecue and to give cash prizes (that winners have to be present to receive).

■ He wants you to look at the most recent performance evaluations of the key union organizers and to terminate the one with the lowest overall evaluation.

■ He wants you to make an announcement that the firm is seriously considering such new benefits as on-site child care, flexible work schedules, telecommuting options, and exercise facilities. Although you know that the firm is indeed looking into these benefits, you also know that, ultimately, your boss will provide far less lavish benefits than he wants you to intimate.

The Dilemma

When you questioned the ethics—and even the legality—of these tactics, your boss responded by saying, "Look, all's fair in love and war, and this is war." He went on to explain that he was seriously concerned that a union victory might actually shut down the company's domestic operations altogether, forcing it to move all of its production capacities to lower-cost foreign plants. He concluded by saying that he was really looking out for the employees, even if he had to play hardball to help them. You easily see through his hypocrisy, but you also realize that there is some potential truth in his warning: If the union wins, jobs may actually be lost.

QUESTIONS FOR DISCUSSION

1 What are the ethical issues in this situation?

2 What are the basic arguments for and against extreme measures to fight unionization efforts?

3 What do you think most managers would do in this situation? What would you do?

 # CRAFTING YOUR BUSINESS PLAN

TAKING THE OCCASION TO DEAL WITH LABOR

The Purpose of the Assignment

1 To acquaint students with the labor and management relations issues faced by a sample start-up firm as it develops its business plan in the framework of the *Business PlanPro (BPP) 2003* software package (Version 6.0).

2 To stimulate students' thinking about the application of the textbook's concepts and methods on labor and management relations to the preparation of a business plan in the *BPP* planning environment.

ASSIGNMENT

After reading Chapter 8 in the textbook, open the BPP *software and search for information about labor and management relations as it applies to a sample firm:* Occasions, The Event Planning Specialists. *To find* Occasions, *do the following:*

Open the Business PlanPro. *Go to the toolbar and click on the "Sample Plans" icon. In the* **Sample Plan Browser**, *do a search using the* **search category** Personal services. *From the resulting list, select the category entitled* **Event Planning—Personal**, *which is the location for* Occasions, The Event Planning Specialists. *The screen you are looking* *at is the introduction page for the* Occasions *business plan. Next, scroll down until you reach the* **Table of Contents** *for* Occasions' *business plan.*

NOW RESPOND TO THE FOLLOWING ITEMS:

1 Explore the business plan for this company, paying special attention to its product line and the types of clients who will be buying its products. Do you suspect that there will be union members among the employees of some *Occasions* customers? [Sites to see in *BPP* for this item: On the Table of Contents page, click on each of the following in turn: **1.0 Executive Summary, 1.1 Objectives**, and **1.2 Mission**. After returning to the Table of Contents page, examine each of the following: **Table 2.2: Startup** (beneath **2.2 Startup Summary**), **3.0 Products and Services, 3.1 Competitive Comparison**, and **4.1 Market Segmentation**.]

2 Considering *Occasions'* growth projections, do you foresee increasing likelihood for unionization of its employees? Why or why not? What should *Occasions* do to accommodate clients' unions? [Sites to see in *BPP*: In the Table of Contents page, click on *1.1 Objectives*. Also look at both *2.0 Company Summary* and *6.1 Organizational Structure*.]

3 Explain why some experience with labor laws and management–union contract issues would be valuable for *Occasions'* salespeople in their dealings with clients. [Sites to see in *BPP* for this item: In the Table of Contents page, click on each of the following in turn: **1.0 Executive Summary, 3.0 Products and Services**, and **4.1 Market Segmentation**. After returning to the Table of Contents page, examine each of the following: **4.2 Target Market Segment Strategy** and **4.3 Industry Analysis**. After returning once again to the Table of Contents page, click on **1.3 Keys to Success**.]

 # VIDEO EXERCISE

MANAGING THE HUMAN SIDE OF BUSINESS: PARK PLACE ENTERTAINMENT

Learning Objectives
The purpose of this video is to help you:
1 Recognize the ways in which human resource management contributes to organizational performance.
2 Understand how and why HR managers make plans and decisions about staffing.
3 Identify some of the ways that HR managers handle staff evaluation and development.

Synopsis
Park Place Entertainment owns and operates resorts and casinos around the world. Its human resource department is responsible for hiring, training, and managing a diverse group of more than 52,000 employees. Because its customers come from many countries and speak many languages, the company seeks out employees from diverse backgrounds, varying the recruitment process for different properties in different areas. HR managers have created specific job descriptions for each position, instituted programs for employee and management development, and established incentive programs to reward good performance. Park Place's 360-degree evaluation method allows supervisors to get performance feedback from the employees they supervise.

DISCUSSION QUESTIONS
1 **For analysis:** What are the advantages and disadvantages of centralizing the recruiting process at a company such as Park Place Entertainment?
2 **For analysis:** Why did Park Place begin the restructuring of its HR department by standardizing training for supervisors?
3 **For application:** What steps might Park Place HR managers take to reduce employee turnover at particular resorts?
4 **For application:** How might Park Place encourage employees to refer friends as candidates for open positions?
5 **For debate:** Rather than hiring employees when business booms and then laying them off when it slumps, should Park Place temporarily rehire retired supervisors and employees during peak periods? Support your chosen position.

Online Exploration
Visit the Park Place Entertainment Web site at *(www.ballys.com)* and browse the home page to find the names and locations of the company's resorts and casinos. Then follow the company information link to find information on career opportunities and company benefits. What kinds of jobs are featured on the Web site? Why does Park Place arrange jobs by region? How does the firm make it convenient for applicants to submit résumés online? Why would Park Place put so much emphasis on Internet recruiting?

After reading this chapter,
you should be able to:

1 Describe the nature and importance of *psychological contracts* in the workplace.

2 Discuss the importance of *job satisfaction* and *employee morale* and summarize their roles in human relations in the workplace.

3 Identify and summarize the most important *theories of employee motivation*.

4 Describe some of the strategies used by organizations to improve *job satisfaction* and *employee motivation*.

5 Discuss different managerial styles of *leadership* and their impact on human relations in the workplace.

BRINGING THE BOUNTY BACK TO P&G

As the 1990s drew to a close, consumer products powerhouse Procter & Gamble (P&G) *(www.pg.com)* found itself in an unfamiliar a rut. Fueled by such megabrands as Tide, Crest, Charmin, Downy, Pampers, Folgers, Bounty, and Pringles, the 1980s had been a decade of phenomenal growth, but in the 1990s—for the first time ever—P&G failed to meet its goal of doubling sales growth each decade. Part of the problem was clear—

MOTIVATING, SATISFYING, AND LEADING EMPLOYEES

> "If there were 15 people sitting around the conference table, it wouldn't be obvious that he was the CEO."
>
> —Industry analyst on P&G CEO Alan Lafley

turnover at the top. P&G had gone through three different CEOs during the 1990s, each with his own unique personality and individual view of how the firm should be run.

The last of the three, Durk Jager, was appointed in 1998. Jager was an avid reorganizer who moved no fewer than 110,000 workers into new jobs. His strategy also called for focusing attention on new products rather than best-sellers. Unfortunately, the innovations that he championed, such as Olay cosmetics, often bombed. He also liked the idea of putting American brand names on P&G's global products, but shoppers in Germany and Hong Kong didn't recognize such brands as "Pantene" and "Dawn," and overseas sales plummeted. Jager tried to acquire drugmakers Warner-Lambert and American Home Products but dropped the idea under pressure from investors who thought the prices too high.

Under Jager's leadership, P&G missed earnings targets and lost $70 billion in market value. To make matters worse, his aggressive personality didn't endear Jager to P&G employees. Insiders reported that morale was falling daily, and many senior managers felt as if they no longer knew what they were supposed to be doing. "I was lost," said one vice president. "It was like no one knew how to get anything done anymore." Jager was fired in mid-2000, after only 17 months on the job.

The announcement of his replacement, 25-year P&G veteran Alan Lafley, was met with yawns and a $4 per share drop in share price. According to conventional wisdom, Durk Jager had saddled the company with so many problems that only a dynamic, strong-willed successor stood a chance of turning things around. And by most accounts, that wasn't Alan Lafley, whose low-key style and bespectacled appearance caused one industry analyst to comment that "If there were 15 people sitting around the conference table, it wouldn't be obvious that he was the CEO." *Fortune* magazine dubbed him "the un-CEO."

But to the surprise of many—and the shock of some—the quiet and unassuming Lafley has succeeded in turning around the stumbling manufacturer when other, more flamboyant leaders might well have failed. In some ways, he's even made it seem easy, demonstrating the virtues of back-to-basics strategy and honest, straightforward leadership. Lafley has also succeeded in restoring a sense of pride in the company and its products and lifted employee morale in dramatic style.

Our opening story continues on page 282.

PSYCHOLOGICAL CONTRACTS IN ORGANIZATIONS

psychological contract
Set of expectations held by an employee concerning what he or she will contribute to an organization (referred to as contributions) and what the organization will in return provide the employee (referred to as inducements)

Whenever we buy a car or sell a house, both buyer and seller sign a contract that specifies the terms of the agreement—who pays what to whom, when it's paid, and so forth. In some ways, a psychological contract resembles a legal contract. On the whole, however, it's less formal and less rigidly defined. A **psychological contract** is the set of expectations held by employees concerning what they will contribute to an organization (referred to as contributions) and what the organization will provide the employees (referred to as inducements) in return.[1]

For example, consider Christine Choi, a programmer for BMC Software in Houston. Choi contributes her education, skills, effort, time, and energy. In return for these contributions, BMC provides various inducements for her to remain with the firm—a good place to work, nice benefits, and a competitive salary. Both BMC and Choi seem to be satisfied with the relationship and are thus likely to maintain it—at least for the time being.

In other situations, however, things might not work out as well. If either party perceives an inequity in the contract, that party may seek a change. The employee, for example, might ask for a pay raise, promotion, or a bigger office. Also, the employee might put forth less effort or look for a better job elsewhere. The organization can also initiate change by training workers to improve their skills, transferring them to new jobs, or terminating them.

All organizations face the basic challenge of managing psychological contracts. They want value from their employees, and they must give employees the right inducements. Valuable but underpaid employees may perform below their capabilities or leave for better jobs. Conversely, overpaying employees who contribute little incurs unnecessary costs. The foundation of good human relations—the interactions between employers and employees and their attitudes toward one another—is a satisfied and motivated workforce.[2]

When Curtis Barthold needed seven months to stay at home with a terminally ill wife and two children, he got help from his employer, investment broker Charles Schwab & Co. *(www.schwab.com)*. As a member of Schwab's Life-Threatening Illness program, Barthold received a two-month sabbatical and five months of unused sick and vacation days donated by coworkers. The program obviously promotes loyalty among Schwab employees, 90 percent of whom say that they can count on coworkers for help in time of need.

If psychological contracts are created, maintained, and managed effectively, the result is likely to be workers who are satisfied and motivated. On the other hand, poorly managed psychological contracts may result in dissatisfied, unmotivated workers. Although most people have a general idea of what job satisfaction is, both job satisfaction and high morale can be elusive in the workplace. Because they are critical to an organization's success, we now turn our attention to discussing their importance.

■ THE IMPORTANCE OF SATISFACTION AND MORALE

Broadly speaking, **job satisfaction** is the degree of enjoyment that people derive from performing their jobs. If people enjoy their work, they are relatively satisfied; if they do not enjoy their work, they are relatively dissatisfied. In turn, satisfied employees are likely to have high **morale**—the overall attitude that employees have toward the workplace. Morale reflects the degree to which they perceive that their needs are being met by their jobs. It is determined by a variety of factors, including job satisfaction and satisfaction with such things as pay, benefits, coworkers, and promotion opportunities.[3]

Companies can improve morale and job satisfaction in a variety of ways. Some large firms, for example, have instituted companywide programs designed specifically to address employees' needs. Some of *Fortune*'s "100 Best Companies to Work For" offer take-home meals for employees who don't have time to cook. Others provide personal concierge services to help harried employees with everything from buying birthday gifts and organizing social events to planning vacations and maintaining cars.[4]

Managers at Hyatt Hotels *(www.hyatt.com)* report that conducting frequent surveys of employee attitudes, soliciting employee input, and—most important—acting on that input give the company an edge in recruiting and retaining productive workers. Managers of smaller businesses realize that the personal touch can reap big benefits in employee morale. For example, First Tennessee *(www.ftb.com)*, a midsize regional bank, believes that work and family are so closely related that family considerations should enter into job design. Thus, it offers such benefits as on-site child care.

job satisfaction
Degree of enjoyment that people derive from performing their jobs

morale
Overall attitude that employees have toward their workplace

Unfortunately, today's tough economic times have caused some firms to rethink the benefits they offer to employees, and many have reduced some of the benefits they provide. But others, especially those committed to remaining one of *Fortune*'s "100 Best Companies to Work For" are still convinced that a comprehensive benefits program makes good business sense.

When workers are satisfied and morale is high, the organization benefits in many ways. Compared with dissatisfied workers, for example, satisfied employees are more committed and loyal. Such employees are more likely to work hard and to make useful contributions. In addition, they tend to have fewer grievances and engage in fewer negative behaviors (complaining, deliberately slowing their work pace, and so forth) than dissatisfied counterparts. Finally, satisfied workers tend not only to come to work every day but also to remain with the organization. By promoting satisfaction and morale, then, management is working to ensure more efficient operations.

Conversely, the costs of dissatisfaction and poor morale are high.[5] Dissatisfied workers are far more likely to be absent for minor illnesses, personal reasons, or a general disinclination to go to work. Low morale may also result in high **turnover**— the percentage of an organization's workforce that leaves and must be replaced. High levels of turnover have many negative consequences, including the disruption of production schedules, high retraining costs, and decreased productivity. On the other hand, a moderate level of turnover may be beneficial: Organizations can eliminate the jobs of low-performing workers and/or bring in new ideas and fresh talent.

turnover
Annual percentage of an organization's workforce that leaves and must be replaced

Recent Trends in Managing Satisfaction and Morale

Achieving high levels of job satisfaction and morale seems like a reasonable organizational goal, especially given their potential impact on organizational performance. But managing satisfaction and morale in light of economic fluctuations poses continuing problems. For example, during the late 1990s dramatic job growth coupled with a chronic shortage of workers in some areas led to higher wages, the increasing array of benefits noted earlier, and even signing bonuses. For the last couple of years, though, because of a sluggish economy, many big firms have laid off workers.

Morale at Enron Corp. reached a low point in January 2002, about a month after the giant energy trader filed for bankruptcy. For one thing, there were suddenly 4,000 employees in the 50-story headquarters instead of 7,000. "It's been dead here for a while," reported one survivor who found himself the lone occupant of the 27th floor. Sonia Garcia, who went job hunting in rush-hour Houston traffic, wasn't even one of the 4,000 survivors of the first round of layoffs.

Say WHAT YOU MEAN

SIGNALING SENSITIVITY

These days, there's a lot of pressure placed on global companies to be "good corporate citizens"—to treat employees with respect and dignity, to be sensitive to local cultures, and to ensure that the laws of the host country are followed.

It's a rule of thumb that the happier the employee, the more productive and dedicated he or she will be. But *communicating* the fact that a firm has a stake in the satisfaction of its employees and the prosperity of its community is more easily said than done. For one thing, global companies employ people all over the world; there's no one unified group of people who share all the same values and all the same attitudes. In addition, because people take jobs for many different reasons, they may have very different expectations when it comes to pay and benefits and to the degree of commitment they're prepared to make to a corporate entity.

One way companies are trying to communicate more effectively with employees is through Web sites and in-house publications. The aim is to give employees around the world a sense of belonging to a community whose members have shared interests. At the same time, however, companies want to send the message that they're sensitive to employee *differences*—to the cultural and other forms of diversity that characterize their workforces and the communities in which they operate. Many global firms, for example, sponsor extensive local outreach programs in which they provide assistance to various groups in the communities where they conduct business.

There are still a lot of questions about the role of the corporation in an increasingly globalized world, and of course, there have always been questions about the degree to which companies should exercise social responsibility in host communities. One thing, however, seems certain: Global companies are going to become a good deal more sophisticated in the way they communicate to both groups of stakeholders.

In 2003, for instance, United Airlines, Ford Motor Co., and Kodak each had major job cuts. And most firms were reluctant to add jobs or hire new workers. Not surprisingly, then, satisfaction and morale plummeted in many companies. Workers feared for their job security, and even those who kept their jobs were unhappy about their less fortunate colleagues and friends.[6] As a result, most workers today are satisfied just to have a job. When the economy begins to grow again, their attitudes may become more negative, and employers might again be forced to reinstate benefit programs that have recently been phased out.

SELF-CHECK QUESTIONS 1–3

You should now be able to answer Self-Check Questions 1–3.*

1 **True/False** A *psychological contract* consists of employee contributions and organizational inducements.

2 **Multiple Choice** Which of the following describes the level of enjoyment that people derive from their jobs? [select one]: **(a)** morale; **(b)** job enjoyment; **(c)** job satisfaction; **(d)** job empowerment; **(e)** human relations.

3 **True/False** Job cuts and the elimination of employee benefits have had which of the following effects on *morale?* [select one]: **(a)** increased it; **(b)** maintained it; **(c)** affected it in unpredictable ways; **(d)** reduced it; **(e)** none of these.

*****Answers to Self-Check Questions 1–3 can be found on pp. 508–509.**

■ MOTIVATION IN THE WORKPLACE

motivation
The set of forces that cause people to behave in certain ways

Although job satisfaction and morale are important, employee motivation is even more critical to a firm's success. As we saw in Chapter 5, motivation is one part of the managerial function of directing. Broadly defined, **motivation** is the set of forces that cause people to behave in certain ways. One worker may be motivated to work hard to produce as much as possible, whereas another may be motivated to do just enough to survive. Managers must understand these differences in behavior and the reasons for them.

Over the years, a steady progression of theories and studies has attempted to address these issues. In this section, we survey the major studies and theories of employee motivation. In particular, we focus on three approaches to human relations in the workplace that reflect a basic chronology of thinking in the area: (1) *classical theory* and *scientific management*, (2) *behavior theory*, and (3) *contemporary motivational theories.*[7]

Classical Theory

classical theory of motivation
Theory holding that workers are motivated solely by money

According to the so-called **classical theory of motivation**, workers are motivated solely by money. In his seminal 1911 book, *The Principles of Scientific Management,* industrial engineer Frederick Taylor proposed a way for both companies and workers to benefit from this widely accepted view of life in the workplace. If workers are motivated by money, Taylor reasoned, then paying them more should prompt them to produce more. Meanwhile, the firm that analyzed jobs and found better ways to perform them would be able to produce goods more cheaply, make higher profits, and thus pay and motivate workers better than its competitors.

Taylor's approach is known as *scientific management.* His ideas captured the imagination of many managers in the early twentieth century. Soon, plants across the United States were hiring experts to perform time-and-motion studies: Industrial engineering techniques were applied to each facet of a job in order to determine how to perform it most efficiently. These studies were the first scientific attempts to break down jobs into easily repeated components and to devise more efficient tools and machines for performing them.

Behavior Theory: The Hawthorne Studies

In 1925, a group of Harvard researchers began a study at the Hawthorne works of Western Electric outside Chicago. With an eye to increasing productivity, they wanted to examine the relationship between changes in the physical environment and worker output.

The results of the experiment were unexpected, even confusing. For example, increased lighting levels improved productivity. For some reason, however, so did lower lighting levels. Moreover, against all expectations, increased pay failed to increase productivity. Gradually, the researchers pieced together the puzzle. The explanation lay in the workers' response to the attention that they were receiving. The researchers concluded that productivity rose in response to almost any management action that workers interpreted as special attention. This finding, known widely today as the **Hawthorne effect**, had a major influence on human relations theory, although in many cases it amounted simply to convincing managers that they should pay more attention to employees.

Contemporary Motivational Theories

Following the Hawthorne studies, managers and researchers alike focused more attention on the importance of good human relations in motivating employee performance. Stressing the factors that cause, focus, and sustain workers' behavior, most motivation theorists are concerned with the ways in which management thinks about and treats employees. The major motivation theories include the *human resources model,* the *hierarchy of needs model, two-factor theory, expectancy theory,* and *equity theory.*

Human Resources Model: Theories X and Y
In an important study, behavioral scientist Douglas McGregor concluded that managers had radically different beliefs about how best to use the human resources employed by a firm. He classified these beliefs into sets of assumptions that he labeled "Theory X" and "Theory Y." The basic differences between these two theories are highlighted in Table 9.1.

Managers who subscribe to **Theory X** tend to believe that people are naturally lazy and uncooperative and must, therefore, be either punished or rewarded to be made productive. Managers who are inclined to accept **Theory Y** tend to believe that people are naturally energetic, growth oriented, self-motivated, and interested in being productive.

McGregor generally favored Theory Y beliefs. Thus, he argued that Theory Y managers are more likely to have satisfied and motivated employees. Of course, Theory X and Y distinctions are somewhat simplistic and offer little concrete basis for action. Their value lies primarily in their ability to highlight and classify the behavior of managers in light of their attitudes toward employees.

Theory X
Theory of motivation holding that people are naturally irresponsible and uncooperative

Theory Y
Theory of motivation holding that people are naturally responsible, growth oriented, self-motivated, and interested in being productive

Maslow's Hierarchy of Needs Model
Psychologist Abraham Maslow's **hierarchy of human needs model** proposed that people have several different needs that they attempt to satisfy in their work. He classified these needs into five basic types and suggested that they be arranged in the hierarchy of importance as shown in Figure 9.1. According to Maslow, needs are hierarchical because lower-level needs must be met before a person will try to satisfy higher-level needs.

hierarchy of human needs model
Theory of motivation describing five levels of human needs and arguing that basic needs must be fulfilled before people work to satisfy higher-level needs

Theory X	Theory Y
People are lazy.	People are energetic.
People lack ambition and dislike responsibility.	People are ambitious and seek responsibility.
People are self-centered.	People can be selfless.
People resist change.	People want to contribute to business growth and change.
People are gullible and not very bright.	People are intelligent.

TABLE 9.1

Theory X and Theory Y

FIGURE 9.1

Maslow's Hierarchy of Needs

General Examples

Self-fulfillment

Status

Friendship

Stability

Shelter

Self-actualization needs

Esteem needs

Social needs

Security needs

Physiological needs

Organizational Examples

Challenging job

Job title

Friends at work

Pension plan

Salary

Once a set of needs has been satisfied, it ceases to motivate behavior. This is the sense in which the hierarchical nature of lower- and higher-level needs affects employee motivation and satisfaction. For example, if you feel secure in your job, a new pension plan will probably be less important to you than the chance to make new friends and join an informal network among your coworkers.

If, however, a lower-level need suddenly becomes unfulfilled, most people immediately refocus on that lower level. Suppose, for example, that you are seeking to meet your self-esteem needs by working as a divisional manager at a major company. If you learn that your division and, consequently, your job may be eliminated, you might very well find the promise of job security at a new firm as motivating as a promotion once would have been at your old company.

Maslow's theory recognizes that because different people have different needs, they are motivated by different things. Unfortunately, it provides few specific guidelines for action in the workplace. Furthermore, research has found that the hierarchy varies widely, not only for different people but also across different cultures.

Two-Factor Theory After studying a group of accountants and engineers, psychologist Frederick Herzberg concluded that job satisfaction and dissatisfaction depend on two factors: *hygiene factors,* such as working conditions, and *motivation factors*, such as recognition for a job well done.

two-factor theory
Theory of motivation holding that job satisfaction depends on two types of factors, hygiene and motivation

According to the **two-factor theory**, hygiene factors affect motivation and satisfaction only if they are absent or fail to meet expectations. For example, workers will be dissatisfied if they believe that they have poor working conditions. If working conditions are improved, however, they will not necessarily become satisfied; they will simply not be dissatisfied. If workers receive no recognition for successful work, they may be neither dissatisfied nor satisfied. If recognition is provided, they will likely become more satisfied.

Figure 9.2 illustrates the two-factor theory. Note that motivation factors lie along a continuum from *satisfaction* to *no satisfaction.* Hygiene factors, in contrast, are likely to produce feelings that lie on a continuum from *dissatisfaction* to *no dissatisfaction.* Whereas motivation factors are directly related to the work that employees actually perform, hygiene factors refer to the environment in which they perform work.

This theory thus suggests that managers should follow a two-step approach to enhancing motivation. First, they must ensure that hygiene factors—working condi-

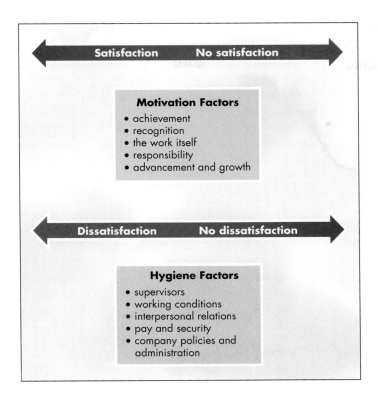

FIGURE 9.2

Two-Factor Theory of Motivation

tions, for example, or clearly stated policies—are acceptable. This practice will result in an absence of dissatisfaction. Then they must offer motivation factors—recognition or added responsibility—as a way to improve satisfaction and motivation.

Research suggests that although two-factor theory works in some professional settings, it is less effective in clerical and manufacturing settings. (Herzberg's research was limited to accountants and engineers.) In addition, one person's hygiene factor may be another person's motivation factor. For example, if money represents nothing more than pay for time worked, it may be a hygiene factor for one person. For another person, however, money may be a motivation factor because it represents recognition and achievement.

Expectancy Theory **Expectancy theory** suggests that people are motivated to work toward rewards that they want and that they believe they have a reasonable chance—or expectancy—of obtaining. A reward that seems out of reach is likely to be undesirable even if it is intrinsically positive. Figure 9.3 illustrates expectancy theory in terms of issues that are likely to be considered by an individual employee.

Consider the case of an assistant department manager who learns that her firm needs to replace a retiring division manager two levels above her in the organization. Even though she wants the job, she does not apply because she doubts that she will

expectancy theory
Theory of motivation holding that people are motivated to work toward rewards that they want and that they believe they have a reasonable chance of obtaining

FIGURE 9.3

Expectancy Theory Model

be selected. In this case, she raises the *performance-to-reward* issue: For some reason, she believes that her performance will not get her the position. Note that she may think that her performance merits the new job but that performance alone will not be enough; perhaps she expects the reward to go to someone with more seniority.

Assume that our employee also learns that the firm is looking for a production manager on a later shift. She thinks that she could get this job but does not apply because she does not want to change shifts. In this instance, she raises the *rewards-to-personal goals* issue. Finally, she learns of an opening one level higher—department manager—in her own division. She may well apply for this job because she both wants it and thinks that she has a good chance of getting it. In this case, her consideration of all the issues has led to an expectancy that she can reach a given goal.

Expectancy theory helps explain why some people do not work as hard as they can when their salaries are based purely on seniority. Paying employees the same whether they work very hard or just hard enough to get by removes the financial incentive for them to work harder. In other words, they ask themselves, "If I work harder, will I get a pay raise?" and conclude that the answer is no. Similarly, if hard work will result in one or more undesirable outcomes—say, a transfer to another location or a promotion to a job that requires unpleasant travel—employees will not be motivated to work hard.

equity theory
Theory of motivation holding that people evaluate their treatment by employers relative to the treatment of others

Equity Theory **Equity theory** focuses on social comparisons—people evaluating their treatment by the organization relative to the treatment of others. This approach holds that people begin by analyzing *inputs* (what they contribute to their jobs in terms of time, effort, education, experience) relative to *outputs* (what they receive in return—salary, benefits, recognition, security). The result is a ratio of contribution to return. Then they compare their own ratios with those of other employees; they ask whether their ratios are *equal to, greater than,* or *less than* those of the people with whom they are comparing themselves. Depending on their assessments, they experience feelings of equity or inequity. Figure 8.4 illustrates the three possible results of such an assessment.

For example, suppose a new college graduate gets a starting job at a large manufacturing firm. His starting salary is $35,000 a year, he gets a compact company car, and he shares an office with another new employee. If he later learns that another

FIGURE 9.4

Equity Theory: Possible
Assessments

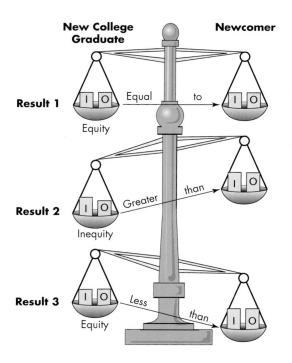

new employee has received the same salary, car, and office arrangement, he will feel equitably treated (Result 1 in Figure 9.4). If the other newcomer, however, has received $40,000, a full-size company car, and a private office, he may feel inequitably treated (see Result 2).

Note, however, that for an individual to feel equitably treated, the two ratios do not have to be the same, only fair. Assume, for instance, that our new employee has a bachelor's degree and two years of work experience. Perhaps he learns subsequently that the other new employee has an advanced degree and 10 years of experience. After first feeling inequity, the new employee may conclude that the person with whom he compared himself is actually contributing more to the organization. That employee is equitably entitled, therefore, to receive more in return (Result 3).

When people feel they are being inequitably treated, they may do various things to restore fairness. For example, they may ask for raises, reduce their efforts, work shorter hours, or just complain to their bosses. They may also rationalize ("Management succumbed to pressure to promote a woman/Asian American"), find different people with whom to compare themselves, or leave their jobs.

Virtually perfect examples of equity theory at work can be found in professional sports. Each year, for example, rookies, sometimes fresh out of college, are often signed to lucrative contracts. No sooner is the ink dry than veteran players start grumbling about raises or revised contracts.

STRATEGIES FOR ENHANCING JOB SATISFACTION AND MORALE

Deciding what provides job satisfaction and motivates workers is only one part of human resource management. The other part is applying that knowledge. Experts have suggested—and many companies have implemented—a range of programs designed to make jobs more interesting and rewarding and to make the work environment more pleasant.

Reinforcement/Behavior Modification Theory

Many companies try to control—and even alter or modify—workers' behavior through systematic rewards and punishments for specific behaviors. In other words, such companies first try to define the specific behaviors that they want their employees to exhibit (working hard, being courteous to customers, stressing quality) and the specific behaviors they want to eliminate (wasting time, being rude to customers, ignoring quality). Then they try to shape employee behavior by linking reinforcement with desired behaviors and punishment with undesired behaviors.

Reinforcement is used when a company pays *piecework* rewards—when workers are paid for each piece or product completed. In reinforcement strategies, rewards refer to all the positive things that people get for working (pay, praise, promotions, job security, and so forth). When rewards are tied directly to performance, they serve as *positive reinforcement.* For example, paying large cash bonuses to salespeople who exceed quotas prompts them to work even harder during the next selling period. John Deere *(www.deere.com)* has adopted a reward system based on positive reinforcement. The firm gives pay increases when its workers complete college courses and demonstrate mastery of new job skills.

reinforcement
Theory that behavior can be encouraged or discouraged by means of rewards or punishments

ENTREPRENEURSHIP and New Ventures

Keeping Pleasant Company

Pleasant Rowland was looking for a Christmas gift for her two nieces. It was 1985 and Cabbage Patch dolls were hot that year, but Rowland felt that her nieces, ages 8 and 10, were too grown-up for baby dolls (though maybe not quite old enough for Barbie). She wanted something to spark the kids' imaginations, and when she couldn't find anything suitable, Rowland got the idea of a doll for "tweens"—preteen girls who are neither little children or teenagers. The result was the American Girl collection of dolls, which is now a $700 million toy empire.

Rowland's extraordinary success was motivated by a number of factors. Her deep-seated convictions played a big part. She wanted to furnish role models for young girls that weren't too "babyish" or too mature. She was looking for an image that was wholesome *and* empowering. "Here I was," she recalls, "in a generation of women at the forefront of redefining women's roles, and yet our daughters were playing with dolls that celebrated being a teen queen or a mommy. I knew I couldn't be the only woman in America who was unhappy with those choices. . . . Mothers," she adds, "yearned for a product that would both capture children's interest and allow little girls to be little girls for a little longer."

Then Rowland took a trip to Williamsburg, Virginia, where she was excited by the celebration of colonial America. "I remember . . . reflecting on what a poor job schools do of teaching history," she explains, "and how sad it was that more kids couldn't visit this fabulous classroom of living history." The two ideas—teaching history and designing better toys for preteens—collided, and as Rowland recalls, "The concept literally exploded in my brain. Once the idea had formed, I could think of nothing else. In one weekend, I wrote out the concept in great detail." Her concept was a series of books about girls growing up in different places and times in American history. The books would be accompanied by dolls, accessories, and toys.

Developing the American Girl concept allowed Rowland to draw on her background in education and writing. She

> *"For all the money the company made subsequently, none of it was as fun or rewarding as that first million dollars."*
>
> *—Pleasant Rowland, founder of American Girl books and dolls*

had begun her career in the 1960s as an elementary school teacher but was dismayed by the poor quality of classroom materials. So she became a writer of books for children—a very successful one. When she came up with the idea of the American Girl, business advisers told her that there was no profit in selling educational toys or dolls. Rowland, however, was confident that her line of unique educational products would sell. And she was right: In the first four months, the Pleasant Co. sold $1.7 million of dolls and books.

Office workers had to help with the sewing, and because the start-up's cramped old warehouse was barely heated, they had to do it in mittens. Rowland thrived on the chaos. "For all the money the company made subsequently," she reports, "none of it was as fun or rewarding as that first million dollars." Money, however, was never the most important motivator for Rowland. She was already a millionaire from her book royalties and worked more for love than for money, and when she was diagnosed with cancer in 1989, work became her source of strength. "I never missed a day of work, and work is probably what saved me. I loved what I was doing."

In 1995, Rowland sold Pleasant Co. to Mattel (*www.mattel.com*) for $700 million. "Finally," she explains, "my vision was complete, my original business plan had been executed, and I was tired. It was time to sell the company." Some people criticized her for selling out to the company whose Barbie products had stimulated her original quest for a better concept, but Rowland saw former Mattel CEO Jill Barad as a kindred spirit—a smart, tough, ambitious, passionate businesswoman. Has Rowland regretted the sale? Not at all. "As I walked out the door, I stopped and looked around at all I had built, expecting to be overwhelmed by sadness or loss. But no emotion came. . . . It was then that I realized that I had never felt I 'owned' American Girl. I had been its steward, and I had given it my best during the prime of my career. It was time for someone else to take care of it."

Punishment is designed to change behavior by presenting people with unpleasant consequences if they fail to change in desirable ways. Employees who are repeatedly late for work, for example, may be suspended or have their pay docked. Similarly, when the National Football League or Major League Baseball fines or suspends players found guilty of substance abuse, the organization is seeking to change players' behavior.

"O.K., I messed up. He didn't have to rub my nose in it."

Extensive rewards work best when people are learning new behavior, new skills, or new jobs. As workers become more adept, rewards can be used less frequently. Because such actions contribute to positive employer–employee relationships, managers generally prefer giving rewards and placing positive value on performance. Conversely, most managers dislike doling out punishment, partly because workers may respond with anger, resentment, hostility, or even retaliation. To reduce this risk, many managers couple punishment with rewards for good behavior.

Management by Objectives

Management by objectives (MBO) is a system of collaborative goal setting that extends from the top of an organization to the bottom. As a technique for managing the planning process, MBO is concerned mainly with helping managers implement and carry out their plans. As you can see from Figure 9.5, MBO involves managers and subordinates in setting goals and evaluating progress. Once the program is set up, the first step is establishing overall organizational goals. It is also these goals that will ultimately be evaluated to determine the success of the program. At the same time, however, collaborative activity—communicating, meeting, controlling, and so forth—is the key to MBO. Therefore, it can also serve as a program for improving satisfaction and motivation.

According to many experts, motivational impact is the biggest advantage of MBO. When employees sit down with managers to set upcoming goals, they learn more

management by objectives (MBO) Set of procedures involving both managers and subordinates in setting goals and evaluating progress

FIGURE 9.5

Management by Objectives

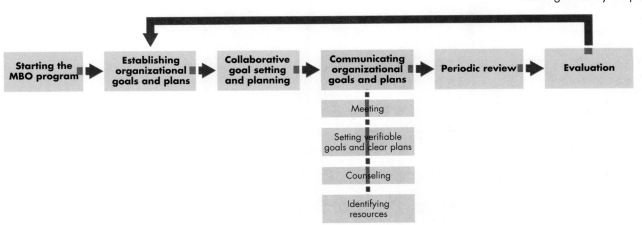

about companywide objectives, come to feel that they are an important part of a team, and see how they can improve companywide performance by reaching their own goals. If an MBO system is used properly, employees should leave meetings not only with an understanding of the value of their contributions but also with fair rewards for their performances. They should also accept and be committed to the moderately difficult and specific goals they have helped set for themselves.

Participative Management and Empowerment

participative management and empowerment
Method of increasing job satisfaction by giving employees a voice in the management of their jobs and the company

In **participative management and empowerment**, employees are given a voice in how they do their jobs and in how the company is managed—they become empowered to take greater responsibility for their own performance. Not surprisingly, participation and empowerment make employees feel more committed to organizational goals they have helped to shape.

Participation and empowerment can be used in large firms or small firms, both with managers and operating employees. For example, managers at General Electric *(www.ge.com)* who once needed higher-level approval for any expenditure over $5,000 have the autonomy to make their own expense decisions up to as much as $50,000. At Adam Hat Co., a small firm that makes men's dress, military, and cowboy hats, workers who previously had to report all product defects to supervisors now have the freedom to correct problems themselves or even return products to the workers who are responsible for them.

Team Management

At one level, employees may be given decision-making responsibility for certain narrow activities, such as when to take lunch breaks or how to divide assignments with coworkers. On a broader level, employees are also being consulted on such decisions as production scheduling, work procedures and schedules, and the hiring of new employees. Among the many organizations actively using teams today are Texas Instruments *(www.ti.com)*, Lucent Technologies *(www.lucent.com)*, and Ford Motor Co. *(www.ford.com)*.

When employees of the Beck Group *(www.beckgroup.com)*, a Dallas-based construction and real estate development company, go to work on a project, they enjoy a great deal of autonomy in applying their decision-making and other skills. The approach works because the company encourages continuous training, reimbursing workers up to $4,500 a year for higher-education courses. Bonuses are paid out when customers are happy, and apparently the job satisfaction of Beck employees translates into customer satisfaction: 80 percent of the firm's clients are repeats.

Although some employees thrive in participative programs, such programs are not for everyone. Many people will be frustrated by responsibilities they are not equipped to handle. Moreover, participative programs may actually result in dissatisfied employees if workers see the invitation to participate as more symbolic than substantive. One key, say most experts, is to invite participation only to the extent that employees want to have input and only if participation will have real value for an organization.

Managers, therefore, should remember that teams are not for everyone. Levi Strauss *(www.levi.com)*, for example, encountered major problems when it tried to use teams. Individual workers previously performed repetitive, highly specialized tasks, such as sewing zippers into jeans, and were paid according to the number of jobs they completed each day. In an attempt to boost productivity, company management reorganized everyone into teams of 10 to 35 workers and assigned tasks to the entire group. Each team member's pay was determined by the team's level of productivity. In practice, however, faster workers became resentful of slower workers because they reduced the group's total output. Slower workers, meanwhile, resented the pressure put on them by faster-working coworkers. As a result, motivation, satisfaction, and morale all dropped, and Levi's eventually abandoned the teamwork plan altogether.

By and large, however, participation and empowerment in general, and team management in particular, continue to be widely used as enhancers of employee motivation and company performance. Although teams are often less effective in traditional and rigidly structured bureaucratic organizations, they often help smaller, more flexible organizations make decisions more quickly and effectively, enhance companywide communication, and encourage organizational members to feel more like a part of an organization. In turn, these attitudes usually lead to higher levels of both employee motivation and job satisfaction.

Job Enrichment and Job Redesign

Whereas MBO programs and empowerment can work in a variety of settings, *job enrichment* and *job redesign* programs are generally used to increase satisfaction in jobs significantly lacking in motivating factors.[8]

Job Enrichment Programs **Job enrichment** is designed to add one or more motivating factors to job activities. For example, *job rotation* programs expand growth opportunities by rotating employees through various positions in the same firm. Workers gain not only new skills but also broader overviews of their work and their organization. Other programs focus on increasing responsibility or recognition. At Continental Airlines *(www.continental.com)*, for example, flight attendants now have more control over their own scheduling. The jobs of flight service managers were enriched when they were given more responsibility and authority for assigning tasks to flight crewmembers.

job enrichment
Method of increasing job satisfaction by adding one or more motivating factors to job activities

Job Redesign Programs Job redesign acknowledges that different people want different things from their jobs. By restructuring work to achieve a more satisfactory fit between workers and their jobs, **job redesign** can motivate individuals with strong needs for career growth or achievement. Job redesign is usually implemented in one of three ways: through *combining tasks, forming natural work groups,* or *establishing client relationships.*

job redesign
Method of increasing job satisfaction by designing a more satisfactory fit between workers and their jobs

Combining Tasks The job of combining tasks involves enlarging jobs and increasing their variety to make employees feel that their work is more meaningful. In turn, employees become more motivated. For example, the job done by a programmer who maintains computer systems might be redesigned to include some system design and system development work. While developing additional skills, then, the programmer also gets involved in the overall system package.

Forming Natural Work Groups People who do different jobs on the same projects are candidates for natural work groups. These groups are formed to help employees see the place and importance of their jobs in the total structure of the firm. They are valuable to management because the people working on a project are usually the most knowledgeable about it and thus the most capable problem solvers.

Establishing Client Relationships Establishing client relationships means letting employees interact with customers. This approach increases job variety. It gives workers both a greater sense of control and more feedback about performance than they get when their jobs are not highly interactive.

For example, software writers at Microsoft *(www.microsoft.com)* watch test users work with programs and discuss problems with them directly rather than receive feedback from third-party researchers. In Fargo, North Dakota, Great Plains Software *(www.greatplains.com)* has employee turnover of less than 7 percent, compared with an industry average of 15 to 20 percent. The company recruits and rewards in large part according to candidates' customer service skills and their experience with customer needs and complaints.

Modified Work Schedules

As another way of increasing job satisfaction, many companies are experimenting with *modified work schedules*—different approaches to working hours and the workweek. The two most common forms of modified scheduling are *work-share programs* and *flextime programs,* including *alternative workplace strategies.*[9]

work sharing (or **job sharing**)
Method of increasing job satisfaction by allowing two or more people to share a single full-time job

Work-Share Programs At Steelcase Inc. *(www.steelcase.com)*, the country's largest maker of office furnishings, two very talented women in the marketing division both wanted to work only part-time. The solution: They now share a single full-time job. With each working 2.5 days a week, both got their wish and the job gets done—and done well. In another situation, one person might work mornings and the other afternoons. The practice, known as **work sharing** (or **job sharing**), has "brought sanity back to our lives," according to at least one Steelcase employee.

Job sharing usually benefits both employees and employers. Employees, for instance, tend to appreciate the organization's attention to their personal needs. At the same time, the company can reduce turnover and save on the cost of benefits. On the negative side, job-share employees generally receive fewer benefits than their full-time counterparts and may be the first to be laid off when cutbacks are necessary.

flextime programs
Method of increasing job satisfaction by allowing workers to adjust work schedules on a daily or weekly basis

Flextime Programs and Alternative Workplace Strategies Flextime programs allow people to choose their working hours by adjusting a standard work schedule on a daily or weekly basis. Indeed, there was a significant boom in flextime programs in the late 1990s as part of the escalation of employee benefits that we mentioned before. There are, of course, limits. The Steelcase program, for instance, requires all employees to work certain core hours. This practice allows everyone to reach coworkers at a specified time of day. Employees can then decide whether to make up the rest of the standard eight-hour day by coming in and leaving early (by working 6:00 A.M. to 2:00 P.M. or 7:00 A.M. to 3:00 P.M.) or late (9:00 A.M. to 5:00 P.M. or 10:00 A.M. to 6:00 P.M.).

Figure 9.6 shows a hypothetical flextime system that could be used by three different people. The office is open from 6:00 A.M. until 7:00 P.M. Core time is 9:00 A.M.

FIGURE 9.6

Sample Flextime Schedule

to 11:00 A.M. and 1:00 P.M. to 3:00 P.M. Joe, an early riser, comes in at 6:00, takes an hour for lunch between 11:00 and noon, and finishes his day by 3:00. Sue, a working mother, prefers a later day. She comes in at 9:00, takes a long lunch from 11:00 to 1:00, and then works until 7:00. Pat works a more traditional 8-to-5 schedule.

In one variation, companies may also allow employees to choose four, five, or six days on which to work each week. Some, for instance, may choose Monday through Thursday, others Tuesday through Friday. Still others may work Monday–Tuesday and Thursday–Friday and take Wednesday off. By working 10 hours over four workdays, employees still complete 40-hour weeks.

Telecommuting and Virtual Offices Kelly Ramsey-Dolson is an accountant employed by Ernst & Young *(www.ey.com)*. Because she has a young son, she does not want to be away from home more than she absolutely must. Ramsey-Dolson and the company have worked out an arrangement whereby she works at home two or three days a week and comes into the office the other days. Her home office is outfitted with a PC, modem, and fax machine, and she uses this technology to keep abreast of everything going on at the office.

Ramsey-Dolson is one of a rapidly growing number of U.S. workers who do a significant portion of their work on the basis of a relatively new version of flextime known as **telecommuting**—performing some or all of a job away from standard office settings. Among salaried employees, the telecommuter workforce grew by 21.5 percent in 1994—to 7.6 million—and then to 11 million in 1997; the number of telecommuters in 2002 exceeded 27.5 million employees.

The key to telecommuting is technology. The availability of networked computers, fax machines, cellular telephones, and overnight-delivery services makes it possible for many professionals to work at home or while traveling. Cisco Systems *(www.cisco.com)*, the Internet networking giant, is at the forefront of telecommuting arrangements for its workers. The firm estimates that by allowing employees to do some of their work at home, it has boosted productivity by 25 percent, lowered overhead costs by $1 million, and achieved a higher retention rate among key knowledge workers who might have otherwise left for more flexibility elsewhere.[10]

telecommuting
Form of flextime that allows people to perform some or all of a job away from standard office settings

Martin Gertel used to commute three hours a day, five days a week from Virginia to Washington, DC, to work as an auditor for the Transportation Department *(www.dot.gov)*. Now he telecommutes, working on Mondays and Fridays from his home office. Gertel's arrangement is unusual: Telecommuting among government workers lags behind private-sector practices because much government work doesn't adapt very well, the costs of home offices are high, and federal managers have been slow to encourage change. Congress is now looking at legislation that would make more government employees eligible to telecommute.

"Sometimes one's best thinking is done in a conference room with other people. Other times it's done on a ski slope or driving to a client's office."

—Adelaide Horton, director of operations, TBWA/Chiat/Day Advertising

Other companies have experimented with so-called virtual offices. They have redesigned conventional office space to accommodate jobs and schedules that are far less dependent on assigned spaces and personal apparatus. At the advertising firm of TBWA/Chiat/Day *(www.chiatday.com)* in Los Angeles, California, only about one-third of the salaried workforce is in the office on any given day. The office building features informal work carrels or nooks and open areas available to every employee. "The work environment," explains Director of Operations Adelaide Horton, "was designed around the concept that one's best thinking isn't necessarily done at a desk or in an office. Sometimes it's done in a conference room with other people. Other times it's done on a ski slope or driving to a client's office."

Advantages and Disadvantages of Modified Schedules and Alternative Workplaces

Flextime gives employees more freedom in their professional and personal lives. It allows workers to plan around the work schedules of spouses and the school schedules of young children. Studies show that the increased sense of freedom and control reduces stress and thus improves individual productivity.

Companies also benefit in other ways. In urban areas, for example, such programs can reduce traffic congestion and similar problems that contribute to stress and lost work time. Furthermore, employers benefit from higher levels of commitment and job satisfaction. John Hancock Insurance *(www.jhancock.com)*, Hewlett-Packard, IBM, and Metropolitan Life *(www.metlife.com)* are among the major American corporations that have successfully adopted some form of flextime.

Conversely, flextime sometimes complicates coordination because people are working different schedules. In the schedules shown in Figure 9.6, for instance, Sue may need some important information from Joe at 4:30 P.M., but because Joe is working an earlier schedule, he leaves for the day at 3:00. In addition, if workers are paid by the hour, flextime may make it difficult for employers to keep accurate records of when employees are actually working.

As for telecommuting and virtual offices, although they may be the wave of the future, they may not be for everyone. For example, consultant Gil Gordon points out that telecommuters are attracted to the ideas of "not having to shave and put on makeup or go through traffic, and sitting in their blue jeans all day." However, he suggests that would-be telecommuters ask themselves several other questions: "Can I manage deadlines? What will it be like to be away from the social context of the office five days a week? Can I renegotiate the rules of the family, so my spouse doesn't come home every night expecting me to have a four-course meal on the table?" One study has shown that even though telecommuters may be producing results, those with strong advancement ambitions may miss networking and rubbing elbows with management on a day-to-day basis.

> **"Managers always ask, 'How can I tell if someone is working when I can't see them?' That's based on the erroneous assumption that if you *can* see them, they *are* working."**
>
> **—HR consultant on managerial qualms about telecommuting**

Another obstacle to establishing a telecommuting program is convincing management that it can be beneficial for all involved. Telecommuters may have to fight the perception from both bosses and coworkers that if they are not being supervised, they are not working. Managers, admits one experienced consultant, "usually have to be dragged kicking and screaming into this. They always ask, 'How can I tell if someone is working when I can't see them?'" By the same token, he adds, "That's based on the erroneous assumption that if you *can* see them, they *are* working." Most experts agree that re-education and constant communication are requirements of a successful telecommuting arrangement. Both managers and employees must determine expectations in advance.

SELF-CHECK QUESTIONS 4–6

You should now be able to answer Self-Check Questions 4–6.*

4 **Multiple Choice** Which of the following is **not** a popular *motivational theory?* [select one]: **(a)** equity theory; **(b)** expectancy theory; **(c)** two-factor theory; **(d)** hierarchy of needs model; **(e)** all are popular motivational theories.

5 **Multiple Choice** In Maslow's *hierarchy of needs model,* an important job title can generally help sat-isfy which of the following set of needs? **(a)** self-actualization needs; **(b)** esteem needs; **(c)** social needs; **(d)** security needs; **(e)** physiological needs.

6 **True/False** *Team management* is an important form of *job enrichment.*

***Answer to Self-Check Questions 4–6 can be found on p. 509.**

■ MANAGERIAL STYLES AND LEADERSHIP

In trying to enhance morale, job satisfaction, and motivation, managers can use many different styles of leadership. **Leadership** is the process of motivating others to work to meet specific objectives. Leading is also one of the key aspects of a manager's job and an important component of the directing function.[11] Consider, for example, the odyssey of one successful leader.

leadership
Process of motivating others to work to meet specific objectives

Andrall (Andy) Pearson, former chairman and new director of Yum! Brands Inc. (formerly Tricon Global Restaurants), the parent company of Pizza Hut, Taco Bell, and KFC (Kentucky Fried Chicken), has evolved from feared dictator to beloved guru. A graduate of USC with a Harvard M.B.A., Pearson sums up the managerial approach of the old Andy by admitting, "I proved that I was smart by finding fault with other people's ideas." After rising to the post of senior director at the consulting firm McKinsey & Co., Pearson began a 14-year stint as president and COO of PepsiCo, where he built a reputation for being abrasive, numbers oriented, and hard to please. *Fortune* named him one of the top 10 toughest bosses in 1980, in part because he often drove employees to tears or out the door if they failed to meet his expectations. In fact, he greased the hinges on the corporate door: His policy called for firing the lowest-performing 10 to 20 percent of all employees every year.

While a tenured professor at Harvard (where he published such articles as "Tough-Minded Ways to Get Innovative"), he was invited to join Tricon by CEO David Novak, who felt that Pearson's no-nonsense style would complement his own people-oriented approach. "He was brutal," recalls former Tricon COO Aylwin Lewis. "One time he told us, 'A room full of monkeys could do better than this!'"

Now, however, there's a new Andy. Some employees still weep because of him, but now it's usually with gratitude. Managers who've been mentored by Pearson tell him that the experience has been life-changing. "I get letters that would just bring tears to your eyes," says Pearson, who rates cheers when he tells audiences why his experience at Tricon "represents the capstone of my career." What happened to turn the old Andy into the new Andy? At the outset, Novak told Pearson, "We can learn from each other," and when Pearson arrived at Tricon headquarters, a band played while employees cheered. "All the time I was at Pepsi," marveled Pearson, "nothing remotely like this had ever happened. It was overwhelming. I knew something was going on that was fundamentally very powerful. If we could learn how to harness that spirit with something systematic, then we would have something unique."

Pearson, it seems, has been transformed by the effort to harness such positive energy. "If I could only unleash the power of everybody in the organization, instead of just a few people . . . we'd be a much better company," he says, and he seems convinced of the role to be played by employees in transforming a company. Along the way, his thinking about leadership has also matured: "Great leaders," he argues, "find a balance between getting results and how they get them. A lot of people make the mistake of thinking that getting results is all there is to a job. . . . Your real job is to get results and to do it in a way that makes your organization a great place to work."[12]

> "Great leaders find a balance between getting results and how they get them. A lot of people make the mistake of thinking that getting results is all there is to a job."
>
> —Andrall Pearson, Director of Yum! Brands Inc.

In this section, we begin by describing some of the basic features of and differences in managerial styles. We then focus on an approach to managing and leading that recognizes, like Andy Pearson, that management and leadership must change and evolve in response to a variety of complex situations.

Managerial Styles

managerial style
Pattern of behavior that a manager exhibits in dealing with subordinates

Early theories of leadership tried to identify specific traits associated with strong leaders. For example, physical appearance, intelligence, and public speaking skills were once thought to be leadership traits. Indeed, it was once believed that taller people made better leaders than shorter people. The trait approach, however, proved to be a poor predictor of leadership potential. Ultimately, attention shifted from managers' traits to their behaviors, or **managerial styles**—patterns of behavior that a manager exhibits in dealing with subordinates. Managerial styles run the gamut from autocratic to democratic to free rein. Naturally, most managers do not clearly conform to any one style, but these three major types of styles involve very different kinds of responses to human relations problems. Under different circumstances, any given style or combination of the following three styles may prove appropriate.[13]

■ Managers who adopt an **autocratic style** generally issue orders and expect them to be obeyed without question. The military commander prefers and usually needs the autocratic style on the battlefield. Because no one else is consulted, the autocratic style allows for rapid decision making. It may, therefore, be useful in situations testing a firm's effectiveness as a time-based competitor.

■ Managers who adopt a **democratic style** generally ask for input from subordinates before making decisions, but they retain final decision-making power. For example, the manager of a technical group may ask other group members to interview and offer opinions about job applicants. The manager, however, will ultimately make the hiring decision.

■ Managers who adopt a **free-rein style** typically serve as advisers to subordinates who are allowed to make decisions. The chairperson of a volunteer committee to raise funds for a new library may find a free-rein style most effective.

autocratic style
Managerial style in which managers generally issue orders and expect them to be obeyed without question

democratic style
Managerial style in which managers generally ask for input from subordinates but retain final decision-making power

free-rein style
Managerial style in which managers typically serve as advisers to subordinates who are allowed to make decisions

According to many observers, the free-rein style of leadership is currently giving rise to an approach that emphasizes broad-based employee input into decision making and the fostering of workplace environments in which employees increasingly determine what needs to be done and how.

Regardless of theories about the ways in which leaders ought to lead, the relative effectiveness of any leadership style depends largely on the desire of subordinates to share input or to exercise creativity. Whereas some people, for example, are frustrated by autocratic managers, others prefer them because they don't want a voice in making decisions. The democratic approach, meanwhile, can be disconcerting both to people who want decision-making responsibility and to those who do not. A free-rein style lends itself to employee creativity and thus to creative solutions to pressing problems. This style also appeals to employees who like to plan their own work. Not all subordinates, however, have the necessary background or skills to make creative decisions. Others are not sufficiently self-motivated to work without supervision.

The Contingency Approach to Leadership

Because each managerial style has both strengths and weaknesses, most managers vary their responses to different situations. Flexibility, however, has not always characterized managerial style or responsiveness. For most of the twentieth century, in fact, managers tended to believe that all problems yielded to preconceived, pretested solutions. If raising pay reduced turnover in one plant, for example, it followed that the same tactic would work equally well in another.

More recently, however, managers have begun to adopt a **contingency approach to managerial style**. They have started to view appropriate managerial behavior in any situation as dependent, or contingent, on the elements unique to that situation. This change in outlook has resulted largely from an increasing appreciation of the complexity of managerial problems and solutions. For example, pay raises may reduce turnover when workers have been badly underpaid. The contingency approach, however, recognizes that raises will have little effect when workers feel adequately paid but ill treated by management. This approach also recommends that training managers in human relations skills may be crucial to solving the problem in the second case.[14]

contingency approach to managerial style
Approach to managerial style holding that the appropriate behavior in any situation is dependent (contingent) on the unique elements of that situation

The contingency approach also acknowledges that people in different cultures behave differently and expect different things from their managers. A certain managerial style, therefore, is more likely to be successful in some countries than in others. Japanese workers, for example, generally expect managers to be highly participative and to give them input in decision making. In contrast, many South American workers actually balk at participation and want take-charge leaders. The basic idea, then, is that managers will be more effective when they adapt their styles to the contingencies of the situations they face.

Motivation and Leadership in the Twenty-First Century

Motivation and leadership remain critically important areas of organizational behavior. As times change, however, so do the ways managers motivate and lead their employees.

Changing Patterns of Motivation From the motivational side, today's employees want rewards that are often quite different from those valued by earlier generations. Money, for example, is no longer the prime motivator for most people. In addition, because businesses today cannot offer the degree of job security that many workers want, motivating employees to strive toward higher levels of performance requires skillful attention from managers.

One recent survey asked workers to identify those things they most wanted at work. Among the things noted were flexible working hours (67%), casual dress (56%), unlimited Internet access (51%), opportunities to telecommute (43%), nap time (28%), massages (25%), day care (24%), espresso machines (23%), and the opportunity to bring a pet to work (11%). In another study focusing on fathers, many men also said they wanted more flexible working hours in order to spend more time with their families. Managers, then, must recognize the fact that today's workers have a complex set of needs and must be motivated in increasingly complicated ways.

Finally, the diversity inherent in today's workforce also makes motivating behavior more complex. The reasons why people work reflect more varying goals than ever before, and the varying lifestyles of diverse workers mean that managers must first pay closer attention to what their employees expect to get for their efforts and then try to link rewards with job performance.[15]

Changing Patterns of Leadership Leadership, too, is taking different directions in the twenty-first century. For one thing, today's leaders are finding it necessary to change their own behavior. As organizations become flatter and workers more empowered, managers naturally find it less acceptable to use the autocratic approach to leadership. Instead, many are becoming more democratic—functioning more as coaches than as bosses. Just as an athletic coach teaches athletes how to play and then steps back to let them take the field, many leaders now try to provide workers with the skills and resources they need to perform at their best before backing off to let them do their work with less supervision.

Diversity, too, is also affecting leadership processes. In earlier times, most leaders were white males who were somewhat older than the people they supervised—people who were themselves relatively similar to one another. But as organizations become more and more diverse, leaders are also becoming increasingly diverse—women, African Americans, and Hispanics are entering the managerial ranks in ever greater numbers. They are also increasingly likely to be younger than some of the people they are leading. Leaders, therefore, must have greater sensitivity to the values, needs, and

These female executives are all clients of the Growth and Leadership Center *(www.glcweb.com)* in Mountain View, California, because the same toughness that got them up the corporate ladder is keeping them from climbing any higher. Or so say their employers (mostly men). Program founder Jean A. Hollands recommends that female executives back off from the assertive stance they were taught in the 1980s and return to a "softer" approach to interpersonal relationships. Many people, of course, think that Hollands's approach is all wrong. "I think women in many cases need to be more aggressive," says Alexandra Lebenthal, CEO of the brokerage firm Lebenthal & Co.

motives of a diverse group of people as they examine their own behavior in relation to other people.

Finally, leaders must also adopt more of a network mentality than a hierarchical one. As long as people worked in the same place at the same time, the organizational hierarchy had a clear vertical chain of command and lines of communication. But now people work in different places and at different times. New forms of organization design may call for one person to be the leader on one project and a team member on another. Thus, people need to get comfortable with leadership based more on expertise than on organizational position and with interaction patterns not tied to specific places or times. The leader of tomorrow, then, will need a different set of skills and a different point of view than did the leader of yesterday.[16]

SELF-CHECK QUESTIONS 7–9

You should now be able to answer Self-Check Questions 7–9*

7 **Multiple Choice** Which of the following is a common *managerial style?* [select one]: **(a)** autocratic; **(b)** democratic; **(c)** free-rein; **(d)** all of these are common managerial styles; **(e)** none of these are common managerial styles.

8 **True/False** According to the *contingency approach to leadership,* there is usually one approach to leadership that should always be used.

9 **Multiple Choice** When Sam supervises Mike, he uses an *autocratic style* because he knows that Mike wants to be told what to do. But when he supervises Ashley, he uses a *democratic style* because he knows she wants to have a voice in how she does her work. To which of the following theories of workplace behavior is Sam adhering? [select one]: **(a)** contingency approach to leadership; **(b)** trait approach to leadership; **(c)** expectancy theory of motivation; **(d)** equity theory of motivation; **(e)** behavioral approach to leadership.

***Answers to Self-Check Questions 7–9 can be found on p. 509.**

Continued from page 260

TURNING THE TIDE

From day one as CEO, Alan Lafley knew that P&G could do a better job of selling its proven winners. One of his first acts was to allocate more resources to the managers of the company's top 10 brands. "The trick," he recalls, "was to find the few things that were really going to sell, and sell as many of them as you could. . . . The essence of our strategy," he adds, "is incredibly simple, but I believe the simplicity is its power. . . . It's Sesame Street–simple, but it works." For example, hair-care managers reinvented the way they marketed Pantene, the company's top-selling hair-care brand. Rather than position products by hair type (for oily hair or fine hair), new campaigns focused on the looks that customers wanted—say, more curls or more volume. Sales went up by 8 percent.

Instead of insisting that new products be developed internally, Lafley also started acquiring small, idea-driven firms. He announced that 50 percent of the company's product innovations should come through such acquisitions. If the strategy proves successful, Lafley explains, "We would double the productivity of our current investment in R&D." Lafley also demands more marketability in new products, reminding researchers, "Innovation is in the consumer's eyes. . . . It isn't a great innovation until [the customer] loves it and purchases it."

Lafley is shaking up P&G's staid culture in other ways, too. "I have made a lot of symbolic, very physical changes," he says, "so people understand we are in the business of change." At the company's Cincinnati headquarters, product managers have moved out of executive suites to work more closely with employees. Wood paneling and oil paintings are coming down so that top managers can work as teams in modern, open spaces. The penthouse floor is now a learning center, where top executives conduct lessons and share knowledge with the workforce. "I really believe knowledge is power," says Lafley, "and translating knowledge into action in the marketplace is one of the things that distinguishes leadership."

> " **K**nowledge is power, and translating knowledge into action in the marketplace is one of the things that distinguishes leadership."
>
> —Alan Lafley, CEO of Procter & Gamble

Not surprisingly, communication between managers, workers, board members, and even competitors has opened up. "You can tell him bad news or things you'd be afraid to tell other bosses," says one vice president of Lafley. The CEO also rewards managers for financial results and is harsh on poor performers—half of the top team is new.

With a series of small changes, Alan Lafley has had a powerful impact on P&G's performance. Since he took over, earnings regularly beat expectations, and stock price has risen 70 percent. Profits are up 49 percent over last year. As for Lafley himself, he continues to emphasize the basics. "Nearly 2 billion times a day," he reminds his employees, "P&G products are put to the test when consumers use [them]. . . . When we get this right . . . then we begin to earn the trust on which great brands are built."

Questions for Discussion

1 Discuss the role of psychological contracts at Procter & Gamble.
2 How important are job satisfaction and morale to a large firm such as P&G?
3 Show how various theories of motivation apply to P&G.
4 What does this case illustrate about the nature of leadership?
5 Compare and contrast the leadership approaches used by Durk Jager and Alan Lafley.

■ SUMMARY OF LEARNING OBJECTIVES

1 Describe the nature and importance of *psychological contracts* in the workplace.

The foundation of good **human relations**—the interactions between employers and employees and their attitudes toward one another—is a satisfied and motivated workforce. Satisfaction and motivation depend on a **psychological contract** between organizations and employees: the set of expectations held by employees concerning what they will contribute and what the organization will provide in return. If contracts are managed effectively, workers will probably be satisfied and motivated. If not, they are likely to be dissatisfied and unmotivated.

2 Discuss the importance of *job satisfaction* and *employee morale* and summarize their roles in human relations in the workplace.

Job satisfaction is the degree of enjoyment that people get from doing their jobs. **Morale** reflects the degree to which they perceive that their needs are being met by their jobs. When workers are satisfied and morale is high, the organization benefits in many ways. Satisfied employees are more committed and loyal and more likely to make useful contributions. They tend to have fewer grievances and engage in fewer negative behaviors (complaining, deliberately slowing their work pace, and so forth). Satisfied workers tend to come to work every day and to remain with the organization. By promoting satisfaction and morale, then, management helps to ensure more efficient operations.

3 Identify and summarize the most important theories of *employee motivation*.

Motivation is the set of forces that cause people to behave in certain ways. The three major approaches to human relations in the workplace are (1) **classical theory**, (2) **behavior theory**, and (3) **contemporary theories**. There are five motivation theories: (1) **Theories X and Y**; (2) **Maslow's hierarchy of needs**; (3) **two-factor theory**; (4) **expectancy theory**; and (5) **equity theory**.

4 Describe some of the strategies used by organizations to improve *job satisfaction* and *employee motivation*.

There are five major programs designed to make jobs more interesting and rewarding: (1) **reinforcement/behavior modification theory**; (2) **management by objectives (MBO)**; (3) **participative management and empowerment**; (4) **job enrichment and job redesign**; and (5) **modified work schedules**, including (i) **work sharing** (or job sharing), (ii) **flextime programs**, and (iii) **telecommuting**.

5 Discuss different managerial styles of *leadership* and their impact on human relations in the workplace.

An important component of the manager's directing function, **leadership** is the process of motivating others to work to meet specific objectives. Contemporary theories of leadership focus on **managerial styles**—patterns of behavior that a manager exhibits in dealing with subordinates. Managers who adopt an **autocratic style** issue orders and expect them to be followed. This style allows for rapid decision making. Managers who adopt a **democratic style** ask for input from subordinates before making decisions, but they retain final decision-making power. Managers who adopt a **free-rein style** advise subordinates who are allowed to make decisions. Managers have begun to adopt a **contingency approach to managerial style**: viewing appropriate managerial behavior in any situation as dependent, or contingent, on the elements unique to that situation. This approach recognizes the complexity of managerial problems and acknowledges that people in different cultures expect different things from their managers.

■ KEY TERMS

psychological contract (p. 260)
job satisfaction (p. 261)
morale (p. 261)
turnover (p. 262)
motivation (p. 264)
classical theory of motivation (p. 264)
Hawthorne effect (p. 265)

Theory X (p. 265)
Theory Y (p. 265)
hierarchy of human needs model (p. 265)
two-factor theory (p. 266)
expectancy theory (p. 267)
equity theory (p. 268)

reinforcement (p. 269)
management by objectives (MBO) (p. 271)
participative management and empowerment (p. 272)
job enrichment (p. 273)
job redesign (p. 273)

work sharing (or job sharing) (p. 274)
flextime programs (p. 274)
telecommuting (p. 275)

leadership (p. 277)
managerial style (p. 278)
autocratic style (p. 279)
democratic style (p. 279)

free-rein style (p. 279)
contingency approach to managerial style (p. 279)

■ QUESTIONS AND EXERCISES

Questions for Review

1 Describe the psychological contract you currently have or have had in the past with an employer. If you have never worked, describe the psychological contract that you have with the instructor in this class.

2 Do you think that most people are relatively satisfied or dissatisfied with their work? Why are they mainly satisfied or dissatisfied?

3 Compare and contrast Maslow's hierarchy of needs with the two-factor theory of motivation.

4 How can participative management programs enhance employee satisfaction and motivation?

Questions for Analysis

5 Some evidence suggests that recent college graduates show high levels of job satisfaction. Levels then drop dramatically as they reach their late twenties, only to increase gradually once they get older. What might account for this pattern?

6 As a manager, under what sort of circumstances might you apply each of the theories of motivation discussed in this chapter? Which would be easiest to use? Which would be hardest? Why?

7 Suppose you realize one day that you are dissatisfied with your job. Short of quitting, what might you do to improve your situation?

8 List five U.S. managers who you think would also qualify as great leaders.

Application Exercises

9 At the library or using the Internet, research the manager or owner of a company in the early twentieth century and the manager or owner of a company in the 1990s. Compare and contrast the two in terms of their times, leadership styles, and views of employee motivation.

10 Interview the manager of a local manufacturing company. Identify as many different strategies for enhancing job satisfaction at that company as you can.

 BUILDING YOUR BUSINESS SKILLS

TOO MUCH OF A GOOD THING

This exercise enhances the following SCANS workplace competencies: demonstrating basic skills, demonstrating thinking skills, exhibiting interpersonal skills, working with information, and applying systems knowledge.

Goal
To encourage students to apply different motivational theories to a workplace problem involving poor productivity.

Background
For years, working for the George Uhe Co., a small chemicals broker in Paramus, New Jersey, made employees feel as if they were members of a big family. Unfortunately, this family was going broke because too few members were working hard enough to make money for it. They were happy, comfortable, complacent—and lazy.

With sales dropping in the pharmaceutical and specialty-chemicals division, Uhe brought in management consultants to analyze the situation and to make recommendations. The outsiders quickly identified a motivational problem affecting the sales force: Reps were paid a handsome salary and received automatic, year-end bonuses regardless of performance. They were also treated to bagels every Friday and regular group birthday lunches that cost as much as $200. Employees felt satisfied but had little incentive to work very hard. Eager to return to profitability, Uhe's owners waited to hear the consultants' recommendations.

Method

Step 1
In groups of four, step into the role of Uhe's management consultants. Start by analyzing your client's workforce-motivation problems from the following perspectives (our questions focus on key motivational issues):

■ **Job satisfaction and morale.** As part of a 77-year-old family-owned business, Uhe employees were happy and loyal, in part, because they were treated so well. Can high morale have a downside? How can it breed stagnation, and what can managers do to prevent stagnation from taking hold?

■ **Theory X versus Theory Y.** Although the behavior of these workers seems to make a case for Theory X, why is it difficult to draw this conclusion about a company that focuses more on satisfaction than on sales and profits?

■ **Two-factor theory.** Analyze the various ways in which improving such motivational factors as recognition, added responsibility, advancement, and growth might reduce the importance of hygiene factors, including pay and security.

■ **Expectancy theory.** Analyze the effect on productivity of redesigning the company's sales force compensation structure—namely, by paying lower base salaries while offering greater earnings potential through a sales-based incentive system. Why would linking performance with increased pay that is achievable through hard work motivate employees? Why would the threat of a job loss also motivate greater effort?

Step 2

Writing a short report based on your analysis, make recommendations to Uhe's owners. The goal of your report is to change the working environment in ways that will motivate greater effort and generate greater productivity.

FOLLOW-UP QUESTIONS

1 What is your group's most important recommendation? Why do you think it is likely to succeed?
2 Changing the corporate culture to make it less paternalistic may reduce employees' sense of belonging to a family. If you were an employee, would you consider a greater focus on profits to be an improvement or a problem? How would it affect your motivation and productivity?
3 What steps would you take to improve the attitude and productivity of longtime employees who resist change?

 ## EXERCISING YOUR ETHICS

PRACTICING CONTROLLED BEHAVIOR

The Situation

As we noted in the text, some companies try to control—and even alter—workers' behavior through systematic rewards and punishments for specific behaviors. In other words, they first try to define the specific behaviors that they want their employees to exhibit (such as working hard, being courteous to customers, stressing quality) and the specific behaviors they want to eliminate (wasting time, being rude to customers, ignoring quality). Then they try to shape employee behavior by linking reinforcement to desired behaviors and punishment to undesired behaviors.

The Dilemma

Assume that you are the new human resources manager in a medium-size organization. Your boss has just ordered you to

implement a behavior-modification program by creating an intricate network of rewards and punishments to be linked to specific desired and undesired behaviors. You, however, are uncomfortable with this approach. You regard behavior-modification policies to be too much like experiments on laboratory rats. Instead, you would prefer to use rewards in a way that is consistent with expectancy theory—that is, by letting employees know in advance how they can most effectively reach the rewards they most want. You have tried to change your boss's mind but to no avail. She says to proceed with behavior modification with no further discussion.

QUESTIONS FOR DISCUSSION

1 What are the ethical issues in this case?
2 What do you think most managers would do in this situation?
3 What would you do?

 ## CRAFTING YOUR BUSINESS PLAN

MAKING RESERVATIONS AND OTHER PLANS

The Purpose of the Assignment

1 To familiarize students with the ways in which employee considerations (morale, motivation, and job satisfaction)

enter into the development of a sample business plan, using the planning framework of the *Business PlanPro (BPP) 2003* software package (Version 6.0).

2 To stimulate students' thinking about the application of textbook information on employee morale, motivation,

job satisfaction, and leadership to the preparation of a *BPP* business plan.

Assignment

After reading Chapter 9 in the textbook, open the BPP *software and look around for information about the plans being made by a sample firm,* Puddle Jumpers Airlines Inc. *To find* Puddle Jumpers, *do the following:*

Open *Business PlanPro.* Go to the toolbar and click on the "*Sample Plans*" icon. In the **Sample Plan Browser,** do a search using the **search category** *Transportation by air.* From the resulting list, select the category entitled *Airline— Regional,* which is the location for *Puddle Jumpers Airlines Inc.* The screen that you are looking at is the introduction page with the business plan for *Puddle Jumpers.* Next, scroll down until you reach the **Table of Contents** for the company's business plan. Familiarize yourself with this firm by clicking on **1.0 Executive Summary.**

THEN RESPOND TO THE FOLLOWING ITEMS:

1 Consider *Puddle Jumpers'* plans to lower costs by using its flight crews more effectively than its competition does. If implemented, how might these plans affect employee morale? Job satisfaction? [Sites to see in *BPP* for this item: On the Table of Contents page, click on each of the following in turn: **1.2 Mission** and **1.3 Keys to Success.** After returning to the Table of Contents page, click on **3.2 Competitive Comparison.** Finally, return to the Table of Contents page, and explore any listed categories in which you would expect to find information about employee motivation and job satisfaction.]

2 Consider both *Puddle Jumpers'* plans for dealing with the high turnover among airline reservationists and its plans for training reservationists. Do you think the planned redesign will enrich the reservationist's job? Will it affect job satisfaction? Explain. [Sites to see in *BPP* for this item: On the Table of Contents page, click on each of the following in turn: **3.2 Competitive Comparison** and **3.5 Technology.** After returning to the Table of Contents page, click on **5.0 Strategy and Implementation Summary.**]

3 Consider the qualifications of Judy Land, director of reservations. Based on her background, would you say that she is qualified to lead and motivate employees under the new reservations system? Explain. [Sites to see in *BPP:* From the Table of Contents page, click on **6.2 Management Team.**]

 VIDEO EXERCISE

COMPUTING FAMILY VALUES: KINGSTON TECHNOLOGY

Learning Objectives
The purpose of this video is to help you:
1 Understand the importance of motivating employees.
2 Consider ways in which financial and nonfinancial rewards can motivate employees.
3 Explain how high morale can positively affect organizational performance.

Synopsis
California-based Kingston Technology is the world's largest independent manufacturer of computer memory products. Founded by John Tu and David Sun, Kingston employs more than 1,500 people but makes each employee feel like part of the family. The company returns 10 percent of its profits to employees every year through a profit-sharing program. Equally important is the policy of fostering mutual trust and respect between employees and management. Senior managers stay in touch with employees at all levels and conduct surveys to obtain employee feedback. For their part, employees report high job satisfaction and develop both personal and professional connections with their colleagues— boosting morale and motivation.

DISCUSSION QUESTIONS
1 **For analysis:** After Kingston's sale to Softbank, employees learned from news reports that Kingston's $100 million profit-sharing distribution was one of the largest in U.S. history. What was the likely effect of this publicity on employee morale?
2 **For analysis:** Are Kingston's managers applying Theory X or Theory Y in their relations with employees? How do you know?
3 **For application:** What kinds of questions should Kingston ask in order to gauge satisfaction and morale through employee surveys?
4 **For application:** What might Kingston management do to help employees satisfy higher-level needs such as self-actualization?
5 **For debate:** Do you agree with Kingston's policy of giving new employees profit-sharing bonuses even when they join the company just one week before profits are distributed? Support your position.

Online Exploration

Visit Kingston Technology's Web site at *(www.kingston.com)* and follow the links to company information about its awards. From the company information page, follow the links to learn about the organization's values. How do these values support the founders' intention to create a family feeling within the company? How do they support employee satisfaction of higher-level needs? Why would Kingston post a list of corporate milestones (including the company's founding and honors bestowed on it by *Fortune* and others) on its Web site?

PLANNING FOR YOUR CAREER

MANAGING YOUR HUMAN RESOURCES

As we saw in Chapter 8, human resource management is concerned with the ways in which an organization attracts, develops, and maintains its workforce. Of course, HR management is really a two-way street: While companies are trying to recruit and hire the best employees, talented people are busy trying to choose the best companies to work for. This exercise will help you better understand your role in this process as you look forward to starting or advancing in your own career.

Assignment

Start by reviewing Chapter 7-9 in *Beginning Your Career Search*, 3d ed., by James S. O'Rourke IV. These chapters cover the interviewing process and discuss the things you need to do when you're offered a job. Also review Chapter 9 in this text to make sure that you recall the various elements of the HR management process.

To complete this exercise, do the following:

1 Review the text discussion on the ways organizations recruit. Now describe the ways you might go about looking for a job. Be sure to compare your approach with what you know about organizational recruiting methods.

2 Review the text discussion on the means by which organizations select human resources. List the questions you have regarding application forms, tests, and other techniques. Compare your questions and concerns with O'Rourke's detailed description of interviewing.

3 What do you see as your current personal strengths and weaknesses that might affect an employment interview? What can you do to overcome your weaknesses?

4 If you were offered more than one job, what role might a company's policies on training and performance appraisal play in helping you make a choice?

5 Although it's advisable to not focus on compensation in the early stages of an employment discussion, what role would pay and benefits play in helping you make your decision? Would you automatically pick the job with the highest salary? Why or why not?

6 Do you think you might have an interest in being an HR manager? Why or why not?

10

After reading this chapter, you should be able to:

1 Explain the concept of *marketing* and describe the five forces that constitute the *external marketing environment*.

2 Explain the purpose of a *marketing plan* and identify the four components of the *marketing mix*.

3 Explain *market segmentation* and show how it is used in *target marketing*.

4 Describe the key factors that influence the *consumer buying process*.

5 Discuss the three categories of *organizational markets*.

6 Explain the definition of a product as a *value package*.

7 Explain the importance of *branding* and *packaging*.

XBOX SPOTS THE MARKET

Once the domain of teenage boys, interactive games now lure a much broader audience, including younger kids and adults. It's easy to become addicted: With cinematically realistic graphics and challenging action sequences, games require split-second timing

UNDERSTANDING MARKETING PROCESSES AND CONSUMER BEHAVIOR

"I used to tell my mother it would improve my hand–eye coordination."

— Josh Bell
Violinist and electronic gamer

and rapid-fire reactions. Today's communications technology allows real-time interaction among gaming enthusiasts, either in side-by-side competition or among opponents anywhere in the world.

Consider one such enthusiast, Josh Bell, a Grammy Award–winning violinist and one of *People* magazine's "50 Most Beautiful People" for 2001. Bell spends 20 hours a week gaming, sometimes at the expense of violin practice. He uses a wireless keyboard hooked into a 50-inch plasma wall TV. Six speakers provide surround sound for total immersion in such virtual games as "Quake III" and "Defense," an Internet game. To justify time away from the violin, admits Bell, "I used to tell my mother it would improve my hand–eye coordination." At 32, Bell is at the older end of the gaming-enthusiast spectrum. The mainstream is in its mid 20s, late and early teens, and, at the youngest end of the demographic spectrum, 10 years old.

Computer- and video-game sales have grown 15 percent a year for four years. By 2001, they had caught up with sales of DVDs and videotapes. Sales of game hardware and software in the three biggest markets—the United States, Europe, and Japan—reached $16.5 billion in 2001 and will top $20 billion in 2003. It's no surprise that the prospect of such a vast market has attracted the attention of Microsoft.

Before its launch in November 2001, Xbox—Microsoft's entry into console gaming—was one of the industry's most anticipated products. Its $500 million marketing budget included a prelaunch Web site *(www.xbox.com)* to tantalize players with the most advanced hardware and hottest graphics in the industry. Microsoft designed its site to become the gathering place for players and to promote enthusiasm among gamers everywhere. Thus far, Xbox.com has succeeded both in establishing relationships among gamers and in forming new bonds between gamers and the Xbox brand. Microsoft wants gamers to become loyal members of an Xbox community.

But industry experts know that it takes more than relationship building and nifty hardware to succeed in this market. Success depends on a steady flow of exciting software—games that capture players' imaginations. Xbox hardware, reports Phaedra Boinodiris, head of Womengamers.com, "far outweighs the competition for speed and memory," but she adds that "there's a serious problem with the lineup [of games] so far." The initial launch featured 12 to 20 games, most of them action and sports oriented. By early 2002, the list had grown to 56 but included only two—"Shrek" and "Rise of Parethi"—that cater to the market for adventure and strategy games.

Nevertheless, Microsoft's start-up marketing has already had an impact: By December 2001, more than 1.4 million Xbox units had been sold, many of them even before reaching store shelves.

Our opening story continues on page 315.

■ WHAT IS MARKETING?

marketing
The process of planning and executing the conception, pricing, promotion, and distribution of ideas, goods, and services to create exchanges that satisfy individual and organizational objectives

What comes to mind when you think of marketing? Most of us think of marketing as advertisements for detergents and soft drinks. Marketing, however, encompasses a much wider range of activities. The American Marketing Association *(www.ama.org)* defines **marketing** as "the process of planning and executing the conception, pricing, promotion, and distribution of ideas, goods, and services to create exchanges that satisfy individual and organizational goals."[1] In this section, we begin by looking at how marketing focuses on providing value and utility for consumers. We then explore the marketing environment and the development of marketing strategy. Finally, we focus on the four activities that comprise the *marketing mix:* developing, pricing, placing, and promoting products.

Providing Value and Satisfaction

What attracts buyers to one product instead of another? Although our desires for the many goods and services available to us may be unbounded, limited financial resources force most of us to be selective. Accordingly, consumers buy products that offer the best value when it comes to meeting their needs and wants.

Value and Benefits **Value** compares a product's benefits with its costs. The benefits of a *high-value* product are much greater than its costs. *Benefits* include not only the functions of the product but also the emotional satisfactions associated with owning, experiencing, or possessing it. But, of course, every product has costs, including sales price, the expenditure of the buyer's time, and even the emotional costs of making a purchase decision. The satisfied buyer perceives the benefits derived from the purchase to be greater than its costs. Thus the simple but important ratio for value:

$$Value = \frac{Benefits}{Cost}$$

value
Relative comparison of a product's benefits with its costs

The marketing strategies of leading firms focus on increasing value for customers. Marketing resources are deployed to add value to products in order to satisfy customers' needs and wants. Satisfying customers may mean developing an entirely new product that performs better (provides greater benefits) than existing products. Or it may entail keeping a store open extra hours during a busy season (adding the benefit of greater shopping convenience). Some firms simply offer price reductions (the benefit of lower cost). Customers may also gain benefits from an informational promotion that explains how a product can be used in new ways.

Value and Utility To understand how marketing creates value for customers, we need to know the kind of benefits that buyers get from a firm's goods or services. As we discussed in Chapter 7, products provide consumers with **utility**—the ability of a product to satisfy a human want or need. Marketing strives to provide four kinds of utility: time utility, place utility, ownership utility, and form utility. Marketing plays a role in all four areas—determining the timing, place, terms of sale, and product features that provide utility and add value for customers. Marketers, therefore, must begin with an understanding of customers' wants and needs. Their methods for creating utility are described in this and the following chapter.

utility
Ability of a product to satisfy a human want or need

Goods, Services, and Ideas

The marketing of tangible goods is obvious in everyday life. You walk into a department store and a woman with a clipboard asks if you would like to try a new cologne. A pharmaceutical company proclaims the virtues of its new cold medicine. Your local auto dealer offers an economy car at an economy price. These products—the cologne, the cold medicine, and the car—are all **consumer goods**: products that you, the consumer, may buy for personal use. Firms that sell products to consumers for personal consumption are engaged in *consumer marketing.*

consumer goods
Products purchased by consumers for personal use

Marketing also applies to **industrial goods**: products used by companies to produce other products. Surgical instruments and earthmovers are industrial goods, as are such components and raw materials as integrated circuits, steel, and unformed plastic. Firms that sell products to other manufacturers are engaged in *industrial marketing.*

industrial goods
Products purchased by companies to produce other products

Marketing techniques can also be applied to **services**—intangible products such as time, expertise, or some activity that you can purchase. *Service marketing* has become a major growth area in the United States. Insurance companies, airlines, investment counselors, health clinics, and public accountants all engage in service marketing, both to individuals and to other companies.

services
Intangible products, such as time, expertise, or an activity that can be purchased

Finally, marketers also promote ideas. Television ads, for example, can remind us that teaching is an honorable profession and that teachers are "heroes." Other ads stress the importance of driving only when sober and the advantages of not smoking.

Relationship Marketing Although marketing often focuses on single transactions for products, services, or ideas, marketers also take a longer-term perspective. Thus, **relationship marketing** emphasizes lasting relationships with customers and suppliers. Stronger relationships—including stronger economic and social ties—can result in greater long-term satisfaction and customer loyalty.[2]

relationship marketing
Marketing strategy that emphasizes lasting relationships with customers and suppliers

Commercial banks, for example, offer economic incentives to encourage longer-lasting relationships. Customers who purchase a certain number of the bank's products (for example, checking accounts, savings accounts, and loans) accumulate credits toward free or reduced-price services, such as free traveler's checks.

The Marketing Environment

Marketing strategies are not determined unilaterally by any business, not even by marketers as experienced as Coca-Cola *(www.coke.com)* and Procter & Gamble *(www.pg.com)*. Rather, they are strongly influenced by powerful outside forces. As you can see in Figure 10.1, every marketing program must recognize the factors in a company's **external environment**. In this section, we describe five of these environmental factors: the *political-legal, social-cultural, technological, economic,* and *competitive environments.*

external environment
Outside factors that influence marketing programs by posing opportunities or threats

Political and Legal Environment Political activities, both foreign and domestic, have profound effects on marketing. Legislation on the use of cell phones in cars and the Clean Air Act have determined the destinies of entire industries. Marketing managers thus try to maintain favorable political-legal environments in several ways. To gain public support for products and activities, marketers use ad campaigns to

FIGURE 10.1

The External Marketing Environment

raise public awareness of local, regional, or national issues. Companies contribute to political candidates and frequently support the activities of political action committees (PACs) maintained by their respective industries.

Social and Cultural Environment More people are working in home offices, the number of single-parent families is increasing, and food preferences reflect a growing concern for healthy lifestyles. These and other trends reflect the values, beliefs, and ideas that shape U.S. society.

Changing social values force companies to develop and promote new products for both individual consumers and industrial customers. For example, although most of us value privacy, Web surfers are discovering that a loss of privacy is often a price for the convenience of Internet shopping. Dot-com sites regularly collect personal information that they use for marketing purposes and that they often sell to other firms. Responding to the growing demand for better privacy protection, firms like iNetPrivacy *(www.inetprivacy.com)* offer such new products as Anonymity 4 Proxy software, which allows you to surf the Net anonymously.

Technological Environment New technologies create new goods (the satellite dish) and services (home television shopping). New products make existing products obsolete (compact disks are replacing audiotapes), and many products change our values and lifestyles. In turn, lifestyle changes often stimulate new products not directly related to the new technologies themselves. Cell phones, for example, not only facilitate business communication but free up time for recreation and leisure. The Internet is a new medium for selling, buying, and distributing products from your own home to customers around the world.

Economic Environment Because they determine spending patterns by consumers, businesses, and governments, economic conditions influence marketing plans for product offerings, pricing, and promotional strategies. Marketers are concerned with such economic variables as inflation, interest rates, and recession. Thus, they must monitor the general business cycle, which typically features a pattern of transition from periods of prosperity to recession to recovery. Not surprisingly, consumer spending increases as consumer confidence in economic conditions grows during periods of prosperity.

Traditionally, economic analysis focused on the national economy. Increasingly, however, as nations form more complex economic connections, the global economy is becoming more prominent in the thinking of marketers everywhere.[3] At Wal-Mart *(www.walmartstores.com)*, for example, 17 percent of all sales revenue comes from the retailer's international division. Although overall international sales were up 41 percent for 2001, sales in some Latin American countries stalled. Why? Because economic conditions in such markets as Argentina and Brazil differ significantly from those in Mexico, which, in turn, differ from those in China, South Korea, and Germany.

Competitive Environment In a competitive environment, marketers must convince buyers that they should purchase one company's products rather than those of some other seller. Because both consumers and commercial buyers have limited resources, every dollar spent on one product is no longer available for other purchases. Each marketing program, therefore, seeks to make its product the most attractive. Theoretically, a failed program loses the buyer's dollar forever (or at least until it is time for the next purchase decision).

The *euro,* the common currency of the European Union, is a variable in Great Britain's economic environment. On the one hand, for member-nation companies doing international business, it eliminates *exchange rate risk*—the risk that changes in rates might adversely affect a firm's transactions. That's why multinationals and banks in England—a non-euro nation—favor the euro. On the other hand, protestors fear that in order to keep the British economy in line with those of euro nations, Britain would have to enact labor and other regulation like those of other EU countries.

substitute product
Product that is dissimilar to those of competitors but that can fulfill the same need

brand competition
Competitive marketing that appeals to consumer perceptions of similar products

international competition
Competitive marketing of domestic products against foreign products

marketing manager
Manager who plans and implements the marketing activities that result in the transfer of products from producer to consumer

marketing plan
Detailed strategy for focusing marketing efforts on consumer needs and wants

marketing mix
The combination of product, pricing, promotion, and distribution strategies used to market products

product
Good, service, or idea that is marketed to fill consumer needs and wants

Marketers must decide how to position products for three types of competition:

■ **Substitute products** are dissimilar from those of competitors but can fulfill the same need. For example, your cholesterol level may be controlled with either a physical fitness program or a drug regimen. The fitness program and the drugs compete as substitute products.

■ **Brand competition** occurs between similar products, such as the auditing services provided by the large accounting firms of Ernst & Young *(www.ey.com)* and KPMG Peat Marwick *(www.kpmg.com).* The competition is based on buyers' perceptions of the benefits of products offered by particular companies.

■ **International competition** matches the products of domestic marketers against those of foreign competitors—a flight on Swissair *(www.swissair.com)* versus Delta Airlines *(www.delta-air.com).* The intensity of international competition has, of course, been heightened by the formation of alliances such as the European Union and NAFTA.

Strategy: The Marketing Mix

A company's **marketing managers** are responsible for planning and implementing all the activities that result in the transfer of goods or services to its customers. These activities culminate in the **marketing plan**—a detailed strategy for focusing marketing efforts on consumer needs and wants. Therefore, marketing strategy begins when a company identifies a consumer need and develops a product to meet it.

In planning and implementing strategies, marketing managers develop the four basic components (often called the "Four P's") of the **marketing mix**. In this section, we describe each of those components: *product, pricing, place,* and *promotion.*

Product Marketing begins with a **product**—a good, a service, or an idea designed to fill a consumer need or want. Conceiving and developing new products is a constant challenge for marketers, who must always consider the factor of change—changing technology, changing consumer wants and needs, and changing economic conditions. Meeting consumer needs, then, often means changing existing products to keep pace with emerging markets and competitors.

Product Differentiation Producers often promote particular features of products in order to distinguish them on the marketplace. **Product differentiation** is the creation of a feature or image that makes a product differ enough from existing products to attract consumers. For example, Volvo automobiles *(www.volvo.com)* provide newer, better safety features to set them apart from competitors. Customers of E*Trade™ *(www.etrade.com)*, the online investment service, gain value from after-hours trading not offered by conventional investment service firms.

product differentiation
Creation of a product or product image that differs enough from existing products to attract consumers

Pricing

Pricing a product—selecting the best price at which to sell it—is often a balancing act. On the one hand, prices must support a variety of costs—operating, administrative, and research costs as well as marketing costs. On the other hand, prices can't be so high that consumers turn to competitors. Successful pricing means finding a profitable middle ground between these two requirements.

Both low- and high-price strategies can be effective in different situations. Low prices, for example, generally lead to larger sales volumes. High prices usually limit market size but increase profits per unit. High prices may also attract customers by implying that a product is of high quality. We discuss pricing in more detail in Chapter 11.

Place (Distribution)

In the marketing mix, *place* refers to **distribution**. Placing a product in the proper outlet—say, a retail store—requires decisions about several activities, all of which are concerned with getting the product from the producer to the consumer. Decisions about warehousing and inventory control are distribution decisions, as are decisions about transportation options.

distribution
Part of the marketing mix concerned with getting products from producers to consumers

Firms must also make decisions about the *channels* through which they distribute products. Many manufacturers, for instance, sell goods to other companies that, in turn, distribute them to retailers. Others sell directly to major retailers such as Sears,

Jann Wenner started *Rolling Stone* magazine in 1967, and it's been the cash cow of Wenner Media *(www.rollingstone.com)* ever since. In 1985, Wenner bought *Us* magazine and set out to compete with *People*, perhaps the most successful magazine ever published. Wenner's latest strategy calls for greater differentiation between the two products. *People* is news driven, reporting on ordinary people as well as celebrities, and Wenner intends to punch up *Us* with more coverage of celebrity sex and glitter. So far, he hasn't been successful: *People* reaches 3.7 million readers, *Us* about 900,000.

Wal-Mart, and Safeway. Still others sell directly to final consumers. We explain distribution decisions further in Chapter 11.

Promotion The most highly visible component of the marketing mix is no doubt promotion, which refers to techniques for communicating information about products. The most important promotional tools include advertising, personal selling, sales promotions, and public relations. We describe promotional activities more fully in Chapter 11. Here we briefly describe the most important promotional tools.

Advertising Advertising is any form of paid nonpersonal communication used by an identified sponsor to persuade or inform potential buyers about a product. For example, The MonyGroup *(www.mony.com)*, a financial adviser that provides investment and securities products, reaches its customer audience by advertising its services in *Fortune* magazine.

Personal Selling Many products (for example, insurance, clothing, and real estate) are best promoted through personal selling, or person-to-person sales. Industrial goods receive the bulk of personal selling. When companies buy from other companies, purchasing agents and others who need technical and detailed information are usually referred to the selling company's sales representatives.

Sales Promotions Relatively inexpensive items are often marketed through sales promotions, which involve one-time direct inducements to buyers. Premiums (usually free gifts), coupons, and package inserts are all sales promotions meant to tempt consumers to buy products.

Public Relations Public relations includes all communication efforts directed at building goodwill. It seeks to build favorable attitudes toward the organization and its products. The Ronald McDonald House program *(www.rmhc.com)* is a well-known example of public relations.

SELF-CHECK QUESTIONS 1–3

You should now be able to answer Self-Check Questions 1–3.*

1 **Multiple Choice** Marketers know that consumers buy products that offer the best *value.* Which of the following is **not** true regarding *value* for the buyer? [select one]: **(a)** It is related to the buyer's wants and needs. **(b)** It is the comparison of a product's benefits versus its costs. **(c)** It is intangible and cannot be measured. **(d)** It depends on the product's price. **(e)** Market strategies focus on increasing it.

2 **Multiple Choice** A program in which a bank offers free services to long-standing customers is an example of which of the following? [select one]: **(a)** industrial marketing; **(b)** services marketing; **(c)** brand competition; **(d)** product differentiation; **(e)** relationship marketing.

3 **Multiple Choice** All of the following are elements in the *marketing mix (the "Four P's" of marketing)* except [select one]: **(a)** product differentiation; **(b)** place (or distribution); **(c)** promotion; **(d)** product; **(e)** pricing.

*Answers to Self-Check Questions 1–3 can be found on p. 509.

■ TARGET MARKETING AND MARKET SEGMENTATION

Marketers have long known that products cannot be all things to all people. Buyers have different tastes, goals, lifestyles, and so on. The emergence of the marketing concept and the recognition of consumer needs and wants led marketers to think in terms of **target markets**—groups of people with similar wants and needs. Selecting target markets is usually the first step in the marketing strategy.

target market
Group of people that has similar wants and needs and that can be expected to show interest in the same products

Target marketing requires **market segmentation**—dividing a market into categories of customer types or "segments." Once they have identified segments, companies may adopt a variety of strategies. Some firms market products to more than one segment. General Motors *(www.gm.com)*, for example, offers compact cars, vans, trucks, luxury cars, and sports cars with various features and at various price levels. GM's strategy is to provide an automobile for nearly every segment of the market.

market segmentation
Process of dividing a market into categories of customer types

In contrast, some businesses offer a narrower range of products, each aimed toward a specific segment. Note that segmentation is a strategy for analyzing consumers, not products. The process of fixing, adapting, and communicating the nature of the product itself is called *product positioning.*

Identifying Market Segments

By definition, members of a market segment must share some common traits that affect their purchasing decisions. In identifying segments, researchers look at several different influences on consumer behavior. Three of the most important are *geographic, demographic,* and *psychographic variables.*

Geographic Variables Many buying decisions are affected by the places people call home. The heavy rainfall in Washington State, for instance, means that people there buy more umbrellas than people in the Sun Belt. Urban residents don't need agricultural equipment, and sailboats sell better along the coasts than on the Great Plains. **Geographic variables** are the geographical units, from countries to neighborhoods, that may be considered in a segmentation strategy.

geographic variables
Geographical units that may be considered in developing a segmentation strategy

These patterns affect decisions about marketing mixes for a huge range of products. For example, consider a plan to market down-filled parkas in rural Minnesota. Demand will be high and price competition intense. Local newspaper ads may be

"I'd get out of children and into older people."

effective, and the best retail location may be one that is easily reached from several small towns.

Although the marketability of some products is geographically sensitive, others enjoy nearly universal acceptance. Coke, for example, gets more than 70 percent of its sales from international markets. It is the market leader in Great Britain, China, Germany, Japan, Brazil, and Spain. Pepsi's international sales are about 15 percent of Coke's. In fact, Coke's chief competitor in most countries is some local soft drink, not Pepsi, which earns 78 percent of its income at home.

demographic variables
Characteristics of populations that may be considered in developing a segmentation strategy

Demographic Variables **Demographic variables** describe populations by identifying such traits as age, income, gender, ethnic background, marital status, race, religion, and social class. For example, several general consumption characteristics can be attributed to certain age groups (18–25, 26–35, 36–45, and so on). A marketer can, thus, divide markets into age groups. Table 10.1 lists some possible demographic breakdowns. Depending on the marketer's purpose, a segment can be a single classification (*aged 20–34*) or a combination of categories (*aged 20–34, married with children, earning* $25,000–$34,999). Foreign competitors, for example, are gaining market share in U.S. auto sales by appealing to young buyers (under age 30) with limited incomes (under $30,000). Whereas companies such as Hyundai *(www.hyundai.net)*, Kia *(www.kia.com)*, and Daewoo *(www.daewoous.com)* are winning entry-level customers with high quality and generous warranties, Volkswagen *(www.vw.com)* targets under-35 buyers with its entertainment-styled VW Jetta.[4]

psychographic variables
Consumer characteristics, such as lifestyles, opinions, interests, and attitudes, that may be considered in developing a segmentation strategy

Psychographic Variables Markets can also be segmented according to such **psychographic variables** as lifestyles, interests, and attitudes. Take, for example, Burberry *(www.burberry.com)*, whose raincoats have been a symbol of British tradition since 1856. Burberry has repositioned itself as a global luxury brand, like Gucci *(www.gucci.com)* and Louis Vuitton *(www.vuitton.com)*. The strategy, which recently resulted in a 31-percent sales increase, calls for attracting a different type of customer—the top-of-the-line, fashion-conscious individual—who shops at such stores as Neiman Marcus and Bergdorf Goodman.[5]

Psychographics are particularly important to marketers because, unlike demographics and geographics, they can be changed by marketing efforts. For example, Polish companies have overcome consumer resistance by promoting the safety and desirability of using credit rather than depending solely on cash. One product of changing attitudes is a booming economy and the emergence of a robust middle class.

TABLE 10.1

Demographic Variables

Age	Under 5, 5–11, 12–19, 20–34, 35–49, 50–64, 65+
Education	Grade school or less, some high school, graduated high school, some college, college degree, advanced degree
Family life cycle	Young single, young married without children, young married with children, older married with children under 18, older married without children under 18, older single, other
Family size	1, 2–3, 4–5, 6+
Income	Under $9,000, $9,000–$14,999, $15,000–$24,999, $25,000–$34,999, $35,000–$45,000, over $45,000
Nationality	African, American, Asian, British, Eastern European, French, German, Irish, Italian, Latin American, Middle Eastern, Scandinavian
Race	Native American, Asian, Black, White
Religion	Buddhist, Catholic, Hindu, Jewish, Muslim, Protestant
Sex	Male, female

Although Nike *(www.nike.com)* leads the $15.5 billion athletic footwear industry and had revenues of $9 billion last year, it still has a serious problem: Women's footwear accounts for 33 percent of industrywide sales but generates only 20 percent of Nike's. Nike is going after this demographic segment with a marketing campaign that focuses on differences between the way men and women think about sports and the way they shop for clothing. According to Nike marketers, for example, women are more interested in image trends and active lifestyles than in athletic competition and sports celebrities.

The increasing number of Polish households with TVs, appliances, automobiles, and houses is defining the status of Poland's middle class as the most stable in the former Soviet bloc.[6]

■ UNDERSTANDING CONSUMER BEHAVIOR

Although marketing managers can tell us what features people want in a new VCR, they cannot tell us *why* they buy particular VCRs. What desire are consumers fulfilling? Is there a psychological or sociological explanation for why they purchase one product and not another? These questions and many others are addressed in the study of **consumer behavior**—the study of the decision process by which people buy and consume products.

consumer behavior
Various facets of the decision process by which customers come to purchase and consume products

Influences on Consumer Behavior

To understand consumer behavior, marketers draw heavily on such fields as psychology and sociology. The result is a focus on four major influences on consumer behavior: *psychological, personal, social,* and *cultural.* By identifying which influences are most active in certain circumstances, marketers try to explain consumer choices and predict future buying behavior.

1 *Psychological influences* include an individual's motivations, perceptions, ability to learn, and attitudes.
2 *Personal influences* include lifestyle, personality, and economic status.
3 *Social influences* include family, opinion leaders (people whose opinions are sought by others), and such reference groups as friends, coworkers, and professional associates.

4 *Cultural influences* include culture (the way of living that distinguishes one large group from another), subculture (smaller groups, such as ethnic groups, with shared values), and social class (the cultural ranking of groups according to such criteria as background, occupation, and income).

Although these factors can have a strong impact on a consumer's choices, their effect on actual purchases is sometimes weak or negligible. Some consumers, for example, exhibit high **brand loyalty**—they regularly purchase products because they are satisfied with their performance. Such people (for example, users of Maytag appliances) are less subject to influence and stick with preferred brands. On the other hand, the clothes you wear and the food you eat often reflect social and psychological influences on your consumer behavior.

brand loyalty
Pattern of regular consumer purchasing based on satisfaction with a product

The Consumer Buying Process

Students of consumer behavior have constructed various models to help show how consumers decide to buy products. Figure 10.2 presents one such model. At the core of this and similar models is an awareness of the psychosocial influences that lead to consumption. Ultimately, marketers use this information to develop marketing plans.

■ **Problem/need recognition** The process begins when the consumer recognizes a problem or need. After strenuous exercise, for example, you may realize that you are thirsty. Need recognition also occurs when you have a chance to change your buying habits. When you obtain your first job after graduation, your new income may let you purchase items that were once too expensive for you. You may find that you need professional clothing, apartment furnishings, and a car. American

FIGURE 10.2
The Consumer Buying Process

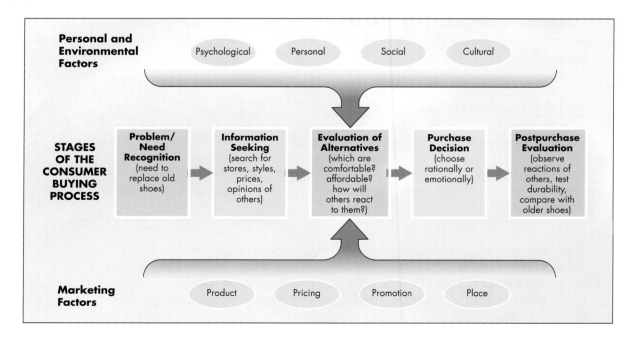

Express and Sears cater to such shifts in needs when they market credit cards to college seniors.

■ **Information seeking** Having recognized a need, consumers often seek information. The search is not always extensive, but before making major purchases, most people seek information from personal sources, public sources, and experience. Before buying an exercise bike, you may read about bikes in *Consumer Reports (www.consumerreports.org)* or you may test-ride several bikes.

■ **Evaluation of alternatives** If you are in the market for skis, you probably have some idea of who makes skis and how they differ. Perhaps accumulated knowledge during the information-seeking stage is combined with what you knew beforehand. By analyzing product attributes (color, price, prestige, quality, service record), you will compare products before deciding which one best meets your needs.

■ **Purchase decision** Ultimately, consumers make purchase decisions. "Buy" decisions are based on rational motives, emotional motives, or both.[7] **Rational motives** involve the logical evaluation of product attributes: cost, quality, and usefulness. **Emotional motives** involve nonobjective factors and include sociability, imitation of others, and aesthetics. For example, you might buy the same brand of jeans as your friends to feel comfortable in a certain group, not because your friends happen to have the good sense to prefer durable, comfortably priced jeans.

■ **Postpurchase evaluations** Marketing does not stop with the sale of a product. What happens *after* the sale is important. Marketers want consumers to be happy after buying products so that they are more likely to buy them again. Because consumers do not want to go through a complex decision process for every purchase, they often repurchase products they have used and liked. Not all consumers, of course, are satisfied with their purchases. These buyers are not likely to purchase the same product(s) again and are much more apt to broadcast their experiences than are satisfied customers.

rational motives
Reasons for purchasing a product that are based on a logical evaluation of product attributes

emotional motives
Reasons for purchasing a product that are based on nonobjective factors

Data Warehousing and Data Mining

Almost everything you do leaves a trail of information about you. Your preferences in movie rentals, television viewing, Internet sites, and groceries; the destinations of your phone calls, your credit card charges, your financial status; personal information about age, gender, marital status, and even health—these are just a few of the items in a huge cache of data that are stored about each of us. The collection, storage, and retrieval of such data in electronic files is called **data warehousing**. For marketing researchers, the data warehouse is a gold mine of clues about consumer behavior.[8]

data warehousing
Process of collecting, storing, and retrieving data in electronic files

The Uses of Data Mining After collecting information, marketers use **data mining**—the application of electronic technologies for searching, sifting, and reorganizing pools of data to uncover useful marketing information and to plan for new products that will appeal to target segments in the marketplace. Using data mining, for example, the insurance company Farmers Group discovered that a sports car is not an exceptionally high insurance risk if it's not the only family car. The company thus issued more liberal policies on Corvettes and Porches and so generated more revenue without significantly increasing payout claims. Among retailers, Wal-Mart has long been a data-mining pioneer, maintaining perhaps the world's

data mining
Application of electronic technologies for searching, sifting, and reorganizing data in order to collect marketing information and target products in the marketplace

largest privately held data warehouse. Data include demographics, markdowns, returns, inventory, and other data for forecasting sales and the effects of marketing promotions.[9]

ORGANIZATIONAL MARKETING AND BUYING BEHAVIOR

In the consumer market, buying and selling transactions are visible to the public. Equally important, though far less visible, are *organizational* (or *commercial*) *markets.* Some 23 million U.S. organizations buy goods and services to be used in creating and delivering consumer products. Marketing to these buyers involves various kinds of markets and buying behaviors different from those in consumer markets.

Organizational Markets

Organizational or commercial markets fall into three categories: *industrial, reseller,* and *government/institutional markets.* Taken together, these markets do about $8 trillion in business annually—approximately three times the amount done in the U.S. consumer market.

industrial market
Organizational market consisting of firms that buy goods that are either converted into products or used during production

Industrial Market The **industrial market** includes businesses that buy goods to be converted into other products or goods that are used up during production. It includes farmers, manufacturers, and some retailers. For example, Seth Thomas *(www.seththomas.com)* buys electronics, metal components, and glass to make clocks for the consumer market. The company also buys office supplies, tools, and factory equipment—items never seen by clock buyers—that are used during production.

reseller market
Organizational market consisting of intermediaries that buy and resell finished goods

Reseller Market Before products reach consumers, they pass through a **reseller market** consisting of intermediaries, including wholesalers and retailers, that buy and resell finished goods. As a leading distributor of parts and accessories for the pleasure boat market, The Coast Distribution System buys lights, steering wheels, and propellers and resells them to marinas and boat-repair shops. On resold products, 750,000 U.S. wholesalers have annual sales of $2.4 trillion. Some 2.5 million U.S. retailers purchase merchandise that, when resold, is valued at $2.6 trillion per year.[10]

Government and Institutional Market In addition to federal and state governments, there are some 87,000 local governments (municipalities, counties, and school districts) in the United States. State and local governments annually spend $1.3 trillion for durable goods, nondurables, services, and construction. The **institutional market** consists of nongovernmental organizations, such as hospitals, churches, museums, and charities, which also use supplies and equipment as well as legal, accounting, and transportation services.

institutional market
Organizational market consisting of such nongovernmental buyers of goods and services as hospitals, churches, museums, and charitable organizations

Organizational Buying Behavior

In some respects, organizational buying behavior bears little resemblance to consumer buying practices. Differences include the buyers' purchasing skills and an emphasis on buyer–seller relationships.

Differences in Buyers Unlike most consumers, organizational buyers are professional, specialized, and expert (or at least well informed):

- As *professionals,* organizational buyers are trained in methods for negotiating purchase terms. Once buyer–seller agreements have been reached, they also arrange for formal contracts.
- As a rule, industrial buyers are company *specialists* in a line of items. As one of several buyers for a large bakery, for example, you may specialize in food ingredients. Another buyer may specialize in baking equipment (industrial ovens and mixers), whereas a third may buy office equipment and supplies.
- Industrial buyers are often *experts* about the products they buy. On a regular basis, organizational buyers study competing products and alternative suppliers by attending trade shows, by reading trade magazines, and by conducting technical discussions with sellers' representatives.

Differences in the Buyer–Seller Relationship Consumer–seller relationships are often impersonal, short-lived, one-time interactions. In contrast, industrial situations often involve frequent and enduring buyer–seller relationships. The development of a long-term relationship provides each party with access to the technical strengths of the other as well as the security of knowing what future business to expect. Thus, a buyer and a supplier may form a design team to create products of benefit to both. Accordingly, industrial sellers emphasize personal selling by trained representatives who understand the needs of each customer.

SELF-CHECK QUESTIONS 4–6

You should now be able to answer Self-Check Questions 4–6.*

4 **True/False** *Target marketing* requires *market segmentation.*

5 **Multiple Choice** The following is **not** a stage in the *consumer buying process* [select one]: **(a)** substitution purchase; **(b)** evaluation of alternatives; **(c)** postpurchase evaluation; **(d)** information seeking; **(e)** problem/need recognition.

6 **True/False** In terms of market size, *organizational buying* in the United States is economically much more significant than *consumer buying.*

***Answers to Self-Check Questions 4–6 can be found on p. 509.**

■ WHAT IS A PRODUCT?

In developing the marketing mix for any product, whether goods or services, marketers must consider what consumers really buy when they purchase products. Only then can these marketers plan strategies effectively. We begin this section where product strategy begins: by understanding that every product is a *value package* that provides benefits to satisfy the needs and wants of customers. Next, we describe the major *classifications of products,* both consumer and industrial. Finally, we discuss the most important component in the offerings of any business: its *product mix.*

The Value Package

feature
Tangible quality that a company builds into a product

Whether it is a physical good, a service, or some combination of the two, customers get value from the various benefits, features, and even intangible rewards associated with a product. Product **features** are the qualities, tangible and intangible, that a company builds into its products, such as a 12-horsepower motor on a lawn mower. But to attract buyers features also must provide *benefits:* The mower must produce an attractive lawn. The owner's pleasure in knowing that the mower is nearby when needed is an intangible reward.

value package
Product marketed as a bundle of value-adding attributes, including reasonable cost

Today's consumer regards a product as a bundle of attributes that, taken together, marketers call the **value package**. Increasingly, buyers expect to receive products with greater *value*—with more benefits at reasonable costs. Consider, for example, the possible attributes in a personal computer value package:

- Easy access to understandable prepurchase information
- Choices in keyboards, monitors, and processing capacities
- Choices of color
- Attractive software packages
- Attractive prices
- Fast, simple ordering via the Internet
- Protection for credit card purchasing
- Assurance of speedy delivery
- Warranties
- Easy access to around-the-clock postpurchase technical support
- Internet chat room capability
- Prestige of owning a state-of-the art system

Although the computer includes physical *features*—processing devices and other hardware—most items in the value package are services or intangibles that, collectively, add value by providing *benefits* that increase the customer's satisfaction. Reliable data processing is certainly a benefit, but so too are pride of ownership, access to technical support, and a feeling of security. Today, more and more firms compete on the basis of enhanced value packages. They find that the addition of a simple new service often pleases customers far beyond the cost of providing it. Just making the purchase transaction more convenient, for example, adds value by sparing customers long waits and cumbersome paperwork.[11]

Look carefully at the ad in Figure 10.3 for SAS Institute *(www.sas.com)*, a major designer of statistical software. SAS emphasizes not the technical features of its products and not even the criteria that companies use in selecting software—efficiency, compatibility, support. Rather, the ad focuses on the customer-oriented benefits that a buyer of SAS software can expect from using the firm's products: "Only SAS provides you with a complete view of your customers." These benefits are being marketed as part of a complete value package.

Classifying Goods and Services

We can classify products according to expected buyers, who fall into two groups: buyers of *consumer products* and buyers of *industrial products.* As we saw earlier in this chapter, the consumer and industrial buying processes differ significantly. Not surprisingly, marketing products to consumers is vastly different from marketing products to other companies.

FIGURE 10.3

The Product: Features and
Benefits

Classifying Consumer Products Consumer products are commonly divided
into three categories that reflect buyer behavior:

- **Convenience goods** (such as milk and newspapers) and **convenience services** (such as those offered by fast-food restaurants) are consumed rapidly and regularly. They are inexpensive and are purchased often and with little output of time and effort.

  convenience good/service
  Inexpensive product purchased and
  consumed rapidly and regularly

- **Shopping goods** (such as stereos and tires) and **shopping services** (such as insurance) are more expensive and are purchased less often than convenience products. Consumers often compare brands, sometimes in different stores. They may also evaluate alternatives in terms of style, performance, color, price, and other criteria.

  shopping good/service
  Moderately expensive, infrequently
  purchased product

- **Specialty goods** (such as wedding gowns) and **specialty services** (such as catering for wedding receptions) are extremely important and expensive purchases. Consumers usually decide on precisely what they want and will accept no substitutes. They often go from store to store, sometimes spending a great deal of money and time to get a specific product.

  specialty good/service
  Expensive, rarely purchased product

Classifying Industrial Products Depending on how much they cost and how
they will be used, industrial products can be divided into two categories:

- **Expense items** are goods or services that are consumed within a year by firms producing other goods or supplying other services. The most obvious expense items are industrial goods used directly in the production process (for example, bulkloads of tea processed into tea bags).

  expense item
  Industrial product purchased and
  consumed rapidly and regularly for
  daily operations

- **Capital items** are permanent (expensive and long-lasting) goods and services. They have expected lives of more than a year and, typically, of several years. Buildings (offices, factories), fixed equipment (water towers, baking ovens), and accessory equipment (computers, airplanes) are *capital goods. Capital services* are

  capital item
  Expensive, long-lasting, infrequently
  purchased industrial product such as
  a building

those for which long-term commitments are made, such as building and equipment maintenance or legal services. Because capital items are expensive and purchased infrequently, they often involve decisions by high-level managers.

The Product Mix

product mix
Group of products that a firm makes available for sale

The group of products that a company makes available for sale, whether consumer, industrial, or both, is its **product mix**. Black & Decker *(www.blackanddecker.com)*, for example, makes toasters, vacuum cleaners, electric drills, and a variety of other appliances and tools. 3M Corp. *(www.3m.com)* makes everything from Post-it notes to laser optics.

Product Lines Many companies begin with a single product, such as simple iced tea. Over time, they find that the initial product fails to suit every consumer shopping for the product type. To meet market demand, they introduce similar products—such as flavored teas—designed to reach more consumers. ServiceMaster *(www.servicemaster.com)* was among the first successful home services that offered mothproofing and carpet cleaning. Subsequently, the company expanded into other home services—lawn care (TruGreen, ChemLawn), pest control (Terminix), and cleaning (Merry Maids). A group of similar products intended for a group of similar buyers who will use them in similar ways is a **product line**.

product line
Group of similar products intended for a similar group of buyers who will use them in similar ways

Companies may extend their horizons and identify opportunities outside existing product lines. The result—*multiple* (or *diversified*) *product lines*—is evident at firms such as ServiceMaster. After years of serving residential customers, ServiceMaster has added business and industry services (landscaping and janitorial), education services (management of schools and institutions, including physical facilities and financial and personnel resources), and health-care services (management of support services—plant operations, asset management, laundry/linen supply—for long-term–care facilities). Multiple product lines allow a company to grow rapidly and can help to offset the consequences of slow sales in any one product line.

■ DEVELOPING NEW PRODUCTS

To expand or diversify product lines—in fact, just to survive—firms must develop and introduce streams of new products. Faced with competition and shifting consumer preferences, no firm can count on a single successful product to carry it forever. Even products that have been popular for decades need constant renewal.

Consider one of America's most popular brands—Levi's *(www.levistrauss.com)*. Its riveted denim styles were once market leaders, but the company failed to keep pace with changing tastes, fell behind new products from competitors, and lost market share among 14- to 19-year-old males during the 1990s. By 1999, at least one industry analyst was forced to report that Levi's "hasn't had a successful new product in years." More recently, the company may have gotten back on track by recognizing that female consumers in various sizes need special attention. In 2001, instead of trying to market women's jeans merely as variations on denim pants for men, Levi's introduced the Superlow line of jeans that emphasized femininity.[12]

In the next section, we focus on the process by which companies develop new goods and services.

The New Product Development Process

The demand for food and beverage ingredients has grown more than 6 percent per year, reaching $5 billion in the year 2000. Flavors and flavor enhancers are the biggest part of that growth, especially artificial sweeteners. However, companies that develop and sell these products face a big problem: It costs between $30 million and $50 million and can take as long as 8 to 10 years to get a new product through the approval process at the Food and Drug Administration (FDA) *(www.fda.gov)*. Testing, both for FDA approval and for marketing, can be the most time-consuming stage of development. Acesulfame K beverage sweetener, which is made by Hoechst Celanese Corp. *(www.hoechst.com)*, has been through more than 90 safety studies and 1,000 technical studies to see how it performs in various kinds of beverages. After the testing process, additional stages include advertising and demonstration to food producers.[13] Cashing in on the growth of the food- and beverage-ingredients market requires an immense amount of time, patience, and money.

Product development is a long and expensive process, and like Hoechst, many firms have research and development (R&D) departments for exploring new product possibilities. Why do they devote so many resources to exploring product possibilities, rejecting many seemingly good ideas along the way? In this section, we focus on two answers to this question. First, we see that high *mortality rates* for new ideas mean that only a few new products reach the market. Second, for many companies, *speed to market* with a product is as important as care in developing it.

Product Mortality Rates It is estimated that it takes 50 new product ideas to generate one product that finally reaches the market. Even then, only a few of these survivors become *successful* products. Many seemingly great ideas have failed as

At Equity Marketing *(www.equity-marketing.com)* in Los Angeles, engineers like Mike Barbato and Frank Kautzman used to design toys by sculpting models out of lumps of clay. Now they design promotional toys by means of "rapid prototyping," using technology that allows several employees to work simultaneously on three-dimensional "models" that can then be printed and faxed for review by clients anywhere in the world. It now takes five days instead of three weeks to make an initial sculpture, and problems can be spotted and corrected much more quickly.

products. Indeed, creating a successful new product has become increasingly more difficult—even for the most experienced marketers. Why? The number of new products hitting the market each year has increased dramatically: More than 25,000 new household, grocery, and drugstore items are introduced annually. In 2001, the beverage industry alone launched 3,800 new products.[14] At any given time, however, the average supermarket carries a total of only 20,000 to 25,000 different items. Because of lack of space and customer demand, about 9 out of 10 new products will fail. Those with the best chances are innovative and deliver unique benefits.

Speed to Market The more rapidly a product moves from the laboratory to the marketplace, the more likely it is to survive. By introducing new products ahead of competitors, companies establish market leadership. They become entrenched in the market before being challenged by newer competitors. How important is **speed to market**—that is, a firm's success in responding to customer demand or market changes? One study reports that a product that is only three months late to market (three months behind the leader) loses 12 percent of its lifetime profit potential. At six months, it will lose 33 percent.

speed to market
Strategy of introducing new products to respond quickly to customer or market changes

The Product Life Cycle

product life cycle (PLC)
Series of stages in a product's profit-producing life

When a product reaches the market, it enters the **product life cycle (PLC)**: a series of stages through which it passes during its profit-producing life. Depending on the product's ability to attract and keep customers, its PLC may be a matter of months, years, or decades. Strong, mature products (such as Clorox bleach and H&R Block tax preparation) have had long productive lives.

Stages in the Product Life Cycle The life cycle for both goods and services is a natural process in which products are born, grow in stature, mature, and finally decline and die. Look at the two graphics in Figure 10.4. In Figure 10.4(a), the four phases of the PLC are applied to several products with which you are familiar:

1 **Introduction.** This stage begins when the product reaches the marketplace. Marketers focus on making potential consumers aware of the product and its benefits. Extensive promotional and development costs erase all profits.
2 **Growth.** If the new product attracts enough consumers, sales start to climb rapidly. The product starts to show a profit, and other firms move rapidly to introduce their own versions.
3 **Maturity.** Sales growth starts to slow. Although the product earns its highest profit level early in this stage, increased competition eventually forces price cutting and lower profits. Toward the end of the stage, sales start to fall.
4 **Decline.** Sales and profits continue to fall, as new products in the introduction stage take away sales. Firms end or reduce promotional support (ads and salespeople) but may let the product linger to provide some profits.

Figure 10.4(b) plots the relationship of the PLC to a product's typical sales, costs, and profits. Although the early stages of the PLC often show negative cash flows, successful products usually recover those losses and, in fact, continue to generate profits until the decline stage. For most products, profitable life spans are short—thus the importance placed by so many firms on the constant replenishment of product lines.

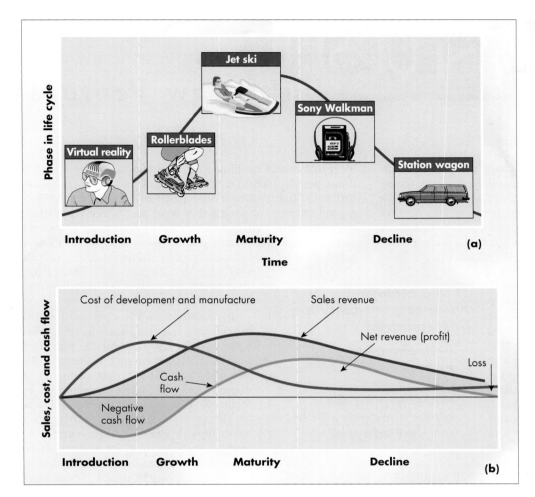

FIGURE 10.4

Products in the Life Cycle: Stages, Sales, Cost, and Profit

IDENTIFYING PRODUCTS

As we noted earlier, developing a product's features is only part of a marketer's job. Marketers must also identify products so that consumers recognize them. Two important tools for this task are *branding* and *packaging*.

Branding Products

Coca-Cola *(www.coca-cola.com)* is the best-known brand in the world. Indeed, some Coke executives claim that if all the company's other assets were obliterated, they could go to the bank and borrow $100 billion on the strength of the brand name alone. Brand names such as Coca-Cola and emblems such as the McDonald's golden arches are symbols that characterize products and distinguish them from one another. **Branding** is a process of using symbols to communicate the qualities of a particular product made by a particular producer. Brands are designed to signal uniform quality: Customers who try and like a product can return to it by remembering its name.

Several benefits result from successful branding, including *brand loyalty* (which we discussed earlier in this chapter) and **brand awareness**—the brand name that first comes to mind when you consider a particular product category.[15] What company, for

branding
Process of using symbols to communicate the qualities of a product made by a particular producer

brand awareness
Extent to which a brand name comes to mind when the consumer considers a particular product category

ENTREPRENEURSHIP and *New Ventures*

The Patriotic Entrepreneur

Serious discussions about biotechnology seldom touch on Malaysia. That situation, however, may soon change as Malaysia takes its first steps toward what officials hope will be world-class status in the biotech sector. The Malaysian vision calls for developing not one dominant product, but rather families or streams of biologically based products to compete on world markets.

Unfortunately, Malaysians are starting from scratch: Malaysia, critics scoff, doesn't have the science community necessary to compete with Europe and the United States in attracting the needed investment. In fact, experts question whether Malaysia can even compete with regional neighbors such as Singapore, which has similar ambitions and more money to lure talent from abroad. Malaysia's response to seemingly insurmountable odds is simple: Bring in Kim Tan, regarded by many as the world's top biochemistry entrepreneur.

Tan has already built three major biotech companies, with facilities in Canada, China, Britain, and the United States, while amassing a personal fortune estimated at $500 million. He has decided to collaborate with the Malaysian government to set up the country's first biotech venture fund—dubbed Springhill Biotech Ventures. As founding father of the country's biotech industry, Tan will manage Malaysia's planned life-sciences activities from its new biotech hub—called Biovalley—near the capital of Kuala Lumpur. The plan calls for Springhill to invest in new technologies from abroad that are almost ready to hit the market and that hold promise for future Biovalley research. The fund will also form joint ventures with companies that agree to locate facilities and conduct research in Malaysia.

Just how valuable is Tan's participation? Born in Malaysia and educated in Britain in the 1970s, Tan is an

> *"I'm a Malaysian. One has a responsibility to [his] country."*
>
> *—Biochemist-entrepreneur Kim Tan, on why he's underwriting the biotech industry in his native Malaysia*

ideal role model for biotech entrepreneurs. "We really need more people like him to jump-start this industry," says Gurinder Shahi, a Singapore-based biotech consultant. "He's a good example of people that were part of the brain drain that now are returning and combining science and business skills that pay off." Tan's patents have already led to new drugs for treatment of cancer and chronic illnesses, and his research in genetic engineering has developed hormones for treating diabetes and arthritis.

In addition to his contributions of money and scientific knowledge to Biovalley, Tan also brings to Biovalley biotech-management and business skills. In 1986, he sold his first company, a diagnostics firm, using the proceeds to form KS Biomedics to commercialize his ideas for growing cancer-fighting antibodies in sheep. More recently, he formed TranXenoGen for genetic engineering in chickens to produce eggs containing therapeutic proteins for use in drugs. Yet another company—Genemedix—mass-produces low-cost generic drugs for reducing the fatal side effects of chemotherapy.

Tan has no illusions about the monumental task ahead: Biovalley starts with an inexperienced scientific base, few patents, and little venture capital. So, after all his success, why is Tan risking yet another start-up project? "Nationalism," he says. "I could make far more money and it's easier over there [in Britain]. The main reason: I'm a Malaysian. One has a responsibility to [his] country." Significantly, the country did not recruit Tan for the job; rather, it was Tan who took the initiative: "I took it to them. I've been waiting to see what the government was going to do [about building the sector]. They are committed. So I decided, right, let's do something."

example, comes to mind when you need to ship a document a long way on short notice? For many people, FedEx has the necessary brand awareness.

E-Business Branding It takes a long time to establish national or global brand recognition.[16] After years of work, Cisco Systems Inc. *(www.cisco.com)*, the network-equipment manufacturer, reached new heights in branding for business-to-business, or B2B, e-commerce. The company's "Cisco Internet Generation" promotional campaign for 2001 stressed reliability and innovation, and in analyzing the campaign,

Cisco found that its brand awareness increased by 80 percent (boosting it past rivals Lucent Technologies and Nortel Networks). The campaign also lifted Cisco's reputation as an Internet expert above that of Microsoft, IBM, and Lucent.[17]

Collectively, the top Internet brands—America Online, Yahoo!, and Amazon.com—spend billions a year even though they have just barely cracked the ranks of the top 60 global brands. Moreover, the costs of branding promotions are hitting all dot-coms at a time when they are trying to survive the near collapse of the industry. The mounting costs of brand identity mean that many more would-be e-businesses will probably fail.

Types of Brand Names Just about every product has a brand name. Generally, different types of brand names—national, licensed, or private—increase buyers' awareness of the nature and quality of competing products. When consumers are satisfied with a product, marketers try to build brand loyalty among the largest possible segment of repeat buyers.

National Brands **National brands** are produced by, widely distributed by, and carry the name of the manufacturer. These brands (for example, Scotch tape or Scope mouthwash) are often widely recognized by consumers because of national advertising campaigns, and they are, therefore, valuable assets. Because the costs of developing a national brand are high, some companies use a national brand on several related products. Procter & Gamble *(www.pg.com)* now markets Ivory shampoo, capitalizing on the name of its bar soap and dishwashing liquid.

national brand
Brand-name product produced by, widely distributed by, and carrying the name of a manufacturer

Licensed Brands We have become used to companies (and even personalities) selling the rights to put their names on products. These are called **licensed brands**. The logo "2002 Winter Olympic Games—Salt Lake City" generated millions in revenues for the International Olympic Committee, which licensed its name on license plates, clothing, tableware, coins, and countless other merchandise items. Harley-Davidson's famous logo—emblazoned on boots, eyewear, gloves, purses, lighters, and watches—brings the motorcycle maker more than $150 million annually. Along with brands such as Coors and Ferrari, licensing for character-based brands—Blade, Spiderman, Pokémon—are equally lucrative. Marketers exploit brands because of their public appeal—the image and status that consumers hope to gain by associating with them. The free advertising that comes with some licensing, such as T-shirts and other clothing, is an added bonus.

licensed brand
Brand-name product for whose name the seller has purchased the right from an organization or individual

Private Brands When a wholesaler or retailer develops a brand name and has a manufacturer put it on a product, the resulting name is a **private brand** (or **private label**). Sears, which carries such lines as Craftsman tools *(www.craftsman.com)*, Canyon River Blues denim clothing, and Kenmore appliances *(www.kenmore.com)*, is a well-known seller of private brands.

private brand (or **private label**)
Brand-name product that a wholesaler or retailer has commissioned from a manufacturer

Packaging Products

With a few exceptions (such as fresh fruits and vegetables and structural steel), products need some form of **packaging**. A package also serves as an in-store advertisement that makes the product attractive, displays the brand name, and identifies features and benefits. It also reduces the risk of damage, breakage, or spoilage, and it increases the difficulty of stealing small products. Recent advances in materials have created added uses for packaging. A paper-based material that doubles as a cooking container has made Budget Gourmet dinners *(www.budgetgourmet.com)* a low-cost entry in the dinner-entrée market. No-drip bottles have enhanced sales of Clorox bleach *(www.clorox.com)*.

packaging
Physical container in which a product is sold, advertised, or protected

It's pronounced a little differently—STAH-buks-zu—but the brand means pretty much the same: large cups of gourmet coffee served in comfortable surroundings to the sound of hip-hop and reggae. In Japan, Starbucks *(www.starbucks.co.jp/en/home .htm)* has opened 300 stores since 1996 and plans another 180 over the next three years. In a depression-ridden country of traditional tea drinkers, volume per store is twice that of U.S. outlets. The brand has become so popular that Starbucks earned $242 million there last year (twice the previous year's total) even though it has yet to advertise in Japan.

■ THE INTERNATIONAL MARKETING MIX

Marketing internationally means mounting a strategy to support global business operations. Foreign customers, for example, differ from domestic buyers in language, customs, business practices, and consumer behavior. If they go global, marketers must reconsider each element of the marketing mix—product, pricing, place, and promotion.

International Products Some products can be sold abroad with virtually no changes. Budweiser, Coca-Cola, and Marlboros are exactly the same in Peoria, Illinois, and Paris, France. In other cases, U.S. firms have had to create products with built-in flexibility—for instance, electric shavers that adapt to either 115- or 230-volt outlets.

Sometimes a redesigned product will satisfy foreign buyers. To sell computers in Japan, for example, Apple had to develop a Japanese-language operating system. Whether they are designed for unique or universal markets, the branding and labeling of products are especially important for communicating global messages.

International Pricing When pricing for international markets, marketers must consider the higher costs of transporting and selling products abroad. Because of the higher costs of buildings, rent, equipment, and imported meat, a McDonald's Big Mac that sells for $2.43 in the United States has a price tag of $3.58 in Denmark.

International Distribution In some industries, delays in starting new distribution networks can be costly. Therefore, companies with existing systems often enjoy an advantage. Likewise, many companies have gained advantages by buying existing businesses. Procter & Gamble, for example, bought Revlon's Max Factor and Betrix cosmetics, both of which have distribution and marketing networks in foreign markets.

International Promotion Occasionally, a good ad campaign is a good campaign just about anywhere. Quite often, however, U.S. promotional tactics do not succeed in other countries. In fact, many Europeans believe that a product must be inherently shoddy if a company resorts to any advertising, particularly the American hard-sell variety.

International marketers must also be aware that cultural differences can cause negative reactions to improperly advertised products. Some Europeans, for example, are offended by television commercials that show weapons or violence. Meanwhile, cigarette commercials that are banned from U.S. television thrive in many Asian and European markets. Product promotions must be carefully matched to local customs and cultural values.

Because of the need to adjust the marketing mix, success in international markets is hard won. But whether a firm markets in domestic or international markets, the basic principles of marketing still apply; only their implementation changes.

■ SMALL BUSINESS AND THE MARKETING MIX

Many of today's largest firms were yesterday's small businesses. Behind the success of many small firms lies a skillful application of the marketing concept and an understanding of each element in the marketing mix.[18]

Small-Business Products Some new products and firms are doomed at the start because few consumers want or need what they have to offer. Many fail to estimate realistic market potential, and some offer new products before they have clear pictures of their target segments.

In contrast, a thorough understanding of what customers want has paid off for many small firms. Take, for example, the case of Little Earth Productions Inc. *(www.littlearth.com)*, a company that makes fashion accessories such as handbags. Originally, the company merely considered how consumers would use its handbags. But after examining shopping habits, Little Earth redesigned for better store display. Because stores can give handbags better visibility by hanging them instead of placing them on floors or low countertops, Little Earth added small handles specifically for that purpose.

Small-Business Pricing Haphazard pricing can even sink a firm with a good product. Small-business pricing errors usually result from a failure to estimate operating expenses accurately. Owners of failing businesses have often been heard to say, "I didn't realize how much it costs to run the business!" But when small businesses set prices by carefully assessing costs, many earn satisfactory profits.

Small-Business Distribution Perhaps the most critical aspect of distribution for small businesses is facility location, especially for new service businesses. The ability of many small businesses to attract and retain customers depends partly on the choice of location.

In distribution as in other aspects of the marketing mix, however, smaller companies may have advantages over larger competitors, even in highly complex industries. Everex Systems Inc. of Fremont, California *(www.everex.com)*, sells personal computers to wholesalers and dealers through a system that the company calls *zero response time.* Because Everex is small and flexible, phone orders can be reviewed every two hours and factory assembly adjusted to match demand.

Say WHAT YOU MEAN

NEVER GIVE A GERMAN A YELLOW ROSE

Good things come in small packages—right? Not in cultures in which the size of the package says a lot about its value. More is better in some places, while big is wasteful in others. Color is important, too. White signifies death and mourning in China, while red means good luck and prosperity. Never give a German an even number of roses; it's bad luck. And don't give a German any number of yellow roses because yellow is associated with jealousy. In Japan the number four is bad luck; avoid putting any four things in any single package.

What does all of this superstition have to do with business? Packaging, color, quantity, and the way a product is presented can determine whether something's going to sell or sit on the shelf.

Almost all cultures have an unwritten set of rules when it comes to using words, colors, numbers, and images. Displaying images of animate objects—humans or otherwise—is frowned on in some Islamic cultures, while in Italy and Brazil, nakedness (or even near nakedness) always sells. Americans like to see their flag on packages; it's a good way of displaying one's patriotism. In some cultures, however, commercializing the national emblem is in bad taste.

If you're giving someone a package in Japan, don't expect the recipient to open it in front of you; it's not polite. But if someone gives you something in the United States, it's rude not to show your delight immediately. Be careful of what you call things, too. Even in English-speaking countries, you can get into a lot of trouble by using culturally inaccurate names. If you want to market flip-flops in New Zealand, you'd better call them *jandals*. How about cookies in England? Put *biscuits* on the label.

And finally, speaking of food, beef in a hamburger in India is taboo, but you can't go wrong with a lamb burger in Saudi Arabia. Americans use chopsticks in Thai restaurants, but you won't find too many Thais using them. If you want to keep something cool in Australia, put it in an *eskie*—which is what Americans call a *cooler*. Sometimes the name says it all, and sometimes it doesn't.

Know the culture and you'll know something about its market. Nothing beats a little research and a lot of cultural sensitivity.

Small-Business Promotion Successful small businesses plan for promotional expenses as part of start-up costs. Some hold down costs by using less expensive promotional methods. Local newspapers, for example, are sources of publicity when they publish articles about new or unique businesses. Other small businesses identify themselves and their products with associated groups, organizations, and events. Thus, a crafts gallery might join with a local art league to organize public showings of their combined products.

SELF-CHECK QUESTIONS 7–9

You should now be able to answer Self-Check Questions 7-9.*

7 Multiple Choice When viewed as a *value package* for the buyer, a product is a bundle of attributes consisting of the following [select one]: **(a)** benefits; **(b)** features; **(c)** intangible rewards; **(d)** reasonable price; **(e)** all of the above.

8 True/False The *product mix* is the group of products that a company makes available for sale and within which it may have several *product lines.*

9 Multiple Choice Which of the following is **not** true of the *international marketing mix?* [select one]: **(a)** Products that sell for a given price in the United States may sell at a different price in another country. **(b)** The International Standards Act ensures the existence of uniform advertising practices in most countries. **(c)** A company can speed up its international distribution activities by buying an existing business in another country. **(d)** Some products can be sold abroad with virtually no changes. **(e)** Cultural differences can cause negative reactions to products that are advertised improperly.

***Answers to Self-Check Questions 7–9 can be found on p. 509.**

Continued from page 290

MICROSOFT'S GREAT XPECTATIONS

Xbox is Microsoft's first venture into game consoles, and the company's marketing strategy differs from that of competitors, especially Nintendo, which targets the younger end of the market. Xbox, says product team leader Robbie Rash, targets a different audience. "Let's face it," he says, "Nintendo's system is for kids. We're for sophisticated gamers. I don't know any 30-year-olds who want a GameCube [by Nintendo]." Both Xbox and PlayStation 2 (by Sony) are aimed at the 16- to 26-year-old audience. Nintendo, however, wants to shed its "kids only" image and attract more players in the 20s age group, too. Both Xbox and GameCube would like to bump Sony's PlayStation 2 (PS2) from the top spot in the console market. In January 2003, Xbox was outselling GameCube on console sales by a 2-to-1 margin.

With its current selling price of $199, the revenue from each Xbox doesn't begin to cover the cost of making it. In fact, Microsoft will lose about $125 on every box it sells. Because the consoles cost so much to make, the profits for console makers—Sony and Nintendo as well as Microsoft—depend on software sales. Thus, the console maker that fails to supply a constant stream of new titles is doomed. In early 2003 Microsoft had more than 200 Xbox games available with an additional 300 titles in development. For international appeal, Sega's participation also gives Xbox an important boost: Many Japanese gamers doubted Xbox's credibility until they learned of Microsoft's alliance with Sega's respected game publishers.

The Xbox product itself is also different from competing products. Sony's PS2 plays music CDs and DVD movies right out of the box. Xbox can also play music and movies—in

intendo's system is for kids. We're for sophisticated gamers. I don't know any 30-year-olds who want a Nintendo GameCube."

—Robbie Rash, Xbox product team leader

fact, it delivers theater-quality 3D sound—but if you want DVD, you need a separate remote controller. Nintendo plays games only—no movies or CDs. Xbox also offers broadband multiplayer gaming and lets players take advantage of high-speed networks by playing online. By uniting gamers on the Internet via the Xbox, Microsoft is laying the groundwork for a future home-networking strategy that will use Xbox console as a hub.

Questions for Discussion

1 What social and technological factors have influenced the growth of the interactive entertainment market?
2 What demographics would you use to define the Xbox target market? How about the target market for Nintendo's GameCube?
3 Do you agree or disagree with Microsoft's strategy of featuring hardware, sound, and graphics rather than immediately offering lots of game titles?
4 Which is more important to Xbox's success—the product itself or Microsoft's marketing program for it? Explain your reasoning.
5 Why do you suppose Sega's participation was so meaningful for Japanese customers?

■ SUMMARY OF LEARNING OBJECTIVES

1 Explain the concept of *marketing* and describe the five forces that constitute the *external marketing environment.*

Marketing is "the process of planning and executing the conception, pricing, promotion, and distribution of ideas, goods, and services to create exchanges that satisfy individual and organizational goals." Consumers buy products that offer the best **value**—the comparison of a product's benefits to its costs—when it comes to meeting their needs and wants. The satisfied buyer perceives that the benefits derived from a purchase outweigh its costs.

Five outside factors comprise a company's external environment and influence its marketing programs by posing opportunities or threats: (1) *political and legal environment;* (2) *social and cultural environment;* (3) *technological environment;* (4) *economic environment;* (5) *competitive environment.*

2 Explain the purpose of a *marketing plan* and identify the four components of the *marketing mix.*

Marketing managers plan and implement all the marketing activities that result in the transfer of products to customers. These activities culminate in the **marketing plan**—a detailed strategy for focusing the effort to meet consumer needs and wants. Marketing managers rely on the "Four P's" of marketing, or the **marketing mix.** (1) *Product:* Marketing begins with a **product,** a good, a service, or an idea designed to fill a consumer need or want. **Product differentiation** is the creation of a feature or image that makes a product differ from competitors. (2) *Pricing:* Pricing is the strategy of selecting the most appropriate price at which to sell a product. (3) *Place (Distribution):* All **distribution** activities are concerned with getting a product from the producer to the consumer. (4) *Promotion:* Promotion refers to techniques for communicating information about products and includes advertising.

3 Explain *market segmentation* and show how it is used in *target marketing.*

Marketers think in terms of **target markets**—groups of people who have similar wants and needs and who can be expected to show interest in the same products. Target marketing requires **market segmentation**—dividing a market into customer types or "segments."

Members of a *market segment* must share some common traits that influence purchasing decisions. Following are three of the most important influences: (1) **Geographic variables** are the geographical units that may be considered in developing a segmentation strategy. (2) **Demographic variables** describe populations by identifying such traits as age, income, gender, ethnic background, marital status, race, religion, and social class. (3) Members of a market can be segmented according to such **psychographic variables** as lifestyles, interests, and attitudes.

4 Describe the key factors that influence the *consumer buying process.*

Students of consumer behavior have constructed various models to help marketers understand how consumers decide to purchase products. One model considers five influences that lead to consumption: (1) *Problem/need recognition:* The buying process begins when the consumer recognizes a problem or need. (2) *Information seeking:* Having recognized a need, consumers seek information. (3) *Evaluation of alternatives:* By analyzing the attributes that apply to a given product, consumers compare products in deciding which product best meets their needs. (4) *Purchase decision:* "Buy" decisions are based on rational motives, emotional motives, or both. **Rational motives** involve the logical evaluation of product attributes such as cost, quality, and usefulness. **Emotional motives** involve nonobjective factors and include sociability, imitation of others, and aesthetics. (5) *Postpurchase evaluations:* Marketers want consumers to be happy after the consumption of products so that they are more likely to buy them again.

5 Discuss the three categories of *organizational markets.*

Organizational (or *commercial*) markets, in which organizations buy goods and services to be used in creating and delivering consumer products, fall into three categories. (1) The **industrial market** consists of businesses that buy goods to be converted into other products or goods that are used during production. (2) Before products reach consumers, they pass through a **reseller market** consisting of intermediaries that buy finished goods and resell them. (3) *Government and institutional market:* Federal, state, and local governments buy durable and nondurable products. The **institutional market** consists of nongovernmental buyers such as hospitals, churches, museums, and charities.

6 Explain the definition of a product as a *value package.*

A *product* is a good, service, or idea that is marketed to fill consumer needs and wants. Customers buy products because of the *value* that they offer. Thus, a successful product is a **value package**—a bundle of attributes that, taken together, provides the right *features* and offers the right *benefits*. Attributes include such characteristics as ease of use, prestige of ownership, warranties, and technical support. Features are the qualities, tangible and intangible, that a company builds into its products (such as a 12-horsepower motor on a lawn mower). To be sellable, features also must provide benefits (say, an attractive lawn). The items in the value package are services and features that, collectively, add value by providing benefits that increase the customer's satisfaction.

7 Explain the importance of *branding* and *packaging*.

Each product is given an identity by its brand and the way it is packaged. The goal in developing *brands*—symbols to dis-tinguish products and signal their uniform quality—is to increase *brand loyalty* (the preference that consumers have for a product with a particular brand name). **National brands** are produced, widely distributed by, and carry the name of the manufacturer; they are often widely recognized because of national advertising campaigns. (2) **Licensed brands** are brand names purchased from the organizations or individuals who own them. (3) When a wholesaler or retailer develops a brand name and has a manufacturer place it on a product, the product name is a **private brand** (or **private label**). With a few exceptions, a product needs some form of **packaging**—a physical container in which it is sold, advertised, or protected. A package makes the product attractive, displays the brand name, and identifies features and benefits. It also reduces the risk of damage, breakage, or spoilage, and it lessens the likelihood of theft.

■ KEY TERMS

marketing (p. 290)
value (p. 291)
utility (p. 291)
consumer goods (p. 291)
industrial goods (p. 291)
services (p. 291)
relationship marketing (p. 292)
external environment (p. 292)
substitute product (p. 294)
brand competition (p. 294)
international competition (p. 294)
marketing manager (p. 294)
marketing plan (p. 294)
marketing mix (p. 294)
product (p. 294)
product differentiation (p. 295)
distribution (p. 295)

target market (p. 297)
market segmentation (p. 297)
geographic variables (p. 297)
demographic variables (p. 298)
psychographic variables (p. 298)
consumer behavior (p. 299)
brand loyalty (p. 300)
rational motives (p. 301)
emotional motives (p. 301)
data warehousing (p. 301)
data mining (p. 301)
industrial market (p. 302)
reseller market (p. 302)
institutional market (p. 302)
feature (p. 304)
value package (p. 304)
convenience good/service (p. 305)

shopping good/service (p. 305)
specialty good/service (p. 305)
expense item (p. 305)
capital item (p. 305)
product mix (p. 306)
product line (p. 306)
speed to market (p. 308)
product life cycle (PLC) (p. 308)
branding (p. 309)
brand awareness (p. 309)
national brand (p. 311)
licensed brand (p. 311)
private brand (or private label)
   (p. 311)
packaging (p. 311)

■ QUESTIONS AND EXERCISES

Questions for Review

1 What are the key similarities and differences between consumer buying behavior and organizational buying behavior?

2 Why and how is market segmentation used in target marketing?

3 How are data mining and data warehousing useful in finding new information for marketing to consumers?

4 What are the various classifications of consumer and industrial products? Give an example of a good and a service for each category other than those discussed in the text.

Questions for Analysis

5 Select an everyday product (books, CDs, skateboards, dog food, or shoes, for example). Show how different

versions of your product are aimed toward different market segments. Explain how the marketing mix differs for each segment.

6 Select a second everyday product and describe the consumer buying process that typically goes into its purchase.

7 Consider a service product, such as transportation, entertainment, or health care. What are some ways that more customer value might be added to this product? Why would your improvements add value for the buyer?

8 How would you expect the branding and packaging of convenience, shopping, and specialty goods to differ? Why? Give examples to illustrate your answers.

Application Exercises

9 Interview the marketing manager of a local business. Identify the degree to which this person's job is focused on each element in the marketing mix.

10 Select a product made by a foreign company and sold in the United States. What is the product's target market? What is the basis on which the target market is segmented? Do you think that this basis is appropriate? How might another approach, if any, be beneficial? Why?

Extra Exercise

Break the class into small groups and assign each group a specific industry. Have each group discuss the strategies that it believes are important to the marketing of products in that industry.

BUILDING YOUR BUSINESS SKILLS

DEALING WITH VARIABLES

This exercise enhances the following SCANS workplace competencies: demonstrating basic skills, demonstrating thinking skills, exhibiting interpersonal skills, and working with information.

Goal

To encourage students to analyze the ways in which various market segmentation variables affect business success.

The Situation

You and four partners are thinking of purchasing a heating and air conditioning (H/AC) dealership that specializes in residential applications priced between $2,000 and $40,000. You are now in the process of deciding where that dealership should be located. You are considering four locations: Miami, Florida; Westport, Connecticut; Dallas, Texas; and Spokane, Washington.

Method

Step 1

Working with your partnership group, do library research to learn how H/AC makers market residential products. Check for articles in the *Wall Street Journal, Business Week, Fortune,* and other business publications.

Step 2

Continue your research. Now focus on the specific marketing variables that define each prospective location. Check

Census Bureau and Department of Labor data at your library and on the Internet and contact local chambers of commerce (by phone and via the Internet) to learn about the following factors for each location:

1 Geography
2 Demography (especially age, income, gender, family status, and social class)
3 Psychographic factors (lifestyles, interests, and attitudes)

Step 3

As a group, determine which location holds the greatest promise as a dealership site. Base your decision on your analysis of market segment variables and their effects on H/AC sales.

FOLLOW-UP QUESTIONS

1 Which location did you choose? Describe the segmentation factors that influenced your decision.

2 Identify the two most important variables that you believe will affect the dealership's success. Why are these factors so important?

3 Which factors were least important? Why?

4 When equipment manufacturers advertise residential H/AC products, they often show them in different climate situations (winter, summer, or high-humidity conditions). Which market segments are these ads targeting? Describe these segments in terms of demographic and psychographic characteristics.

EXERCISING YOUR ETHICS

DRIVING A LEGITIMATE BARGAIN

The Situation

A firm's marketing methods are sometimes at odds with the consumer's buying process. This exercise illustrates how ethical issues can become entwined with personal selling activities, product pricing, and customer relations.

The Dilemma

In buying his first-ever new car, Matt visited showrooms and Web sites for every make of SUV. After weeks of reading and test-driving, he settled on a well-known Japanese-made vehicle with a manufacturer's suggested retail price of $34,500 for the 2002 model. The price included accessories and options that Matt considered essential. Because he planned to own the car for at least five years, he was willing to wait for just the right package rather than accept a lesser-equipped car already on the lot. Negotiations with Gary, the sales representative, continued for two weeks. Finally, a sales contract was signed for $30,600, with delivery due no more than two or three months later if the vehicle had to be special-ordered from the factory and earlier if Gary found the exact car when he searched other dealers around the country. On April 30, to close the deal, Matt had to write a check for $1,000.

Matt received a call on June 14 from Angela, Gary's sales manager: "We cannot get your car before October," she reported, "so it will have to be a 2003 model. You will have to pay the 2003 price." Matt replied that the agreement called for a stated price and delivery deadline for 2002, pointing out that money had exchanged hands for the contract. When asked what the 2003 price would be, Angela responded that it had not yet been announced. Angrily, Matt replied that he would be foolish to agree now on some unknown future price. Moreover, he didn't like the way the dealership was treating him. He told Angela to send back to him everything he had signed; the deal was off.

QUESTIONS FOR DISCUSSION

1 Given the factors involved in the consumer buying process, how would you characterize the particular ethical issues in this situation?

2 From an ethical standpoint, what are the obligations of the sales rep and the sales manager regarding the pricing of the product in this situation?

3 If you were responsible for maintaining good customer relations at the dealership, how would you handle this matter?

CRAFTING YOUR BUSINESS PLAN

PICKING AND PACKAGING THE RIGHT PRODUCTS

The Purpose of the Assignment

1 To familiarize students with the various marketing issues that a sample firm faces in developing its business plan in the framework of *Business PlanPro (BPP) 2003* software package (Version 6.0).

2 To demonstrate how four chapter topics—consumer versus organizational marketing, relationship marketing, market segmentation, and product differentiation—can be integrated as components of the *BPP* planning environment.

Assignment

After reading Chapter 10 in the textbook, open the BPP *software and look around for information about the*

marketing plan for a sample firm, a promotional products manufacturer called Elsewares Promotional Products & Packaging. *To find* Elsewares, *do the following:*

Open *Business PlanPro.* Go to the toolbar and click on the *"Sample Plans"* icon. In the **Sample Plan Browser,** do a search using the **search category** *Wholesale trade—nondurable goods.* From the resulting list, select the category entitled **Promotional Products Mfr.,** which is the location for *Elsewares Promotional Products & Packaging.* The screen you are looking at is the introduction page for the *Elsewares* business plan. Next, scroll down this page until you reach the **Table of Contents** for the *Elsewares* business plan.

NOW RESPOND TO THE FOLLOWING ITEMS:

1 Is *Elsewares* involved in consumer marketing or organizational marketing? [Sites to see in *BPP* (for this item): On the Table of Contents page, click on and read **1.0**

Executive Summary. After returning to the Table of Contents page, click on and read each of the following: **1.1 Objectives**, **1.2 Mission**, and **1.3 Keys to Success**.]

2 Identify *Elsewares'* strategy and methods for building relationships with its customers. [Sites to see in *BPP:* On the Table of Contents page, click on and read **5.0 Strategy and Implementation Summary**. Also visit **5.1.4 Service and Support**. Then read **1.0 Executive Summary** and **1.3 Keys to Success**.]

3 What basis—geographic, demographic, or psychographic—does *Elsewares* plan to use for its market seg-

mentation strategy? [Sites to see in *BPP:* On the Table of Contents page, click on and read each of the following in turn: **4.0 Market Analysis Summary** and **4.1 Market Segmentation**.]

4 Describe *Elsewares'* plans for differentiating its product. Is the plan clear enough on this matter? Why or why not? [Sites to see in *BPP:* On the Table of Contents page, click on and read **4.0 Market Analysis Summary**. Then go to **4.2 Industry Analysis**, and explore the information in that section.]

 VIDEO EXERCISE

PUTTING YOURSELF IN THE CONSUMER'S SHOES: SKECHERS USA

Learning Objectives

The purpose of this video is to help you:

1 Describe the role of the "Four P's" in a company's marketing mix.

2 Explain how a company shapes its market research to fit its marketing goals.

3 Discuss the effectiveness of target marketing and segmentation in analyzing consumers.

Background Information

Skechers USA *(www.skechers.com)* enjoys a reputation for producing footwear that combines comfort with innovative design. It has built its product line into a globally recognized brand distributed in more than 110 countries. From its corporate headquarters in Manhattan Beach, California, Skechers has engineered steady growth in market share while competing against some powerful players in the high-ticket, branded athletic shoe industry.

Since its start in 1992, Skechers has burnished its image as a maker of hip footwear through a savvy marketing strategy that calls for catering to a closely targeted consumer base. Maintaining brand integrity and its reputation for innovation is a crucial goal in all of Skechers' product development and marketing activities.

The Video

Director of public relations Kelly O'Connor discusses her work and the marketing activities that are critical to maintaining Skechers' edge in the highly competitive footwear marketplace. She describes the company's goal of creating a

megabrand with an image, personality, and "feel" that can be translated and marketed globally. Skechers has been successful in brand building by means of an "Ask, Don't Tell" approach to product development and marketing: It aims to find out what the market wants and then appeal to customers' wants rather than trying to influence the market with the products that it makes available.

DISCUSSION QUESTIONS

1 **For analysis:** Which of the "Four P's" of the marketing mix seems to govern Skechers' marketing strategy? Why? How do you suppose Skechers alters elements of its American marketing mix to attract consumers in international markets?

2 **For application:** Skechers collects a lot of primary data in its market research. What kinds of primary data does the company prefer to gather? Why do these kinds of data suit its marketing goals? How do the data suit the firm's consumer base? Given Skechers' fairly limited consumer base, are there other types of research data that you would recommend?

3 **For analysis:** Describe Skechers' target market and explain how company marketers segment it. How effective is this strategy in analyzing customers? How successful are Skechers' marketing efforts among 12- to 24-year-olds (and consumers wishing they were in that demographic segment)?

4 **For application:** Discuss the impact of brand loyalty on the sale of Skechers products. Building brand loyalty is a major effort that presents both opportunities and challenges to marketers and product developers. What are some of the opportunities and challenges encountered by Skechers' marketing managers?

5 **For application:** How do you think Skechers might expand its current product lines? What other new products might Skechers research, such as clothing or accessories? How could the company go about investigating the market potential for such products?

Online Exploration

Go online to find out about the product lines and target markets of such companies as Nike *(www.nike.com)*, Reebok *(www.reebok.com)*, Lady Foot Locker *(www. ladyfootlocker.com)*, and FUBU *(wwwl.fubu.com)*. How does the approach to segmentation at these companies compare with Skechers' approach?

**After reading this chapter,
you should be able to:**

1 Identify the various *pricing objectives* that govern pricing decisions and describe the *price-setting tools* used in making these decisions.

2 Explain the *distribution mix* and identify the different *channels of distribution*.

3 Identify the different types of *retailing* and *retail stores*.

4 Define *physical distribution* and describe the major activities in the physical distribution process.

5 Identify the important objectives of *promotion*, discuss the considerations entailed in selecting a *promotional mix*, and describe the key *advertising media*.

6 Outline the tasks involved in *personal selling* and describe the various types of *sales promotions*.

CONGESTED? STUFFED UP? TRY DTC

There was a time when patients didn't care about the name of the drug that the doctor prescribed—so long as it cured the ailment. Not so in today's consumer-empowered environment. If you watch television, you know the names of such medicines as Vioxx, Prilosec,

PRICING, DISTRIBUTING, AND PROMOTING PRODUCTS

" **T**he Zyban ads began and all of a sudden people came to me and said: 'Help me stop smoking.' "

—Stuart Gitlow, addiction psychiatrist

Zocor, Viagra, Celebrex, and Allegra whether you need them or not. What's more, a lot of people want to know more about them. It's all part of a revolutionary marketing movement known as direct-to-consumer (DTC) marketing.

DTC is a form of "pull" marketing in which ads tell consumers about a prescription drug and encourage them to ask their doctors about it. Some ads, for example, target the approximately 45 million allergy sufferers in the United States: "Congested? Stuffed Up? Watery Eyes? Talk to your doctor about Allegra-D, send in for your rebate, and start enjoying real relief today."

In using DTC, drug makers are appealing to end users—today's informed health-care consumers—who, instead of passively entrusting themselves to a doctor's care, not only expect educational information about available treatments but also often engage in self-diagnosis. The concept behind DTC is to motivate the consumer, rather than the doctor, to initiate the consumption of a specific drug. Ads are designed to increase consumer awareness, thereby stimulating more inquiries to doctors who, in turn, will prescribe the advertised drug more often than its competitors.

It works. Since 1997, industry spending on DTC ads has tripled and now tops $2.5 billion annually. At the same time, of course, prescription takers are feeling the side effects of higher prices at the pharmacy. Why? To help defray the cost of DTC advertising. During the same period, spending on prescription drugs tripled, topping $116 billion in 2000. Major media growth has been in television, whose share of DTC spending is now 64 percent.

Generating a flurry of spiraling ad expenditures and skyrocketing drug prices, DTC advertising is the most prominent and expensive—and controversial—promotional method in the history of pharmaceuticals. Drug companies argue that DTC encourages patients to see their doctors and informs them about the latest health news. Critics counter that DTC drives up prices and stimulates excessive spending on drugs. They also charge that ads often contain incomplete or misleading information that could lead to misuse.

And how do physicians feel about such changes in promotional conditions? In many cases, they are less than enthusiastic. "It's catastrophic in my office, with people coming in and demanding a drug they saw on television," Dr. David Priver of San Diego told a meeting of the American Medical Association (AMA). Other doctors complain that ads are biased, circulate incomplete information, and have already degenerated into a competition to see who can sell the most antihistamines or nasal sprays. The patient, says New Jersey Dr. Angelo Agro, "is at best incompletely informed and at worst . . . deluded." Agro also argues that DTC ads undermine the doctor's credibility, especially if the doctor disagrees with the patient's choice among advertised drugs.

The medical profession has considered a resolution asking the Food and Drug Administration (FDA) to ban DTC ads, but health-care professionals can't seem to agree among themselves. The proposed resolution was defeated at the 2001 meeting of the AMA. "It's too late to ban direct-to-consumer advertising," laments Dr. Sandra Adamson Fryhofer. "The cat's out of the bag." Moreover, some doctors point to the upside of DTC. Ads, they say, help patients remember to take their medicine. They also prompt more patients to talk about health conditions. "I like DTC advertising," says Stuart Gitlow, an addiction psychiatrist in Providence, Rhode Island. "The Zyban ads began and all of a sudden people came to me and said: 'Help me stop smoking.' "

Some physicians not only approve of DTC advertising, but they also actively support it with computer-interactive kiosks in their waiting rooms. Moments before entering the office, patients are exposed to ads on consumer-friendly touch-screen displays sponsored by pharmaceutical companies. In effect, drug makers are betting that customers familiar with on-site ads are more likely to request a particular product. "It's location, location, location," says Mark Pavao, vice president of marketing for Helios Healthcare's eStations. "We're reaching people when they're thinking about their health care—when they're sitting in the doctor's office."

Controversy and confusion continue to surround DTC advertising. One thing, however, is clear: Physician–patient relationships are being redefined. Ad expenditures and health-care costs are climbing, while consumer access to health-care information is at an all-time high. As of mid-2002, both Congress and a number of state legislatures were investigating the fallout from DTC advertising, looking at both the public-health benefits and health-care costs. Critics are adamant in pointing to the drawbacks of DTC, while advocates proclaim its benefits. The question, however, may not be whether DTC is a cure-all or a prescription for disaster. Many observers contend that it works both ways.

Says Drew Altman, president of the Kaiser Family Foundation, a California think tank, "Drug ads may drive up [health-care] costs and drug company profits. But the drugs people get may also make them healthier."

Our opening story continues on page 348.

■ DETERMINING PRICES

As we saw in Chapter 10, product development managers decide what products a company will offer to customers. In **pricing**, the second major component of the marketing mix, managers decide what the company will get in exchange for its products. In this section, we first discuss the objectives that influence a firm's pricing decisions. Then we describe the major tools that companies use to meet those objectives.

pricing
Process of determining what a company will receive in exchange for its products

Pricing to Meet Business Objectives

Companies often price products to maximize profits, but they often hope to satisfy other **pricing objectives** as well. Some firms want to dominate the market or secure high market share. Pricing decisions are also influenced by the need to compete in the marketplace, by social and ethical concerns, and even by corporate image.

pricing objectives
Goals that producers hope to attain in pricing products for sale

Profit-Maximizing Objectives
Pricing to maximize profits is tricky. If prices are set too low, the company will probably sell many units of a product but may miss the chance to make additional profits on each unit (and may even lose money on each exchange). If prices are set too high, the company will make a large profit on each item but will sell fewer units. Again, the firm loses money. It may also be left with excess inventory and may have to reduce or even close production operations. To avoid these problems, companies try to set prices to sell the number of units that will generate the highest possible total profits.

In calculating profits, managers weigh sales revenues against costs for materials and labor. However, they also consider the capital resources (plant and equipment) that the company must tie up to generate a given level of profit. The costs of marketing (such as maintaining a large sales staff) can also be substantial. To use these resources efficiently, many firms set prices to achieve a targeted level of return on sales or capital investment.

E-Business Objectives
When pricing for Internet sales, marketers must consider different kinds of costs and different forms of consumer awareness. Many e-businesses reduce both costs and prices because of the Web's unique marketing capabilities. Because the Web provides a more direct link between producer and consumer, buyers avoid the added costs of wholesalers and retailers. Another factor is the ease of comparison shopping: Obviously, point-and-click shopping is much more efficient than driving from store to store in search of the best price. Moreover, both consumers and business buyers can get lower prices by joining together for greater purchasing power. Numerous small businesses, for example, are joining forces on the Web to negotiate lower prices for employee health care.

Market Share Objectives
In the long run, a business must make a profit to survive. Even so, companies often set initially low prices for new products. Because they

"O.K., who can put a price on love? Jim?"

market share
As a percentage, total of market sales for a specific company or product

are willing to accept minimal profits, even losses, to get buyers to try products, they use pricing to establish **market share**—a company's percentage of total market sales for a specific product type. Even with established products, market share may outweigh profit as a pricing objective. For a product such as Philadelphia Brand Cream Cheese, dominating a market means that consumers are more likely to buy because they are familiar with a well-known, highly visible product. Market domination means the continuous sales of more units and thus higher profits even at lower unit prices.

Price-Setting Tools

Whatever a company's objectives, managers must measure the potential impact before deciding on final prices. Two tools may be used for this purpose: *cost-oriented*

In the northeastern United States, where more than a third of all houses are heated by oil, homeowners can take out fixed-price contracts in the spring to lock in the heating oil prices they'll pay during the winter. In some years, it's a good bet; in others, it's not. Two years ago, the homeowner receiving this delivery locked in $1.15 per gallon and saved about $1,000 over the winter because open-market prices went up to $1.80. The next year, she locked at $1.25 in June. Unfortunately, prices dropped to about 85 cents. "It's like buying insurance," says one analyst. "When you buy a fixed-price deal, you're saying you want the peace of mind."

pricing and *breakeven analysis*. They are combined to determine prices that will allow the company to reach its objectives.

Cost-Oriented Pricing Cost-oriented pricing considers the firm's desire to make a profit and its need to cover production costs. A music store manager would price CDs by calculating the cost of making them available to shoppers. He or she would include the costs of store rent, employee wages, utilities, product displays, insurance, and, of course, the manufacturer's price.

Let's assume that the manufacturer's price is $8 per CD. If the store sells CDs for $8, it won't make any profit. Nor will it make a profit if it sells CDs for $8.50 each—or even $10 or $11. The company must charge enough to cover product and other costs in order to make a profit. Together, these factors determine the **markup**. In this case, a reasonable markup of $7 over costs means a $15 selling price. Markup is usually stated as a percentage of selling price and is calculated as follows:

markup
Amount added to an item's cost to sell it at a profit

$$\text{Markup percentage} = \frac{\text{Markup}}{\text{Sales price}}$$

For our CD retailer, the markup percentage is 46.7:

$$\text{Markup percentage} = \frac{\$7}{\$15} = 46.7\%$$

Out of every dollar taken in, $0.467 will be gross profit. Out of this profit, the store must still pay rent, utilities, insurance, and all other costs. Markup can also be expressed as a percentage of cost: The $7 markup is 87.5 percent of the $8 cost of a CD ($7/$8).

Breakeven Analysis: Cost-Volume-Profit Relationships Using cost-oriented pricing, a firm will cover **variable costs**—costs that change with the number of units of a product produced and sold. It will also make some money to pay **fixed costs**: costs that are unaffected by the number of units produced and sold. But how many units must the company sell before all costs, both variable and fixed, are covered and it begins to make a profit? What if too few units are sold? And what happens if sales are greater than expected? The answers depend on costs, selling price, and number of units sold. **Breakeven analysis** assesses costs versus revenues for various sales volumes. It shows, at any particular selling price, the financial result—the amount of loss or profit—for each possible volume of sales.[1]

variable cost
Cost that changes with the quantity of a product produced or sold

fixed cost
Cost unaffected by the quantity of a product produced or sold

breakeven analysis
For a particular selling price, assessment of the seller's costs versus revenues at various sales volumes

To continue our music store example, suppose that the *variable cost* for each CD (in this case, the cost of buying the CD from the producer) is $8. This means that the store's annual variable costs depend on how many CDs are sold—the number of CDs sold times the $8 cost for each CD. Say that *fixed costs* for keeping the store open for one year are $100,000. The number of CDs sold does not affect these costs. Costs for lighting, rent, insurance, and salaries are steady no matter how many CDs are sold. Therefore, what we want to know is this: How many CDs must be sold *so that revenues exactly cover both* fixed and variable costs? The answer is the **breakeven point**, which is 14,286 CDs. We arrive at this number through the following equation:

breakeven point
Sales volume at which the seller's total revenue from sales equals total costs (variable and fixed) with neither profit nor loss

$$\text{Breakeven point (in units)} = \frac{\text{Total fixed costs}}{\text{Price} - \text{Variable Cost}} = \frac{\$100,000}{\$15 - \$8} = 14,286 \text{ CDs}$$

FIGURE 11.1

Breakeven Analysis

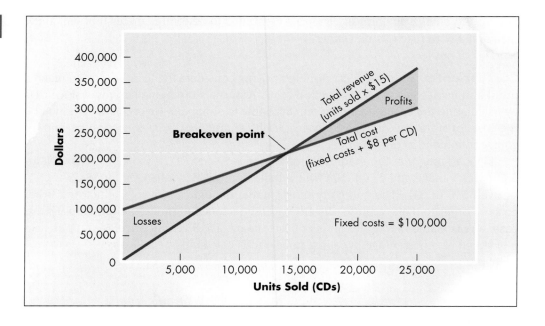

Look at Figure 11.1. If the store sells fewer than 14,286 CDs, it loses money for the year. If sales go over 14,286, profits grow by $7 for each additional CD. If the store sells exactly 14,286 CDs, it will cover all its costs but earn zero profit.

Zero profitability at the breakeven point can also be seen by using the profit equation:

Profit = Total revenue − (Total fixed cost + Total variable cost)
      = (14,286 CDs × $15) − ($100,000 Fixed cost + [14,286 CDs × $8 Variable cost])
$0 = ($214,290) − ($100,000 + $114,288) (rounded to the nearest whole CD)

PRICING STRATEGIES AND TACTICS

The pricing tools discussed in the previous section help managers set prices on specific goods. They do not, however, help them decide on pricing philosophies. In this section, we discuss pricing *strategy*—pricing as a planning activity. We then describe some basic pricing *tactics*: ways in which managers implement a firm's pricing strategies.

Pricing Strategies

How important is pricing as an element in the marketing mix and in the marketing plan? Because pricing has a direct impact on revenues, it is extremely important. Moreover, it is a very flexible tool. It is certainly easier to change prices than to change products or distribution channels. In this section, we focus on the ways in which pricing strategies can result in widely differing prices for very similar products.

Pricing Existing Products A firm has three options for pricing existing products:

- Pricing above prevailing market prices for similar products
- Pricing below market prices
- Pricing at or near market prices

Pricing above the market takes advantage of the common assumption that higher price means higher quality. In contrast, pricing below prevailing market price works if a firm offers a product of acceptable quality while keeping costs below those of higher-priced competitors.

Pricing New Products When introducing new products, companies must often choose between two pricing policy options: very high prices or very low prices. **Price skimming**—setting an initially high price to cover costs and generate a profit—may generate a large profit on each item sold. The revenue is often needed to cover development and introduction costs. Skimming works only if marketers can convince consumers that a new product is truly different from existing products. In contrast, **penetration pricing**—setting an initially low price to establish a new product in the market—seeks to create consumer interest and stimulate trial purchases.[2]

price skimming
Setting an initially high price to cover new product costs and generate a profit

penetration pricing
Setting an initially low price to establish a new product in the market

Fixed Versus Dynamic Pricing for E-Business The electronic marketplace has introduced a highly variable pricing system as an alternative to more conventional—and more stable—pricing structures for both consumer and B2B products. *Dynamic pricing* works because information flow on the Web notifies millions of buyers of instantaneous changes in product availability. In order to attract sales that might be lost under traditional fixed-price structures, sellers can alter prices privately, on a one-to-one, customer-to-customer basis.[3]

At present, fixed pricing is still the most common option for cybershoppers. E-tail giant Amazon.com has maintained the practice as the pricing strategy for its 16 million retail items. That situation, however, is beginning to change as dynamic-price challengers, such as eBay (the online, person-to-person auction Web site) and Priceline.com (the online clearinghouse for person-to-business price negotiation), grow in popularity.

An even more novel approach is taken by NexTag.com Inc. Instead of asking buyers to bid up prices against each other, NexTag asks customers to state the prices that they are willing to pay for products. Merchants then compete for the sales. Unlike Priceline customers, NexTag customers do not commit in advance to sale prices: They wait to see how low the price goes. NexTag gathers offers from merchants, each of whom decides how low to price a product. The customer then chooses the lowest price. According to one expert, NexTag's dynamic pricing may be the trend of the future. "Fixed prices," she points out, "are only a 100-year-old phenomenon. I think they will disappear online, simply because it is possible—cheap and easy—to vary prices online."

> **"Fixed prices will disappear online, simply because it is possible—cheap and easy—to vary prices online."**
>
> **—Patti Maes, MIT Media Lab**

Pricing Tactics

Regardless of its pricing strategy, a company may adopt one or more *pricing tactics*. Companies selling multiple items in a product category often use **price lining**—offering all items in certain categories at a limited number of prices. With price lining, a store predetermines three or four *price points* at which a particular product will be sold. If price points for men's suits are $175, $250, and $400, all men's suits will be priced at one of these three levels.

Psychological pricing takes advantage of the fact that customers are not completely rational when making buying decisions. One type of psychological pricing, **odd-even pricing**, is based on the theory that customers prefer prices that are not stated in even dollar amounts. Thus, customers regard prices of $1,000, $100, $50,

price lining
Setting a limited number of prices for certain categories of products

psychological pricing
Pricing tactic that takes advantage of the fact that consumers do not always respond rationally to stated prices

odd-even pricing
Psychological pricing tactic based on the premise that customers prefer prices not stated in even dollar amounts

discount
Price reduction offered as an incentive to purchase

and $10 as significantly higher than $999.95, $99.95, $49.95, and $9.95, respectively. Finally, sellers must often resort to price reductions—**discounts**—to stimulate sales.

SELF-CHECK QUESTIONS 1–3

You should now be able to answer Self-Check Questions 1–3.*

1 **Multiple Choice** Suppose your main *pricing objective* is twofold: to establish a new product in the market and to gain market share. The appropriate *pricing strategy* for this objective is [select one]: **(a)** market-share pricing; **(b)** dynamic pricing; **(c)** fixed pricing; **(d)** psychological pricing; **(e)** penetration pricing.

2 **True/False** With *dynamic pricing for e-business,* buyers do not bid up prices by bidding against one

another. Rather, they tell sellers the price they are willing to pay so that sellers can lower selling prices as they bid against one another to make the sale.

3 **True/False** Consider the *pricing tactics* in the clothing department of a department store. If the department uses *price lining*, then it cannot also use *odd-even pricing*.

***Answers to Self-Check Questions 1–3 can be found on p. 509.**

■ THE DISTRIBUTION MIX

distribution mix
The combination of distribution channels by which a firm gets its products to end users

intermediary
Individual or firm that helps to distribute a product

We have already seen that a company needs a good *product mix* and effective *pricing*. But the success of any product also depends on its **distribution mix**: the combination of distribution channels by which a firm gets products to end users. In this section, we will consider some of the many factors in the distribution mix. First, we will look at the role of the target audience and explain the need for intermediaries. Then we will discuss basic distribution strategies.

Intermediaries and Distribution Channels

wholesaler
Intermediary who sells products to other businesses for resale to final consumers

Once called *middlemen*, **intermediaries** help to distribute a producer's goods, either by moving them or by providing information that stimulates their movement from sellers to customers. **Wholesalers** are intermediaries who sell products to other businesses for resale to final consumers. **Retailers** sell products directly to consumers. Whereas some firms rely on independent intermediaries, others employ their own distribution networks and sales forces.[4]

retailer
Intermediary who sells products directly to consumers

Distribution of Consumer Products A **distribution channel** is the path that a product follows from producer to end user. Figure 11.2 shows how eight primary distribution channels can be identified according to the kinds of channel members involved in getting products to buyers. Note first that all channels begin with a producer and end either with a consumer or an industrial (business) user. Channels 1 through 4 are most often used to distribute consumer products.

distribution channel
Network of interdependent companies through which a product passes from producer to end user

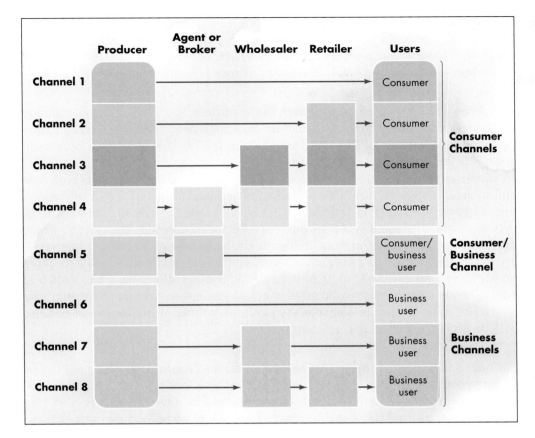

FIGURE 11.2

Channels of Distribution

Channel 1: Direct Distribution of Consumer Products In a **direct channel**, the product travels from the producer to the consumer without intermediaries. Using their own sales forces, companies such as Avon, Fuller Brush, and Tupperware use this channel. This direct channel is also prominent on the Internet for thousands of products ranging from books and automobiles to insurance and vacation packages sold directly by producers to consumers.

direct channel
Distribution channel in which a product travels from producer to consumer without intermediaries

Channel 2: Retail Distribution of Consumer Products In Channel 2, producers distribute products through retailers. Goodyear, for example, maintains its own system of retail outlets. Levi's has its own outlets but also produces jeans for other retailers such as Gap. Many retailers offer Internet sales.

Channel 3: Wholesale Distribution of Consumer Products Once the most widely used method of nondirect distribution, Channel 2 requires a large amount of floor space, both for storing merchandise and for displaying it in stores. Faced with the rising cost of store space, many retailers found that they could not afford both retail and storage space. Thus, wholesalers entered the distribution network to take over more of the storage function. The combination convenience store/gas station is an example of Channel 3. With approximately 90 percent of the space used to display merchandise, only 10 percent is left for storage and office facilities. Wholesalers store merchandise and restock it frequently.

Channel 4: Distribution Through Sales Agents or Brokers Channel 4 uses **sales agents**, or **brokers**, who represent producers and sell to wholesalers, retailers, or both. They receive commissions based on the prices of the goods they sell. Agents

sales agent/broker
Independent intermediary who usually represents many manufacturers and sells to wholesalers or retailers

generally deal in the related product lines of a few producers and work on a long-term basis. Travel agents, for example, represent airlines, car-rental companies, and hotels. In contrast, brokers match sellers and buyers as needed. The real estate industry relies on brokers to match buyers and sellers of property.

The Pros and Cons of Nondirect Distribution Each link in the distribution chain makes a profit by charging a markup or commission. Thus, nondirect distribution means higher prices: The more members in the channel—the more intermediaries—the higher the final price.

Intermediaries, however, can provide *added value* by saving consumers both time and money. Moreover, the value accumulates with each link in the supply chain. Intermediaries provide time-saving information and make the right quantities of products available where and when consumers need them. Consider Figure 11.3, which illustrates the problem of making chili without the benefit of a common intermediary—the supermarket. As a consumer/buyer, you would obviously spend a lot more time, money, and energy if you tried to gather all the ingredients from one retailer at a time. In any case, even if we did away with intermediaries, you would not eliminate either their tasks or the costs entailed by performing those tasks. They exist because they do necessary jobs in cost-efficient ways.

Channel 5: Distribution by Agents to Consumers and Businesses Channel 5 differs from previous channels in two ways: (1) An agent functions as the sole intermediary and (2) the agent distributes to both consumers and business customers. Consider Vancouver-based Uniglobe Travel International, a travel agency representing airlines, car-rental companies, and hotels. Uniglobe books flight reservations and arranges complete recreational travel services for consumers. The firm also services companies whose employees need lodging and transportation for business travel.

Distribution of Business Products Industrial channels are important because every company is also a customer that buys other companies' products. **Industrial (business) distribution**, therefore, is the network of channel members involved in the flow of manufactured goods to business customers. Unlike consumer products, business products are traditionally distributed through Channels 6, 7, and 8, as shown in Figure 11.2.

industrial (business) distribution
Network of channel members involved in the flow of manufactured goods to industrial customers

FIGURE 11.3

The Value-Adding Intermediary

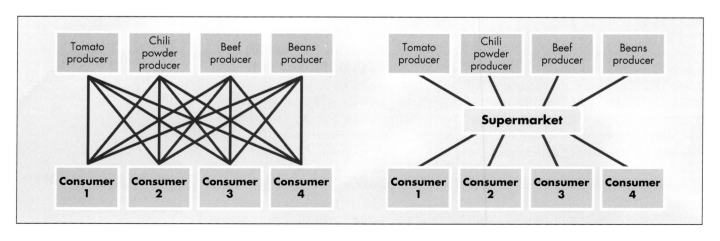

Say WHAT YOU MEAN

KEEPING CHANNELS CLEAR

Merely securing a major distributor is not a guarantee of success in any market. Distributors often carry a huge range of products and usually have different incentives for getting different products to market. Using intermediaries to distribute products around the world requires an understanding of cultural differences, especially when it comes to communicating with channel partners whose cultural values—such as what's an incentive and what's not—are not the same as your own.

Most communication with distributors is written—e-mails, faxes, letters, and so forth. Obviously, your distributor must be able to understand what you need, so here are a few tips for communicating with foreign members of your distribution channel. Don't be too casual or informal when you're e-mailing businesspeople in Germany; you may give them the wrong idea about your commitment to the partnership and even turn them off to you and your firm. German businesspeople expect to be addressed by *Mr., Mrs.,* and other appropriate titles, and they will expect you to observe a certain level of formality in all communications. Latin Americans, on the other hand, tend to appreciate a personal touch—say, a reference to family or health early in the communication. If you're an American, you probably expect succinct, matter-of-fact messages; you don't even mind bulleted lists of things to be discussed.

If distributors don't understand the value or benefits of your new product features, they're less likely to market them successfully. In many cases, explaining things in culturally specific slang or jargon just confuses foreign distributors. Do not, however, expect Singaporeans or Filipinos to tell you voluntarily that they don't understand your technical terms. They'd lose face. You're better off anticipating communication challenges and focusing on such questions as how they would recommend improving your sales in their markets. You're bound to get a list of polite suggestions that may not only be useful but that also should help you determine whether your communications are effective.

Finally, remember that your distributor is probably the best person to ask about the local market. Thus, you may want to consider translating your marketing and product materials to ensure that foreign distributors understand the features and benefits of your products. Typically, they're representing numerous products, and communicating clearly with them will make it easier for them to represent your products.

Channel 6: Direct Distribution of Business Products Most business goods are sold directly by the manufacturer to the industrial buyer. Intermediaries are often unnecessary because goods distributed through Channel 6 are usually purchased in large quantities. In some cases, however, brokers or agents may enter the chain between manufacturers and buyers. Finally, e-commerce technologies have also popularized Channel 6. Dell Computer Corp. *(www.dell.com)*, a pioneer in direct Internet sales, now gets about two-thirds of its $32 billion in sales from other businesses, governments, and schools.[5]

Channel 7: Wholesale Distribution of Industrial Products Wholesalers function in only a few industrial channels. Brokers and agents are even rarer. Channel 7 mostly handles accessory equipment (computers, fax machines, and other office equipment) and supplies (floppy disks, pencils, copier paper). Manufacturers produce these items in large quantities, but companies buy them in small quantities. For example, few companies order truckloads of paper clips. Intermediaries, then, help end users by breaking down large quantities into smaller sales units. Thus, the traditional office-supply store wholesales a variety of goods to other businesses.

Channel 8: Wholesale Distribution to Business Retailers In some industries, the roles of channel members are changing. In the office-products industry, Channel 7 is

At the Flint, Michigan, plant of Delphi Automotive Systems (*www.delphi.com*), the world's largest auto parts supplier, Jessica V. Prince assembles fuel pumps according to a process that she helped engineers and consultants design. Radically increased efficiency has become an absolute necessity in the direct distribution of auto parts to car makers: There are now about 12,000 auto parts makers, down from 30,000 in 1980, and the number may plummet to about 200 in just a few decades.

being displaced by a channel that looks very much like Channel 3 for consumer products: Instead of buying office supplies from wholesalers (Channel 7), many businesses are now shopping at office discount stores such as Staples, Office Depot, and Office Max. Before selling to large companies, these warehouse-like superstores originally targeted retail consumers and small businesses that bought supplies at retail stores (and at retail prices). Today, however, small-business buyers shop at discount stores designed for industrial users, selecting from 7,000 items at prices 20 to 75 percent lower than retail.

WHOLESALING

Now that you know something about distribution channels, we can consider more closely the role of intermediaries. Wholesalers, for example, provide a variety of services to buyers of products for resale or business use. In addition to storing and providing an assortment of products, some wholesalers offer delivery, credit, and product information.

Merchant Wholesalers

merchant wholesaler
Independent wholesaler who takes legal possession of goods produced by a variety of manufacturers and then resells them to other businesses

Most wholesalers are independent operations that sell various consumer or business goods produced by a variety of manufacturers. The largest group, **merchant wholesalers**, buys products from manufacturers and sells them to other businesses. They own the goods that they resell and usually provide storage and delivery.

Agents and brokers, including Internet e-agents, serve as independent sales representatives for many companies' products. They work on commission, usually about 4 to 5 percent of net sales. They often provide a wide range of services, including shelf and display merchandising. Many supermarket products are handled through brokers.

The Advent of the E-Intermediary

The ability of e-commerce to bring together millions of widely dispersed consumers and businesses is changing the types and roles of intermediaries. **E-intermediaries** are Internet-based channel members who perform one or both of two functions: (1) They collect information about sellers and present it to consumers, or (2) they help deliver Internet products to buyers.[6] We will examine three types of e-intermediaries: *syndicated sellers*, *shopping agents*, and *business-to-business brokers*.

Syndicated Sellers **Syndicated selling** occurs when one Web site offers another a commission for referring customers. Here's how it works. With 9.2 million users each month, Expedia.com is a heavily visited travel-services Web site. Expedia has given Dollar Rent A Car *(www.dollarcar.com)* a special banner on its Web page. When Expedia customers click on the banner for a car rental, they are transferred from the Expedia site to the Dollar site. Dollar pays Expedia a fee for each booking that comes through this channel. Although the new intermediary increases the cost of Dollar's supply chain, it adds value for customers. Travelers avoid unnecessary cyberspace searches and are efficiently guided to a car-rental agency.[7]

Shopping Agents **Shopping agents** (or **e-agents**) help Internet consumers by gathering and sorting information. Although they don't take possession of products, they know which Web sites and stores to visit, give accurate comparison prices, identify product features, and help consumers complete transactions by presenting information in a usable format—all in a matter of seconds. PriceScan *(www.pricescan.com)* is a well-known shopping agent for computer products. For CDs and tapes, evenbetter.com searches for vendors, does price comparisons, lists prices from low to high, and then transfers you to the Web sites of 50 different e-stores.

Business-to-Business Brokers E-commerce intermediaries have also emerged for business customers. The start-up Internet company Efdex (which stands for *electronic food and drink exchange*) is a massive food exchange for buying and selling foodstuffs among food manufacturers, restaurants, grocers, and farmers. Established first in the United Kingdom in early 2000, the Web site *(www.efdex.com)* provides up-to-date market information and price and product data from both suppliers and buyers. Efdex lets businesses buy and sell from one another and confirm transactions electronically. As a broker, Efdex does not take possession of products. Rather, it brings together timely information and links businesses to one another.[8]

e-intermediary
Internet distribution channel member that assists in moving products through to customers or that collects information about various sellers to be presented in convenient format for Internet customers

syndicated selling
E-commerce practice whereby a Web site offers other Web sites commissions for referring customers

shopping agent (or **e-agent**)
E-intermediary (middleman) in the Internet distribution channel that assists users in finding products and prices but that does not take possession of products

■ RETAILING

There are more than 1.6 million retail establishments in the United States. Most of them are small, often consisting of owners and part-time help. Indeed, over one-half of the nation's retailers account for less than 10 percent of all retail sales. Retailers also include huge operations such as Wal-Mart, the largest employer in the United States, and Sears. Although there are large retailers in many other countries—Kaufhof *(www.kaufhof.de)* in Germany, Carrefour *(www.carrefour.com)* in France, and Daiei *(www.cybercitykobe.com/daiei/index.htm)* in Japan—most of the world's largest retailers are U.S. businesses.

It took a few years after the fall of communism before entrepreneurs braved the uncertain economic climate of Russia and opened supermarkets and other retail chains. IKEA, the Swedish home-furnishings seller, has been successful in Moscow, as has Kopeika *(www.kopeika.ru)*, a home-owned discount chain that models itself after Wal-Mart. Russian shoppers (who used to go to drab stores called "Food" and "Furniture") are enthusiastic, and more companies are opening outlets in Moscow, a city that has more people than the country of Belgium.

Types of Retail Outlets

department store
Large product line retailer characterized by organization into specialized departments

supermarket
Large product line retailer offering a variety of food and food-related items in specialized departments

specialty store
Small retail store carrying one product line or category of related products

bargain retailer
Retailer carrying a wide range of products at bargain prices

discount house
Bargain retailer that generates large sales volume by offering goods at substantial price reductions

catalog showroom
Bargain retailer in which customers place orders for catalog items to be picked up at on-premises warehouses

U.S. retail operations vary widely by type as well as size. We can classify them in various ways: by pricing strategies, location, range of services, or range of product lines. Choosing the right types of retail outlets is a crucial aspect of every seller's distribution strategy. In this section, we describe U.S. retail stores by using two classifications: *product line retailers* and *bargain retailers.*

Product Line Retailers Retailers featuring broad product lines include **department stores**, which are organized into specialized departments: shoes, furniture, women's petite sizes, and so on. Stores are usually large, handle a wide range of goods, and offer a variety of services, such as credit plans and delivery. Similarly, **supermarkets** are divided into departments of related products: food products, household products, and so forth. They stress low prices, self-service, and wide selection.

In contrast, **specialty stores** are small stores that carry one line of related products. They serve specific market segments with full product lines in narrow product fields and often feature knowledgeable sales personnel. Sunglass Hut International *(www.sunglasshut.com)*, for instance, has 1,600 outlets with a deep selection of competitively priced sunglasses.

Bargain Retailers **Bargain retailers** carry wide ranges of products and come in many forms. The first **discount houses** sold large numbers of items (such as televisions and other appliances) at substantial price reductions to certain customers. As name-brand items became more common, they offered better product assortments while still transacting cash-only sales in low-rent facilities. As they became firmly entrenched, they began moving to better locations, improving decor, and selling better-quality merchandise at higher prices. They also began offering a few department store services, such as credit plans and noncash sales.

Catalog showrooms mail catalogs to attract customers into showrooms to view display samples, place orders, and wait briefly while clerks retrieve orders from attached warehouses. **Factory outlets** are manufacturer-owned stores that avoid wholesalers and retailers by selling merchandise directly from factory to consumer. The **warehouse club** (or **wholesale club**) offers large discounts on a wide range of brand-name merchandise to customers who pay annual membership fees. Neighborhood food retailers such as 7-Eleven and Circle K stores are **convenience store** chains, which offer ease of purchase: They stress easily accessible locations, extended store hours, and speedy service. They differ from most bargain retailers in that they do not feature low prices. Like bargain retailers, they control prices by keeping in-store service to a minimum.

Nonstore and Electronic Retailing

Some of the nation's largest retailers sell all or most of their products without brick-and-mortar stores. Certain types of consumer goods—soft drinks, candy, and cigarettes—sell well from vending machines. But even at $107 billion per year, vending machine sales still make up less than 4 percent of all U.S. retail sales. In e-retailing, sales reached $42 billion in 2001, as some 63 million households with PCs went online to shop.

Nonstore retailing also includes **direct-response retailing**, in which firms contact customers directly to inform them about products and to receive sales orders. **Mail order** (or **catalog marketing**), such as that practiced by Spiegel *(www.spiegel.com)* and its Eddie Bauer *(www.eddiebauer.com)* subsidiary, is a form of direct-response retailing. So is **telemarketing**—the use of the telephone to sell directly. Telemarketing is growing rapidly in the United States, Canada, and Great Britain, and experts estimate that U.S. sales alone could top $800 billion in 2004. Finally, more than 600 U.S. companies use direct selling to sell door-to-door or through home-selling parties. Avon Products has 465,000 independent U.S. sales reps.[9]

The Boom in Electronic Retailing **Electronic retailing** is made possible by communications networks that let sellers post product information on consumers' PCs. With more than 3.6 million subscribers, Prodigy Communications Corp. *(www.prodigy.com)* is among the largest home networks. As an *Internet service provider (ISP)*, Prodigy employs a network of more than 850 U.S. locations that can be accessed by 90 percent of the population with a local telephone call. Prodigy gives members access to the Internet and displays of products ranging from travel packages to financial services to consumer goods. Home PC users can examine detailed descriptions, compare brands, send for free information, or purchase by credit card.[10]

Internet-Based Stores Use of the Internet to interact with customers—to inform, sell to, and distribute to them—is booming. Internet use by American small businesses doubled in 1998, nearly doubled again in 1999, and added another 2.1 million Web sites during 2000. Figure 11.4 tells the story of this growth by showing the percentages of small businesses with Web sites (Figure 11.4[a]), of those planning to post Web sites (Figure 11.4[b]), and of the marketing functions that owners expect sites to perform (Figure 11.4[c]).[11]

The rampant growth of e-commerce is undoubtedly just the beginning. B2B e-commerce is already a $1.2 *trillion* industry and is expected to reach $4.8 trillion in 2004. In addition, although e-retail sales were 15 times higher in 2001 than in 1997, at $42 billion they were still less than 4 percent of total retail sales. There is a lot of room for growth, and huge growth prospects are spurring the scramble among firms to go into e-business.[12]

factory outlet
Bargain retailer owned by the manufacturer whose products it sells

warehouse club (or **wholesale club**)
Bargain retailer offering large discounts on brand-name merchandise to customers who have paid annual membership fees

convenience store
Retail store offering easy accessibility, extended hours, and fast service

direct-response retailing
Nonstore retailing by direct interaction with customers to inform them of products and to receive sales orders

mail order (or **catalog marketing**)
Form of nonstore retailing in which customers place orders for catalog merchandise received through the mail

telemarketing
Nonstore retailing in which the telephone is used to sell directly to consumers

electronic retailing
Nonstore retailing in which information about the seller's products and services is connected to consumers' computers, allowing consumers to receive the information and purchase the products in the home

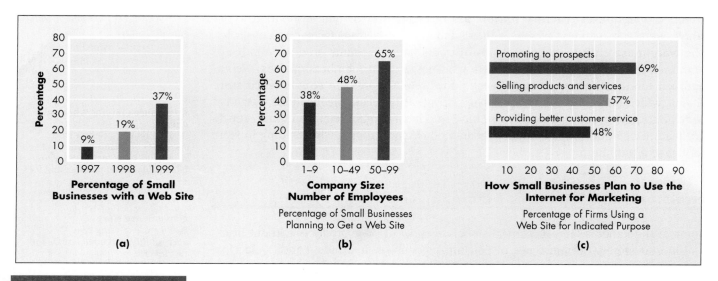

FIGURE 11.4

Small Business and the Web

e-catalog
Nonstore retailing in which the Internet is used to display products

Electronic Catalogs E-catalogs use the Internet to display products for both retail and business customers. By sending electronic versions (instead of traditional mail catalogs), firms give millions of users instant access to pages of product information. The seller avoids mail-distribution and printing costs, and once an online catalog is in place, there is little cost in maintaining and accessing it. Recognizing these advantages, about 85 percent of all catalogers are now on the Internet, with sales via Web sites accounting for 10 percent of all catalog sales. The top 10 consumer e-catalogs include JCPenney (#1), Fingerhut (#3), L. L. Bean (#7), and Victoria's Secret (#8). Top B2B e-catalogs include Dell Computer (#1) and Office Depot (#5).[13]

electronic storefront
Commercial Web site in which customers gather information about products, buying opportunities, placing orders, and paying for purchases

Electronic Storefronts and Cybermalls Today, a seller's Web site is an **electronic storefront** (or *virtual storefront*) from which consumers collect information about products and buying opportunities, place orders, and pay for purchases. Producers of large product lines, such as Dell Computer *(www.dell.com)*, dedicate storefronts to their own product lines. Other sites, such as CDNOW *(www.cdnow.com)*, which offers CDs and audio and video tapes, are category sellers whose storefronts feature products from many manufacturers.

cybermall
Collection of virtual storefronts (business Web sites) representing a variety of products and product lines on the Internet

Search engines like Yahoo! *(www.yahoo.com)* serve as **cybermalls**: collections of virtual storefronts representing diverse products. After entering a cybermall, shoppers can navigate by choosing from a list of stores (Eddie Bauer or Macy's), product listings (Pokémon or MP3 players), or departments (apparel or bath/beauty). When your virtual shopping cart is full, you check out and pay your bill. The value-added properties of cybermalls are obvious: speed, convenience, 24-hour access, and, most importantly, efficient searching that avoids the "click-'til-you-drop" syndrome—the endless wandering through cyberspace experienced by early Internet users.[14]

interactive marketing
Nonstore retailing that uses a Web site to provide real-time sales and customer service

Interactive and Video Marketing Today, both retail and B2B customers interact with multimedia Web sites using voice, graphics, animation, film clips, and access to live human advice. One good example of **interactive marketing** is LivePerson *(www.liveperson.com)*, a leading provider of real-time sales and customer service for over 450 Web sites. When customers log on to the sites of e-Loan, Playboy, CBS Sportsline's IgoGolf, or USABancShares—all of which are LivePerson clients—they enter a live chat room where a service operator initiates a secure one-on-one text chat. Questions and answers go back and forth to help customers with answers to specific questions that must be answered before they decide on a product. Another form of interaction is the so-called *banner ad* that changes as the user's mouse moves about the page, revealing new drop-down, check, and search boxes.

Video marketing, a long-established form of interactive marketing, lets viewers shop at home from TV screens. Most cable systems offer video marketing through home-shopping channels that display and demonstrate products and allow viewers to phone in or e-mail orders. One U.S. network, QVC *(www.qvc.com)*, also operates in the United Kingdom, Germany, Mexico, and South America and has also launched iQVC as an interactive Web site.

video marketing
Nonstore retailing to consumers via standard and cable television

PHYSICAL DISTRIBUTION

Physical distribution refers to the activities needed to move products from manufacturer to consumer. Its purpose is to make goods available when and where consumers want them, keep costs low, and provide services that keep customers satisfied. Thus, physical distribution includes *warehousing* and *transportation operations*.

physical distribution
Activities needed to move a product efficiently from manufacturer to consumer

Warehousing Operations

Storing, or **warehousing**, is a major part of distribution management. In selecting a strategy, managers must keep in mind both the different characteristics and costs of warehousing operations. **Private warehouses** are owned by a single manufacturer, wholesaler, or retailer. Most are run by large firms that deal in mass quantities and need regular storage. JCPenney, for example, facilitates the movement of products to retail stores by maintaining its own warehouses.

Public warehouses are independently owned and operated. Because companies rent only the space they need, these facilities are popular with firms needing storage only during peak periods. They are also used by manufacturers who need multiple storage locations to get products to multiple markets.

warehousing
Physical distribution operation concerned with the storage of goods

private warehouse
Warehouse owned by and providing storage for a single company

public warehouse
Independently owned and operated warehouse that stores goods for many firms

Transportation Operations

Because the highest cost faced by many companies is that of physically moving a product, cost is a major factor in choosing transportation methods. But firms must also consider other factors: the nature of the product, the distance it must travel, the speed with which it must be received, and customer wants and needs.

Transportation Modes The major transportation modes are trucks, railroads, planes, water carriers, and pipelines. Differences in cost are most directly related to delivery speed. Air, for instance, is the fastest mode of transportation. It boasts much lower costs in handling and packing and unpacking. Inventory carrying costs can also be reduced by eliminating the need to store items that might deteriorate. Shipments of

Specializing in long-haul shipping, U.S. Xpress Enterprises *(www.usxpress.com)* employs nearly 6,000 drivers to operate 5,300 trucks and 12,000 trailers. The company has used satellite technology to communicate with drivers since the 1980s, and trucks now have anticollision radar, vehicle-detection sensors, and computers for shifting through 10 speeds. Roomy cabs have sleepers, refrigerators, and microwaves because driver comfort is a top priority. "Drivers," explains a company executive, "can lose you a $100 million account with words, actions, and how they do business."

fresh fish, for example, can be picked up by restaurants each day, avoiding the risk of spoilage from packaging and storing. Air freight, however, is the most expensive form of transportation. Water, by contrast, is the least expensive mode but, unfortunately, also the slowest.

Physical Distribution and E-Customer Satisfaction

order fulfillment
All activities involved in completing a sales transaction, beginning with making the sale and ending with on-time delivery to the customer

New e-commerce companies often focus on sales, only to discover that delays in after-sale distribution cause customer dissatisfaction. Any delay in physical distribution is a breakdown in fulfillment. **Order fulfillment** begins when the sale is made: It involves getting the product to each customer in good condition and on time. But the volume of a firm's transactions can be huge—Web retailers shipped 300 million packages in 2001—and fulfillment performance has been disappointing for many e-businesses.

To improve on-time deliveries, many businesses, such as Amazon.com, maintain distribution centers and ship from their own warehouses. Other e-tailers, however, entrust order filling to distribution specialists such as the giant UPS e-logistics *(www.e-logistics.ups.com)* and the much smaller Atomic Box *(www.atomicbox.com)*. Both Atomic Box and UPS e-logistics process customer orders, ship goods, provide information about product availability, inform customers about the real-time status of orders, and handle returns. To perform these tasks, the client's computer system must be integrated with that of the distribution specialist.

Distribution as a Marketing Strategy

Distribution is an increasingly important way of competing for sales. Instead of just offering advantages in product features and quality, price, and promotion, many firms have turned to distribution as a cornerstone of business strategy. This approach means assessing and improving the entire stream of activities—wholesaling, warehousing, and transportation—involved in getting products to customers.

Consider, for example, the distribution system of National Semiconductor *(www.national.com)*, one of the world's largest computer-chip makers. Finished silicon microchips are produced in plants around the world and shipped to customers such as IBM, Toshiba, Siemens, Ford, and Compaq, which also run factories around the globe. Chips originally sat waiting at one location after another—on factory floors, at customs, in distributors' facilities, and in customers' warehouses. Typically, they traveled 20,000 different routes on as many as 12 airlines and spent time in 10 warehouses before reaching customers. National has streamlined the system by shutting down six warehouses and now airfreights chips worldwide from a single center in Singapore. Every activity—storage, sorting, and shipping—is run by Federal Express *(www.fedex.com)*. As a result, distribution costs have fallen, delivery times have been reduced by half, and sales have increased.

SELF-CHECK QUESTIONS 4–6

You should now be able to answer Self-Check Questions 4–6.*

4 True/False The *distribution mix* is the combination of products that a firm offers for distribution to end users.

5 Multiple Choice Which of the following is **not true** regarding *intermediaries* and *distribution channels*? [select one]: **(a)** Wholesalers sell products to other businesses, which resell them to final customers. **(b)** Intermediaries are retailers who move goods or information to customers. **(c)** Intermediaries provide added value for customers. **(d)** Distribution channels for consumer products are often different from those for industrial products.

6 Multiple Choice Which of the following is **false** regarding *retailing* and *retail outlets*? [select one]: **(a)** Factory outlets and warehouse clubs, but not specialty stores, are examples of bargain retailers. **(b)** Department stores offer a wide range of goods and customer services. **(c)** Mail-order retailers, such as catalog showrooms, offer deep price discounts. **(d)** Electronic retailing relies on communication networks connecting sellers to buyers' computers.

*Answers to Self-Check Questions 4–6 can be found on p. 509.

■ THE IMPORTANCE OF PROMOTION

As we noted in Chapter 10, **promotion** is any technique designed to sell a product. It is part of the *communication mix*: the total message any company sends to consumers about its product. Promotional techniques, especially advertising, must communicate the uses, features, and benefits of products. Sales promotions also include various programs that add value beyond the benefits inherent in the product. It's nice to get a quality product at a good price but even better when you get a rebate or a bonus pack

promotion
Aspect of the marketing mix concerned with the most effective techniques for selling a product

with "20 percent more free." In promoting products, then, marketers have an array of tools at their disposal.

Promotional Objectives

The ultimate objective of any promotion is to increase sales. In addition, marketers may use promotion to *communicate information, position products, add value*, and *control sales volume*. Promotion is effective for communicating information from one person or organization to another. Consumers cannot buy products unless they know about them. Information may thus advise customers that a product exists, or it may educate them about the product's features.

positioning
Process of establishing an identifiable product image in the minds of consumers

As we noted in Chapter 10, **positioning** is the process of establishing an easily identifiable product image in the minds of consumers. First, the firm must identify which segments are likely to purchase its product and who are its competitors. Only then can it focus its strategy on differentiating its product while still appealing to its target audience.[15]

Promotional mixes are often designed to communicate a product's *value-added benefits*. Burger King *(www.burgerking.com)* shifted its promotional mix by cutting back on advertising dollars and using the money for customer discounts: Getting the same food at a lower price is a value-added benefit. Finally, by increasing promotions during slow periods, firms that experience seasonal sales patterns (say, greeting-card companies) can keep production and distribution systems *running evenly* and stabilize sales volume throughout the year.

The Promotional Mix

promotional mix
Combination of tools used to promote a product

We observed in Chapter 10 that there are four types of promotional tools: *advertising, personal selling, sales promotions*, and *publicity and public relations*. The best combination of these tools—the best **promotional mix**—depends on many factors. The most important is the target audience.

The Target Audience: Promotion and the Buyer Decision Process In establishing a promotional mix, marketers match promotional tools with the five stages in the buyer decision process:

1 Buyers must first recognize the need to make a purchase. At this stage, marketers must make sure that buyers are aware of their products. Advertising and publicity, which can reach many people quickly, are important.

2 Buyers also want to learn more about available products. Advertising and personal selling are important because both can be used to educate consumers.

3 Buyers compare competing products. Personal selling can be vital. Sales representatives can demonstrate product quality and performance in comparison with competitors' products.

4 Buyers choose products and purchase them. Sales promotion is effective because it can give consumers an incentive to buy. Personal selling can help by bringing products to convenient purchase locations.

5 Buyers evaluate products after purchase. Advertising, or even personal selling, is sometimes used to remind consumers that they made wise purchases.

Figure 11.5 summarizes the effective promotional tools for each stage of the consumer buying process.

FIGURE 11.5

The Consumer Buying Process and the Promotional Mix

Advertising Promotions

Advertising is paid, nonpersonal communication, by which an identified sponsor informs an audience about a product. In 2000, U.S. firms spent $243 billion on advertising—$83 billion of it by just 100 companies.[16] In this section, we will begin by describing the different types of advertising media, noting some of the advantages and limitations of each.

advertising
Promotional tool consisting of paid, nonpersonal communication used by an identified sponsor to inform an audience about a product

Advertising Media Consumers tend to ignore the bulk of advertising messages that bombard them. Marketers must find out who their customers are, which media they pay attention to, what messages appeal to them, and how to get their attention. Thus, marketers use several different **advertising media**—specific communication devices for carrying a seller's message to potential customers.

With 24 percent of all advertising outlays, television is the most widely used medium. Figure 11.6 shows network-TV advertising expenditures for some U.S. firms.[17] In addition to the major networks, cable television increased ad revenues from $3.4 billion in 1995 to more than $14 billion in 2000.[18] Information on viewer demographics for particular programs allows advertisers to use sight, sound, and motion for aiming their commercials at target audiences.

advertising media
Variety of communication devices for carrying a seller's message to potential customers

Newspapers account for about 20 percent of all advertising outlays. Because each local market has at least one daily newspaper, newspapers provide excellent coverage, reaching more than 171 million U.S. adults daily. Newspaper ads are flexible—they can easily be changed from day to day. By the same token, newspapers are generally thrown out after one day, and because their readership is so broad, they don't allow advertisers to target audiences very well.

Direct-mail advertisements, which account for 18 percent of all advertising outlays, involve printed ads mailed directly to consumers' homes or places of business. Direct mail allows a company to select its audience and personalize its message. Although many people discard junk mail, advertisers can predict in advance how many recipients will take a mailing seriously. These recipients display stronger-than-average interest in an advertised product and are more likely than most to buy it.

direct mail
Advertising medium in which messages are mailed directly to consumers' homes or places of business

About 8 percent of all advertising outlays go to radio. Ads on the airwaves are inexpensive and, because stations are usually segmented into categories such as rock 'n' roll, country and western, jazz, talk, or news, audiences are largely segmented. The huge variety of magazines provides a high level of ready market segmentation, and magazine ads account for roughly 5 percent of all advertising. Outdoor advertising—billboards, signs, and advertisements on buses, street furniture, taxis, stadiums, and subways—makes up about 1 percent of all advertising, but at 8 percent per year,

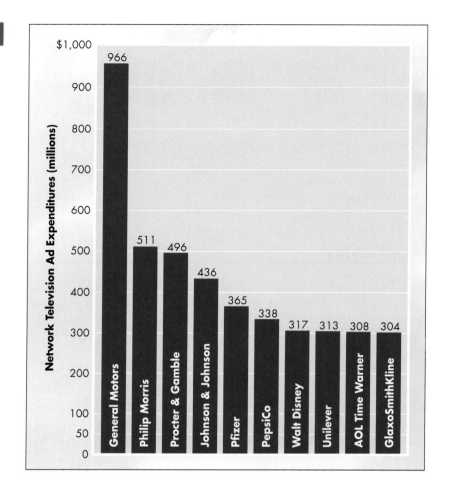

FIGURE 11.6

Top 10 Network TV Advertisers

it's growing faster than newspapers, magazines, and television. These ads are inexpensive, face little competition for consumers' attention, and provide high repeat exposure.

A combination of other media, including catalogs, sidewalk handouts, Yellow Pages, skywriting, telephone calls, special events, and door-to-door communication, make up the remaining 22 percent of all U.S. advertising. The combination of media through which a company advertises is called its **media mix**.

media mix
Combination of advertising media chosen to carry message about a product

Internet Advertising The most recent advertising medium is the Internet, where such well-known names as 3M Corp., Burlington Coat Factory, Miller Genuine Draft, MCI Communications, Reebok, and thousands of lesser-known firms have all placed ads. Although Internet advertising is still in its infancy and has great potential, many marketers recognize its limitations. In particular, consumers don't want to wade through electronic pages looking at hundreds of products. Some experts contend that most commercial ads on the Internet are never read by anyone, but Internet advertising accounts for nearly 2 percent of U.S. ad expenditures.[19]

Targeted advertising, however, is appealing because Internet advertisers can measure the success of messages: They count how many people see each ad and track the number of click-throughs to the advertiser's own Web site. Electronic tracking devices relay such information as which ads generate more purchases, what sales margins result from each sale, and which ads attract the most attention from target audiences. DoubleClick *(www.doubleclick.com)*, a global Internet advertising firm, was one of the first companies to help other advertisers take advantage of the Web's unique capacity for tailoring ad messages and tracking user behavior online.

Data Mining and Data Warehousing for Internet Advertising The Internet fosters targeting because volumes of data can be gathered electronically from users. The behavior patterns of millions of users can be traced by analyzing files of information gathered over time. By means of *data mining* and *data warehousing* (see Chapter 10), vast pools of data on user behavior reveal who has bought which products and how many, over what Web site individuals bought products, how they paid, and so on. By analyzing what consumers actually do, e-marketers can determine what subsequent purchases they are likely to make and then send them tailor-made ads.

> "All we're doing is using information we have on our customers . . . to enhance our knowledge of them and market back to them."
>
> —Advertising executive Howard Draft, on the use of data mined from the Internet

"All we're doing," says Howard Draft, chairman of Draft Worldwide in Chicago *(www.draftworldwide.com)*, "is using information we have on our customers, with overlays of demographic or psychographic information, to enhance our knowledge of them and market back to them." Instead of using one advertisement to blanket all consumers, data mining makes it feasible to use niche advertising that is targeted to individual consumers.

Personal Selling

In **personal selling**, a salesperson communicates one-to-one with potential customers to identify their needs and align them with the seller's products. As the oldest form of selling, it lends credibility to a firm because it allows buyers to interact with and ask questions of the seller.

personal selling
Promotional tool in which a salesperson communicates one-on-one with potential customers

Personal Selling Tasks An important aspect of sales force management is overseeing salespeople as they perform three basic tasks of personal selling. In **order processing**, a salesperson receives an order and sees to its handling and delivery. Route salespeople, who call on regular customers to check inventories, are often order processors. When the benefits of a product are not entirely clear, creative selling can help to persuade buyers. **Creative selling** is crucial for high-priced consumer products, such as homes and cars, for which buyers comparison shop.

order processing
Personal selling task in which salespeople receive orders and see to their handling and delivery

creative selling
Personal selling task in which salespeople try to persuade buyers to purchase products by providing information about their benefits

Finally, a company may use **missionary selling** when it wants to promote itself and its products rather than simply to close a sale. Drug company representatives promote drugs to doctors who, in turn, prescribe them to patients. The sale, then, is actually made at the drugstore. Depending on the product and company, sales jobs usually require individuals to perform all three tasks to some degree.

missionary selling
Personal selling tasks in which salespeople promote their firms and products rather than try to close sales

Telemarketing and Personal Sales Costs have prompted many companies to turn to *telemarketing*: using telephone solicitations to conduct the personal selling process. Telemarketing is useful in handling any stage of this process and in arranging appointments for salespeople. For example, it cuts the cost of personal sales visits to industrial customers, each of whom requires about four visits to complete a sale. Telemarketing has saved some sellers $1,000 or more in sales visits. Such savings are stimulating the growth of telemarketing, which, in the United States, placed 40 billion phone calls and sold $668 billion in goods and services in 2001. Employing some 6 million people in the United States, the industry's growth makes sense. It averages more than a $7 return for every dollar invested.[20]

ENTREPRENEURSHIP and *New Ventures*

Capitalizing on the VirTus of Experience

When Marian Marchese and Joseph Barone joined forces to create VirTu Inc.—a strategic marketing company that has pioneered the integration of branding and communications—they had no inkling that Lifecycle Success Framework™ would become the backbone of their own company's strategy. Today, VirTu *(www.virtuinc.com)* shows clients—including the Franklin Institute, Penn Mutual Life Insurance, and Sunoco Logistics—how to combine traditional or offline services (such as direct-response retailing) and interactive or online services (such as Web site development) for conducting both business-to-business and business-to-consumer marketing activities.

Starting with strategic planning, VirTu helps clients in developing multichannel marketing systems and methods for online and offline branding. Then it gives them help in designing and programming processes for reaching their business goals. VirTu's three competencies—marketing, creative design, and technology—work together to provide each client company with a unified approach to reaching its customers.

The Lifecycle Success Framework™ (LSF) has proved to be a highly effective outline to help clients conceive, design, and implement integrated marketing plans. LSF has three main stages. The discovery phase ensures that the client establishes clear objectives for each marketing project. It involves conducting marketing research, clarifying target audiences, identifying competitors, and assessing Web site potential. In the design/implementation phase, VirTu executes all the marketing, creative, and technology improvements that have been developed in the discovery phase. During the final stage, the continuity marketing phase, VirTu implements the marketing program, adapting it over time as changes occur in the client's needs, target audience, and evolving markets.

> *"I resolved at that moment that I would never allow anyone to do this to me again."*
>
> *—Entrepreneur Marian Marchese, on why she started her own company after getting fired for earning too much money*

Like many entrepreneurial ventures, VirTu did not have immediate success with its innovative approach to doing business. Rather, LSF emerged through trial and error and took advantage of some hard-learned lessons in failure as well as success. The founders pooled their experiences from early-career jobs and watched for opportunities to use them in turning their vision of LSF into reality. Marian Marchese, for example, didn't start off planning to be in business for herself. As vice president of account services at an ad agency, she discovered that her boss had a peculiar way of holding down costs: When people rose to certain salary levels, he fired them and replaced them with younger employees. That was why one day Marchese, who had just scraped together the down payment on a house, found herself jobless on the streets of Philadelphia.

"I resolved at that moment," she recalls, "that I would never allow anyone to do this to me again." So she took a chance and started her own ad agency, which later became part of a very successful partnership. In 1995, Marchese and Joe Barone, convinced that the Internet was transforming the advertising and marketing industries, founded a new partnership—an Internet company called VirTu—that was more profitable within eight months than the ad agency had been in 11 years. That's when they merged the two partnerships to create the new media firm that they called VirTu Inc.

In applying past experiences to new ideas, Marchese and Barone not only recognized the possibilities for a new venture but also went on to implement those ideas. Right now, VirTu's possibilities include going public and joining forces with other companies that are interested in the secrets to VirTu's success.

Sales Promotions

sales promotion
Short-term promotional activity designed to stimulate consumer buying or cooperation from distributors and sales agents

Sales promotions are short-term promotional activities designed to stimulate either consumer buying or cooperation from distributors, sales agents, or other members of the trade. They are important because they increase the likelihood that buyers will try products. They also enhance product recognition and can increase purchase size and amount.

Types of Sales Promotions Most consumers have taken part in a variety of sales promotions. For example, when you use a certificate entitling you to savings off regular prices, you are participating in a **coupon** promotion. It may be used to encourage customers to try new products, to lure customers away from competitors, or to induce customers to buy more of a product.

To grab customers' attention as they move through stores, companies use **point-of-purchase (POP) displays**. Located at the ends of aisles or near checkout counters, POP displays make it easier for customers to find products and easier for sellers to eliminate competitors from consideration. *Purchasing incentives* include free samples that let customers try products without risk. **Premiums** are free or reduced-price items, such as pens, pencils, calendars, and coffee mugs, given to consumers in return for buying a specified product. **Trade shows** allow companies to rent booths to display and demonstrate products to customers who have a special interest or who are ready to buy. In *contests*, consumers may win prizes by entering their cats in the Purina Cat Chow calendar contest, for example, by submitting entry blanks from the backs of cat food packages.

Publicity and Public Relations

To the delight of marketers with tight budgets, **publicity** is free. However, marketers usually have little control over publicity and, because it is presented in a news format, consumers often regard it as objective and credible.[21] In 2002, for example, the entire accounting industry suffered a loss of respect and trust from negative publicity about Arthur Andersen Company's corrupt accounting practices.

In contrast to publicity, **public relations** is company-influenced publicity that seeks either to build good relations with the public or to deal with unfavorable events. A firm will try to establish goodwill with customers (and potential customers) by performing and publicizing its public-service activities.

coupon
Sales promotion technique in which a certificate is issued entitling the buyer to a reduced price

point-of-purchase (POP) display
Sales promotion technique in which product displays are located in certain areas to stimulate purchase

premium
Sales promotion technique in which offers of free or reduced-price items are used to stimulate purchases

trade show
Sales promotion technique in which various members of an industry gather to display, demonstrate, and sell products

publicity
Promotional tool in which information about a company or product is transmitted by general mass media

public relations
Company-influenced publicity directed at building goodwill with the public or dealing with unfavorable events

Best Buy *(www.bestbuy.com)*, a 1,900-store chain once known for consumer electronics and appliances, has added software and entertainment to its inventory and is now the country's biggest retailer of CDs and DVDs. To promote its entertainment products, Best Buy uses promotional tie-ins, such as deals to become the exclusive retailer of U2's latest DVD. In return, Best Buy spent $10 million to put U2 *(www.u2.com)* in newspaper circulars and on the sides of buses. Meanwhile, CEO Richard Schultze (right) pursues his strategy of putting electronics and entertainment under one roof. "Consumers," he explains, "are telling us they want to depend increasingly on one guy."

SELF-CHECK QUESTIONS 7–9

You should now be able to answer Self-Check Questions 7–9.*

7 Multiple Choice In regard to *marketing promotions*, all of the following are correct **except** [select one]: **(a)** The ultimate objective of any promotion is to provide information. **(b)** The promotional mix can provide value-added benefits. **(c)** The positioning of a product cannot be accomplished until a specific market segment has been identified. **(d)** The choice of a promotional mix should consider the target audience. **(e)** Personal selling can be effective when potential buyers have questions about the seller's products.

8 Multiple Choice Which of the following is **true** about *advertising media*? [select one]: **(a)** TV is the most-used medium and reaches the most people.

(b) TV ads are more effective than radio ads. **(c)** Advertisers who want fast, immediate impact prefer magazines. **(d)** The success of an Internet ad cannot be measured as easily as the success of ads in other media.

9 Multiple Choice Suppose your chief *personal selling strategy* is to *persuade* buyers that there are benefits to your company's product, especially buyers who are unfamiliar with its features and uses. The appropriate name for this type of selling is [select one]: **(a)** order extraction; **(b)** missionary selling; **(c)** prospecting; **(d)** psychological selling; **(e)** creative selling.

***Answers to Self-Check Questions 7–9 can be found on p. 509.**

Continued from page 325

DO WE NEED RELIEF FROM DTC?

The pharmaceuticals business is risky because it involves expensive research and development (R&D) for new drugs. Sales revenues must recover not only the costs of developing successful drugs but also the costs of unsuccessful research. To stimulate sales, drug companies have historically relied on various methods for persuading doctors to prescribe products, such as sponsoring educational events, providing promotional gifts, and funding medical research. But the shift to DTC promotions is an expensive multimedia thrust that embraces TV—national and cable—radio, telephone (for instance, 1-800-for-Nexium), Internet *(www.purplepill.com)*, magazines, newspapers, Sunday supplements, and outdoor advertising. Both advertising costs and drug prices are skyrocketing, whereas product information—sometimes informative, sometimes misleading—is at an all-time high.

In 2002, the National Health Council (NHC), a nonprofit group of 118 U.S. health-related organizations, concluded that, on balance, DTC marketing is more beneficial than detrimental to most patients and doctors. Says the NHC report, "The Council recognizes that DTC advertising provides important information to consumers and patients, which often is beneficial to their health." It adds, however, that whereas some ads are merely unclear about the conditions that drugs are supposed to treat, others fail to report product risks. Some even make drugs seem more effective than they are. The NHC also reports that one-third of doctors are concerned about the negative effects of DTC advertising on physician–patient relationships.

Aside from questions of consumer motivation and physician–patient relationships, controversy rages over how to curb the rising prices of prescription drugs. A 2002 study of health-care managers reported that DTC advertising—the fastest-growing expense in the industry's promotional budget—is the number-one factor in the explosion of drug costs. It is greater even than the cost of developing new drugs. The study overwhelmingly singles out pharmaceutical companies—rather than consumers, government, or health-care organizations—as responsible for high drug costs.

At the same time, it advises caution in dealing with the problem. Most respondents dislike the idea of government management of prices, arguing that bureaucrats aren't qualified to set prices and would just make matters worse. Let the free market, say these experts, correct itself. A dissenting minority, however, noted that runaway costs must be kept down—and that the only way to do this is to regulate the industry. DTC advertising, they contend, should be banned, and price controls should be put in place. The FDA, they suggest, should loosen regulations governing the introduction of new drugs so that more choices become available to consumers.

How do matters look to observers outside the United States? Foreign observers are wary about the U.S. experience and the danger posed by DTC to health care inside their own borders. In Canada, for example, DTC ads are banned. Officials in the European Union (EU) have also banned DTC ads, but they are experimenting with a pilot plan to "ensure the availability of better, clear, and reliable information" on authorized drugs. The EU allows drug makers to supply limited information—and only when patients request it. Although protecting the public from misleading information is a prime goal, officials also worry that U.S.-style DTC advertising could spur both higher prescription costs and the use of unsafe and unnecessary drugs. Gradually, the ban on DTC broadcast ads may be softened because health-conscious Europeans are already getting doses of medical information from other sources, especially from the Internet.

Even the proponents of DTC ads recognize the dangers of misleading or biased information. Every year, the U.S. FDA demands that drug makers alter certain ads. Recently, for example, Pharmacia Corp., maker of the arthritis medicine Celebrex, was chided for television ads claiming "powerful 24-hour relief." The ad, charged the FDA, "suggests that Celebrex is more effective than has been demonstrated by substantial evidence." The allergy drugs Claritin, Flonase, and Flovent have been cited 10 or more times each.

So is DTC advertising good, bad, or a little of both? The FDA isn't sure and wants more information before making additional decisions. Accordingly, the FDA's Division of Drug Marketing, Advertising & Communications (DDMAC) launched a 2002 survey to get the views of doctors and patients. Although the results may help, industry experts expect to see a mixture of pros and cons rather than a sure cure for any DTC malady.

Questions for Discussion

1 Why do you suppose TV is the industry's medium of choice for DTC promotions?

2 In addition to prescription drugs, can you think of any other industry that uses a DTC promotional strategy? What elements must be present in the marketing environment for such a strategy to be successful?

3 Why are physicians concerned about the effect of DTC advertising on doctor–patient relationships? List some ways in which those relationships might be changed. Are the changes you listed good or bad?

4 List at least four measures that drug companies might take to hold down consumer prices. What are the disadvantages and advantages of each measure?

5 What might the federal government do to prevent the rise of prescription drug prices? Outline the pros and cons for each action you identify. Which action(s) do you recommend?

6 Has the emergence of DTC advertising created any ethical or social-responsibility issues for physicians? Explain why or why not.

■ SUMMARY OF LEARNING OBJECTIVES

1 Identify the various *pricing objectives* that govern pricing decisions and describe the *price-setting tools* used in making these decisions.

In pricing, managers decide what the company will get in exchange for its products. **Pricing objectives** refer to the goals that producers hope to attain as a result of pricing decisions. These objectives can be divided into two major categories: (1) *Pricing to maximize profits:* If prices are too low, the company will probably sell many product units but miss the chance to make additional profits on each one. If prices are set too high, it will make a large profit on each

unit but will sell fewer units. (2) *Market share objectives:* Many companies are willing to accept minimal profits, even losses, to get buyers to try products. They may use pricing to establish **market share**—a company's percentage of the total market sales for a specific product type.

Managers must measure the potential impact before deciding on final prices. For this purpose, they use two basic tools (which are often combined): (1) *Cost-oriented pricing:* Managers price products by calculating the cost of making them available to shoppers; when they total these costs and add a figure for profit, they arrive at a markup. (2) *Breakeven analysis:* **Breakeven analysis** assesses total costs versus revenues for various sales volumes. It shows, at any particular sales price, the financial result—the amount of loss or profit—for each possible sales volume. The number of units that must be sold for total revenue to equal total costs is the **breakeven point**.

2 Explain the *distribution mix* and identify the different *channels of distribution*.

The success of any product depends on its **distribution mix**: the combination of distribution channels that a firm uses to get products to end users. **Intermediaries** help to distribute a producer's goods: **Wholesalers** sell products to other businesses, which resell them to final consumers. **Retailers** sell products directly to consumers.

Among the eight **distribution channels**, the first four are aimed at getting products to consumers, the fifth is for consumers or business customers, and the last three are aimed at getting products to business customers. Channel 1 involves direct sales to consumers. Channel 2 includes a *retailer*. Channel 3 involves both a retailer and a *wholesaler*, and Channel 4 includes an *agent* or *broker*. Channel 5 includes only an agent between the producer and consumer. Channel 6, which is used extensively for e-commerce, involves a direct sale to an industrial user. Channel 7 entails selling to business users through wholesalers. Channel 8 includes retail superstores that get products from producers or wholesalers (or both) for reselling to business customers.

3 Identify the different types of *retailing* and *retail stores*.

U.S. retail operations fall under two classifications. *Product line retailers* featuring broad product lines include **department stores** and **supermarkets**. Small **specialty stores** serve clearly defined market segments by offering full product lines in narrow product fields. *Bargain retailers* carry wide ranges of products and come in many forms, including **discount houses, catalog showrooms, factory outlets, warehouse clubs** (or **wholesale clubs**), and **convenience stores**.

Nonstore retailing includes direct-response retailing, in which firms make direct contact with customers to inform them about products and take sales orders. **Mail order** (or **catalog marketing**) is a form of **direct-response retailing**, as is **telemarketing**. **Electronic retailing** uses communications networks that allow sellers to connect to consumers' computers. Internet retail shopping includes **electronic storefronts** where customers can examine a store's products, place orders, and make payments electronically. Customers can also visit **cybermalls**—a collection of virtual storefronts representing a variety of product lines on the Internet.

4 Define *physical distribution* and describe the major activities in the physical distribution process.

Physical distribution refers to all the activities needed to move products from producers to consumers, so that products are available when and where customers want them at reasonable cost. Physical distribution activities include providing *customer services*, **warehousing**, and *transportation* of products. Warehouses provide storage for products and may be either *public* or *private*. Transportation operations physically move products from suppliers to customers. Trucks, railroads, planes, water carriers (boats and barges), and pipelines are the major *transportation modes* used in the distribution process.

5 Identify the important objectives of *promotion*, discuss the considerations entailed in selecting a *promotional mix*, and describe the key *advertising media*.

Although the ultimate goal of **promotion** is to increase sales, other goals include *communicating information, positioning a product, adding value*, and *controlling sales volume*. In deciding on the appropriate **promotional mix**—the best combination of promotional tools (e.g., advertising, personal selling, public relations)—marketers must consider the good or service being offered, characteristics of the target audience and the buyer's decision process, and the promotional mix budget.

Advertising media include television, newspapers, direct mail, radio, magazines, outdoor advertising, and the Internet, as well as other channels such as *Yellow Pages*, movies, special events, and door-to-door selling. The combination of media that a company chooses is called its *media mix*.

6 Outline the tasks involved in *personal selling* and describe the various types of *sales promotions*.

Personal selling tasks include **order processing, creative selling** (activities that help persuade buyers), and **missionary selling** (activities that promote firms and products). **Point-of-purchase (POP) displays** are intended to grab attention and help customers find products in stores. Purchasing incentives include *samples* (which let customers try products without having to buy them) and **premiums** (rewards for buying products). At **trade shows**, sellers rent booths to display products to customers who already have an interest in buying. **Contests** are intended to increase sales by stimulating buyers' interest in products.

■ KEY TERMS

pricing (p. 325)
pricing objectives (p. 325)
market share (p. 326)
markup (p. 327)
variable cost (p. 327)
fixed cost (p. 327)
breakeven analysis (p. 327)
breakeven point (p. 327)
price skimming (p. 329)
penetration pricing (p. 329)
price lining (p. 329)
psychological pricing (p. 329)
odd-even pricing (p. 329)
discount (p. 330)
distribution mix (p. 330)
intermediary (p. 330)
wholesaler (p. 330)
retailer (p. 330)
distribution channel (p. 330)
direct channel (p. 331)
sales agent/broker (p. 331)
industrial (business) distribution (p. 332)
merchant wholesaler (p. 334)

e-intermediary (p. 335)
syndicated selling (p. 335)
shopping agent (e-agent) (p. 335)
department store (p. 336)
supermarket (p. 336)
specialty store (p. 336)
bargain retailer (p. 336)
discount house (p. 336)
catalog showroom (p. 336)
factory outlet (p. 337)
warehouse club (wholesale club) (p. 337)
convenience store (p. 337)
direct-response retailing (p. 337)
mail order (catalog marketing) (p. 337)
telemarketing (p. 337)
electronic retailing (p. 337)
e-catalog (p. 338)
electronic storefront (p. 338)
cybermall (p. 338)
interactive marketing (p. 338)
video marketing (p. 339)
physical distribution (p. 339)

warehousing (p. 339)
private warehouse (p. 339)
public warehouse (p. 339)
order fulfillment (p. 340)
promotion (p. 341)
positioning (p. 342)
promotional mix (p. 342)
advertising (p. 343)
advertising media (p. 343)
direct mail (p. 343)
media mix (p. 344)
personal selling (p. 345)
order processing (p. 345)
creative selling (p. 345)
missionary selling (p. 345)
sales promotion (p. 346)
coupon (p. 347)
point-of-purchase (POP) display (p. 347)
premium (p. 347)
trade show (p. 347)
publicity (p. 347)
public relations (p. 347)

■ QUESTIONS AND EXERCISES

Questions for Review

1 How does breakeven analysis help managers measure the potential impact of prices?

2 What is the overall goal of price skimming? Of penetration pricing?

3 Identify the eight channels of distribution. In what key ways do the four channels used only for consumer products differ from the channels used only for industrial products?

4 Explain how the activities of e-agents (Internet shopping agents) or brokers differ from those of traditional agents/brokers.

5 Compare the advantages and disadvantages of different advertising media.

Questions for Analysis

6 Suppose that a small publisher selling to book distributors has fixed operating costs of $600,000 each year and variable costs of $3.00 per book. How many books must the firm sell to break even if the selling price is $6.00? If the company expects to sell 50,000 books next year and decides on a 40-percent markup, what will the selling price be?

7 Take a look at some of the advertising conducted by locally based businesses in your area. Choose two campaigns: one that you think is effective and one that you think is ineffective. What differences in the campaigns make one better than the other?

8 Consider the various kinds of nonstore retailing. Give examples of two products that typify the products sold to at-home shoppers through each form of nonstore retailing. Explain why different products are best suited to each form of nonstore retailing.

Application Exercises

9 Select a product with which you are familiar, and analyze various possible pricing objectives for it. What

information would you want to have if you were to adopt a profit-maximizing objective? A market-share objective? An image objective?

10 Select a product that is sold nationally. Identify as many media used in its promotion as you can. Which medium is used most? On the whole, do you think the campaign is effective? Why or why not?

 BUILDING YOUR BUSINESS SKILLS

QUESTIONS AND EXERCISES

This exercise enhances the following SCANS workplace competencies: demonstrating basic skills, demonstrating thinking skills, exhibiting interpersonal skills, and working with information.

Goal

To encourage students to analyze the potential usefulness of two promotional methods—personal selling and direct mail—for a start-up greeting card company.

Situation

You are the marketing adviser for a local start-up company that makes and sells specialty greeting cards in a city of 400,000. Last year's sales totaled 14,000 cards, including personalized holiday cards, birthday cards, and special-events cards for individuals. Although revenues increased last year, you see a way of further boosting sales by expanding into card shops, grocery stores, and gift shops. You see two alternatives for entering these outlets:

1 Use direct mail to reach more individual customers for specialty cards.

2 Use personal selling to gain display space in retail stores.

Your challenge is to convince the owner of the start-up company which alternative is the more financially sound decision.

Method

Step 1

Get together with four or five classmates to research the two kinds of product segments: *personalized cards* and *retail store cards*. Find out which of the two kinds of marketing promotions will be more effective for each of the two segments. What will be the reaction to each method of customers, retailers, and card company owners?

Step 2

Draft a proposal to the company owner. Leaving budget and production details to other staffers, list as many reasons as possible for adopting direct mail. Then list as many reasons as possible for adopting personal selling. Defend each reason. Consider the following reasons in your argument:

■ **Competitive environment:** Analyze the impact of other card suppliers that offer personalized cards and cards for sale in retail stores.

■ **Expectations of target markets:** Who buys personalized cards and who buys ready-made cards from retail stores?

■ **Overall cost of the promotional effort:** Which method, direct mail or personal selling, will be more costly?

■ **Marketing effectiveness:** Which promotional method will result in greater consumer response?

FOLLOW-UP QUESTIONS

1 Why do you think some buyers want personalized cards? Why do some consumers want ready-made cards from retail stores?

2 Today's computer operating systems provide easy access to software for designing and making cards on home PCs. How does the availability of this product affect your recommendation?

3 What was your most convincing argument for using direct mail? For using personal selling?

4 Can a start-up company compete in retail stores against industry giants such as Hallmark and American Greetings?

EXERCISING YOUR ETHICS

THE CHAIN OF RESPONSIBILITY

The Situation

Because several stages are involved when distribution chains move products from supply sources to end consumers, the process offers ample opportunity for ethical issues to arise. This exercise encourages you to examine some of the ethical issues that can emerge during transactions among suppliers and customers.

The Dilemma

A customer bought an expensive wedding gift at a local store and asked that it be shipped to the bride in another state. Several weeks after the wedding, the customer contacted the bride because she had sent no word confirming the arrival of the gift. In fact, it hadn't arrived. Charging that the merchandise had not been delivered, the customer requested a refund. The store manager uncovered the following facts:

- All shipments from the store are handled by a well-known national delivery firm.
- The delivery firm verified that the package had been delivered to the designated address two days after the sale.

- Normally, the delivery firm does not obtain recipient signatures; deliveries are made to the address of record, regardless of the name on the package.

The gift giver argued that even though the package had been delivered to the right address, it had not been delivered to the named recipient. It turns out that, unbeknownst to the gift giver, the bride had moved. It stood to reason, then, that the gift was in the hands of the new occupant of the bride's former address. The manager informed the gift giver that the store had fulfilled its obligation. The cause of the problem, she explained, was the incorrect address given by the customer. She refused to refund the customer's money and suggested that the customer might want to recover the gift by contacting the stranger who received it at the bride's old address.

QUESTIONS FOR DISCUSSION

1 What are the responsibilities of each party—the customer, the store, the delivery firm—in this situation?
2 From an ethical standpoint, in what ways is the store manager's action right? In what ways is it wrong?
3 If you were appointed to settle this matter, what actions would you take?

 CRAFTING YOUR BUSINESS PLAN

GETTING THE CAFFEINE INTO YOUR CUP

The Purpose of the Assignment

1 To acquaint students with product distribution issues that a sample firm addresses in developing its business plan in the framework of the *Business PlanPro (BPP) 2003* software package (Version 6.0).
2 To demonstrate how channels of distribution, supply chains, and warehousing can be integrated as components in the *BPP* planning environment.

Assignment

After reading Chapter 11 in the textbook, open the BPP *software and look around for information about plans for supply chains and channels of distribution as they apply to a sample firm, a coffee exporter:* Silvera & Sons Ltd. *To find* Silvera, *do the following:*

Open *Business PlanPro*. Go to the toolbar and click on the *"Sample Plans"* icon. In the **Sample Plan Browser**, do a search using the **search category** *Food and kindred products*. From the resulting list, select the category entitled **Export— Coffee**, which is the location for *Silvera & Sons Ltd.* The screen you are looking at is the introduction page for the *Silvera* business plan. Next, scroll down from this page until you reach the Table of Contents for the *Silvera* business plan.

NOW RESPOND TO THE FOLLOWING ITEMS:

1 Describe *Silvera*'s products and customers. Then identify the steps in the supply chain, beginning from raw materials to the final consumer. [Sites to see in *BPP* for this item: In the Table of Contents page, click on **1.0 Executive Summary**. Then click on each of the following in turn: **1.1 Objectives, 2.0 Company Summary, 2.2 Company History,** and **3.0 Products**.]

2 Where is *Silvera*'s main warehouse located? What are its activities? [Sites to see in *BPP*: In the Table of Contents page, click on **2.3 Company Locations and Facilities**. After returning to the Table of Contents page, click on **3.0 Products**.]

3 Describe the equipment and warehousing activities that are needed to prepare coffee beans for shipment. [Sites to see in *BPP*: From the Table of Contents page,

click on each of the following in turn: **3.1 Competitive Comparison** and **3.4 Technology**.]

4 What steps are involved in getting the product from *Silvera*'s plant in Ouro Fino to Miami? Who is responsible for paying the distribution charges? [Sites to see in *BPP*: In the Table of Contents page, click on **4.2.2 Distribution Patterns**. After returning to the Table of Contents page, click on **5.3.4 Distribution Strategy**.]

 VIDEO EXERCISE

THROUGH THE GRAPEVINE: CLOS DU BOIS WINERY

Learning Objectives

The purpose of this video is to help you:

1 Understand how a company works with wholesalers and retailers to make its products available to consumers.

2 Discuss the factors that affect a company's distribution strategy.

3 Consider physical distribution goals and challenges.

Synopsis

Riding a tidal wave of U.S. consumer interest in California wines, Clos du Bois Winery sells its wines from coast to coast. The company now produces and ships more than 1 million cases of wine every year, although less than 20 percent is sold in California. The winery works through a network of statewide and regional distributors that sell to retailers and restaurants which, in turn, serve the wine to consumers. For efficient order fulfillment and inventory management, Clos du Bois ships from a central warehouse to more than 300 wholesaler warehouses around the United States. To ensure that quality is not compromised by temperature extremes, the company also pays close attention to the details of physical distribution. Now the company is tapping the infrastructure of parent company Allied Domecq to arrange for wider distribution in Europe.

DISCUSSION QUESTIONS

1 **For analysis:** Why does Clos du Bois sell through wholesalers rather than sell to retailers and restaurants?

2 **For analysis:** How does the U.S. pattern of table wine consumption affect the winery's domestic distribution strategy?

3 **For application:** What might Clos du Bois do when its supply of a certain vintage is quite limited?

4 **For application:** What effect does the cost of storing and shipping Clos du Bois wine have on the prices paid by retailers and, ultimately, consumers?

5 **For debate:** Given its long-term relationships with established wholesalers, should Clos du Bois lobby against direct sales of wine to U.S. consumers through Internet channels? Support your position.

Online Exploration

Visit the Web site of the Clos du Bois Winery at (*www.closdubois.com/home.html*) and (if you are of legal drinking age in your state) enter and read what the company says about its wines, winery, and wine club. Also follow the link to explore the trade site and find out where Clos du Bois wines are sold. Considering the winery's dependence on distributors, why would it invest so heavily in a consumer-oriented Web site? What channel conflict might be caused by this site? If you cannot legally enter the winery's Web site, use your favorite search engine (such as Google.com) to see whether other online retailers are selling this wine. If so, why would Clos du Bois make its wine available through these intermediaries?

PLANNING FOR YOUR CAREER

SELLING YOURSELF

We've seen how marketing managers apply the principles discussed in Chapters 10 and 11 in order to sell products to target markets. At the same time, as you prepare for your career, you're searching for useful skills and tools to help sell yourself to prospective employers. This exercise gives you an opportunity to look more closely at basic marketing principles as potential career-building tools.

Assignment

Recall from Chapter 10 that as a customer, you buy a product because you like what it can do for you—because it has the right features and benefits to satisfy your needs. Try thinking of yourself as a product—a business professional—and visualize potential employers as customers in the market for business professionals. Your objective in this exercise is to evaluate the product-customer match and use your findings to improve your Career Portfolio (*Beginning Your Career Search*, 3d ed. by James S. O'Rourke IV).

To complete this exercise, do the following:

1 Make a list of product *features* (tangible and intangible) that you possess (or intend to possess) as a business professional.

2 Make a list of product *benefits* that your features provide (or will provide) potential employers.

3 Identify an industry or organization(s) that you are considering for your career. This is your target market. List key *characteristics* of the customers in this target market. What are some specific needs that they expect employees to satisfy?

4 Compare your features and benefits lists in items 1 and 2 with your target-market–needs list in item 3. Are your features and benefits well matched with your target market's needs? Do you detect any gaps that might indicate a mismatch?

5 What changes in your career plans might improve the match between you and your target customers?

6 Reconsider your findings in the context of *Beginning Your Career Search*, 3d ed. In particular, which of your Career Portfolio documents might benefit from the results of this exercise? Try to make two or more specific improvements to your Portfolio.

12

**After reading this chapter,
you should be able to:**

1 Explain why businesses must manage *information* and show how computer systems and communication technologies have revolutionized *information management.*

2 Identify and briefly describe three elements of *data communication networks*—the Internet, the World Wide Web, and intranets.

3 Describe five *new options for organizational design* that have emerged from the rapid growth of information technologies.

4 Discuss different information system *application programs* that are available for users at various organizational levels.

5 Briefly describe the content and role of a *database* and the purpose of *database software* for information systems.

MORE PRODUCTIVE THAN A SPEEDING LOCOMOTIVE

Locomotive manufacturing: Is it a twilight industry? Yes and no. At GE Transportation Systems, a unit of General Electric Co., the core business of making locomotives is in a severe downturn. Sales of 911 locomotives in 1999 had plummeted to 350 by 2002. So

MANAGING INFORMATION SYSTEMS AND COMMUNICATION TECHNOLOGY

why is CEO John Krenicki Jr. so upbeat about the future? One reason is an industrywide shift toward improving railroad services rather than just buying more trains.

Railroads want to raise productivity, improve on-time delivery, and cut costs—and GE is in a position to help with its *remote monitoring diagnostics*. Developed at GE's corporate R&D center, the technology has been used in GE Medical Systems products and aircraft engines. Now it's being customized for the locomotive business. For 2002, revenues from Transportation Systems services, including remote diagnostics applications, was $1.5 billion—triple the 1996 total. New technologies, reports Krenicki, are changing the industry. "We're also digitizing all of our workflows— not just in our own factories but in customers' service shops. We want to run service shops like an Indianapolis pit crew." If shops run smoothly, freight rolls on time and at lower cost.

What does remote diagnostics do? It's designed to anticipate breakdowns before they happen. An unexpected breakdown can cost hundreds of thousands of dollars in lost operations, rescheduling, and unhappy customers. Remote sensing—sensing from afar—transmits signals from equipment to a satellite and then to the Internet, where specialists anywhere can view data, perform tests, predict maintenance needs, and troubleshoot equipment operating in out-of-the-way places. Monitoring key components can catch failures ahead of time so that they can be repaired less expensively, with less disruption to schedules, and with shorter downtimes. The ideal is just-in-time maintenance: performing work when it's needed, not before or too late. "There are two kinds of mistakes," says Gerald Hahn, retired founder of GE's Applied Statistics Program. "Replacing too soon and replacing too late. We want to minimize both."

Remote monitoring is possible because of two advances in technology. First is the miniaturization of sensors—the devices that attach to components and detect system characteristics (temperature, pressure, and so forth). New devices are easier to install, take up little room, and don't interfere with normal operation. Second, advanced computing power makes it easier to process data for diagnosis. Today's 6,000-horsepower locomotive engine is controlled by two dozen microprocessors that monitor such variables as speed, horsepower output, and voltage. Sensor data are relayed from a satellite to GE's service center in Erie, Pennsylvania, where technicians monitor 300 locomotives around the country.

Let's say that GE's diagnostics team detects a clogged fuel filter, which can cut horsepower by 30 percent. Even the engineer wouldn't detect the loss if the train were pulling a light load, but it would slow down a heavily loaded train on an uphill grade, and the effect would soon be felt throughout the entire rail system. Other trains would fall behind, and the rescheduling would be expensive. With remote monitoring, technicians can check real-time data on hundreds of variables and detect problems that would otherwise go unsuspected. Much of the rail industry's increase in effectiveness, therefore, is due not to bigger or even better equipment, but rather to advanced technology and better information.

Our opening story continues on page 377.

■ INFORMATION MANAGEMENT: AN OVERVIEW

Business today relies on information management in ways that no one could foresee a decade ago. Managers now treat digital technology as a basic organizational resource for conducting daily business. At major firms, every activity—designing services, ensuring product delivery and cash flow, evaluating personnel—is linked to information systems. Managing systems is a core business activity that can no longer be delegated to technical personnel.

information manager
Manager responsible for designing and implementing systems to gather, organize, and distribute information

information management
Internal operations for arranging a firm's information resources to support business performance and outcomes

Most businesses also regard their information as a private resource—an asset that's planned, developed, and protected. It's not surprising that they have **information managers**, who operate systems for gathering, organizing, and distributing information, just as they have production, marketing, and finance managers. **Information management** is the internal operation that arranges information resources to support business performance and outcomes. At Chaparral Steel (*www.chaparralsteel.com*), delivery times, sales, profits, and (last, but by no means least) customer service and loyalty have been boosted by an information system that gives customers electronic access to the mill's inventories. The technology that lets customers shop electronically through its storage yards makes Chaparral more agile in responding to their needs, and because it responds faster than its competitors, Chaparral enjoys more sales.

To find information, managers must often sift through mountains of reports, memos, and phone messages. Thus, the question facing so many businesses today is how to channel useful information to the right people at the right time. In this section, we will explore the ways in which companies manage information with computers and related information technologies.

Information Systems

One response to this challenge has been the growth of the **information system (IS)**— a system for transforming raw data into information and transmitting it for use in decision making. **Data** are raw facts and figures that, by themselves, may not have much meaning. **Information** is the meaningful, useful interpretation of data. IS managers must first determine what information is needed. Then they must gather the data and apply the technology to convert data into information. They must also control the flow of information so that it goes only to those people who need it.[1]

Supplied information varies according to such factors as the functional areas in which people work (say, accounting or marketing) and their management levels. At all levels, informational quality depends on an organization's technological resources and on the people who manage them. In the following section, we discuss the evolution of information-processing technology and then describe the information requirements of today's organization.

information system (IS)
System for transforming raw data into information that can be used in decision making

data
Raw facts and figures

information
Meaningful, useful interpretation of data

NEW BUSINESS TECHNOLOGIES IN THE INFORMATION AGE

Employees at every level—from operational specialists to top executives—use the IS to improve performance. Information systems aid in scheduling trips, evaluating employees, and formulating strategy. The widening role of IS is due to rapid developments in electronic technologies that allow faster and broader communications and information flows. But as we shall see, the networked enterprise is more than a firm equipped with the latest technology. Technology has inspired new organizational designs, innovative relationships with other organizations, and new management processes for improved competitiveness.

The Expanding Scope of Information Systems

The relationship between the IS and the organization is among the fastest-changing aspects of business. At one time, IS applications were narrow in scope and technically oriented—processing payroll data, simulating engineering designs, compiling advertising expenditures. But as you can see in Figure 12.1, managers soon began using IS not merely to solve technical problems but also to analyze management problems, especially for control purposes—applying quality standards to production, comparing costs against budgets, and keeping records on absences and turnover.

FIGURE 12.1

Evolution of IS Scope

Scope of IS Application

Isolated technical problems — Low-level management problems — Higher-level management questions — Organizationwide planning and implementation

1950s–1960s   1960s–1970s   1970s–1980s   1990s–2000s

Today, information systems are also crucial in planning. Managers routinely use the IS to decide on products and markets for the next 5 to 10 years. The same database that helps marketing analyze demographics is used for financial planning, materials handling, and electronic funds transfers with suppliers and customers.

Another basic change is greater interdependence between a company's strategy and its IS. In addition to choosing a strategy—say, to be the lowest-cost, most flexible, or highest-quality provider—the firm needs an IS that can support that strategy. Consider a strategy that calls for the rapid receipt of customer orders and fast order fulfillment. Unless IS components are specifically designed to handle these tasks, the best-laid plans are probably doomed to failure.

Electronic Business and Communication Technologies

The need for better communications and information systems is growing as competition intensifies and as companies go global and expand into e-business. Firms like Ralston Purina Co. *(www.ralston.com)* need instantaneous communications among managers in countries where they either sell products or buy raw materials, including China, Colombia, Canada, and Brazil. Such needs are being met by new electronic information technologies and advanced data communication networks.

electronic information technologies (EIT)
Information-systems applications, based on telecommunications technologies, that use networks of appliances or devices to communicate information by electronic means

Electronic Information Technologies Electronic information technologies **(EIT)** are IS applications based on telecommunications technologies. EITs use networks of devices (such as computers and satellites) to communicate information by electronic means. They enhance performance and productivity by serving two functions:

1 By providing coordination and communication within the firm
2 By speeding up transactions with other firms

Following are two of the most widely used innovations in digital business systems: *electronic conferencing* and *groupware*.

electronic conferencing
Computer-based system that allows people to communicate simultaneously from different locations via software or telephone

Electronic Conferencing Electronic conferencing allows groups of people to communicate simultaneously from various locations via e-mail or phone. One form, called *dataconferencing,* allows people in remote locations to work simultaneously on one document: Working as a team, they can revise a marketing plan or draft a press release. *Videoconferencing* allows participants to see one another on video screens while the conference is in progress. Teleconferencing is attractive because it eliminates travel and thus saves money.[2]

"Ah, here is your fax now."

Groupware Collaborative work is made easier by **groupware**—software that connects group members for e-mail distribution, electronic meetings, message storing, appointments and schedules, and group writing. Linked by groupware, people can collaborate from their own desktop PCs even if they're remotely located. It is especially useful when people work together regularly and rely heavily on information sharing. Groupware products include Lotus Development Corp.'s Lotus Notes *(www.lotus.com/home.nsf/welcome/lotusnotes)* and Netscape Communicator *(http://home.netscape.com/communicator/v4.5/index.html).*

groupware
Software that connects members of a group for shared e-mail distribution, electronic meetings, appointments, and group writing

Data Communication Networks Data communication networks carry streams of digital data (electronic documents and other forms of video and sound) back and forth over telecommunication systems. The most prominent network, the Internet, and its companion system, the World Wide Web, have emerged as powerful communication technologies. Let's look a little more closely at each of these networks.

data communication network
Global network (such as the Internet) that permits users to send electronic messages and information quickly and economically

The Internet The largest public data communications network, the **Internet** (or "the Net") is a gigantic system of networks that both serves millions of computers with information on business, science, and government and provides communication flows among more than 170,000 separate networks around the world.[3] Originally commissioned by the Pentagon *(www.defenselink.mil)* as a wartime communication tool, the Internet allows personal computers in virtually any location to be linked. Because it can transmit information fast and at lower cost than long-distance phone service and postal delivery, the Net is also the most important e-mail system in the world. For thousands of businesses, it has joined—and is even replacing—the telephone, fax machine, and express mail as a communications tool.

Internet
Global data communication network serving millions of computers with information on a wide array of topics and providing communication flows among certain private networks

Individuals can't connect directly to the Internet, but for small monthly usage fees, they can subscribe to the Net via an **Internet service provider (ISP)**, such as Prodigy *(www.prodigy.com)*, America Online, or Earthlink *(www.earthlink.com)*. An ISP is a commercial firm that maintains a permanent connection to the Net and sells temporary connections to subscribers.

Internet service provider (ISP)
Commercial firm that maintains a permanent connection to the Net and sells temporary connections to subscribers

A sluggish economy (and a lingering post-9/11 reluctance to fly) is hampering business travel. More companies are thus turning to video-conferencing as a means of holding meetings among people located in distant places. In the weeks following September 11, the law firm of Mintz, Levin, Cohen, Feris, Glovsky & Popeo managed to "virtually" link its Boston, Washington, and New York offices through teleconferencing. The firm's human resource director notes that the technology allows her to analyze participants' body language—something she couldn't do over the telephone or through e-mail.

By 2002, more than 700 million Net users were active in more than 180 countries. In North America, more than 95 million users over the age of 16 were on the Net every day. Its power to change the way business is conducted has been amply demonstrated in both large and small firms. Consider how it's changing just one industry—financial markets. In 2003, 25 million U.S. households traded stocks and 32 million U.S. households banked online with many online brokerages appearing to meet the growing demand.[4]

World Wide Web
Subsystem of computers providing access to the Internet and offering multimedia and linking capabilities

The World Wide Web Thanks to the subsystem of computers known as the **World Wide Web** (WWW or "the Web"), the Internet allows users around the world to communicate electronically with little effort. The Web is a system with universally accepted standards for storing, retrieving, formatting, and displaying information.[5] It provides the common language that allows us to surf the Net and makes it available to a general audience, not merely to technical users such as computer programmers. To access a Web site, the user specifies the *Uniform Resource Locator (URL)* that points to the unique Web address of the resource. Thus, American Airlines' URL is *www.aa.com*—a designation that specifies the storage location of American's Web pages.

Web server
Dedicated workstation customized for managing, maintaining, and supporting Web sites

SERVERS AND BROWSERS Each Web site opens with a *home page*—a screen display that introduces the visitor and may include graphics, sound, and visual enhancements. Additional *pages* present the sponsor's products and explain how to get help in using the site. They often furnish URLs for related Web sites that the user can link into by simply pointing and clicking. The person who is responsible for maintaining an organization's Web site is usually called a *Webmaster.* Large sites use dedicated workstations—large computers—known as **Web servers**, which are customized for managing and supporting such sites.

ENTREPRENEURSHIP and *New Ventures*

When to Put Your Incubator on Life Support

Is Bill Gross a new-venture visionary or just a scoundrel? Once touted as an Internet superstar, Gross is often credited with popularizing the concept of the *incubator* when, in 1996, he founded Idealab *(www.idealab.com)*, a Pasadena-based firm for generating new companies from scratch. Gross's master plan for mass-producing start-ups sounds simple enough: find good ideas, turn them into Internet companies, recruit executives to run them, and raise start-up capital. In return for these services, Idealab takes an ownership stake in the new firms.

As CEO, Gross himself is a serial entrepreneur whose endless stream of start-up ideas forms the basis of Idealab's current portfolio, which includes more than 15 companies, including CarsDirect.com, Cooking.com, Overature, Evolution Robotics, and a host of legacy companies—CitySearch, eToys, GoTo.com, HomesDirect, Tickets.com, and PETsMART.com—that are no longer part of the Idealab network.

Gross, testifies business journalist Joseph Nocera, is "the most amazing entrepreneur I've met in 20 years covering business." Unfortunately, adds Nocera, he's also "a stupendously poor manager." Nocera isn't alone in having observed Gross's unorthodox, sometimes nonsensical business style: According to some, he always seems to have more ideas than he knows what to do with. Others say that he knows far more about starting a business than running one. Still others find him a captivating talker who has a habit of shifting from topic to topic but who is willing to try things—sometimes seemingly loony ideas—that others wouldn't dream of touching.

In any case, Gross emerged as a hero in the heyday of the Internet, and his impact on the incubator industry has been profound: Since 1996, hosts of wannabe imitators have converged on Pasedena to observe Idealab in operation and copy its business model. Between 1996 and 2001, Gross's success inspired dozens of new incubator firms, including eCompanies, CMGI Inc., Internet Capital Group, and DivineInterVentures.

At the height of the tech boom, investors were enthusiastic, too: Idealab attracted $35 million in 1996, $70 million in 1997, $170 million in 1999, and a whopping $1 billion more in 2000. Dell Computer ventured $100 million, as did T. Rowe Price and the Japanese wireless company Hikari Tsushin. Five ex-Microsoft executives contributed $2.5 to $5 million each, while Travelers Insurance invested $15 million. When Hollywood talent agents, excited about Idealab's entertainment site (Z.com), insisted that they be allowed to invest, the William Morris Agency's $1.9 million was quickly overshadowed by United Talent Agency's $2.5 million. Other Hollywood notables pitched in various sums ranging from $100,000 to $4.2 million each.

But then the e-business bubble burst and many of Idealab's start-ups were on the fast track to failure. In early 2002, Gross's reputation took another hit when he was charged with squandering $800 million of investors' money in just eight months. Angry investors say he used their money to buy controlling interest in losing propositions such as cosmetics e-tailer Eve.com (not to mention Z.com itself).

Some accuse Gross and Idealab President Marcia Goodstein with mismanagement of the company's funds. So bad are so many of Idealab's current companies that investors are pressuring Gross to liquidate Idealab; most are willing to accept 35 cents on the dollar. (Gross has made a counteroffer of 10 cents on the dollar.) A group that includes Dell Computer and T. Rowe Price has filed suit to liquidate and distribute the $500 million remaining in Idealab's account. The litigation is still pending. Responds Teresa Bridwell, Idealab vice president of corporate communications: "Our belief is that there is much unrealized value in Idealab today that we would like to mature and return [funds] to all investors." Bridwell adds that the Internet market went sour for everyone and that Idealab isn't the only business incubator on life support. New ventures, she suggests, are risky, and perhaps the faint of heart should consider investments other than Internet incubators.

With hundreds of thousands of new Web pages appearing each day, cyberspace now posts billions of pages of information. Sorting through this maze would be impossible without a Web **browser**—the software that permits users to access information on the Web. A browser runs on the user's PC and supports the graphics and linking capabilities needed to navigate the Web. Netscape Navigator *(home.netscape.com/browsers/index.html)* once enjoyed an 80-percent market share but is now being challenged by other browsers, including its own Netscape Communicator and Microsoft's Internet Explorer *(www.microsoft.com/windows/ie)*.

browser
Software supporting the graphics and linking capabilities necessary to navigate the World Wide Web

search engine
Tool that searches Web pages containing the user's search terms and then displays pages that match

DIRECTORIES AND SEARCH ENGINES Browsers offer additional tools—Web site directories and search engines—for navigating on the Web. Among the most successful cyberspace enterprises are companies such as Yahoo! *(www.yahoo.com)* that maintain free-to-use *directories* of Web content. When Yahoo! is notified about new Web sites, it classifies them in its directory. Users enter one or two keywords (for example, "compact disk"), and the directory retrieves a list of sites with titles containing those words.

In contrast, a **search engine** scans millions of Web pages without preclassifying them into a directory. It merely searches for pages containing the same words as the user's search terms, displaying addresses for those that come closest to matching, then the next closest, and so on. A search engine, such as AltaVista *(www.altavista.com)* or Lycos *(www.lycos.com)*, may respond to more than 10 million inquiries a day. Not surprisingly, both directories and search engines are packed with paid ads.[6]

intranet
Private network of internal Web sites and other sources of information available to a company's employees

Intranets Many companies have extended Net technology internally by maintaining internal Web sites linked throughout the firm.[7] These private networks, or **intranets**, are accessible only to employees through electronic **firewalls**—hardware and software security systems inaccessible to outsiders.[8] The Ford Motor Co. *(www.ford.com)* intranet connects 120,000 workstations in Asia, Europe, and the United States to thousands of Ford Web sites containing private information on Ford activities in production, engineering, distribution, and marketing. Sharing information has reduced the lead time for getting models into production from 36 to 24 months, and it has shortened customer delivery times. Ford expects to save billions in inventory and fixed costs.[9]

firewall
Software and hardware system that prevents outsiders from accessing a company's internal network

extranet
Internet allowing outsiders access to a firm's internal information system

Extranets Extranets allow outsiders limited access to a firm's internal information system. The most common application allows buyers to enter a system to see which products are available for sale and delivery, thus providing convenient product-availability information. Industrial suppliers are often linked into customers' intranets so that they can see planned production schedules and prepare supplies for customers' upcoming operations.

SELF-CHECK QUESTIONS 1–3

You should now be able to answer Self-Check Questions 1–3.*

1 **Multiple Choice** All of the following are true regarding *electronic information technologies* **except** [select one]: **(a)** They are based on telecommunications technologies. **(b)** They provide coordination within the firm. **(c)** They rely on face-to-face interaction among users. **(d)** They speed up transactions with other firms.

2 **Multiple Choice** All of the following are **true** of the *World Wide Web* **except** [select one]: **(a)** It uses Uniform Resource Locators (URLs) to identify unique Web addresses. **(b)** It has uniform standards for formatting and displaying information. **(c)** It maintains orderly flows by prohibiting Web sites from listing URLs for related sites. **(d)** Its accessibility is facilitated by Web browsers.

3 **True/False** A *search engine,* such as AltaVista or Lycos, will search millions of Web pages and then classify them into free-to-use directories of Web content.

*****Answers to Self-Check Questions 1–3 can be found on p. 509.**

Say WHAT YOU MEAN

"ARE YOU E-MAILING *ME*?"

Just because we have international communication tools such as the Internet, we can't simply ignore local culture when we're communicating with someone in another country. It's always a good idea to remember who's on the other end of the T-3 line.

Americans are notoriously informal when talking to one another. The same goes for our e-mail communications, and the Internet enables us to spread the message of informality all over the world. Unfortunately, however, being too informal in your e-mail can send the wrong message. In some places, you'll come across as too familiar (or even too aggressive). In some cultures, including the United Kingdom, Germany, and Japan, people like a little formality, even in their e-mail.

For example, be careful about using first names or a casual tone of voice (yes, you do have a tone of voice when you're writing). Pay attention to your grammar: Sloppy language is often a turn-off, and many people automatically regard it as a sign of poor education. Try to organize your message in a logical way. In some cultures, an Internet message is perceived as a letter with a formal structure.

Don't always expect people to reply immediately. Different cultures have different concepts of time, and a person's concept of time plays a big part in his or her sense of when to respond to messages. Demanding an immediate response in Brazil or Mexico is a good way to send your message to the bottom of the electronic pile. Finally, remember that a lot of people are bombarded with e-mail and many of them regard dealing with a constant barrage of communications as a strain on their time. Communicate electronically only when you have something that needs to be said sooner rather than later or when you need a question answered.

As usual, the bottom line in communications is knowing the culture in which your message is going to be received. Find out something about the culture of the person you're dealing with before you engage him or her in electronic conversation.

New Options for Organizational Design: The Networked Enterprise

The rapid growth of information technologies has changed the very structure of business organizations. We begin this section by discussing changes wrought by technology in the workforces and structures of many organizations. We then examine ways that electronic networks contribute to greater flexibility in dealing with customers. After discussing the growing importance of workplace collaboration, we look at ways in which information networks help to free the workplace from the constraints of physical location. Finally, we describe new management processes inspired by the availability of electronic networks.

Leaner Organizations Information networks are leading to leaner companies with fewer employees and simpler structures. Because a networked firm can maintain information links among both employees and customers, more work can be accomplished with fewer people. Bank customers can dial into a 24-hour information system and find out their current balances from a digital voice. Assembly workers at IBM once got instructions from supervisors or special staff. Now these instructions are delivered to workstations electronically.

Reducing middle-management spots and eliminating layers of organizational structure are possible because information networks provide direct communications between the top managers and lower-level workers. The operating managers who once forwarded policies, procedures, or instructions to lower-level employees are being replaced by information networks.

More Flexible Operations Electronic networks let businesses offer customers greater variety and faster delivery cycles. Products such as cellular phones, PCs, and audio systems can be custom-ordered, with choices of features and next-day delivery. The principle is called **mass-customization**: Although companies produce in large volumes, each unit features the unique options preferred by the customer.[10] As you can see in Figure 12.2, flexible production and fast delivery depend on an integrated network to coordinate all the transactions and processes needed to make quick adjustments in production. The ability to organize and store massive volumes of information is crucial, as are the electronic links among customers, manufacturers, suppliers, and shippers.

mass-customization
Flexible production process that generates customized products in high volumes at low cost

Increased Collaboration Collaboration, both among internal units and with outside firms, is on the rise because networked systems make it cheaper and easier to contact everyone. Aided by intranets, companies are learning that complex problems can be better solved through collaboration, either by means of formal teams or spontaneous interaction. Decisions once made by individuals are now shared among people and departments. The design of new products, for example, was once an engineering responsibility. Now it can be shared because so much information is available from and accessible to people in different functional areas: Marketing, finance, production, engineering, and purchasing can share stores of information and determine the best design.[11]

FIGURE 12.2

Networking for
Mass-Customization

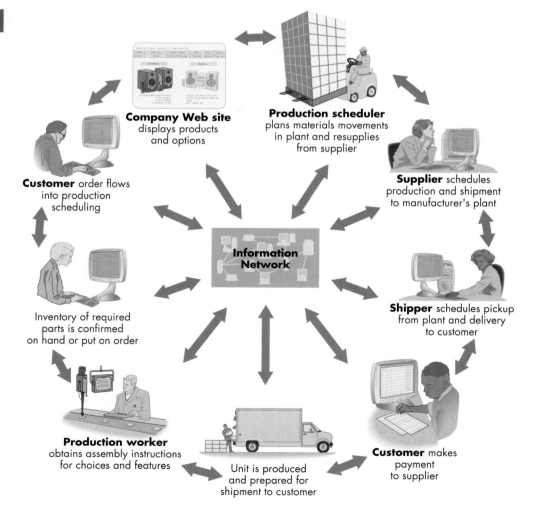

Company Web site displays products and options

Production scheduler plans materials movements in plant and resupplies from supplier

Customer order flows into production scheduling

Supplier schedules production and shipment to manufacturer's plant

Information Network

Inventory of required parts is confirmed on hand or put on order

Shipper schedules pickup from plant and delivery to customer

Production worker obtains assembly instructions for choices and features

Unit is produced and prepared for shipment to customer

Customer makes payment to supplier

Networking and the Virtual Company Networked systems can also improve collaboration between organizations through the so-called *virtual company.* We noted in Chapter 6 that this can be a temporary team assembled by a single organization, but a virtual company can also be created by several allied firms. Each contributes different skills and resources that collectively result in a competitive business that wouldn't be feasible for any one of them working alone. A company with marketing and promotional skills, for example, may team up with firms with expertise in warehousing and distribution, engineering, and production. Networking lets collaborators exchange ideas, plan strategy, share customer information, and otherwise coordinate efforts, even if their respective facilities are far apart.

Greater Independence of Company and Workplace

Geographic separation of the workplace from headquarters is now more common. Employees no longer work only at the office or the factory, nor are all of a company's operations performed at one place. A sales manager for an ad agency may visit the New York office twice a month, preferring instead to use the firm's electronic network from home in Florida.

Likewise, company activities may be geographically scattered but highly coordinated through a networked system. Many e-businesses conduct no activities at one centralized location. When you order furniture from an Internet storefront—say, a chair, a sofa, a table, and two lamps—the chair may come from a warehouse in Philadelphia and the lamps from a manufacturer in California; the sofa and table may be direct-shipped from different mills in North Carolina. Every activity begins instantaneously with the customer's order and is coordinated through the network just as if the whole order were being processed at one place.

Improved Management Processes

Networked systems have changed the nature of the management process. The activities and methods of today's manager differ significantly from those that were common just a few years ago. At one time, upper-level managers didn't concern themselves with all of the detailed information filtering upward in the workplace. Why? Because it was expensive to gather, it was slow in coming, and it quickly became out of date. Workplace management was delegated to middle and first-line managers.

With networked systems, however, instantaneous information is accessible and useful. Consequently, more upper managers use it routinely for planning, leading, directing, and controlling operations. Today, a top manager can find out the current status of any customer order, inspect productivity statistics for each workstation, and analyze the delivery performance of any vehicle. More important, managers can better coordinate companywide performance. They can identify departments that are working well together and those that are creating bottlenecks.

Enterprise Resource Planning One type of networked system is **enterprise resource planning (ERP)**—a large information system for integrating the activities of all of a company's units.[12] It is supported by one large database through which everyone shares the same information when any transaction occurs. The biggest supplier of commercial ERP packages is Germany's SAP AG *(www.sap.com)*, followed by Oracle *(www.oracle.com)*. Hershey Foods *(www.hersheys.com)* uses the SAP system. It identifies the status of any order and traces its progress from order entry through customer delivery and receipt of payment. Progress and delays at intermediate stages—materials ordering, inventory availability, production scheduling, packaging, warehousing, distribution—can be checked continuously to determine which operations should be more closely coordinated with others to improve overall performance.

enterprise resource planning (ERP)
Large information system for integrating all the activities of a company's business units

■ TYPES OF INFORMATION SYSTEMS

In a sense, the term *information system* may be a misnomer. It suggests that there is one system when, in fact, employees have many different responsibilities and decision-making needs. One IS can't handle such a range of requirements. In reality, the information system is a complex of several information systems that share information while serving different levels of the organization, different departments, or different operations.

User Groups and System Requirements

knowledge worker
Employee who uses information and knowledge as raw materials and who relies on information technology to design new products or business systems

Four user groups are identified in Figure 12.3, which also indicates the kinds of systems best suited to each user level. We include **knowledge workers**—employees for whom information and knowledge are the raw materials of their work. They are specialists, usually professionally trained and certified—engineers, scientists, information technology specialists—who rely on information technology to design new products or create new processes.

Managers at Different Levels Because they work on different kinds of problems, top managers, middle managers, knowledge workers, and first-line managers have different information needs. First-line (or operational) managers need information to oversee the day-to-day details of departments or projects. Knowledge workers need information in order to conduct technical projects. Middle managers need summaries and analyses for setting intermediate and long-range goals for activities under

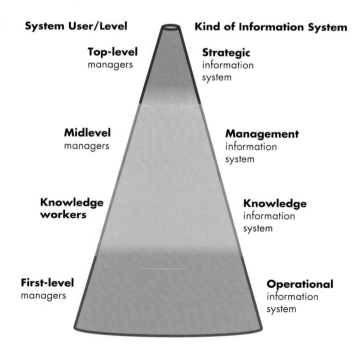

FIGURE 12.3

Matching Information Users and Systems

System User/Level	Kind of Information System
Top-level managers	**Strategic** information system
Midlevel managers	**Management** information system
Knowledge workers	**Knowledge** information system
First-level managers	**Operational** information system

their supervision. Top management analyzes trends in the business environment and overall company performance in order to make long-range plans.

Consider the information needs for a flooring manufacturer. Sales managers (first-level managers) supervise salespeople and handle customer service and delivery problems. They need current information on the sales and delivery of products: lists of incoming customer orders and daily delivery schedules. Regional managers (middle managers) set sales quotas for sales managers and prepare budgets. They need information on monthly sales by product and region. To develop new materials, knowledge workers need information on the chemical properties of adhesives. Top managers need both external and internal information. Internally, they compare current sales data, summarized by product and geographic region, to data from previous years. Equally important is external information on consumer trends and economic forecasts.

Functional Areas and Business Processes Each business *function*—marketing, human resources, accounting, production, finance—has its own information needs. In addition, in businesses organized according to business processes, process groups need special information. Each user group and department are represented by an IS. Now add to these systems the four systems needed by the four levels of users that we just discussed: The total number of systems and applications increases significantly.

Each cell on the left side of Figure 12.4 represents a potential IS associated with a given functional group. Top-level finance managers, for instance, plan long-range spending for facilities and equipment, and they determine sources of capital. The arrows on the right side of Figure 12.4 show that a business-process group will include users, both managers and employees, drawn from all organizational levels. The supply chain management group, for instance, may need to cut the number of suppliers. The IS supporting this project would contain information cutting across

FIGURE 12.4

Matching User Levels with Functional Areas and Business Processes

	Organization Function			Business Process			
	Marketing	**Finance**	**Production**	**Strategic planning**	**Product development**	**Order fulfillment**	**Supply chain management**
Top-level managers				↑	↑	↑	↑
Midlevel managers							
Knowledge workers							
First-level managers				↓	↓	↓	↓

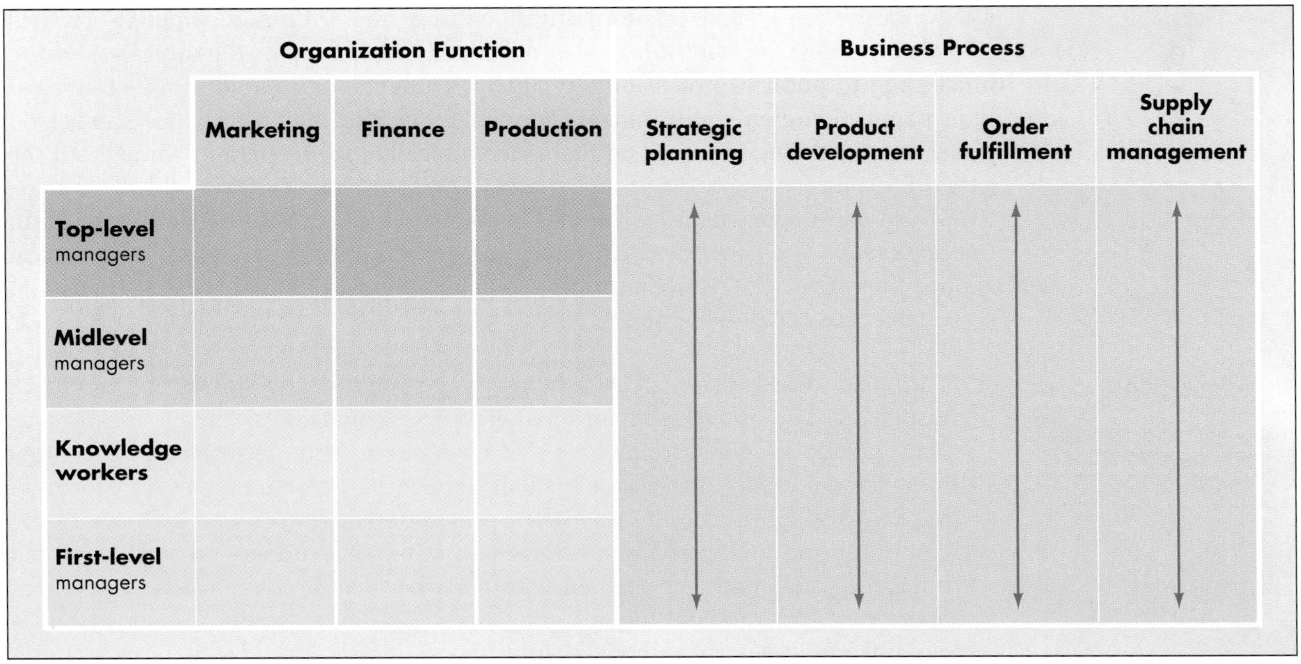

different functions and management levels. The group will need information on and expertise in marketing, warehousing and distribution, production, communications technology, purchasing, and finance. It will also need input on operational, technical, and managerial issues—say, technical requirements for new suppliers and future financial requirements.

Systems for Knowledge Workers and Office Applications

Many systems and office applications support the activities of both knowledge workers and clerical workers. They aid in data processing and other activities, including the creation of communications documents. Like other departments, the IS department includes both *knowledge workers* and *data workers.*

IS Knowledge Workers IS knowledge workers include both systems analysts and application or systems programmers:

- *Systems analysts* deal with the entire computer system. They learn users' requirements and design systems that meet them, deciding on types and sizes of computers and how to set up links to form a network.
- *Programmers* write the software instructions that tell computers what to do. Application programmers, for example, write instructions to address particular problems. Systems programmers ensure that a system can handle the requests made by application programs.

system operations personnel
Information-systems employees who run a company's computer equipment

Operations Personnel (Data Workers) **System operations personnel** run the company's computer equipment. They make sure that the right programs are run in the correct sequence and monitor equipment to see that it's operating properly. Many organizations also have personnel to enter data for processing in the system.

Knowledge-Level and Office Systems

New support systems—word processing, desktop publishing, computer-aided design, simulation modeling—have increased the productivity of both office and knowledge workers. We will discuss *word processing*—systems for formatting, editing, and storing documents—later in this chapter. *Desktop publishing,* also discussed later, combines graphics and word processing to publish professional-quality documents. *Document imaging systems* scan paper documents and images, convert them into digital form for storage on disks, retrieve them, and transmit them electronically to workstations throughout the network.

World-class firms such as Harley-Davidson *(www.harley-davidson.com)*, John Deere *(www.deere.com)*, and GE *(www.ge.com)* rely on knowledge-level system applications that help reduce product-design times and production-cycle times and make faster customer deliveries.[13]

computer-aided design (CAD)
Computer-based electronic technology that assists in designing products by simulating a real product and displaying it in three-dimensional graphics

- **Computer-aided design (CAD)** helps design products by simulating them and displaying them in three-dimensional graphics. Immersion's MicroScribe-3D software *(www.immersion.com)* uses a penlike tool to scan the surface of any three-dimensional object, such as a football helmet, and electronically transforms it into a 3D graphic. The designer then tries different shapes and surfaces in the computer and analyzes them on a video monitor. Products ranging from cell phones to auto parts are created with CAD because it creates faster designs at lower cost than manual modeling methods. The older method—making hand-crafted prototypes (trial models) from wood, plastic, or clay—is replaced with *rapid prototyping (RP):* The CAD system electronically transfers instructions to a computer-controlled machine that builds the prototype.

- **Computer-aided manufacturing (CAM)** is used to design facilities, layouts, and equipment for better product flows. *Computer operations control* refers to any system for managing day-to-day production activities. Hospitals use computer-based scheduling to prepare patients' meals, just as manufacturers do for making cars, clocks, and paper products.

computer-aided manufacturing (CAM)
Computer system used to design and control equipment needed in the manufacturing process

Management Information Systems

Management information systems (MIS) support managers by providing daily reports, schedules, plans, and budgets that can then be used for making decisions. Each manager's information activities vary according to his or her functional area (accounting or marketing and so forth) and management level. Whereas midlevel managers focus on internal activities and information, higher-level managers are also engaged in external activities. Middle managers, the largest MIS user group, need information to plan such activities as personnel training, materials movements, and cash flows. They also need to know the status of the jobs and projects assigned to their departments. What stage is a job at now? When will it be finished? Is there an opening so we can start the next job? Many management information systems—cash flow, sales, production scheduling, shipping—are indispensable for helping managers find answers to such questions.[14]

management information system (MIS)
System used for transforming data into information for use in decision making

Decision Support Systems

Middle- and top-level managers get assistance from **decision support systems (DSS)**—interactive systems that find and present information needed for the decision-making process. Whereas some DSSs handle specific problems, others are general purpose, allowing managers to analyze different types of problems. A firm faced with decisions on plant capacity may have a *capacity DSS.* The manager inputs data on anticipated sales, working capital, and customer-delivery requirements. Then built-in transaction processors manipulate the data and make recommendations on the best levels of plant capacity for each future time period.

decision support system (DSS)
Interactive computer-based system that locates and presents information needed to support decision making

Even as late as the 1980s, computing hadn't had much impact on industrial automation, largely because there were no good software programs for computer operated manufacturing. Working in the 1970s to help set up Unix operating systems for various manufacturers, Myron Zimmerman recognized a need, and in 1980, he founded VenturCom (*www.plantautomation.com/ storefronts/venturcominc.html*), which develops programs for controlling industrial production equipment like this metal-cutting machine at Hillside Industries in Middletown, Connecticut.

executive support system (ESS)
Quick-reference information-system application designed specially for instant access by upper-level managers

Executive Support Systems An **executive support system (ESS)** is an easy-access IS application specially designed for upper-level managers. ESSs are designed to assist with executive-level problems ranging from "What lines of business should we be in five years from now?" to "Based on forecasted developments in electronic technologies, to what extent should our firm be globalized in five years? In 10 years?" The ESS uses a wide range of both internal and external sources, such as industry reports, global economic forecasts, and reports on competitors.

artificial intelligence (AI)
Computer-system application that imitates human behavior by performing physical tasks, using thought processes, sensing, and learning

Artificial Intelligence and Expert Systems **Artificial intelligence (AI)** is the construction of computer systems to imitate human behavior—in other words, systems that perform physical tasks, use thought processes, and learn. In developing AI systems, business specialists, modelers, and information-technology experts try to design computer-based systems capable of reasoning so that computers, instead of people, can perform certain activities. A credit-evaluation system may decide which loan applicants are creditworthy and which are too risky, and it may then compose acceptance and rejection letters accordingly.[15]

robotics
Combination of computers and industrial robots for use in manufacturing operations

Robotics—the combination of computers with industrial robots—is a category of AI. With certain reasoning capabilities, robots can "learn" repetitive tasks such as painting, assembling components, and inserting screws. They also avoid repeating mistakes by "remembering" the causes of past mistakes and, when those causes reappear, adjusting or stopping until adjustments are made.

expert system
Form of artificial intelligence that attempts to imitate the behavior of human experts in a particular field

Expert Systems A special form of AI, the **expert system**, is designed to imitate the thought processes of human experts in a particular field. Expert systems incorporate the rules that an expert applies to specific types of problems, such as a doctor's judgments in diagnosing illness. In effect, they endow everyday users with instant expertise.

SELF-CHECK QUESTIONS 4–6

You should now be able to answer Self-Check Questions 4–6.*

4 **Multiple Choice** Suppose you are a *knowledge worker* in a major industrial firm. Which of the following types of information do you most likely need from an IS? [select one]: **(a)** data on broad economic trends and overall company performance information for long-range planning; **(b)** summaries and analyses for setting intermediate-range goals for a group of departments; **(c)** special information for conducting technical projects on specific problems; **(d)** daily production schedules and work-shift assignments.

5 **True/False** The development of next year's business plan is an example of an activity that can be conducted by a *computer-aided design (CAD) system.*

6 **Multiple Choice** The *networked enterprise*—one that adopts information technologies—can be expected to have all of the following characteristics except [select one]: **(a)** shrinkage of layers in organizational structure; **(b)** more departments and firms participating in designing products; **(c)** more employees working at home rather than at the office, **(d)** upper-level managers' avoidance of detailed information about specific operations; **(e)** increased likelihood of participating with other firms in a virtual company.

Answers to Self-Check Questions 4–6 can be found on p. 509.

■ DATABASES AND SOFTWARE FOR THE INFORMATION SYSTEM

We know that an IS is a group of interconnected devices that exchange information from different locations. We also know that *networking*—connecting these devices—allows decentralized computers to exchange data quickly and easily. A key component of the IS is its **computer network**—all the computer and information technology devices that, working together, drive the flow of digital information through the system. This includes all the **hardware**—the physical components such as keyboards, video monitors, scanners, and printers—of a computer system.

computer network
All the computer and information technology devices that, by working together, drive the flow of digital information throughout a system

Although the hardware is essential, it is only one part of the information system. Data must be organized so they are conveniently accessible to users throughout the network. Likewise, programs (software) must be available to process the data. In this section we will describe the kinds of databases and software that enable the networked information system to function effectively. We will reserve our discussion of telecommunications for the next section.

hardware
Physical components of a computer system

Databases and Program Software

As we have noted, all computer processing is the processing of data. This processing is carried out by **software**—program instructions that tell the system to perform specified functions. In this section we begin by briefly describing the nature of computer data and databases. We then discuss IS software, including a few of the specialized application programs designed for business use.

software
Programs that instruct a computer in what to do

Data and Databases Computers convert data into information by organizing them in some meaningful manner. Within the system, chunks of data—numbers, words, and sentences—are stored in a series of related collections called *fields, records,* and *files.* Together, data files constitute a **database**—a central, organized collection of related data.

database
Centralized, organized collection of related data

System Programs One type of software, called **system programs**, tells the computer what resources to use and how. For example, an *operating* system program tells the computer how and when to transfer data from secondary to primary storage and return information to the user.

system program
Software that tells the computer what resources to use and how to use them

Application Programs Most computer users do not write programs but rather use **application programs**: software packages written by others. Each different type of application (such as financial analysis, word processing, or Web browsing) uses a program that meets that need. Programs are available for a huge variety of business-related tasks. Some address such common, long-standing needs as accounting and inventory control, whereas others have been developed for an endless variety of specialized needs. Most business programs fall into one of four categories—*word processing, spreadsheets, database management,* and *graphics.* Of all PC software applications, 70 percent are designed for the first three types of programs.

application program
Software (such as Word for Windows) that processes data according to a user's special needs

Word Processing Popular **word-processing programs**, such as Microsoft Word for Windows *(www.microsoft.com/windows)* and Lotus's Word Pro *(www.lotus.com/home/nsf/welcome/smartsuite),* allow computer users to store, edit, display, and print documents. Sentences and paragraphs can be added or

word-processing program
Applications program that allows computers to store, edit, and print letters and numbers for documents created by users

deleted without retyping or restructuring an entire document, and mistakes are easily corrected.

electronic spreadsheet
Applications program with a row-and-column format that allows users to store, manipulate, and compare numeric data

Spreadsheets **Electronic spreadsheets** spread data across and down the page in rows and columns. Users enter data, including formulas, at row and column intersections, and the computer automatically performs the necessary calculations. Payroll records, sales projections, and a host of other financial reports can be prepared in this manner.

Spreadsheets are good planning tools because they let managers see how making a change in one item affects related items. For example, you can insert operating-cost percentages, tax rates, or sales revenues into the spreadsheet. The computer will automatically recalculate all the other figures and determine net profit. Popular spreadsheet packages include Lotus 1-2-3, Quattro Pro *(www.corel/products/wordperfect/cqp)*, and Microsoft Excel for Windows.

database management program
Applications program for creating, storing, searching, and manipulating an organized collection of data

Database Management Another popular type of personal-productivity software is a **database management program**. Such programs as Microsoft Access for Windows and Borland's InterBase *(www.borland.com)* are popular for desktop applications. Oracle9i *(www.oracle.com)* is a popular database for Internet computing. These systems can create, store, sort, and search through data and integrate a single piece into several different files.

computer graphics program
Applications program that converts numeric and character data into pictorial information such as graphs and charts

Graphics **Computer graphics programs** convert numeric and character data into pictorial information, such as charts and graphs. They make computerized information easier to use and understand in two ways. First, graphs and charts summarize data and allow managers to detect problems, opportunities, and relationships more easily. Second, graphics contribute to clearer and more persuasive reports and presentations.

presentation graphics software
Applications that enable users to create visual presentations that can include animation and sound

Presentation graphics software, such as CorelDRAW, Microsoft PowerPoint for Windows, and Microsoft Visio 2002, lets users assemble graphics for visual displays, slides, video, and even sound splices for professional presentations. Varying color and size, using pictures and charts with three-dimensional effects, and shading with animation and sound make for far more visually interesting presentations.

Computer graphics capabilities go beyond data presentation. They also include stand-alone programs for artists, designers, and special effects engineers. Everything from simple drawings to motion picture special effects are now created by computer graphics software. The sinking ship in *Titanic,* the aliens in *Men in Black II,* and the dog in *Scooby-Doo* were all created with computer graphics.

desktop publishing
Process of combining word-processing and graphics capability to produce virtually typeset-quality text from personal computers

Some software allows firms to publish sales brochures, in-house magazines, and annual reports. The latest **desktop publishing** packages for the PC combine word processing and graphics to produce typeset-quality text with stimulating visual effects. They also eliminate printing costs for reports and proposals. QuarkXPress *(www.quark.com)*, which can manipulate text, tables of numbers, graphics, and full-color photographs, is used by ad agencies such as J. Walter Thompson because its computer-generated designs offer greater control over color and format. Other packages include Microsoft Publisher and Adobe Systems PageMaker *(www.adobe.com/products/pagemaker/main.html)*.

graphical user interface (GUI)
Software that provides a visual display to help users select applications

Graphical User Interface An important software development is the **graphical user interface (GUI)**—the user-friendly visual display that helps users select from among the computer applications. The screen displays numerous **icons** (small images) representing such choices as word processing, graphics, fax, printing, CD, or

icon
Small image in a GUI that enables users to select applications or functions

Star Wars: Episode I: The Phantom Menace was recorded on traditional film. Then nearly all of the film's 2,200 separate shots were digitally scanned into a computer for editing. *Star Wars: Episode II: Attack of the Clones* was shot entirely with a digital videotape system developed in partnership by Sony *(www.sony.com)* and Panavision *(www.panavision.com)*. At director George Lucas's film effects company, Industrial Light and Magic *(www.ilm.com)*, videotaped images were transferred to the hard drives of special computers for editing and special effects. Newly developed laser printers then exposed the footage onto photographic paper.

games. The user tells the computer what to do by moving a pointing device (usually an arrow) around the screen to activate the desired icon. Simple printed instructions explain activated features.

■ TELECOMMUNICATIONS AND NETWORKS

Communications systems are constantly evolving, but certain basic elements are well established: computers, communications devices, and networking. The most powerful vehicle for using these elements to their full potential is the marriage of computers and communication technologies.

A *network* organizes telecommunications components into an effective system. When a company decides how to organize its equipment and facilities, it also determines how its information resources will be shared, controlled, and applied by network users. In this section, we will first discuss *multimedia communications technologies* and some of the devices found in today's systems. We will then describe different ways of organizing information resources into networks.

Multimedia Communication Systems

Today's IS includes not only computers but also **multimedia communication systems**—connected networks of communication appliances, such as faxes, televisions, sound equipment, cell phones, printers, and photocopiers, that may also be linked by satellite with other networks. The integration of these elements is changing the way we manage our businesses. A good example is the modern grocery store. The checkout scanner reads the bar code on the product you buy. Data are then transmitted to the store's inventory-control system, which updates the number of available units. If inventory falls below a given level, more product is ordered. Meanwhile, the correct price is added to your bill and appropriate checkout coupons

multimedia communication system
Connected network of communication appliances (such as faxes or TVs) that may be linked to other forms of mass media (such as print publications or TV programming)

are printed. Your debit card transfers funds, sales reports are generated for store management, and all the while, satellite transmissions are dispatching trucks loaded with replacement inventory.

Communication Devices Today's technology lets people conduct business across large distances and from places where communications were once unavailable. *Global positioning systems (GPSs),* for example, use satellite transmissions to track the geographic locations of targets, such as boats or even people. When you're linked to a GPS network, your firm can know your whereabouts at all times. *Personal digital assistants (PDAs)* are tiny handheld computers with wireless telecommunications capabilities. Many can access the Internet, even receiving and sending e-mail messages from the most primitive locations. *Paging systems* and *cellular telephones* connect us instantly with distant networks.

Communication Channels *Communication channels,* including wired and wireless transmission, are the media that make all these transmissions possible.[16] Most of us use communication channels when we use wired telephone systems, but today most telephone transmissions are data, not conversations. Fax data account for 90 percent of all telephone signals between the United States and Japan.

Meanwhile, microwave systems transmit wireless radio signals between transmission stations. Satellite communication has also gained popularity with the growth in demand for wireless transmission. Accessible through satellite networks built by McCaw *(www.mccaw.com),* Hughes *(www.hns.com),* Motorola *(www.gi.com),* AT&T *(www.attws.com),* and Loral *(www.loral.com),* the Net is available in remote areas where underground cable isn't feasible.

System Architecture

There are several ways to organize computer and network components. As we see in the next section, one way to classify networks is according to *geographic scope.*[17]

Local and Wide Area Networks Networked systems may be either local or wide area networks. Computers may be linked statewide or even nationwide through telephone lines, microwave, or satellite communications, as in a **wide area network (WAN)**. Firms can lease lines from communications vendors or maintain private WANs. Wal-Mart, for example, depends heavily on a private satellite network that links more than 2,000 retail stores to its Bentonville, Arkansas, headquarters.

wide area network (WAN)
Network of computers and workstations located far from one another and linked by telephone wires or by satellite

Limited internal networks may link all of a firm's nearby computers, as in a **local area network (LAN)**. Computers within a building, for example, can be linked by cabling (fiber-optic, coaxial, or twisted wire) or by wireless technology. Internally networked computers share processing duties, software, storage areas, and data. On cable TV's *Home Shopping Network (www.hsn.com),* hundreds of operators are united by a LAN for entering call-in orders. The arrangement requires only one computer system with one database and software system.

local area network (LAN)
Network of computers and workstations, usually within a company, that are linked together by cable

Wireless Networks Wireless technologies use airborne electronic signals for linking network appliances. In addition to mobile phones, wireless technology extends to laptops, handheld computers, and applications in cars (including Internet access and music players, map terminals, and game machines). Businesses benefit by avoiding webs of wires crisscrossing facilities. Ford, for example, uses an innovative industrial information system—WhereNet—for tracking inventory by means of identification tags that transmit radio waves. Antennas mounted on the factory ceiling receive transmissions and send information to a central computer that locates tags in the plant. The system saves time and money by coordinating the delivery of hundreds of parts to assembly lines.[18]

Client-Server Systems　An obvious advantage of networks is resource sharing—and thus avoiding costly duplication. In a **client-server network**, clients are the users of services. They are the points of entry, usually laptop or desktop computers or workstations. The server provides the services shared by users.

Larger and more sophisticated than your PC, a powerful minicomputer at the network hub may be the server for client PCs in an office network. As a file server, the minicomputer has a large-capacity disk for storing the database and word-processing, graphics, and spreadsheet programs used by all network PCs. As a print server, it controls the printer, stores printing requests from client PCs, and routes jobs as the printer becomes available. As the fax server, it receives and sends and controls fax activities. Thus, an entire system of users needs only one disk drive, one printer, and one fax. Internet computing uses the client-server arrangement.

client-server network
Information-technology system consisting of clients (users) that are electronically linked to share network resources provided by a server, such as a host computer

---

SELF-CHECK QUESTIONS 7–9

You should now be able to answer Self-Check Questions 7–9.*

7 Multiple Choice All of the following are *popular components of the information system* **except** [select one]: **(a)** hardware; **(b)** software, including system and application programs; **(c)** software programs written by system users; **(d)** a database; **(e)** the people at various levels who use and prepare the system.

8 True/False If you're preparing a professional presentation for a business audience, an information system can be helpful by providing *application pro-*

grams such as word processing, electronic spreadsheets, and computer graphics software.

9 Multiple Choice Suppose your pickup-and-delivery vehicles cover the countryside making trips to and from customers' facilities. Which of the following telecommunications devices and characteristics would be most helpful for continuous tracking of truck locations? [select one]: **(a)** a wide area network (WAN); **(b)** fiber-optic cable; **(c)** a client-server network; **(d)** a paging system; **(e)** a global positioning system (GPS).

*Answers to Self-Check Questions 7–9 can be found on p. 509.

Continued from page 358.

REMOTE DAMAGE CONTROL

As it flies from Tokyo to San Francisco, the jet engines on an Airbus 340 are monitored and readings are collected by onboard computers transmitted to a GE monitoring station in Cincinnati, Ohio. By detecting impending component failures, airlines can avoid not only expensive repairs but also flight diversions and delays. An aircraft engine costs $5 million to $10 million, and remote monitoring also helps with maintenance scheduling. Each engine needs an overhaul—costing between $500,000 and $2 million—every three to five years. Using software that runs statistical tests on monitored data, GE's Engine Services team can predict when engines will deteriorate to the point at which servicing is justified. By forecasting how many engines will need repair, service teams can anticipate how many spare engines and parts will be needed, thereby avoiding delays from shortages and the costs of storing too many expensive extras. In factories, too, remote monitoring tools are used for advanced maintenance programs on pumps, motors, machining centers, assembly lines, and automated painting systems.

The goal of remote monitoring is early detection. In the trucking industry, wireless communications combine data from onboard sensors with real-time data gathered from global positioning systems (GPSs). Detecting low pressure in tire number seven of a fleet truck in Montana, a dispatcher in Chicago may signal the driver that a repair station is located 15 miles ahead, thus avoiding tire failure and lost road time. Diagnostics also monitor other potential breakdowns—low coolant, alternator failure, engine oil or lube depletion, and electrical system deterioration.

There will soon be similar applications for consumer products, not only for household appliances—washers, dryers, refrigerators, and air conditioners—but also for cars and home alarm systems. Studded with computing chips, tiny sensors, and communications ports, your refrigeration compressor will detect and report potential failures before breakdown spoils a week's worth of food. GE, Whirlpool, Samsung, IBM, and several carmakers are working on systems that will detect and report maintenance problems over the Internet.

Whatever the application, the key is the diagnostics center, including data inflow and the software needed to extract useful information from it. Specialists must create the diagnostics software that receives data, discovers and stores correlations among variables, interprets the data, and reports findings in a format that's useful to maintenance personnel. As applications expand, don't be surprised if signals from your new car, television set, or refrigerator are being monitored at some diagnostics center far, far away.

Questions for Discussion

1 What role, if any, does human judgment play in GE's remote monitoring diagnostics system?
2 What are the financial risks, if any, in subscribing to the GE system? What are the risks of not subscribing?
3 Consider the kinds of software that might be useful in remote monitoring and diagnosis. What kinds of software might be needed, and what functions would it have to perform?
4 Do you foresee any potential ethical issues in the use of remote monitoring and diagnostics? Explain.
5 Recall some equipment and conveniences on which you rely in your everyday activities. What are some potential applications for remote monitoring and diagnostics?

■ SUMMARY OF LEARNING OBJECTIVES

1 Explain why businesses must manage *information* and show how computer systems and communication technologies have revolutionized *information management*.

Because businesses are faced with an overwhelming amount of **data** and **information** about customers, competitors, and their own operations, the ability to manage this resource can mean the difference between success and failure. The management of its information system is a core activity because all of a firm's business activities are linked to it. With intensified competition and expanded global and e-business operations, companies need more advanced **data communication networks** and new **electronic information technologies (EITs)**—IS applications based on telecommunications technologies. EITs use networks of devices (such as computers and satellites) to communicate information and enhance productivity by serving two functions: (1) by providing coordination and communication within the firm; and (2) by speeding up transactions with other firms.

2 Identify and briefly describe three elements of *data communication networks*—the Internet, the World Wide Web, and intranets.

Data communication networks are global networks that use telecommunication systems to carry streams of digital data back and forth quickly and economically. The largest communications network, the **Internet** (or "the Net"), is a system of networks serving millions of computers, offering a vast range of information, and providing communication flows among more than 170,000 separate networks. It allows PCs virtually anywhere to be linked and has also become the most important e-mail system in the world. Individuals can't connect directly, but monthly usage fees permit them to subscribe to it via an **Internet service provider (ISP)**—a commercial firm that maintains a permanent connection to the Net and sells temporary connections.

The **World Wide Web** (WWW or "the Web") lets users around the world communicate with little effort. The Web supports standards for storing, retrieving, formatting, and displaying information. It provides the "common language" that makes the Internet available to a general audience and not just technical users. **Intranets** allow users to browse internal sites containing a firm's information. Only employees can get in by penetrating electronic **firewalls**—hardware and software security systems that can't be breached by outsiders.

3 Describe five *new options for organizational design* that have emerged from the rapid growth of information technologies.

Information networks are leading to *leaner* organizations— businesses with fewer employees and simpler organizational structures—because networked firms can maintain electronic, rather than just face-to-face or voice, information linkages among employees and customers. Operations are *more flexible* because electronic networks allow businesses to offer greater product variety and faster delivery cycles. Aided by intranets and the Internet, *greater collaboration* is possible, both among internal units and with outside firms. *Geographic separation* of the workplace and company headquarters is more common because electronic linkages are replacing the need for physical proximity between the company and its workstations. *Improved management processes* are feasible because managers have rapid access to more information about the current status of company activities and easier access to electronic tools for planning and decision making.

4 Discuss different information-system *application programs* that are available for users at various organizational levels.

System requirements for **knowledge workers** vary because they often face specialized problems. IS applications for

middle- or top-level management decisions must also be flexible because they depend on a broader range of information collected from both external and internal sources. **Application programs** for knowledge workers and office applications include personal productivity tools such as **word processing, desktop publishing,** and **computer-aided design. Management information systems (MISs)** support an organization's managers by providing daily reports, schedules, plans, and budgets. Middle managers, the largest MIS user group, need networked information to plan upcoming activities and to track current activities. **Decision support systems (DSSs)** are interactive applications that assist the decision-making processes of middle- and top-level managers. **Executive support systems (ESSs)** are quick-reference, easy-access programs to assist upper-level managers. **Artificial intelligence (AI)** and **expert systems** are designed to imitate human behavior and provide computer-based assistance in performing specialized business activities.

5 Briefly describe the content and role of a *database* and the purpose of *database software* for information systems.

The **database** is a centralized, organized collection of related data, in digital form, within a computer system. The database is the storehouse of all the system data that are classified into fields, records, and files having numerical storage locations. The purpose of the database and **database software** is to make the data accessible on demand for system users. **Database management programs** are software applications that enable data to be conveniently stored, retrieved, sorted, and searched. This software allows system users to integrate a single piece of data into several different files within the system so that useful information is created.

■ KEY TERMS

information manager (p. 358)
information management (p. 358)
information system (IS) (p. 359)
data (p. 359)
information (p. 359)
electronic information technologies (EIT) (p. 360)
electronic conferencing (p. 360)
groupware (p. 361)
data communication network (p. 361)
Internet (p. 361)
Internet service provider (ISP) (p. 361)

World Wide Web (p. 362)
Web server (p. 362)
browser (p. 363)
search engine (p. 364)
intranet (p. 364)
firewall (p. 364)
extranet (p. 364)
mass-customization (p. 366)
enterprise resource planning (ERP) (p. 367)
knowledge worker (p. 368)
system operations personnel (p. 370)

computer-aided design (CAD) (p. 370)
computer-aided manufacturing (CAM) (p. 371)
management information system (MIS) (p. 371)
decision support system (DSS) (p. 371)
executive support system (ESS) (p. 372)
artificial intelligence (AI) (p. 372)
robotics (p. 372)
expert system (p. 372)

■ QUESTIONS AND EXERCISES

Questions for Review

1 Why must a business manage information as a resource?

2 How can an electronic conferencing system increase productivity and efficiency?

3 Why do the four levels of user groups in an organization need different kinds of information from the IS?

4 In what ways are local area networks (LANs) different from or similar to wide area networks (WANs)?

5 What are the main types of electronic information technologies being applied in business information systems?

Questions for Analysis

6 Give two examples (other than those in this chapter) for each of the major types of business application programs.

7 Describe three or four activities in which you regularly engage that might be made easier by multimedia technology.

8 Give three examples (other than those in this chapter) of how a company can become leaner by adopting a networked IS.

Application Exercises

9 Describe the IS at your school. Identify its components and architecture. What features either promote or inhibit collaboration?

10 Visit a small business in your community to investigate the ways it's using communication technologies and the ways it plans to use them in the future. Prepare a report for class presentation.

▶ BUILDING YOUR BUSINESS SKILLS

THE ART AND SCIENCE OF POINT-AND-CLICK RESEARCH

This exercise enhances the following SCANS workplace competencies: demonstrating basic skills, demonstrating thinking skills, exhibiting interpersonal skills, working with information, applying system knowledge, and using technology.

Goal
To introduce students to World Wide Web search sites.

Background
In a recent survey of nearly 2,000 Web users, two-thirds said they used the Web to obtain work-related information. With an estimated 320 million pages of information on the Web,

the challenge for business users is fairly obvious: how to find what they're looking for.

Method
You'll need a computer and access to the World Wide Web to complete this exercise.

Step 1
Get together with three classmates and decide on a business-related research topic. Choose a topic that interests you—for example, "Business Implications of the Year 2000 Census," "Labor Disputes in Professional Sports," or "Marketing Music Lessons and Instruments to Parents of Young Children."

Step 2

Search the following sites for information on your topic (dividing them among group members to speed the process):

- Yahoo! *(www.yahoo.com)*
- Hotbot *(www.hotbot.lycos.com)*
- Alta Vista *(www.altavista.com)*
- Excite *(www.excite.com)*
- Infoseek *(www.infoseek.go.com)*
- Lycos *(www.lycos.com)*
- Metacrawler *(www.metacrawler.com)*
- Dogpile *(www.dogpile.com)*
- Ask Jeeves *(www.askjeeves.com)*
- Northern Light *(www.northernlight.com)*

Take notes as you search so that you can explain your findings to other group members.

Step 3

Working as a group, answer the following questions about your collective search:

1 Which sites were the easiest to use?
2 Which sites offered the most helpful results? What specific factors made these sites better than the others?

3 Which sites offered the least helpful results? What were the problems?
4 Why is it important to learn the special code words or symbols, called *operators,* that target a search? (Operators are words like AND, OR, and NOT that narrow search queries. For example, using AND in a search tells the system that all words must appear in the results—American AND Management AND Association.)

FOLLOW-UP QUESTIONS

Research the differences between *search engines* and *search directories.* Then place the sites listed in Step 2 in the proper category. Did you find search engines or directories more helpful in this exercise?

1 Why is it important to learn how to use the search-site "Help" function?
2 Based on your personal career goals, how do you think that mastering Web-research techniques might help you in the future?
3 How has the Web changed the nature of business research?

EXERCISING YOUR ETHICS

SUPPLYING THE RIGHT ANSWERS

The Situation

Networked systems facilitate information sharing among companies and often involve sensitive customer data. This exercise asks you to consider ethical issues that might arise when firms are developing information technologies for use in networked systems.

The Dilemma

Home Sweet Home-e (HSH-e) was an e-business start-up that sold virtually everything in home furnishings—from linens and towels to cleaning supplies and furniture. From home computers, HSH-e members could shop in virtual storefronts, chat online with other shoppers, talk live with virtual store clerks, and pay electronically at a one-stop Web site. In reality, HSH-e was a *virtual store:* a network of numerous suppliers located around the country, each specializing in a particular line of goods. The network was connected by a centrally controlled information technology that HSH-e developed, owned, and operated. Once a customer's order was placed, suppliers instantaneously received information on what to ship, where to ship it, and how much to charge.

HSH-e chose only suppliers who guaranteed fast, reliable deliveries and promised to supply HSH-e exclusively. The linen supplier, for example, could not supply products to other home-furnishings e-businesses. In return, the supplier was guaranteed all HSH-e orders for linen products. As HSH-e grew, suppliers stood to gain more business and prosper in an expanding e-tail industry. As it turns out, some prospective suppliers refused to join the network and others in the network were discontinued by HSH-e for failing to expand fast enough to keep up with demand.

QUESTIONS FOR DISCUSSION

1 For a potential HSH-e supplier of a specialized product line, what are the ethical issues in this situation?
2 Consider past suppliers who have been discontinued or have withdrawn from the HSH-e network. Do they face any ethical issues involving HSH-e customers? Involving HSH-e operations? Involving other HSH-e suppliers?
3 Suppose you work at HSH-e and discover a nonnetwork supplier that is more attractive than one of the company's existing suppliers. What ethical considerations do you face in deciding whether or not to replace an existing supplier?

CRAFTING YOUR BUSINESS PLAN

GETTING WIRED FOR BETTER INFORMATION

The Purpose of the Assignment

1 To acquaint students with issues involving information systems that a sample firm faces in developing its business plan in the framework of *Business PlanPro (BPP) 2003* software package (Version 6.0).

2 To demonstrate how communications technologies, the Internet, and database considerations can be integrated as components in the *BPP* planning environment.

Assignment

After reading Chapter 12 in the textbook, open the BPP *software and look around for information about plans for computer and communication technologies as they apply to a sample firm, a travel agency called* Adventure Travel International (ATI). *To find* Adventure Travel, *do the following:*

Open *Business PlanPro.* Go to the toolbar and click on the *"Sample Plans"* icon. In the **Sample Plan Browser,** do a search using the **search category** *Transportation services.* From the resulting list, select the category entitled **Travel Agency—Adventure,** which is the location for *ATI.* The screen that you are looking at is the introduction page for

the *ATI* business plan. Next, scroll down from this page until you reach the Table of Contents for the *ATI* business plan.

NOW RESPOND TO THE FOLLOWING ITEMS:

1 How have the Internet and related communications technologies changed the travel agency industry? [Sites to see in *BPP* for this question: On the Table of Contents page, click in turn on each of the following: **3.2 Competitive Comparison** and **4.3.1 Business Participants.**]

2 How might databases be used to advantage at *ATI*? [Sites to see in *BPP*: On the Table of Contents page, click in turn on each of the following: **3.3 Sales Literature, 3.5 Technology, 4.1 Market Segmentation, 5.0 Strategy and Implementation Summary,** and **5.3.5 Marketing Programs.**]

3 What are the advantages in *ATI*'s computerized reservation system? [Sites to see in *BPP*: From the Table of Contents page, click in turn on each of the following: **3.5 Technology** and **4.3.2 Distributing a Service.**]

4 How can *ATI*'s distribution system benefit from the Web? After exploring the *ATI* plan, what suggestions would you make about using the Web? [Sites to see in *BPP*: In the Table of Contents page, click on **5.3.4 Distribution Strategy** and **5.5 Strategic Alliances.**]

VIDEO EXERCISE

SPACE AGE INFORMATION SYSTEMS: BOEING SATELLITE SYSTEMS

Learning Objectives

The purpose of this video is to help you:

1 Understand why a business must manage information.

2 Consider the role of information systems in an organization.

3 Understand how information systems and communications technology contribute to efficiency and performance.

Synopsis

The world's leading manufacturer of commercial communications satellites, Boeing Satellite Systems is a wholly owned subsidiary of Boeing and serves customers in 14

countries. Boeing's information system collects and analyzes data from all departments and then disseminates the results to help management make decisions for boosting performance, productivity, and competitiveness. The chief information officer also oversees security precautions, disaster recovery plans, and procedures for safeguarding valuable data. In addition, each of the company's more than 8,000 employees is equipped with a personal computer or laptop that can also serve as a television to receive broadcasts about company activities.

DISCUSSION QUESTIONS

1 **For analysis:** What role do information systems play at Boeing Satellite Systems?

2 **For analysis:** What are some of the ways in which information technology can improve productivity and performance at Boeing Satellite Systems?

3 **For application:** What potential problems might Boeing Satellite Systems have encountered when introducing computer kiosks into factory operations?

4 **For application:** In addition to scenes of Boeing-made satellite launches, what else should the company broadcast over employee computers? Why?

5 **For debate:** Should Boeing Satellite Systems try to prevent potential abuses by using software for monitoring employee use of company PCs and laptops? Support your position.

Online Exploration

Visit the Boeing Satellite Systems Web site at *(www.boeing.com/satellite)* and search for more information about the firm's state-of-the-art integration and test facility. Also browse the site to see what the company says about its use of information systems and communication technology. Why would the company discuss technology in detail on a public Web site? What specific benefits of IS does Boeing Satellite Systems highlight? Why are these benefits important to customers who buy satellites?

After reading this chapter,
you should be able to:

1 Explain the role of accountants and distinguish between the kinds of work done by *public* and *private accountants.*

2 Discuss the *CPA Vision Project* and explain how the CPA profession is changing.

3 Explain how the following concepts are used in accounting: the *accounting equation* and *double-entry accounting.*

4 Describe the three basic *financial statements,* show how they reflect the activity and financial condition of a business, and explain the key standards and principles for reporting them.

5 Show how computing key *financial ratios* can help in analyzing the financial strengths of a business and explain some of the special issues that arise in international accounting.

HUMPTY-DUMPTY TIME AT ARTHUR ANDERSEN

Rarely does a single event shake a whole industry as dramatically as Arthur Andersen's failed attempts to cover up the role of accounting in aiding and abetting the dubious and self-destructive activities of oil-trading giant Enron. With employee and stock-

UNDERSTANDING PRINCIPLES OF ACCOUNTING

"They brought all the king's horses and all the king's men, and they couldn't put Humpty together again."

—U.S. Prosecutor Samuel Buell, on Enron executives' last-ditch effort to clean up their accounting mess

holder losses totaling tens of billions of dollars, the Enron breakdown certainly caused monumental damage to this country's business psyche. But in many ways, it's really small stuff compared with the widespread failure of confidence that Andersen has spawned. As Enron's auditors, Andersen's CPAs were supposed to assess Enron's financial status, evaluate its financial statements, and report on its adherence to generally accepted accounting practices. Had it done what it was supposed to do, how could Andersen have failed to see through the bookkeeping sleight of hand that soon led to Enron's mammoth collapse? And what if Andersen *did* foresee the collapse? What if its accountants had actually *helped* Houston-based Enron hide its financial shortfalls and ethical shortcomings?

In March 2002, the Department of Justice (DOJ) filed obstruction-of-justice charges against Andersen, accusing the firm of shredding tons of Enron documents that should have been preserved as legal records. Andersen executives denied that any crimes had been committed. Prosecutors argued that months before Enron's collapse, Andersen knew that its second-biggest client was in an accounting mess. To implement damage control, Chicago-based Andersen executives moved to Houston, but it was too late. "It was Humpty Dumpty time for Arthur Andersen," says U.S. Prosecutor Samuel Buell. "They brought all the king's horses and all the king's men, and they couldn't put Humpty together again. Enron's accounting was made up of eggshells."

Meanwhile, a pall of cynicism has fallen over the accounting industry: If it can happen at Andersen, what's to keep it from happening to anyone else in the accounting industry? Such questions lead, at best, to a profound skepticism about the profession's methods and mores, and, at worst, to further questions of possible corruption. As of mid-2002, suspicious investors were questioning the accounting practices of thousands of firms, and people are still extremely skeptical about the honesty of independent auditors who are supposed to keep clients honest. Without unbiased audits, how much can investors know about a company's financial health and trust its financial reports? Long among the world's most trusted professionals, accountants have been regarded as providers of valid information on corporate performance and as watchdogs of the public interest. Almost single-handedly, Andersen has changed all that. The public is suspicious. If a firm with Andersen's reputation can't be trusted, how much confidence can be placed in the paperwork spewing from anywhere else in Corporate America?

Loss of confidence—on the part of investors, employees, retirees, unions, and government—has contributed to a plunging stock market, with losses in the hundreds of billions since Enron's demise. Corporate mischief and the willingness of accountants to cover it up have done untold damage to public trust. "We all too often forget," said one securities analyst, "that markets depend on trust to operate. Enron and the . . . corporate scandals that followed have all but destroyed that trust. What it all means is that the U.S. must get its house in order and fast."

Our opening story continues on page 409.

■ WHAT IS ACCOUNTING AND WHO USES ACCOUNTING INFORMATION?

accounting
Comprehensive system for collecting, analyzing, and communicating financial information

bookkeeping
Recording of accounting transactions

accounting information system (AIS)
Organized means by which financial information is identified, measured, recorded, and retained for use in accounting statements and management reports

Accounting is a comprehensive system for collecting, analyzing, and communicating financial information. It measures business performance and translates the findings into information for management decisions. Accountants also prepare performance reports for owners, the public, and regulatory agencies. To perform these functions, they keep records of taxes paid, income received, and expenses incurred, and they assess the effects of these transactions on business activities. By sorting and analyzing thousands of such transactions, accountants can determine how well a business is being managed and how financially strong it is.[1] **Bookkeeping** is just one phase of accounting—the recording of transactions. Accounting itself is much more comprehensive than bookkeeping because it involves more than merely recording information.

Because businesses engage in thousands of transactions, ensuring consistent, dependable financial information is mandatory. This is the job of the **accounting information system (AIS)**—an organized procedure for identifying, measuring, recording, and retaining financial information so that it can be used in accounting statements and management reports. The system includes all of the people, reports, computers, procedures, and resources that are needed to compile financial transactions.[2]

There are numerous users of accounting information:

- *Business managers* use it to develop goals and plans, set budgets, and evaluate future prospects.
- *Employees and unions* use it to plan for and receive compensation and such benefits as health care, vacation time, and retirement pay.
- *Investors and creditors* use it to estimate returns to stockholders, determine growth prospects, and decide whether a firm is a good credit risk.
- *Tax authorities* use it to plan for tax inflows, determine the tax liabilities of individuals and businesses, and ensure that correct amounts are paid on time.
- *Government regulatory agencies* rely on it to fulfill their duties toward the public. The Securities and Exchange Commission (SEC), for example, requires firms to file financial disclosures so that potential investors have valid information about their financial status.

■ WHO ARE ACCOUNTANTS AND WHAT DO THEY DO?

At the head of the AIS is the **controller**, who manages a firm's accounting activities. As chief accounting officer, the controller ensures that the AIS provides the reports and statements needed for planning, controlling, decision making, and other management activities. This range of activities requires different types of accounting specialists. In this section, we begin by distinguishing between the two main fields of accounting: *financial* and *managerial*. Then we discuss the different functions and activities of *certified public accountants* and *private accountants*.

controller
Person who manages all of a firm's accounting activities (chief accounting officer)

Financial Versus Managerial Accounting

In any company, two fields of accounting—financial and managerial—can be distinguished by the users they serve. It is both convenient and accurate to classify users as those outside the company and those inside the company. We can use this same distinction to classify accounting systems as *financial* or *managerial*.[3]

Financial Accounting A firm's **financial accounting system** is concerned with external information users: consumer groups, unions, stockholders, and government agencies. It regularly prepares income statements and balance sheets as well as other financial reports published for shareholders and the public. All of these documents focus on the activities of the company as a whole rather than on individual departments or divisions.[4]

financial accounting system
Field of accounting concerned with external users of a company's financial information

Managerial Accounting Managerial (or **management**) **accounting** serves internal users. Managers at all levels need information to make departmental decisions, monitor projects, and plan future activities. Other employees also need accounting information. Engineers need to know certain costs in order to make product or operations improvements. To set performance goals, salespeople need past

managerial (or **management**) **accounting system**
Field of accounting that serves internal users of a company's financial information

sales data by geographic region. Purchasing agents use information on materials costs to negotiate terms with suppliers.

Certified Public Accountants

certified public accountant (CPA)
Accountant licensed by the state and offering services to the public

Certified public accountants (CPAs) offer accounting services to the public. They are licensed by the state after passing an exam prepared by the American Institute of Certified Public Accountants (AICPA) *(www.aicpa.org)*, which also provides technical support and discipline in matters of ethics.

Professional Practice Whereas some CPAs work as individual practitioners, many form partnerships or professional corporations. There are more than 40,000 CPA firms in the United States, but one-half of the total revenues go to the four biggest firms: Deloitte Tohmatsu Touche *(www.deloitte.com)*, Ernst & Young *(www.ey.com)*, KPMG LLP *(www.kpmg.com)*, and Price WaterhouseCoopers *(www.pwcglobal.com)*. In addition to their prominence in the United States, international operations are important for all four of these companies.

CPA Services Virtually all CPA firms, whether large or small, provide auditing, tax, and management services. Larger firms earn up to 60 percent of their revenue from auditing services, and consulting services constitute a major growth area. Smaller firms earn most of their income from tax and management services.

audit
Systematic examination of a company's accounting system to determine whether its financial reports fairly represent its operations

generally accepted accounting principles (GAAP)
Accepted rules and procedures governing the content and form of financial reports

Auditing An **audit** examines a company's AIS to determine whether financial reports reliably represent its operations.[5] Organizations must provide audit reports when applying for loans or selling stock or when going through a major restructuring. Auditors ensure that clients' accounting systems follow **generally accepted accounting principles (GAAP)**—rules and procedures governing the content and form of financial reports. GAAP is formulated by the Financial Accounting Standards Board (FASB) of the AICPA and should be used to determine whether a firm has controls to prevent errors and fraud.[6] Ultimately, the auditor will certify whether the client's reports comply with GAAP.

Tax Services Tax services include assistance not only with tax return preparation but also with tax planning. A CPA's advice can help a business structure (or restructure) operations and investments and perhaps save millions of dollars in taxes. Staying abreast of tax law changes is no simple matter. Legislators made more than 70 pages of technical corrections to the 1986 Tax Reform Act before it even became law.

management advisory services
Specialized accounting services to help managers resolve a variety of business problems

Management Advisory Services As consultants, accounting firms provide **management advisory services** ranging from personal financial planning to planning corporate mergers. Other services include production scheduling, computer-feasibility studies, and AIS design. Some firms even assist in executive recruitment. On the staffs of the largest CPA firms are engineers, architects, mathematicians, and psychologists, who are available for consulting.

Noncertified Public Accountants Many accountants don't take the CPA exam; others work in the field while getting ready for it or while meeting requirements for state certification. Many small businesses, individuals, and even larger firms rely on these noncertified public accountants for income tax preparation, payroll accounting, and financial-planning services.

Although employees at telecommunications giant WorldCom *(www.worldcom.com)* were surprised to hear about the company's $3.8 billion restatement of 2002 earnings, many were even more shocked when they were laid off a short time later: The largest bankruptcy in U.S. history put some 17,000 people out of work. Many of them blamed auditor Arthur Andersen *(www.arthurandersen.com)* for failing to uncover WorldCom's accounting problems. Government officials and financial analysts questioned whether Andersen could have maintained any objectivity as an auditor while collecting millions of dollars in consulting fees from the same client.

Private Accountants

To ensure integrity in reporting, CPAs are always independent of the firms they audit. A CPA firm, for example, cannot serve as auditor for a firm that it owns. As employees of accounting firms, CPAs provide services for outside clients. However, many businesses also hire their own salaried employees—**private accountants**—to perform day-to-day activities.

private accountant
Salaried accountant hired by a business to carry out its day-to-day financial activities

Private accountants perform numerous jobs. An internal auditor at Phillips Petroleum might fly to the North Sea to confirm the accuracy of oil-flow meters on offshore drilling platforms. A supervisor responsible for $2 billion in monthly payouts to vendors and employees may never leave the executive suite. Large businesses employ specialized accountants in such areas as budgets, financial planning, internal auditing, payroll, and taxation. In small businesses, a single person may handle all accounting tasks.

Most private accountants are management accountants who provide services to support managers in various activities (marketing, production, engineering, and so forth). Many hold the **certified management accountant (CMA)** designation, awarded by the Institute of Management Accountants (IMA), recognizing qualifications of professionals who have passed IMA's experience and examination requirements.

certified management accountant (CMA)
Professional recognition of management qualifications awarded by the Institute of Management Accountants

The CPA Vision Project

The CPA Vision Project *(www.cpavision.org)* is a professionwide program that was established to assess the future of accounting.[7] A prime reason for the project is a disturbing decline in the number of young people who entered the profession in the 1990s. The talent shortage has forced the profession to rethink its culture and lifestyle. With grassroots participation from CPAs, educators, and industry leaders, the AICPA has undertaken a comprehensive long-term project to define the role of the accountant in the world economy of the twenty-first century. In recognizing a rapidly changing business world, the project focuses on certain desired goals for the profession and identifies the changes that will be needed to accomplish them.

Identifying Issues for the Future First, the Vision Project has identified key forces, both domestic and global, affecting the profession. Why are fewer students choosing to become CPAs? Technology is replacing many traditional CPA skills, the new borderless business world requires that accountants (like everybody else) offer new skills and services, and the perceived value of some traditional accounting services, including auditing and tax preparation, is declining. In addition, an increasing number of non-CPA competitors are not bound by the accounting profession's code of standards. In considering these forces, the Vision Project has identified the most important issues in the profession's future:

- Success will depend on public perceptions of the CPA's abilities and roles.
- CPAs must respond to market needs rather than rely on regulation to keep them in business.
- The market demands more high-value consulting and fewer auditing and accounting services.
- Specialization will be vital.
- CPAs must be familiar with global strategies and business practices.

Global Forces as Drivers of Change The Vision Project explains how the six classes of global forces shown in Figure 13.1 are driving the profession's

FIGURE 13.1

Global Forces in the Changing CPA Profession

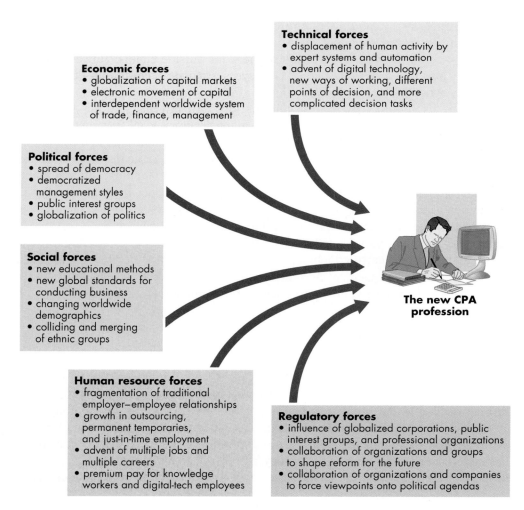

Economic forces
- globalization of capital markets
- electronic movement of capital
- interdependent worldwide system of trade, finance, management

Technical forces
- displacement of human activity by expert systems and automation
- advent of digital technology, new ways of working, different points of decision, and more complicated decision tasks

Political forces
- spread of democracy
- democratized management styles
- public interest groups
- globalization of politics

Social forces
- new educational methods
- new global standards for conducting business
- changing worldwide demographics
- colliding and merging of ethnic groups

Human resource forces
- fragmentation of traditional employer–employee relationships
- growth in outsourcing, permanent temporaries, and just-in-time employment
- advent of multiple jobs and multiple careers
- premium pay for knowledge workers and digital-tech employees

Regulatory forces
- influence of globalized corporations, public interest groups, and professional organizations
- collaboration of organizations and groups to shape reform for the future
- collaboration of organizations and companies to force viewpoints onto political agendas

The new CPA profession

reorientation. The wide range of these forces touches on nearly all aspects of CPA work—everything from working hours and knowledge requirements to cultural flexibility.

Recommendations for Change What, precisely, needs to be done? The Vision Project indicates that accounting educators and accounting professionals must make changes in the functioning of the profession. Among the top recommendations for change are these:

- The profession should adopt a broader focus beyond "numbers" that includes "strategic thinking."
- The profession should provide more value to society by expanding knowledge, education, and experience.
- CPA education must be revitalized to meet the demands of the future.
- To attract qualified members, the profession must increase opportunities for advancement, rewards, and lifestyle preferences.

A New Direction Responses from participants in the Vision Project reveal the profession's views of its own future. They are summarized in two categories—*Core Services* and *Core Competencies*—that are designed to shape and guide the CPA profession in the twenty-first century.

Core Services *Core services* refer to the work that the CPA performs. The Vision Project reports a stark departure from the traditional range of accounting activities and strongly recommends a broader perspective that encompasses areas traditionally outside the accounting realm. As you can see in Table 13.1, CPAs must develop new skills to deal with the range of business activities that affect performance. Financial planning, for instance, arguably falls beyond accounting's traditional role of reporting on historical financial performance. The distinction is largely one of perspective: futuristic outlook (financial planning) versus the historical (financial performance reporting). But many companies feel that they could get a clearer picture of their competitive health if the two areas were integrated. It will

---

TABLE 13.1

Core Services in Accounting

Assurance and Information Integrity

A variety of services that improve and assure the quality of information for business activities

Technology

Services that utilize technology—new business applications in knowledge management, system security, and new business practices—to improve business activities.

Management Consulting and Performance Management

Broad business knowledge and judgment to supply advice on an organization's strategic, operational, and financial performance

Financial Planning

Various services—in tax planning, financial transactions, investment portfolio structuring, financial statement analysis—that help clients better understand, interpret, and utilize the full range of financial information

International Business

Services that enhance performance in global operations and facilitate global commerce

TABLE 13.2

Core Competencies in
Accounting

Strategic and Critical Thinking Skills

The accountant can provide competent advice for strategic action by combining data, knowledge, and insight

Communications and Leadership Skills

The accountant can exchange information meaningfully in a variety of business situations with effective delivery and interpersonal skills

Focus on the Customer, Client, and Market

The accountant can meet the changing needs of clients, customers, and employers better than the competition and can anticipate those needs better than competitors

Skills in Interpreting Converging Information

The accountant can interpret new meaning by combining financial and nonfinancial information into a broader understanding that adds more business value

Technology Skills

The accountant can use technology to add value to activities performed for employers, customers, and clients

require a major commitment of organizational resources for a CPA firm to move in this direction.

Core Competencies The Vision Project identifies a unique combination of skills, technology, and knowledge—called *core competencies*—that will be necessary for the future CPA. As Table 13.2 shows, those skills go far beyond the ability to "crunch numbers." They include certain communications skills, along with skills in critical thinking and leadership. Indeed, the Vision Project foresees CPAs who combine specialty skills with a broad-based orientation in order to communicate more effectively with people in a wide range of business activities.

SELF-CHECK QUESTIONS 1–3

You should now be able to answer Self-Check Questions 1–3.*

1 **True/False** *Auditing services*, as provided by CPA firms for client companies, are primarily concerned with managerial accounting.

2 **Multiple Choice** *CPA firms* provide all of the following services **except** [select one]: **(a)** auditing for clients owned by the CPA firm; **(b)** financial planning for government and business firms; **(c)** management advisory services for companies and individuals; **(d)** tax services; **(e)** advice on accounting system design.

3 **Multiple Choice** Which of the following is **not** a motivating factor for development of the *CPA Vision*

Project? [select one]: **(a)** an increasing number of non-CPA competitors who are not bound by the accounting profession's standards; **(b)** fewer students choosing to become CPAs; **(c)** a variety of forces—economic, political, regulatory, cultural—that urge a reorientation; **(d)** today's accounting systems, which require fundamental revisions in generally accepted accounting principles (GAAP) for auditing; **(e)** professionals who believe that new core CPA services and core CPA competencies will be required in the future.

*****Answers to Self-Check Questions 1–3 can be found on p. 509.**

■ TOOLS OF THE ACCOUNTING TRADE

All accountants rely on record keeping, either manual or electronic, to enter and track transactions. Underlying all record-keeping procedures are the two key concepts of accounting: the *accounting equation* and *double-entry accounting*.

The Accounting Equation

At various points in the year, accountants use the following equation to balance the data pertaining to financial transactions:

$$\text{Assets} = \text{Liabilities} + \text{Owners' equity}$$

To understand the importance of this equation, we must first understand the terms *assets*, *liabilities*, and *owners' equity*.[8]

Assets and Liabilities An **asset** is any economic resource that is expected to benefit a firm or an individual who owns it. Assets include land, buildings, equipment, inventory, and payments due the company (accounts receivable). A **liability** is a debt that the firm owes to an outside party.

asset
Any economic resource expected to benefit a firm or an individual who owns it

Owners' Equity You may have heard of the *equity* that a homeowner has in a house—that is, the amount of money that could be made by selling the house and paying off the mortgage. Similarly, **owners' equity** is the amount of money that owners would receive if they sold all of a company's assets and paid all of its liabilities. We can rewrite the accounting equation to highlight this definition:

liability
Debt owed by a firm to an outside organization or individual

$$\text{Assets} - \text{Liabilities} = \text{Owners' equity}$$

If a company's assets exceed its liabilities, owners' equity is *positive*; if the company goes out of business, the owners will receive some cash (a gain) after selling assets and paying off liabilities. If liabilities outweigh assets, owners' equity is *negative*; assets are insufficient to pay off all debts. If the company goes out of business, the owners will get no cash and some creditors won't be paid. Owners' equity is meaningful for both investors and lenders. Before lending money to owners, for example, lenders want to know the amount of owners' equity in a business. Owners' equity consists of two sources of capital:

owners' equity
Amount of money that owners would receive if they sold all of a firm's assets and paid all of its liabilities

1 The amount that the owners originally invested
2 Profits earned by and reinvested in the company

When a company operates profitably, its assets increase faster than its liabilities. Owners' equity, therefore, will increase if profits are retained in the business instead of paid out as dividends to stockholders. Owners' equity also increases if owners invest more of their own money to increase assets. However, owners' equity can shrink if the company operates at a loss or if owners withdraw assets.

The inventory at this Boston-area Volkswagen dealership is among the company's *assets*: The cars constitute an economic resource because the firm will benefit financially as it sells them. When (and if) they are sold, at the end of the company's accounting period, the dealership will convert the cost of the cars as *expenses* and show them as *cost of goods sold.*

Double-Entry Accounting

If your business buys inventory with cash, you decrease your cash and increase your inventory. Similarly, if you buy supplies on credit, you increase your supplies and increase your accounts payable. If you invest more money in your business, you increase the company's cash and increase your owners' equity. In other words, *every transaction affects two accounts.* Accountant thus use a **double-entry accounting system** to record the dual effects of transactions.[9] This practice ensures that the accounting equation always balances. If it doesn't balance, an accounting error has occurred.

double-entry accounting system
Bookkeeping system that balances the accounting equation by recording the dual effects of every financial transaction

■ FINANCIAL STATEMENTS

As we noted earlier, the job of accounting is to summarize the results of a firm's transactions and to issue reports to help managers make informed decisions. Among the most important reports are **financial statements**, which fall into three broad categories—*balance sheets, income statements*, and *statements of cash flows*.[10] In this section, we will discuss these three types of financial statements, as well as the function of the budget as an internal financial statement. We'll conclude by explaining the most important reporting practices and the standards that guide accountants in drawing up financial statements.

financial statement
Any of several types of reports summarizing a company's financial status and measuring its financial health

Balance Sheets

Balance sheets supply detailed information about the accounting equation factors: *assets, liabilities,* and *owners' equity.* Because they also show a firm's financial condition at one point in time, they are sometimes called *statements of financial position.* Figure 13.2 is the balance sheet for a hypothetical wholesaler called Perfect Posters.

balance sheet
Financial statement detailing a firm's assets, liabilities, and owners' equity

□□□□□□□□□□□ **Perfect Posters**, ɪɴᴄ.
555 RIVERVIEW, CHICAGO, IL 60606

Perfect Posters, Inc.
Balance Sheet
As of December 31, 2003

Assets

Current Assets:
Cash		$7,050
Marketable securities		2,300
Accounts receivable	$26,210	
Less: Allowance for doubtful	(650)	25,560
accounts		
Merchandise inventory		21,250
Prepaid expenses		1,050
Total current assets		**$ 57,210**

Fixed assets:
Land		18,000
Building	65,000	
Less: Accumulated depreciation . .	(22,500)	42,500
Equipment	72,195	
Less: Accumulated depreciation . .	(24,815)	47,380
Total fixed assets		**$ 107,880**

Intangible assets:
Patents	7,100	
Trademarks	900	
Total intangible assets		**8,000**

Total assets **$173,090**

Liabilities and Owners' Equity

Current liabilities:
Accounts payable	$16,315	
Wages payable	3,700	
Taxes payable	1,920	
Total current liabilities		**$ 21,935**

Long-term liabilities:
Notes payable, 8% due 2005 .	10,000	
Bonds payable, 9% due 2007 .	30,000	
Total long-term liabilities . . .		**40,000**

Total liabilities . . . . **$ 61,935**

Owners' Equity:
Common stock, $5 par	40,000	
Additional paid-in capital	15,000	
Retained earnings	56,155	
Total owners' equity		**$ 111,155**

Total liabilities and owners' equity . . **$173,090**

FIGURE 13.2

Perfect Posters' Balance Sheet

Perfect Posters' balance sheet as of December 31, 2003. Perfect Posters' balance sheet shows clearly that the firm's total assets equal its total liabilities and owners' equity.

Assets As we have seen, an asset is any economic resource that a company owns and from which it expects to get some future benefit. From an accounting standpoint, most companies have three types of assets: *current, fixed*, and *intangible*.

Current Assets **Current assets** include cash and assets that can be converted into cash within a year. They are normally listed in order of **liquidity**—the ease of converting them into cash. Debts, for example, are usually paid in cash. A company that needs but cannot generate cash—a company that's not liquid—may be forced to sell assets at reduced prices or even go under.

By definition, cash is completely liquid. *Marketable securities* purchased as short-term investments are slightly less liquid but can be sold quickly. These include stocks or bonds of other companies, government securities, and money market certificates. Many companies hold three other important nonliquid assets: *accounts receivable, merchandise inventory*, and *prepaid expenses*.

1 **Accounts Receivable:** **Accounts receivable** (or **receivables**) are amounts due from customers who have purchased goods on credit. Most businesses expect to receive payment within 30 days of a sale. In our example, the entry *Less: Allowance for doubtful accounts* in Figure 13.2 indicates $650 in receivables that Perfect Posters doesn't expect to collect. Total receivable assets are decreased accordingly.

2 **Merchandise Inventory:** Following accounts receivable on the Perfect Posters' balance sheet is **merchandise inventory**—the cost of merchandise that's been acquired for sale to customers and is still on hand.[11] Accounting for the value of inventories is difficult because they're always flowing in and out. We must, therefore, make assumptions about which ones were sold and which ones remain in storage.

current asset
Asset that can or will be converted into cash within the following year

liquidity
Ease with which an asset can be converted into cash

account receivable (or **receivable**)
Amount due from a customer who has purchased goods on credit

merchandise inventory
Cost of merchandise that has been acquired for sale to customers and is still on hand

prepaid expense
Expense, such as prepaid rent, that is paid before the upcoming period in which it is due

fixed asset
Asset with long-term use or value, such as land, buildings, and equipment

depreciation
Process of distributing the cost of an asset over its life

intangible asset
Nonphysical asset, such as a patent or trademark, that has economic value in the form of expected benefit

goodwill
Amount paid for an existing business above the value of its other assets

current liability
Debt that must be paid within the year

account payable (or **payable**)
Current liability consisting of bills owed to suppliers, plus wages and taxes due within the upcoming year

long-term liability
Debt that is not due for more than one year

paid-in capital
Additional money, above proceeds from stock sale, paid directly to a firm by its owners

retained earnings
Earnings retained by a firm for its use rather than paid as dividends

income statement (or **profit-and-loss statement**)
Financial statement listing a firm's annual revenues and expenses so that a bottom line shows annual profit or loss

3 Prepaid Expenses: Prepaid expenses include supplies on hand and rent paid for the period to come. They are assets because they've been paid for and are available to the company. In all, Perfect Posters' current assets as of December 31, 2003, totaled $57,210.

Fixed Assets **Fixed assets** (such as land, buildings, and equipment) have long-term use or value. But as buildings and equipment wear out or become obsolete, their value decreases, and accountants use **depreciation** to spread the cost of an asset over the years of its useful life. To reflect decreasing value, they calculate its useful life in years, divide its worth by that many years, and subtract the resulting amount each year. Every year, therefore, the remaining value decreases on the books. In Figure 13.2, Perfect Posters shows fixed assets of $107,880 after depreciation.

Intangible Assets Although their worth is hard to set, **intangible assets** have monetary value in the form of expected benefits. These usually include the cost of obtaining rights or privileges such as patents, trademarks, copyrights, and franchise fees. **Goodwill** is the amount paid for an existing business beyond the value of its other assets. A purchased firm, for example, may have a particularly good reputation or location.[12]

Perfect Posters has no goodwill assets, but it does own trademarks and patents for specialized storage equipment. These intangible assets are worth $8,000. Larger companies, of course, have much more valuable intangible assets.

Liabilities Like assets, liabilities are often separated into different categories. **Current liabilities** are debts that must be paid within one year. These include **accounts payable** (or **payables**)—unpaid bills to suppliers for materials as well as wages and taxes that must be paid in the coming year. Perfect Posters has current liabilities of $21,935.

Long-term liabilities are debts that are not due for at least a year. These normally represent borrowed funds on which the company must pay interest. Perfect Posters' long-term liabilities are $40,000.

Owners' Equity The final section of the balance sheet in Figure 13.2 shows owners' equity broken down into *common stock, paid-in capital*, and *retained earnings*. When Perfect Posters was formed, the declared legal value of its common stock was $5 per share. By law, this $40,000 ($5 × 8,000 shares) can't be distributed as dividends. **Paid-in capital** is additional money invested by owners. Perfect Posters has $15,000 in paid-in capital.

Retained earnings are net profits kept by a firm rather than paid out as dividend payments to stockholders. They accumulate when profits, which can be distributed to stockholders, are kept instead for the company's use. At the close of 2003, Perfect Posters had retained earnings of $56,155.[13]

Income Statements

The **income statement** is sometimes called a **profit-and-loss statement** because its description of revenues and expenses results in a figure showing the firm's annual profit or loss. In other words,

$$\text{Revenues} - \text{Expenses} = \text{Profit (or Loss)}$$

Popularly known as "the bottom line," profit or loss is probably the most important figure in any business enterprise. Figure 13.3 shows the 2003 income statement

□□□□□□□□□□□□□□ **Perfect Posters, INC.**
555 RIVERVIEW, CHICAGO, IL 60606

Perfect Posters, Inc.
Income Statement
Year Ended December 31, 2003

Revenues (gross sales)		**$256,425**
Cost of goods sold:		
Merchandise inventory, January 1, 2003	$22,380	
Merchandise purchases during year	103,635	
Goods available for sale		$126,015
Less: Merchandise inventory		
December 31, 2003	21, 250	
Cost of goods sold		**104,765**
Gross profit		**151,660**
Operating expenses:		
Selling and repackaging expenses:		
Salaries and wages	49,750	
Advertising	6,380	
Depreciation—warehouse and repackaging		
equipment	3,350	
Total selling and repackaging expenses		59,480
Administrative expenses:		
Salaries and wages	55,100	
Supplies	4,150	
Utilities	3,800	
Depreciation—office equipment	3,420	
Interest expense	2,900	
Miscellaneous expenses	1,835	
Total administrative expenses		71,205
Total operating expenses		**130,685**
Operating income (income before taxes)		20,975
Income taxes		8,390
Net income		**$12,585**

Perfect Posters' income statement for year ended December 31, 2003. The final entry on the income statement, the bottom line, reports the firm's profit or loss.

FIGURE 13.3
Perfect Posters' Income Statement

for Perfect Posters, whose bottom line was $12,585. Like the balance sheet, the income statement is divided into three major categories: *revenues, cost of goods sold*, and *operating expenses*.

Revenues   When a law firm receives $250 for preparing a will or a supermarket collects $65 from a grocery shopper, both are receiving **revenues**—the funds that flow into a business from the sale of goods or services. In 2003, Perfect Posters reported revenues of $256,425 from the sale of art prints and other posters.

revenues
Funds that flow into a business from the sale of goods or services

Cost of Goods Sold   In Perfect Posters' income statement, the **cost of goods sold** section shows the costs of obtaining materials to make the products sold during the year. Perfect Posters began 2003 with posters valued at $22,380. Over the year, it spent $103,635 on materials to make posters. During 2003, then, it had $126,015 worth of merchandise available to sell. By the end of the year, it had sold all but $21,250 of those posters, which remained as merchandise inventory. The cost of obtaining the goods that it sold was thus $104,765.

cost of goods sold
Total cost of obtaining materials for making the products sold by a firm during the year

Gross Profit (or Gross Margin)   To calculate **gross profit** (or **gross margin**), subtract cost of goods sold from revenues obtained from goods sold. Perfect Posters' gross profit in 2003 was $151,660 ($256,425 − $104,765). Expressed as a percentage of sales, gross profit is 59.1 percent ($151,660 / $256,425).

gross profit (or **gross margin**)
Revenues obtained from goods sold minus cost of goods sold

Gross profit percentages vary widely across industries. In retailing, Home Depot (*www.homedepot.com*) reports 30 percent. In manufacturing, Harley-Davidson

At the end of its accounting period, this pharmaceuticals company will subtract the cost of making the goods that it sold from the revenues received from sales. The difference will be its *gross profit* (or *gross margin*). *Cost of goods sold* does not include the firm's *operating expenses*, including such selling expenses as advertising and sales commissions. In part, gross margins in the pharmaceuticals industry are high because they do not account for high *selling expenses*.

(www.harley-davidson.com) reports 34 percent; and in pharmaceuticals, American Home Products *(www.ahp.com)* reports 75 percent. For companies with low gross margins, product costs are a big expense. If a company has a high gross margin, it probably has low cost of goods sold but high selling and administrative expenses.

operating expenses
Costs, other than the cost of goods sold, incurred in producing a good or service

Operating Expenses In addition to costs directly related to acquiring goods, every company has general expenses ranging from erasers to the CEO's salary. Like cost of goods sold, **operating expenses** are resources that must flow out of a company if it is to earn revenues. As you can see from Figure 13.3, Perfect Posters had 2003 operating expenses of $130,685—$59,480 in selling and repackaging expenses and $71,205 in administrative expenses.

Selling expenses result from activities related to selling goods or services, such as sales force salaries and advertising expenses. *General and administrative expenses*, such as management salaries and maintenance costs, are related to the general management of the company.

operating income
Gross profit minus operating expenses

Operating and Net Income Operating income compares the gross profit from operations against operating expenses. This calculation for Perfect Posters ($151,660 − $130,685) reveals an operating income, or income before taxes, of $20,975. Subtracting income taxes from operating income ($20,975 − $8,390) reveals **net income** (also called **net profit** or **net earnings**). In 2003, Perfect Posters' net income was $12,585.

net income (or **net profit** or **net earnings**)
Gross profit minus operating expenses and income taxes

Statements of Cash Flows

statement of cash flows
Financial statement describing a firm's yearly cash receipts and cash payments

Some companies prepare only balance sheets and income statements. The Securities and Exchange Commission *(www.sec.gov)*, however, requires all firms whose stock is publicly traded to issue a third report: The **statement of cash flows** describes yearly cash receipts and cash payments.[14] It shows the effects on cash of three activities:

This concession stand at Dodger Stadium is operated by the Los Angeles Dodgers Inc. *(www.dodgers.com)*. It sells products manufactured mostly by members of the Sporting Goods Manufacturers Association (SGMA) *(www.sportlink.com)*, which make apparel, footwear, and equipment. Much of this merchandise is licensed from Major League Baseball Properties Inc. *(www.mlb.com)*, which distributes licensing revenues to the sport's 30 franchises. Both MLB teams (which own logos and uniform designs) and MLB Properties treat sales of licensed products as cash flows from operations.

■ **Cash flows from operations.** This part of the statement concerns main operating activities: cash transactions involved in buying and selling goods and services. It reveals how much of the year's profits result from the firm's main line of business (for example, Jaguar's sales of automobiles) rather than from secondary activities (say, licensing fees paid to Jaguar by a clothing firm that puts the Jaguar logo on shirts).

■ **Cash flows from investing.** This section reports net cash used in or provided by investing. It includes cash receipts and payments from buying and selling stocks, bonds, property, equipment, and other productive assets.

■ **Cash flows from financing.** The final section reports net cash from all financing activities. It includes cash inflows from borrowing or issuing stock as well as outflows for payment of dividends and repayment of borrowed money.

The overall change in cash from these three sources provides information to lenders and investors. When creditors and stockholders know how a firm obtained and used funds during the course of a year, it's easier for them to interpret year-to-year changes in the balance sheet and income statement.

The Budget: An Internal Financial Statement

For planning, controlling, and decision making, the most important internal financial statement is the **budget**—a detailed report on estimated receipts and expenditures for a future period of time.[15] Although that period is usually one year, some companies also prepare three- or five-year budgets, especially when considering major capital expenditures.

Budgets are also useful for keeping track of weekly or monthly performance. Procter & Gamble evaluates business units monthly by comparing actual financial results with monthly budgets. Discrepancies signal potential problems and spur action to improve financial performance.

budget
Detailed statement of estimated receipts and expenditures for a period of time in the future

FIGURE 13.4

Perfect Posters' Sales Budget

□□□□□□□□□□□ **Perfect Posters, INC.**
555 RIVERVIEW, CHICAGO, IL 60606

Perfect Posters, Inc.
Sales Budget
First Quarter, 2004

	January	February	March	Quarter
Budgeted sales (units)	7,500	6,000	6,500	20,000
Budgeted selling price per unit	$3.50	$3.50	$3.50	$3.50
Budgeted sales revenue	**$26,250**	**$21,000**	**$22,750**	**$70,000**
Expected cash receipts:				
From December sales	$26,210[a]			$26,210
From January sales	17,500[b]	$8,750		26,250
From February sales		14,000	$7,000	21,000
From March sales			15,200	15,200
Total cash receipts:	**$43,710**	**$22,750**	**$22,200**	**$88,660**

[a]This cash from December sales represents a collection of the accounts receivable appearing on the December 31, 2003, balance sheet.
[b]The company estimates that two-thirds of each month's sales revenues will result in cash receipts during the same month. The remaining one-third is collected during the following month.

Although the accounting staff coordinates the budget process, it needs input from many areas regarding proposed activities and required resources. In preparing a sales budget like the one in Figure 13.4, accounting must obtain from the sales group projections for units to be sold and expected expenses for the coming year. Then accounting draws up the final budget and, throughout the year, compares the budget to actual expenditures and revenues.

Reporting Standards and Practices

Accountants follow standard reporting practices and principles when they prepare external reports. The common language dictated by standard practices is designed to give external users confidence in the accuracy and meaning of financial information. Spelled out in GAAP, these principles cover a range of issues, such as when to recognize revenues from operations, how to *match* revenues and expenses, and how to make full public disclosure of financial information. Without such standards, users of financial statements wouldn't be able to compare information from different companies and thus they would misunderstand—or be led to misconstrue—a company's true financial status.

Revenue Recognition As we noted earlier, revenues are funds that flow into a business as a result of operating activities during an accounting period. Revenue recognition is the formal recording and reporting of revenues in financial statements.[16] Although a firm earns revenues continuously as it makes sales, earnings are not reported until the *earnings cycle* is completed. This cycle is complete under two conditions:

1 The sale is complete and the product delivered.
2 The sale price has been collected or is collectible (accounts receivable).

ENTREPRENEURSHIP and *New Ventures*

How Can You Account for a Good Beer?

Denison's, lamented a recent article in the Canadian trade journal *World of Beer*, "has closed, and with it has gone our sole opportunity to enjoy Canada's finest Bavarian-style wheat beer and some of the best lagers in the land." The failure of Denison's Brewing Co., a favorite among brewpub aficionados in Toronto, Ontario, issued a stark warning to all local brewers: Even a great-tasting beer will go sour if you can't produce and sell it profitably.

The lesson of Denison's rise and fall has been studied seriously at Black Oak Brewing Co., where founders Ken Woods and John Gagliardi may be the perfect pair to survive in Canada's highly competitive beer market. Although each brings different skills to the joint venture, they share a vision: to make—and sell—the highest-quality beer possible. Gagliardi, certified as a brewmaster by the world-renowned Siebel Institute in 1993, is the quality-control expert whose responsibilities include ensuring the consistency and character of every batch of Black Oak. He admits that as a businessman, he is "first and foremost" a beer lover, and he continues to refresh the company's brand mix by releasing seasonal brews, such as Oktoberfest and Christmas Nutcracker—a practice that permits him to conduct brewing experiments without too much risk. "We're bent on making the highest-quality beer possible," says Gagliardi. "It's got to have the right taste and the perfect clarity and quality. We won't settle for anything less than the best, because we know our customers are going to be expecting a high-quality beer."

Woods, meanwhile, is a Certified Management Accountant (CMA) and a member of the Society of Management Accountants of Canada, but he shares his partner's enthusiastic interest in beer and brewing. For 10 years, he devoted his evenings to developing both his bartending skills and his business contacts, while both would-be entrepreneurs refined their concepts of beers and brewery operations. Since opening Black Oak in 1999, they've managed to develop award-winning beers such as Black Oak Nut Brown Ale, Pale Ale, and Premium Lager, which *The Bar Towel*, a Web site for Toronto beer lovers, calls "fine, flavourful brews."

Just as importantly, they've also managed to cultivate successful business operations. Woods's accounting background enables him to set up and monitor management and financial procedures, such as the cost controls that made it possible for the company to buy a vintage 1940s labeling machine. "It doesn't matter that it's old," explains Woods. "It's a great piece of equipment and we got it at the right price." Woods and Gagliardi also take care to buy high-quality raw materials at the right price. That's why toasted wheat comes from the nearby town of Fergus while malt is imported from western Canada.

Accounting expertise is especially important because the company's cash flows are affected by the terms of payment negotiated with suppliers and by its procedures for collecting sales revenues. Working in finance and purchasing departments while earning his CMA credentials, Woods learned a lot about payables and receivables. He also produced staff expense reports and tax documents and set up standards for keeping operating costs under control. Finally, his management-accountant training has been especially useful in dealing with the numerous guidelines and rafts of government forms that characterize Ontario's highly regulated beer industry. Being a CMA, says Woods, "is really helpful because it firms up everything you need to know in the marketplace."

The end of the earning cycle determines the timing for revenue recognition in a firm's financial statements. Revenues are recorded for the accounting period in which sales are completed and collectible (or collected). This practice assures the users that the statement gives a fair comparison of what was gained in return for the resources that were given up.

Matching Net income is calculated by subtracting expenses from revenues. The *matching principle* states that expenses will be matched with revenues to determine net income for an accounting period.[17] Why is this principle important? It permits the statement user to see how much net gain resulted from the assets that had to be given up in order to generate revenues during a given period. Thus, when we match revenue recognition with expense recognition, we get net income for the period.

Consider the hypothetical case of Little Red Wagon Co. Let's see what happens when the books are kept in two different ways:

1 **Correct method:** Revenue recognition is matched with expense recognition to determine net income when the earnings cycle is *completed*.
2 **Incorrect method:** Revenue recognition occurs *before* the earnings cycle is completed.

Suppose that 500 wagons are produced and delivered to customers at $20 each during 2002. In the next year, 600 wagons are produced and delivered. In part (A) of Table 13.3, we use the correct matching method: Revenues are recorded for the period in which sales are completed and collectible from customers. So are the expenses of producing and delivering the products that were sold. When sales revenues are matched against the expenses of making sales, we see how much better off the company is at the end of each accounting period as a result of that period's operations. Little Red Wagon earned $2,000 net income for the first year and did even better in 2003.

In part (B) of Table 13.3, the principles of revenue recognition and matching have been violated. Certain activities of the two accounting periods are disguised and mixed together rather than separated by period. The result is a distorted performance report showing (incorrectly) that 2002 was better than 2003.

Here's what Red Wagon's accountants did wrong. The sales department sold 200 wagons (with revenues of $4,000) to a customer late in 2002. Those *revenues* are included in the $14,000 for 2002. But because the 200 wagons were produced and delivered to the customer in 2003, the *expenses* are recorded, as in (A), for 2003. The result is a distorted picture of operations: It looks as if expenses for 2003 are very high for such a low sales level and as if expenses (compared to revenues) were better kept under control during 2002.

Accountants violated the matching principle by ignoring *the period during which the earnings cycle was completed*. Although $4,000 in sales of wagons occurred in 2002, the earnings cycle for those wagons is not completed until they were produced and delivered, which occurred in 2003. Accordingly, both revenues and expenses for those 200 wagons should have been reported *in the same period*—namely, in 2003.

TABLE 13.3

Revenue Recognition and the Matching Principle

(A) The Correct Method Reveals Each Accounting Period's Activities and Results

	Year Ended December 31, 2002	Year Ended December 31, 2003
Revenues	$10,000	$12,000
Expenses	8,000	9,000
Net income	$ 2,000	$ 3,000

(B) The Incorrect Method Disguises Each Accounting Period's Activities and Results

	Year Ended December 31, 2002	Year Ended December 31, 2003
Revenue	$14,000	$ 8,000
Expenses	8,000	9,000
Net income	$ 6,000	$(1,000)

They were properly reported in part (A), where we can see clearly what was gained and what was lost on activities completed in an accounting period. By requiring this practice, the matching principle avoids financial distortions.

Full Disclosure Full disclosure means that financial statements should not include just numbers. They should also furnish management's interpretations and explanations of those numbers so that users can better understand information in the statements. Because they know about events inside the company, the people in management prepare additional information to explain certain events or transactions or to disclose the circumstances behind certain results.

SELF-CHECK QUESTIONS 4–6

You should now be able to answer Self-Check Questions 4–6.*

4 Multiple Choice The end-of-year *financial statement* for Millie's fruit stand includes the following data: assets = $20,000; owner's equity = $4,500; liabilities = $17,500. Given this information, which of the following is **true**? [select one]: **(a)** Assets are increasing faster than liabilities. **(b)** Profits are being reinvested in the firm. **(c)** Assets are mostly fixed rather than current. **(d)** An accounting error has occurred. **(e)** Retained earnings for the year have increased.

5 Multiple Choice Which of the following is **not** true regarding *assets on the balance sheet*? [select

one]: **(a)** Next year's book value for a fixed asset will be less than this year's value after depreciation is subtracted. **(b)** Cash is the most liquid of all current assets. **(c)** Merchandise inventory is a current asset. **(d)** Prepaid expenses are increased by paying next year's rent this year. **(e)** Allowance for doubtful accounts increases the book value of accounts receivable.

6 True/False Because *gross profit* (or gross margin) is calculated by subtracting the cost of goods sold from revenues, the result (gross profit) must always be a positive number.

*Answers to Self-Check Questions 4–6 can be found on p. 509.

■ ANALYZING FINANCIAL STATEMENTS

Financial statements present a lot of information, but what does it all *mean*? How, for example, can statements help investors decide what stock to buy or help lenders decide whether to extend credit? Statements provide data, which can in turn be applied to various *ratios* (comparative numbers). We can then use these ratios to analyze a firm's financial health or to check its progress by comparing current and past statements.[18]

Ratios are normally grouped into three major classifications:

■ **Solvency ratios**, both short- and long-term, estimate risk.
■ **Profitability ratios** measure potential earnings.
■ **Activity ratios** reflect management's use of assets.

Depending on the decisions to be made, a user may apply none, some, or all of the ratios in a classification.

solvency ratio
Financial ratio, either short or long term, for estimating the risk in investing in a firm

profitability ratio
Financial ratio for measuring a firm's potential earnings

activity ratio
Financial ratio for evaluating management's use of a firm's assets

Short-Term Solvency Ratios

liquidity ratio
Solvency ratio measuring a firm's ability to pay its immediate debts

In the short run, survival depends on a company's ability to pay its immediate debts. Such payments require cash. Short-term solvency ratios measure a company's relative liquidity and thus its ability to pay immediate debts. The higher a firm's **liquidity ratios**, the lower the risk to investors.

current ratio
Solvency ratio that determines a firm's creditworthiness by measuring its ability to pay current liabilities

Current Ratio The most commonly used liquidity ratio, the current ratio or "banker's ratio," concerns a firm's creditworthiness. The **current ratio** measures a company's ability to meet current obligations out of current assets. It thus reflects a firm's ability to generate cash to meet obligations through the normal, orderly process of selling inventories and collecting accounts receivable. It is calculated by dividing current assets by current liabilities.

As a rule, a current ratio is satisfactory at 2:1 or higher—that is, if current assets more than double current liabilities. A smaller ratio may indicate that a firm will have trouble paying its bills. Note, however, that a larger ratio may imply that assets are not being used productively and should be invested elsewhere.

How does Perfect Posters measure up? Look again at the balance sheet in Figure 13.2. Judging from current assets and current liabilities at the end of 2003, we see that

$$\frac{\text{Current assets}}{\text{Current liabilities}} = \frac{\$57,210}{\$21,935} = 2.61$$

How does this ratio compare with those of other companies? Not bad: It's lower than O'Reilly Automotive *(www.oreillyauto.com)* (2.94) and higher than those of Gillette *(www.gillette.com)* (1.56), Cisco Systems *(www.cisco.com)* (2.14), and Starwood Hotels & Resorts Worldwide *(www.sheraton.com)* (0.23). Perfect Posters may be holding too much uninvested cash, but it looks like a good credit risk.

working capital
Difference between a firm's current assets and current liabilities

Working Capital A related measure is **working capital**—the difference between a firm's current assets and current liabilities. Working capital indicates a firm's ability to pay short-term debts (liabilities) owed to outsiders. At the end of 2003, Perfect Posters' working capital was $35,275 (that is, $57,210 − $21,935). Because current liabilities must be paid off within one year, current assets are more than enough to meet current obligations.

Long-Term Solvency Ratios

debt ratio
Solvency ratio measuring a firm's ability to meet its long-term debts

To survive in the long run, a company must meet both its short-term (current) debts and its long-term liabilities. These latter debts usually involve interest payments. A firm that can't meet them is in danger of collapse or takeover—a risk that makes creditors and investors quite cautious.

debt-to-owners' equity ratio (or debt-to-equity ratio)
Solvency ratio describing the extent to which a firm is financed through borrowing

Debt-to-Owners' Equity Ratio To measure a company's risk of running into this problem, we use **debt ratios**. The most common debt ratio is the **debt-to-owners' equity ratio** (or **debt-to-equity ratio**), which describes the extent to which a firm is financed through borrowed money. It is calculated by dividing **debt**—total liabilities—by owners' equity. Companies with debt-to-equity ratios above 1 are probably relying too much on debt. Such firms may find themselves owing so much debt that they lack the income needed to meet interest payments or to repay borrowed money.

debt
A firm's total liabilities

In the case of Perfect Posters, we can use the balance sheet in Figure 13.2 to work out the debt-to-equity ratio as follows:

$$\frac{\text{Debt}}{\text{Owners' equity}} = \frac{\$61,935}{\$111,155} = 0.56$$

Leverage Sometimes, however, a high debt-to-equity ratio can be not only acceptable but also desirable. Borrowing funds gives a firm **leverage**—the ability to make otherwise unaffordable investments. In *leveraged buyouts (LBOs)*, firms have willingly taken on sometimes huge debt in order to buy out other companies. But when owning the purchased company generates profits above the cost of borrowing the purchase price, leveraging makes sense, even if it raises the buyer's debt-to-equity ratio. Unfortunately, many buyouts have caused problems because profits fell short of expected levels or because rising interest rates increased payments on the buyer's debt.

leverage
Ability to finance an investment through borrowed funds

Profitability Ratios

It's important to know whether a company is solvent in both the long and the short term, but risk alone is not an adequate basis for investment decisions. Investors also want some measure of the returns they can expect. *Return on equity* and *earnings per share* are two common profitability ratios.

Return on Equity Investors want to know the net income earned for each dollar invested. **Return on equity** measures this performance by dividing net income (recorded in the income statement, Figure 13.3) by total owners' equity (recorded in the balance sheet, Figure 13.2).[19] For Perfect Posters, we calculate 2003 return on equity as follows:

return on equity
Profitability ratio measuring income earned for each dollar invested

$$\frac{\text{Net income}}{\text{Total owners' equity}} = \frac{\$12,585}{\$11,155} = 11.3\%$$

Earnings per Share Defined as net income divided by the number of shares of common stock outstanding, **earnings per share** determines the size of the dividend that a firm can pay shareholders. Investors use this ratio to decide whether to buy or sell a company's stock. As the ratio goes up, stock value increases because investors know that the firm can better afford to pay dividends. Naturally, stock loses market value if financial statements report a decline in earnings per share. For Perfect Posters, we can use the net income total from the income statement in Figure 13.3 to calculate earnings per share as follows:

earnings per share
Profitability ratio measuring the size of the dividend that a firm can pay shareholders

$$\frac{\text{Net income}}{\text{Number of common shares outstanding}} = \frac{\$12,585}{8,000} = \$1.57 \text{ per share}$$

As a baseline for comparison, note that Gucci's *(www.gucci.com)* recent earnings were $3.31 per share. Phillips Petroleum Co. *(www.phillips66.com)* earned $7.26.

Activity Ratios

The efficiency with which a firm uses resources is linked to profitability. As a potential investor, then, you want to know which company gets more mileage from its resources. Activity ratios measure this efficiency. Let's say, for example, that two firms use the same amount of resources or assets. If Firm A generates greater profits or sales, it's more efficient and so enjoys a better activity ratio.

Say WHAT YOU MEAN

TECHNICALLY SPEAKING

The meeting for department heads began when the general manager asked, "Well, how did we do last month compared to the budget?" "On a static-budget basis," replied the head of accounting, "unfavorable variances were realized for variable expenses and total expenses. Favorable budget variances were realized for units sold, sales revenues, and operating income." She paused and then continued: "On a flexible-budget basis, unfavorable variances were realized on variable expenses, fixed expenses, total expenses, and operating income." After a moment of silence, the general manager said, "What does all that mean?"

An interesting situation. The key element—and the problem—is specialization. Companies form specialized units—whether departments, teams, or other groups—to foster expertise. But specialization can be both a blessing and a curse. On the one hand, specialists tend to develop their own languages so that they can communicate with one another efficiently and clearly. Communicating with outsiders, however—nonspecialists and specialists with other specialties—presents problems, because specialists then have to communicate in the foreign languages of other specialists. What happens when, say, a team includes engineers and accountants and people from sales, purchasing, and production? Team effectiveness depends on specialists finding a common language.

In our sample meeting, the general manager asked for information from a specialist (an accountant) in front of other specialists. The answer, though technically accurate, didn't inform anyone who didn't understand the special language of accountants. Matters could have gotten worse if, in heeding a call for clarification, the accountant had launched into even more technical detail—perhaps by offering a quick course on static versus flexible budgets and favorable versus unfavorable variances. Obviously, this meeting was neither the time nor the place for a tutorial on budgeting technicalities. In fact, it was probably called to focus on budgeting as a tool for managing performance across the entire organization—to explain, for instance, why budgets are important in every department. The technical detail just sidetracked everyone.

How could this situation have been avoided from the outset? The first step is recognizing the existence of specialized languages and working to foster communications across specialty areas. Second, the general manager should have let accounting know beforehand the purpose of the meeting, perhaps giving the accountant advance notice of the question with which he intended to start things off. This way, the accountant could have come up with alternative answers based on the manager's purpose in asking the question. The third step—adopting a language to be used by everyone—is optional. It suggests that there are occasions when specialized language should be spoken throughout the organization. This approach, for example, would have been useful if our general manager had decided that all of his departments should know more about the technicalities of the budgets for which they're responsible.

inventory turnover ratio
Activity ratio measuring the average number of times that inventory is sold and restocked during the year

Inventory Turnover Ratio Certain specific measures can be used to explain how one firm earns more profit than another. The **inventory turnover ratio** measures the average number of times that inventory is sold and restocked during the year—that is, how quickly it is produced and sold.[20] To find this ratio, you first need to know your *average inventory*—the typical amount of inventory on hand during the year. You can calculate average inventory by adding end-of-year inventory to beginning-of-year inventory and dividing by 2. You can now find your inventory turnover ratio, which is expressed as the cost of goods sold divided by average inventory:

$$\frac{\text{Cost of goods sold}}{\text{Average inventory}} = \frac{\text{Cost of goods sold}}{(\text{Beginning inventory} + \text{Ending inventory}) / 2}$$

High inventory turnover means efficient operations. Because less investment money is tied up in inventory, funds can be put to work elsewhere to earn greater

"It's up to you now, Miller. The only thing that can save us is an accounting breakthrough."

returns. But inventory turnover must be compared with both prior years and industry averages. A rate of 5, for example, might be excellent for an auto supply store but disastrous for a supermarket, where a rate of about 15 is common. Rates can also vary within a company that markets a variety of products. To calculate Perfect Posters' inventory turnover ratio for 2003, we take the merchandise inventory figures for the income statement in Figure 13.3. The ratio can be expressed as follows:

$$\frac{\$104,765}{(\$22,380 + \$21,259) / 2} = 4.8 \text{ times}$$

In other words, new merchandise replaces old merchandise every 76 days (365 days/4.8). The 4.8 ratio is below the average of 7.0 for comparable operations, indicating that the business is slightly inefficient.

Inventory turnover ratio measures the average number of times that a store sells and restocks its inventory in one year. The higher the ratio, the more products that get sold and the more revenue that comes in. Supermarkets— even upscale outlets like this Whole Foods Market *(www.wholefoodsmarket.com)* in New York City—must have a much higher turnover ratio than, say, auto-supply or toy stores. In almost all retail stores, products with the highest ratios get the shelf spaces that generate the most customer traffic and sales.

■ INTERNATIONAL ACCOUNTING

More U.S. companies are buying and selling in other countries. Coca-Cola and Boeing receive large portions of their revenues from overseas sales, whereas Sears and Kmart buy goods from other countries for sale in the United States. In addition, more and more companies own foreign subsidiaries. Obviously, accounting for foreign transactions involves special procedures. One of the most basic is translating the values of the different currencies.

Foreign Currency Exchange

A unique consideration in international accounting is the value of currencies and exchange rates.[21] As we saw in Chapter 4, the value of any country's currency is subject to change. Political and economic conditions, for instance, affect the stability of a currency and its value relative to other currencies.

foreign currency exchange rate
Value of a nation's currency as determined by market forces

As it's traded around the world, a currency's value is determined by market forces—what buyers are willing to pay for it. The resulting values are called **foreign currency exchange rates**. When a currency becomes unstable—that is, when its value changes frequently—it is regarded as a *weak currency*. The value of the Brazilian real, for example, fluctuated between 0.416 and 0.957—a variation range of 130 percent in U.S. dollars—during the period from 1997 to 2002. On the other hand, a *strong currency* historically rises or holds steady in comparison to the U.S. dollar. As changes occur, they must be considered by accountants when recording international transactions. They will affect, perhaps profoundly, the amount that a firm pays for foreign purchases and the amount it gains from sales to foreign buyers.

International Transactions

International purchases, credit sales, and accounting for foreign subsidiaries all involve transactions affected by exchange rates. When a U.S. company called Village Wine and Cheese Shops imports Bordeau wine from a French company called Pierre Bourgeois, its accountant must be sure that Village's books reflect its true costs. The amount owed to Pierre Bourgeois changes daily along with the exchange rate between euros and dollars. Thus, our accountant must identify the actual rate *on the day that payment in euros is made* so that the correct U.S.-dollar cost of the purchase is recorded.

International Accounting Standards

Professional accounting groups from about 80 countries are members of the International Accounting Standards Board (IASB) *(www.iasb.org.uk)*, which is trying to eliminate national differences in financial reporting procedures.[22] Bankers, investors, and managers want procedures that are comparable from country to country and applicable to all firms regardless of home nation. Standardization is occurring in some areas but is far from universal. IASB financial statements include an income statement, balance sheet, and statement of cash flows similar to those issued by U.S. accountants. International standards, however, do not require a uniform format, and variety abounds.

SELF-CHECK QUESTIONS 7–9

You should now be able to answer Self-Check Questions 7–9.*

7 **True/False** In 2002, Kiddie Kar Kompany received orders for 400 red wagons at a purchase price of $80 per wagon. The wagons were delivered to customers in 2003. According to the *revenue recognition principle*, Kiddie Kars should report the $32,000 as revenue for year 2003 rather than for 2002.

8 **True/False** *Earnings per share* is a more reliable indicator of profitability than is *return on equity*.

9 **Multiple Choice** Which of the following statements about *financial ratios* is **not true**? [select one]: **(a)** An *inventory turnover ratio* of 6.5 means that the firm has enough inventory on hand to supply its sales requirements for the next 6.5 months. **(b)** A *current ratio* of 10.4 strongly suggests that the firm is able to meet immediate (short-term) debts. **(c)** A company with a *debt-to-equity ratio* of 4.8 is probably risky because it's relying too much on debt. **(d)** A *return on equity* of 16 percent indicates that the firm is earning net income of 16 percent on each dollar invested. **(e)** *Solvency ratios*, both short and long term, estimate risk.

*Answers to Self-Check Questions 7–9 can be found on p. 510.

Continued from page 386

IS ANYBODY HOLDING AUDITORS ACCOUNTABLE?

Although Andersen executives claimed that no one had committed any crimes, that story turned to fiction when a former partner pleaded guilty to obstruction charges. As a witness for the government, David Duncan admitted that he'd broken the law by destroying documents. Even more damning for Andersen was news that the Enron affair wasn't its first brush with charges of shady auditing. Four years earlier, the firm's Fort Lauderdale office had destroyed sensitive documents when the SEC came to look into Andersen's restatement of Sunbeam's earnings following a barrage of lawsuits by Sunbeam stockholders. According to another Andersen partner, employees were ordered to destroy anything that didn't agree with the CPA's final statement of Sunbeam's earnings.

In a case involving another client—Waste Management—Andersen agreed in 2001 to pay $7 million to settle federal charges of filing false auditing reports dating back to before the Sunbeam case. In assessing the largest civil penalty ever levied against a major accounting firm, the SEC claimed that Andersen had filed false audits of its client's books from 1992 to 1996. Andersen claimed that all financial statements were prepared according to GAAP, but income was, in fact, overstated by more than $1 billion.

In an even larger action—one of the largest nonprofit frauds in history—Andersen agreed in 2002 to a $217 million settlement involving the Baptist Foundation of Arizona. The Foundation, with Andersen as its auditor, allegedly swindled elderly people out of $590 million. The suit accused Andersen of ignoring danger signs, falsifying documents, and destroying records.

In June 2002, Andersen was convicted of obstructing justice in the Enron case by destroying files while on notice of a federal investigation. Both accountants and clients began leaving Andersen once its entanglement with Enron came to light. Hundreds of accountants, many of them partners in the firm, have jumped to other major firms, and many others have started their own consulting or accounting firms. Even before the conviction in June, more than 500 clients, including the 15 biggest publicly traded firms that Andersen had audited the year before, had found new CPAs.

Before long, wrongdoing at Enron, Tyco, WorldCom, Rite Aid, Adelphia Communications, Dynegy, and ImClone Systems—including a wide range of practices that should have been noticed by vigilant CPAs—had spooked investors and strained public trust to the breaking point. By late June 2002, the U.S. stock market, buried under an avalanche of reports of fraud and deceit, had lost more than 20 percent of its value—amounting to hundreds of billions in losses for retirees and other investors.

What can we do to recover? As part of the settlement in the Baptist Foundation case, one Andersen partner and one auditing manager had to give up their CPA licenses. The Arizona Board of Accountancy appointed a three-person panel to monitor Andersen's audits of Arizona companies for two years. In effect, this last action reveals the sad state of affairs in contemporary accounting: We need auditors to monitor auditors. And unfortunately, we don't yet have an answer to the next obvious question: How many layers of monitors monitoring monitors will we need to restore public trust in the accounting profession?

Questions for Discussion

1 Why do you suppose Andersen auditors were reluctant to disclose deficiencies in clients' financial statements and accounting practices?

2 Do you think that Arizona authorities were overly harsh with the penalties they imposed on Andersen? Why or why not?

3 Consider the obligations of CPAs employed by Arthur Andersen. Is the CPA's first obligation to Andersen or to the accounting profession? Explain your reasoning.

4 Suppose that you're a CPA at a major accounting firm, where you suspect that a client isn't abiding by GAAP. You also get the impression that your boss would prefer you to keep your suspicions under wraps. How would you handle this situation?

5 What changes, if any, do you recommend the accounting profession or regulatory agencies make to restore public confidence in the business of financial reporting?

■ SUMMARY OF LEARNING OBJECTIVES

1 **Explain the role of accountants, and distinguish between the kinds of work done by *public* and *private accountants.***

Accounting is a comprehensive system for collecting, analyzing, and communicating financial information. It measures business performance and translates the results into information for management decisions. It also prepares performance reports for owners, the public, and regulatory agencies, thereby providing an accurate picture of the firm's financial health.

There are two main fields in accounting: (1) **Financial accounting** deals with external information users (consumer groups, unions, stockholders, and government agencies). It prepares income statements, balance sheets, and other financial reports published for shareholders and the public. (2) **Managerial** (or **management**) **accounting** serves internal users, such as managers at all levels.

Certified public accountants (CPAs) are licensed professionals who provide auditing, tax, and management advisory services for other firms and individuals. CPAs are always independent of the firms they audit. Many businesses hire their own salaried employees—**private accountants**—to perform internal accounting activities. **Certified management accountants (CMAs)** are certified professionals who provide services to support managers in such areas as taxation, budgeting, internal auditing, and cost analysis.

2 **Discuss the *CPA Vision Project,* and explain how the CPA profession is changing.**

The Vision Project is a professionwide assessment to see what the future of the accounting profession will be like. It was initiated because of the declining number of students entering the accounting profession and because of rapid changes in the business world. Practicing CPAs and other industry leaders participated in identifying key forces that are affecting the profession. Then they developed recommendations for change, including a set of *core services* that the profession should offer clients and a set of *core competencies* that CPAs should possess. Overall, the new vision reflects changes in the CPA's culture and professional lifestyle.

3 **Explain how the following concepts are used in accounting: the *accounting equation* and *double-entry accounting.***

Accountants use the following equation to balance the data pertaining to financial transactions:

$$\text{Assets} = \text{Liabilities} + \text{Owners' equity}$$

We can rewrite the **accounting equation** to show the value of the firm to the owners:

$$\text{Assets} - \text{Liabilities} = \text{Owners' equity}$$

In the accounting equation, if **assets** exceed **liabilities**, **owners' equity** is positive; if the firm goes out of business, owners will receive some cash (a gain) after selling assets and paying off liabilities. If liabilities outweigh assets, owners' equity is negative; assets aren't enough to pay off debts. If the company goes under, owners will get no cash and some creditors won't be paid.

Because every transaction affects two accounts, accountants use a *double-entry accounting system* to record the dual effects. Because the double-entry system requires at least two bookkeeping entries for each transaction, it keeps the accounting equation in balance. These tools serve as double-checks for accounting errors.

4 **Describe the three basic *financial statements*, show how they reflect the activity and financial condition of a business, and explain the key standards and principles for reporting them.**

Accounting summarizes the results of a firm's transactions and issues reports to help managers make informed decisions. The class of reports known as **financial statements** is divided into three categories. (1) **Balance sheets** (sometimes called *statements of financial position*) supply detailed information about the accounting-equation factors: assets, liabilities, and owners' equity, at a given point in time. (2) The **income statement** (sometimes called a **profit-and-loss statement**) describes revenues and expenses to show a firm's annual profit or loss. (3) A publicly traded firm must issue a **statement of cash flows**, which describes its yearly cash receipts and payments. It shows the effects on cash of three activities: (1) cash flows from operations, (2) cash flows from investing, and (3) cash flows from financing.

Accountants follow standard reporting practices and principles when they prepare financial statements. Otherwise, users wouldn't be able to compare information from different companies, and they might misunderstand—or be led to misconstrue—a company's true financial status. The following are three of the most important standard reporting practices and principles: (1) *Revenue recognition* is the formal recording and reporting of revenues in the financial statements. All firms earn revenues continuously as they make sales, but earnings are not reported until the earnings cycle is completed. This cycle is complete under two conditions: (i) The sale is complete and the product delivered; (ii) the sale price has been collected or is collectible. This practice assures interested parties that the statement gives a fair comparison of what was gained for the resources that were given up.

(2) The *matching principle* states that expenses will be matched with revenues to determine net income. It permits users to see how much net gain resulted from the assets that had to be given up in order to generate revenues. (3) Because they have inside knowledge, management prepares additional information that explains certain events or transactions or discloses the circumstances behind certain results. *Full disclosure* means that financial statements include management interpretations and explanations to help external users understand information contained in statements.

5 **Show how computing key *financial ratios* can help in analyzing the financial strengths of a business and explain some of the special issues that arise in international accounting.**

Financial statements provide data that can be applied to ratios (comparative numbers). Ratios can then be used to analyze the financial health of one or more companies. Ratios can help creditors, investors, and managers assess a firm's finances. They can also be used to check a firm's progress by comparing current with past statements.

Solvency ratios, such as the **current ratio**, estimate risk by measuring the ability to meet current obligations out of current assets. Long-term solvency ratios, such as the **debt-to-owners' equity ratio** (or **debt-to-equity ratio**), describe the extent to which a firm is financed through borrowed money. High indebtedness can be risky because it requires payment of interest and repayment of borrowed funds. **Profitability ratios—return on equity** and **earnings per share**—measure potential earnings. **Activity ratios** reflect management's use of assets by measuring the efficiency with which a firm uses its resources. The **inventory turnover ratio**, for example, measures the average number of times that inventory is sold and restocked annually—that is, how quickly it is produced and sold. A high inventory turnover ratio means efficient operations: Because a smaller amount of investment is tied up in inventory, the firm's funds can be put to work elsewhere to earn greater returns.

Accounting for foreign transactions involves special procedures, such as translating the values of different countries' currencies and accounting for the effects of exchange rates. Moreover, currencies are subject to change: As they're traded each day around the world, their values are determined by market forces—what buyers are willing to pay for them. The resulting values are **foreign currency exchange rates**, which can be fairly volatile.

International purchases, sales on credit, and accounting for foreign subsidiaries all involve transactions affected by exchange rates. When a U.S. company imports a French product, its accountant must be sure that its books reflect its true costs. The amount owed to the French seller changes daily along with the exchange rate between euros and dollars. The American accountant must therefore identify the actual rate on the day that payment in euros is made so that the correct U.S.-dollar cost of the product is recorded.

■ KEY TERMS

accounting (p. 386)

bookkeeping (p. 386)

accounting information system (AIS) (p. 386)

controller (p. 387)

financial accounting system (p. 387)

managerial (or management) accounting system (p. 387)

certified public accountant (CPA) (p. 388)

audit (p. 388)

generally accepted accounting principles (GAAP) (p. 388)

management advisory services (p. 388)

private accountant (p. 389)

certified management accountant (CMA) (p. 389)

asset (p. 393)

liability (p. 393)

owners' equity (p. 393)

double-entry accounting system (p. 394)

financial statement (p. 394)

balance sheet (p. 394)

current asset (p. 395)

liquidity (p. 395)

account receivable (or receivables) (p. 395)

merchandise inventory (p. 395)

prepaid expense (p. 396)

fixed asset (p. 396)

depreciation (p. 396)

intangible asset (p. 396)

goodwill (p. 396)

current liability (p. 396)

accounts payable (or payables) (p. 396)

long-term liability (p. 396)

paid-in capital (p. 396)

retained earnings (p. 396)

income statement (or profit-and-loss statement) (p. 396)

revenues (p. 397)

cost of goods sold (p. 397)

gross profit (or gross margin) (p. 397)

operating expenses (p. 398)

operating income (p. 398)

net income (or net profit or net earnings) (p. 398)

statement of cash flows (p. 398)

budget (p. 399)

solvency ratio (p. 403)

profitability ratio (p. 403)

activity ratio (p. 403)

liquidity ratio (p. 404)

current ratio (p. 404)

working capital (p. 404)

debt ratio (p. 404)

debt-to-owners' equity ratio (or debt-to-equity ratio) (p. 404)

debt (p. 404)

leverage (p. 405)

return on equity (p. 405)

earnings per share (p. 405)

inventory turnover ratio (p. 406)

foreign currency exchange rate (p. 408)

■ QUESTIONS AND EXERCISES

Questions for Review

1 Identify the three types of services performed by CPAs.

2 How does the double-entry system reduce the chances of mistakes or fraud in accounting?

3 What are the three basic financial statements, and what major information does each contain?

4 Identify the three major classifications of financial statement ratios, and give an example of one ratio in each category.

5 Explain how financial ratios allow managers to monitor efficiency and effectiveness.

6 Explain the ways in which financial accounting differs from managerial (management) accounting.

Questions for Analysis

7 If you were planning to invest in a company, which of the three types of financial statements would you most want to see? Why?

8 Dasar Co. reports the following data in its September 30, 2002, financial statements:

Gross sales	$225,000
Current assets	40,000
Long-term assets	100,000
Current liabilities	16,000
Long-term liabilities	44,000
Owners' equity	80,000
Net income	7,200

Compute the following ratios: current ratio, debt-to-equity ratio, and return on owners' equity.

Application Exercises

9 Interview an accountant at a local manufacturing firm. Trace the process by which the company develops budgets. How does it use them? How does budgeting help managers plan business activities? How does budgeting help them control activities? Give examples.

10 Interview the manager of a local retail or wholesale business about taking inventory. What is the firm's primary purpose in taking inventory? How often is it done?

BUILDING YOUR BUSINESS SKILLS

PUTTING THE BUZZ IN BILLING

This exercise enhances the following SCANS workplace competencies: demonstrating basic skills, demonstrating thinking skills, exhibiting interpersonal skills, working with information, and applying system knowledge.

Goal
To encourage students to think about the advantages and disadvantages of using an electronic system for handling accounts receivable and accounts payable.

Method

Step 1
Study Figure 13.5. The outside circle depicts the seven steps involved in the issuance of paper bills to customers, the payment of these bills by customers, and the handling by banks of debits and credits for the two accounts. The inside circle shows the same bill process handled electronically.

Step 2
As the chief financial officer of a midwestern utility company, you are analyzing the feasibility of switching from a paper to an electronic system. You decide to discuss the ramifications of the choice with three associates (choose three classmates to take on these roles). Your discussion requires that you research electronic payment systems now being developed. Specifically, using online and library research, you must find out as much as you can about the electronic bill-paying systems being developed by Visa International, Intuit, IBM, and the Checkfree Corp. After you have researched this information, brainstorm the advantages and disadvantages of switching to an electronic system.

FOLLOW-UP QUESTIONS
1 What cost savings are inherent in the electronic system for both your company and its customers? In your answer, consider such costs as handling, postage, and paper.
2 What consequences would your decision to adopt an electronic system have on others with whom you do business, including manufacturers of check-sorting equipment, the U.S. Postal Service, and banks?
3 Switching to an electronic system would mean a large capital expense for new computers and software. How could analyzing the company's income statement help you justify this expense?
4 How are consumers likely to respond to paying bills electronically? Are you likely to get a different response from individuals than from business customers?

EXERCISING YOUR ETHICS

CONFIDENTIALLY YOURS

The Situation
Accountants are often entrusted with private, sensitive information that should be used confidentially. In this exercise, you're encouraged to think about ethical considerations that might arise when an accountant's career choices come up against a professional obligation to maintain confidentiality.

The Dilemma
Assume that you're the head accountant in a large electronics firm. Your responsibilities include preparing income statements and balance sheets for financial reporting to stockholders. In addition, you regularly prepare confidential budgets for internal use by managers responsible for planning departmental activities, including future investments in new assets. You've also worked with auditors and supplied sensitive information to consultants from a CPA firm that assesses financial problems and suggests solutions.

Now let's suppose that you're approached by another company—one of the electronics industry's most successful firms—and offered a higher-level position. If you accept, your new job will include developing financial plans and serving on the strategic planning committee. Thus, you'd be

FIGURE 13.5

Two Ways of Handling Accounts
Receivable

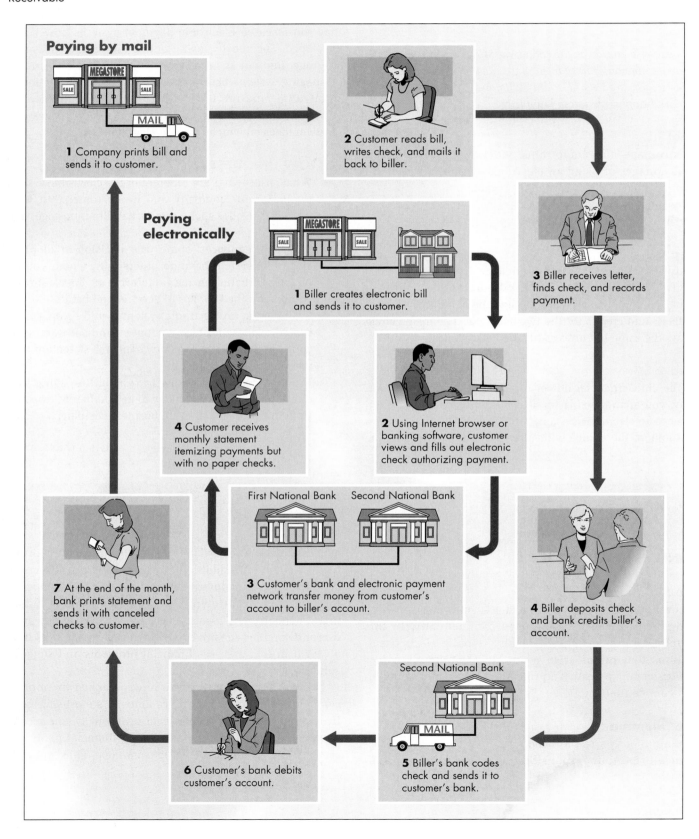

involved not only in developing strategy but also in evaluating the competition. You'll undoubtedly be called on to use your knowledge of your previous firm's competitive strengths and weaknesses. You realize that your insider knowledge could be useful in your new job.

1 What are the roles of financial accounting, managerial accounting, and accounting services in this scenario?

2 What are the chief ethical issues in this situation?

3 As the central figure in this scenario, how would you handle this situation?

 ## CRAFTING YOUR BUSINESS PLAN

THE PROFITABILITY OF PLANNING

The Purpose of the Assignment

1 To acquaint students with accounting issues faced by a sample firm in developing its business plan in the framework of *Business PlanPro (BPP) 2003* software package (Version 6.0).

2 To demonstrate how three chapter topics—accounting skills, financial data reports, and the profit-and-loss statement—can be integrated as components in the *BPP* planning environment.

Assignment

After reading Chapter 13 in the textbook, open the BPP *software and search for information about plans for accounting as it applies to a sample firm:* AMT Computer Store (American Management Technology). *To find* AMT Computer Store, *do the following:*

Open *Business PlanPro*. Go to the toolbar and click on the "*Sample Plans*" icon. In the **Sample Plan Browser**, do a search using the **search category** *Wholesale trade—durable goods*. From the resulting list, select the category entitled **Computer Hardware—Reseller**, which is the location for *AMT Computer Store*. The screen that you're now looking at

is the introduction page for the *AMT Computer Store* business plan. Next, scroll down until you reach the **Table of Contents** for *AMT's* business plan.

NOW RESPOND TO THE FOLLOWING ITEMS:

1 What is your assessment of the accounting skills possessed by AMT's management team? What do you recommend? [Sites to see in *BPP* for this item: On the Table of Contents page, click on each of the following, in turn: **6.1 Organizational Structure, 6.2 Management Team**, and **6.3 Management Team Gaps**.]

2 Use *BPP*'s computer graphics to explore *AMT*'s financial data reports. Describe the kinds of accounting information you find in the charts. [Sites to see in *BPP*: Beginning on the **Table of Contents** page, go to the outline section entitled **7.2 Key Financial Indicators**, including **Benchmarks Comparison Chart**.]

3 At the time of this plan, *AMT Computer Store* was expecting large changes in annual net profits during the next three years. Based on the company's planned profit-and-loss statement, identify the key factors—changes in revenues and expenses—that account for changes in expected net profits from year to year. [Sites to see in *BPP*: From the **Table of Contents** page, click on **7.4 Projected Profit and Loss**, including **Table: Profit and Loss (Planned)**.]

 ## VIDEO EXERCISE

ACCOUNTING FOR BILLIONS OF BURGERS: MCDONALD'S

Learning Objectives

The purpose of this video is to help you

1 Understand the challenges that a company may face in managing financial information from operations in multiple countries.

2 Consider ways in which managers and investors use financial information reported by a public company.

3 Understand how different laws and monetary systems can affect the accounting activities of a global corporation.

Synopsis

Collecting, analyzing, and reporting financial data from 27,000 restaurants in 119 countries is no easy task, as the accounting experts at McDonald's are well aware. Every month, individual restaurants send their sales figures to be consolidated with data from other restaurants at the local or country level. From there, the figures are sent to country-group offices and then to one of three major regional offices before going to their final destination at McDonald's headquarters in Oak Brook, Illinois. In the past, financial information arrived in Illinois in bits and pieces, sent by courier, mail, or fax. Today, local and regional offices enter month-end figures into a special secure Web site, enabling the corporate controller to produce financial statements and projections for internal and external use.

DISCUSSION QUESTIONS

1 **For analysis:** Why does McDonald's use "constant currency" comparisons when reporting its financial results?

2 **For analysis:** What types of assets might McDonald's list under depreciation in its financial statements?

3 **For application:** What effect do corporate income tax rates in the countries where it operates have on the income statements prepared at McDonald's local offices?

4 **For application:** What problems might arise if individual restaurants were required to enter sales data directly on the company's centralized accounting Web site instead of following the current procedure of sending it through country and regional channels?

5 **For debate:** To help investors and analysts better assess the company's worldwide financial health, should McDonald's be required to disclose detailed financial results for every country and region? Support your position.

Online Exploration

Visit the McDonald's corporate Web site at *(www.mcdonalds.com/corporate)*. Locate the most recent financial report (quarterly or annual) and examine both overall and regional results. What aspects of its results does McDonald's highlight in this report? Which regions are doing particularly well? Which are lagging? How does management explain any differences in performance? What does McDonald's say about its use of constant currency reporting?

PLANNING FOR YOUR CAREER

PRESENTING YOURSELF ONLINE

We saw in Chapters 12 and 13 that information and communication technology are valuable resources for increasing any firm's competitiveness. In preparing for your career, you'll find that information and technology resources can also be helpful to you. You can use them, for example, when going online to present yourself to prospective employers. This exercise gives you the opportunity to look more closely at various online career-information resources, including announcements of vacancies, methods for job hunting, and practices in employee hiring.

Assignment

Recall from Chapter 12 that geographic separation of workplaces from company headquarters is more common than ever because of networked organizations. For the same reasons, both job seekers and businesses searching for employees rely more heavily on digital contact than on face-to-face and land-mail communication. Although some traditional methods—such as sending out printed résumés—are still effective, innovative online possibilities are too important to ignore. Your objective in this exercise is to evaluate online sources for career information and to explore ways in which you can use online technology for job hunting.

To complete this exercise, do the following:

1 Examine the activities for online career planning presented in Chapter 6, "Marketing Yourself Online," of *Beginning Your Career Search*, 3d ed., by James S. O'Rourke IV.

2 Explore one of the general-career sites on the Internet, such as *(www.job.com)*, that O'Rourke discusses. Identify three (or more) of the career-planning services that would be more difficult to obtain using off-line sources.

3 Consider O'Rourke's suggestions for online job searches in a career field that interests you. Use three different tools to search for jobs in your selected field: (1) an online newspaper source, (2) a general-career Web site, and (3) any of the general-purpose search engines available on the Internet. Which source provides the most useful information?

4 Using any means you choose, identify a potential employer in your career field. Explore the organization's career opportunities by visiting its Web site. Do its employment listings contain information that might help you adapt your résumé for a better match with this particular organization?

5 Compare two methods for entering the job market: (1) sending out printed résumés versus (2) responding to online postings. List the résumé-design skills for each method that are most important for job-search success. Explain the key differences in the skills requirements entailed by the two methods.

6 O'Rourke cautions job seekers against using free Web-hosting services that flash ads alongside your résumé. Why does he post this warning?

14

After reading this chapter, you should be able to:

1 Define *money* and identify the different forms that it takes in the nation's money supply.

2 Describe the different kinds of *financial institutions* that comprise the U.S. financial system and explain the services they offer.

3 Explain how banks *create* money and describe the means by which they are regulated.

4 Discuss the functions of the *Federal Reserve System* and describe the tools that it uses to control the money supply.

5 Identify three important ways the financial industry is changing.

6 Understand some of the key concepts and activities in *international banking and finance.*

ARGENTINES NO LONGER BANK ON THE PESO

They get in line before dawn. Peaceful at first, they become unruly when they have to protect their places in line. No, they're not jockeying for seats at a rock concert or a World Cup soccer game. These frenzied people are customers at one of the largest banks

UNDERSTANDING MONEY AND BANKING

> **"I'm going to put everything in Uruguay where there is a much more serious banking system."**
>
> **—Argentine bank customer disgruntled by the freezing of his assets**

in Buenos Aires, a bank that, like every other bank in the country's depleted system, has to say no to angry account holders. Denied access to their life savings, many will return tomorrow (and be rejected again). In one day, panicked depositors had yanked $2 billion, and to stop the bleeding, the government has temporarily limited withdrawals to $250 a week regardless of the size of the account. Transfers abroad are limited to $1,000 a month, and even the accounts of the wealthiest patrons are frozen. The result? Not surprisingly, a serious shortage of money. "As long as I live, I shall never again put a peso in a bank in Argentina," says Buenos Aires real estate agent Pablo Pechague. "I'm going to put everything in Uruguay where there is a much more serious banking system."

Argentina's currency—the peso—was long known as the most stable in Latin America. The country's free-market economy, South America's second largest (after Brazil), was the darling of emerging markets with its fast-paced economic growth during the 1990s. Billions of investment dollars flowed in from abroad as Argentina undertook the privatization of state industries by selling off hundreds of inefficient businesses.

A healthy 9 percent growth rate and low unemployment meant economic prosperity—until a turnaround started in the late 1990s, with a recession that worsened into 2002. With unemployment reaching 18 percent, investors from the United States and Europe feared that Argentina would devalue the peso to help the economy and, by doing so, would slash investors' profits and, perhaps, even cause the government to protect local industry by reverting back to old policies that are less market friendly than the recent privatization movement.

As the recession lingered, the peso, long considered the foundation of Argentina's steady economy, gradually came to be viewed as overvalued, making the country's exports too expensive and uncompetitive in foreign markets. In late 2001, worried investors and savers started a run on the banks in hopes of reclaiming their money rather than risking financial loss if the economy failed. By year-end 2001, Argentines had withdrawn 17 percent of all bank deposits, or $14.5 billion, causing a sharp decline in the central bank reserves. In early 2002, Economy Minister Jorge Remes Lenicov broke the news: "We are devaluing; we are in collapse. Argentina is bankrupt."

The currency devaluation could cause further job cuts and inflation for Argentina's citizens. As the threat of further instability continued, fears mounted that a steep drop in the peso's value could trigger huge losses for foreign companies in telecommunications, oil, banks, and utilities. And those fears were justified: By mid-2002, foreign creditors, too, were taking a financial beating. Citigroup, for example, the New York–based financial giant, reported losses of $470 million in one calendar quarter from economic problems in Argentina. J.P. Morgan Chase & Co. was hurt even worse, and FleetBoston Financial Corp. took the rare step of postponing its regularly scheduled earnings report until it could sort out the full financial impact of its Argentine losses. Meanwhile, frustrated Argentines, starved for cash, have to rely on bank debit cards, credit cards, and checks to pay for day-to-day purchases.

Our opening story continues on page 441.

■ WHAT IS MONEY?

When someone asks you how much money you have, do you count the dollar bills and coins in your pockets? Do you include your checking and savings accounts? What about stocks and bonds? Do you count your car? Taken together, the value of all these things is your personal wealth. Not all of it, however, is "money." In this section, we consider more precisely what *money* is and what it does.

The Characteristics of Money

money
Any object that is portable, divisible, durable, and stable and serves as a medium of exchange, a store of value, and a unit of account

Modern money often takes the form of stamped metal or printed paper—U.S. dollars, British pounds, Japanese yen—issued by governments. Theoretically, however, just about any object can serve as **money** if it is *portable, divisible, durable*, and *stable*. To appreciate these qualities, imagine using something that lacks them—say, a 70-pound salmon:

- **Portability.** Try lugging 70 pounds of fish from shop to shop. In contrast, modern currency is light and easy to handle.
- **Divisibility.** Suppose that you want to buy a hat, a book, and some milk from three different stores. How would you divide your fish-money? Is a pound of its head worth as much as, say, two gills? Modern currency is easily divisible into smaller parts, each with a fixed value. A dollar, for example, can be exchanged for four quarters. More important, units of money can be easily matched with the value of all goods.
- **Durability.** Regardless of whether you "spend" it, your salmon will lose value every day (in fact, it will eventually be too smelly to be worth anything). Modern currency, however, neither dies nor spoils, and if it wears out, it can be replaced. It is also hard to counterfeit—certainly harder than catching more salmon.
- **Stability.** If salmon were in short supply, you might be able to make quite a deal for yourself. In the middle of a salmon run, however, the market would be flooded with fish. Sellers of goods would soon have enough fish and would refuse to produce anything for which they could get only salmon. Goods would become scarcer, but the salmon would continue (or cease) running, regardless of the plenitude or scarcity of buyable goods. The value of our paper money also fluctuates, but it is considerably more stable than salmon. Its value is related to what we can buy with it.

The Functions of Money

Imagine a successful fisherman who needs a new sail for his boat. In a barter economy—one in which goods are exchanged directly for one another—he would have to find someone who not only needs fish but who is also willing to exchange a sail for it. If no sail maker wants fish, the fisherman must find someone else—say, a shoemaker—who does want fish. Then the fisherman must hope that the sail maker will trade for his new shoes. Clearly, barter is inefficient in comparison with money. In a money economy, the fisherman would sell his catch, receive money, and exchange the money for such goods as a new sail.

Money serves three functions:[1]

- **Medium of exchange.** Like the fisherman "trading" money for a new sail, we use money as a way of buying and selling things. Without money, we would be bogged down in a system of barter.
- **Store of value.** Pity the fisherman who catches a fish on Monday and wants to buy a few bars of candy on, say, the following Saturday, by which time the fish would have spoiled and lost its value. In the form of currency, however, money can be used for future purchases and so "stores" value.
- **Unit of account.** Money lets us measure the relative values of goods and services. It acts as a unit of account because all products can be valued and accounted for in terms of money. For example, the concepts of "$1,000 worth of clothes" and "$500 in labor costs" have universal meaning because everyone deals with money every day.

The Spendable Money Supply: M-1

For money to serve its basic functions, both buyers and sellers must agree on its value. That value depends in part on its *supply*—on how much money is in circulation. When the money supply is high, the value of money drops. When it is low, that value increases.

In the modern world, we've become used to highly structured monetary systems. But in some places, centuries-old systems still survive. In Quetta, Pakistan, for example. traders like Mohammad Essa transfer funds through handshakes and code words. The system is called *hawala*, which means "trust" in Arabic. The worldwide hawala system, though illegal in most countries, moves billions of dollars past regulators annually and is alleged to be the system of choice for terrorists because it leaves no paper trail.

M-1
Measure of the money supply that includes only the most liquid (spendable) forms of money

currency
Government-issued paper money and metal coins

check
Demand deposit order instructing a bank to pay a given sum to a specified payee

demand deposit
Bank account funds that may be withdrawn at any time

M-2
Measure of the money supply that includes all the components of M-1 plus the forms of money that can be easily converted into spendable form

time deposit
Bank funds that cannot be withdrawn without notice or transferred by check

Unfortunately, it is not easy to measure the supply of money. In the United States, one of the most commonly used measures, known widely as **M-1**, counts only the most liquid, or spendable, forms of money: currency, demand deposits, and other checkable deposits. These are all non-interest-bearing or low-interest-bearing forms of money. As of May 2002, M-1 totaled $1.18 trillion.[2]

Paper money and metal coins are **currency** issued by the government. Currency is widely used for small exchanges, and the law requires creditors to accept it in payment of debts. As of May 2002, currency in circulation in the United States amounted to $605 billion, or about 51 percent of M-1.[3]

A **check** is essentially an order instructing a bank to pay a given sum to a "payee." Although not all sellers accept them as payment, many do. Checks are usually acceptable in place of cash because they are valuable only to specified payees and can be exchanged for cash. Checking accounts, which are known as **demand deposits**, are counted in M-1 because their funds may be withdrawn at any time—"on demand." In May 2002, demand deposits in the United States totaled $306 billion (26 percent of M-1).[4]

M-1 Plus the Convertible Money Supply: M-2

M-2 includes everything in M-1 plus items that cannot be spent directly but are easily converted to spendable forms. The major components of M-2 are M-1, *time deposits, money market mutual funds*, and *savings deposits*. Totaling over $5.5 trillion in May 2002, M-2 accounts for nearly all of the nation's money supply.[5] Thus, it measures the store of monetary value available for financial transactions. As this overall level of money increases, more is available for consumer purchases and business investment. When the supply is tightened, less money is available, and financial transactions, spending, and business activity, thus, slow down.

Unlike demand deposits, **time deposits**, such as certificates of deposit (CDs) and savings certificates, require prior notice of withdrawal and cannot be transferred by check. However, time deposits pay higher interest rates. Time deposits in M-2 include only accounts of less than $100,000 that can be redeemed on demand with small penalties.

Operated by investment companies that bring together pools of assets from many investors, **money market mutual funds** buy a collection of short-term, low-risk financial securities. Ownership of and profits (or losses) from the sale of these securities are shared among the fund's investors. In May 2002, these funds held $942 billion in assets.[6] In the wake of new, more attractive investments, traditional savings deposits, such as passbook savings accounts, have declined in popularity. Totaling a little over $2.5 trillion, savings deposits represented 44 percent of M-2 in May 2002.[7]

Figure 14.1 shows how the two measures of money, M-1 and M-2, have grown since 1959. For many years, M-1 was the traditional measure of liquid money. Because it was closely related to gross domestic product, it served as a reliable predictor of the nation's economic health. As you can see, however, this situation changed in the early 1980s, with the introduction of new types of investments and the easier transfer of money among investment funds to gain higher interest returns. As a result, M-2 today is a more reliable measure than M-1 and is often used by economists for economic planning.

money market mutual fund
Fund of short-term, low-risk financial securities purchased with the assets of investor-owners pooled by a nonbank institution

Credit Cards: Plastic Money?

Citi Cards *(www.citigroup.com)* is the world's largest credit card issuer, with more than 100 million accounts in North America alone. It is estimated that more than 160 million U.S. cardholders carry 1.5 billion cards. Spending with general-purpose credit cards in the United States is estimated at $1.7 trillion—almost half of all transactions—for the year 2001.[8] Indeed, the use of cards such as Visa *(www.visa.com)*, MasterCard *(www.mastercard.com)*, American Express *(www.americanexpress.com)*, Discover *(www.discover.com)*, and Diners Club *(www.dinersclub.com)* has become so widespread that many people refer to them as "plastic money." Credit cards, however, are not money and, accordingly, are not included in M-1 or M-2 when measuring the nation's money supply.

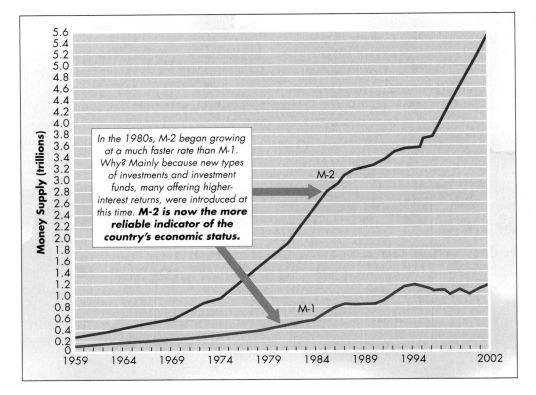

FIGURE 14.1

Money-Supply Growth

In the 1980s, M-2 began growing at a much faster rate than M-1. Why? Mainly because new types of investments and investment funds, many offering higher-interest returns, were introduced at this time. **M-2 is now the more reliable indicator of the country's economic status.**

Say WHAT YOU MEAN

MONEY TALKS

Money makes the world go round. Or so they say. But in different cultures, people put different spins on monetary transactions. In some countries—Japan is a good example—money is exchanged with a good deal of respect, even down to the way it's physically handled. You'll often find little trays and dishes next to cash registers where notes and coins are placed for people to pick up. Rarely is money passed from hand to hand. In Japan, too, it's not good form to talk too much about how much you make or have in the bank. These are private matters. The same goes in the United Kingdom, where it's often considered bad manners to talk about money.

In some places, of course—and the United States is one of them—attitudes toward money and talking about it are far more relaxed. You'll find people freely discussing how much they make, how much they paid for their houses, and how much they're worth. Notes and coins themselves are exchanged with very little formality. Typically, peo-ple pitch bills on a counter or slap them into someone's hand with little ceremony.

In many countries—America included—money is an important element of national identity: It helps to distinguish a country from its neighbors, and people often feel a touch of pride toward their national currencies. A lot of people don't like to see denominations of national currency removed from circulation or altered in design.

Ironically, that's just what happened in Europe beginning in January 2002, when the currencies of 12 nations were replaced by a new currency called the *euro.* Officials worried that many Europeans would be reluctant to give up their unique currencies in favor of common notes and coins. After all, the German deutschmark and the French franc were important symbols of national identity. But when the time came to make the switch, old currencies disappeared swiftly, and Europeans quickly became used to the cash and coinage. Ultimately, of course, what's important is what you can buy with your money.

Credit cards are big business for two basic reasons. First, they are convenient. Second, they are extremely profitable for issuing companies. Profits derive from two sources:

1 Some cards charge annual fees to holders. All charge interest on unpaid balances. Depending on the issuer—and on certain state regulations—cardholders pay interest rates ranging from 11 to 20 percent.
2 Merchants who accept credit cards pay fees to card issuers. Depending on the merchant's agreement with the issuer, 2 to 5 percent of total credit sales dollars goes to card issuers.

SELF-CHECK QUESTIONS 1–3

You should now be able to answer Self-Check Questions 1–3*

1 **Multiple Choice** Suppose you possess paper money on which the printing will eventually be so faint that merchants won't accept it. In terms of its *characteristics*, we would say that your money does not possess the following [select one]: **(a)** stability; **(b)** durability; **(c)** divisibility; **(d)** portability.

2 **True/False** "I can use my $2,000 to buy the new stereo system, or I can buy a new suit of clothes for $600 and the deluxe road bike for $1,400." In this example, we say that money is serving its function as a *medium of exchange*.

---

3 Multiple Choice The following is not true regarding the U.S. *money supply* [select one]: **(a)** M-2 is a more reliable measure of the money supply than M-1. **(b)** Credit cards ("plastic money") are included in M-2 but not in M-1. **(c)** Checking accounts are also known as demand deposits. **(d)** As measured by M-2, the money supply is always greater than when measured by M-1. **(e)** Time deposits and savings deposits are included in M-2.

***Answers to Self-Check Questions 1–3 can be found on p. 510.**

■ THE U.S. FINANCIAL SYSTEM

Many forms of money, especially demand deposits and time deposits, depend on the existence of financial institutions to provide a broad spectrum of services to both individuals and businesses. Just how important are these financial institutions to both businesses and individuals? In the sections that follow, we describe the major types of financial institutions, explain how they work, and survey some of the special services that they offer. We also explain their role as creators of money and discuss the regulation of the U.S. banking system.

Financial Institutions

The main function of financial institutions is to ease the flow of money from sectors with surpluses to those with deficits. They do this is claims against themselves and using the proceeds to buy the assets of—and thus invest in—other organizations. A bank, for instance, can issue financial claims against itself by making available funds for checking and savings accounts. In turn, its assets will be mostly loans invested in individuals and businesses and perhaps government securities. In this section, we discuss each of the major types of financial institutions: *commercial banks, savings and loan associations, mutual savings banks, credit unions*, and various organizations known as *nondeposit institutions*.

Commercial Banks The United States today boasts nearly 10,000 **commercial banks**—companies that accept deposits that they use to make loans and earn profits. Commercial banks range from the very largest institutions in New York, such as Bank of America and Chase Manhattan, to tiny banks dotting the rural landscape. Bank liabilities include checking accounts and savings accounts. Assets consist of a wide variety of loans to individuals, businesses, and governments.

> **commercial bank**
> Federal- or state-chartered financial institution accepting deposits that it uses to make loans and earn profits

Diversification and Mergers Many observers today believe that traditional banking has become a mature industry, one whose basic operations have expanded as broadly as they can. For instance, 1993 marked the first year in which the money invested in mutual funds—almost $2 trillion—equaled the amount deposited in U.S. banks. Thus, financial industry competitors in areas such as mutual funds are growing, sometimes rapidly.

As consumers continue to look for alternatives to traditional banking services, commercial banks and savings and loan associations find themselves with a dwindling share of the market. The investment bank Merrill Lynch *(www.ml.com)* has originated billions of dollars in commercial loans, formerly the province of commercial banks. Savers, too, have been putting their savings into money market funds, stocks, and bonds that are offered by companies such as Charles Schwab *(www.schwab.com)* instead of into the traditional savings accounts offered by banks. Many observers contend that to

> "The only way banks can compete is to transform themselves into successful retailers of financial services, which involves dramatic, not incremental change."
>
> —Thomas Brown, banking analyst

compete, banks, too, must diversify their offerings. The only way that they can compete, says banking analyst Thomas Brown, "is to transform themselves into successful retailers of financial services, which involves dramatic, not incremental change."

A related option seems to be to get bigger. In efforts to regain competitiveness, banks were merging at a record-setting pace in the 1990s. When commercial banks merge with investment banks, the resulting companies hold larger shares of the financial market, and the lines become blurred between traditional banking and nonbank financial institutions. Citigroup Inc. *(www.citigroup.com)*, for example, was formed as the result of a 1998 merger between Citicorp (a commercial bank) and Travelers Group, which includes investment bank Salomon Smith Barney *(www.smithbarney.com)*. Still, Citicorp is the largest U.S. retail bank, with $902 billion in assets in 2001. Citigroup, the parent company, offers one-stop shopping on a global scale for both consumers and businesses, including private banking, credit card services, mortgages, mutual funds, stock brokerage services, insurance, and loans.

Mergers are the trend, and fewer but larger banks are offering a wide range of financial products. The strategy streamlines operations to reduce costs and focuses on providing products that will win back customers from nonbank competitors.

Commercial Interest Rates Every bank receives a major portion of its income from interest paid on loans by borrowers. As long as terms and conditions are clearly revealed to borrowers, banks are allowed to set their own interest rates. Traditionally, the lowest rates were made available to the bank's most creditworthy commercial customers. That rate is called the **prime rate**. Most commercial loans are set at markups over prime. However, the prime rate is no longer a strong force in setting loan rates. Borrowers can now get funds less expensively from other sources, including foreign banks that set lower interest rates. To remain competitive, U.S. banks now offer some commercial loans at rates below prime.[9] Figure 14.2 shows the changes in the prime rate since 1992.[10]

prime rate
Interest rate available to a bank's most creditworthy customers

Think your bank is robbing you blind? Actually, it's often just the opposite in rural America, where robberies at small-town banks are on the rise, thanks in part to an increase in suburban sprawl and all the changes that have come with it. Better roads, for example, make for easier getaways. "It's easier to hit and run," explains one expert in rural crime. This bank in Plevna, Kansas, went 99 years without a robbery, only to be hit twice in a span of two months in 2001 and 2002. Despite cutting back its Friday afternoon hours and hiring an armed guard, the bank eventually went out of business.

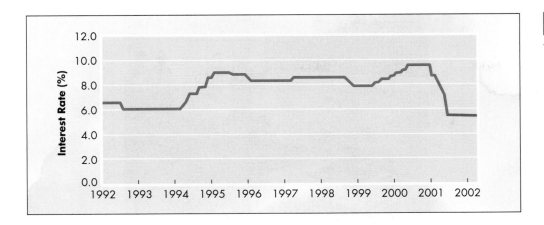

FIGURE 14.2

The Prime Rate

Savings and Loan Associations Like commercial banks, **savings and loan associations (S&Ls)** accept deposits and make loans. They lend money primarily for home mortgages. Most S&Ls were created to provide financing for homes. Many of them, however, have ventured into other investments, with varying degrees of success. S&Ls in the United States now hold $1.2 trillion in assets and deposits of $738 billion.[11]

savings and loan association (S&L)
Financial institution accepting deposits and making loans primarily for home mortgages

Mutual Savings Banks and Credit Unions In **mutual savings banks**, all depositors are considered owners of the bank. All profits, therefore, are divided proportionately among depositors, who receive dividends. Like S&Ls, mutual savings banks attract most of their funds in the form of savings deposits, and funds are loaned out in the form of mortgages.

mutual savings bank
Financial institution whose depositors are owners sharing in its profits

In **credit unions**, deposits are accepted only from members who meet specific qualifications, usually working for a particular employer. Most universities run credit unions, as do the U.S. Navy (*www.navy.mil*) and the Pentagon (*www.defenselink.mil*). Credit unions make loans for automobiles and home mortgages as well as other types of personal loans. Currently, U.S. credit unions hold $442 billion in assets.[12]

credit union
Financial institution that accepts deposits from, and makes loans to, only its members, usually employees of a particular organization

Nondeposit Institutions A variety of other organizations take in money, provide interest or other services, and make loans. Four of the most important are *pension funds, insurance companies, finance companies,* and *securities dealers.*

A **pension fund** is essentially a nondeposit pool of funds managed to provide retirement income for its members. *Public pension funds* include Social Security (*www.ssa.gov*) and $3.1 trillion in retirement programs for state and local government employees. *Private pension funds*, operated by employers, unions, and other private groups, cover about 100 million people and have total assets of $9 trillion.[13]

pension fund
Nondeposit pool of funds managed to provide retirement income for its members

Insurance companies collect large pools of funds from the premiums charged for coverage. Funds are invested in stocks, real estate, and other assets. Earnings pay for insured losses, such as death benefits, automobile damage, and health-care expenses.

insurance company
Nondeposit institution that invests funds collected as premiums charged for insurance coverage

Finance companies are nondeposit institutions that specialize in making loans to businesses and consumers. *Commercial finance companies* lend to businesses needing capital or long-term funds. They may, for instance, lend to a manufacturer that needs new assembly-line equipment. *Consumer finance companies* devote most of their resources to small noncommercial loans to individuals.

finance company
Nondeposit institution that specializes in making loans to businesses and consumers

Securities investment dealers (brokers), such as Merrill Lynch (*www.ml.com*) and A.G. Edwards & Sons (*www.agedwards.com*), buy and sell stocks and bonds on the New York and other stock exchanges for client-investors. They also invest in securities—they buy stocks and bonds for their own accounts in hopes of reselling them later at a profit. These companies hold large sums of money for transfer

securities investment dealer (broker)
Nondeposit institution that buys and sells stocks and bonds both for investors and for its own accounts

*"And, hey, don't kill yourself trying to pay it back.
You know our motto—'What the hell, it's only money.'"*

between buyers and sellers. (We discuss the activities of brokers and investment bankers more fully in Chapter 15.)

Special Financial Services

The finance business today is a highly competitive industry. No longer is it enough for commercial banks to accept deposits and make loans. Most, for example, now offer bank-issued credit cards and safe-deposit boxes. In addition, many offer pension, trust, international, and brokerage services and financial advice. Most offer ATMs and electronic money transfer.

Pension and Trust Services Most banks help customers establish savings plans for retirement. **Individual retirement accounts (IRAs)** are tax-deferred pension funds that wage earners and their spouses can set up to supplement other retirement funds. All wage earners can invest up to $2,000 of earned income annually in an IRA. IRAs offer a significant tax benefit: Under many circumstances, taxes on principal and earnings are deferred until funds are withdrawn upon retirement. Under the 1997 tax changes, some IRAs are entirely tax-free. Banks serve as financial intermediaries by receiving funds and investing them as directed by customers. They also provide customers with information on investment vehicles available for IRAs (deposit accounts, mutual funds, stocks, and so forth).[14]

Many commercial banks offer **trust services**—the management of funds left "in the bank's trust." In return for a fee, the trust department will perform such tasks as making your monthly bill payments and managing your investment portfolio. Trust departments also manage the estates of deceased persons.

International Services The three main international services offered by banks are *currency exchange, letters of credit*, and *banker's acceptances*. Suppose a U.S. company wants to buy a product from a British supplier. For a fee, it can use one or more of three services offered by its bank:

1 It can exchange U.S. dollars for British pounds at a U.S. bank and then pay the British supplier in pounds.

---

individual retirement account (IRA)
Tax-deferred pension fund with which wage earners supplement other retirement funds

trust services
Bank management of an individual's investments, payments, or estate

2 It can pay its bank to issue a **letter of credit**—a promise by the bank to pay the British firm a certain amount if specified conditions are met.

3 It can pay its bank to draw up a **banker's acceptance**, which promises that the bank will pay some specified amount at a future date.

A banker's acceptance requires payment by a particular date. Letters of credit are payable only after certain conditions are met. The British supplier, for example, may not be paid until shipping documents prove that the merchandise has been shipped from England.

Financial Advice and Brokerage Services Many banks, both large and small, help their customers manage their money. Depending on the customer's situation, the bank may recommend different investment opportunities. The recommended mix might include CDs, mutual funds, stocks, and bonds. Many banks also serve as securities intermediaries, using their own stockbrokers to buy and sell securities and their own facilities to hold them. Bank advertisements often stress the role of banks as financial advisers.

Automated Teller Machines Electronic **automated teller machines (ATMs)** allow customers to withdraw money and make deposits 24 hours a day, seven days a week. They also allow transfers of funds between accounts and provide information on account status. Some banks offer cards that can be used in affiliated nationwide systems. About 324,000 machines are now located at U.S. bank buildings, grocery stores, airports, shopping malls, and other locations. Bank of America, with 12,000 units, is this country's leading owner of ATMs. U.S. bank customers conduct more than 13 billion ATM transactions a year, with each machine being used an average of 3,500 times a month.[15]

Increasingly, ATMs are also becoming global fixtures. In fact, among the world's nearly 1 million ATMs, 68 percent are located outside the United States. Asia, with 32 percent of the world's total, is the leading region for ATMs, followed by North America (31 percent), Western Europe (25 percent), and Latin America (8 percent). Many U.S. banks now offer international ATM services. Citicorp installed Shanghai's first 24-hour ATM and is the first foreign bank to receive approval from the People's Bank of China to issue local currency through ATMs. Elsewhere, Citibank machines feature touch screens that take instructions in any of 10 languages.

letter of credit
Bank promise, issued for a buyer, to pay a designated firm a certain amount of money if specified conditions are met

banker's acceptance
Bank promise, issued for a buyer, to pay a designated firm a specified amount at a future date

automated teller machine (ATM)
Electronic machine that allows customers to conduct account-related activities 24 hours a day, 7 days a week

Citibank (www.citibank.com) now has consumer banking outlets in 41 countries, where it strives to make once specialized products universal. One of the key functions of overseas ATMs is to attract customers to the bank's retail branches, and the strategy has been particularly successful in Japan. Since 1986, Citibank Japan (www.citibank.co.jp/en/) has offered Japanese customers such services as free ATM and telephone banking and multicurrency accounts. Aftertax profits in Asia now top $700 million a year.

electronic funds transfer (EFT)
Communication of fund-transfer information over wire, cable, or microwave

Electronic Funds Transfer ATMs are the most popular form of **electronic funds transfer (EFT)**. These systems transfer many kinds of financial information via electrical impulses over wire, cable, or microwave. In addition to ATMs, EFT systems include automatic payroll deposit, bill payment, and automatic funds transfer. Such systems can help a businessperson close an important business deal by transferring money from San Francisco to Miami within a few minutes.[16]

Banks as Creators of Money

In the course of their activities, financial institutions provide a special service to the economy—they create money. This is not to say that they mint bills and coins. Rather, by taking in deposits and making loans, they expand the money supply.[17]

As Figure 14.3 shows, the money supply expands because banks are allowed to loan out most (although not all) of the money they take in from deposits. Suppose that you deposit $100 in your bank. If banks are allowed to loan out 90 percent of all their deposits, then your bank will hold $10 in reserve and loan $90 of your money to borrowers. (You, of course, still have $100 on deposit.) Meanwhile, borrowers—or the people they pay—will deposit the $90 loan in their own banks. Together, the borrowers' banks will then have $81 (90 percent of $90) available for new loans. Banks, therefore, have turned your original $100 into $271 ($100 + $90 + $81). The chain continues, with borrowings from one bank becoming deposits in the next.

Regulation of Commercial Banking

Because commercial banks are critical to the creation of money, the government regulates them to ensure a sound and competitive financial system. Later in this chapter, we will see how the Federal Reserve System regulates many aspects of U.S. banking. Other federal and state agencies also regulate banks to ensure that the failure of some banks as a result of competition will not cause the public to lose faith in the banking system itself.

Federal Deposit Insurance Corporation (FDIC)
Federal agency that guarantees the safety of all deposits up to $100,000 in the financial institutions that it insures

Federal Deposit Insurance Corporation The **Federal Deposit Insurance Corporation (FDIC)** insures deposits in member banks. More than 99 percent of the nation's commercial banks pay fees for membership in the FDIC (*www.fdic.gov*). In return, the FDIC guarantees, through its Bank Insurance Fund (BIF), the safety of all deposits up to the current maximum of $100,000. If a bank collapses, the FDIC promises to pay its depositors—through the BIF—for losses up to $100,000 per

FIGURE 14.3

How Banks Create Money

Deposit	Money Held in Reserve by Bank	Money to Lend	Total Supply
$100.00	$10.00	$90.00	**$190.00**
90.00	9.00	81.00	**271.00**
81.00	8.10	72.90	**343.90**
72.90	7.29	65.61	**409.51**
65.61	6.56	59.05	**468.56**

account. (A handful of the nation's 10,000 commercial banks are insured by states rather than by the BIF.)

To insure against multiple bank failures, the FDIC maintains the right to examine the activities and accounts of all member banks. Such regulation was effective from 1941 through 1980, when fewer than 10 banks failed per year. At the beginning of the 1980s, however, banks were deregulated, and between 1981 and 1990, losses from nearly 1,100 bank failures depleted the FDIC's reserve fund. In recent years, the FDIC has thus raised the premiums charged to member banks to keep up with losses incurred by failed banks.

SELF-CHECK QUESTIONS 4–6

You should now be able to answer Self-Check Questions 4–6*

4 **True/False** *Loans* are available from all of the following financial institutions: credit unions, mutual savings banks, savings and loan associations, commercial banks, and finance companies.

5 **Multiple Choice** Suppose you have accumulated substantial wealth that you want to leave to your now-infant children when they reach age 40. Which of the following *financial services* is most appropriate for your purposes? [select one]: **(a)** individual retirement account (IRA); **(b)** pension fund; **(c)** banker's acceptance; **(d)** banker's trust; **(e)** commercial loan.

6 **Multiple Choice** Suppose that you deposit $250 in your local bank, which is allowed to loan out 85 percent of its deposits. Suppose, further, that the following events occur: Your bank loans out the maximum allowable money to borrowers who, in turn, deposit the borrowed money in their banks. These banks also loan out the maximum allowable funds. In total, banks, as *creators of money*, have turned your original $250 into which of the following amounts? [select one]: **(a)** $643.12; **(b)** $319.75; **(c)** $750.00; **(d)** $487.37; **(e)** none of the above.

*Answers to Self-Check Questions 4–6 can be found on p. 510.

■ THE FEDERAL RESERVE SYSTEM

Perched atop the U.S. financial system and regulating many aspects of its operation is the Federal Reserve System. Established by Congress in 1913, the **Federal Reserve System** (or **the Fed**) *(www.federalreserve.gov)* is the nation's central bank. In this section, we describe the structure of the Fed, its functions, and the tools that it uses to control the nation's money supply.

Federal Reserve System (the Fed) Central bank of the United States, which acts as the government's bank, serves member commercial banks, and controls the nation's money supply

The Structure of the Fed

The Federal Reserve System consists of a board of governors, a group of reserve banks, and member banks. As originally established by the Federal Reserve Act of 1913, the system consisted of 12 relatively autonomous banks and a seven-member committee whose powers were limited to coordinating the activities of those banks. By the 1930s, however, both the structure and function of the Fed had changed dramatically.

The Board of Governors The Fed's board of governors consists of seven members appointed by the president for overlapping terms of 14 years. The chair of the board serves on major economic advisory committees and works actively with the administration to formulate economic policy. The board plays a large role in controlling the money supply. It alone determines the reserve requirements, within statutory limits, for depository institutions. It also works with other members of the Federal Reserve System to set discount rates and handle the Fed's sale and purchase of government securities.

Reserve Banks The Federal Reserve System consists of 12 administrative areas and 12 banks. Each Federal Reserve bank holds reserve deposits from and sets the discount rate for commercial banks in its region. Reserve banks also play a major role in the nation's check-clearing process.

Member Banks All nationally chartered commercial banks are members of the Federal Reserve System, as are some state-chartered banks. The accounts of all member bank depositors are automatically covered by the FDIC/BIF. Although many state-chartered banks do not belong to the Federal Reserve System, most pay deposit insurance premiums and are covered by the FDIC.

The Functions of the Fed

In addition to chartering national banks, the Fed serves as the federal government's bank and the "bankers' bank," regulating a number of banking activities. Most important, it controls the money supply. In this section, we describe these functions in some detail.

The Government's Bank Two of the Fed's activities are producing the nation's paper currency and lending money to the government. The Fed decides how many bills to produce and how many to destroy. To lend funds to the government, the Fed buys bonds issued by the Treasury Department *(www.ustreas.gov)*. The borrowed money is then used to help finance the national deficit.

The Bankers' Bank Individual banks that need money can borrow from the Federal Reserve and pay interest on the loans. In addition, the Fed provides storage for commercial banks, which are required to keep funds on reserve at a Federal Reserve bank.

Check Clearing The Fed also clears checks, some 69 million of them each day, for commercial banks. To understand the check-clearing process, imagine that you are a photographer living in New Orleans. To participate in a workshop in Detroit, you must send a check for $50 to the Detroit studio. Figure 14.4 traces your check through the clearing process:

1. You send your check to the Detroit studio, which deposits it in its Detroit bank.
2. The Detroit bank deposits the check in its own account at the Federal Reserve Bank of Chicago.
3. The check is sent from Chicago to the Atlanta Federal Reserve Bank for collection because you, the check writer, live in the Atlanta district.
4. Your New Orleans bank receives the check from Atlanta and deducts the $50 from your personal account.
5. Your bank then has $50 deducted from its deposit account at the Atlanta Federal Reserve Bank.
6. The $50 is shifted from Atlanta to the Chicago Federal Reserve Bank. The studio's Detroit bank gets credited, whereupon the studio's account is then credited $50. Your bank mails the canceled check back to you.

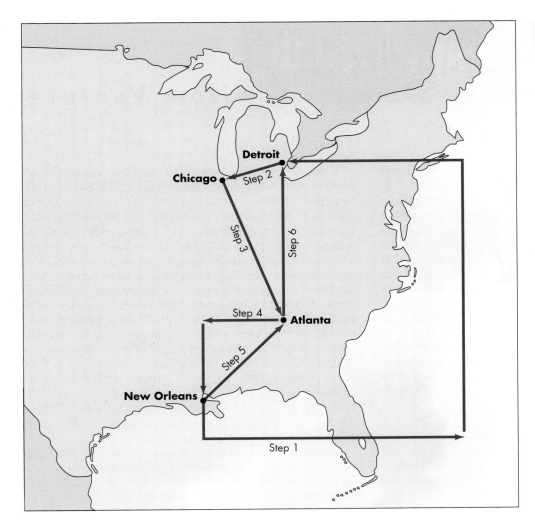

FIGURE 14.4
Clearing a Check

Depending on the number of banks and the distances between them, a check will clear in two to six days. Until the process is completed, the studio's Detroit bank cannot spend the $50 deposited there. Meanwhile, your bank's records will continue to show $50 in your account. Each day, approximately $1 billion in checks is processed by the system. The term **float** refers to all of the checks in the process at any one time.

float
Total amount of checks written but not yet cleared through the Federal Reserve

Controlling the Money Supply The Federal Reserve System is responsible for the conduct of U.S. **monetary policy**—the management of the nation's economic growth by managing money supply and interest rates. By controlling these two factors, the Fed influences the ability and willingness of banks throughout the country to loan money.

monetary policy
Policies by which the Federal Reserve manages the nation's money supply and interest rates

Inflation Management As we defined it in Chapter 1, *inflation* is a period of widespread price increases throughout an economic system. It occurs if the money supply grows too large. Demand for goods and services increases, and the prices of everything rise. (In contrast, too little money means that an economy will lack the funds to maintain high levels of employment.) Because commercial banks are the main creators of money, much of the Fed's management of the money supply takes the form of regulating the supply of money through commercial banks.

ENTREPRENEURSHIP and *New Ventures*

"Your Check Is Not in the Mail"

Pete Kight recognized the advantages of electronic funds transfer (EFT) when, at age 24, he started CheckFree Corp. in his grandmother's basement. Now, as CEO of the dominant firm in the world of electronic bill-payments systems, Kight's goal is to change a traditional way of life by replacing check writing with electronic payments. Eliminating the movement of checks and clearing them faster will save billions of dollars in the Federal Reserve's check-clearing process alone. Far greater advantages, however, are in store for millions of households and businesses once they get accustomed to the idea of abandoning checkbooks and manual recordkeeping. "When consumers understand the benefits, they will want it," Kight insists. Until the masses sign on, however, Kight has to balance rising revenues (most recently, a quarterly increase of 12 percent, to $135 million) against mounting losses ($17.4 million for the same quarter). CheckFree needs more revenue, and the only way that Kight can get it is by inducing more people to switch to electronic bill paying.

CheckFree (*www.checkfree.com*) has pioneered electronic bill paying by using the Internet to provide hundreds of companies with behind-the-scenes software and networking technologies. Consumers who sign up for CheckFree's basic *e-Bill Service* receive and pay selected bills electronically to more than 260 participating companies, including Bloomingdale's, the *Wall Street Journal*, Texaco, and Florida Power and Light. *E-Bill Service* is free, but if you want expanded service, CheckFree offers *Online Payment Service* (OPS) for online billing and payments of any bill, to any company, from any person. OPS is available (for a fee of up to $15 per month) from any of 657 providers—including banks, credit unions, brokerages, and Internet portals—powered by CheckFree technology.

If you sign up with a preferred provider, such as Yahoo!, Bank of America, Fidelity Investments, or CheckFree itself, you specify the companies and individuals whose bills you want to receive and view online. In turn, your billing—say, for utilities, car payments, credit cards, cable TV, or the mortgage—comes with CheckFree. Your personalized account displays e-bills for online viewing, including amount owed and due date, and it even sends e-mail reminders for upcoming due dates. You choose dates of payment, dollar amounts, and which bills to pay. Instead of stacking a closet or your attic with boxes of paper records, you can retrieve, view, and print past transactions from electronic storage files. The system tracks all your bills from one central location, with no envelopes, no stamps, and no check writing. You pay your online bills through an approved bank account, money market account, or credit card accepted by the biller. Billers, meanwhile, benefit from the flow of electronic funds while avoiding slower, more costly paperwork transactions.

In growing from a one-person start-up to a six-state firm with more than 1,800 employees, Kight's expanded vision for the future is to "enable anyone to pay for anything, anywhere electronically over the Internet." He hopes to attract more customers with a marketing strategy aimed at educating people about online bill payment. As of 2003, however, consumers have been slow to adopt the concept: The American Bankers Association estimates that just 13 million of the nation's 90-plus million banking households pay bills online. Undaunted, however, and encouraged by steady growth, huge market potential, and its leadership position in the industry, CheckFree continues its quest to revolutionize the U.S. banking system by making the checkbook obsolete.

The Tools of the Fed

According to the Fed's original charter, its primary duties were to supervise banking and to manage both the currency and commercial paper. The duties of the Fed evolved, however, along with a predominant philosophy of monetary policy. That policy includes an emphasis on the broad economic goals as discussed in Chapter 1, especially growth and stability. The Fed's role in controlling the nation's money supply stems from its role in setting policies to help reach these goals. To control the money supply, the Fed uses four primary tools: *reserve requirements, discount rate controls, open-market operations*, and *selective credit controls*.[18]

reserve requirement
Percentage of its deposits that a bank must hold in cash or on deposit with the Federal Reserve

Reserve Requirements The **reserve requirement** is the percentage of its deposits that a bank must hold, in cash or on deposit, with a Federal Reserve bank.

High requirements mean that banks have less money to lend. Thus, a high reserve requirement reduces the money supply. Conversely, low requirements permit the supply to expand. Because the Fed sets requirements for all depository institutions, it can adjust them to make changes to the overall supply of money in the economy.

Discount Rate Controls As the "bankers' bank," the Fed loans money to banks. The interest rate on these loans is known as the **discount rate**. If the Fed wants to reduce the money supply, it increases the discount rate, making it more expensive for banks to borrow money and less attractive for them to loan it. Conversely, low rates encourage borrowing and lending and expand the money supply. The Fed used a series of discount rate decreases—from 6.0 percent beginning in May 2000 down to 1.25 percent in December 2001—to speed up the sagging U.S. economy.[19]

> **discount rate**
> Interest rate at which member banks can borrow money from the Federal Reserve

Open-Market Operations The third instrument for monetary control is probably the Fed's most important tool. **Open-market operations** refer to the Fed's sale and purchase of securities (usually U.S. Treasury notes and bonds) in the open market. Open-market operations are particularly effective because they act quickly and predictably on the money supply. How so? The Fed buys securities from dealers. Because the dealer's bank account is credited for the transaction, its bank has more money to lend, and so this transaction expands the money supply. The opposite happens when the Fed sells securities.[20]

> **open-market operations**
> The Federal Reserve's sales and purchases of securities in the open market

Selective Credit Controls The Federal Reserve can exert considerable influence over business activity by exercising **selective credit controls**. The Fed may set special requirements for consumer stock purchases as well as credit rules for other consumer purchases.

As we will see in Chapter 15, investors can set up credit accounts with stockbrokers to buy stocks and bonds. A margin requirement set by the Fed stipulates the amount of credit that the broker can extend to the customer. For example, a 60-percent margin rate means that approved customers can purchase stocks having $100,000 market value with $60,000 in cash (60 percent of $100,000) and $40,000 in loans from the dealer. If the Fed wants to increase securities transactions, it can lower the margin requirement. Customers can then borrow greater percentages of their purchase costs

> **selective credit controls**
> Federal Reserve authority to set both margin requirements for consumer stock purchases and credit rules for other consumer purchases

In 2001, the Fed (*www.federalreserve.gov*) cut the discount rate 11 times in an effort to bolster a sagging U.S. economy. Although it's hard to calculate the effects on the overall economy, the immediate impact on the housing market was profound. Because banks could lower mortgage rates, the number of people who could afford to buy houses went up by 3 million. "People keep buying the darn things," reported one economist, and in so doing they strengthened the economy by adding $2 trillion to $3 trillion to total homeowner wealth.

from dealers, thus increasing their purchasing power and the amount of securities that they can buy.

Within stipulated limits, the Fed is also permitted to specify the conditions of certain credit purchases. This authority extends to such conditions as allowable down payment percentages for appliance purchases and repayment periods on automobile loans. The Fed has chosen not to use these powers in recent years.

■ THE CHANGING MONEY AND BANKING SYSTEM

The U.S. money and banking systems have changed in recent years and continue to change today. Deregulation and interstate banking, for example, have increased competition not only among banks but also between banks and other financial institutions. Electronic technologies affect how you obtain money and how much interest you pay for it.

Deregulation

The Depository Institutions Deregulation and Monetary Control Act (DIDMCA) of 1980 brought many changes to the banking industry. Before its passage, there were clear distinctions between the types of services offered by different institutions. Although all institutions could offer savings accounts, only commercial banks could offer checking accounts, and S&Ls and mutual savings banks generally could not make consumer loans. The DIDMCA and subsequent laws sought to promote competition by eliminating many such restrictions.

Under deregulation, many banks were unable to survive in the new competitive environment. In the 1980s, more than 1,000 banks—more than 7 percent of the total—failed, as did 835 savings and loans. Many economists, however, regard some bank closings as a beneficial weeding out of inefficient competitors.

Interstate Banking

Although interstate banking is commonplace, it is a relatively new development. The Interstate Banking Efficiency Act was passed into law in September 1994, thus allowing banks to enter (gradually) into interstate banking—the operation of banks or branches across state lines. It also mandates regulation by government agencies to ensure proper operation and competition. The key provisions in this act include the following:

■ Limited nationwide banking is permitted, beginning in 1995. Bank holding companies can acquire subsidiaries in any state.

■ The ultimate *size* of any company is limited. No one company can control more than 10 percent of nationwide insured deposits. No bank can control more than 30 percent of a state's deposits (each state is empowered to set its own limit).

■ Beginning in 1995, banks can provide limited transactions for affiliated banks in other states. They can thus accept deposits, close loans, and accept loan payments on behalf of other affiliated banks. (They cannot, however, originate loans or open deposit accounts for affiliates.)

■ Beginning in June 1997, banks can convert affiliates into full-fledged interstate branches.

Interstate banking offers certain efficiencies. For example, it allows banks to consolidate services and eliminate duplicated activities. Opponents, however, remain concerned that some banks will gain undue influence, dominate other banks, and hinder competition.

The Impact of Electronic Technologies

Like so many other businesses, banks are increasingly investing in technology as a way to improve efficiency and customer service levels. Many banks offer ATMs and EFT systems. Some offer TV banking, in which customers use television sets and terminals—or home computers—to make transactions. The age of electronic money has arrived. Digital money is replacing cash in stores, taxicabs, subway systems, and vending machines. Each business day, more than $2 trillion exists in and among banks and other financial institutions in purely electronic form. Each year, the Fed's Fedwire funds transfer system transfers electronically more than $390 trillion in transactions.

Debit Cards One of the electronic offerings from the financial industry that has gained popularity is the debit card. Unlike credit cards, **debit cards** allow only the transfer of money between accounts. They do not increase the funds at an individual's disposal. They can, however, be used to make retail purchases. The number of cards in use more than doubled from 173 million in 1990 to more than 400 million in 2001, with transactions exceeding $400 billion. Debit card purchases are expected to reach $1 trillion in 2005.

debit card
Plastic card that allows an individual to transfer money between accounts

In stores with **point-of-sale (POS) terminals**, customers insert cards that transmit to terminals information relevant to their purchases. The terminal relays the information directly to the bank's computer system. The bank automatically transfers funds from the customer's account to the store's account.

point-of-sale (POS) terminal
Electronic device that allows customers to pay for retail purchases with debit cards

Smart Cards The so-called **smart card** is a credit-card-size plastic card with an embedded computer chip that can be programmed with "electronic money." Also known as electronic purses or stored-value cards, smart cards have existed for more than a decade. Phone callers and shoppers in Europe and Asia are the most avid users, holding the majority of the nearly 2 billion cards in circulation in 2001. Although small by European standards, card usage in North America has grown by more than 40 percent since 2000, reaching more than 50 million cards in 2002. They are most popular in financial services, followed by prepaid long-distance or wireless phone cards.[21]

smart card
Credit-card-size plastic card with an embedded computer chip that can be programmed with electronic money

Why are smart cards increasing in popularity today? For one thing, the cost of producing them has fallen dramatically, from as much as $10 to as little as $1. Convenience is equally important, notes Donald J. Gleason, president of Smart Card Enterprise, a division of Electronic Payment Services *(www.eps.com.hk)*. "What consumers want," Gleason contends, "is convenience, and if you look at cash, it's really quite inconvenient."

Smart cards can be loaded with money at ATM machines or, with special telephone hookups, even at home. After using your card to purchase an item, you can then check an electronic display to see how much money your card has left. Analysts predict

> **"What consumers want is convenience, and if you look at cash, it's really quite inconvenient."**
>
> **—Donald J. Gleason, president, Smart Card Enterprise**

that in the near future, smart cards will function as much more than electronic purses. For example, travel industry experts predict that people will soon book travel plans at home on personal computers and then transfer their reservations onto their smart cards. The cards will then serve as airline tickets and boarding passes. As an added benefit, they will allow travelers to avoid waiting in lines at car rental agencies and hotel front desks.

e-cash
Electronic money that moves between consumers and businesses via digital electronic transmissions

"Banking is essential to the modern economy, but banks are not."

—Investment banker

E-Cash A new, revolutionary world of electronic money has begun to emerge with the rapid growth of the Internet. Electronic money, known as **e-cash**, is money that moves along multiple channels of consumers and businesses via digital electronic transmissions. E-cash moves outside of the established network of banks, checks, and paper currency overseen by the Federal Reserve. Companies as varied as new start-up Mondex *(www.mondex.com)* and giant Citicorp are developing their own forms of electronic money that allow consumers and businesses to spend money more conveniently, quickly, and cheaply than they can through the banking system. In fact, some observers predict that by the year 2005, as much as 20 percent of all household expenditures will take place on the Internet. "Banking," comments one investment banker, "is essential to the modern economy, but banks are not."

How does e-cash work? Traditional currency is used to buy electronic funds, which are downloaded over phone lines into a PC or a portable "electronic wallet" that can store and transmit e-cash. E-cash is purchased from any company that issues (sells) it, including companies such as Mondex, Citicorp, and banks. When shopping online—for example, to purchase jewelry—a shopper sends digital money to the merchant instead of using traditional cash, checks, or credit cards. Businesses can purchase supplies and services electronically from any merchant that accepts e-cash. It flows from the buyer's into the seller's e-cash funds, which are instantaneously updated and stored on a microchip. One system, operated by CyberCash *(www.cybercash.com)*, tallies all e-cash transactions in the customer's account and, at the end of the day, converts the e-cash balance back into dollars in the customer's conventional banking account.

Although e-cash transactions are cheaper than handling checks and the paper records involved with conventional money, there are some potential problems.[22] Hackers, for example, may break into e-cash systems and drain them instantaneously. Moreover, if the issuer's computer system crashes, it is conceivable that money "banked" in memory may be lost forever. Finally, regulation and control of e-cash systems remain largely nonexistent; there is virtually none of the protection that covers government-controlled money systems.

INTERNATIONAL BANKING AND FINANCE

Along with international banking networks, electronic technologies now permit nearly instantaneous financial transactions around the globe. The economic importance of international finance is evident from both the presence of foreign banks in the U.S. market and the sizes of certain banks around the world. In addition, each nation tries to influence its currency exchange rates for economic advantage in international trade. The subsequent country-to-country transactions result in an *international payments process* that moves money between buyers and sellers on different continents.

The International Payments Process

When transactions are made between buyers and sellers in different countries, exactly how are payments made? Payments are simplified through the services provided by their banks.[23] For example, payments from buyers flow through a local bank that converts them from the local currency into the foreign currency of the seller. The local bank receives and converts incoming money from the banks of foreign buyers. The payment process is shown in Figure 14.5.

■ **Step 1.** Let's say that some time before Greece converted to the euro, a U.S. olive importer withdraws $1,000 from its checking account to buy olives from a Greek exporter. The local U.S. bank converts those dollars into Greek drachmas at the current exchange rate (230 drachmas per dollar).

■ **Step 2.** The U.S. bank sends a check for 230,000 drachmas (230 × 1,000) to the exporter in Greece.

■ **Steps 3 and 4.** The exporter sends olives to its U.S. customer and deposits the check in its local Greek bank. The exporter now has drachmas that can be spent in Greece, and the importer has olives to sell in the United States.

At the same time, a separate transaction is being made between a U.S. machine exporter and a Greek olive oil producer. This time, importer/exporter roles are reversed between the two countries: The Greek firm needs to import a $1,000 olive oil press from the United States.

■ **Steps 5 and 6.** Drachmas (230,000) withdrawn from a local Greek bank account are converted into U.S. $1,000 and sent via check to the U.S. exporter.

■ **Steps 7 and 8.** The olive oil press is sent to the Greek importer, and the importer's check is deposited in the U.S. exporter's local bank account.

In this example, trade between the two countries is in balance. Money inflows and outflows are equal for both countries. When such a balance occurs, *money does*

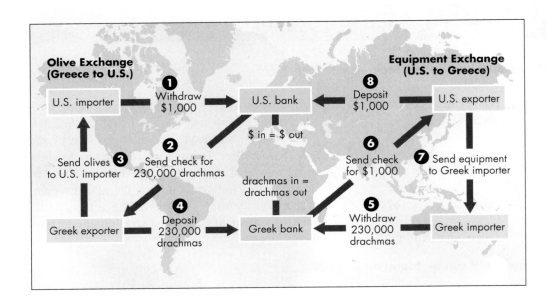

FIGURE 14.5

International Payments Process

not actually have to flow between the two countries. Within each bank, the dollars spent by local importers offset the dollars received by local exporters. In effect, therefore, the dollars have simply flowed from U.S. importers to U.S. exporters. Similarly, the drachmas have moved from Greek exporters to Greek importers.

International Bank Structure

There is no worldwide banking system that is comparable, in terms of policy making and regulatory power, to the system of any industrialized nation. Rather, worldwide banking stability relies on a loose structure of agreements among individual countries or groups of countries.

World Bank
United Nations agency that provides a limited scope of financial services, such as funding national improvements in undeveloped countries

International Monetary Fund (IMF)
United Nations agency consisting of about 150 nations that have combined resources to promote stable exchange rates, provide temporary short-term loans, and serve other purposes

The World Bank and the IMF Two United Nations agencies, the World Bank and the International Monetary Fund, help to finance international trade.[24] Unlike true banks, the **World Bank** (technically the International Bank for Reconstruction and Development) *(www.worldbank.org)*, a U.N. agency, provides only a very limited scope of services. For instance, it funds national improvements by making loans to build roads, schools, power plants, and hospitals. The resulting improvements eventually enable borrowing countries to increase productive capacity and international trade.

Another U.N. agency, the **International Monetary Fund (IMF)** *(www.imf.org)*, is a group of some 150 nations that have combined resources for the following purposes:

■ To promote the stability of exchange rates
■ To provide temporary, short-term loans to member countries
■ To encourage members to cooperate on international monetary issues
■ To encourage development of a system for international payments

The IMF makes loans to nations suffering from temporary negative trade balances. By making it possible for these countries to continue buying products from other countries, the IMF facilitates international trade. However, some nations have declined IMF funds rather than accept the economic changes that the IMF demands. For example, some developing countries reject the IMF's requirement that they cut back social programs and spending in order to bring inflation under control.

SELF-CHECK QUESTIONS 7–9

You should now be able to answer Self-Check Questions 7–9*

7 Multiple Choice Suppose the Fed decides that the nation's *money supply* is too large and takes action to reduce it. Which of the following Fed actions is **not** appropriate for reducing the money supply? [select one]: **(a)** sell securities; **(b)** increase the reserve requirement; **(c)** decrease the discount rate; **(d)** increase the margin rate for stock purchases; **(e)** increase the discount rate.

8 Multiple Choice Which of the following electronic technologies allows money to move among consumers and businesses *outside the established network of banks and money supplies* overseen by the Fed? [select one]: **(a)** debit cards; **(b)** e-cash; **(c)** smart cards; **(d)** credit cards; **(e)** ATMs.

9 True/False The *World Bank* is the global regulatory authority that supervises the international banking system and monitors the international payments process.

*Answers to Self-Check Questions 7–9 can be found on p. 510.

Continued from page 420

THERE'S NO ACCOUNTING FOR FINANCIAL SYSTEMS

As the run on Argentina's banks continued into 2002, unpopular banking restrictions were tightened even further, triggering widespread street protests. Bank accounts were frozen by the government. All checking accounts with money over $10,000 were switched into fixed-term deposits, meaning the money was not available to depositors for at least a year. The same was true for savings accounts of $3,000 or more. "We want our money and we want it now," shouted Rubin Orlando, a 46-year-old doctor, as he slammed two trash can lids together. Angry vandals set fires in downtown Buenos Aires, shattered windows, and destroyed ATMs. The economic and social chaos led to a government turnover that included five presidents in two weeks. So intense and violent was public unrest that Roque Maccarone, the head of Argentina's central bank, resigned.

As economist Raul Buonuome of SBS Brokerage noted, however, "Simply changing the head of the bank would not be enough by itself to bolster confidence of Argentines in the banking system." Overall, he says, the government has two main tasks: revamping Argentina's financial system and restructuring debt. President Eduardo Duhalde's government has taken two steps to rescue the country: First, devaluing the currency should help increase Argentina's exports, and second, temporarily halting debt payments should help stabilize the domestic economy.

In a move to assist in the crisis, the IMF granted Argentina a one-year extension for repaying a nearly $1 billion loan due early in 2002, hoping the reprieve will help restart the economy and calm social unrest. Meanwhile, Horst Koehler, managing director of IMF, is offering more than just short-term assistance for getting Argentina's economy back on track: "We have been in close contact with the government of President Duhalde from the beginning. We have sent technical experts for the banking sector there, for the debt operation and for fiscal measures, so everything is offered to Argentina if [it wants] to get our technical assistance to work on a comprehensive strategy."

In addition to the government defaulting on its $132 billion debt, companies, too, are joining in nonpayment on obligations. In the country's biggest corporate default to date,

Telecom Argentina, the nation's number-two phone carrier, announced it would suspend principal payments on its $3.2 billion debt. Most of the debt is in the form of bonds and bank loans. Telecom Argentina issued most of its debt in dollars during the past decade, while the peso was stable. When the Argentine government devalued the peso by 30 percent to 1.4 pesos per dollar in January 2002, it continued to fall on the world markets and quickly lost 65 percent of its value as the recession deepened, so there are not enough funds to pay what is owed. It is paying interest—$200 million in interest is due in 2002—but it will not be paying the $900 million in principal that is due. And the firm cannot raise prices to cover its debt because the government froze prices—in pesos—that utility companies can charge customers.

As the downslide continues, additional defaults include $1 billion by Argentina's wireless unit of Verizon, $1 billion by CTI Holdings, and $425 million by Metrogas SA, a giant natural gas company.

Questions for Discussion

1 Assume for a moment that you're a consumer of retail goods in Argentina. Can you identify any problems you might expect to encounter during your country's transition to the devalued peso?

2 Suppose you are manager of an Argentine retail store that sells imported clothing. What preparations would you make to ensure that your business is ready for the transition to the devalued peso?

3 Identify the advantages to be gained—for both individuals and companies—by the payment of all debt by the Argentine government and businesses, instead of both sectors defaulting on debt payments. What are the disadvantages?

4 Consider the actions taken by the government to stop the run on cash from the Argentine banking system. Do you think the actions were effective? Can you propose alternative actions that might have been better than those that were implemented?

5 Consider the risks that foreign banks and businesses took by investing in Argentina. In consideration of their financial losses and other economic and political factors, do you expect those businesses will invest again in Argentine-based ventures? Explain why or why not.

■ SUMMARY OF LEARNING OBJECTIVES

1 Define *money* and identify the different forms that it takes in the nation's money supply.

Any item that is portable, divisible, durable, and stable satisfies the four basic characteristics of **money**. Money also serves three functions: It is a medium of exchange, a store of value, and a unit of account. The nation's money supply is often determined by two measures. **M-1** includes liquid (or spendable) forms of money: **currency** (bills and coins), **demand deposits**, and other checkable deposits (such as ATM account balances and NOW accounts). **M-2** includes M-1 plus items that cannot be directly spent but can be converted easily to spendable forms: **time deposits, money market funds,** and savings deposits. Credit must also be considered as a factor in the money supply.

2 Describe the different kinds of *financial institutions* that comprise the U.S. financial system and explain the services they offer.

The U.S. financial system includes federal- and state-chartered commercial banks, savings and loan associations, mutual savings banks, credit unions, and nondeposit institutions such as pension funds and insurance companies. **Commercial banks** accept deposits that they use to make loans and earn profits. **Savings and loan associations (S&Ls)** also accept deposits and make loans, primarily for home mortgages. In **mutual savings banks**, all depositors are owners of the bank, and all profits are divided proportionately among them. In **credit unions**, deposits are accepted only from members.

Numerous other organizations called **nondeposit institutions**—pension funds, insurance companies, finance companies, and securities investment dealers—take in money, provide interest or other services, and make loans. In the competitive finance business, most commercial banks offer a wide range of special services: (1) pension and trust services, (2) international services, (3) financial advice and brokerage services, and (4) **automated teller machines (ATMs)**.

3 Explain how banks *create* money, and describe the means by which they are regulated.

The money supply expands because banks can loan out most (although not all) of the money they take in from deposits. Out of a deposit of $100, the bank may hold $10 in reserve and loan 90 percent—$90—to borrowers. There will still be $100 on deposit, and borrowers will also deposit the

$90 loan in their banks. Now the borrowers' banks have $81 (90 percent of $90) available for new loans. Banks, therefore, have turned the original $100 into $271 ($100 + $90 + $81).

The government regulates commercial banks to ensure a sound financial system. The **Federal Deposit Insurance Corporation (FDIC)** insures deposits and guarantees, through its Bank Insurance Fund (BIF), the safety of all deposits up to the current maximum of $100,000. It also examines the activities and accounts of all member banks.

4 Discuss the functions of the *Federal Reserve System* and describe the tools that it uses to control the money supply.

The **Federal Reserve System** (or the **Fed**) is the nation's central bank. As the government's bank, the Fed produces currency and lends money to the government. As the bankers' bank, it lends money (at interest) to member banks, stores required reserve funds for banks, and clears checks for them. The Fed is empowered to audit member banks and sets U.S. **monetary policy** by controlling the country's money supply. To control the money supply, the Fed specifies **reserve requirements** (the percentage of its deposits that a bank must hold with the Fed). It sets the **discount rate** at which it lends money to banks and conducts **open-market operations** to buy and sell securities. It also exerts influence through **selective credit controls** (such as margin requirements governing the credit granted to buyers by securities brokers).

5 Identify three important ways the financial industry is changing.

(1) *Deregulation:* The Depository Institutions Deregulation and Monetary Control Act (DIDMCA) of 1980 and subsequent laws promote competition by eliminating many restrictions on banking services. (2) *Interstate banking*: The Interstate Banking Efficiency Act (1994) allows banks to operate across state lines. (3) *The impact of electronic technologies:* Banks are increasingly investing in technology as a way to improve efficiency and customer service: (i) **Debit cards** allow the transfer of money between accounts and can be used to make retail purchases at **point-of-sale (POS) terminals**, which relay purchase information directly to the bank's computer system for automatic transfer to the store's account. (ii) The **smart card** can be programmed with "electronic money" at ATM machines. (iii) **E-cash** is money that moves along multiple channels via digital electronic trans-

missions. It moves outside the established network of banks, checks, and paper currency overseen by the Fed. Traditional currency is used to buy electronic funds, which are downloaded over phone lines into a PC or a portable "electronic wallet" that can store and transmit e-cash. The online shopper pays by sending digital money into the seller's e-cash funds, which are instantaneously updated.

6 Understand some of the key concepts and activities in *international banking and finance.*

Electronic technologies now permit speedy global financial transactions to support the growing importance of international finance. Country-to-country transactions are conducted according to an international payments process

that moves money between buyers and sellers in different nations. The payment process recognizes the current exchange rates of currencies for all countries involved in international exchange.

Two United Nations agencies help to finance international trade: (1) The **World Bank** funds national improvements by making loans to build roads, schools, and so forth. Improvements enable borrowers to increase productive capacity and international trade. (2) In the **International Monetary Fund (IMF)**, some 150 nations have combined resources for the following purposes: (i) to promote the stability of exchange rates; (ii) to provide temporary, short-term loans to member countries; (iii) to encourage cooperation on international monetary issues; and (iv) to encourage development of a system for international payments.

■ KEY TERMS

money (p. 420)
M-1 (p. 422)
currency (p. 422)
check (p. 422)
demand deposit (p. 422)
M-2 (p. 422)
time deposit (p. 422)
money market mutual fund (p. 423)
commercial bank (p. 425)
prime rate (p. 426)
savings and loan association (S&L) (p. 427)
mutual savings bank (p. 427)
credit union (p. 427)
pension fund (p. 427)

insurance company (p. 427)
finance company (p. 427)
securities investment dealer (broker) (p. 427)
individual retirement account (IRA) (p. 428)
trust services (p. 428)
letter of credit (p. 429)
banker's acceptance (p. 429)
automated teller machine (ATM) (p. 429)
electronic funds transfer (EFT) (p. 430)
Federal Deposit Insurance Corporation (FDIC) (p. 430)

Federal Reserve System (the Fed) (p. 431)
float (p. 433)
monetary policy (p. 433)
reserve requirement (p. 434)
discount rate (p. 435)
open-market operations (p. 435)
selective credit controls (p. 435)
debit card (p. 437)
point-of-sale (POS) terminal (p. 437)
smart card (p. 437)
e-cash (p. 438)
World Bank (p. 440)
International Monetary Fund (IMF) (p. 440)

■ QUESTIONS AND EXERCISES

Questions for Review
1 What are the components of M-1? Of M-2?
2 Explain the roles of commercial banks, savings and loan associations, and nondeposit institutions in the U.S. financial system.
3 Explain the types of pension services that commercial banks provide for their customers.
4 Describe the structure of the Federal Reserve System.

5 Show how the Fed uses the discount rate to manage inflation in the U.S. economy.

Questions for Analysis
6 Do you think credit cards should be counted in the money supply? Why or why not? Support your argument by using the definition of money.

7 Should commercial banks be regulated, or should market forces be allowed to determine the money supply? Why?

8 Identify a purchase made by you or a family member in which payment was made by check. Draw a diagram to trace the steps in the clearing process followed by that check.

Application Exercises

9 Start with a $1,000 deposit and assume a reserve requirement of 15 percent. Now trace the amount of money created by the banking system after five lending cycles.

10 Interview the manager of a local commercial bank. Identify several ways in which the Fed either helps the bank or restricts its operations.

▶ BUILDING YOUR BUSINESS SKILLS

FOUR ECONOMISTS IN A ROOM

This exercise enhances the following SCANS workplace competencies: demonstrating basic skills, demonstrating thinking skills, exhibiting interpersonal skills, working with information, and applying system knowledge.

Goal
To encourage students to understand the economic factors considered by the Federal Reserve Board in determining current interest rates.

Background
One of the Federal Reserve's most important tools in setting monetary policy is the adjustment of the interest rates it charges member banks to borrow money. To determine interest rate policy, the Fed analyzes current economic conditions from its 12 districts. Its findings are published eight times a year in a report commonly known as the *Beige Book.*

Method

Step 1
Working with three other students, access the Federal Reserve Web site at *(www.federalreserve.gov)*. Look for the heading "Monetary Policy," and then look for "Federal Open Market Committee." Next, click on the subheading "Beige Book." When you reach that page, click on "Summary of the Current Report."

Step 2
Working with group members, study each of the major summary sections:
- Consumer spending
- Manufacturing
- Construction and real estate
- Banking and finance
- Nonfinancial services
- Labor market, wages, and pricing
- Agriculture and natural resources

Working with team members, discuss ways in which you think that key information contained in the summary might affect the Fed's decision to raise, lower, or maintain interest rates.

Step 3
At your library, find back issues of *Barron's (www.barrons.com)*, the highly respected weekly financial publication. Look for the issue published immediately following the appearance of the most recent *Beige Book.* Search for articles analyzing the report. Discuss with group members what the articles say about current economic conditions and interest rates.

Step 4
Based on your research and analysis, what factors do you think the Fed will take into account to control inflation? Working with group members, explain your answer in writing.

Step 5
Working with group members, research what the Federal Reserve chairperson says about interest rates. Do the chairperson's reasons for raising, lowering, or maintaining rates agree with your group's analysis?

FOLLOW-UP QUESTIONS

1 What are the most important factors in the Fed's interest rate decision?

2 Consider the old joke about economists that goes like this: When there are four economists in a room analyzing current economic conditions, there are at least eight different opinions. Based on your research and analysis, why do you think economists have such varying opinions?

EXERCISING YOUR ETHICS

TELLING THE ETHICAL FROM THE STRICTLY LEGAL

The Situation

When upgrading services for convenience to customers, commercial banks are concerned about setting prices that cover all costs so that, ultimately, they make a profit. This exercise challenges you to evaluate one banking service—ATM transactions—to determine if there are also ethical issues that should be considered in a bank's pricing decisions.

The Dilemma

A regional commercial bank in the western United States has more than 300 ATMs serving the nearly 400,000 checking and savings accounts of its customers. Customers are not charged a fee for their 30 million ATM transactions each year, so long as they use their bank's ATMs. For issuing cash to noncustomers, however, the bank charges a $2 ATM fee. The bank's officers are reexamining their policies on ATM surcharges because of public protests against other banks in Santa Monica, New York City, and Chicago. Iowa has gone even further, becoming the first state to pass legislation that bans national banks from charging ATM fees for noncus-

tomers. To date, the courts have ruled that the access fees are legal, but some organizations—such as the U.S. Public Interest Research Group (PIRG)—continue to fight publicly against them.

In considering its current policies, our western bank's vice president for community relations is concerned about more than mere legalities. She wants to ensure that her company is "being a good citizen and doing the right thing." Any decision on ATM fees will ultimately affect the bank's customers, its image in the community and industry, and its profitability for its owners.

QUESTIONS FOR DISCUSSION

1 From the standpoint of a commercial bank, can you find any economic justification for ATM access fees?

2 Based on the scenario described for our bank, do you find any ethical issues in this situation? Or do you find the main issues to be legal and economic rather than ethical?

3 As an officer for this bank, how would you handle this situation?

CRAFTING YOUR BUSINESS PLAN

HOW TO BANK ON YOUR MONEY

The Purpose of the Assignment

1 To familiarize students with banking issues that a sample firm faces in developing its business plan, in the framework of *Business PlanPro (BPP) 2003* software package (Version 6.0).

2 To demonstrate how two chapter topics—bank services and interest rates—can be integrated as components in the *BPP* planning environment.

Assignment

After reading Chapter 14 in the textbook, open the BPP *software and search for information about the financial plans of a sample firm:* Fantastic Florals Inc. *To find* Fantastic Florals, *do the following:*

Open *Business PlanPro.* Go to the toolbar and click on the "*Sample Plans*" icon. In the **Sample Plan Browser**, do a search using the **search category**, *Wholesale trade—nondurable goods.* From the resulting list, select the category entitled, **Import—Artificial Flowers**, which is the location for *Fantastic Florals Inc.* (FFI). The screen you are looking at is the introduction page for the *Fantastic Florals* business plan. Now scroll down until you reach the **Table of Contents** for the *Fantastic Florals* business plan.

NOW RESPOND TO THE FOLLOWING ITEMS:

1 Consider interest rates that are assumed in the business plan. Are the short-term and long-term rates reasonable in today's economy? Explain. [Sites to see in *BPP* for this item: On the Table of Contents page, click on **7.1 Important Assumptions.**]

2 Identify some international banking services that would benefit *FFI* in its daily operations. [Sites to see in *BPP*: On the Table of Contents page, click on **1.0 Executive Summary**. Return to the Table of Contents page, and click on each of the following in turn: **3.4 Sourcing** and **3.6 Future Products.**]

3 From *FFI's* financial plan, can you see any need for bank credit? When, during the planning horizon, might the firm need a line of credit, and how much might it need? [Sites to see in *BPP*: From the Table of Contents page, click on each of the following in turn: **7.0 Financial Plan** and **7.5 Projected Cash Flow.**]

4 Does *FFI* plan to have excess cash that can be deposited in the bank to earn interest? When, during the planning horizon, might the firm accumulate excess cash, and how much might it have? [Sites to see in *BPP*: On the Table of Contents page, click on **5.2.1 Sales Forecast**. Return to the Table of Contents page, and click on **7.5 Projected Cash Flow**. Observe the cash balance at the bottom of the table.]

VIDEO EXERCISE

FUNDING THE BUSINESS WORLD: COAST BUSINESS CREDIT

Learning Objectives

The purpose of this video is to help you to:

1 Recognize how and why banks use customer deposits as the basis of loans.

2 Understand the role of banks and financial services firms in providing funding for business expansion, operations, and acquisitions.

3 Identify the risks that financial services firms take when loaning money to businesses.

Synopsis

Coast Business Credit, a division of Southern Pacific Bank, provides money for business. When evaluating the risk that a loan will not be repaid, Coast carefully considers the borrower's collateral, cash flow, and management. Business customers may apply for a short-term line of credit, a long-term loan, or other types of financing for a variety of purposes. One company may need operating capital; another may need money to make a major acquisition or to expand. Coast analyzes each lending opportunity in terms of potential risk, potential profit, and—in some cases—the ability to create or save jobs and, thus, benefit the community at large.

DISCUSSION QUESTIONS

1 **For analysis:** How might the amount of time deposits gathered by parent company Southern Pacific Bank affect the loans made by Coast Business Credit?

2 **For analysis:** If the Federal Reserve lowers the discount rate by a significant amount, what would be the likely effect on business loan rates?

3 **For application:** What type of collateral might Coast Business Credit prefer when considering a loan application?

4 **For application:** In addition to collateral, Coast Business Credit looks at cash flow and management when considering a loan application. Why is management such an important element?

5 For debate: Should Coast Business Credit establish a separate lending department specifically for financing Internet start-ups? Support your chosen position.

Online Exploration

Visit the Coast Business Credit Web site at *(www. coastbusinesscredit.com)*. After browsing the home page, follow the links to learn more about Coast Business Credit. What types of loans will Coast make? To what types of businesses? Why does Coast explain its financial offerings in such detail? Why would it mention the names of its parent company, its affiliates, and its FDIC coverage on its Web site? How does Coast make it easy for businesses to make contact?

15

After reading this chapter, you should be able to:

1 Explain the difference between *primary* and *secondary securities markets.*

2 Discuss the value to shareholders of *common* and *preferred stock* and describe the secondary market for each type of security.

3 Distinguish among various types of *bonds* in terms of their issuers, safety, and retirement.

4 Describe the investment opportunities offered by *mutual funds.*

5 Explain the process by which securities are bought and sold.

6 Explain how securities markets are regulated.

THE STREET HITS THE WALL

In the late 1990s, tens of thousands of U.S. investors became new millionaires in a booming economy spurred by a vibrant stock market. Annual returns of 15 to 25 percent were commonplace as investors pumped money into the market at a record pace. Major market indexes—the Dow Jones Industrials, the Nasdaq Composite, and the S&P 500—continued an unstinting climb to record highs. Dot-coms and other beneficiaries of

UNDERSTANDING SECURITIES AND INVESTMENTS

the new economy led a parade toward record levels of wealth and prosperity. Government revenues grew so fast that legislators struggled to figure out how to spend the nation's newfound wealth. As investor assets accumulated, older workers began planning for early retirement. Young parents could rest assured that their kids' educations would be paid for.

Then something happened: A slowdown that had first surfaced in late 1999 gradually gained momentum and began to dampen stock prices in mid-2000. Soon the slowdown became a calm but unmistakable retreat. With unprofitable dot-coms failing, unemployment started to climb and the stock market was hit by further economic downturns that continued throughout 2001, even before the devastating blow of September 11.

To further depress an already downcast market, more setbacks came in a series of corporate scandals involving well-known firms—Global Crossings, Enron, Arthur Andersen, ImClone, WorldCom, and a host of others—that struck both fear and anger in retirees, employees, investors, and the entire U.S. public. As reports rolled in, the public's trust dwindled until, by fall 2002, the market had tumbled to its lowest level in years as wary investors pulled money out of stocks and went looking for safer investments. "It's very volatile out there," commented one executive at UBS Warburg. "There seems to be a disaster a day, and investors are frustrated."

In the wake of Wall Street's precipitous fall, many erstwhile millionaires began assessing the damage. How bad was it? One prominent publication pointed out that if you owned 500 shares of JDS Uniphase Corp., a California producer of components for fiber-optic networks, in March 2000, you could have bought a new Porsche 911 Carrera. By July 2002, those same shares would have bought you a 1990 Dodge Omni Hatchback with 100,000 miles and no air conditioning. Aside from millionaires, blue-collar investors were also hit hard. Some would-be early retirees began replanning to delay retirements. Others were left with no retirement funds at all. Young parents started saving all over again for their children's education; legislators scrambled to figure out how to cover suddenly growing government deficits.

Our opening story continues on page 473.

SECURITIES MARKETS

securities
Stocks and bonds representing secured, or asset-based, claims by investors against issuers

Stocks and bonds are known as **securities** because they represent *secured*, or *asset-based*, claims on the part of investors. In other words, holders of stocks and bonds have a stake in the business that issued them. As we saw in Chapter 1, stockholders have claims on some of a corporation's assets (and a say in how the company is run) because each share of stock represents part ownership.

In contrast, *bonds* represent strictly financial claims for money owed to holders by a company. Companies sell bonds to raise long-term funds. The markets in which stocks and bonds are sold are called *securities markets*.[1]

Primary and Secondary Securities Markets

primary securities market
Market in which new stocks and bonds are bought and sold

In **primary securities markets**, new stocks and bonds are bought and sold by firms and governments. Sometimes new securities are sold to single buyers or small groups of buyers. These so-called *private placements* are desirable because they allow issuers to keep their plans confidential.[2]

Securities and Exchange Commission (SEC)
Federal agency that administers U.S. securities laws to protect the investing public and maintain smoothly functioning markets

In 2001, more than $9 billion in new private placements were purchased in the United States by large pension funds and other institutions that privately negotiate prices with sellers.[3] Because private placements cannot be resold in the open market, buyers generally demand higher returns from the issuers.

investment bank
Financial institution engaged in issuing and reselling new securities

Investment Banking Most new stocks and some bonds are sold on the wider public market. To bring a new security to market, the issuing firm must get approval from the **Securities and Exchange Commission (SEC)** *(www.sec.gov)*—the government agency that regulates securities markets. It also needs the services of an **investment bank**—a financial institution that specializes in issuing and reselling new securities. Such investment banking firms as Merrill Lynch *(www.ml.com)* and Morgan Stanley *(www.msdw.com)* provide three important services:

1 They advise companies on the timing and financial terms of new issues.
2 By *underwriting*—that is, buying—new securities, they bear some of the risks of issuing them.
3 They create the distribution networks for moving new securities through groups of other banks and brokers into the hands of individual investors.

In 2001, U.S. investment bankers brought to the market $128 billion in new corporate stocks and $1.2 trillion in new corporate bonds.[4] New securities, however, represent only a minute portion of traded securities. Existing stocks and bonds are sold in the **secondary securities market**, which is handled by such familiar bodies as the New York Stock Exchange. We consider the activities of these markets later in this chapter.

secondary securities market
Market in which stocks and bonds are traded

■ STOCKS

Each year, financial managers, with millions of individual investors, buy and sell the stocks of thousands of companies. This widespread ownership has become possible because of the availability of different types of stocks and because markets have been established that enable individuals to conveniently buy and sell them. In this section, we focus on the value of *common* and *preferred stock* as securities. We also describe the *stock exchanges* on which they are bought and sold.

Common Stocks

Individuals and other companies purchase a firm's common stock in the hope that it will increase in value, provide dividend income, or both. But how is the value of a common stock determined? Stock values are expressed in three different ways—as par, market, and book value.

1 The face value of a share of stock at the time it is originally issued is the **par value**. To receive their corporate charters, all companies must declare par values for their stocks. Each company must preserve the par value money in its retained earnings, and it cannot be distributed as dividends.
2 A stock's real value is its **market value**—the current price of a share in the stock market. Market value reflects buyers' willingness to invest in a company.
3 Recall from Chapter 13 our definition of *owners' equity*—the sum of a company's common stock par value, retained earnings, and additional paid-in capital. The **book value** of common stock represents *owners' equity* (see Chapter 13) divided by the number of shares. Book value is used as a comparison indicator because, for successful companies, the market value is usually greater than its book value. Thus, when market price falls to near book value, some investors buy the stock on the principle that it is underpriced and will increase in the future.

par value
Face value of a share of stock, set by the issuing company's board of directors

market value
Current price of a share of stock in the stock market

book value
Value of a common stock expressed as total owners' equity divided by the number of shares of stock

Investment Traits of Common Stock Common stocks are among the riskiest of all securities. Uncertainties about the stock market itself, for instance, can quickly change a given stock's value. Furthermore, when companies have unprofitable years,

At Cerner Corp. *(www.cerner.com)*, a healthcare software company, CEO Neal L. Patterson e-mailed managers to complain that empty parking lots at 8 A.M. and 5 P.M. reflected a lazy workforce: "You have a problem and you will fix it, or I will replace you," warned Patterson. "You have two weeks. Tick, tock." Unfortunately, the message found its way onto the Internet. When investors and analysts read it, they deduced that Cerner was struggling to make its quarterly goals by working overtime. In a three-day period, Cerner stock went down 22 percent.

blue-chip stock
Common stock issued by a well-established company with a sound financial history and a stable pattern of dividend payouts

they often cannot pay dividends. Shareholder income, therefore—and perhaps share price—drops. At the same time, however, common stocks offer high growth potential. Naturally, the prospects for growth in various industries change from time to time, but the **blue-chip stocks** of well-established, financially sound firms such as Ralston Purina *(www.ralston.com)* and ExxonMobil *(www.exxon.mobil.com)* have historically provided investors steady income through consistent dividend payouts.

The "Old" Economy Versus the "New": What's a "Blue Chip" Now? Because the very nature of the stock market is continuously changing, the future performance of any stock is often unpredictable. With the proliferation of Internet and start-up dot-coms, experts realize that many of the old rules for judging the market prospects of stocks are changing. Conventional methods don't seem to apply to the surprising surges in "new economy" stock prices. Old performance yardsticks—a company's history of dividend payouts, steady growth in earnings per share, and a low price-earnings ratio (current stock price divided by annual earnings per share)—do not seem to measure the value of new economy stocks. In some cases, market prices are soaring for start-ups that have yet to earn a profit.

Although some of the newcomers—America Online, Amazon, eBay, Yahoo!—are regarded by many on Wall Street as Internet blue chips, their financial performance is quite different from that of traditional blue-chip stocks. Let's compare Yahoo! and Wal-Mart. If you had invested $10,000 in Wal-Mart stock in July 1997, the market value of this blue chip would have increased to more than $35,000 in just five years (see Figure 15.1). The same investment in Yahoo! would have also grown to about $35,000. At peak value during the five-year period, however, the Yahoo! investment surged to nearly $600,000 versus Wal-Mart's nearly $40,000.

Could this gigantic difference be predicted from indicators traditionally used by market experts? Hardly. The initial public offering (IPO) of Yahoo! stock in 1996 was priced at $13 per share. It quickly jumped to $43, then settled down to close the day at $33 even though the company had not yet turned a profit. Subsequently, because Yahoo! was the leading Internet portal brand name, investors were betting that it would become a profitable business in the future—a bet that many traditionalists would view as extremely risky.

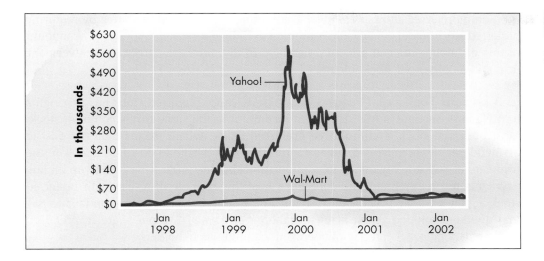

FIGURE 15.1
Market Value Growth:
Wal-Mart Versus Yahoo!

Consider the fact that Wal-Mart's book value is more than double that of Yahoo!. Even more glaring is the fact that entering 2002, Yahoo! has had zero or negative earnings per share for the last six years, whereas Wal-Mart's net earnings have grown steadily during the previous 10 years. The comparison is similar for dividends: Whereas Wal-Mart has a steady history of payouts to stockholders, Yahoo! has never paid a cash dividend. Overall, then, the traditional performance yardsticks favor Wal-Mart heavily. Nevertheless, investors are betting the future on Yahoo!. As recently as July 2000, the original $10,000 investment had accumulated in three years to a market value more than 10 times that of the same investment in Wal-Mart.[5]

Preferred Stock

Preferred stock is usually issued with a stated par value, and dividends are typically expressed as a percentage of par value. If a preferred stock with a $100 par value pays a 6 percent dividend, holders will receive an annual dividend of $6 per share.

Back in 1998, when Henry Blodget, an analyst at brokerage firm Merrill Lynch (www.ml.com), predicted (correctly) that the stock of Amazon.com would climb from $240 to $400 a share, Merrill's leading Internet analyst laughed. But the laugh, it turns out, was on every other analyst, as the value of Amazon—and that of hundreds of dot-coms—soared until early 2000. Then came the so-called "dot-com crash." In March 2001, Amazon.com had dropped to $9.56; as of this writing, it was at $36.32. Still a leading analyst, Blodget maintains that he and Merrill Lynch rode but did not fuel the Internet euphoria of the late 1990s.

Some preferred stock is *callable*. The issuing firm can call in shares by requiring preferred stockholders to surrender them in exchange for cash payments. The amount of this payment—the call price—is specified in the purchase agreement between the firm and its preferred stockholders.

Investment Traits of Preferred Stock Because preferred stock has first rights to dividends, income is less risky than income from the same firm's common stock. Most preferred stock is **cumulative preferred stock**, which means that any missed dividend payments must be paid as soon as the firm is able to do so. In addition, the firm cannot pay any dividends to common stockholders until it has made up all late payments to preferred stockholders. Let's take the example of a firm with preferred stock having a $100 par value and paying a 6 percent dividend. If the firm fails to pay that dividend for two years, it must make up arrears of $12 per share to preferred stockholders before it can pay dividends to common stockholders.

cumulative preferred stock
Preferred stock on which dividends not paid in the past must be paid to stockholders before dividends can be paid to common stockholders

Stock Exchanges

Most of the secondary market for stocks is handled by organized stock exchanges. In addition, a dealer in the over-the-counter market handles the exchange of some stocks. A **stock exchange** is an organization of individuals formed to provide an institutional setting in which stock can be bought and sold. The exchange enforces certain rules to govern its members' trading activities. Most exchanges are nonprofit corporations established to serve their members.

stock exchange
Organization of individuals formed to provide an institutional setting in which stock can be traded

To become a member, an individual must purchase one of a limited number of memberships, called *seats,* on the exchange. Only members (or their representatives) are allowed to trade on the exchange. In this sense, because all orders to buy or sell must flow through members, members of the exchange have a legal monopoly. Memberships can be bought and sold like other assets.

The Trading Floor Each exchange regulates the places and times at which trading may occur. Trading is allowed only at an actual physical location called the trading floor. The floor is equipped with a vast array of electronic communications equipment for conveying buy-and-sell orders or confirming completed trades. A variety of news services furnish up-to-the-minute information about world events and business developments. Any change in these factors, then, may be swiftly reflected in share prices.

"Our stock just went up ten points on the rumor that I was replacing you all with burlap sacks stuffed with straw."

Say WHAT YOU MEAN

SWIMMING AGAINST THE TIDE OF TRUST

These are tough times for both global financial markets and corporate America. Over the last few years, there's been a dramatic drop in public confidence, both in the ability of financial markets to perform at desired levels and in the capacity of corporate America to perform in ethically responsible ways. The assault on the public trust has been two-pronged.

Financial markets, of course, have always fluctuated. The difference is that never before have so many people had a stake in the system. Over the past few years, millions of Americans have invested their life savings in 401(k) retirement plans and other financial instruments. In fact, the latest data suggest that over 50 percent of all U.S. households now own shares of stock. Unfortunately, some of the companies they've invested in haven't done much to bolster their confidence in Corporate America. Among other practices, issuing bogus balance sheets and false financial-health reports has prefigured some spectacular declines in stock prices and corresponding losses of investors' money.

In addition, the always volatile world of business and finance has been further agitated by an enormous amount of media attention. Since the early 1990s, our supply of investment information has exploded, especially with the advent of new media outlets devoted entirely to market analysis and other business coverage. The media attention means that corporations must communicate with larger stakeholder audiences, ranging from individual investors to large pension funds that control huge blocks of company stock. It's not easy to get a coherent message across to an audience with widely differing expectations. That's why many large corporations employ financial communications experts whose job is to project an accurate and up-to-date image of the company. They're also responsible for ensuring that certain legal obligations are met in the reporting of financial statements.

In the end, of course, it's hard for companies to buck financial trends, and even the best financial communications specialists have a hard time convincing investors that things are going well when sentiment about the state of the market—not to mention public opinion of corporate ethics—is against them.

Brokers Some of the people on the trading floor are employed by the exchange. Others are trading stocks for themselves. Many, however, are **brokers**, who earn commissions by executing buy-and-sell orders from nonexchange members. Although they match buyers with sellers, brokers do not own the securities. They earn commissions from the individuals and organizations for whom they place orders.

broker
Individual or organization who receives and executes buy-and-sell orders on behalf of other people in return for commissions

Discount Brokers Like many products, brokerage assistance can be purchased at either discount or at full-service prices. Buying 200 shares of a $20 stock in 2002 cost the investor $8 at Ameritrade *(www.ameritrade.com)*, $14.99 to $19.99 at E*Trade *(www.etrade.com)*, $29.95 at Charles Schwab *(www.schwab.com)*, and more than $100 at a full-service brokerage firm. Price differences are obvious even among the discount brokers—Ameritrade, E*Trade, and Schwab—but the highest discount price is well below the price of the full-service broker.[6]

Discount brokers offer well-informed individual investors a fast, low-cost way to participate in the market. Charles Schwab's customers are do-it-yourself investors. They know what they want to buy or sell, and they usually make trades by using personal computers or Schwab's automated telephone order system without talking with a broker. Why are discount brokerage services low cost? For one thing, sales personnel receive fees or salaries, not commissions. Unlike many full-service brokers, they do not offer investment advice or person-to-person sales consultations. They do, however, offer automated online services, such as stock research, industry analysis, and screening for specific types of stocks.

Online Trading The popularity of online trading stems from convenient access to the Internet, fast no-nonsense transactions, and the opportunity for self-directed investors to manage their own portfolios while paying low fees for trading. Although only 14 percent of all equity trades were executed online in 1998, that number was growing rapidly until the market slowdown in the 2000–2002 period. The Internet, says Gideon Sasson, head of Schwab's electronic brokerage unit, "is fundamentally changing the story of investing."[7] As you can see in Figure 15.2, the volume of online trading is increasing as competition among brokers drives prices further downward.

> **"The Internet is fundamentally changing the story of investing."**
>
> **—Gideon Sasson, head of electronic brokerage, Charles Schwab & Co.**

Full-Service Brokers Despite the growth in online investing, there remains an important market for full-service brokerages, both for new, uninformed investors and for experienced investors who don't have time to keep up with all the latest developments. When you deal with busy people who want to invest successfully, says Joseph Grano of UBS PaineWebber *(www.ubspainewebber.com)*, "you can't do it through a telephone response system. In a world that's growing more and more complicated, the advice and counsel of a broker will be more important, not less important."

With full lines of financial services, firms such as Merrill Lynch can offer clients consulting advice in personal financial planning, estate planning, and tax strategies, along with a wider range of investment products. IPOs of stock, for example, are generally not available to the public through online retail brokers. Rather, a full-service broker, who is also the investment banker that sells the IPO shares, can sell IPO shares to its clients. Financial advisers also do more than deliver information: They offer interpretations of and suggestions on investments that clients might overlook when trying to sift through an avalanche of online financial data.

The Major Exchanges and the OTC Market The two major stock exchanges that operate on trading floors in the United States are the New York and American stock exchanges. The New York Stock Exchange, for many years the largest exchange in the United States, has recently begun to face stiff competition from both the electronic market in the United States and large foreign exchanges, especially in London and Tokyo.

FIGURE 15.2

Growth of Online Trading

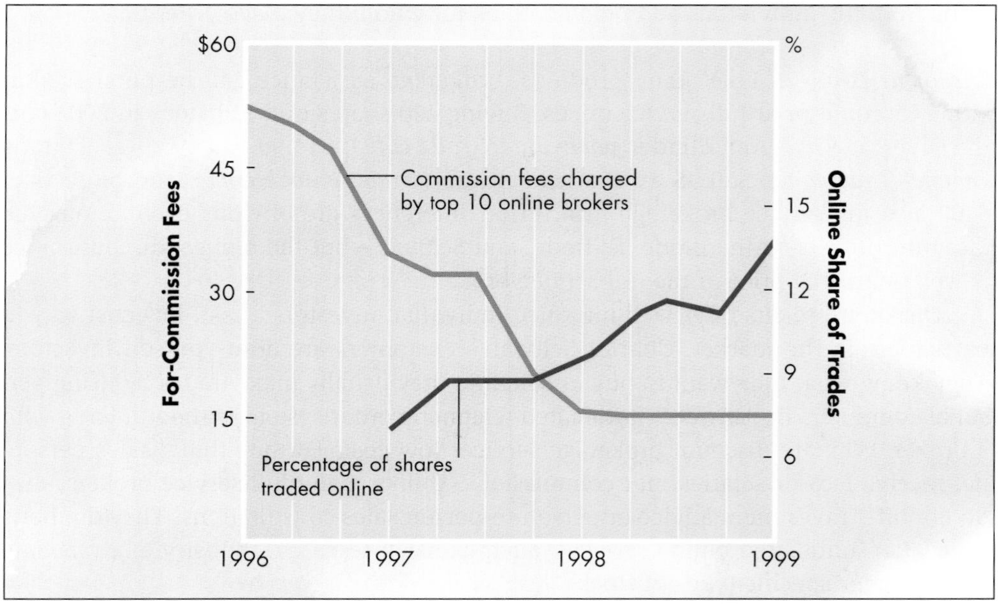

The most important differences between exchanges and the electronic market are (1) the activity of *dealers* and (2) the geographic location of the market. On the trading floor of an exchange, one dealer, called a *specialist*, is appointed by the exchange to control trading for each stock. The specialist not only buys and sells that stock for his or her own inventory but also acts as exclusive auctioneer for it. The electronic market, on the other hand, conducts trades electronically among thousands of dealers in remote locations around the world.

The New York Stock Exchange For many people, "the stock market" means the New York Stock Exchange (NYSE) *(www.nyse.com)*. Founded in 1792 and located at the corner of Wall and Broad Streets in New York City, the largest of all U.S. exchanges is the model for exchanges worldwide. An average of 1.24 billion shares valued at $42.3 billion changes hands each day. About 41 percent of all shares traded on U.S. exchanges are traded here. Only firms meeting certain minimum requirements—earning power, total value of outstanding stock, and number of shareholders—are eligible for listing on the NYSE.[8]

The American Stock Exchange The second-largest floor-based U.S. exchange, the American Stock Exchange (AMEX) *(www.amex.com)*, is also located in New York City. It accounts for about 2 percent of all shares traded on U.S. exchanges and, like the NYSE, has minimum requirements for listings. They are, however, less stringent. The minimum number of publicly held shares, for example, is 500,000—versus 1.1 million for the NYSE.

Regional Stock Exchanges Established long before the advent of modern communications, the seven regional stock exchanges were organized to serve investors in places other than New York. The largest regional exchanges are the Chicago (formerly the Midwest) Stock Exchange and the Pacific Stock Exchange in Los Angeles and San Francisco. Other exchanges are located in Philadelphia, Boston, Cincinnati, and Spokane, Washington. Many corporations list their stocks both regionally and on either the NYSE or the AMEX.

Foreign Stock Exchanges As recently as 1980, the U.S. market accounted for more than half the value of the world market in traded stocks. Indeed, as late as 1975, the

On September 17, 2001, the trading floor of the New York Stock Exchange *(www.nyse.com)* reopened after a six-day shutdown following the September 11 attacks. As experts looked on to see whether the market would rebound, trading followed the day's news events: Prices fell just after President Bush announced that he wanted Osama bin Laden "dead or alive," prompting fears of future violence. At closing, stocks had slid 7 percent but still remained above what many investors had feared. "Bad Numbers," said a *New York Times* headline, "Still Felt Good."

equity of IBM alone *(www.ibm.com)* was greater than the national market equities of all but four countries. Market activities, however, have shifted as the value of shares listed on foreign exchanges continues to grow. The annual dollar value of trades on exchanges in London, Tokyo, and other cities is in the trillions. In fact, the London exchange exceeds even the NYSE in number of stocks listed. In market value, however, transactions on U.S. exchanges remain larger than those on exchanges in other countries. Relatively new exchanges are also flourishing in cities from Shanghai to Warsaw.

over-the-counter (OTC) market
Organization of securities dealers formed to trade stock outside the formal institutional setting of the organized stock exchanges

Over-the-Counter Market The **over-the-counter (OTC) market** is so called because its original traders were somewhat like retailers. They kept supplies of shares on hand and, as opportunities arose, sold them over the office counter to interested buyers. Even today, the OTC market has no trading floor. Rather, it consists of many people in different locations who hold an inventory of securities that are not listed on any of the national U.S. securities exchanges. The over-the-counter market consists of independent dealers who own the securities that they buy and sell at their own risk. Although OTC activities are of interest from an historical perspective, trading volume is small in comparison to other markets.[9]

National Association of Securities Dealers Automated Quotation (Nasdaq) system
Organization of securities dealers who own, buy, and sell their own securities over a network of electronic communications

Nasdaq and NASD In the 1960s, an SEC study reported that the OTC, on which the shares of thousands of companies were traded, was unduly fragmented. One proposal recommended automation of the OTC, calling for a new system to be implemented by the National Association of Securities Dealers Inc. (NASD). The resulting automated OTC system, launched in 1971, is known as the **National Association of Securities Dealers Automated Quotation—or Nasdaq—system**, the world's first electronic stock market. In 2001, NASD became a separate organization from the Nasdaq system so that NASD could focus solely on securities regulation.

With more than 5,500 member firms, NASD *(www.nasd.com)* is the largest private-sector securities-regulation organization in the world. Every broker/dealer in the United States who conducts securities business with the public is required by law to be a member of the NASD. NASD includes dealers (not just brokers) who must pass qualification exams and meet certain standards for financial soundness. The privilege of trading in the market is granted by federal regulators and by NASD.

Meanwhile, the Nasdaq telecommunications system operates the Nasdaq Stock Market by broadcasting trading information on an intranet to over 350,000 terminals worldwide. Whereas orders at the NYSE are paired on the trading floor, Nasdaq orders are paired and executed on a computer network. Currently, Nasdaq is working with officials in an increasing number of countries who want to replace the trading floors of traditional exchanges with electronic networks like Nasdaq.

The stocks of nearly 4,100 companies are traded by Nasdaq. Newer firms are often listed here when their stocks first become available in the secondary market. Current listings include Starbucks and such well-known technology stocks as Intel *(www.intel.com)*, Dell Computer *(www.dell.com)*, Oracle Technology *(www.oracle.com)*, and Microsoft *(www.microsoft.com)*.

In early 2001, Nasdaq, the fastest-growing U.S. stock market, set a record volume of over 3 billion shares traded in one day. Its 2001 volume of 471 billion shares traded was the industry leader, and it is the leading U.S. market for non-U.S. listings, with a total of 461 non-U.S. companies. Although the volume of shares traded surpasses that of the New York Stock Exchange, the total market value of Nasdaq's U.S. stocks is only about one-half that of the NYSE.

Steps Toward a Global Stock Market With its electronic telecommunication system, Nasdaq possesses an infrastructure that could eventually lead to a truly global stock market—one that would allow buyers and sellers to interact from any point in the world. Currently, Nasdaq provides equal access to both the market and market information via simultaneous broadcasts of quotes from more than 1,000 participating firms. Nasdaq communication networks enter customer orders and then display new quotes reflecting those orders.

In laying the groundwork for a system that would connect listed companies and investors for worldwide 24-hour-a-day trading, Nasdaq is taking the following steps:

- The Nasdaq Japan Market was launched in 2000 in partnership with the Osaka Securities Exchange *(www.ose.or.jp/e)*. In 2001, it captured nearly 30 percent of Japan's new public stock offerings. This electronic securities market uses a technology that can eventually link Europe and the United States as well.
- Nasdaq-Europe, an Internet-accessible stock market patterned after Nasdaq, was opened in June 2001. It offers European traders access to the stocks of listed U.S. and Asian companies.
- In 2001, Nasdaq opened offices in Shanghai, China, primarily for educational purposes, and in Bangladore, India.
- It has agreed to a deal with the government of Quebec to launch Nasdaq Canada.
- An agreement with the Hong Kong Stock Exchange allows some of Nasdaq's shares to trade in Hong Kong and some of Hong Kong's shares to trade in the United States.
- News reports indicate that Nasdaq has established relationships with Sydney, Australia's, stock market and that negotiations are underway with South Korea's stock market.[10]

Although these initiatives are promising, it will take several years to resolve differences in market regulation and trading practices that currently separate various countries.

SELF-CHECK QUESTIONS 1–3

You should now be able to answer Self-Check Questions 1–3.*

1 **Multiple Choice** Suppose your firm has decided to raise capital by *issuing new securities*. Which of the following services or institutions will be most useful for your purposes? [select one]: **(a)** a discount broker; **(b)** a full-service broker; **(c)** New York Stock Exchange; **(d)** an investment bank; **(e)** secondary securities market.

2 **True/False** Suppose you're thinking about buying 100 common shares of a particular stock on the secondary securities market. Is the following statement true or false? The *par value* of a share of that stock is a good indicator of the purchase price you will have to pay.

3 **Multiple Choice** Which of the following items regarding *organized stock exchanges* is **not** true? [select one]: **(a)** Buy-and-sell orders at the New York Stock Exchange are paired on the trading floor; **(b)** trading volume on the NYSE far exceeds that on the American Exchange; **(c)** the number of shares traded on the floor at the Nasdaq Stock Market is greater than at the NYSE; **(d)** the over-the-counter market has no trading floor; **(e)** the NYSE is facing increasing competition from electronic and foreign stock exchanges.

*Answers to Self-Check Questions 1–3 can be found on p. 510.

■ BONDS

bond
Security through which an issuer promises to pay the buyer a certain amount of money by a specified future date

A **bond** is an IOU—a promise by the issuer to pay the buyer a certain amount of money by a specified future date, usually with interest paid at regular intervals. The U.S. bond market is supplied by three major sources—the U.S. government, municipalities, and corporations. Bonds differ in terms of maturity dates, tax status, and level of risk versus potential yield.[11]

To aid bond investors in making purchase decisions, several services rate the quality of bonds. Table 15.1, for example, shows the systems of two well-known services, Moody's *(www.moodys.com)* and Standard & Poor's *(www.standardpoors.com)*. Ratings measure default risk—the chance that one or more promised payments will be deferred or missed altogether. The highest grades are *AAA* and *Aaa,* the lowest are *C* and *D.* Low-grade bonds are usually called *junk bonds.*

U.S. Government Bonds

The U.S. government is the world's largest debtor. New federal borrowing from the public actually decreased by $90 billion in 2001. In other words, the federal government's repayments of loans exceeded the funds it raised in new loans. Nevertheless, the total U.S. debt at the beginning of 2002 hovered near $6 trillion.[12] To finance its debt, the federal government issues a variety of government bonds. The U.S. Treasury issues Treasury bills (T-bills), Treasury notes, and Treasury bonds (including U.S. savings bonds). Many government agencies (for example, the Federal Housing Administration, or FHA) also issue bonds.

government bond
Bond issued by the federal government

Government bonds, issued by the federal government, are among the safest investments available. Securities with longer maturities are somewhat riskier than short-term issues because their longer lives expose them to more political, social, and economic changes. All federal bonds, however, are backed by the U.S. government. Government securities are sold in large blocks to institutional investors who buy them to ensure desired levels of safety in their portfolios. As investors' needs change, they may buy or sell government securities to other investors.

Municipal Bonds

municipal bond
Bond issued by a state or local government

State and local governments issue **municipal bonds** to finance school and transportation systems and a variety of other projects. In 2001, new municipal bonds were issued at a value of more than $270 billion.

Some bonds, called *obligation bonds,* are backed by the issuer's taxing power. A local school district, for example, may issue $50 million in obligation bonds to fund

TABLE 15.1

Bond Rating Systems

	High Grades	Medium Grades (Investment Grades)	Speculative	Poor Grades
Moody's	Aaa, Aa	A, Baa	Ba, B	Caa to C
Standard & Poor's	AAA, AA	A, BBB	BB, B	CCC to D

new elementary and high schools. The issuer intends to retire the bonds from future tax revenues. In contrast, *revenue bonds* are backed only by the revenue generated by a specific project.

The most attractive feature of municipal bonds is the fact that investors do not pay taxes on interest received. Commercial banks invest in bonds nearing maturity because they are relatively safe, liquid investments. Pension funds, insurance companies, and even private citizens also make longer-term investments in municipals.

Corporate Bonds

Although the U.S. government and municipalities are heavy borrowers, corporate long-term borrowing is even greater. **Corporate bonds** issued by U.S. companies are a large source of financing, involving more money than government and municipal bonds combined.[13] U.S. companies raised nearly $1.4 trillion from new bond issues in 2001. Bonds have traditionally been issued with maturities ranging from 20 to 30 years. In the 1980s, 10-year maturities came into wider use.

corporate bond
Bond issued by a company as a source of long-term funding

Like municipal bonds, longer-term corporate bonds are somewhat riskier than shorter-term bonds. To help investors evaluate risk, Standard & Poor's and Moody's rate both new and proposed issues on a weekly basis. Remember, however, that negative ratings do not necessarily keep issues from being successful. Rather, they raise the interest rates that issuers must offer. Corporate bonds may be categorized in terms of the method of interest payment or in terms of whether they are *secured* or *unsecured.*

Interest Payment: Registered and Bearer Bonds **Registered bonds** register the names of holders with the company, which simply mails out checks. Certificates are of value only to registered holders. **Bearer** (or **coupon**) **bonds** require bondholders to clip coupons from certificates and send them to the issuer to receive an interest payment. Coupons can be redeemed by anyone, regardless of ownership.

registered bond
Bond bearing the name of the holder and registered with the issuing company

bearer (or **coupon**) **bond**
Bond requiring the holder to clip and submit a coupon to receive an interest payment

Secured Bonds With **secured bonds**, issuers can reduce the risk to holders by pledging assets in case of default. Bonds can be backed by first mortgages, other mortgages, or other specific assets. In 1994, the Union Pacific Railroad Co. *(www.uprr.com)* issued $76 million in bonds to finance the purchase and renovation of equipment. Rated *Aaa* (prime) by Moody's and maturing in 2012, the bonds are secured by the newly purchased and rehabilitated equipment itself—80 diesel locomotives, 1,300 hopper cars, and 450 auto-rack cars.

secured bond
Bond backed by pledges of assets to the bondholders

Debentures Unsecured bonds are called **debentures**. No specific property is pledged as security. Rather, holders generally have claims against property not otherwise pledged in the company's other bonds. Thus, debentures are said to have inferior claims on a corporation's assets. Financially strong firms often use debentures. An example is the $175 million debenture issued by Boeing *(www.boeing.com)* in 1993, with maturity on April 15, 2043. Similar issues by weaker companies often receive low ratings and may have trouble attracting investors.

debenture
Unsecured bond for which no specific property is pledged as security

Secondary Markets for Bonds Nearly all secondary trading in bonds occurs in the OTC market rather than on organized exchanges. Thus, precise statistics about annual trading volumes are not recorded. As with stocks, however, market values and prices change daily. Bond prices and interest rates move in opposite directions. As interest rates move up, bond prices tend to go down. The prices of riskier bonds fluctuate more widely than those of higher-grade bonds.

■ MUTUAL FUNDS

mutual fund
Company that pools investments from individuals and organizations to purchase a portfolio of stocks, bonds, and other securities

Companies called **mutual funds** pool investments from individuals and organizations to purchase a portfolio of stocks, bonds, and other securities. Investors are thus part owners of the portfolio. If you invest $1,000 in a mutual fund with a portfolio worth $100,000, you own 1 percent of that portfolio. Investors in **no-load funds** are not charged sales commissions when they buy into or sell out of funds. Investors in **load funds** generally pay commissions of 2 to 8 percent.

no-load fund
Mutual fund in which investors pay no sales commissions when they buy in or sell out

Reasons for Investing The total assets invested in U.S. mutual funds grew significantly every year from 1991 to 2000—to a total of $7 trillion in more than 10,000 different funds. The total fell, however, to $6.9 trillion with the economic downturn and reports of corporate scandals by mid-2002.[14] Why do investors find mutual funds so attractive? Remember first of all that they vary in their investment goals. Naturally, different funds are designed to appeal to the different motives and goals of investors. Funds stressing safety often include money market mutual funds and other safe issues offering immediate income. Investors seeking higher current income must generally sacrifice some safety. Typically, these people look to long-term municipal bonds, corporate bonds, and income mutual funds that invest in common stocks with good dividend-paying records.

load fund
Mutual fund in which investors are charged sales commissions when they buy in or sell out

Mutual funds that stress growth include *balanced mutual funds*—portfolios of bonds and preferred and common stocks, especially the common stocks of established firms. Aggressive growth funds seek maximum capital appreciation. They sacrifice current income and safety and invest in stocks of new (and even troubled) companies and other high-risk securities.

SELF-CHECK QUESTIONS 4–6

You should now be able to answer Self-Check Questions 4–6*

4 **Multiple Choice** Which of the following is **not** true about *bonds?* [select one]: **(a)** Government bonds are among the safest investments available. **(b)** Corporate bonds issued by U.S. companies involve less money than U.S. government and municipal bonds. **(c)** Secured bonds can reduce risk to holders because the issuing firms pledge assets in case of default. **(d)** Bonds can be traded on the secondary market.

5 **True/False** Suppose a well-respected corporation has decided to issue bonds for raising capital but also does not want to pledge specific prop-

erty as security. Is the following statement true or false? A *debenture* is well suited to this firm's objectives.

6 **Multiple Choice** Suppose you have $20,000 to invest. Your goal is to maximize capital appreciation over the next 20 years. Which of the following would be the **most suitable** kind of *mutual fund* for meeting your objectives? [select one]: **(a)** municipal bond fund; **(b)** balanced fund; **(c)** money market fund; **(d)** corporate bond fund; **(e)** aggressive growth fund.

*Answers to Self-Check Questions 4–6 can be found on p. 510.

Making Choices for Diversification, Asset Allocation, and Risk Reduction

Stocks, bonds, and mutual funds offer diverse opportunities for financial gain and involve different risks as well. In striking the right balance for risk among investment alternatives, financial managers seldom take an extreme approach—total risk or total risk avoidance—in selecting their investments. Extreme positions attract extreme results, and most investors have a preference toward either risk or risk avoidance, but they are not totally immersed at either end of the risk spectrum. Instead, they select a mixture, or *portfolio*, of investments—some riskier and some more conservative—that, collectively, provides the right balance between risk and financial stability at which they are comfortable. They do this in two ways: through *diversification* and *asset allocation.*

Diversification Diversification means buying several different kinds of investments rather than just one. Diversification as applied to common stocks means, for example, that you invest in stocks of several different companies, such as IBM, Cisco Systems, and Boeing, rather than put all your money into just one of them. The risk of loss is reduced by spreading the total investment across more stocks because, although any one stock may tumble, there is less chance that all of them will fall. Even more diversification is gained when funds are spread across more kinds of investment alternatives—stocks, bonds, mutual funds, real estate, and so on. Among the tragedies resulting from the scandals at Enron and WorldCom were the lifelong employees who did not diversify their 401(k) investments and, instead, had all their retirement funds invested in their firm's stock. This was an extremely risky position, as they sorrowfully learned. When their firm's stock took a free fall to near zero, their retirement funds disappeared.

diversification
Purchase of several different kinds of investments rather than just one

Asset Allocation Asset allocation is the proportion—the relative amounts—of funds invested in (or allocated to) each of the investment alternatives. You may decide, for example, to allocate $20,000 to common stocks, $10,000 to a money market mutual fund, and $10,000 to a U.S. Treasury bond mutual fund. Ten years later, you may decide on a less risky asset allocation of $10,000, $15,000, and $15,000 in the same investment categories, respectively. As investment objectives change, in this example from moderate risk to lower risk for capital preservation, the asset allocation must be changed accordingly.

asset allocation
Relative amount of funds invested in (or allocated to) each of several investment alternatives

■ BUYING AND SELLING SECURITIES

The process of buying and selling securities is complex. First, you need to find out about possible investments and match them to your investment objectives. Then you must select a broker and open an account. Only then can you place orders and make different types of transactions.

Financial Information Services

Have you ever looked at the financial section of your daily newspaper and wondered what all those tables and numbers mean? It is a good idea to know how to read stock,

ENTREPRENEURSHIP and *New Ventures*

The Personality of a Risk Taker

Thanks to the risks entailed in setting up and growing her own business, Lucy Marcus, founder of London-based Marcus Venture Consulting *(www.marcusventures.com)*, has become an expert at assessing the risk involved in starting up a new business, investing in it, and managing it. In many ways, risk is the mainstay of Marcus's business. Her clients—mostly venture capital investors—want answers to such questions as, "If I invest in XYZ Venture Capital Fund, how well will it be managed? How well does it treat entrepreneurial clients? What kind of financial return can I expect?" Her clients include individuals, companies, and pension funds—investors seeking a clear picture of the risks posed by potential investment opportunities. Her assessments help them determine the right balance between prospective gains and losses.

As one of a handful of senior female executives in the private equity industry, Marcus has to gain the trust of all sorts of clients by demonstrating dependable judgment about risk. It's a business with few women in leadership roles, but Marcus says it's just a matter of time until more women get into venture capital. "Private equity is all about managing risk," she says. "An investor will be drawn to what is familiar, where there is common ground, and familiarity—be it because two people are the same sex or from the same neighborhood—is a way of eliminating some of that risk."

To encourage women in the equities industry, Marcus set up a network called HighTech Women—a 2,500-member discussion group for women to meet and mentor one another. "HighTech Women was something I had to do," she explains. "I kept going to conferences and being one of four women in a roomful of 200 CEOs. I found that I'd meet the most interesting people in the ladies' room."

> *"I kept going to conferences and being one of four women in a roomful of 200 CEOs. I found that I'd meet the most interesting people in the ladies' room."*
>
> *—Lucy Marcus, head of Marcus Venture Consulting*

Marcus's success—she was selected as a World Economic Forum Global Leader for Tomorrow in 2002—stems from diverse career-building experiences, self-developed personal practices designed to sharpen creativity, and energetic drive. A native New Yorker, she attended Wellesley College and did a summer internship with U.S. Senator Edward Kennedy. Before getting a master's degree in political philosophy from the University of Cambridge, she worked in public policy for the U.S. Treasury Department and Price Waterhouse. She later held positions in various U.S. and European technology companies before opening Marcus Venture Consulting.

As an entrepreneur advising other entrepreneurs, Marcus's outlook is also influenced by a number of personal characteristics. For professional reasons, she won't tell anyone her age: "I'm too young for some people and too old for others." She regards herself as a maverick who's too outspoken for the average corporate environment, and she thinks people should be judged on what they achieve. She admires people who do different and interesting work, who buck trends, and who know what they're talking about. She prides herself on an ability to walk in other people's shoes and appreciate different points of view. She claims to be a quick judge of character and admits that she has to work hard at networking because she doesn't make friends with everybody. She refuses to live in California because she wants to spend time with people in completely different industries. She avoids focusing solely on the business she's in, but that doesn't mean that she's not passionate about what she does. "I couldn't do something I wasn't passionate about," she says, "because I couldn't put the energy into it."

bond, and mutual fund quotations if you want to invest in issues. Fortunately, this skill is easily mastered.

Stock Quotations Daily transactions for NYSE and Nasdaq common stocks are reported in most city newspapers. Figure 15.3 shows part of a listing from the *Wall Street Journal*, with columns numbered 1 through 11. Let us analyze the listing for the company at the top, Gap Inc. *(www.gap.com)*:

❶	❷	❸	❹	❺	❻	❼	❽	❾	❿	⓫
YTD	52 Weeks					Yld		Vol		Net
% Chg	High	Low	Stock	Sym	Div	%	PE	100s	Last	Chg
– 1.4	30.68	11.12	Gap Inc	GPS	.09	.7	dd	27593	13.74	–0.20
– 11.5	28	18.35	GardnrDenvr	GDI		...	14	279	19.75	...
– 24.0	13.70	8.20	Gartner	IT		...	dd	2657	8.88	–0.29
– 23.6	13.50	8.05	GartnerB	ITB		...	...	346	8.56	–0.44
– 49.0	16.20	3.80	Gateway	GTW		...	dd	18600	4.10	0.11
– 18.4	29.26	18.49	GaylEnt	GET		...	dd	160	20.08	–1.17
– 15.7	16.25	10.50	GenCorp	GY	.12	1.0	4	1413	11.90	–0.21
– 45.2	58.95	25.10	Genentech	DNA		...	dd	33696	29.75	1.61
– 53.8	19.24	5.59	GenlCbl	BGC	.20	3.3	dd	1699	6.05	–0.20
20.9	111.18	74.90	GenDynam	GD	1.20	1.2	21	28126	96.31	–2.29
– 28.6	47.75	26.40	GenElec	GE	.72	2.5	20	479987	28.60	1.25

FIGURE 15.3

Reading a Stock Quotation

- The first column ("YTD % Chg") shows the stock price percentage change for the calendar year to date. Gap's common stock price decreased 1.4 percent for 2002 (as of mid-July).

- The next two columns ("High" and "Low") show the highest and lowest prices paid for one share of Gap stock *during the past year*. Note that stock prices throughout are expressed in dollars per share. In the past 52 weeks, then, Gap's stock ranged in value from $30.68 to $11.12 per share. This range reveals a fairly volatile stock price.

- The fourth column ("Stock") is the abbreviated company name.

- The NYSE *symbol* for the stock is listed in column 5 ("Sym").

- The sixth column ("Div") indicates that Gap pays an annual *cash dividend* of $0.09 per share. This amount can be compared with payouts by other companies.

- Column 7 ("Yld %") is the *dividend yield* expressed as a percentage of the stock's current price (shown in column 10). Gap's dividend yield is 0.7 percent (0.09/13.74, rounded). Potential buyers can compare this yield with returns they might get from alternative investments.

- Column 8 ("PE") shows the **price-earnings ratio**—the current price of the stock divided by the firm's current annual earnings per share. On this day, Gap's PE is indicated as *dd,* a code meaning that Gap had negative earnings for the past four quarters. If, in contrast, Gap's PE had been 20, for example, it means that investors are willing to pay $20 for each dollar of reported profits to own Gap stock. This figure can be compared with PE ratios of other stocks when deciding which is the best investment.

- The last three columns detail the day's trading. Column 9 ("Vol 100s") shows the *number of shares* (in hundreds) that were traded—in this case, 27,593. Some investors interpret increases in trading volume as an indicator of forthcoming price changes in a stock.

- Column 10 ("Last") shows that Gap's *last sale of the day* was for $13.74.

- The final column ("Net Chg") shows the *difference between the previous day's close and the close on the day being reported.* The closing price of Gap stock is $0.20 lower than it was on the previous business day. Day-to-day changes are indicators of recent price stability or volatility.

price-earnings ratio
Current price of a stock divided by the firm's current annual earnings per share

The listings also report unusual conditions of importance to investors. An *s* next to the stock symbol, for example, would indicate either a *stock split* (a division of stock that gives stockholders a greater number of shares but that does not change each individual's proportionate share of ownership) or an *extra stock dividend* paid by the company during the past 52 weeks. An *n* accompanying a stock symbol would indicate that this stock was *newly issued* during the past 52 weeks. A downward-pointing marker (▼) next to a stock symbol would indicate a new 52-week low in the price of that stock. The stock listings contain an index explaining the various codes for unusual conditions.

Reports on daily transactions for preferred stocks use a format similar to that for common stocks.

Bond Quotations   Daily quotations on corporate bonds from the NYSE are also widely published. Bond quotations contain essentially the same type of information as stock quotations. One difference is that the year in which it is going to mature is listed beside each bond.

Mutual Funds Quotations   Selling prices for mutual funds are reported daily in most city newspapers. Additional investor information is also available in the financial press. Figure 15.4 shows how to read a typical weekly mutual funds quotation.

- Column 1 is the *net asset value* (NAV), or the value of a single share as calculated by the fund.
- Column 2 shows the *net asset value change*—the gain or loss based on the previous day's NAV.
- Column 3 lists the *fund family* at the top and the individual fund names beneath the family name.

FIGURE 15.4

Reading a Mutual Fund Quotation

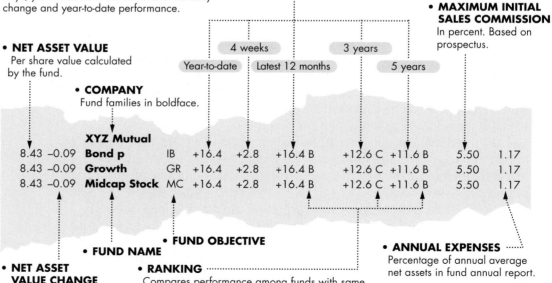

Performance calculations assume reinvestment of all distributions and are after subtracting annual expenses. But figures don't reflect sales charges ("loads") or redemption fees.
These expanded tables appear Fridays. Other days, you'll find net asset value and the daily change and year-to-date performance.

• **TOTAL RETURN**
NAV change plus accumulated income for the period, in percent. Assumes reinvestment of all distributions. Percentages are annualized for periods exceeding one year. Calculations are based on latest data from fund.

• **MAXIMUM INITIAL SALES COMMISSION**
In percent. Based on prospectus.

• **NET ASSET VALUE**
Per share value calculated by the fund.

• **COMPANY**
Fund families in boldface.

			Year-to-date	4 weeks	Latest 12 months	3 years	5 years		
XYZ Mutual									
8.43	–0.09	**Bond p**	IB	+16.4	+2.8	+16.4 B	+12.6 C	+11.6 B	5.50	1.17
8.43	–0.09	**Growth**	GR	+16.4	+2.8	+16.4 B	+12.6 C	+11.6 B	5.50	1.17
8.43	–0.09	**Midcap Stock**	MC	+16.4	+2.8	+16.4 B	+12.6 C	+11.6 B	5.50	1.17

• **FUND OBJECTIVE**

• **FUND NAME**

• **NET ASSET VALUE CHANGE**
Gain or loss, based on prior day's NAV.

• **RANKING**
Compares performance among funds with same investment objectives and then ranked for time periods listed. Performance is measured from either the closest Thursday or month-end for periods of more than 3 years. A = top 20%; B = next 20%; C = middle 20%; D = next 20%; E = bottom 20%

• **ANNUAL EXPENSES**
Percentage of annual average net assets in fund annual report.

■ Column 4 reports each *fund's objective.* The "IB" code stands for an intermediate-term bond fund; "GR" indicates a growth stock fund. This allows readers to compare the performance of funds with similar objectives.

■ The next five columns report *each fund's recent and long-term performance,* and they rank the funds within each investment objective. These numbers reflect the percentage change in NAV plus accumulated income for each period, assuming that all distributions are reinvested in the fund. These five columns show the return of the fund for the year to date, the last 4 weeks, 12 months, 3 years, and 5 years. The numbers for periods exceeding a year show an average annual return for the period, and they are followed by letters indicating the fund's performance relative to other funds with the same objective. "A" means the fund was among the top 20 percent of funds in that category, "B" indicates the second 20 percent, and so on.

■ The next column reports the *maximum initial sales commission,* expressed as a percentage, which the investor would have to pay to purchase shares in the fund.

■ The last column shows the fund's *average annual expenses* as a percentage of the fund's assets, paid annually by investors in the fund.

Market Indexes Although they do not indicate the status of particular securities, **market indexes** provide useful summaries of price trends, both in specific industries and in the stock market as a whole. Market indexes, for example, reveal bull and bear market trends. **Bull markets** are periods of rising stock prices. Periods of falling stock prices are called **bear markets**.

As Figure 15.5 shows, the years 1981 to the beginning of 2000 boasted a strong bull market, the longest in history. Inflation was under control as business

market index
Summary of price trends in a specific industry and/or the stock market as a whole

bull market
Period of rising stock prices

bear market
Period of falling stock prices

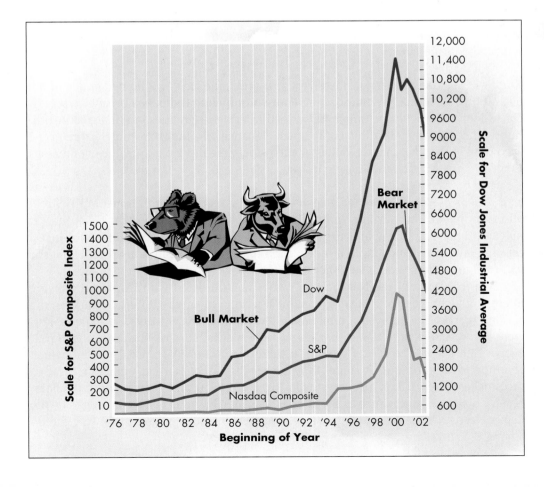

FIGURE 15.5

Bull and Bear Markets

flourished in a healthy economy. In contrast, the period 2000 to 2002 was characterized by a bear market. Financial failures closed many dot-com firms, sluggish sales abroad decreased U.S. exports, terrorism on September 11, 2001, brought a halt to business activity, and corporate misconduct led to a downcast mood among investors. As you can see, the data that characterize such periods are drawn from three leading market indexes—the Dow Jones, Standard & Poor's, and the Nasdaq Composite.

Dow Jones Industrial Average (DJIA)
Market index based on the prices of 30 of the largest industrial firms listed on the NYSE

The Dow The **Dow Jones Industrial Average (DJIA)** is the most widely cited American index. The Dow measures the performance of U.S. financial markets by focusing on 30 blue-chip companies as reflectors of economic health. The Dow is an average of the stock prices for these 30 large firms and, by tradition, traders and investors use it as a barometer of the market's overall movement. Because it includes only 30 of the thousands of companies on the market, the Dow is only an approximation of the overall market's price movements.

Over the decades, the Dow has been revised and updated to reflect the changing composition of U.S. companies and industries. The most recent modification occurred in November 1999, when four companies were added—Home Depot *(www.homedepot.com)*, Intel, Microsoft, and SBC Communications *(www.sbc.com)*—replacing Chevron *(www.chevron.com)*, Goodyear *(www.goodyear.com)*, Sears *(www.sears.com)*, and Union Carbide *(www.unioncarbide.com)*. These changes not only reflect the increasing importance of technology stocks but also include for the first time two stocks from the Nasdaq market rather than only companies listed on the NYSE.

The Dow average is computed as the sum of the current prices of the 30 stocks divided not by 30 (as might be expected) but rather by a number that compensates for stock splits and each stock's available number of shares. On July 15, 2002, the value of that divisor was 0.14445. Each day, the divisor's value is printed in the *Wall Street Journal,* as is the DJIA.

Standard & Poor's Composite Index
Market index based on the performance of 400 industrial firms, 40 utilities, 40 financial institutions, and 20 transportation companies

The S&P 500 Because it considers very few firms, the Dow is a limited gauge of the overall U.S. stock market. **Standard & Poor's Composite Index** is a broader report. It consists of 500 stocks, including 400 industrial firms, 40 utilities, 40 financial institutions, and 20 transportation companies. Because the index average is weighted according to the total market values of each stock, the more highly valued companies exercise a greater influence on the index.

Nasdaq Composite Index
Value-weighted market index that includes all Nasdaq-listed companies, both domestic and foreign

The Nasdaq Composite Because it considers more stocks, some Wall Street observers regard the **Nasdaq Composite Index** as the most important of all market indexes. Unlike the Dow and the S&P 500, all Nasdaq-listed companies not just a selected few, are included in the index, for a total of over 4,000 firms (both domestic and foreign)—more than most other indexes.

The popularity of the Nasdaq Index goes hand-in-hand with investors' growing interest in technology and small-company stocks. Compared with other markets, the Nasdaq market has enjoyed a remarkable level of activity. By 1998, so many shares were being traded on Nasdaq that its share-of-market surpassed that of the NYSE. Figure 15.6 shows the steady growth in the dollar volume of Nasdaq trades, which continue to capture market share. In a further display of Nasdaq's emerging role in the stock market, it has also overtaken the NYSE in terms of investor awareness. NYSE's historical dominance as the market's flagship brand is being challenged by the newer Nasdaq, which, according to one study, even enjoys greater name recognition among U.S. investors.

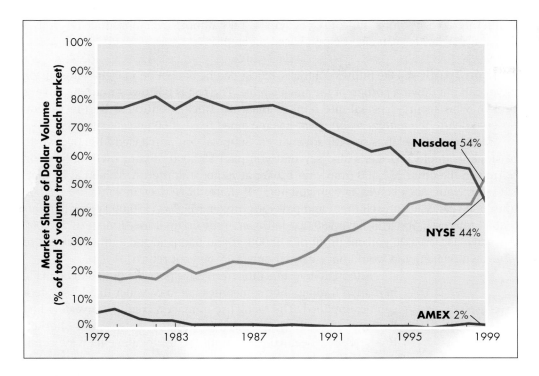

FIGURE 15.6

The Stock Markets: Comparative Dollar Volume of Trades

market order
Order to buy or sell a security at the market price prevailing at the time the order is placed

Placing Orders

After doing your own research and getting recommendations from your broker, you can choose to place several different types of orders:[15]

- A **market order** requests that a broker buy or sell a certain security at the prevailing market price at the time of the order. For example, look again at Figure 15.3. On that day, your broker would have sold your Gap stock at a price near $13.74.
- Note that when you gave your order to sell, you did not know exactly what the market price would be. This situation can be avoided with limit and stop orders, which allow for buying and selling only if certain price conditions are met.

  A **limit order** authorizes the purchase of a stock only if its price is less than or equal to a specified limit. For example, an order to buy at $15 a share means that the broker is to buy if and only if the stock becomes available for a price of $15 or less. A **stop order** instructs the broker to sell if a stock price falls to a certain level. For example, an order of $10 on a particular stock means that the broker is to sell that stock if and only if its price falls to $10 or below.
- Orders also differ by *size*. An order for a **round lot** requests 100 shares of a particular stock or some multiple thereof. Fractions of round lots are called **odd lots**. Because an intermediary—an *odd-lot broker*—is often involved, odd-lot trading is usually more expensive than round-lot trading.

limit order
Order authorizing the purchase of a stock only if its price is equal to or less than a specified amount

stop order
Order authorizing the sale of a stock if its price falls to or below a specified level

round lot
Purchase or sale of stock in units of 100 shares

odd lot
Purchase or sale of stock in fractions of round lots

Financing Purchases

When you place a buy order of any kind, you must tell your broker how you will pay for the purchase. For example, you might maintain a cash account with your broker. Then, as you buy and sell stocks, your broker adds proceeds to your account while

margin
Percentage of the total sales price that a buyer must put up to place an order for stock of futures contracts

deducting commissions and purchase costs. Like almost every product in today's economy, securities can also be purchased on credit.

Margin Trading Like futures contracts, stocks can be bought on **margin**—that is, the buyer can put down a portion of the stock's price. The rest is borrowed from the buyer's broker, who secures special-rate bank loans with stock. Controlled by the Federal Reserve Board, the *margin requirement* has remained fixed at 50 percent since 1974.

Margin trading offers several advantages. Suppose you purchased $100,000 worth of stock in Intel Corp. Let's also say that you paid $50,000 of your own money and borrowed the other $50,000 from your broker at 10 percent interest. Valued at its market price, your stock serves as your collateral. If shares have risen in value to $115,000 after one year, you can sell them and pay your broker $55,000 ($50,000 principal plus $5,000 interest). You will have $60,000 left over. Your original investment of $50,000 will have earned a 20 percent profit of $10,000. If you had paid the entire price out of your own pocket, you would have earned only a 15 percent return.

Although investors often recognize possible profits to be made in margin trading, they sometimes fail to consider that losses, too, can be amplified. The rising use of margin credit by investors had become a growing concern during the recent bull market. Investors who seemed focused on the upside benefits were confident that the market trend would continue upward, and they were less sensitive to the downside risks of margin trading. Especially at online brokerages, inexperienced traders were borrowing at an alarming rate, and some were using the borrowed funds for risky and speculative day trading. So-called *day traders* visited Web sites online to buy and sell a stock in the same day (so-called *intraday trades*), seeking quick in-and-out fractional gains on large volumes (many shares) of each stock. Although some day traders were successful, most ended up financial losers. With more investors buying on debt, more of them were headed for a serious accelerated crash. Bradley Skolnick, president of the North American Securities Administrators Association, voices the opinion held by many investment experts: "A lot of people are purchasing rather speculative, high-risk stocks with borrowed money, and that's a source of concern for me. In a volatile market, trading on margin can find you in a whole lot of hurt very quickly."[16]

> **"In a volatile market, trading on margin can find you in a whole lot of hurt very quickly."**
>
> **—Bradley Skolnick, president, North American Securities Administrators Association**

In a packed Orlando classroom, customers have paid $595 each for a one-day class with Toni Turner *(www.toniturner.com)*. What special message makes Turner worth that much? Turner teaches a type of day trading called "swing trading": She discourages buying and selling stocks in a matter of minutes (the strategy of the typical day trader) and explains when and why it's better to study prices and patterns over the course of days. If you're interested in day trading, there are a number of Web sites that can tell you about the perils and perks. See *(www.daytradingworld.com/)* as a start.

Short Sales In addition to lending money, brokerages also lend securities. A **short sale** begins when you borrow a security from your broker and sell it (one of the few times that it is legal to sell something that you do not own). At a given point in the future, you must restore an equal number of shares of that issue to the brokerage, along with a fee.

We now return to our Gap example. Suppose that in January, you believe the price of Gap stock will soon fall. You, therefore, order your broker to "sell short" 100 shares at the market price of $13.74 per share. Your broker will make the sale and credit $1,374 to your account. If Gap's price falls to $8 per share in July, you can buy 100 shares for $800 and use them to repay your broker. You will have made a $574 profit (before commissions). Your risk, of course, is that Gap's price will not fall. If it holds steady or rises, you will take a loss.

short sale
Stock sale in which an investor borrows securities from a broker to be sold and then replaced at a specified future date

■ SECURITIES MARKET REGULATION

In addition to regulation by government agencies, both the NASD and the NYSE exercise self-regulation to maintain the public trust and to ensure professionalism in the financial industry. A visible example is the NYSE's actions in establishing so-called circuit breakers—trading rules for reducing excessive market volatility and promoting investor confidence—that suspend trading for a preset length of time. Adopted first in October 1988, with the approval of the SEC, the rules suspend trading on the NYSE whenever the market begins spiraling out of control during a single day. The 1988 rules stipulated that trading would halt for one hour on any day when the Dow Jones Industrial Average dropped 250 points and would close for two hours with any 400-point decline. The interruption provides a "cooling off" period that slows trading activity, gives investors time to reconsider their trading positions, and allows computer programs to be revised or shut down.[17]

Because circuit-breaker thresholds are updated periodically to keep up with the Dow's growth, as of April 2000 the following single-day declines will halt trading marketwide:

■ A 1,050-point drop in the DJIA before 2 P.M. halts trading for one hour.
■ A 2,100-point drop before 1 P.M. halts trading for two hours.
■ A 3,150-point drop at any time halts trading for the day.

Although circuit breaker rules were initiated in response to severe market plunges in October 1987 and October 1988, they have been triggered only once—on October 27, 1997, when the DJIA fell 350 points at 2:35 P.M. and 550 points at 3:30 P.M., for an overall 7 percent plunge that shut down trading for the day.

One oft-cited cause of sudden market fluctuations is **program trading**—the portfolio trading strategy involving the sale or purchase of a group of stocks valued at $1 million or more, often triggered by computerized trading programs that can be launched without human supervision or control. It works in the following way. As market values change and economic events transpire during the course of a day, computer programs are busy recalculating the future values of stocks. Once a calculated value reaches a critical point, the program automatically signals a buy or sell order. Because electronic trading could cause the market to spiral out of control, it has contributed to the establishment of circuit breakers.

program trading
Large purchase or sale of a group of stocks, often triggered by computerized trading programs that can be launched without human supervision or control

The Securities and Exchange Commission

To protect the investing public and to maintain smoothly functioning markets, the SEC oversees many phases of the process through which securities are issued. The SEC regulates the public offering of new securities by requiring that all companies file prospectuses before proposed offerings commence. To protect investors from fraudulent issues, a **prospectus** contains pertinent information about both the offered security and the issuing company. False statements are subject to criminal penalties.

prospectus
Registration statement filed with the SEC before the issuance of a new security

Insider Trading The SEC also enforces laws against **insider trading**—the use of special knowledge about a firm for profit or gain. In June 2002, for example, the SEC filed suit in federal court in New York against Samuel Waksal, the former CEO of ImClone Systems Inc., on charges of using insider information to gain illegal profits. The suit charged that Waksal received disappointing news in late December 2001 that the U.S. Food and Drug Administration (FDA) would soon reject ImClone's application to market its cancer treatment drug, Erbitux. The next day, before the FDA was scheduled to notify ImClone of its rejection, Waksal's family members sold more than $9 million in ImClone stock. For two days, Waksal himself tried to sell his shares, which were worth nearly $5 million, but two brokerage firms refused to execute the orders. The following day, after the stock market had closed, ImClone publicly announced the FDA decision. The next trading day, ImClone's stock price dropped 16 percent—from $55.25 to $46.46. By mid-2002, it had plummeted to $8 per share.[18] Family members, according to the SEC suit, avoided millions in losses by illegally using the insider information. In June 2003, federal prosecutors indicted Martha Stewart, the home décor entrepreneur and a friend of Waksal, who sold 3,900 shares at $58 per share the day before ImClone made its public announcement.

insider trading
Illegal practice of using special knowledge about a firm for profit or gain

The SEC also offers a bounty to any person who provides information leading to a civil penalty for illegal insider trading. The courts can render such a penalty of up to three times the illegal profit that was gained, and the bounty can, at most, be 10 percent of that penalty.

Along with the SEC's enforcement efforts, the stock exchanges and securities firms, as members of NASD, cooperate in detecting and stopping insider action. In any given year, NASD may refer more than 100 cases to the SEC for charges of possible insider trading. In addition, NASD's self-regulation results in actions ranging from fining member firms and officers to barring or suspending them.

blue-sky laws
Laws requiring securities dealers to be licensed and registered with the states in which they do business

Blue-Sky Laws State governments also regulate the sale of securities. For example, commenting that some promoters would sell stock "to the blue sky itself," one legislator's speech led to the phrase **blue-sky laws** and the passage of statutes requiring securities to be registered with state officials. In addition, securities dealers must be registered and licensed by the states in which they do business. Finally, states may prosecute for the sale of fraudulent securities.

SELF-CHECK QUESTIONS 7–9

You should now be able to answer Self-Check Questions 7–9.*

7 Multiple Choice Which of the following is **not** true about printed *stock quotations,* like those published in the *Wall Street Journal?* [select one]: **(a)** The percentage change in the stock's price for the year is shown. **(b)** The company's annual cash dividend is reported. **(c)** A stock's high and low prices for any given day are reported. **(d)** The difference between closing prices on successive days is shown. **(e)** The stock's closing price for the day is given.

8 True/False The *Dow Jones Industrial Average* is the most widely cited American index because it approximates the market's overall price movements more accurately than other indexes.

9 Multiple Choice Suppose you want to *buy a particular stock* at a price lower than current market value. Once it's purchased, you intend to hold it for future price gains. After you buy shares, however, you also want to protect yourself by being able to sell quickly if the market price should suddenly fall. To accomplish all of this, which of the following arrangements should you use with your broker? [select one]: **(a)** Place a limit order and a stop order. **(b)** Trade only in round lots. **(c)** Place a market order now and another market order later. **(d)** Use margin trading. **(e)** Place an order to sell short.

***Answers to Self-Check Questions 7–9 can be found on p. 510.**

Continued from page 450

BEARING UP

Many investors, having experienced only bull market years during the 1970s to 1999, were unprepared for the bear that greeted them in the 2001–2002 period. By mid-July 2002, losses in U.S. market values amounted to a resounding $7.7 trillion—more than $28,000 for every woman, man, and child in the United States. Dazed traders and market analysts were using words like "crash" and "panic," and the numbers bore them out: The Nasdaq Composite Index fell from a record high 5,100 in 2000 to just above 1,300 in mid-July 2002, losing 74 percent of its value. In that same period, the Dow fell 32 percent, the S&P 500 44 percent. In just one week in mid-July 2002, the Dow fell 7.7 percent, the Nasdaq 4 percent, and the S&P 500 8 percent.

So, what will it take for the market to recover? How do you restore the public's faith in corporations and the market? There was some talk about the Fed stepping in to cut interest rates to generate money for investment, but many analysts argued that any Fed action would only stoke concerns about the market. President George W. Bush and Fed Chairman Alan Greenspan cited positive economic signs— increases in sales and industrial production, low inflation, strong consumer spending—but investors continued to retreat to safer ground as new reports surfaced about conniving CEOs cooking corporate books. On August 14, 2002, more than 1,000 U.S. corporations were required to resubmit financial statements revised to reflect financial conditions as certified by CEOs, who can now be held criminally liable for misstatements. Unfortunately, the impact of this policy has not yet registered on overall economic activity.

Meanwhile, individual investors still have their own problems. After more than two years of losses, those still brave enough to remain in the market faced the possibility of sinking even further or pulling out. Should they hang on or get out? Should they put their money in money market mutual funds? Should they gamble on further downfalls by selling short? How about taking the stance that currently low prices present bargain buying opportunities? Although the answers to these and other questions are by no means clear, there is general agreement that an important lesson has been learned: Because it's volatile and unpredictable, the market is a comfortable home for some investors but a very disturbing place for those who can't deal with economic uncertainty.

Questions for Discussion

1 In a volatile stock market, why is it important for investors to assess their reactions to financial risk and to put together short-term and long-term financial plans?

2 What do you think about the media's role in stock market volatility?

3 As the market was falling during the 2000–2002 period, why do you suppose that some market indexes experienced larger changes than others?

4 What factors will be most significant—economic, social, political, or psychological—for reversing the market crash of 2002?

5 Suppose your retirement account had reached $500,000 in 2000 and was invested equally in a bond mutual fund and an S&P 500 index mutual fund. By mid-July 2002, the index fund had fallen to $150,000 in market value, whereas the bond fund was worth $280,000. At mid-July 2002, what would be your investment strategy?

■ SUMMARY OF LEARNING OBJECTIVES

1 Explain the difference between *primary* and *secondary securities markets.*

Primary securities markets involve the buying and selling of new securities, either in public offerings or through private placements (sales to single buyers or small groups of buyers). **Investment bankers** specialize in issuing securities in primary markets. **Secondary markets** involve the trading of stocks and bonds through such familiar bodies as the New York Stock Exchange, the American Stock Exchange, and the Nasdaq market.

2 Discuss the value to shareholders of *common* and *preferred stock* and describe the secondary market for each type of security.

Common stock affords investors the prospect of capital gains and/or dividend income. Common stock values are expressed in three ways: as **par value** (the face value of a share when it is issued), **market value** (the current market price of a share), and **book value** (the value of shareholders' equity divided by the number of shares). Market value is most important to investors. **Preferred stock** is less risky. Cumulative preferred stock entitles holders to missed dividends as soon as the company is financially capable of paying. It also offers the prospect of steadier income. Shareholders of preferred stock must be paid dividends before shareholders of common stock.

Both common stock and preferred stock are traded on **stock exchanges** (institutions formed to conduct the trading of existing securities) including floor-based exchanges, electronic markets, and in **over-the-counter (OTC) markets** (dealer organizations formed to trade securities outside stock exchange settings). "Members" who hold seats on exchanges act as brokers—agents who execute buy-and-sell orders—for nonmembers. Floor-based exchanges include the New York, American, and regional and foreign exchanges. **Nasdaq** is the world's first and largest electronic stock market.

3 Distinguish among various types of *bonds* in terms of their issuers, safety, and retirement.

A **bond** is an IOU—a promise by the issuer to pay the buyer a certain amount of money by a specified future date, usually with interest paid at regular intervals. U.S. **government bonds** are backed by government institutions and agencies such as the Treasury Department or the Federal Housing Administration. **Municipal bonds**, which are offered by state and local governments to finance a variety of projects, are also usually safe, and the interest is ordinarily tax exempt. **Corporate bonds** are issued by companies to gain long-term funding. They may be secured (backed by pledges of the issuer's assets) or unsecured, and offer varying degrees of safety. The safety of bonds issued by various borrowers is rated by Moody's and Standard & Poor's.

4 Describe the investment opportunities offered by *mutual funds.*

Mutual funds pool investments from individuals and organizations to purchase portfolios of securities. Investors are, thus, part owners of the portfolio. Investors in **no-load funds** are not charged sales commissions when they buy in or sell out. Those in **load funds** pay commissions of 2 to 8 percent. Different funds are designed to appeal to the different goals of investors. Those that stress growth include balanced mutual funds—portfolios of bonds and preferred and common stocks, especially those of established firms.

Investors often select a mixture, or portfolio, of mutual funds—some riskier and some more conservative—in one of two ways. (1) **Diversification** means buying several different kinds of funds rather than just one. (2) **Asset allocation** refers to the relative amounts of funds invested in (or allocated to) each alternative mutual fund. As your investment objectives change, you can change your asset allocation accordingly.

5 Explain the process by which securities are bought and sold.

First, you need to match investments to your investment objectives. Then you must select a broker and open an account so that you can make transactions. It's also a good idea to know how to read stock, bond, and mutual fund quotations. Daily transactions are reported in newspapers.

Investors generally use such *financial information services* as newspaper and online stock, bond, and OTC quotations to learn about possible investments. **Market indexes** such as the **Dow Jones Industrial Average**, the **Standard & Poor's Composite Index**, and the **Nasdaq Composite Index** provide useful summaries of trends, both in specific industries and in the market as a whole. Investors can then place different types of orders. **Market orders** are orders to buy or sell at current prevailing prices. Because investors do not know exactly what prices will be when market orders are executed, they may issue **limit** or **stop orders** that are to be executed only if prices rise to or fall below specified levels. **Round lots** are purchased in multiples of 100 shares. **Odd lots** are purchased in fractions of round lots. Securities can be bought on margin or as part of **short sales**—sales in which investors sell securities that are borrowed from brokers and returned at a later date.

6 Explain how securities markets are regulated.

In addition to government regulation, both the NASD and the NYSE exercise self-regulation. For example, one cause of sudden market fluctuations is **program trading**—a strategy involving the sale or purchase of a group of stocks valued at $1 million or more, often triggered by computerized trading programs with no human supervision. Because such trading could cause the market to spiral out of control, it has led to *circuit breakers*—trading rules for reducing excessive volatility and promoting investor confidence.

The SEC protects investors from fraudulent issues by requiring all companies to file prospectuses before proposed offerings commence. A **prospectus** contains information about both the offered security and the issuing company. The SEC also enforces laws against **insider trading**—the use of special knowledge for profit or gain. The stock exchanges help in stopping insider action, fining member firms and officers and barring or suspending them. State governments enforce so-called **blue-sky laws,** and securities dealers must be licensed by the states in which they do business.

■ KEY TERMS

securities (p. 450)
primary securities market (p. 450)
Securities and Exchange Commission (SEC) (p. 450)
investment bank (p. 450)
secondary securities market (p. 451)
par value (p. 451)
market value (p. 451)
book value (p. 451)
blue-chip stock (p. 452)
cumulative preferred stock (p. 454)
stock exchange (p. 454)
broker (p. 455)
over-the-counter (OTC) market (p. 458)
National Association of Securities Dealers Automated Quotation (Nasdaq) system (p. 458)

bond (p. 460)
government bond (p. 460)
municipal bond (p. 460)
corporate bond (p. 461)
registered bond (p. 461)
bearer (or coupon) bond (p. 461)
secured bond (p. 461)
debenture (p. 461)
mutual fund (p. 462)
no-load fund (p. 462)
load fund (p. 462)
diversification (p. 463)
asset allocation (p. 463)
price-earnings ratio (p. 465)
market index (p. 467)
bull market (p. 467)
bear market (p. 467)

Dow Jones Industrial Average (DJIA) (p. 468)
Standard & Poor's Composite Index (p. 468)
Nasdaq Composite Index (p. 468)
market order (p. 469)
limit order (p. 469)
stop order (p. 469)
round lot (p. 469)
odd lot (p. 469)
margin (p. 470)
short sale (p. 471)
program trading (p. 471)
prospectus (p. 472)
insider trading (p. 472)
blue-sky laws (p. 472)

■ QUESTIONS AND EXERCISES

Questions for Review

1 What are the purposes of the primary and secondary markets for securities?
2 Which one of the three measures of common stock value is most important? Why?
3 How do government, municipal, and corporate bonds differ from one another?
4 How might an investor lose money in a short sale (selling short) of a security?
5 How does the Securities and Exchange Commission regulate securities markets?

6 Which U.S. stock market has the largest volume of trade?

Questions for Analysis

7 Suppose you decide to invest in common stocks as a personal investment. Which kind of broker—full service or online discount—would you use for buying and selling? Why?
8 Which type of mutual fund would be most appropriate for your investment purposes at this time? Why?

9 Using a newspaper, select an example of a recent day's transactions for each of the following: a stock on the NYSE, a stock on the AMEX, a Nasdaq stock, a bond on the NYSE, and a mutual fund. Explain the meaning of each element in the listing.

Application Exercises

10 Interview the financial manager of a local business or your school. What are the investment goals of this person's organization? What securities does it use?

What advantages and disadvantages do you see in its portfolio?

11 Either in person or through a toll-free number, contact a broker and request information about setting up a personal account for trading securities. Prepare a report on the broker's policies regarding the following: buy/sell orders, credit terms, cash account requirements, services available to investors, and commissions or fees schedules.

BUILDING YOUR BUSINESS SKILLS

MARKET UPS AND DOWNS

This exercise enhances the following SCANS workplace competencies: demonstrating basic skills, demonstrating thinking skills, exhibiting interpersonal skills, and working with information.

Goal

To encourage students to understand the forces that affect fluctuations in stock prices.

Background

Investing in stocks requires an understanding of the various factors that affect stock prices. These factors may be intrinsic to the company itself or part of the external environment.

- Internal factors relate to the company itself, such as an announcement of poor or favorable earnings, earnings that are more or less than expected, major layoffs, labor problems, management issues, and mergers.

- External factors relate to world or national events, such as a threatened war in the Persian Gulf, the Asian currency crisis, weather conditions that affect sales, the Federal Reserve Board's adjustment of interest rates, and employment figures that were higher or lower than expected.

By analyzing these factors, you will often learn a lot about why a stock did well or why it did poorly. Being aware of these influences will help you anticipate future stock movements.

Method

Step 1

Working alone, choose a common stock that has experienced considerable price fluctuations in the past few years. Here are several examples (but there are many others): IBM, J.P. Morgan, AT&T, Amazon.com, Oxford Health Care, and

Apple Computer. Find the symbol for the stock (for example, J.P. Morgan is JPM) and the exchange on which it is traded (JPM is traded on the New York Stock Exchange).

Step 2

At your library, find the *Daily Stock Price Record,* a publication that provides an historical picture of daily stock closings. There are separate copies for the New York Stock Exchange, the American Stock Exchange, and the Nasdaq markets. Find your stock, and study its trading pattern.

Step 3

Find four or five days over a period of several months or even a year when there have been major price fluctuations in the stock. (A two- or three-point price change from one day to the next is considered major.) Then research what happened on that day that might have contributed to the fluctuation. The best place to begin is with the *Wall Street Journal* or on the business pages of a national newspaper, such as the *New York Times* or the *Washington Post.*

Step 4

Write a short analysis that links changes in stock price to internal and external factors. As you analyze the data, be aware that it is sometimes difficult to know why a stock price fluctuates.

Step 5

Get together with three other students who studied different stocks. As a group, discuss your findings, looking for fluctuation patterns.

FOLLOW-UP QUESTIONS

1 Do you see any similarities in the movement of the various stocks during the same period? For example, did the stocks move up or down at about the same time? If so, do you think the stocks were affected by the same factors? Explain your thinking.

2 Based on your analysis, did internal or external factors have the greater impact on stock price? Which factors had the more long-lasting effect? Which factors had the shorter effect?

3 Why do you think it is so hard to predict changes in stock price on a day-to-day basis?

 EXERCISING YOUR ETHICS

ARE YOU ENDOWED WITH GOOD JUDGMENT?

The Situation

Every organization faces decisions about whether to make conservative or risky investments. Let's assume that you have been asked to evaluate the advantages and drawbacks of conservative versus risky investments, including all relevant ethical considerations, by Youth Dreams Charities (YDC), a local organization that assists low-income families in gaining access to educational opportunities. YDC is a not-for-profit firm that employs a full-time professional manager to run daily operations. Overall governance and policy making reside with a board of directors—10 part-time community-minded volunteers who are entrusted with carrying out YDC's mission.

For the current year, 23 students receive tuition totaling $92,000 paid by YDC. Tuition comes from annual fund-raising activities (a white-tie dance and a seafood carnival) and from financial returns from YDC's $2.1 million endowment. The endowment has been amassed from charitable donations during the past 12 years, and this year it has yielded some $84,000 for tuitions. The board's goal is to increase the endowment to $4 million in five years in order to provide $200,000 in tuition annually.

The Dilemma

Based on the Finance Committee's suggestions, the board is considering a change in YDC's investment policies. The current, rather conservative approach invests the endowment in CDs and other low-risk instruments that have consistently yielded a 6 percent annual return. This practice has allowed the endowment to grow modestly (at about 2 percent per year). The remaining investment proceeds (4 percent) flow out for tuitions. The proposed plan would invest one-half of the endowment in conservative instruments and the other half in blue-chip stocks. Finance Committee members believe that with market growth, the endowment has a good chance of reaching the $4 million goal within five years. Although some board members like the prospects of faster growth, others think the proposal is too risky. What happens if, instead of increasing, the stock market collapses and the endowment shrinks? What will happen to YDC's programs then?

QUESTIONS FOR DISCUSSION

Your opinion has been asked on the following issues:

1 Why might a conservative versus risky choice be different at a not-for-profit organization than at a for-profit organization?

2 What are the main ethical issues in this situation?

3 What action should the board take?

 CRAFTING YOUR BUSINESS PLAN

A CAPITAL IDEA

The Purpose of the Assignment

1 To familiarize students with securities and investment issues that a sample firm may face in developing its business plan, in the framework of *Business PlanPro (BPP) 2003* software package (Version 6.0).

2 To demonstrate how three chapter topics—issuing stock, issuing bonds, and making securities-market transactions—can be integrated as components in the *BPP* planning environment.

Assignment

After reading Chapter 15 in the textbook, open the BPP *software and search for information about financial plans, equity financing (stocks), and debt financing via bonds as they apply to a sample firm:* Sample Software Company. (Sample Software Inc.). *To find* Sample Software, *do the following:*

Open *Business PlanPro.* Go to the toolbar and click on the "*Sample Plans*" icon. In the **Sample Plan Browser,** do a search using the **search category** *Business services.* From the resulting list, select the category entitled, **Software Publishing—UK,** which is the location for *Sample Software Company.* The screen you are looking at is the introduction page for the *Sample Software* business plan. Scroll down until you reach the **Table of Contents** for the company's business plan.

NOW RESPOND TO THE FOLLOWING ITEMS:

1 Evaluate *Sample Software*'s plans for financing its operations. Does the company have any outstanding stock? Does it plan to issue stock or bonds in the future? [Sites to see in *BPP* for this question: On the Table of Contents page, click on **7.0 Financial Plan.**]

2 What sources of capital have been used to meet *Sample Software*'s financial requirements? What equity (stock) sources are available for meeting the firm's financial needs? What debt sources are available? [Sites to see in *BPP:* On the Table of Contents page, click on **1.0 Executive Summary.** Return to the Table of Contents page, and click on each of the following in turn: **2.1 Company Ownership, 2.2 Company History,** and **7.1 Important Assumptions.**]

3 Based on the company's net profit projections, at what points in time will *Sample Software* be able to pay dividends or repay its debt obligations? How much financing will be needed according to this plan, and at what points in time? [Sites to see in *BPP:* From the Table of Contents page, click on **7.4 Projected Profit and Loss.**]

 VIDEO EXERCISE

INFORMATION PAYS OFF: MOTLEY FOOL

Learning Objectives

The purpose of this video is to help you to:

1 Identify the wide variety of investments available to individuals.

2 Describe the process by which securities are bought and sold.

3 Recognize the risks involved in commodities and other investments.

Synopsis

Despite news reports about lottery winners and other overnight millionaires, individuals have a better chance of getting rich if they learn to select investments that are appropriate for their long-term financial goals. Experts advise looking for investments that will beat inflation and keep up with or—ideally—beat general market returns. You can invest in preferred or common stock, newly issued stock from IPOs, managed or index mutual funds, bonds, or commodities. These investments, however, are far from risk free. Commodities and IPOs can be particularly risky. Thus, if you're planning to invest, you might want to educate yourself about securities and investment strategies by surfing Web sites such as the Motley Fool *(www.fool.com).*

DISCUSSION QUESTIONS

1 **For analysis:** Why is the SEC concerned about stock rumors that circulate on the Internet?

2 **For application:** What should you consider when deciding whether to buy and sell stock through a broker, through a Web-based brokerage, or directly through the company issuing the stock?

3 **For application:** If you were about to retire, why might you invest in preferred stock rather than common stock?

4 **For debate:** Should stock rumors that circulate on the Internet be covered by the individual's constitutional right to freedom of speech rather than be regulated by the SEC? Support your chosen position.

Online Exploration

Mutual funds that seek out environmentally and socially conscious firms in which to invest are becoming more popular because they offer investors a way to earn returns that don't offend their principles. Investigate the following Web sites: *(www.efund.com), (www.ethicalfunds.com),* and *(www.domini.com).* What types of firms does each fund avoid? What type does each prefer? Would you choose one of these funds if you wanted to invest in a mutual fund? Explain your answer.

THE APPLICATION LETTER

In Chapters 14 and 15, we explained the U.S. banking system, described the activities of various financial institutions, and explored markets for buying and selling securities. Financial organizations, of course, rely on employees to provide services for customers, and so they're all prospective employers. This exercise gives you an opportunity not only to look into entry-level job possibilities in banking, but also to sharpen a specific job-hunting and career-building tool: application-letter writing.

Assignment

Recall from Chapter 14 that the responsibilities of the Federal Reserve System include such diverse activities as producing currency, lending money to the government, controlling the money supply, clearing checks, and auditing banks. Think of yourself as a potential employee who's looking for an entry-level job in an interesting area of activity at the Fed. Your objective in this exercise is to write an effective job-specific application letter to the Fed using the methods described by James O'Rourke IV in Chapter 4, "Employment Correspondence," of *Beginning Your Career Search,* 3d ed.

To complete this exercise, do the following:

1 Suppose you're applying for a summer internship. Start by visiting the Fed's Web site at *www.federalreserve.gov.* Under **Career Opportunities,** select "Summer Internships." Then choose an area in which to apply by identifying the field that interests you most (Information Technology, Banking Regulation, etc.).

2 Using the guidelines furnished by O'Rourke, draw up an outline for your letter.

3 Write your letter using the three-paragraph structure recommended by O'Rourke. Be sure that your letter is tailored specifically for the internship area that you've targeted. Save this draft of your letter for later use in this exercise.

4 Compare your letter with the sample letters in "Appendix A" of O'Rourke. Evaluate your draft using O'Rourke's lists of suggestions for good cover letters and common mistakes to avoid. Identify those areas of your letter that need improvement.

5 Rewrite your letter by making necessary improvements. Now compare your revised draft with the original. How did the changes improve the letter? In what ways—specifically—is the revised version better? Is there any room for further improvement?

6 Suppose you're applying for a part-time job as a teller at a local bank. Write a letter applying for the position. Compare it with the letter you wrote for the internship at the Fed. In what specific ways do the letters differ, and why?

UNDERSTANDING FINANCIAL RISK AND RISK MANAGEMENT

■ THE ROLE OF THE FINANCIAL MANAGER

The business activity known as **finance** (or **corporate finance**) typically entails four responsibilities:

- Determining a firm's long-term investments
- Obtaining funds to pay for those investments
- Conducting the firm's everyday financial activities
- Helping to manage the risks that the firm takes

finance (or **corporate finance**) Activities concerned with determining a firm's long-term investments, obtaining the funds to pay for them, conducting the firm's everyday, financial activities, and managing the firm's risks

As we saw in Chapter 7, production managers plan and control the output of goods and services. In Chapter 10, we saw that marketing managers plan and control the development and marketing of products. Similarly, **financial managers** plan and control the acquisition and dispersal of a firm's financial resources. In this section, we will see in some detail how those activities are channeled into specific plans for protecting—and enhancing—a firm's financial well-being.

financial manager Manager responsible for planning and controlling the acquisition and dispersal of a firm's financial resources

Responsibilities of the Financial Manager

Financial managers collect funds, pay debts, establish trade credit, obtain loans, control cash balances, and plan for future financial needs. But a financial manager's overall objective is to increase a firm's value—and thus stockholders' wealth. Whereas accountants create data to reflect a firm's financial status, financial managers make decisions for improving that status. Financial managers, then, must ensure that a company's earnings exceed its costs—in other words, that it earns a profit. In sole proprietorships and partnerships, profits translate directly into increases in owners' wealth. In corporations, profits translate into an increase in the value of common stock.

The various responsibilities of the financial manager in increasing a firm's wealth fall into two general categories: *cash-flow management* and *financial planning*.

Cash-Flow Management To increase a firm's value, financial managers must ensure that it always has enough funds on hand to purchase the materials and human resources that it needs to produce goods and services. At the same time, of course, there may be funds that are not needed immediately. These must be invested to earn more money for the firm. This activity—**cash-flow management**—requires careful

cash-flow management Management of cash inflows and outflows to ensure adequate funds for purchases and the productive use of excess funds

planning. If excess cash balances are allowed to sit idle instead of being invested, a firm loses the cash returns that it could have earned.

How important to a business is the management of its idle cash? One study has revealed that companies averaging $2 million in annual sales typically hold $40,000 in non-interest-bearing accounts. Larger companies hold even larger sums. More and more companies, however, are learning that these idle funds can become working funds. By locating idle cash and putting it to work, for instance, they can avoid borrowing from outside sources. The savings on interest payments can be substantial.

financial plan
A firm's strategies for reaching some future financial position

Financial Planning The cornerstone of effective financial management is the development of a financial plan. A **financial plan** describes a firm's strategies for reaching some future financial position. In constructing the plan, a financial manager must ask several questions:

- What amount of funds does the company need to meet immediate needs?
- When will it need more funds?
- Where can it get the funds to meet both its short- and long-term needs?

To answer these questions, a financial manager must develop a clear picture of why a firm needs funds. Managers must also assess the relative costs and benefits of potential funding sources. In the sections that follow, we will examine the main reasons for which companies generate funds and describe the main sources of business funding, both for the short term and the long term.

◼ WHY DO BUSINESSES NEED FUNDS?

Every company must spend money to survive: According to the simplest formula, funds that are spent on materials, wages, and buildings eventually lead to the creation of products, revenues, and profits. In planning for funding requirements, financial managers must distinguish between two different kinds of expenditures: *short-term (operating)* and *long-term (capital) expenditures*.

Short-Term (Operating) Expenditures

Short-term expenditures are incurred regularly in a firm's *everyday business activities*. To manage these outlays, managers must pay special attention to *accounts payable*, *accounts receivable*, and *inventories*. We will also describe the measures used by some firms in managing the funds known as working capital.

Accounts Payable In Chapter 13, we defined *accounts payable* as unpaid bills owed to suppliers plus wages and taxes due within the upcoming year. For most companies, this is the largest single category of short-term debt. To plan for funding flows, financial managers want to know *in advance* the amounts of new accounts payable as well as when they must be repaid. For information about such obligations and needs—say, the quantity of supplies required by a certain department in an upcoming period—financial managers must rely on other managers.

Accounts Receivable As we also saw in Chapter 13, *accounts receivable* consist of funds due from customers who have bought on credit. A sound financial plan requires financial managers to project accurately both how much and when buyers will make payments on these accounts. For example, managers at Kraft Foods must know how many dollars' worth of cheddar cheese Kroger's supermarkets will order each month; they must also know Kroger's payment schedule. Because they represent an investment in products for which a firm has not yet received payment, accounts receivable temporarily tie up its funds. Clearly, the seller wants to receive payment as quickly as possible.

Inventories Between the time a firm buys raw materials and the time it sells finished products, it ties up funds in **inventory**—materials and goods that it will sell within the year. Failure to manage inventory can have grave financial consequences. Too little inventory of any kind can cost a firm sales. Too much inventory means tied-up funds that cannot be used elsewhere. In extreme cases, a company may have to sell excess inventory at low profits simply to raise cash.

> **inventory**
> Materials and goods that are held by a company but that will be sold within the year

Working Capital Basically, **working capital** consists of a firm's current assets on hand. It is a liquid asset out of which current debts can be paid. A company calculates its working capital by adding up the following:

> **working capital**
> Liquid current assets out of which a firm can pay current debts

- Inventories—that is, raw materials, work-in-process, and finished goods on hand
- Accounts receivable (minus accounts payable)

How much money is tied up in working capital? *Fortune* 500 companies typically devote 20 cents of every sales dollar—about $800 billion total—to working capital. What are the benefits of reducing these sums? There are two very important pluses:

1 Every dollar that is not tied up in working capital becomes a dollar of more useful cash flow.
2 Reduction of working capital raises earnings permanently.

The second advantage results from the fact that money costs money (in interest payments and the like). Reducing working capital, therefore, means saving money.

Long-Term (Capital) Expenditures

In addition to needing funds for operating expenditures, companies need funds to cover long-term expenditures on fixed assets. As we saw in Chapter 13, *fixed assets* are items with long-term use or value, such as land, buildings, and machinery.

Long-term expenditures are usually more carefully planned than short-term outlays because they pose special problems. They differ from short-term outlays in the following ways, all of which influence the ways that long-term outlays are funded:

- Unlike inventories and other short-term assets, they are not normally sold or converted into cash.
- Their acquisition requires a very large investment.
- They represent a binding commitment of company funds that continues long into the future.

■ SOURCES OF SHORT-TERM FUNDS

Firms can call on many sources for the funds they need to finance day-to-day operations and to implement short-term plans. These sources include *trade credit* and secured and *unsecured loans*.

Trade Credit

Accounts payable are not merely expenditures. They also constitute a source of funds for the buying company. Until it pays its bill, the buyer has the use of *both* the purchased product and the price of the product. This situation results when the seller

trade credit
Granting of credit by one firm to another

open-book credit
Form of trade credit in which sellers ship merchandise on faith that payment will be forthcoming

secured loan
Loan for which the borrower must provide collateral

collateral
Borrower-pledged legal asset that may be seized by lenders in case of nonpayment

pledging accounts receivable
Using accounts receivable as loan collateral

unsecured loan
Loan for which collateral is not required

line of credit
Standing arrangement in which a lender agrees to make available a specified amount of funds upon the borrower's request

revolving credit agreement
Arrangement in which a lender agrees to make funds available on demand and on a continuing basis

commercial paper
Short-term securities, or notes, containing a borrower's promise to pay

grants **trade credit**, which is effectively a short-term loan from one firm to another. The most common form of trade credit, **open-book credit**, is essentially a "gentlemen's agreement." Buyers receive merchandise along with invoices stating credit terms. Sellers ship products on faith that payment will be forthcoming.

Secured Short-Term Loans

For most firms, bank loans are a very important source of short-term funding. Such loans almost always involve promissory notes in which the borrower promises to repay the loan plus interest. In **secured loans**, banks also require **collateral**: a legal interest in certain assets that can be seized if payments are not made as promised.

Secured loans allow borrowers to get funds when they might not qualify for unsecured credit. Moreover, they generally carry lower interest rates than unsecured loans. Collateral may be in the form of inventories or accounts receivable, and most businesses have other types of assets that can be pledged. Some, for instance, own marketable securities, such as stocks or bonds of other companies (see Chapter 15). Many more own fixed assets, such as land, buildings, or equipment. Fixed assets, however, are generally used to secure long-term rather than short-term loans. Most short-term business borrowing is secured by inventories and accounts receivable.

When a loan is made with inventory as a collateral asset, the lender loans the borrower some portion of the stated value of the inventory. When accounts receivable are used as collateral, the process is called **pledging accounts receivable**. In the event of nonpayment, the lender may seize the receivables—that is, funds owed the borrower by its customers.

Unsecured Short-Term Loans

With an **unsecured loan**, the borrower does not have to put up collateral. In many cases, however, the bank requires the borrower to maintain a *compensating balance*: The borrower must keep a portion of the loan amount on deposit with the bank in a non-interest-bearing account.

The terms of the loan—amount, duration, interest rate, and payment schedule—are negotiated between the bank and the borrower. To receive an unsecured loan, then, a firm must ordinarily have a good banking relationship with the lender. Once an agreement is made, a promissory note will be executed and the funds transferred to the borrower. Although some unsecured loans are one-time-only arrangements, many take the form of *lines of credit, revolving credit agreements*, or *commercial paper*.

Lines of Credit and Credit Agreements
A **line of credit** is a standing agreement between a bank and a business in which the bank promises to lend the firm a specified amount of funds on request. **Revolving credit agreements** are similar to consumer bank cards. A lender agrees to make some amount of funds available on demand and on a continuing basis. The lending institution guarantees that these funds will be available when sought by the borrower. In return for this guarantee, the bank charges the borrower a *commitment fee* for holding the line of credit open. This fee is payable even if the customer does not borrow any funds. It is often expressed as a percentage of the loan amount (usually 0.5 to 1 percent of the committed amount).

Commercial Paper
Finally, some firms can raise short-term funds by issuing **commercial paper**—short-term securities, or notes, containing the borrower's promise to pay. Because it is backed solely by the issuing firm's promise to pay, commercial paper is an option for only the largest and most creditworthy firms.

How does commercial paper work? Corporations issue commercial paper with a certain face value. Buying companies pay less than that value. At the end of a specified period (usually 30 to 90 days, but legally up to 270 days), the issuing company buys back the paper—*at face value*. The difference between the price paid and the face value is the buyer's profit. For the issuing company, the cost is usually lower than prevailing interest rates on short-term loans.

■ SOURCES OF LONG-TERM FUNDS

Firms need long-term funding to finance expenditures on fixed assets: the buildings and equipment necessary for conducting their business. They may seek long-term funds through *debt financing* (that is, from outside the firm) or through *equity financing* (by drawing on internal sources). We will discuss both options in this section, as well as a middle ground called hybrid financing. We will also analyze some of the options that enter into decisions about long-term financing, as well as the role of the *risk-return relationship* in attracting investors to a firm.

Debt Financing

Long-term borrowing from sources outside the company—**debt financing**—is a major component of most firms' long-term financial planning. Long-term debts are obligations that are payable more than one year after they were originally issued. The two primary sources of such funding are *long-term loans* and the sale of *corporate bonds*.

debt financing
Long-term borrowing from sources outside a company

Long-Term Loans Most corporations get long-term loans from commercial banks, usually those with which they have developed long-standing relationships. Credit companies (such as Household Finance Corp.), insurance companies, and pension funds also grant long-term business loans.

Long-term loans are attractive to borrowers for several reasons:

● Because the number of parties involved is limited, loans can often be arranged very quickly.
● The firm need not make public disclosure of its business plans or the purpose for which it is acquiring the loan. (In contrast, the issuance of corporate bonds requires such disclosure.)
● The duration of the loan can easily be matched to the borrower's needs.
● If the firm's needs change, loans usually contain clauses making it possible to change terms.

Long-term loans also have some disadvantages. Borrowers, for instance, may have trouble finding lenders to supply large sums. Long-term borrowers may also face restrictions as conditions of the loan. For example, they may have to pledge long-term assets as collateral or agree to take on no more debt until the loan is paid.

Corporate Bonds As we saw in Chapter 15, a *corporate bond*, like commercial paper, is a contract—a promise by the issuer to pay the holder a certain amount of money on a specified date. Unlike issuers of commercial paper, however, bond issuers do not pay off quickly. In many cases, bonds may not be redeemable for 30 years. Also, unlike commercial paper, most bonds pay bondholders a stipulated sum of annual or semiannual interest. If the company fails to make a bond payment, it is said to be *in default*.

Bonds are the major source of long-term debt financing for most corporations. They are attractive when firms need large amounts for long periods of time. The issuing company also gains access to large numbers of lenders through nationwide bond markets and stock exchanges. On the other hand, bonds entail high administrative and selling costs. They may also require stiff interest payments, especially if the issuing company has a poor credit rating.

Equity Financing

Although debt financing often has strong appeal, looking inside the company for long-term funding is sometimes preferable. In small companies, for example, founders may increase personal investments in their own firms. In most cases, **equity financing** means issuing common stock or retaining the firm's earnings. Both options involve putting the owners' capital to work.

equity financing
Use of common stock and/or retained earnings to raise long-term funding

Common Stock People who purchase common stock seek profits in two forms—dividends and appreciation. Overall, shareholders hope for an increase in the market value of their stock (appreciation) because the firm has profited and grown. By issuing shares of stock, the company gets the funds it needs for buying land, buildings, and equipment.

Consider, for example, a hypothetical company called Sunshine Tanning. Suppose the company's founders invested $10,000 by buying the original 500 shares of common stock (at $20 per share) in 1996. The company used these funds to buy equipment, and it succeeded financially. By 2003, then, it needed funds for expansion. A pattern of profitable operations and regularly paid dividends now allows Sunshine to raise $50,000 by selling 500 new shares of stock at $100 per share. This $50,000 would constitute *paid-in capital*—additional money, above the par value of its original stock sale, paid directly to a firm by its owners. As Table AI.1 shows, this additional paid-in capital would increase total stockholders' equity to $60,000.

retained earnings
Earnings retained by a firm for its use rather than paid out as dividends

Retained Earnings **Retained earnings** are profits retained for the firm's use rather than paid out in dividends. If a company uses retained earnings as capital, it will not have to borrow money and pay interest. If a firm has a history of reaping profits by reinvesting retained earnings, it may be very attractive to some investors. Retained earnings, however, mean smaller dividends for shareholders. In this sense, then, the practice may decrease the demand for—and thus the price of—the company's stock.

For example, if Sunshine Tanning had net earnings of $50,000 in 2003, it could pay a $50-per-share dividend on its 1,000 shares of common stock. Let's say, however, that Sunshine plans to remodel at a cost of $30,000, intending to retain $30,000 in

TABLE AI.1

Stockholders' Equity for Sunshine Tanning

Common Stockholders' Equity, 1996	
Initial common stock (500 shares issued @ $20 per share, 1996)	$10,000
Total stockholders' equity	$10,000
Common Stockholders' Equity, 2003	
Initial common stock (500 shares issued @ $20 per share, 1996)	$10,000
Additional paid-in capital (500 shares issued @ $100 per share, 2003)	50,000
Total stockholders' equity	$60,000

earnings to finance the project. Only $20,000—$20 per share—will be available for shareholders.

Hybrid Financing: Preferred Stock

A middle ground between debt financing and equity financing is the use of preferred stock (see Chapter 15). Preferred stock is a "hybrid" because it has some of the features of both corporate bonds and common stocks. As with bonds, for instance, payments on preferred stock are fixed amounts such as $6 per share per year. Unlike bonds, however, preferred stock never matures; like common stock, it can be held indefinitely. In addition, preferred stocks have first rights (over common stock) to dividends.

A major advantage to the issuer is the flexibility of preferred stock. Because preferred stockholders have no voting rights, the stock secures funds for the firm without jeopardizing corporate control of its management. Furthermore, corporations are not obligated to repay the principal and can withhold payment of dividends in lean times.

Choosing Between Debt and Equity Financing

Needless to say, an aspect of financial planning is striking a balance between debt and equity financing. Because a firm relies on a mix of debt and equity to raise the cash needed for capital outlays, that mix is called its **capital structure**. Financial plans, thus, contain targets for capital structure; an example would be 40 percent debt and 60 percent equity. But choosing a target is not easy. A wide range of mixes is possible, and strategies range from conservative to risky.

capital structure
Relative mix of a firm's debt and equity financing

The most conservative strategy is all-equity financing and no debt: A company has no formal obligations to make financial payouts. As we have seen, however, equity is an expensive source of capital. The riskiest strategy is all-debt financing. Although less expensive than equity funding, indebtedness increases the risk that a firm will be unable to meet its obligations (and even go bankrupt). Somewhere between the two extremes, financial planners try to find mixes that will increase stockholders' wealth with a reasonable exposure to risk.

The Risk-Return Relationship

While developing plans for raising capital, financial managers must be aware of the different motivations of individual investors. Why, for example, do some individuals and firms invest in stocks while others invest only in bonds? Investor motivations, of course, determine who is willing to buy a given company's stocks or bonds. Investors give money to firms and, in return, anticipate receiving future cash flows. Thus, everyone who invests money is expressing a personal preference for safety versus risk.

In other words, some cash flows are more certain than others. Investors generally expect to receive higher payments for higher uncertainty. They do not generally expect large returns for secure investments like government-insured bonds. Each type of investment, then, has a **risk-return relationship** reflecting the principle that whereas safer investments tend to offer lower returns, riskier investments tend to offer higher returns.

risk-return relationship
Principle that, whereas safer investments tend to offer lower returns, riskier investments tend to offer higher returns

Risk-return differences are recognized by financial planners, who try to gain access to the greatest funding at the lowest possible cost. By gauging investors' perceptions of their riskiness, a firm's managers can estimate how much they must pay to attract funds to their offerings. Over time, a company can reposition itself on the risk continuum by improving its record on dividends, interest payments, and debt repayment.

■ FINANCIAL MANAGEMENT FOR SMALL BUSINESS

New business success and failure are often closely related to adequate or inadequate funding. For example, one study of nearly 3,000 new companies revealed a survival rate of 84 percent for new businesses with initial investments of at least $50,000. Unfortunately, those with less funding have a much lower survival rate. Why are so many start-ups underfunded? For one thing, entrepreneurs often underestimate the value of establishing *bank credit* as a source of funds and use trade credit ineffectively. In addition, they often fail to consider *venture capital* as a source of funding, and they are notorious for not planning *cash-flow needs* properly.

Establishing Bank and Trade Credit

Some banks have liberal credit policies and offer financial analysis, cash-flow planning, and suggestions based on experiences with other local firms. Some provide loans to small businesses in bad times and work to keep them going. Some, of course, do not. Obtaining credit, therefore, begins with finding a bank that can—and will—support a small firm's financial needs. Once a line of credit is obtained, the small business can seek more liberal credit policies from other businesses. Sometimes, for instance, suppliers give customers longer credit periods—say, 45 or 60 days rather than 30 days. Liberal trade credit terms with their suppliers let firms increase short-term funds and avoid additional borrowing from banks.

Long-Term Funding Naturally, obtaining long-term loans is more difficult for new businesses than for established companies. With unproven repayment ability, start-up firms can expect to pay higher interest rates than older firms. If a new enterprise displays evidence of sound financial planning, however, the Small Business Administration (see Chapter 3) may support a guaranteed loan.

Venture Capital

venture capital
Outside equity financing provided in return for part ownership of the borrowing firm

Many newer businesses—especially those undergoing rapid growth—cannot get the funds they need through borrowing alone. They may, therefore, turn to **venture capital**: outside equity funding provided in return for part ownership of the borrowing firm. *Venture capital firms* actively seek chances to invest in new firms with rapid growth potential. Because failure rates are high, they typically demand high returns, which are now often 20 to 30 percent.

Planning for Cash-Flow Requirements

Although all businesses should plan for their cash flows, this planning is especially important for small businesses. Success or failure may hinge on anticipating those times when either cash will be short or excess cash can be expected.

Figure AI.1 shows possible cash inflows, cash outflows, and net cash position (inflows minus outflows) month by month for Slippery Fish Bait Supply—a highly seasonal business. As you can see, bait stores buy heavily from Slippery during the spring and summer months. Revenues outpace expenses, leaving surplus funds that can be invested. During the fall and winter, however, expenses exceed revenues. Slippery must borrow funds to keep going until revenues pick up again in the spring. Comparing predicted cash inflows from sales with outflows for expenses shows the firm's expected monthly cash-flow position.

Such knowledge can be invaluable for the small business manager. By anticipating shortfalls, for example, a financial manager can seek funds in advance and mini-

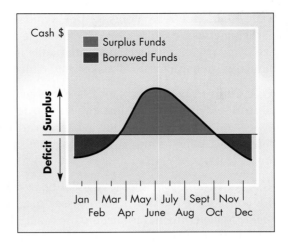

FIGURE AI.1
Projected Cash Flow for Slippery Fish Bait Supply Co.

mize their cost. By anticipating excess cash, a manager can plan to put the funds to work in short-term, interest-earning investments.

■ RISK MANAGEMENT

Financial risks are not the only risks faced every day by companies (and individuals). In this section, we will describe various other types of risks that businesses face and analyze some of the ways in which they typically manage them.

Coping with Risk

Businesses constantly face two basic types of **risk**—that is, uncertainty about future events. **Speculative risks**, such as financial investments, involve the possibility of gain or loss. **Pure risks** involve only the possibility of loss or no loss. Designing and distributing a new product, for example, is a speculative risk. The product may fail, or it may succeed and earn high profits. In contrast, the chance of a warehouse fire is a pure risk.

For a company to survive and prosper, it must manage both types of risk in a cost-effective manner. We can thus define the process of **risk management** as conserving the firm's earning power and assets by reducing the threat of losses due to uncontrollable events. In every company, each manager must be alert for risks to the firm and their impact on profits. The risk-management process usually entails five steps.

Step 1: Identify Risks and Potential Losses Managers analyze a firm's risks to identify potential losses. For example, a firm with a fleet of delivery trucks can expect that one of them will eventually be involved in an accident. The accident may cause bodily injury to the driver or others, may cause physical damage to the truck or other vehicles, or both.

Step 2: Measure the Frequency and Severity of Losses and Their Impact To measure the frequency and severity of losses, managers must consider both past history and current activities. How often can the firm expect the loss to occur? What is the likely size of the loss in dollars? For example, our firm with the fleet of delivery trucks may have had two accidents per year in the past. If it adds trucks, however, it may reasonably expect the frequency of accidents to increase.

Step 3: Evaluate Alternatives and Choose the Techniques That Will Best Handle the Losses Having identified and measured potential losses, managers are in a better position to decide how to handle them. With this third step, they generally have four choices: *risk avoidance, control, retention,* or *transfer.*

risk
Uncertainty about future events

speculative risk
Risk involving the possibility of gain or loss

pure risk
Risk involving only the possibility of loss or no loss

risk management
Process of conserving the firm's earning power and assets by reducing the threat of losses due to uncontrollable events

risk avoidance
Practice of avoiding risk by declining or ceasing to participate in an activity

risk control
Practice of minimizing the frequency or severity of losses from risky activities

risk retention
Practice of covering a firm's losses with its own funds

risk transfer
Practice of transferring a firm's risk to another firm

Risk Avoidance A firm opts for **risk avoidance** by declining to enter or by ceasing to participate in a risky activity. For example, the firm with the delivery trucks could avoid any risk of physical damage or bodily injury by closing down its delivery service. Similarly, a pharmaceutical maker may withdraw a new drug for fear of liability suits.

Risk Control When avoidance is not practical or desirable, firms can practice **risk control**—say, the use of loss-prevention techniques to minimize the frequency of losses. A delivery service, for instance, can prevent losses by training its drivers in defensive-driving techniques, mapping out safe routes, and conscientiously maintaining its trucks.

Risk Retention When losses cannot be avoided or controlled, firms must cope with the consequences. When such losses are manageable and predictable, they may decide to cover them out of company funds. The firm is thus said to assume or retain the financial consequences of the loss: hence, the practice known as **risk retention**. For example, our firm with the fleet of trucks may find that vehicles suffer vandalism totaling $100 to $500 per year. Depending on its coverage, the company may find it cheaper to pay for repairs out of pocket rather than to submit claims to its insurance company.

Risk Transfer When the potential for large risks cannot be avoided or controlled, managers often opt for **risk transfer**. They transfer the risk to another firm—namely, an insurance company. In transferring risk to an insurance company, a firm pays a sum called a premium. In return, the insurance company issues an insurance policy—a formal agreement to pay the policyholder a specified amount in the event of certain losses. In some cases, the insured party must also pay a deductible—an agreed-upon amount of the loss that the insured must absorb prior to reimbursement. Thus, our hypothetical company may buy insurance to protect itself against theft, physical damage to trucks, and bodily injury to drivers and others involved in an accident.

Step 4: Implement the Risk-Management Program The means of implementing risk-management decisions depend on both the technique chosen and the activity being managed. For example, risk avoidance for certain activities can be implemented by purchasing those activities from outside providers—say, hiring delivery services instead of operating delivery vehicles. Risk control might be implemented by training employees and designing new work methods and equipment for on-the-job safety. For situations in which risk retention is preferred, reserve funds can be set aside out of revenues. When risk transfer is needed, implementation means selecting an insurance company and buying the right policies.

Step 5: Monitor Results Because risk management is an ongoing activity, follow-up is always essential. New types of risks, for example, emerge with changes in customers, facilities, employees, and products. Insurance regulations change, and new types of insurance become available. Consequently, managers must continually monitor a company's risks, reevaluate the methods used for handling them, and revise them as necessary.

Insurance as Risk Management

To deal with some risks, both businesses and individuals may choose to purchase one or more of the products offered by insurance companies. Buyers find insurance appealing for a very basic reason: In return for a relatively small sum of money, they are protected against certain losses, some of them potentially devastating. In this sense, buying insurance is a function of risk management. To define it as a management activity dealing with insurance, we can expand our definition of *risk management* to say that it is the logical development and implementation of a plan to deal with chance losses.

With insurance, then, individuals and businesses share risks by contributing to a fund out of which those who suffer losses are paid. But why are insurance companies willing to accept these risks for other companies? Insurance companies make profits by taking in more **premiums** than they pay out to cover policyholders' losses. Quite simply, although many policyholders are paying for protection against the same type of loss, by no means will all of them suffer such a loss.

premium
Fee paid by a policyholder for insurance coverage

Insurable Versus Uninsurable Risks Like every business, insurance companies must avoid certain risks. Insurers thus divide potential sources of loss into *insurable* and *uninsurable risks*. Obviously, they issue policies only for insurable risks. Although there are some exceptions, an insurable risk must meet the four criteria described in the following sections.

Predictability The insurer must be able to use statistical tools to forecast the likelihood of a loss. For example, an auto insurer needs information about the number of car accidents in the past year to estimate the expected number of accidents for the following year. With this knowledge, the insurer can translate expected numbers and types of accidents into expected dollar losses. The same forecast, of course, also helps insurers determine premiums charged to policyholders.

Casualty A loss must result from an accident, not from an intentional act by the policyholder. Obviously, insurers do not have to cover damages if a policyholder deliberately sets fire to corporate headquarters. To avoid paying in cases of fraud, insurers may refuse to cover losses when they cannot determine whether policyholders' actions contributed to them.

Unconnectedness Potential losses must be random and must occur independently of other losses. No insurer can afford to write insurance when a large percentage of those who are exposed to a particular kind of loss are likely to suffer such a loss. One insurance company, for instance, would not want all the hurricane coverage in Miami or all the earthquake coverage in Los Angeles. By carefully choosing the risks that it will insure, an insurance company can reduce its chances of a large loss or even insolvency.

Verifiability Finally, insured losses must be verifiable as to cause, time, place, and amount. Did an employee develop emphysema because of a chemical to which she was exposed or because she smoked 40 cigarettes a day for 30 years? Did the policyholder pay the renewal premium before the fire destroyed his factory? Were the goods stolen from company offices or from the president's home? What was the insurable value of the destroyed inventory? When all these points have been verified, payment by the insurer goes more smoothly.

The Insurance Product Insurance companies are often distinguished by the types of insurance coverage they offer. Whereas some insurers offer only one area of coverage—life insurance, for example—others offer a broad range. In this section, we describe the four major categories of business insurance: *liability, property, life,* and *health.*

Liability Insurance As we will see in Appendix II, liability means responsibility for damages in case of accidental or deliberate harm to individuals or property. **Liability insurance** covers losses resulting from damage to people or property when the insured party is judged liable.

liability insurance
Insurance covering losses resulting from damage to people or property when the insured is judged responsible

workers' compensation coverage
Coverage provided by a firm to employees for medical expenses, loss of wages, and rehabilitation costs resulting from job-related injuries or disease

property insurance
Insurance covering losses resulting from physical damage to or loss of the insured's real estate or personal property

business interruption insurance
Insurance covering income lost during times when a company is unable to conduct business

life insurance
Insurance paying benefits to the policyholder's survivors

group life insurance
Insurance underwritten for a group as a whole rather than for each individual in it

health insurance
Insurance covering losses resulting from medical and hospital expenses as well as income lost from injury or disease

disability income insurance
Insurance providing continuous income when disability keeps the insured from gainful employment

Workers' Compensation   A business is liable for any injury to an employee when the injury arises from activities related to occupation. When workers are permanently or temporarily disabled by job-related accidents or disease, employers are required by law to provide **workers' compensation coverage** for medical expenses, loss of wages, and rehabilitation services. U.S. employers now pay out approximately $60 billion in workers' compensation premiums each year, much of it to public insurers.

Property Insurance   Firms purchase **property insurance** to cover injuries to themselves resulting from physical damage to or loss of real estate or personal property. Property losses may result from fire, lightning, wind, hail, explosion, theft, vandalism, or other destructive forces. Losses from fire alone in the United States come to over $10 billion per year.

Business Interruption Insurance   In some cases, loss to property is minimal in comparison to loss of income. A manufacturer, for example, may have to close down for an extended time while repairs to fire damage are being completed. During that time, of course, the company is not generating income. Even so, however, certain expenses—such as taxes, insurance premiums, and salaries for key personnel—may continue. To cover such losses, a firm may buy **business interruption insurance**.

Life Insurance   Insurance can also protect a company's human assets. As part of their benefits packages, many businesses purchase **life insurance** for employees. Life insurance companies accept premiums in return for the promise to pay beneficiaries after the death of insured parties. A portion of the premium is used to cover the insurer's own expenses. The remainder is invested in various types of financial instruments such as corporate bonds and stocks.

Group Life Insurance   Most companies buy **group life insurance**, which is underwritten for groups as a whole rather than for each individual member. The insurer's assessment of potential losses and its pricing of premiums are based on the characteristics of the whole group. Johnson & Johnson's benefit plan, for example, includes group life coverage with a standard program of protection and benefits—a master policy purchased by J & J—that applies equally to all employees.

Health Insurance   **Health insurance** covers losses resulting from medical and hospital expenses as well as income lost from injury or disease. It is, of course, no secret that the cost of health insurance has skyrocketed in recent years. In one recent year, for example, companies paid an average of $7,308 per employee on health insurance premiums to both commercial insurers such as Prudential, Metropolitan, and Nationwide and special health insurance providers such as Blue Cross/Blue Shield and other organizations called *health maintenance organizations* and *preferred provider organizations*.

Disability Income Insurance   **Disability income insurance** provides continuous income when disability keeps the insured from gainful employment. Many health insurance policies cover short-term disabilities, sometimes up to two years. Coverage for permanent disability furnishes some stated amount of weekly income—usually 50 to 70 percent of the insured's weekly wages—with payments beginning after a six-month waiting period. Group policies account for over 70 percent of all disability coverage in the United States.

Special Health Care Providers   Instead of reimbursement for a health professional's services, Blue Cross/Blue Shield, which is made up of nonprofit health care membership groups, provides specific service benefits to its subscribers. Many other commercial insurers do the same. What is the advantage to the subscriber or policyholder? No matter what the service actually costs, the special health care provider will cover the cost. In contrast, when policies provide reimbursement for services received, the policyholder may pay for a portion of the expense if the policy limit is exceeded. Other important options include *HMO*s and *PPO*s:

- A **health maintenance organization (HMO)** is an organized health care system providing comprehensive medical care to its members for a fixed, prepaid fee. In an HMO, all members agree that, except in emergencies, they will receive their health care through the organization.
- A **preferred provider organization (PPO)** is an arrangement whereby selected hospitals and/or doctors agree to provide services at reduced rates and to accept thorough review of their recommendations for medical services. The objective of the PPO is to help control health care costs by encouraging the use of efficient providers' health care services.

health maintenance organization (HMO)
Organized health care system providing comprehensive care in return for fixed membership fees

preferred provider organization (PPO)
Arrangement whereby selected professional providers offer services at reduced rates and permit thorough review of their service recommendations

Special Forms of Business Insurance Many forms of insurance are attractive to both businesses and individuals. For example, homeowners are as concerned about insuring property from fire and theft as are businesses. Businesses, however, have some special insurable concerns. In this section, we will discuss two forms of insurance that apply to the departure or death of key employees or owners.

Key Person Insurance Many businesses choose to protect themselves against loss of the talents and skills of key employees. For example, if a salesperson who annually rings up $2.5 million dies or takes a new job, the firm will suffer loss. It will also incur recruitment costs to find a replacement and training expenses once a replacement is hired. **Key person insurance** is designed to offset both lost income and additional expenses.

key person insurance
Special form of business insurance designed to offset expenses entailed by the loss of key employees

Business Continuation Agreements Who takes control of a business when a partner or associate dies? Surviving partners are often faced with the possibility of having to accept an inexperienced heir as a management partner. This contingency can be handled in **business continuation agreements**, whereby owners make plans to buy the ownership interest of a deceased associate from his or her heirs. The value of the ownership interest is determined when the agreement is made. Special policies can also provide survivors with the funds needed to make the purchase.

business continuation agreement
Special form of business insurance whereby owners arrange to buy the interests of deceased associates from their heirs

UNDERSTANDING THE LEGAL CONTEXT OF BUSINESS

In this appendix, we describe the basic tenets of U.S. law and show how these principles work through the court system. We will also survey a few major areas of business-related law. By focusing on the learning objectives of this appendix, you will see that laws may create opportunities for business activity just as readily as they set limits on them.

■ THE U.S. LEGAL AND JUDICIAL SYSTEMS

If people could ignore contracts or drive down city streets at any speed, it would be unsafe to do business on Main Street—or even to set foot in public. Without law, people would be free to act "at will," and life and property would constantly be at risk. **Laws** are the codified rules of behavior enforced by a society. In the United States, laws fall into three broad categories according to their origins: *common, statutory,* and *regulatory.* After discussing each of these types of laws, we will briefly describe the three-tier system of courts through which the judicial system administers the law in the United States.

laws
Codified rules of behavior enforced by a society

Types of Law

Law in the United States originates primarily with English common law. Its sources include the U.S. Constitution, state constitutions, federal and state statutes, municipal ordinances, administrative agency rules and regulations, executive orders, and court decisions.

Common Law Court decisions follow *precedents,* or the decisions of earlier cases. Following precedent lends stability to the law by basing judicial decisions on cases anchored in similar facts. This principle is the keystone of **common law**: the body of decisions handed down by courts ruling on individual cases. Although some facets of common law predate the American Revolution (and even hearken back to medieval Europe), common law continues to evolve in the courts today.

common law
Body of decisions handed down by courts ruling on individual cases

Statutory Law Laws created by constitutions or by federal, state, or local legislative acts constitute **statutory law**. For example, Article I of the U.S. Constitution is a statutory law that empowers Congress to pass laws on corporate taxation, the zoning

statutory law
Law created by constitutions or by federal, state, or local legislative acts

authority of municipalities, and the rights and privileges of businesses operating in the United States.

State legislatures and city councils also pass statutory laws. Some state laws, for example, prohibit the production or sale of detergents containing phosphates, which are believed to be pollutants. Nearly every town has ordinances specifying sites for certain types of industries or designating areas where cars cannot be parked during certain hours.

regulatory (or **administrative**) **law**
Law made by the authority of administrative agencies

Regulatory Law Statutory law and common law have long histories. Relatively new is **regulatory** (or **administrative**) **law**: law made by the authority of administrative agencies. By and large, the expansion of U.S. regulatory law has paralleled the nation's economic and technological development. Lacking the technical expertise to develop specialized legislation for specialized business activities, Congress established the first administrative agencies to create and administer the needed laws in the late 1800s. Before the early 1960s, most agencies concerned themselves with the *economic* regulation of specific areas of business—say, transportation or securities. Since then, many agencies have been established to pursue narrower *social* objectives. They focus on issues that cut across different sectors of the economy—clean air, for example, or product testing.

Today a host of agencies, including the Equal Employment Opportunity Commission (EEOC), the Environmental Protection Agency (EPA), the Food and Drug Administration (FDA), the Federal Trade Commission (FTC), and the Occupational Safety and Health Administration (OSHA), regulate U.S. business practices. In this section, we look briefly at the nature of regulatory agencies and describe some of the key legislation that makes up administrative law in this country. We also discuss an area of increasing importance in the relationship between government and business: regulation—or, more accurately, *deregulation*.

Agencies and Legislation Although Congress retains control over the scope of agency action, once passed, regulations have the force of statutory law. Government regulatory agencies act as a secondary judicial system, determining whether regulations have been violated and imposing penalties. A firm that violates OSHA rules, for example, may receive a citation, a hearing, and perhaps a heavy fine. Much agency activity consists of setting standards for safety or quality and monitoring the compliance of businesses. The FDA, for example, is responsible for ensuring that food, medicines, and even cosmetics are safe and effective.

Regulatory laws have been on the books for nearly a century. As early as 1906, for example, the Pure Food and Drug Act mandated minimum levels of cleanliness and sanitation for food and drug companies. More recently, the Children's Television Act of 1990 requires that broadcasters meet the educational and informational needs of younger viewers and limit the amount of advertising broadcast during children's programs. In 1996, a sweeping new law to increase competition in the communications industry required television makers to install a "V-chip," which allows parents to block undesirable programming. And Congress continues to debate the possibility of regulating the Internet.

Congress has created many new agencies in response to pressure to address social issues. In some cases, agencies were established in response to public concern about corporate behavior. The activities of these agencies have sometimes forced U.S. firms to consider the public interest almost as routinely as they consider their own financial performance.

The Move Toward Deregulation Although government regulation has benefited U.S. business in many ways, it is not without its drawbacks. Businesspeople complain—with some justification—that government regulations require too much paperwork.

To comply with just one OSHA regulation for a year, Goodyear once generated 345,000 pages of computer reports weighing 3,200 pounds. It now costs Goodyear $35.5 million each year to comply with the regulations of six government agencies, and it takes 36 employee-years annually (the equivalent of one employee working full time for 36 years) to fill out the required reports.

Not surprisingly, many people in both business and government support broader **deregulation**: the elimination of rules that restrict business activity. Advocates of both regulation and deregulation claim that each acts to control business expansion and prices, increase government efficiency, and right wrongs that the marketplace cannot or does not handle itself. Regulations such as those enforced by the EEOC, for example, are supposed to control undesirable business practices in the interest of social equity. In contrast, the court-ordered breakup of AT&T was prompted by a perceived need for greater market efficiency. For these and other reasons, the federal government began deregulating certain industries in the 1970s.

deregulation
Elimination of rules that restrict business activity

It is important to note that the United States is the only industrialized nation that has deregulated key industries—financial services, transportation, telecommunications, and a host of others. A 1996 law, for instance, allowed the seven "Baby Bells"—regional phone companies created when AT&T was broken up—to compete for long-distance business. It also allowed cable television and telephone companies to enter each other's markets by offering any combination of video, telephone, and high-speed data communications services. Many analysts contend that such deregulation is now and will become an even greater advantage in an era of global competition. Deregulation, they argue, is a primary incentive to innovation.

According to this view, deregulated industries are forced to innovate in order to survive in fiercely competitive industries. Those firms that are already conditioned to compete by being more creative will outperform firms that have been protected by regulatory climates in their home countries. "What's important," says one economist, "is that competition energizes new ways of doing things." The U.S. telecommunications industry, proponents of this view say, is twice as productive as its European counterparts because it is the only such industry forced to come out from under a protective regulatory umbrella.

The U.S. Judicial System

Laws are of little use unless they are enforced. Much of the responsibility for law enforcement falls to the courts. Although few people would claim that the courts are capable of resolving every dispute, there often seem to be more than enough lawyers to handle them all: Indeed, there are 140 lawyers for every 100,000 people in the United States. Litigation is a significant part of contemporary life, and we have given our courts a voice in a wide range of issues, some touching profoundly personal concerns, some ruling on matters of public policy that affect all our lives. In this section, we look at the operations of the U.S. judicial system.

The Court System There are three levels in the U.S. judicial system—*federal, state,* and *local.* These levels reflect the federalist structure of a system in which a central government shares power with state or local governments. Federal courts were created by the U.S. Constitution. They hear cases on questions of constitutional law, disputes relating to maritime laws, and violations of federal statutes. They also rule on regulatory actions and on such issues as bankruptcy, postal law, and copyright or patent violation. Both the federal and most state systems embody a three-tiered system of *trial, appellate,* and *supreme courts.*

trial court
General court that hears cases not specifically assigned to another court

Trial Courts At the lowest level of the federal court system are the **trial courts**, general courts that hear cases not specifically assigned to another court. A case involving contract violation would go before a trial court. Every state has at least one federal trial court, called a district court.

Trial courts also include special courts and administrative agencies. Special courts hear specific types of cases, such as cases involving tax evasion, fraud, international disputes, or claims against the U.S. government. Within their areas of jurisdiction, administrative agencies also make judgments much like those of courts.

Courts in each state system deal with the same issues as their federal counterparts. However, they may rule only in areas governed by state law. For example, a case involving state income tax laws would be heard by a state special court. Local courts in each state system also hear cases on municipal ordinances, local traffic violations, and similar issues.

Appellate Courts A losing party may disagree with a trial court ruling. If that party can show grounds for review, the case may go before a federal or state **appellate court**. These courts consider questions of law, such as possible errors of legal interpretation made by lower courts. They do not examine questions of fact. There are now 13 federal courts of appeal, each with 3 to 15 judges. Cases are normally heard by three-judge panels.

appellate court
Court that reviews case records of trials whose findings have been appealed

Supreme Courts Cases still not resolved at the appellate level can be appealed to the appropriate state supreme courts or to the U.S. Supreme Court. If it believes that an appeal is warranted or that the outcome will set an important precedent, the U.S. Supreme Court also hears cases appealed from state supreme courts. Each year, the U.S. Supreme Court receives about 5,000 appeals but typically agrees to hear fewer than 200.

■ BUSINESS LAW

Most legal issues confronted by businesses fall into one of six basic areas: *contract, tort, property, agency, commercial,* or *bankruptcy law.* These areas cover a wide range of business activity.

Contract Law

contract
Agreement between two or more parties enforceable in court

A **contract** is any agreement between two or more parties that is enforceable in court. As such, it must meet six conditions. If all these conditions are met, one party can seek legal recourse from another if the other party breaches (that is, violates) the terms of the agreement.

1 **Agreement.** Agreement is the serious, definite, and communicated offer and acceptance of the same terms. Let us say that an auto parts supplier offers in writing to sell rebuilt engines to a repair shop for $500 each. If the repair shop accepts the offer, the two parties have reached an agreement.

2 **Consent.** A contract is not enforceable if any of the parties has been affected by an honest mistake, fraud, or pressure. For example, a restaurant manager orders a painted sign, but the sign company delivers a neon sign instead.

capacity
Competence required of individuals entering into a binding contract

3 **Capacity.** To give real consent, both parties must demonstrate legal **capacity** (competence). A person under legal age (usually 18 or 21) cannot enter into a binding contract.

considerations
Any item of value exchanged between parties to create a valid contract

4 **Consideration.** An agreement is binding only if it exchanges **considerations**— that is, items of value. If your brother offers to paint your room for free, you cannot sue him if he changes his mind. Note that items of value do not necessarily entail money. For example, a tax accountant might agree to prepare a home-

builder's tax return in exchange for a new patio. Both services are items of value. Contracts need not be rational, nor must they provide the best possible bargain for both sides. They need only include legally sufficient consideration. The terms are met if both parties receive what the contract details.

5 **Legality.** A contract must be for a lawful purpose and must comply with federal, state, and local laws and regulations. For example, an agreement between two competitors to engage in price fixing—that is, to set a mutually acceptable price—is not legal.

6 **Proper form.** A contract may be written, oral, or implied from conduct. It must be written, however, if it involves the sale of land or goods worth more than $500. It must be written if the agreement requires more than a year to fulfill— say, a contract for employment as an engineer on a 14-month construction project. All changes to written contracts must also be in writing.

Breach of Contract What can one party do if the other fails to live up to the terms of a valid contract? Contract law offers a variety of remedies designed to protect the reasonable expectations of the parties and, in some cases, to compensate them for actions taken to enforce the agreement.

As the injured party to a breached contract, any of the following actions might occur:

● You might cancel the contract and refuse to live up to your part of the bargain. For example, you might simply cancel a contract for carpet shampooing if the company fails to show up.

● You might sue for damages up to the amount that you lost as a result of the breach. Thus, you might sue the original caterer if you must hire a more expensive caterer for your wedding reception because the original company canceled at the last minute.

● If money cannot repay the damage you suffered, you might demand specific performance—that is, require the other party to fulfill the original contract. For example, you might demand that a dealer in classic cars sell you the antique Stutz Bearcat he agreed to sell you and not a classic Jaguar instead.

Tort Law

Tort law applies to most business relationships *not governed by contracts.* A **tort** is a *civil*—that is, noncriminal—injury to people, property, or reputation for which compensation must be paid. For example, if a person violates zoning laws by opening a convenience store in a residential area, he or she cannot be sent to jail as if the act were a criminal violation. But a variety of other legal measures can be pursued, such as fines or seizure of property. Trespass, fraud, defamation, invasion of privacy, and even assault can be torts, as can interference with contractual relations and wrongful use of trade secrets. In this section, we explain three classifications of torts: *intentional, negligence,* and *product liability.*

tort
Civil injury to people, property, or reputation for which compensation must be paid

Intentional Torts **Intentional torts** result from the deliberate actions of another person or organization—for instance, a manufacturer knowingly fails to install a relatively inexpensive safety device on a product. Similarly, refusing to rectify a product design flaw, as in the case of the space shuttle *Challenger* disaster, can render a firm liable for an intentional tort. The actions of employees on the job may also constitute intentional torts—say, an overzealous security guard who wrongly accuses a customer of shoplifting. To remedy torts, courts will usually impose **compensatory damages**: payments intended to redress an injury actually suffered. They may also impose

intentional tort
Tort resulting from the deliberate actions of a party

compensatory damages
Monetary payments intended to redress injury actually suffered because of a tort

punitive damages
Fines imposed over and above any
actual losses suffered by a plaintiff

negligence
Conduct falling below legal
standards for protecting others
against unreasonable risk

product liability tort
Tort in which a company is
responsible for injuries caused by its
products

strict product liability
Principle that liability can result not
from a producer's negligence but
from a defect in the product itself

property
Anything of value to which a person
or business has sole right of
ownership

tangible real property
Land and anything attached to it

punitive damages: fines that exceed actual losses suffered by plaintiffs and that are intended to punish defendants.

Negligence Torts Ninety percent of tort suits involve charges of **negligence**—conduct falling below legal standards for protecting others against unreasonable risk. If a company installs a pollution-control system that fails to protect a community's water supply, it may later be sued by an individual who gets sick from drinking the water.

Negligence torts may also result from employee actions. For example, if the captain of a supertanker runs aground and spills 11 million gallons of crude oil into coastal fishing waters, the oil company may be liable for potentially astronomical damages. Thus, in September 1994, a jury in Alaska ordered Exxon Corp. to pay $5 billion in punitive damages to 34,000 fishermen and other plaintiffs as a consequence of the Exxon *Valdez* disaster of 1989. (Plaintiffs had asked for $15 billion.) A month earlier, the jury had awarded plaintiffs $287 million in compensatory damages. In 1993, the firm responsible for pipeline operations at the Valdez, Alaska, terminal (which is partially owned by Exxon) agreed to pay plaintiffs in the same case $98 million in damages. In a separate case, Exxon paid $20 million in damages to villages whose food supply had been destroyed. A separate state jury will consider another $120 million in claims by Alaskan corporations and municipalities. Even before any of these awards were handed down, Exxon had spent $2.1 billion on the cleanup effort and paid $1.3 billion in civil and criminal penalties.

Product Liability Torts In cases of **product liability**, a company may be held responsible for injuries caused by its products. According to a special government panel on product liability, about 33 million people are injured and 28,000 killed by consumer products each year.

Strict Product Liability Since the early 1960s, businesses have faced a number of legal actions based on the relatively new principle of **strict product liability**: the principle that liability can result not from a producer's negligence but from a defect in the product itself. An injured party need show only that

1 The product was defective.
2 The defect was the cause of injury.
3 The defect caused the product to be unreasonably dangerous.

Many recent cases in strict product liability have focused on injuries or illnesses attributable to toxic wastes or other hazardous substances that were legally disposed of. Because plaintiffs need not demonstrate negligence or fault, these suits frequently succeed. Not surprisingly, the number of such suits promises to increase.

Property Law

As the name implies, *property law* concerns property rights. But what exactly is "property"? Is it the land under a house? The house itself? A car in the driveway? A dress in the closet? The answer in each case is yes: In the legal sense, **property** is anything of value to which a person or business has sole right of ownership. Indeed, property is technically those rights.

Within this broad general definition, we can divide property into four categories. In this section, we define these categories and then examine more fully the legal protection of a certain kind of property—intellectual property.

● **Tangible real property** is land and anything attached to it. A house and a factory are both tangible real property, as are built-in appliances or the machines inside the buildings.

- **Tangible personal property** is any movable item that can be owned, bought, sold, or leased. Examples are automobiles, clothing, stereos, and cameras.
- **Intangible personal property** cannot be seen but exists by virtue of written documentation. Examples are insurance policies, bank accounts, stocks and bonds, and trade secrets.

Protection of Intellectual Rights **Intellectual property** is created through a person's creative activities. Books, articles, songs, paintings, screenplays, and computer software are all intellectual property. The U.S. Constitution grants protection to intellectual property by means of copyrights, trademarks, and patents. Copyrights and patents apply to the tangible expressions of an idea—not to the ideas themselves. Thus, you could not copyright the idea of cloning dinosaurs from fossil DNA. Michael Crichton could copyright his novel, *Jurassic Park,* which is a tangible result of that idea, and sell the film rights to producer-director Steven Spielberg. Both creators are entitled to the profits, if any, that may be generated by their tangible creative expressions.

Copyrights **Copyrights** give exclusive ownership rights to the creators of books, articles, designs, illustrations, photos, films, and music. Computer programs and even semiconductor chips are also protected. Copyrights extend to creators for their entire lives and to their estates for 70 years thereafter. All terms are automatically copyrighted from the moment of creation.

Trademarks Because the development of products is expensive, companies must prevent other firms from using their brand names. Often they must act to keep competitors from seducing consumers with similar or substitute products. A producer can apply to the U.S. government for a **trademark**—the exclusive legal right to use a brand name.

Trademarks are granted for 20 years and may be renewed indefinitely if a firm continues to protect its brand name. If a firm allows the brand name to lapse into common usage, it may lose protection. Common usage takes effect when a company fails to use the ® symbol to indicate that its brand name is a registered trademark. It also takes effect if a company seeks no action against those who fail to acknowledge its trademark. Recently, for example, the popular brand-name sailboard Windsurfer lost its trademark. Like *trampoline, yo-yo,* and *thermos, windsurfer* has become the common term for the product and can now be used by any sailboard company. In contrast, Formica Corp. successfully spent the better part of a decade in court to protect the name *Formica* as a trademark. The Federal Trade Commission had contended that the word had entered the language as a generic name for any similar laminate material.

Patents **Patents** provide legal monopolies for the use and licensing of manufactured items, manufacturing processes, substances, and designs for objects. A patentable invention must be *novel, useful,* and *nonobvious.* Since June 1995, U.S. patent law has been in harmony with that of most developed nations. For example, patents are now valid for 20 years rather than 17 years. In addition, the term now runs from the date on which the application was *filed,* not the date on which the patent itself was *issued.*

Although the U.S. Patent Office issues about 1,200 patents a week, requirements are stringent, and U.S. patents actually tend to be issued at a slow pace. While Japan and most European countries have installed systems to speed up patent filing and research, the U.S. system can extend the process to years. Other observers argue that American firms trail their foreign counterparts in patents because of the sluggishness

---

tangible personal property
Any movable item that can be owned, bought, sold, or leased

intangible personal property
Property that cannot be seen but that exists by virtue of written documentation

intellectual property
Property created through a person's creative activities

copyright
Exclusive ownership right belonging to the creator of a book, article, design, illustration, photo, film, or musical work

trademark
Exclusive legal right to use a brand name or symbol

patent
Exclusive legal right to use and license a manufactured item or substance, manufacturing process, or object design

with which U.S. companies move products through their own research and development programs.

Restrictions on Property Rights Property rights are not always absolute. For example, rights may be compromised under any of the following circumstances:

- Owners of shorefront property may be required to permit anglers, clam diggers, and other interested parties to walk near the water.
- Utility companies typically have rights called easements, such as the right to run wire over private property or to lay cable or pipe under it.
- Under the principle of **eminent domain**, the government may, upon paying owners fair prices, claim private land to expand roads or erect public buildings.

eminent domain
Principle that the government may claim private land for public use by buying it at a fair price

Agency Law

The transfer of property—whether the deeding of real estate or the transfer of automobile title—often involves agents. An **agent** is a person who acts for, and in the name of, another party, called the **principal**. The most visible agents are those in real estate, sports, and entertainment. Many businesses, however, use agents to secure insurance coverage and handle investments. Every partner in a partnership and every officer and director in a corporation are agents of that business. Courts have also ruled that both a firm's employees and its outside contractors may be regarded as its agents.

agent
Individual or organization acting for, and in the name of, another party

principal
Individual or organization authorizing an agent to act on its behalf

Authority of Agents Agents have the authority to bind principals to agreements. They receive that authority, however, from the principals themselves; they cannot create their own authority. An agent's authority to bind a principal can be express, implied, or apparent.

Let's say, for example, that Ellen is a salesperson in Honest Sam's Used Car Lot. Her written employment contract gives her **express authority** to sell cars, to provide information to prospective buyers, and to approve trade-ins up to $2,000. Derived from the custom of used-car dealers, she also has **implied authority** to give reasonable discounts on prices and to make reasonable adjustments to written warranties. Furthermore, Ellen may—in the presence of Honest Sam—promise a customer that she will match the price offered by another local dealer. If Honest Sam assents—perhaps merely nods and smiles—Ellen may be construed to have the **apparent authority** to make this deal.

express authority
Agent's authority, derived from written agreement, to bind a principal to a certain course of action

implied authority
Agent's authority, derived from business custom, to bind a principal to a certain course of action

apparent authority
Agent's authority, based on the principal's compliance, to bind a principal to a certain course of action

Responsibilities of Principals Principals have several responsibilities to their agents. They owe agents reasonable compensation, must reimburse them for related business expenses, and should inform them of risks associated with their business activities. Principals are liable for actions performed by agents *within the scope of their employment.* Thus, if agents make untrue claims about products or services, the principal is liable for making amends. Employers are similarly responsible for the actions of employees. In fact, firms are often liable in tort suits because the courts treat employees as agents.

Businesses are increasingly being held accountable for *criminal* acts by employees. Court findings, for example, have argued that firms are expected to be aware of workers' propensities for violence, to check on their employees' pasts, and to train and supervise employees properly. Suppose, for instance, that a delivery service hires a driver with a history of driving while intoxicated. If the driver has an accident with a company vehicle while under the influence of alcohol, the company may be liable for criminal actions.

Commercial Law

Managers must be well acquainted with the most general laws affecting commerce. Specifically, they need to be familiar with the provisions of the *Uniform Commercial Code,* which sets down rules regarding *warranties.*

The Uniform Commercial Code For many years, companies doing business in more than one state faced a special problem: Laws governing commerce varied, sometimes widely, from state to state. In 1952, however, the National Conference of Commissioners on Uniform State Laws and the American Law Institute drew up the **Uniform Commercial Code (UCC)**. Subsequently accepted by every state except Louisiana, the UCC describes the rights of buyers and sellers in transactions.

For example, buyers who believe that they have been wronged in agreements with sellers have several options. They can cancel contracts, refuse deliveries, and demand the return of any deposits. In some cases, they can buy the same products elsewhere and sue the original contractors to recover any losses incurred. Sellers, too, have several options. They can cancel contracts, withhold deliveries, and sell goods to other buyers. If goods have already been delivered, sellers can repossess them or sue the buyers for purchase prices.

Warranties A **warranty** is a seller's promise to stand by its products or services if a problem occurs after the sale. Warranties may be express or implied. The terms of an **express warranty** are specifically stated by the seller. For example, many stereo systems are expressly warranted for 90 days. If they malfunction within that period, they can be returned for full refunds.

An **implied warranty** is dictated by law. Implied warranties embody the principle that a product should (1) fulfill the promises made by advertisements and (2) serve the purpose for which it was manufactured and sold. If you buy an advertised frost-free refrigerator, the seller implies that the refrigerator will keep your food cold and that you will not have to defrost it. It is important to note, however, that warranties, unlike most contracts, are easily limited, waived, or disclaimed. Consequently, they are the source of more and more tort action, as dissatisfied customers seek redress from producers.

Bankruptcy Law

At one time, individuals who could not pay their debts were jailed. Today, however, both organizations and individuals can seek relief by filing for **bankruptcy**—the court-granted permission not to pay some or all debts.

Hundreds of thousands of individuals and tens of thousands of businesses file for bankruptcy each year, and their numbers continue to increase. Why do individuals and businesses file for bankruptcy? Cash-flow problems and drops in farm prices caused many farmers, banks, and small businesses to go bankrupt. In recent years, large enterprises such as Continental Airlines and R. H. Macy have sought the protection of bankruptcy laws as part of strategies to streamline operations, cut costs, and regain profitability.

Three main factors account for the increase in bankruptcy filings:

1 The increased availability of credit
2 The "fresh-start" provisions in current bankruptcy laws
3 The growing acceptance of bankruptcy as a financial tactic

In some cases, creditors force an individual or firm into **involuntary bankruptcy** and press the courts to award them payment of at least part of what they are owed. Far more often, however, a person or business chooses to file for court protection

Uniform Commercial Code (UCC)
Body of standardized laws governing the rights of buyers and sellers in transactions

warranty
Seller's promise to stand by its products or services if a problem occurs after the sale

express warranty
Warranty whose terms are specifically stated by the seller

implied warranty
Warranty, dictated by law, based on the principle that products should fulfill advertised promises and serve the purposes for which they are manufactured and sold

bankruptcy
Permission granted by the courts to individuals and organizations not to pay some or all of their debts

involuntary bankruptcy
Bankruptcy proceedings initiated by the creditors of an indebted individual or organization

voluntary bankruptcy
Bankruptcy proceedings initiated by an indebted individual or organization

against creditors. In general, individuals and firms whose debts exceed total assets by at least $1,000 may file for **voluntary bankruptcy**.

Business Bankruptcy A business bankruptcy may be resolved by one of three plans:

● Under a *liquidation plan,* the business ceases to exist. Its assets are sold and the proceeds used to pay creditors.
● Under a *repayment plan,* the bankrupt company simply works out a new payment schedule to meet its obligations. The time frame is usually extended, and payments are collected and distributed by a court-appointed trustee.
● *Reorganization* is the most complex form of business bankruptcy. The company must explain the sources of its financial difficulties and propose a new plan for remaining in business. Reorganization may include a new slate of managers and a new financial strategy. A judge may also reduce the firm's debts to ensure its survival. Although creditors naturally dislike debt reduction, they may agree to the proposal, since 50 percent of one's due is better than nothing at all.

Legislation passed since 1994 has made some major revisions in bankruptcy laws. For example, it is now easier for individuals with up to $1 million in debt to make payments under installment plans instead of liquidating assets immediately. In contrast, the new law restricts how long a company can protect itself in bankruptcy while continuing to do business. Critics have charged, for instance, that many firms have succeeded in operating for many months under bankruptcy protection. During that time, they were able to cut costs and prices, not only competing with an unfair advantage but dragging down overall industry profits. The new laws place time limits on various steps in the filing process. The intended effect is to speed the process and prevent assets from being lost to legal fees.

■ THE INTERNATIONAL FRAMEWORK OF BUSINESS LAW

Laws can vary dramatically from country to country, and many businesses today have international markets, suppliers, and competitors. It follows that managers need a basic understanding of the international framework of business law that affects the ways in which they can do business.

National laws are created and enforced by countries. The creation and enforcement of international law are more complicated. For example, if a company shipping merchandise between the United States and Mexico breaks an environmental protection law, to whom is that company accountable? The answer depends on several factors. Which country enacted the law in question? Where did the violation occur? In which country is the alleged violator incorporated?

international law
Set of cooperative agreements and guidelines established by countries to govern actions of individuals, businesses, and nations

Issues such as pollution across borders are matters of **international law**: the very general set of cooperative agreements and guidelines established by countries to govern the actions of individuals, businesses, and nations themselves. In this section, we examine the various sources of international law. We then discuss some of the important ways in which international trade is regulated and place some key U.S. trade laws in the international context in which they are designed to work.

Sources of International Law

International law has several sources. One source is custom and tradition. Among countries that have been trading with each other for centuries, many customs and traditions governing exchanges have gradually evolved into practice. Although some trading practices still follow ancient unwritten agreements, there has been a clear trend in more recent times to approach international trade within a more formal legal framework. Key features of that framework include a variety of formal trade agreements.

Trade Agreements In addition to subscribing to international rules, virtually every nation has formal trade treaties with other nations. A *bilateral agreement* is one involving two countries; a *multilateral agreement* involves several nations.

GATT and the WTO The **General Agreement on Tariffs and Trade (GATT)** was first signed shortly after the end of World War II. Its purpose is to reduce or eliminate trade barriers, such as tariffs and quotas. It does so by encouraging nations to protect domestic industries within internationally agreed-upon limits and to engage in multilateral negotiations.

> **General Agreement on Tariffs and Trade (GATT)**
> International trade agreement to encourage the multilateral reduction or elimination of trade barriers

In December 1994, the U.S. Congress ratified a revision of GATT that had been worked out by 124 nations over a 12-year period. Still, many issues remain unresolved—for example, the opening of foreign markets to most financial services. Governments may still provide subsidies to manufacturers of civil aircraft, and no agreement was reached on limiting the distribution of American cultural exports—movies, music, and the like—in Europe.

The **World Trade Organization (WTO)** came into being on January 1, 1995, as the result of a complex round of GATT negotiations lasting from 1986 to 1994. The 140 member countries are required to open their markets to international trade, and the WTO is empowered to pursue three goals:

> **World Trade Organization (WTO)**
> Organization through which member nations negotiate trading agreements and resolve disputes about trade policies and practices

1 Promote trade by encouraging member nations to adopt fair trade policies and practices
2 Reduce trade barriers by promoting multilateral negotiations among member nations
3 Establish fair procedures for resolving disputes among member nations

North American Free Trade Agreement The **North American Free Trade Agreement (NAFTA)** was negotiated to remove tariffs and other trade barriers among the United States, Canada, and Mexico. NAFTA also included agreements to monitor environmental and labor abuses. It took effect on January 1, 1994, and immediately eliminated some tariffs; others will disappear after 5-, 10-, or 15-year intervals.

> **North Amercian Free Trade Agreement (NAFTA)**
> Agreement to gradually eliminate tariffs and other trade barriers among the United States, Canada, and Mexico

European Union Originally called the *Common Market,* the **European Union (EU)** includes the principal Western European nations. These countries have eliminated most quotas and have set uniform tariff levels on products imported and exported within their group. In 1992, virtually all internal trade barriers were eliminated, making the European Union the largest free marketplace in the world.

> **European Union (EU)**
> Agreement among major Western European nations to eliminate or make uniform most trade barriers affecting group members

ANSWERS TO SELF-CHECK QUESTIONS

CHAPTER 1

1 **(b)** Buildings and equipment (See the section on "Factors of Production" on pages 6–8)
2 **(e)** Input market (See the section on "Input and Output Markets" on pages 9–10)
3 **False** (See the section on "Market Economies" on pages 9–11)
4 **True** (See the section on "The Laws of Demand and Supply" on pages 12–15)
5 **(d)** The law of demand (See the section on "The Laws of Demand and Supply" on pages 12–15)
6 **(c)** Shoppers will buy fewer eggs (See the section on "The Laws of Demand and Supply" on pages 12–15)
7 **(b)** Inflation (See the section on "Economic Growth" on pages 18–21)
8 **(c)** They mean different things but are usually very similar (See the section on "Gross Domestic Product" on pages 18–21)
9 **False** (See the section on "Managing the U.S. Economy" on pages 24–25)

CHAPTER 2

1 **(b)** Employee behavior toward the organization (See the section on "Business and Managerial Ethics" on pages 38–39)
2 **(e)** Regulation (See the section on "Assessing Ethical Behavior" on pages 40–42)
3 **False** (See the section on "Company Practices and Business Ethics" on pages 40–44)
4 **True** (See the section on "Social Responsibility" on pages 45–49)
5 **(e)** All of these (See the section on "The Stakeholder Model of Responsibility" on pages 45–48)
6 **(d)** Growing skepticism and concern regarding responsible corporate governance (See the section on "Contemporary Social Consciousness" on pages 48–49)
7 **(a)** Responsibility toward the board of directors (See the section on "Areas of Social Responsibility" on pages 50–58)
8 **(e)** All of these (See the section on "Approaches to Social Responsibility" on pages 59–61)
9 **False** (See the section on "Social Responsibility and the Small Business" on pages 61–62)

CHAPTER 3

1 **(e)** One that is independently owned and managed and does not dominate its market (See the section on "What Is a 'Small' Business?" on pages 70–73)
2 **(b)** Manufacturing (See the section on "Popular Areas of Small-Business Enterprise" on pages 72–73)
3 **False** (See the section on "Distinctions Between Entrepreneurship and Small Business on page 74)
4 **False** (See the section on "Crafting a Business Plan" on pages 75–76)
5 **(d)** Personal resources (See the section on "Financing the Small Business" on pages 77–78)
6 **(d)** Employee theft or sabotage (See the section on "Reasons for Failure" on pages 83–84)
7 **(d)** All of the above (See the section on "Sole Proprietorships" on page 86)
8 **False** (See the section on "Alternatives to General Partnerships" on page 87)
9 **(c)** Master limited corporation (See the section on "Types of Corporations" on pages 89–90)

CHAPTER 4

1 **(c)** Association of South American Agricultural Producers (See the section on "The Contemporary Global Economy" on pages 102–105)
2 **False** (See the section on "The Major World Marketplaces" on pages 105–109)
3 **(d)** Movies and other filmed entertainment (See the section on "Comparative Advantage" on page 110)
4 **(b)** Exchange rates (See the section on "Going International" on pages 116–117)
5 **True** (See the section on "Exporters and Importers" on page 118)
6 **(a)** Foreign direct investment (See the section on "International Organizational Structures" on pages 118–120)
7 **(e)** Transportation differences (See the section on "Barriers to International Trade" on pages 120–124)
8 **(b)** Exchange rate parameters (See the section on "Legal and Political Differences" on pages 121–124)
9 **False** (See the section on "The Protectionism Debate" on page 123)

CHAPTER 5

1 **(a)** Goals show the government what the firm hopes to achieve (See the section on "Purposes of Goal Setting" on pages 137–138)

2 **False** (See the section on "Kinds of Goals" on page 138)

3 **(d)** Deciding which division to sell if a firm runs short of cash (See the section on "Contingency Planning" on pages 142–143)

4 **(c)** Coordinating (See the section on "The Management Process" on pages 144–147)

5 **True** (See the section on "Levels of Management" on pages 147–148)

6 **(e)** All of these (See the section on "Areas of Management" on pages 148–149)

7 **(c)** Conceptual skills (See the section on "Basic Management Skills" on pages 150–152)

8 **(b)** Global and technology (See the section on "Management Skills for the Twenty-First Century" on pages 152–153)

9 **False** (See the section on "Management and the Corporate Culture" on pages 154–155)

CHAPTER 6

1 **False** (See the section on "What is Organizational Structure?" on pages 166–167)

2 **(c)** Assembly line worker (See the section on "The Building Blocks of Organizational Structure" on pages 168–171)

3 **(a)** Sequence (See the section on "Departmentalization" on pages 169–171)

4 **(d)** Creating obligations (See the section on "Establishing the Decision-Making Hierarchy" on pages 172–179)

5 **(e)** Narrow (See the section on "Span of Control" on pages 175–176)

6 **True** (See the section on "Three Forms of Authority" on pages 177–179)

7 **(b)** Process organization (See the section on "Basic Forms of Organizational Structure" on pages 179–185)

8 **(e)** All of these (See the section on "Organizational Design for the Twenty-First Century" on pages 182–185)

9 **False** (See the section on "Informal Organization" on pages 185–186)

CHAPTER 7

1 **False** (See the section on "Creating Value Through Operations" on pages 196–201)

2 **(d)** Foot surgery is a good example of a low-contact operation (See the section on "Operations Processes" on pages 197–199)

3 **(a)** Whereas manufacturing operations focus on the outcome of the production process, service operations focus on both the transformation process and its outcome (See the section on "Differences Between Service and Manufacturing Operations" on pages 199–201)

4 **True** (See the section on "Capacity Planning for Producing Services" on page 202)

5 **(c)** Cellular layouts are useful for a family of similar (though not identical) products that follow a fixed flow path (See the section on "Layout Planning" on pages 203–204)

6 **(b)** Methods improvements are feasible in goods-producing operations but are often impossible in service operations because of the unpredictability of customer behavior (See the section on "Operations Planning" on pages 201–205)

7 **(b)** In controlling for quality, managers should establish specific standards and measurements (See the section on "Quality Improvement" on pages 211–216)

8 **True** (See the section on "Statistical Process Control" on pages 213–214)

9 **(b)** A company using the supply chain strategy always focuses on the next stage (either incoming or outgoing) in the chain (See the section on "Adding Value Through Supply Chains" on pages 216–218)

CHAPTER 8

1 **False** (See the section on "Job Analysis" on page 229)

2 **(b)** Replacement chart (See the section on "Forecasting HR Demand and Supply" on pages 229–231)

3 **(c)** Polygraph exams (See the section on "Selecting Human Resources" on pages 232–233)

4 **(e)** All of these (See the section on "Training" on page 234)

5 **(a)** Individual incentive (See the section on "Incentive Programs" on pages 236–237)

6 **True** (See the section on "Equal Employment Opportunity" on pages 238–239)

7 **(b)** It is increasing (See the section on "Managing Workforce Diversity" on pages 242–243)

8 **True** (See the section on "Trends in Contingent and Temporary Employment" on page 244)

9 **(d)** Generally, it has steadily declined (See the section on "Unionism Today" on pages 246–248)

CHAPTER 9

1 **True** (See the section on "Psychological Contracts in Organizations" on pages 260–261)

2 **(c)** Job satisfaction (See the section on "The Importance of Satisfaction and Morale" on pages 261–263)

3 **(d)** Reduced it (See the section on "Recent Trends in Managing Satisfaction and Morale" on pages 262–263)

4 **(e)** All are popular motivational theories (See the section on "Contemporary Motivational Theories" on pages 265–269)

5 **(b)** Esteem needs (See the section on "Maslow's Hierarchy of Needs Model" on pages 265–266)

6 False (See the sections on "Team Management" and "Job Enrichment and Job Redesign" on pages 272–274)

7 (d) All of these are common managerial styles (See the section on "Managerial Styles" on pages 278–279)

8 False (See the section on "The Contingency Approach to Leadership" on pages 279–280)

9 (a) Contingency approach to leadership (See the section on "The Contingency Approach to Leadership" on pages 279–280)

CHAPTER 10

1 (c) It is intangible and cannot be measured (See the section on "Providing Value and Satisfaction" on pages 290–291.)

2 (e) Relationship marketing (See the section on "Relationship Marketing" on page 292.)

3 (a) Product differentiation (See the section on "Strategy: The Marketing Mix" on pages 294–296)

4 True (See the section on "Target Marketing and Market Segmentation" on pages 297–299.)

5 (a) Substitution purchase (See the section on "The Consumer Buying Process" on pages 300–301.)

6 True (See the section on "Organizational Markets" on page 302)

7 (e) All of the above (See the section on "The Value Package" on page 304)

8 True (See the section on "The Product Mix" on page 306)

9 (b) The International Standards Act ensures the existence of uniform advertising practices in most countries (See the section on "International Promotion" on page 313)

CHAPTER 11

1 (e) Penetration pricing (See the section on "Pricing Strategies" on pages 328–329)

2 True (See the section on "Fixed versus Dynamic Pricing for E-Business" on page 329)

3 False (See the section on "Pricing Tactics" on pages 329–330)

4 False (See the section on "The Distribution Mix" on pages 330–334)

5 (b) Intermediaries are retailers who move goods or information to customers (See the section on "Intermediaries and Distribution Channels" on pages 330–334)

6 (c) Mail order retailers, such as catalog showrooms, offer deep price discounts (See the sections on "Bargain Retailers" and "Nonstore and Electronic Retailing" on pages 336–339)

7 (a) The ultimate objective of any promotion is to provide information (See the section on "Promotional Objectives" on page 342)

8 (a) TV is the most-used media and reaches the most people (See the section on "Advertising Media" on pages 343–344)

9 (e) Creative selling (See the section on "Personal Selling" on page 345)

CHAPTER 12

1 (c) They rely on face-to-face interaction among users (See the section on "Electronic Information Technologies" on pages 360–361)

2 (c) It maintains orderly flows by prohibiting Web sites from listing URLs for related sites (See the section on "Servers and Browsers" an pages 362–363)

3 False (See the section on "Directories and Search Engines" on page 364)

4 (c) Special information for conducting technical projects on specific problems (See the section on "User Groups and System Requirements" on pages 368–372)

5 False (See the section on "Knowledge-Level and Office Systems" on pages 370–371)

6 (d) Upper-level managers' avoidance of detailed information about specific operations (See the section on "Management Information Systems" on page 371)

7 (c) Software programs written by system users (See the section on "Application Programs" on pages 373–374)

8 True (See the section on "Application Programs" on pages 373–374)

9 (e) A global positioning system (GPS) (See the section on "Communication Devices" on page 376)

CHAPTER 13

1 False (See the sections on "Financial Accounting" and "Auditing" on pages 387 and 388)

2 (a) Auditing for clients owned by the CPA firm (See the section on "Private Accountants" on page 389)

3 (d) Today's accounting systems, which require fundamental revisions in generally accepted accounting principles (GAAP) for auditing (See the section on "The CPA Vision Project" on pages 389–392)

4 (d) An accounting error has occurred (See the sections on "The Accounting Equation" and "Double-Entry Accounting" on pages 393–394)

5 (e) Allowance for doubtful accounts increases the book value of accounts receivable (See the section on "Current Assets" on pages 395–396)

6 False (See the section on "Gross Profit (or Gross Margin)" on pages 397–398)

7 True (See the section on "Revenue Recognition" on pages 400–401)

8 False (See the section on "Profitability Ratios" on page 405)

9 (a) An *inventory turnover ratio* of 6.5 means that the firm has enough inventory on hand to supply its sales requirements for the next 6.5 months (See the section on "Inventory Turnover Ratio" on pages 406–407)

CHAPTER 14

1 **(b)** Durability (See the section on "The Characteristics of Money" on pages 420–421)
2 **False** (See the section on "The Functions of Money" on page 421)
3 **(b)** Credit cards ("plastic money") are included in M-2 but not in M-1 (See the section on "Credit Cards: Plastic Money?" on pages 423–424)
4 **True** (See the section on "Financial Institutions" on pages 425–428)
5 **(d)** Banker's trust (See the section on "Pension and Trust Services" on page 428)
6 **(a)** $643.12 (See the section on "Banks as Creators of Money" on page 430)
7 **(c)** Decrease the discount rate (See the section on "Discount Rate Controls" on page 435)
8 **(b)** E-Cash (See the section on "E-Cash" on page 438)
9 **False** (See the section on "International Bank Structure" on page 440)

CHAPTER 15

1 **(d)** An investment bank (See the section on "Investment Banking" on pages 450–451)
2 **False** (See the section on "Common Stocks" on pages 451–453)
3 **(c)** The number of shares traded on the floor of the Nasdaq Stock Market is greater than at the NYSE (See the section on "Nasdaq and NASD" on page 458)
4 **(b)** Corporate bonds issued by U.S. companies involve less money than U.S. government and municipal bonds (See the section on "Corporate Bonds" on page 461)
5 **True** (See the section on "Debentures" on page 461)
6 **(e)** Aggressive growth fund (See the section on "Mutual Funds" on page 462)
7 **(c)** A stock's high and low prices for any given day are reported (See the section on "Stock Quotations" on pages 464–466)
8 **False** (See the section on "The Nasdaq Composite" on page 468)
9 **(a)** Place a limit order and a stop order (See the section on "Placing Orders" on page 469)

NOTES, SOURCES, AND CREDITS

■ REFERENCE NOTES

CHAPTER 1

[1] See Paul Heyne, Peter J. Boettke, and David L. Prychitko, *The Economic Way of Thinking*, 10th ed. (Upper Saddle River, NJ: Prentice Hall, 2003), 171–76.

[2] See Karl E. Case and Ray C. Fair, *Principles of Economics*, 6th ed., updated (Upper Saddle River, NJ: Prentice Hall, 2003), 47.

[3] See Ronald M. Ayers and Robert A. Collinge, *Economics: Explore and Apply* (Upper Saddle River, NJ: Prentice Hall, 2004), 30–31.

[4] See Marc Gunther, "AOL's Grand Unified Theory of the Media Cosmos," *Fortune*, January 8, 2001, 72, 741; Catherine Yang with Ronald Grover and Ann Therese Palmer, "Showtime for AOL and Time Warner," *Business Week*, January 15, 2001, 56–621.

[5] See Case and Fair, *Principles of Economics*, 103–05.

[6] Peter Burrows, "Personal Computers: Are the Glory Days Over?" *Business Week*, February 14, 2000, 50.

[7] See Case and Fair, *Principles of Economics*, 48–67.

[8] See Gina M. Larson, "bebe Bridges Style Gap" (July 10, 2001), at *(www.office.com/global/0,2724,509-10386_1,FF.html)*; Natural Fibers Information Center, "Ranking of Top U.S. Public Apparel Companies" (June 4, 2001), at *(www.utexas.edu/depts/bbr/natfiber)*; "bebe.com Finishes #1," *FashionWindows.com* (January 14, 2002), at *(www.fashionwindows.com/beauty/2002/bebe.asp)*.

[9] See Henry R. Cheesman, *Business Law: Legal, E-Commerce, Ethical, and International Environments*, 5th ed. (Upper Saddle River, NJ: Prentice Hall, 2004), 920–23, 928–30.

[10] Case and Fair, *Principles of Economics*, 432–33.

[11] See Olivier Blanchard, *Macroeconomics*, 3rd ed. (Upper Saddle River, NJ: Prentice Hall, 2003), 24–26.

[12] See Jay Heizer and Barry Render, *Operations Management*, 7th ed. (Upper Saddle River, NJ: Prentice Hall, 2004), 14.

[13] This section is based on Heyne, Boettke, and Prychitko, *The Economic Way of Thinking*, 491–93.

[14] See Warren J. Keegan, *Global Marketing Management*, 7th ed. (Upper Saddle River, NJ: Prentice Hall, 2002), 39–42.

[15] This section follows Ayres and Collinge, *Economics: Explore and Apply*, 163–67.

[16] See Heyne, Boettke, and Prychitko, *The Economic Way of Thinking*, 403–09, 503–04.

[17] See especially "9.11.02," *Business Week*, September 16, 2002, 22–281.

CHAPTER 2

[1] Constance L. Hays, "Aide Was Reportedly Ordered to Warn Stewart on Stock Sales," *New York Times*, August 6, 2002, C1, C2.

[2] William G. Symonds with Geri Smith, "The Tax Games Tyco Played," *Business Week*, July 1, 2002, 40–41.

[3] "Drug Companies Face Assault on Prices," *Wall Street Journal*, May 11, 2000, B1, B4.

[4] Jeremy Kahn, "Presto Chango! Sales Are Huge," *Fortune*, March 20, 2000, 90–96; "More Firms Falsify Revenue to Boost Stocks," *USA Today*, March 29, 2000, 1B.

[5] This section follows the logic of Gerald F. Cavanaugh, *American Business Values with International Perspectives*, 4th ed. (Upper Saddle River, NJ: Prentice Hall, 1998), Chapter 3.

[6] See Manuel G. Velasquez, *Business Ethics: Concepts and Cases*, 5th ed. (Upper Saddle River, NJ: Prentice Hall, 2002), Chapter 2. See also John R. Boatright, *Ethics and the Conduct of Business*, 4th ed. (Upper Saddle River, NJ: Prentice Hall, 2003), 34–35, 57–59.

[7] See Abagail McWilliams and Donald Siegel, "Corporate Social Responsibility: A Theory of the Firm Perspective," *Academy of Management Review*, 2001, vol. 26, no. 1, 117–27.

[8] Jeffrey S. Harrison and R. Edward Freeman, "Stakeholders, Social Responsibility, and Performance: Empirical Evidence and Theoretical Perspectives," *Academy of Management Journal*, 1999, vol. 42, no. 5, 479–85. See also David P. Baron, *Business and Its Environment*, 4th ed. (Upper Saddle River, NJ: Prentice Hall, 2003), Chapter 18.

[9] Mara Der Hovanesian and Heather Timmons, "For Small Banks, It's a Wonderful Life," *Business Week*, May 6, 2002, 83–84.

[10] Charles Haddad, "Woe Is WorldCom," *Business Week*, May 6, 2002, 86–90.

[11] Queena Sook Kim, "Once Skeptics, Builders See Green in 'Green,'" *Wall Street Journal*, July 10, 2002, B1, B6.

[12] Symonds with Smith, "The Games Tyco Played," 40–41. "Tyco Titan Charged with Tax Violations," *CBSNews.com* (June 4, 2002), at *(www.cbsnews.com/stories/2002/06/04/national/main511051.shtm)*; Nicholas Varchaver, "CEOs Under Fire," *Fortune.com* (December 6, 2002), at *(www.fortune.com/fortune/ceo/articles/0,15114,389957,00.html)*; Melanie Warner, "Exorcism at Tyco," *Fortune.com* (April 14, 2003), at *(www.fortune.com/fortune/ceo/articles/0,15114,442883,00.html)*.

[13] Gerald Seib, "What Could Bring 1930s-Style Reform of U.S. Business?" *Wall Street Journal*, July 24, 2002, A1, A8.

[14] Andrew C. Revkin, "Who Cares About a Few Degrees?" *New York Times*, December 12, 1997, F1, F4.

[15] Marilyn Adams, "Careless Cargo," *Danatec Educational Services* (July 11, 2001), at *(www.danatec.com/freebie9.htm)*; Cat Lazaroff, "American Airlines Guilty of Hazmat Storage, Shipment Violations," *Environment News Service* (July 11, 2001), at *(http://ens.lycos.com/ens/dec99/1999L-12-17-06.html)*.

[16] Richard B. Schmitt and Robert Langreth, "American Home Products Agrees to Pay Up to $3.75 Billion in Diet-Drug Lawsuits," *WSJ Interactive Edition* (July 11, 2001), at *(www.productslaw.com/diet21.html)*. See also Nancy Shute, "Pills Don't Come with a Seal of Approval," *U.S. News Online* (July 11, 2001), at *(www.usnews.com/usnews/issue/970929/29fen.htm)*.

[17] Department of Justice, "F. Hoffmann-La Roche and BASF Agree to Pay Record Criminal Fines for Participating in

International Vitamin Cartel" (July 11, 2001), at *(www.usdoj.gov/atr/public/ press_releases/1999/2450.htm)*; Alain L. Sanders, "The 'C' in Vitamin C No Longer Stands for Cartel," *Time.com* (July 11, 2001), at *(www.time.com/time/ nation/article/0,8599,25068,00.html)*.

[18] Rick Lyman, "A Tobacco Whistle-Blower's Life Is Transformed," *New York Times*, October 15, 1999, A24.

[19] Cora Daniels, "'It's a Living Hell,'" *Fortune*, April 15, 2002, 367–368.

[20] See Henry R. Cheesman, *Business Law: Legal, E Commerce, Ethical, and International Environments*, 5th ed. (Upper Saddle River, NJ: Prentice Hall, 2004), 128–29.

[21] Andy Pasztor and Peter Landers, "Toshiba to Pay $2B Settlement on Laptops," *ZD Net News* (July 12, 2001), at *(www.zdnet.com/zdnn/stories/news/ 0,4586,2385037,00.html)*.

[22] For a recent discussion of these issues, see Amy Hillman and Gerald Keim, "Shareholder Value, Stakeholder Management, and Social Issues: What's the Bottom Line?" *Strategic Management Journal*, 2001, vol. 22, no. 2, 125–39.

[23] David Bank and Martha Brannigan, "Battling 'Donor Dropsy,'" *Wall Street Journal*, July 19, 2002, B1, B4.

[24] See Michael E. Porter and Mark R. Kramer, "Philanthropy's New Agenda: Creating Value," *Harvard Business Review*, November–December 1999, 121–30.

[25] See Sandra Waddock and Neil Smith, "Corporate Responsibility Audits: Doing Well by Doing Good," *Sloan Management Review*, Winter 2000, 75–85.

CHAPTER 3

[1] U.S. Department of Commerce, *Statistical Abstract of the United States: 2001* (TX: Hoover's Business Press Edition, 2002).

[2] Small Business Administration (SBA), "Learn about SBA" (June 10, 2003), at *(www.sba.gov/aboutsba/)*

[3] See Jim McCartney, "Celebrity Endorsement: Vice President Dick Cheney Got Medtronic's Version of the Implantable Cardioverter Defibrillator," *Pioneer Planet* (July 3, 2001), at *(http://mbbnbet.umn. edu/MBBNetNews/cheney.html)*; John Heilemann, "Reinventing the Wheel," *Time.com* (June 10, 2003), at *(www.time.com/time/business/ article/0,8599,186660,00.html)*.

[4] See Thomas W. Zimmerer and Norman M. Scarborough, *Essentials of Entrepreneurship and Small Business*, 3rd ed. (Upper Saddle River, NJ: Prentice Hall, 2002), 4–6.

[5] See Paulette Thomas, "A New Generation Re-Writes the Rules," *Wall Street Journal*, May 22, 2002, R4.

[6] Nicholas Stein, "The Renaissance Man of E-Commerce," *Fortune*, February 7, 2000, 181–82.

[7] See Zimmerer and Scarborough, *Essentials of Entrepreneurship and Small Business*, Chapter 10.

[8] See Zimmerer and Scarborough, *Essentials of Entrepreneurship and Small Business*, Chapter 8; Charles T. Horngren, Srikant M. Datar, and George Foster, *Cost Accounting: A Managerial Emphasis*, 11th ed. (Upper Saddle River, NJ: Prentice Hall, 2003), 195–99.

[9] Jim Hopkins, "Venture Capital Investments Plunge 23%," *USA Today*, May 1, 2002, 1B.

[10] See Efraim Turban et al., *Electronic Commerce: A Managerial Perspective* (Upper Saddle River, NJ: Prentice Hall, 2000), 449–51.

[11] See U.S. Census Bureau, "Surveys of Minority- and Women-Owned Enterprises," *Statistical Abstract of the United States* (June 10, 2003), at *(www.census. gov/csd/mwb)*.

[12] Bill Meyers, "Women Increase Standing as Business Owners," *USA Today*, June 29, 1999, 1B.

[13] See Scarborough and Zimmerer, *Effective Small Business Management*, 412–13.

[14] Jim Hopkins, "Expert Entrepreneur Got Her Show on the Road at an Early Age," *USA Today*, May 24, 2000, 5B.

[15] See Henry R. Cheeseman, *Business Law: Legal, E-Commerce, Ethical, and International Environments*, 5th ed. (Upper Saddle River, NJ: Prentice Hall, 2004), 607–10; Norman M. Scarborough and Thomas W. Zimmerer, *Effective Small Business Management: An Entrepreneurial Approach*, 6th ed. (Upper Saddle River, NJ: Prentice Hall, 2000), 73–76; Department of Commerce, "Statistics about Business Size," *Statistical Abstracts* (June 10, 2003), at *(www.census.gov/epcd/ www/smallbus.html)*.

[16] Department of Commerce, "Statistics about Business Size," *Statistical Abstracts* (June 10, 2003), at *(www.census.gov/ epcd/www/smallbus.html)*.

[17] "Fortune Five Hundred Largest U.S. Corporations," *Fortune*, April 14, 2003, F1–F20.

[18] See John A. Byrne, "How to Fix Corporate Governance," *Business Week*, May 6, 2002, 68–78.

[19] See Matthew Boyle, "The Dirty Half-Dozen: America's Worst Boards," *Fortune*, May 14, 2001, 249–52.

[20] Go to the National Center for Employee Ownership (June 10, 2003), at *(www.nceo.org/)*.

CHAPTER 4

[1] *Hoover's Handbook of World Business 2002* (Austin, TX: Hoover's Business Press, 2002).

[2] See John J. Wild, Kenneth L. Wild, and Jerry C. Y. Han, *International Business*, 2nd ed. (Upper Saddle River, NJ: Prentice Hall, 2003), 14–21.

[3] See Stuart R. Lynn, *Economic Development: Theory and Practice for a Divided World* (Upper Saddle River, NJ: Prentice Hall, 2003), 2–4, 33–36; Ricky W. Griffin and Michael W. Pustay, *International Business: A Managerial Perspective*, 3rd ed. (Upper Saddle River, NJ: Prentice Hall, 2002), 27.

[4] Trade Partners UK, "Automotive Industries Market in Mexico" (May 15, 2003) at *(ww.tradepartners.gov/uk/automotive/ mexico/opportunities/opportunities. shtml)*; Nafta Works, "Mexico Auto Sector Sees $15 Billion Investment in 5 Years" (May 15, 2003) at *(www.naftaworks.org/ papers/2000/automex.htm)*.

[5] See Bruce Einhorn with Cathy Yang, "Portal Combat," *Business Week*, January 17, 2000, 96–97.

[6] Wild, Wild, and Han, *International Business*, 239.

[7] See Griffin and Pustay, *International Business*, 125–27. See also Steven Husted and Michael Melvin, *International Economics*, 5th ed. (Boston: Addison Wesley Longman, 2001), 54–61; and Karl E. Case and Ray C. Fair, *Principles of Economics*, 6th ed. (Upper Saddle River, NJ: Prentice Hall, 2002), 669–77.

[8] This section is based on Michael Porter, *The Competitive Advantage of Nations* (Boston: Harvard Business School Press, 1990), Chs. 3 and 4. See also Wild, Wild, and Han, *International Business*, 155–59; Warren J. Keegan and Mark C. Green, *Global Marketing*, 3rd ed. (Upper Saddle River, NJ: Prentice Hall, 2003), 380–88.

[9] J. Michael Donnelly, "U.S. Merchandise Trade Statistics: 1948–2000," *CRS Report for Congress* (March 15, 20001), at *(www.cnie.org/NLE/CRSreports/ Economics/econ-54.cfm)*; Andrzej Zwaniecki, "U.S. Trade Deficit Down as Imports Slide and Exports Grow" (October 19, 2001), at *(www.usconsulate. org.hk/usinfo/statis/ft/2001/08.htm)*.

[10] *Hoover's Handbook of World Business 2002*, 56.

[11] See Case and Fair, *Principles of Economics*, 675–77; Griffin and Pustay, *International Business*, 189–91; Husted and Melvin, *International Economics*, 306–10.

[12] Robyn Meredith, "Dollar Makes Canada a Land of the Spree," *New York Times*, August 1, 1999, sec. 3, 1, 1. See also Currencies Direct, "Canada—Cautious Optimism" (July 10, 2001) at *(www.currenciesdirect.com/mecklai/ NTFxCanadaReport.html)*; "Interest Rates," *Canada US Investment* (March 2002), at *(www.canadausinvestment. com/Caninfo2.htm)*; "The Canada/U.S. Exchange Rate," *FRB Cleveland* (March

2001), at *(www.clev.frb.org/research/ Et2001/0301/Html/CANEX.htm)*.

[13] *Hoover's Handbook of World Business 2002.*

[14] Paola Hjelt, "The Fortune Global 500," *Fortune,* July 22, 2002, 144–47.

[15] See Wild, Wild, and Han, *International Business,* Ch. 7; Griffin and Pustay, *International Business,* 332–35.

[16] See Robert L. Simison and Scott Miller, "Ford Grabs Big Prize as Steep Losses Force BMW to Sell Rover," *Wall Street Journal,* March 17, 2000, A1, A8; Shelly Branch and Ernest Beck, "For Unilever, It's Sweetness and Light," *Wall Street Journal,* April 13, 2000, B1, B4.

[17] Bureau of Economic Analysis, "Foreign Direct Investment in the U.S." (July 11, 2001) at *(www.bea.doc.gov/ bea/di/di1fdibal.htm)*; Progressive Policy Institute, "Foreign Direct Investment Is on the Rise around the World" (July 11, 2001) at *(www.neweconomyindex.org/ section1_page04.html)*.

[18] World Trade Organization, "Foreign Direct Investment Seen as Primary Motor of Globalization" (July 11, 2001) at *(www.wto.org/english/news_e/ pres96_e/pr042_e.htm)*.

[19] Anthony DePalma, "Chiquita Sues Europeans, Citing Banana Quota Losses," *New York Times,* January 26, 2001, C5; Brian Lavery, "Trade Feud on Bananas Not as Clear as It Looks," *New York Times,* February 7, 2001, W1; David E. Sanger, "Miffed at Europe, U.S. Raises Tariffs for Luxury Goods," *New York Times,* March 4, 1999, A1, A5.

CHAPTER 5

[1] Stanley Reed, "Can Scardino Get Pearson Out of This Pickle?" *Business Week,* July 22, 2002, 50–52.

[2] "The Top 25 Managers of the Year," *Business Week,* January 8, 2001, 62; Michael Ryan, "AmEx Charges Ahead," *ZD Net News* (July 17, 2001), at *(www.zdnet.com/zdnn/stories/news/ 0,4586,2688779,00.html)*.

[3] David Dorsey, "Andy Pearson Finds Love," *Fast Company,* August 2001, 78–86.

[4] See Thomas L. Wheelan and J. David Hunger, *Strategic Management and Business Policy,* 8th ed. (Upper Saddle River, NJ: Prentice Hall, 2002), 13–14; and Mary K. Coulter, *Strategic Management in Action,* 2nd ed. (Upper Saddle River, NJ: Prentice Hall, 2002), 9–12.

[5] Mike Hofman, "Two Guys and a Start-Up: The True-Life Adventures of First-Time Company Founders," *Inc.,* February 2001, 76–81.

[6] See Wheelan and Hunger, *Strategic Management and Business Policy,* 10–14.

[7] Janet Guyon, "Getting the Bugs Out at VW," *Fortune,* March 29, 1999, 96–102; and Dale Jewett, "Running near the Front," *Automotive Industries* (July 18, 2001), at *(www.findarticles.com/m3012/ 4_180/61892631/p1/article.jhtml)*.

[8] See Stephen P. Robbins and Mary Coulter, *Management,* 7th ed. (Upper Saddle River, NJ: Prentice Hall, 2002), 202–04; Wheelan and Hunger, *Strategic Management and Business Policy,* 109.

[9] Melanie Wells, "Red Baron," *Forbes,* July 3, 2000, 150–60; Andrew Ross Sorkin, "Taking Virgin's Brand into Internet Territory," *New York Times,* February 14, 2000, C1, C17.

[10] "Cruise-Ship Delays Leave Guests High and Dry," *Wall Street Journal,* October 24, 1997, B1, B10; *Hoover's Handbook of American Business 2003* (Austin, TX: Hoover's Business Press, 2003), 1512–13.

[11] Peter Burrows, "The Radical—Carly Fiorina's Bold Management Experiment at HP," *Business Week,* February 19, 2001, 70–80; see also George Anders, "The Carly Chronicles," *Fast Company,* February 2003, 66–73.

[12] David Field, "Fliers Give Continental Sky-High Marks," *USA Today,* May 10, 2000, 3B.

[13] See David A. Whetten and Kim S. Cameron, *Developing Management Skills,* 5th ed. (Upper Saddle River, NJ: Prentice Hall, 2002), Chapter 6.

[14] Alex Taylor III, "Porsche's Risky Recipe," *Fortune,* February 17, 2003, 90–94.

[15] See also Whetten and Cameron, *Developing Management Skills,* 113–20.

[16] "Rallying the Troops at P&G," *Wall Street Journal,* August 31, 2000, B1, B4.

CHAPTER 6

[1] Joann S. Lublin, "Place vs. Product: It's Tough to Choose a Management Model," *Wall Street Journal,* June 27, 2001, A1, A4.

[2] Joann Muller, "Ford: Why It's Worse Than You Think," *Business Week,* June 25, 2001, 80–841.

[3] See Gregory Moorhead and Ricky W. Griffin, *Organizational Behavior: Managing People and Organizations,* 6th ed. (Boston: Houghton Mifflin, 2001), 420–79.

[4] See Amy Wrzesniewski and Jane Dutton, "Crafting a Job: Revisioning Employees as Active Crafters of Their Work," *Academy of Management Review,* 2001, vol. 26, no. 2, 179–201.

[5] "Industry Report: Restaurant Industry," *US Business Reporter* (July 19, 2001) at *(www.activemedia-guide.com/ print_restaurant.htm)*; Michael Arndt, "There's Life in the Old Bird Yet," *Business Week,* May 14, 2001, 77–78.

[6] See David A. Whetten and Kim S. Cameron, *Developing Management Skills,* 5th ed. (Upper Saddle River, NJ: Prentice Hall, 2002), 427–35.

[7] Michael E. Raynor and Joseph L. Bower, "Lead From the Center," *Harvard Business Review* (May 2001), 93–102.

[8] Stephanie Forest, "Can an Outsider Fix J.C. Penney?" *Business Week,* February 12, 2001, 56–58.

[9] Joann Muller, "Thinking Out of the Cereal Box," *Business Week,* January 15, 2001, 54–55.

[10] "Multi-Tasking: Cost-Reduction Strategy at Case Corp.," Machinery Systems Inc. (July 20, 2001), at *(www. machinerysystems.com/RavingFan/ CaseCorp.html)*.

[11] Robert Berner and Kevin Helliker, "Heinz's Worry: 4,000 Products, Only One Star," *Wall Street Journal,* September 17, 1999, B1, B4.

[12] Diane Brady, "Martha Inc.," *Business Week,* January 17, 2000, 62–66.

[13] Mitchell Lee Marks and Philip H. Mirvis, "Creating an Effective Transition Structure," *Organizational Dynamics* (Winter 2000), 35–44. See also Helen Deresky, *International Management: Managing across Borders and Cultures,* 3rd ed. (Upper Saddle River, NJ: Prentice Hall, 2000), Chapter 9.

[14] "Wal-Mart Acquires Interspar," *Management Ventures* (July 20, 2001), at *(www.mventures.com/news/Key1998/ flash98/wmtinters.asp)*; Kerry Capell et al., "Wal-Mart's Not-So-Secret British Weapon," *Business Week Online* (July 20, 2001), at *(www.businessweek.com:/ 2000/00_04/b3665095.htm)*.

[15] Gail Edmondson, "Danone Hits Its Stride," *Business Week,* February 1, 1999, 52–53.

[16] Thomas A. Stewart, "See Jack. See Jack Run," *Fortune,* September 27, 1999, 124–271; Geoffrey Colvin, "America's Most Admired Companies," *Fortune,* February 21, 2000, 108–10.

[17] Leslie P. Willcocks and Robert Plant, "Getting from Bricks to Clicks," *Sloan Management Review* (Spring 2001), 50–60.

[18] Ethan Smith, "Business-Driven CUs Take Many Forms," *Corporate University Review* (July 20, 2001), at *(www. traininguniversity.com/magazine/ mar_apr97/starting.html)*.

[19] See, for example, Denise M. Rousseau, "The Idiosyncratic Deal: Flexibility versus Fairness?" *Organizational Dynamics,* 2001, vol. 29, no. 4, 260–73.

CHAPTER 7

[1] Jennifer L. Martel and Laura A. Kelter, "The Job Market Remains Strong in 1999," *Monthly Labor Review* (February 2000), 3–23.

[2] Martel and Kelter, "The Job Market Remains Strong," 3–23. See also *Employment & Earnings* (Washington, DC: U.S. Department of Labor: Bureau of

Labor Statistics, June 2001), 70; and *Survey of Current Business* (Washington, DC: U.S. Department of Commerce, June 2001), D-4.

[3] See Christopher Lovelock and Lauren Wright, *Principles of Services Marketing and Management*, 2nd ed. (Upper Saddle River, NJ: Prentice Hall, 2002), 53–55.

[4] See Judy Strauss, Adel El Ansary, and Raymond Frost, *E-Marketing*, 3rd ed. (Upper Saddle River, NJ: Prentice Hall, 2003), 293–94, 418–19; and Elias Awad, *Electronic Commerce* (Upper Saddle River, NJ: Prentice Hall, 2002), 339–41.

[5] Lee J. Krajewski and Larry P. Ritzman, *Operations Management: Strategy and Analysis*, 6th ed. (Upper Saddle River, NJ: Prentice Hall, 2002), Chapter 8; and Roberta S. Russell and Bernard W. Taylor III, *Operations Management*, 4th ed. (Upper Saddle River, NJ: Prentice Hall, 2003), Chapter 9.

[6] Dawn Kawamoto, "FTC Approves Digital-Intel Deal," News.com (May 7, 2003), at *(http://news.cnet.com/news/ 0-1005-200-328663.html?tag*5 rltdnws).

[7] Barbara McClellan, "Brazilian Revolution," *Ward's Auto World* (September 2000), 69–74.

[8] "ASQ Glossary of Terms," American Society for Quality (May 6, 2003), at *(www.asq.org/info/glossary/ definition.html#q)*.

[9] See Krajewski and Ritzman, *Operations Management*, 153–54, 828–29; Russell and Taylor, *Operations Management*, 221–22, 593–95.

[10] See Russell and Taylor, *Operations Management*, 222–24.

[11] See Krajewski and Ritzman, *Operations Management*, 608–15; and Russell and Taylor, *Operations Management*, 459–64.

[12] See Sherry Alpert, "The Right 'Corporate Culture' Pays Off in Unseen Ways," *Kansas City Infozine* (May 7, 2003), at *(www.infozine.com/news/stories/op/ storiesView/sid/ 662/)*; and Karen M. Kroll, "Container Store a Hit with Customers, Employees," *Shopping Centers Today* (May 5, 2003), at *(www.icsc.org/ srch/sct/current/sct0500/ 07a.html)*.

[13] "Savoring Fine Chocolates" (May 6, 2003), at *(www.godiva.com)*.

[14] John S. McClenahen, "ITT's Value Champion," *Industry Week* (May 2002), 44–49.

[15] Thomas P. Tylutki and Danny G. Fox, "Mooooving toward Six Sigma," *Quality Progress* (February 2002), 34–41; "SPC Produces Big Savings at Steelcase," *Quality* (April 2002), 42.

[16] See S. Thomas Foster Jr., *Managing Quality: An Integrative Approach* (Upper Saddle River, NJ: Prentice Hall, 2001), 354–71.

[17] See Foster, *Managing Quality*, 106–9; and Russell and Taylor, *Operations Management*, 636–42.

[18] "2000 Award Recipients Applications Summaries" (June 8, 2002), at *(www.quality. nist.gov/2000)*.

[19] "ISO 9001 Registration Helps Improve Airport Security," *Quality Digest* (June 9, 2002), at *(www.qualitydigest.com/ currentmag/html/news.html)*; "A Call for Consistency in the Quality of Airline Security Screening Services," *American Society for Quality* (May 6, 2003), at *(www.asq.org/news/interest/ airportsecurity.html)*.

[20] See Russell and Taylor, *Operations Management*, 137–40.

[21] See Anne T. Coughlin et al., *Marketing Channels*, 6th ed. (Upper Saddle River, NJ: Prentice Hall, 2001), 168–72.

[22] See Sunil Chopra and Peter Meindl, *Supply Chain Management: Strategy, Planning, and Operation*, 2nd ed. (Upper Saddle River, NJ: Prentice Hall, 2004), 4–6; Krajewski and Ritzman, *Operations Management*, Chapter 11; Russell and Taylor, *Operations Management*, Chapter 7; and Foster, *Managing Quality*, Chapter 9.

CHAPTER 8

[1] See Angelo S. DeNisi and Ricky W. Griffin, *Human Resource Management* (Boston: Houghton Mifflin, 2001), 34–67.

[2] See Luis R. Gómez-Mejía, David B. Balkin, and Robert L. Cardy, *Managing Human Resources*, 3rd ed. (Upper Saddle River, NJ: Prentice Hall, 2001), 64–71.

[3] Matthew Boyle, "The Not-So-Fine Art of the Layoff," *Fortune*, March 19, 2001, 209–10.

[4] Associated Press, "Unemployment Steady but Hiring Slows," *WFAA.com* (August 21, 2001), at *(www.wfaa.com/ wfaa/articledisplay/1,1002,18294,00. html)*.

[5] Kenneth Brown, "Using Computers to Deliver Training: Which Employees Learn and Why?" *Personnel Psychology*, Summer 2001, 271–96.

[6] Abby Ellin, "Training Programs Often Miss the Point on the Job," *New York Times*, March 29, 2000, C12.

[7] See Richard I. Henderson, *Compensation Management in a Knowledge-Based World*, 8th ed. (Upper Saddle River, NJ: Prentice Hall, 2000), 17–18.

[8] See Gómez-Mejía, Balkin, and Cardy, *Managing Human Resources*, 366–69.

[9] Barbara Carton, "In 24-Hour Workplace, Day Care Is Moving to the Night Shift," *Wall Street Journal*, July 6, 2001, A1, A4.

[10] See Henry R. Cheeseman, *Business Law: Ethical, International, and E-Commerce Environment*, 4th ed. (Upper Saddle River, NJ: Prentice Hall, 2001), Chapter 42.

[11] See Gary Dessler, *Human Resource Management*, 8th ed. (Upper Saddle River, NJ: Prentice Hall, 2000), 44–46.

[12] See Cheeseman, *Business Law*, 843–47; Dessler, *Human Resource Management*, 40–44.

[13] Jeremy Kahn, "Diversity Trumps the Downturn," *Fortune*, July 9, 2001, 114–28.

[14] Matt Richtel, "Need for Computer Experts Is Making Recruiters Frantic," *New York Times*, December 18, 1999, C1.

[15] See Michael R. Carrell and Christina Heavrin, *Labor Relations and Collective Bargaining: Cases, Practice, and Law*, 6th ed. (Upper Saddle River, NJ: Prentice Hall, 2001), Chapter 1.

[16] David Koenig, "Labor Unions Say Recent Victories Signal a Comeback," Associated Press news release published in *The Bryan-College Station Eagle*, June 11, 2000, E1, E6.

[17] See Carrell and Heavrin, *Labor Relations and Collective Bargaining*, 90–91.

[18] See also Carrell and Heavrin, *Labor Relations and Collective Bargaining*, 189–97.

CHAPTER 9

[1] Richard B. Chase and Sriram Dasu, "Want to Perfect Your Company's Service? Use Behavioral Science," *Harvard Business Review*, June 2001, 79–88.

[2] Daniel M. Cable and Charles K. Parsons, "Socialization Tactics and Person–Organization Fit," *Personnel Psychology*, Spring 2001, 1–24.

[3] Gregory Moorhead and Ricky W. Griffin, *Organizational Behavior*, 6th ed. (Boston: Houghton Mifflin, 2001), 95–99.

[4] Jerry Useem, "Welcome to the New Company Town," *Fortune*, January 10, 2000, 62–70.

[5] See Jerald Greenberg and Robert A. Baron, *Behavior in Organizations: Understanding and Managing the Human Side of Work*, 7th ed. (Upper Saddle River, NJ: Prentice Hall, 2000), 177–79.

[6] Anne Fisher, "Surviving the Downturn," *Fortune*, April 2, 2001, 98–106.

[7] See Moorhead and Griffin, *Organizational Behavior*, Chapters 5 and 6.

[8] See Moorhead and Griffin, *Organizational Behavior*, Chapter 7.

[9] See Moorhead and Griffin, *Organizational Behavior*, Chapter 7.

[10] Robert Levering and Milton Moskowitz, "The 100 Best Companies to Work For," *Fortune*, January 8, 2001, 148–66.

[11] See Gary Yukl, *Leadership in Organizations*, 5th ed. (Upper Saddle River, NJ: Prentice Hall, 2002), Chapter 1.

[12] David Dorsey, "Andy Pearson Finds Love," *Fast Company*, August 2001, 78–86.

[13] See Francis J. Yammarino, Fred Danscreau, and Christina J. Kennedy, "A Multiple-Level Multidimensional Approach to Leadership," *Organizational Dynamics*, vol. 29, no. 3, 2001, 149–63.

[14] See Yukl, *Leadership in Organizations*, Chapter 8; Jon P. Howell and Dan L. Costley, *Understanding Behaviors for Effective Leadership* (Upper Saddle River, NJ: Prentice Hall, 2001), Chapter 3.

[15] See Greenberg and Baron, *Behavior in Organizations*, 193–99; Yukl, *Leadership in Organizations*, 418–20.

[16] Frederick F. Reichheld, "Lead for Loyalty," *Harvard Business Review*, July–August 2001, 76–86.

CHAPTER 10

[1] American Marketing Association, "Marketing Services Guide" (August 23, 2001) at *(www.ama.org/about/ama/markdef.asp.)*

[2] See Philip Kotler, *Marketing Management*, 11th ed. (Upper Saddle River, NJ: Prentice Hall, 2003), 76–78.

[3] See Warren J. Keegan and Mark C. Green, *Global Marketing*, 3rd ed. (Upper Saddle River, NJ: Prentice Hall, 2003), 8–15.

[4] Alex Taylor III, "Detroit: Every Silver Lining Has a Cloud," *Fortune*, January 24, 2000, 92–93.

[5] "Burberry Earns Independence," *BBC News* (August 23, 2001) at *(http://newsvote.bbc.co.uk/hi/english/business/newsid 1047000/1047772.stm)*; GUS: The Retail and Services Business Group, "Reports and Accounts" (April 3, 2002), at *(www.gusplc.com)*

[6] Kitty McKinsey, "Poland: Credit and Debit Cards Take Off," *Radio Free Europe* (August 23, 2001) at *(http://www.rferl.org/nca/features/1997/03/F.RU.970303160756. html.)*

[7] See Leon G. Schiffman and Leslie Lazar Kanuk, *Consumer Behavior*, 8th ed. (Upper Saddle River, NJ: Prentice Hall, 2004), Chapter 3; Kotler, *Marketing Management*, 93–94.

[8] See Kenneth C. Laudon and Jane P. Laudon, *Management Information Systems: Managing the Digital Firm*, 7th ed. (Upper Saddle River, NJ: Prentice Hall, 2002), 221–22.

[9] Barbara J. Bashein and M. Lynne Markus, *Data Warehouses* (Morristown, NJ: Financial Executives Research Foundation Inc., 2000), 1.

[10] U.S. Department of Commerce, *Statistical Abstract of the United States: 1998* (Washington, DC: Bureau of the Census, 1999), 305–09, 547, 768, 776.

[11] See Kotler, *Marketing Management*, Chapter 3; Roger J. Best, *Market-Based Management: Strategies for Growing Customer Value and Profitability*, 2nd ed. (Upper Saddle River, NJ: Prentice Hall, 2000), 87–100.

[12] Kelly Barron, "Getting a Rise Out of Levi's," *Forbes*, November 26, 2001, 156–58; "Levi to Cut 3,600 Jobs," *CNNMoney* (April 8, 2002), at *(http:// money.cnn.com/2002/04/08/news/companies/levis)*.

[13] See Chet Zelasko, "Acesulfame-K," *Better Life Institute* (May 17, 2001), at *(http://blionline.com/HDB/Acesulfame-K.htm)*.

[14] "The Best New Products," *Beverage Industry*, February 2002, 35–37.

[15] See Kevin Lane Keller, *Strategic Brand Management: Building, Measuring, and Managing Brand Equity*, 2nd ed. (Upper Saddle River, NJ: Prentice Hall, 2003), 67–70.

[16] See Eloise Coupey, *Marketing and the Internet* (Upper Saddle River, NJ: Prentice Hall, 2001), 174–79.

[17] John Frook, "Cisco Scores with Its Latest Generation of Empowering Tools," *B to B*, August 20, 2001, 20.

[18] See Norman N. Scarborough and Thomas W. Zimmerer, *Effective Small Business Management: An Entrepreneurial Approach*, 7th ed. (Upper Saddle River, NJ: Prentice Hall, 2003), Chapter 7.

CHAPTER 11

[1] See Thomas T. Nagle and Reed K. Holden, *The Strategy and Tactics of Pricing: A Guide to Profitable Decision Making* (Upper Saddle River, NJ: Prentice Hall, 2002), 39–45, 67–72.

[2] See Nagle and Holden, *The Strategy and Tactics of Pricing*, 166–73; Roger J. Best, *Market-Based Management: Strategies for Growing Customer Value and Profitability*, 2nd ed. (Upper Saddle River, NJ: Prentice Hall, 2000), 189–91.

[3] Judy Strauss, Adel El-Ansary, and Raymond Frost, *E-Marketing*, 3rd ed. (Upper Saddle River, NJ: Prentice Hall, 2003), 320–22; Eloise Coupey, *Marketing and the Internet* (Upper Saddle River, NJ: Prentice Hall, 2001), 281–83.

[4] See also Anne T. Coughlan et al., *Marketing Channels*, 6th ed. (Upper Saddle River, NJ: Prentice Hall, 2001), 9–17.

[5] *Dell Annual Report: FY2001 Year in Review* (April 22, 2002) at *(www.dell.com)*; Qiao Song, "Legend Outlines Role in China's Wireless Future," *Ebn*, March 25, 2002, 3; Faith Hung, "Legend Looks to Defend Its Turf—WTO Entry Will Force China's Top PC Maker to Fend Off Unrestricted Rivals," *Ebn*, December 17, 2001, 44.

[6] See esp. Coupey, *Marketing and the Internet*, Chapter 11; Coughlin et al., *Marketing Channels*, 447–69.

[7] "Expedia.com" (July 8, 2002) at *(www.expedia.com)*.

[8] Diane Brady, "From Nabisco to Tropicana to … EFDEX?" *Business Week*, September 20, 1999, 100; "Efdex_" (April 19, 2000) at *(www.efdex.com)*.

[9] See Mary Jo Foley and Tom Steinert-Threlkeld, "The Ultimate CRM Machine," *Baseline* (October 29, 2001), at *(www.baselinemag.com/article/0,3658,a = 17004,00.asp)*.

[10] "Prodigy.com_" (April 8, 2002), at *(www.prodigy.com)*.

[11] "Small Biz Web Sites on the Rise, Yet Many Owners Slow to Embrace the Internet," *Prodigy.com* (April 19, 2000), at *(www.prodigy.com/pcom/business/business/content)*.

[12] Darren Noyce, "eB2B: Analysis of Business-to-Business E-Commerce and How Research Can Adapt to Meet Future Challenges," *International Journal of Market Research*, First Quarter 2002, 71–95.

[13] "Did You Know?" *Catalog News.com* (April 8, 2002), at *(www.catalog-news.com)*.

[14] See Carolyn Brackett, "Setting Up Shop in Cyberspace," *Inc.com* (May 20, 2002), at *(www.inc.com/conducting_commerce/advice/15237.html)*; David Radin, "'Electronic Mall Syndrome' Gives Way to Unified Buying," *e Business News* (May 20, 2002), at *(http://ebusiness.dci.com/articles/1998/05/14radin.htm)*; Garrett Wasny, "Free Electronic Storefronts" (July, 2000), at *(www.howtoconquertheworld.com/gohome111.htm)*.

[15] See Kenneth E. Clow and Donald Baack, *Integrated Advertising, Promotion, and Marketing Communications*, 2nd ed. (Upper Saddle River, NJ: Prentice Hall, 2004), 48–51.

[16] *Advertising Age*, September 24, 2001, S1.

[17] *Advertising Age*, September 24, 2001, S1.

[18] R. Craig Endicott, "100 Leading National Advertisers," *Advertising Age*, September 24, 2001, S1.

[19] See Clow and Baack, *Integrated Advertising*, Chapter 14; Efraim Turban et al., *Electronic Commerce: A Managerial Perspective* (Upper Saddle River, NJ: Prentice Hall, 2000), Chapter 4.

[20] Ira Teinowitz and Cara B. Dipasquale, "Direct Marketers Take Issue with Proposed FTC Rules," *Advertising Age*, January 28, 2002, 3, 29; Larry Neilson, "Look Out for Telemarketing Speed Bumps," *National Underwriter*, September 17, 2001, 12–14.

[21] See Scott M. Cutlip, Allen H. Center, and Glen M. Broom, *Effective Public Relations*, 8th ed. (Upper Saddle River, NJ: Prentice Hall, 2000), 9–10.

CHAPTER 12

[1] See Kenneth C. Laudon and Jane P. Laudon, *Management Information Systems: Managing the Digital Firm*, 7th ed. (Upper Saddle River, NJ: Prentice Hall, 2002), 7–11.

[2] See Laudon and Laudon, *Management Information Systems*, 252–53.

[3] See Larry Long and Nancy Long, *Computers: Information Technology in*

Perspective, 9th ed. (Upper Saddle River, NJ: Prentice Hall, 2002), Chapter 7 and Chapter 8.

[4] "The Internet: Bringing Wall Street to Main Street," *Wall Street & Technology,* September 2001, 52–53.

[5] See Laudon and Laudon, *Management Information Systems,* 273–83.

[6] Steve Jarvis, "Ain't Nothin' for Free," *Marketing News,* April 23, 2001, 3; Alex Salkever and Sheridan Prasso, "Search Engines: Leading US Astray?" *Business Week (Industry/Technology Edition),* August 6, 2001, 8.

[7] See Laudon and Laudon, *Management Information Systems,* 122–27, 276–77.

[8] Jennifer Tanaka, "Don't Get Burned," *Newsweek,* August 20, 2001, 52–53.

[9] Mary J. Cronin, "Ford's Intranet Success," *Fortune,* March 30, 1998, 158; Rick Gurin, "Online System to Streamline Ford's Delivery Process," *Frontline Solutions,* April 2000, 1, 8.

[10] See Lee J. Krajewski and Larry P. Ritzman, *Operations Management: Strategy and Analysis,* 6th ed. (Upper Saddle River, NJ: Prentice Hall, 2002), 46–48.

[11] See Gary W. Dickson and Gerardine DeSanctis, *Information Technology and the Future Enterprise: New Models for Managers* (Upper Saddle River, NJ: Prentice Hall, 2001), Chapter 4.

[12] See Krajewski and Ritzman, *Operations Management: Strategy and Analysis,* 205–10.

[13] See Krajewski and Ritzman, *Operations Management: Strategy and Analysis,* 232–33.

[14] See Laudon and Laudon, *Management Information Systems,* esp. 40–45.

[15] See Laudon and Laudon, *Management Information Systems,* 383–91.

[16] See Laudon and Laudon, *Management Information Systems,* 237–44.

[17] See Laudon and Laudon, *Management Information Systems,* 270–71.

[18] Nathalie Raffray, "Portal Power," *Communications International,* August 2001, 30–35; David Maloney, "The Newest Better Idea at Ford," *Modern Materials Handling,* June 2000, 34–39. See also Laudon and Laudon, *Management Information Systems,* 239–44.

CHAPTER 13

[1] Charles T. Horngren, Walter T. Harrison Jr., and Linda Smith Bamber, *Accounting,* 5th ed. (Upper Saddle River, NJ: Prentice Hall, 2002), 5.

[2] See Marshall B. Romney and Paul John Steinbart, *Accounting Information Systems,* 9th ed. (Upper Saddle River, NJ: Prentice Hall, 2003), Chapter 1; Kumen H. Jones et al., *Introduction to Accounting: A User Perspective* (Upper Saddle River, NJ: Prentice Hall, 2000), F-231.

[3] See Anthony A. Atkinson et al., *Management Accounting* (Upper Saddle River, NJ: Prentice Hall, 2001), 5–6.

[4] See Walter T. Harrison Jr. and Charles T. Horngren, *Financial Accounting,* 4th ed. (Upper Saddle River, NJ: Prentice Hall, 2000), 6.

[5] See Alvin A. Arens, Randal J. Elder, and Mark S. Beasley, *Essentials of Auditing and Assurance Services* (Upper Saddle River, NJ: Prentice Hall, 2003), 10–14.

[6] See Horngren, Harrison, and Bamber, *Accounting,* 9–11.

[7] This section is based on material from the following sources: AICPA, "CPA Vision Project" (August 12, 2002), at *(www.aicpa.org/vision/index.htm);* AICPA, "CPA Vision Project: 2011 and Beyond" (August 12, 2002), at *(www.cpavision.org).*

[8] See Horngren, Harrison, and Bamber, *Accounting,* 11–12, 39–41.

[9] See Horngren, Harrison, and Bamber, *Accounting,* 41–56.

[10] See Horngren, Harrison, and Bamber, *Accounting,* 17–20.

[11] See Lawrence Revsine, Daniel W. Collins, and W. Bruce Johnson, *Financial Reporting and Analysis,* 2nd ed. (Upper Saddle River, NJ: Prentice Hall, 2002), 387.

[12] See Revsine, Collins, and Johnson; *Financial Reporting and Analysis,* 179–81, 468–70.

[13] See Revsine, Collins, and Johnson; *Financial Reporting and Analysis,* Chapter 15.

[14] See Horngren, Harrison, and Bamber, *Accounting,* Chapter 17.

[15] See Horngren, Harrison, and Bamber, *Accounting,* 927–40.

[16] See Jones et al., *Accounting: A User Perspective,* F-187.

[17] See Horngren, Harrison, and Bamber, *Accounting,* 86.

[18] See Jones et al., *Accounting: A User's Perspective,* F-454–F479.

[19] See Horngren, Harrison, and Bamber, *Accounting,* 728–29; Arthur J. Keown et al., *Foundations of Finance: The Logic and Practice of Financial Management,* 3rd ed. (Upper Saddle River, NJ: Prentice Hall, 2001), 118–20.

[20] See Horngren, Harrison, and Bamber, *Accounting,* 186–88.

[21] See Frederick D. S. Choi, Carol Ann Frost, and Gary K. Meek, *International Accounting,* 4th ed. (Upper Saddle River: Prentice Hall, 2002), Chapter 6.

[22] See Choi, Frost, and Meek, *International Accounting,* 267–79.

CHAPTER 14

[1] See Arthur O'Sullivan and Steven M. Sheffrin, *Economics: Principles and Tools,* 2nd ed. (Upper Saddle River, NJ: Prentice Hall, 2001), 566–68.

[2] Federal Reserve Board of Governors, "M1 Money Stock Seasonally Adjusted" (July 2, 2002), at *(www.federalreserve.gov.)*

[3] Federal Reserve Board of Governors, "Currency Component of Money Stock" (July 2, 2002), at *(www.federalreserve.gov.)*

[4] Federal Reserve Board of Governors, "Demand Deposits at Commercial Banks" (July 2, 2002), at *(www.federalreserve.gov.)*

[5] Federal Reserve Board of Governors, "M2 Money Stock" (July 2, 2002), at *(www.federalreserve.gov.)*

[6] Federal Reserve Board of Governors, "Money Market Funds" (June 2, 2002), at *(www.federalreserve.gov.)*

[7] Federal Reserve Board of Governors, "Total Savings Deposits" (June 2, 2002), at *(www.federalreserve.gov).*

[8] See Citigroup, "Global Consumer Business" (July 17, 2001), at *(www.citigroup.com/citigroup/corporate/gcb_m.htm);* and U.S. Census Bureau, *Statistical Abstract of the United States* (2001), 1191, at *(www.census.gov/statab/www.)*

[9] See James C. Van Horne, *Financial Management and Policy,* 12th ed. (Upper Saddle River, NJ: Prentice Hall, 2002), 494–95.

[10] See "Prime Rate," *Money.café* (July 7, 2002), at *(www.nfsn.com/library/prime.htm.)*

[11] U.S. Census Bureau, Statistical Abstract of the United States (2001), 1163, 1183, at *(www.census.gov/statab/www.)*

[12] U.S. Census Bureau, *Statistical Abstract of the United States* (2001), 1163, at *(www.census.gov/statab/www.)*

[13] U.S. Census Bureau, *Statistical Abstract of the United States* (2001), 532, 1218, at *(www.census.gov/statab/www.)*

[14] See Gordon J. Alexander, William F. Sharpe, and Jeffery V. Bailey, *Fundamentals of Investments,* 3rd ed. (Upper Saddle River, NJ: Prentice Hall, 2001), 100–1.

[15] American Bankers Association, "ATM Fact Sheet" (July 8, 2002), at *(www.aba.com/Press1 Room/ATMfacts2001.htm.)*

[16] See Marshall B. Romney and Paul John Steinbart, *Accounting Information Systems,* 8th ed. (Upper Saddle River, NJ: Prentice Hall, 2000), 218–19.

[17] See Karl E. Case and Ray C. Fair, *Principles of Economics,* 6th ed. (Upper Saddle River, NJ: Prentice Hall, 2002), 483–89.

[18] See O'Sullivan and Sheffrin, *Economics,* 574–76.

[19] See "Discount Window," (July 8, 2002), at *(www.frbdisountwindow.org.)*

[20] See Case and Fair, *Principles of Economics,* 497–99.

[21] See Jim Middlemiss, "Banks Get Smart About Computer Chips," *Bank Systems & Technology* (April 2002), 44; and Lisa

Daigle, "Beyond Expectations," *Credit Card Management* (May 2000), 50–52.

[22] See Michael Froomkin, "The Unintended Consequences of E-Cash" (July 16, 2001), at *(www.law.miami.edu/~froomkin/articles/cfp97.htm.)*

[23] See Charles T. Horngren, Walter T. Harrison Jr., and Linda Smith Bamber, *Accounting,* 5th ed. (Upper Saddle River, NJ: Prentice Hall, 2002), 636–37.

[24] See Ricky W. Griffin and Michael W. Pustay, *International Business: A Managerial Perspective,* 3rd ed. (Upper Saddle River, NJ: Prentice Hall, 2002), 159–61.

CHAPTER 15

[1] See Gordon J. Alexander, William F. Sharpe, and Jeffery V. Bailey, *Fundamentals of Investments,* 3rd ed. (Upper Saddle River, NJ: Prentice Hall, 2001), 2–7.

[2] See Arthur J. Keown et al., *Foundations of Finance: The Logic and Practice of Financial Management,* 4th ed. (Upper Saddle River, NJ: Prentice Hall, 2003), 50–51; Alexander, Sharpe, and Bailey, *Fundamentals of Investments,* 261, 478.

[3] *Flow of Funds Accounts of the United States* (Washington, DC: Board of Governors of the Federal Reserve System, June 6, 2002), Table F.2.

[4] *Federal Reserve Bulletin* (May 2002) A31; *Flow of Funds Accounts of the United States* (Washington, DC: Board of Governors of the Federal Reserve System, June 6, 2002), Table F.4.

[5] See Cory Johnson, "The Internet Blue Chip," *The Industry Standard* (August 7, 2001), at *(www.thestandard.com/article/0,1902,4088,00html)*; Chris Nerney "Yahoo: Bargain or Big Trouble?" *The Internet Stock Report* (August 7, 2001), at *(www.internetstockreport.com/column/print/0,,530021,00.html).*

[6] Chilik Wollenberg, "How Does Your Broker Measure Up?" *Medical Economics,* May 28, 2001, 98–100; Leah Nathans Spiro and Edward C. Baig, "Who Needs a Broker?" *Business Week,* February 22, 1999, 113–116.

[7] Borzou Daragahi, "E-Finance Forecast," *Money,* March 2001, 129–33; Joseph Kahn, "Schwab Lands Feet First on Net," *New York Times,* February 10, 1999, C1, C5.

[8] See Alexander, Sharpe, and Bailey, *Fundamentals of Investments,* 36–39.

[9] See Alexander, Sharpe, and Bailey, *Fundamentals of Investments,* 44–46.

[10] *Nasdaq 2001 Annual Report,* (June 25, 2002) at *(www.nasdaq.com/investorrelations/annualreport2001).* "The World in Its Hands," *The Economist,* May 6, 2000, 77; "The Nasdaq Japan Market Launches First Day of Trading; First Step in Creating Nasdaq Global Platform Is Achieved" (June 19, 2000), at *(www.nasdaq.co.uk/reference).* "Global-ization and International Reach" (June 23, 2000), at *Nasdaq Initiatives* at *(www.nasdaq.com.)*

[11] See Frank J. Fabozzi, *Bond Markets, Analysis and Strategies,* 4th ed. (Upper Saddle River, NJ: Prentice Hall, 2000), Chapter 1.

[12] *Federal Reserve Bulletin* (May 2002), A25, A27; *Flow of Funds Accounts of the United States* (Washington, DC: Board of Governors of the Federal Reserve System, June 6, 2002), page 1.

[13] *Federal Reserve Bulletin* (May 2002), A31.

[14] *Wiesenberger Mutual Funds Update* (Rockville, MD: CDA Investment Technologies, August 31, 2000), iv–ix; *Mutual Funds Facts and Figures,* (July 14, 2002), at *(www.ici.org/facts.figures.)*

[15] See Alexander, Sharpe, and Bailey, *Fundamentals of Investments,* 39–43.

[16] Gretchen Morgenson, "Buying on Margin Becomes a Habit," *New York Times,* March 24, 2000, C1, C7; David Barboza, "Wall Street after Dark," *New York Times,* February 13, 2000, BU1, BU14–BU15.

[17] See Alexander, Sharpe, and Bailey, *Fundamentals of Investments,* 37–38.

[18] U.S. Securities Exchange Commission, "SEC Charges Former ImClone CEO Samuel Waksal with Illegal Insider Trading" (June 12, 2002), at *(www.sec.gov/news/press)*; Andrew Pollack, "ImClone's Ex-Chief in Talks with U.S.on Plea Agreement," *The New York Times on The Web* (July 13, 2002), at *(www.nytimes.com/2002/07/13/business)*; "Martha Scrutiny Heats Up," *CNNMoney* (June 14, 2002), at *(www.cnnfn.co.)*

■ SOURCE NOTES

CHAPTER 1

Megawatt Laundering and Other Bright Business Ideas/Blackouts and Other Dark Forces. Chris Taylor, "California Scheming," *Time,* May 20, 2002, 42–44; Richard A. Oppel Jr., "How Enron Got California to Buy Power It Didn't Need," *New York Times,* May 8, 2002, C1, C6; Mark Gimein, "Who Turned the Lights Out?" *Fortune* (February 5, 2001), 110–141; Holman Jenkins Jr., "Enron for Beginners," *Wall Street Journal,* January 23, 2002, A1, A17; Delroy Alexander, "Keener Focus on Enron Deals," *Chicago Tribune,* February 20, 2002, C1; Brock N. Meeks, "Enron Sailed into a Perfect Storm," *OwestLightspeed* (January 23, 2002), at *(www.msnbc.com/news/692391.asp)*; Nelson D. Schwartz, "Is Energy Trading a Big Scam?" *Fortune,* June 10, 2002, 126–281 Neela Banerjee, "Who Will Needle Regulators Now That Enron's Muzzled?" *New York Times,* January 20, 2002, Sec. 3, 1, 12. **Entrepreneurship and New Ventures:** *Grinding Out Com-* *petitive Success* Kevin Helliker and Shirley Leung, "Despite the Jitters, Most Coffeehouses Survive Starbucks," *The Wall Street Journal,* September 24, 2002, pp. A1, A11; Stanley Holmes, "Planet Starbucks," *Business Week,* September 9, 2002, pp. 100–110. **Figure 1.1** Adapted from Karl E. Case and Ray C. Fair, *Principles of Economics,* 6th ed., revised (Upper Saddle River, NJ: Prentice Hall, 2002) 47.

CHAPTER 2

The Rules of Tipping/When Does a Stock Warrant Warrant a Warrant for Arrest? Geeta Anand, Jerry Markon, and Chris Adams, "ImClone's Ex-CEO Arrested, Charged with Insider Trading," *The Wall Street Journal,* June 13, 2002, A1, A8; Greg Farrell, "Waksal Indictment Unsealed," *USA Today,* August 8, 2002, 1B; Amy Barrett, "No Quick Cure," *Business Week,* May 6, 2002, 30–33; Andrew Pollack, "For ImClone Drug Entrepreneur, a Past of Celebrity and Notoriety," *New York Times,* January 24, 2002, C1, C9. Erin McClam, "ImClone Founder Sentenced," Associated Press wire story as reported in *Bryan-College Station Eagle,* June 11, 2003, p. C6; Thomas Mulligan, "Multiple Strategies Open to Stewart Defense Team," *Los Angeles Times,* June 10, 2003, p. A8. **Figures 2.1 & 2.2** Based on Gerald S. Cavanaugh, *American Business Values: With International Perspectives,* 4th ed. (Upper Saddle River, NJ: Prentice Hall, 1998) 71, 84. **Entrepreneurship and New Ventures: The Electronic Equivalent of Paper Shredding** Erika Brown, "To Shred and Protect," *Forbes,* November 25, 2002, pp. 114–118; "Omniva Earns Microsoft.net Connected Logo Premium Level Status," *PRNewswire* (October 22, 2002), at *(www.disappearing.com/news/announcements/02_10_22_dotnet_logo.html)*; "Tumbleweed Granted New Patent for Electronic Communication," *Tumbleweed Communications* (November 26, 2002), at *(www.tumbleweed.com/en/company/news_events/press_releases/2002/pr-1731.html).* **Figure 2.3** David P. Baron, *Business and Its Environment,* 4th ed. (Upper Saddle River, NJ: Prentice Hall, 2003) 768. **Figure 2.5** Based on Andrew C. Revkin, "Who Cares about a Few Degrees?" *The New York Times,* December 12, 1997, F1. **Table 2.1** The Foundation Center, "Fifty Largest Corporate Foundations by Total Giving," *Researching Philanthropy* (August 12, 2002), at *(fdncenter.org/research/trends_analysis/top50giving.html).*

CHAPTER 3

The Competitor from Out of the Blue/ How High Can An Airline Fly? Julia Boorstin, "JetBlue's IPO Takes Off," *Fortune*, April 29, 2002, pp. 96–100; Melanie Wells, "Lord of the Skies," *Forbes*, October 14, 2002, pp. 130–138; Paul C. Judge, "How Will Your Company Adapt?" *Fast Company*, February, 2003, pp. 105–110. **Figures 3.1, 3.2, & 3.6** Data from U.S. Department of Commerce, "Statistics about Business Size (Including Small Business) from the U.S. Census Bureau," *Statistical Abstract of the United States* (September 6, 2001), at *(www.census.gov/epcd/www/ smallbus.html)*. **Figure 3.3** Data from U.S. Department of Commerce, "Statistics about Business Size," *Statistical Abstract of the United States* (Washington, DC: Bureau of the Census, 2001), 491 **Figure 3.4** Norman M. Scarborough and Thomas W. Zimmerer, *Effective Small Business Management: An Entrepreneurial Approach*, 6th ed. (Upper Saddle River, NJ: Prentice Hall, 2000) 15. Data from Forrester Research Inc. **Entrepreneurship and New Ventures: *Food for Thought*** "About Us" and "Michael Stark: Kitchen," *FreshDirect* (November 25, 2002) at *(www.freshdirect.com)*; David Kirkpatrick, "The Online Grocer Version 2.0," *Fortune*, November 25, 2002, pp. 84–86; Florence Fabricant, "Fresh Groceries Right Off the Assembly Line," *New York Times*, November 6, 2002, p. 4B; Jane Black, "Can FreshDirect Bring Home the Bacon?" *Business Week*, September 24, 2002, pp. 87–88. **Figure 3.5** Data from Catalyst; National Foundation for Women Business Owners.

CHAPTER 4

Where Does Management Stand on Beer Breaks?/Mariachi Bands and Other Weapons of the Retail Wars 2002 Annual Report, "International Operations," "Wal-Mart International Operations," "Wal-Mart Stores Inc. at a Glance" (November 27, 2002), at *(www.walmartstores.com)*; Amy Tsao, "Will Wal-Mart Take Over the World?" *Business Week*, November 27, 2002, pp. 76–79; Geri Smith, "War of the Superstores," *Business Week*, September 23, 2002, p. 60; "The 2002 Global 500," *Fortune*, July 8, 2002. **Table 4.1** *Hoover's Handbook of World Business 2002* (Austin, TX: Hoover's Business Press, 2002) 52. Data from *(http://www.ita.doc. gov/td/industry/otea/ustth/tabcon.html)*. **Figure 4.5** Michael E. Porter, *The Competitive Advantage of Nations* (New York: Free Press, 1990) 72. **Entrepreneurship and New Ventures: *Rolling in the Worldwide Dough*** Ron Lieber, "Give Us This Day Our Global Bread," *Fast Company*, March 2001, 164–67. **Table 4.2** Robyn Meredith, "Dollar Makes Canada a Land of the Spree," *New York Times*, August 1, 1999, C11. **Figures 4.6 & 4.7** *Survey of Current Business*, July 2001 (Washington, DC: U.S. Department of Commerce) 88–89. **Building Your Business Skills: *Putting Yourself in Your Place*** Maria Atanasov, "Taking Her Business on the Road," *Fortune*, April 13, 1998, 158–60.

CHAPTER 5

Yellow Delivers the Goods/"Our Business Isn't Really about Moving Freight" Chuck Salter, "Fresh Start 2002: On the Road Again," *Fast Company*, January 2002, 50–58; Matthew Boyle, "America's Most Admired Companies: The Right Stuff," *Fortune*, March 4, 2002; *Yellow Corporation 2000 Annual Report* (March 2001), at *(www.yellowcorp.com)*. **Entrepreneurship and New Ventures: *Sam Adams Makes Headway*** Christopher Edmunds, "Bottom of the Barrel: Boston Beer's Winning Formula," *RealMoney.com* (March 5, 2003), at *(http://www.thestreet.com/realmoney)*; Gary Hammel, "Driving Grassroots Growth," *Fortune*, September 4, 2002, pp. 173–87; Ronald Lieber, "Beating the Odds," *Fortune*, March 31, 2002, pp. 82–90. **Figure 5.1** Based on Thomas L. Wheelen and J. David Hunger, *Strategic Management and Business Policy*, 8th ed. (Upper Saddle River, NJ: Prentice Hall, 2002) 14. **Figure 5.2** Based on Stephen P. Robbins and Mary Coulter, *Management*, 7th ed. (Upper Saddle River, NJ: Prentice Hall, 2002) 199. **Building Your Business Skills: *Speaking with Power*** Information from Justin Martin, "How You Speak Shows Where You Rank," *Fortune*, February 2, 1998, 156.

CHAPTER 6

Cooking Up a New Structure/Is There Synergy between Baked Goods, Shoe Polish, and Underwear? "Our Brands," *Sara Lee* (July 3, 2002), at *(www.saralee. com)*; Deborah Cohen, "Sara Lee Opens Alternative to Victoria's Secret," *Wall Street Journal*, January 3, 2003, p. B4; Julie Forster, "Sara Lee: Changing the Recipe—Again," *Business Week*, September 10, 2001, pp. 87–89; "Sara Lee: Looking Shapely," *Business Week*, October 21, 2002, p. 52. **Entrepreneurship and New Ventures: *The Dragon Lady Comes to the Rescue*** "Hardlines Buying Groups Analysis: TruServ Corp.," *Home Channel News* (June 9, 2003), at *(www. homechannelnews.com)*; Jo Napolitano, "No, She Doesn't Breathe Fire," *New York Times*, September 1, 2002, p. BU2; "Pamela Forbes Lieberman Elected CEO of TruServ Corporation," "TruServ Names New CEO," "TruServ Names New Chief Financial Officer," TruServ press releases (June 15, 2003), at *(www.truserv.com.)*

CHAPTER 7

A Supersonic Project Gets Off the Ground/"We're Using a Lot of Neat Stuff" Bill Breen, "High Stakes, Big Bets," *Fast Company*, April 2002, 66–78; William H. Miller, "Reaching New Heights," *Industry Week*, February 2002, 61–62; Norm Alster, "Managing a Mega Project," *Electronic Business*, February 2002, 47–49; Chuck Moozakis, "Web Powers Fighter Project—Linking All the Contractors in Real Time Would Have Been Impossible without the Web, Says Northrop's Dave Torchia," *Internetweek*, November 12, 2001, 1, 49; Steve Konicki, "Collaboration is Cornerstone of $19 billion Defense Contract," *Informationweek*, November 12, 2001, 30; James Dao with Laura M. Holson, "Lockheed Wins $200 Billion Deal for Fighter Jet," *New York Times*, October 21, 2001, A1, A9; Holson, "Pushing Limits, Finding None," *New York Times*, November 1, 2001, C1, C6; Edward H. Phillips, "LockMart Bracing for JSF Transition Phase," *Aviation Space & Space Technology*, November 19, 2001, 86; Faith Keenan and Spencer E. Ante, "The New Teamwork," *BusinessWeek Online*, February 18, 2002. **Entrepreneurship and New Ventures: *One Businessperson's Trash Is Another's New Venture*** "Compost Facility Process" (February 8, 2003), at *(www. jepsonprairieorganics.com)*; "Food Scraps to Fine Wine," *fashionwindows. com* (January 9, 2003), at *(www. fashionwindows.com)*; "Norcal Waste Systems Inc.," *Hoover's Online* (February 8, 2003), at *(www.hoovers.com.)*

CHAPTER 8

From Hard Bargains to Hard Times/Time Out on the Labor Front David Leonhardt, "Did Pay Incentives Cut Both Ways?" *New York Times*, April 7, 2002, BU1–3; Dean Foust and Michelle Conlin, "A Smarter Squeeze?" *Business Week*, December 31, 2001, 42–44; John Strauss, "Agency Workers Mull Pay Cut for Time Off," *Indianapolis Star*, March 11, 2002; Rick Perera, "Siemens Offers Workers 'Time-Outs' to Save Cash," *The Industry Standard*, August 31, 2001; Tischelle George, "Bye-Bye, Employee Perks," *Information Week*, October 15, 2001. **Entrepreneurship and New Ventures: *The Guru of Fun Takes a Meeting with the V.P. of Buzz*** Eric

Wahlgren, "Online Extra: Goodbye, 'Guru of Fun,'" *Business Week*, February 6, 2003, pp. 74–77; Lee Clifford, "You Get Paid to Do What?" *Fortune*, January 20, 2003, pp. 106–108. **Figure 8.3** *The Wall Street Journal Almanac 1999*, 226. Reprinted by Permission of Dow Jones Inc. via Copyright Clearance Center Inc. © 1999 Dow Jones and Co. Inc. All rights reserved. **Figure 8.4(a)** Adapted from David Whitford, "Labor's Lost Chance," *Fortune*, September 28, 1998, 180. **Figure 8.4(b)** Dan Seligman, "Driving the AFL-CIO Crazy," *Forbes*, November 1, 1999, 106. Data from Leo Troy and Neil Sheflin, *Union Sourcebook* (1985) and Barry T. Hirsch and David A. MacPherson, *Union Membership and Earnings Data Book* (1999).

CHAPTER 9

Bringing the Bounty Back to P&G/Turning the Tide A.G. Lafley, "Letter to Shareholders," Procter & Gamble, *2002 Annual Report: "A Healthy Gamble," Time*, September 16, 2002, pp. 46–48; Katrina Booker, "The Un-CEO," *Fortune*, September 16, 2002, pp. 88–96; Robert Berner, "Procter & Gamble's Renovator-in-Chief," *Business Week*, December 11, 2002, pp. 98–100; Berner, "The Best and Worst Managers: A.G. Lafley, Procter & Gamble," *Business Week*, January 13, 2003, p. 67. **Figure 9.1** A.H. Maslow, *Motivation and Personality*, 2nd ed. (Upper Saddle River, NJ: Prentice Hall, 1970). Reprinted by permission of Prentice Hall Inc. **Entrepreneurship and New Ventures:** ***Keeping Pleasant Company*** "Company Profile," "Welcome to Pleasant Company," *American Girl* (June 17, 2003), at *(www.americangirl.com)*; Heesun Wee, "Barbie Is Turning Heads on Wall Street Again," *Business Week*, February 9, 2003, pp. 67–69; Julie Sloane, "How We Got Started: Pleasant Rowland," *Fortune Small Business*, October 1, 2002, pp. 110–114; "Our Toys: American Girl," *Mattel: The World's Premier Toy Brands* (June 20, 2003), at *(www.mattel.com)*; Pleasant Rowland, "A New Twist on Timeless Toys," *Fortune Small Business*, October 1, 2002, pp. 85–89.

CHAPTER 10

Xbox Spots the Market/Microsoft's Great Xpectations. Chris Gaither, "Microsoft Explores a New Territory: Fun," *New York Times*, November 4, 2001, Sec. 3, 1, 7; Leslie P. Norton, "Toy Soldiers," *Barron's*, May 14, 2001, 25–30; Chris Taylor, "The Battle of Seattle," *Time*, May 21, 2001, 58–59; N'Gai Croal, "Game Wars 5.0," *Newsweek*, May 28, 2001, 651; Tobi Elkin, "The X Factor: Microsoft, Sony Prepare

for E3," *Advertising Age*, April 23, 2001, 41; Bill Powell, "Gamemakers Aren't Racking Up Bonus Points," *Fortune*, April 16, 2001, 58; Danny Bradbury, "Home Free," *Communications International*, February 2001, 41; Tobi Elkin, "Gearing Up for Xbox Lunch," *Advertising Age*, November 20, 2000, 161; Arlene Weintraub, "Video Games: The Sky's the Limit," *Business Week*, January 14, 2002, 100–01; "Xbox Strengthens Grip on No. 2 Position and Widens Lead Over GameCube" Microsoft press release (February 19, 2003), at *(www.microsoft.com/presspass)*. **Figure 10.4** Adapted from Jay Heizer and Barry Render, *Operations Management*, 7th ed. (Upper Saddle River, NJ: Prentice Hall, 2004) 157. **Entrepreneurship and New Ventures:** ***The Patriotic Entrepreneur*** Cris Prystay, "Bio-Boost," *Far Eastern Economic Review*, February 6, 2003, p. 38; Charles Bickers, "Medicine Man Returns," *Far Eastern Economic Review*, August 23, 2001, pp. 30–33.

CHAPTER 11

Congested? Stuffed Up? Try DTC/Do We Need Relief from DTC? Paul Jung, "No Free Lunch," *Health Affairs*, March/April 2002, 226–31; Richard Haugh, "DTC Drug Advertising Soars," *Hospitals & Health Networks*, February 2002, 49; Lindsey Tanner, "U.S. Doctors Seek Ban on Prescription Drug Ads," *C-Health* (June 18, 2001), at *(www.canoe.ca)*; Victoria Stagg Elliott, "Questions Swirl Around Drug Ads for Patients," *Amednews.com* (July 9/16, 2001), at *(www.ama-assn.org)*; *USA Weekend*, April 19–21, 2002, 9; Andra Brichacek and Sibyl Shalo, "Location, Location, Location," *Pharmaceutical Executive*, June 2001, 126; Jill Wechsler, "DDMAC Queries Docs, Patients about DTC Advertising," *Pharmaceutical Executive*, March 2002, 38; "National Health Council Backs DTC Advertising," *Medical Marketing and Media*, March 2002, 8; Sandra Levy, "Survey Says: DTC Advertising, R&D Driving Up Drug Costs," *Drug Topics*, April 1, 2002, 56; Kevin Gopal, Consumer Communication in Europe Stalls," *Pharmaceutical Executive*, February 2002, 38; Jackie Judd, "Truth in Advertising?" *ABCNews com* (January 3, 2002), at *(www.abcnews.go.com)*; Kathleen Blankenhorn, Nancy Duckwitz, and Marjorie Sherr, "Power to the People," *Medical Marketing and Media*, August 2001, 66–70. **Figure 11.4** Prodigy, "Small Biz Web Sites on the Rise, Yet Many Owners Slow to Embrace the Internet" (April 13, 2000) at *(www.prodigy.com/pcombusiness/business_content)*. **Figure 11.6** *Advertising Age*, September 24, 2001, s16. **Entrepreneurship and New Ventures:** ***Capitalizing on the VirTus***

of Experience Dorothy Perrin Moore, "Women: Are You Ready to Be Entrepreneurs?" *Business and Economic Review*, January-March 2003, p. 15; "VirTu Inc." (February 2, 2003) at *(www.virtuinc.com)*.

CHAPTER 12

More Productive Than a Speeding Locomotive/Remote Damage Control Larry Adams, "Diagnostics from Afar," *Quality*, November 2001, 26–28; Robert Pool, "If It Ain't Broke, Fix It," *Technology Review*," September 2001, 64–69; Richard Baxter, "Remote M&D Leverages Expertise," *Power*, March 20, 2002, 44–52; Jim Mele, "Diagnostics on the Fly," *Fleet Owner*, September 2001, 73–78; Chuck Moozakis, "Planes, Trains, Autos, Monitored from Afar," *Internetweek*, March 12, 2001 1, 70; "Working on the Railroad: A Talk with John Krenicki," *Business Week*, April 29, 2002, 28b. **Figure 12.3** Adapted from Kenneth C. Laudon and Jane P. Laudon, *Essentials of Management Information Systems: Managing the Digital Firm*, 5th ed. (Upper Saddle River, NJ: Prentice Hall, 2003) 39. **Entrepreneurship and New Ventures:** ***When to Put Your Incubator on Life Support*** Marc Gunther, "They All Want a Piece of Bill Gross," *Fortune*, November 11, 2002, pp. 139–44; Patty Enrado, "Here Comes the Lynch Mob," *Upside*, June 2002, p. 15; Seth Lubove, "The Final Act," *Forbes*, March 4, 2002, p. 44; Christopher Palmeri and Linda Himelstein, "The Bloom is Off Idealab," *Business Week*, December 31, 2001, p. 10; Joseph Nocera, "Bill Gross Blew through $800 Million in 8 Months (and He's Got Nothing to Show for It). Why is he Still Smiling?" *Fortune*, March 5, 2001, pp. 81–83.

CHAPTER 13

Humpty-Dumpty Time at Arthur Andersen/Is Anybody Holding Auditors Accountable? John A. Byrne, "Fall from Grace," *Business Week*, August 12, 2002, 50–56; Kurt Eichenwald, "Andersen Witnesses Defend Intent of Shredding," *New York Times*, June 1, 2002, C1, C2; Eichenwald, "Andersen Guilty in Effort to Block Inquiry on Enron," *New York Times*, June 16, 2002, 1, 20; Eichenwald, "Andersen Trial Yields Evidence in Enron's Fall," *New York Times*, June 17, 2002, A1, A14; Mark M. Meinaro and Parija Bhatnagar, "Andersen Loses More Partners, Key Clients," *USA Today* (May 21, 2002), at *(www.usatoday.com)*; Alex Berenson and Jonathan D. Glater, "A Tattered Andersen Fights for Its Future," The New York Times, January 13, 2002, Sec. 3, 1, 10; Greg Farrell, "Arthur Andersen Fined $7 Million by SEC for Audits," *USA Today*

(June 19, 2001), at *(www.usatoday.com)*; Edward Iwata, "Andersen to Pay $217M in Baptist Foundation Case," *USA Today* (March 1, 2002), at *(www.usatoday. com)*. **Figure 13.1** Adapted from "CPA Vision Project: 2011 and Beyond" (September 24, 2002) at *(www.cpavision.org/ final_report)* **Tables 13.1 & 13.2** Adapted from "CPA Vision Project: 2011 and Beyond" (September 24, 2002) at *(www.cpavision.org/final_report)* **Entrepreneurship and New Ventures:** *How Can You Account for a Good Beer?* "Brew Tour Update Form," *The Real Beer Page* (February 14, 2003), at *(www.realbeer.com)*; "Black Oak Nut Brown Ale," *Beer Advocate.com* (February 14, 2003), at *(www.beeradvocate.com)*; Stephen Beaumont, "Lament for a Brewpub—February 2003," *Stephen Beaumont's World of Beer* (February 14, 2003), at *(www.worldofbeer.com)*; "Brewery Profile," *The Bar Towel* (February 14, 2003), at *(www.bartowel.com/ breweries/blackoak.phtml)*; John Cooper, "A Pint of Success," *CMA Management*, December 1999/January 2000, pp 44–46.

CHAPTER 14

Argentines No Longer Bank on the Peso/There's No Accounting for Financial Systems Associated Press, "Argentina Devalues Peso," *Columbia Daily Tribune*, January 7, 2002, 2B; Pamela Druckerman, "Telecom Argentina Plans to Suspend Debt Payments," *Wall Street Journal*, April 3, 2002, A16; "Argentina Bank Chief Quits," *CNNMoney* (January 18, 2002), at *(www.cnnfn.com)*; "Argentina Gets Reprieve," *CNNMoney* (January 17, 2002), at *(www.cnnfn.com)*; "Citigroup 4Q Profit Rises," *CNNMoney* (January 17, 2002), at *(www.cnnfn.com)*; "Peso Plan Encourages IMF," *CNNMoney* (January 15, 2002), at *(www.cnnfn.com)*; "Argentina's Currency Test," *CNNMoney* (January 11, 2002), at *(www.cnnfn.com)*; "Argentina Deepens Bank Curbs," *CNNMoney* (January 10, 2002), at *(www.cnnfn.com)*; "Argentina Limits Cash Bank Withdrawals," *USA TODAY* (December 3, 2001), at *(www.usatoday)*. **Figure 14.1** Data compiled from Federal Reserve Board of Governors (July 20, 2002) at *(www.stls.frb. org/fred/data/monetary)*. **Entrepreneurship and New Ventures:** *"Your Check Is Not in the Mail"* Scott Van Camp, "Know Thy Customer's Customer," *Adweek Magazine's Technology Marketing*, September 2002, pp. 26–28; Jeffrey Kutler, "The Online Finance 40," *Institutional Investor*, March 2002, pp. 144–50; Michael Vizard, "Getting Top Billing," *InfoWorld*, June 24/July 1, 2002, p. 58; Amalia D. Pathenios, "E-Billing All the Way," *Telephony*, June 25, 2001, p. 22; *CheckFree Corp.* (February 17, 2003), at *(www.checkfree.*

com); "In the Trench Innovator," *The IndUS Entrepreneurs* (February 17, 2003), at *(www.tie-atlanta.org)*.

CHAPTER 15

The Street Hits the Wall/Bearing Up Justin Lahart, "The Crash of 2002," *CNNMoney* (July 19, 2002), at *(www. cnnfn.com)*; "We All Got Burned—What Now?" *CNNMoney* (July 19, 2002), at *(www.cnnfn.com)*; "Dow Plunges Below Its Post-Terrorist Attack Low," *USATODAY. com* (July 19, 2002), at *(www.usatoday. com)*. **Figure 15.1** "Yahoo Inc (YHOO)/ Wal-Mart Stores Inc (WMT)," *Quicken. com* (July 13, 2002), at *(www.quicken. com/investments/charts)*. **Figure 15.2** Leah Nathans Spiro and Edward C. Baig, "Who Needs a Broker?" *Business Week*, February 22, 1999, 113–161. **Entrepreneurship and New Ventures:** *The Personality of a Risk Taker* Tom Stein, "Every Step You Take, LPs Will Be Watching You," *Venture Capital Journal*, January 1, 2003, p. 1; Yasmine Chinwala, "US Survey Shows Gender Gap," *eFinancial News* (February 25, 2002), at *(www.marcusventures.com/ financialnews.html)*; Alison Maitland, "An Idea From the Ladies Room," *FT.com/Financial Times* (February 2, 2003), at *(www.marcusventures. com/FT.html)*. **Figure 15.5** Data from *Wall Street Journal*. **Figure 15.6** Nasdaq, "Market Performance & Highlights: Section 3," *Nasdaq.com* (June 23, 2000), at *(www.nasdaq.com/about/ NBW2000Sec3.pdf)*.

■ CARTOON, PHOTO, AND SCREEN CREDITS

CHAPTER 1

Pages 3/27: New York Times Pictures. Page 8: Kelly Guenther. Page 10: Gregory Foster Photography. Page 16: New York Times Pictures. Page 25: Travis Bell. Page 26: Getty Images, Inc – Liaison. Page 5: © The New Yorker Collection 1990 Joseph Mirachi from cartoonbank.com. All Rights Reserved.

CHAPTER 2

Page 35/62: The Patrick McMullan Company, Inc. Page 39 (left): New York Times Pictures. Page 39 (right): New York Times Pictures. Page 47: SIPA Press. Page 48: New York Times Pictures. Page 50: AP/Wide World Photos. Page 55: Getty Images, Inc – Liaison. Page 56: Corbis/ SABA Press Photos, Inc., © Greg Smith/ Corbis SABA. Page 43: © The New Yorker

Collection 1997 Frank Cotham from cartoonbank.com. All Rights Reserved.

CHAPTER 3

Page 69/93: Corbis/SABA Press Photos, Inc., © David Butow/CORBIS SABA. Page 73: Norman Y. Lono, Photography by NORMAN Y. LONO. Page 78: New York Times Pictures. Page 80: Tom Strattman. Page 91: New York Times Pictures. Page 79: © The New Yorker Collection 1988 Robert Weber from cartoonbank.com. All Rights Reserved.

CHAPTER 4

Page 101/125: AP/Wide World Photos. Page 105: Namas Bhojani. Page 106: New York Times Pictures. Page 122: Getty Images/Time Life Pictures. Page 123: AP/ Wide World Photos. Page 115: © The New Yorker Collection 2001 Robert Weber from cartoonbank.com. All Rights Reserved.

CHAPTER 5

Page 133/157: Yellow Corporation. Page 144: Katie Murray Photographer. Page 146: Corbis/SABA Press Photos, Inc. Page 149: Business Week. Page 153: Kistone Photography. Page 155: ZUMA Press. Page 151: © The New Yorker Collection 1993 Mike Twohy from cartoonbank.com. All Rights Reserved.

CHAPTER 6

Page 165/187: Jim Whitmer Photography. Page 170: Robert Wright Photography. Page 171: Mark Richards. Page 175: Vincent Prado. Page 184: Bernd Auers. Page 169: © The New Yorker Collection 1991 Charles Barsotti from cartoonbank.com. All Rights Reserved.

CHAPTER 7

Page 193/219: Lockheed Martin. Page 196: David Hartung. Page 200: Diane L. Chrisman. Page 206: Regina Maria Anzenberger. Page 211: LTI New York. Page 218: Brownie Harris Photography. Page 213: © 2003 Aaron Bacall from cartoonbank.com. All rights reserved.

CHAPTER 8

Page 227/252: Getty Images Inc. - Hulton Archive Photos. Page 233: Robin Nelson. Page 237: Alex Brandon. Page 247: Alan Levenson. Page 240: © The New Yorker Collection from cartoonbank.com. All Rights Reserved.

CHAPTER 9

Page 259/282: AP/Wide World Photos. Page 261: Corbis/SABA Press Photos, Inc. Page 262: New York Times Pictures, James Estrin/The New York Times. Page 272: Corbis/SABA Press Photos, Inc. Page 276: Alex Brandon. Page 281: Randi Lynn Beach. Page 271: © The New Yorker Collection from cartoonbank.com. All Rights Reserved.

CHAPTER 10

Page 289/315: Chuck Fishman. Page 294: Getty Images, Inc – Liaison. Page 295: New York Times Pictures, Chester Higgins/The New York Times. Page 299: New York Times Pictures, Shane Young/The New York Times. Page 307: Jill Connelly. Page 312: AP/Wide World Photos. Page 297: © The New Yorker Collection 1992 Bernard Schoenbaum from cartoonbank.com. All rights reserved.

CHAPTER 11

Page 323/348: The Image Works. Page 326: New York Times Pictures. Page 334: Jim West. Page 336: New York Times Pictures. Page 340: Tova R. Baruch. Page 347 (left): Agence France-Presse AFP. Page 347 (right): Knutson Photography Inc. Page 326: © The New Yorker Collection 1991 Jack Ziegler from cartoonbank.com. All rights reserved.

CHAPTER 12

Page 357/377: AP/Wide World Photos. Page 362 (top): Richard B. Levine/Frances M. Roberts, Frances M. Roberts. Page 362 (bottom): Richard B. Levine/Frances M. Roberts, Frances M. Roberts. Page 371: Jonathan Saunders. Page 375: Photofest. Page 361: © The New Yorker Collection 1994 Danny Shanahan from cartoonbank.com. All rights reserved.

CHAPTER 13

Page 385/409: AP/Wide World Photos. Page 389: AP/Wide World Photos. Page 394: AP/Wide World Photos, AP/Wide World Photos. Page 398: Contact Press Images Inc. Page 399: PhotoEdit. Page 407: Getty Images Inc. - Hulton Archive Photos. Page 407: © The New Yorker Collection 1991 Robert Weber from cartoonbank.com. All rights reserved.

CHAPTER 14

Page 419/441: CORBIS BETTMANN. Page 422: New York Times Pictures. Page 426: Larry Smith. Page 429: Corbis/SABA Press Photos, Inc. Page 435: Standing Don. Page 428: © The New Yorker Collection 1997 J.B. Handelsman from cartoonbank.com. All rights reserved.

CHAPTER 15

Page 449/473: AP/Wide World Photos. Page 452: Roy Inman. Page 453: Michael Dwyer. Page 457: New York Times Pictures. Page 470: Robert Wright Photography. Page 454: © The New Yorker Collection 2000 P.C. Vey from cartoonbank.com. All rights reserved.

GLOSSARY

absolute advantage The ability to produce something more efficiently than any other country can [110]

accommodative stance Approach to social responsibility by which a company, if specifically asked to do so, exceeds legal minimums in its commitments to groups and individuals in its social environment [59]

account payable (or payable) Current liability consisting of bills owed to suppliers, plus wages and taxes due within the upcoming year [396]

account receivable (or receivable) Amount due from a customer who has purchased goods on credit [395]

accountability Liability of subordinates for accomplishing tasks assigned by managers [173]

accounting Comprehensive system for collecting, analyzing, and communicating financial information [377]

accounting information system (AIS) Organized means by which financial information is identified, measured, recorded, and retained for use in accounting statements and management reports [386]

acquisition The purchase of one company by another [92]

activity ratio Financial ratio for evaluating management's use of a firm's assets [403]

advertising Promotional tool consisting of paid, nonpersonal communication used by an identified sponsor to inform an audience about a product [342]

advertising media Variety of communication devices for carrying a seller's message to potential customers [343]

affirmative action plan Practice of recruiting qualified employees belonging to racial, gender, or ethnic groups who are underrepresented in an organization [239]

agent Individual or organization acting for, and in the name of, another party [502]

aggregate output Total quantity of goods and services produced by an economic system during a given period [18]

analytic process Production process in which resources are broken down into components to create finished products [197]

apparent authority Agent's authority, based on the principal's compliance, to bind a principal to a certain course of action [502]

appellate court Court that reviews case records of trials whose findings have been appealed [498]

application program Software (such as Word for Windows) that processes data according to a user's special needs [373]

artificial intelligence (AI) Computer-system application that imitates human behavior by performing physical tasks, using thought processes, sensing, and learning [372]

assembly line Product layout in which a product moves step-by-step through a plant on conveyor belts or other equipment until it is completed [204]

asset Any economic resource expected to benefit a firm or an individual who owns it [389]

asset allocation Relative amount of funds invested in (or allocated to) each of several investment alternatives [463]

audit Systematic examination of a company's accounting system to determine whether its financial reports fairly represent its operations [388]

authority Power to make the decisions necessary to complete a task [173]

autocratic style Managerial style in which managers generally issue orders and expect them to be obeyed without question [278]

automated teller machine (ATM) Electronic machine that allows customers to conduct account-related activities 24 hours a day, 7 days a week [429]

balance of payments Flow of all money into or out of a country [112]

balance of trade Economic value of all products a country exports minus the economic value of all products it imports [111]

balance sheet Financial statement detailing a firm's assets, liabilities, and owners' equity [394]

banker's acceptance Bank promise, issued for a buyer, to pay a designated firm a specified amount at a future date [429]

bankruptcy Permission granted by the courts to individuals and organizations not to pay some or all of their debts [503]

bargain retailer   Retailer carrying a wide range of products at bargain prices [336]

bear market   Period of falling stock prices [467]

bearer (or coupon) bond   Bond requiring the holder to clip and submit a coupon to receive an interest payment [461]

benefits   Compensation other than wages and salaries [235]

bill of materials   Production control tool that specifies the necessary ingredients of a product, the order in which they should be combined, and how many of each are needed to make one batch [211]

blue-chip stock   Common stock issued by a well-established company with a sound financial history and a stable pattern of dividend payouts [452]

blue-sky laws   Laws requiring securities dealers to be licensed and registered with the states in which they do business [472]

board of directors   Governing body of a corporation that reports to its shareholders and delegates power to run its day-to-day operations while remaining responsible for sustaining its assets [91]

bond   Security through which an issuer promises to pay the buyer a certain amount of money by a specified future date [460]

bonus   Individual performance incentive in the form of a special payment made over and above the employee's salary [236]

book value   Value of a common stock expressed as total owners' equity divided by the number of shares of stock [451]

bookkeeping   Recording of accounting transactions [386]

boycott   Labor action in which workers refuse to buy the products of a targeted employer [251]

branch office   Foreign office set up by an international or multinational firm [119]

brand awareness   Extent to which a brand name comes to mind when the consumer considers a particular product category [309]

brand competition   Competitive marketing that appeals to consumer perceptions of similar products [294]

brand loyalty   Pattern of regular consumer purchasing based on satisfaction with a product [299]

branding   Process of using symbols to communicate the qualities of a product made by a particular producer [308]

breakeven analysis   For a particular selling price, assessment of the seller's costs versus revenues at various sales volumes [327]

breakeven point   Sales volume at which the seller's total revenue from sales equals total costs (variable and fixed) with neither profit nor loss [327]

broker   Individual or organization who receives and executes buy-and-sell orders on behalf of other people in return for commissions [455]

browser   Software supporting the graphics and linking capabilities necessary to navigate the World Wide Web [362]

budget   Detailed statement of estimated receipts and expenditures for a period of time in the future [398]

bull market   Period of rising stock prices [467]

business   An organization that provides goods or services to earn profits [4]

business continuation agreement   Special form of business insurance whereby owners arrange to buy the interests of deceased associates from their heirs [493]

business cycle   Pattern of short-term ups and downs (expansions and contractions) in an economy [18]

business ethics   Ethical or unethical behaviors by a manager or employer of an organization [37]

business interruption insurance   Insurance covering income lost during times when a company is unable to conduct business [492]

business plan   Document in which the entrepreneur summarizes her or his business strategy for the proposed new venture and how that strategy will be implemented [75]

business practice law   Law or regulation governing business practices in given countries [124]

business process reengineering   Redesigning of business processes to improve quality, performance, and customer service [215]

business (or competitive) strategy   Strategy, at the business-unit or product-line level, focusing on a firm's competitive position [136]

cafeteria benefit plan   Benefit plan that sets limits on benefits per employee, each of whom may choose from a variety of alternative benefits [238]

capacity   In operations management, amount of a product that a company can produce under normal working conditions [201]

capacity   In law, competence required of individuals entering into a binding contract [498]

capital   The funds needed to create and operate a business enterprise [6]

capital item   Expensive, long-lasting, infrequently purchased industrial product such as a building [305]

capital structure   Relative mix of a firm's debt and equity financing [487]

capitalism   Market economy that provides for private ownership of production and encourages entrepreneurship by offering profits as an incentive [9]

cartel   Association of producers whose purpose is to control supply and prices [124]

cash-flow management   Management of cash inflows and outflows to ensure adequate funds for purchases and the productive use of excess funds [481]

catalog showroom   Bargain retailer in which customers place orders for catalog items to be picked up at on-premises warehouses [336]

cellular layout Spatial arrangement of production facilities designed to move families of products through similar flow paths [204]

centralized organization Organization in which most decision-making authority is held by upper-level management [174]

certified management accountant (CMA) Professional recognition of management accounting qualifications awarded by the Institute of Management Accountants [389]

certified public accountant (CPA) Accountant licensed by the state and offering services to the public [387]

chain of command Reporting relationships within a company [167]

check Demand deposit order instructing a bank to pay a given sum to a specified payee [422]

check kiting Illegal practice of writing checks against money that has not yet been credited at the bank on which the checks are drawn [57]

chief executive officer (CEO) Top manager hired by the board of directors to run a corporation [91]

classical theory of motivation Theory holding that workers are motivated solely by money [264]

client-server network Information-technology system consisting of clients (users) that are electronically linked to share network resources provided by a server, such as a host computer [376]

closely held (or private) corporation Corporation whose stock is held by only a few people and is not available for sale to the general public [89]

collateral Borrower-pledged legal asset that may be seized by lenders in case of nonpayment [484]

collective bargaining Process by which labor and management negotiate conditions of employment for union-represented workers [245]

collusion Illegal agreement between two or more companies to commit a wrongful act [54]

commercial bank Federal- or state-chartered financial institution accepting deposits that it uses to make loans and earn profits [423]

commercial paper Short-term securities, or notes, containing a borrower's promise to pay [484]

committee and team authority Authority granted to committees or work teams involved in a firm's daily operations [178]

common law Body of decisions handed down by courts ruling on individual cases [495]

common stock Stock that pays dividends and guarantees corporate voting rights but offers last claims over assets [91]

comparative advantage The ability to produce some products more efficiently than others [110]

compensation system Set of rewards that organizations provide to individuals in return for their willingness to perform various jobs and tasks within the organization [234]

compensatory damages Monetary payments intended to redress injury actually suffered because of a tort [499]

competition Vying among businesses for the same resources or customers [16]

competitive product analysis Process by which a company analyzes a competitor's products to identify desirable improvements [213]

compulsory arbitration Method of resolving a labor dispute in which both parties are legally required to accept the judgment of a neutral party [251]

computer graphics program Applications program that converts numeric and character data into pictorial information such as graphs and charts [374]

computer network All the computer and information technology devices that, by working together, drive the flow of digital information throughout a system [372]

computer-aided design (CAD) Computer-based electronic technology that assists in designing products by simulating a real product and displaying it in three-dimensional graphics [370]

computer-aided manufacturing (CAM) Computer system used to design and control equipment needed in the manufacturing process [370]

conceptual skills Abilities to think in the abstract, diagnose and analyze different situations, and see beyond the present situation [151]

consideration Any item of value exchanged between parties to create a valid contract [498]

consumer behavior Various facets of the decision process by which customers come to purchase and consume products [298]

consumer goods Products purchased by consumers for personal use [291]

consumer price index (CPI) Measure of the prices of typical products purchased by consumers living in urban areas [22]

consumerism Form of social activism dedicated to protecting the rights of consumers in their dealings with businesses [53]

contingency approach to managerial style Approach to managerial style holding that the appropriate behavior in any situation is dependent (contingent) on the unique elements of that situation [279]

contingency planning Identifying aspects of a business or its environment that might entail changes in strategy [142]

contingent worker Employee hired on something other than a full-time basis to supplement an organization's permanent workforce [243]

contract Agreement between two or more parties enforceable in court [498]

control chart Process control method that plots test sample results on a diagram to determine when a process is beginning to depart from normal operating conditions [214]

controller Person who manages all of a firm's accounting activities (chief accounting officer) [386]

controlling   Management process of monitoring an organization's performance to ensure that it is meeting its goals [146]

convenience good/service Inexpensive product purchased and consumed rapidly and regularly [304]

convenience store   Retail store offering easy accessibility, extended hours, and fast service [337]

copyright   Exclusive ownership right belonging to the creator of a book, article, design, illustration, photo, film, or musical work [501]

corporate bond   Bond issued by a company as a source of long-term funding [461]

corporate culture   The shared experiences, stories, beliefs, and norms that characterize an organization [154]

corporate governance   Roles of shareholders, directors, and other managers in corporate decision making [90]

corporate strategy   Strategy for determining the firm's overall attitude toward growth and the way it will manage its businesses or product lines [136]

corporation   Business that is legally considered an entity separate from its owners and is liable for its own debts; owners' liability extends to the limits of their investments [88]

cost of goods sold   Total cost of obtaining materials for making the products sold by a firm during the year [397]

cost-of-living adjustment (COLA)   Labor contract clause tying future raises to changes in consumer purchasing power [246]

coupon   Sales promotion technique in which a certificate is issued entitling the buyer to a reduced price [346]

creative selling   Personal selling task in which salespeople try to persuade buyers to purchase products by providing information about their benefits [345]

credit union   Financial institution that accepts deposits from, and

makes loans to, only its members, usually employees of a particular organization [427]

crisis management Organization's methods for dealing with emergencies [143]

cumulative preferred stock Preferred stock on which dividends not paid in the past must be paid to stockholders before dividends can be paid to common stockholders [454]

currency   Government-issued paper money and metal coins [422]

current asset   Asset that can or will be converted into cash within the following year [394]

current liability   Debt that must be paid within the year [396]

current ratio   Solvency ratio that determines a firm's creditworthiness by measuring its ability to pay current liabilities [404]

customer departmentalization Departmentalization according to types of customers likely to buy a given product [170]

cybermall   Collection of virtual storefronts (business Web sites) representing a variety of products and product lines on the Internet [338]

data   Raw facts and figures [359]

data communication network Global network (such as the Internet) that permits users to send electronic messages and information quickly and economically [359]

data mining   Application of electronic technologies for searching, sifting, and reorganizing data in order to collect marketing information and target products in the marketplace [301]

data warehousing   Process of collecting, storing, and retrieving data in electronic files [301]

database   Centralized, organized collection of related data [373]

database management program   Applications program for creating, storing, searching, and manipulating an organized collection of data [374]

debenture   Unsecured bond for which no specific property is pledged as security [461]

debit card   Plastic card that allows an individual to transfer money between accounts [437]

debt   A firm's total liabilities [404]

debt financing   Long-term borrowing from sources outside a company [485]

debt ratio   Solvency ratio measuring a firm's ability to meet its long-term debts [404]

debt-to-owners' equity ratio (or debt-to-equity ratio) Solvency ratio describing the extent to which a firm is financed through borrowing [404]

decentralized organization Organization in which a great deal of decision-making authority is delegated to levels of management at points below the top [174]

decision support system (DSS) Interactive computer-based system that locates and presents information needed to support decision making [371]

decision-making skills   Skills in defining problems and selecting the best courses of action [151]

defensive stance   Approach to social responsibility by which a company meets only minimum legal requirements in its commitments to groups and individuals in its social environment [59]

delegation   Assignment of a task, responsibility, or authority by a manager to a subordinate [173]

demand   The willingness and ability of buyers to purchase a good or service [12]

demand and supply schedule Assessment of the relationships between different levels of demand and supply at different price levels [12]

demand curve   Graph showing how many units of a product will be demanded (bought) at different prices [12]

demand deposit   Bank account funds that may be withdrawn at any time [422]

democratic style Managerial style in which managers generally ask for input from subordinates but retain final decision-making power [279]

demographic variables Characteristics of populations that may be considered in developing a segmentation strategy [297]

department store Large product line retailer characterized by organization into specialized departments [335]

departmentalization Process of grouping jobs into logical units [169]

depreciation Process of distributing the cost of an asset over its life [396]

depression Particularly severe and long-lasting recession [24]

deregulation Elimination of rules that restrict business activity [497]

desktop publishing Process of combining word-processing and graphics capability to produce virtually typeset-quality text from personal computers [374]

direct channel Distribution channel in which a product travels from producer to consumer without intermediaries [330]

direct mail Advertising medium in which messages are mailed directly to consumers' homes or places of business [343]

directing Management process of guiding and motivating employees to meet an organization's objectives [145]

direct-response retailing Nonstore retailing by direct interaction with customers to inform them of products and to receive sales orders [337]

disability income insurance Insurance providing continuous income when disability keeps the insured from gainful employment [492]

discount Price reduction offered as an incentive to purchase [330]

discount house Bargain retailer that generates large sales volume by

offering goods at substantial price reductions [336]

discount rate Interest rate at which member banks can borrow money from the Federal Reserve [435]

distribution Part of the marketing mix concerned with getting products from producers to consumers [295]

distribution channel Network of interdependent companies through which a product passes from producer to end user [330]

distribution mix The combination of distribution channels by which a firm gets its products to end users [331]

diversification Purchase of several different kinds of investments rather than just one [463]

divestiture Strategy whereby a firm sells one or more of its business units [92]

division Department that resembles a separate business in producing and marketing its own products [180]

divisional organization Organizational structure in which corporate divisions operate as autonomous businesses under the larger corporate umbrella [179]

double taxation Situation in which taxes may be payable both by a corporation on its profits and by shareholders on dividend incomes [89]

double-entry accounting system Bookkeeping system that balances the accounting equation by recording the dual effects of every financial transaction [393]

Dow Jones Industrial Average (DJIA) Market index based on the prices of 30 of the largest industrial firms listed on the NYSE [468]

dumping Practice of selling a product abroad for less than the cost of production [124]

earnings per share Profitability ratio measuring the size of the dividend that a firm can pay shareholders [405]

e-cash Electronic money that moves between consumers and businesses via digital electronic transmissions [438]

e-catalog Nonstore retailing in which the Internet is used to display products [337]

economic strike Strike usually triggered by stalemate over one or more mandatory bargaining items [250]

economic system A nation's system for allocating its resources among its citizens [6]

e-intermediary Internet distribution channel member that assists in moving products through to customers or that collects information about various sellers to be presented in convenient format for Internet customers [334]

electronic conferencing Computer-based system that allows people to communicate simultaneously from different locations via software or telephone [360]

electronic funds transfer (EFT) Communication of fund-transfer information over wire, cable, or microwave [430]

electronic information technologies (EIT) Information-systems applications, based on telecommunications technologies, that use networks of appliances or devices to communicate information by electronic means [361]

electronic retailing Nonstore retailing in which information about the seller's products and services is connected to consumers' computers, allowing consumers to receive the information and purchase the products in the home [337]

electronic spreadsheet Applications program with a row-and-column format that allows users to store, manipulate, and compare numeric data [373]

electronic storefront Commercial Web site in which customers gather information about products, buying opportunities, placing orders, and paying for purchases [338]

embargo Government order banning exportation and/or importation of a particular product or all products from a particular country [122]

eminent domain Principle that the government may claim private land for public use by buying it at a fair price [502]

emotional motives Reasons for purchasing a product that are based on nonobjective factors [301]

employee information system (skills inventory) Computerized system containing information on each employee's education, skills, work experiences, and career aspirations [231]

employee stock ownership plan (ESOP) Arrangement in which a corporation holds its own stock in trust for its employees, who gradually receive ownership of the stock and control its voting rights [92]

employment-at-will Principle, increasingly modified by legislation and judicial decision, that organizations should be able to retain or dismiss employees at their discretion [241]

enterprise resource planning (ERP) Large information system for integrating all the activities of a company's business units [366]

entrepreneur An individual who accepts the risks and opportunities involved in creating and operating a new business venture [6, 74]

environmental analysis Process of scanning the business environment for threats and opportunities [140]

equal employment opportunity Legally mandated nondiscrimination in employment on the basis of race, creed, sex, or national origin [238]

Equal Employment Opportunity Commission (EEOC) Federal agency enforcing several discrimination-related laws [239]

equity financing Use of common stock and/or retained earnings to raise long-term funding [486]

equity theory Theory of motivation holding that people evaluate their treatment by employers relative to the treatment of others [267]

ethical behavior Behavior conforming to generally accepted social norms concerning beneficial and harmful actions [37]

ethics Beliefs about what is right and wrong or good and bad in actions that affect others [37]

euro A common currency shared among most of the members of the European Union (excluding Denmark, Sweden, and the United Kingdom) [112]

European Union (EU) Agreement among major Western European nations to eliminate or make uniform most trade barriers affecting group members [105, 505]

exchange rate Rate at which the currency of one nation can be exchanged for the currency of another country [112]

executive support system (ESS) Quick-reference information-system application designed specially for instant access by upper-level managers [371]

expectancy theory Theory of motivation holding that people are motivated to work toward rewards that they want and that they believe they have a reasonable chance of obtaining [266]

expense item Industrial product purchased and consumed rapidly and regularly for daily operations [305]

expert system Form of artificial intelligence that attempts to imitate the behavior of human experts in a particular field [372]

export Product made or grown domestically but shipped and sold abroad [102]

exporter Firm that distributes and sells products to one or more foreign countries [118]

express authority Agent's authority, derived from written agreement, to bind a principal to a certain course of action [502]

express warranty Warranty whose terms are specifically stated by the seller [503]

external environment Outside factors that influence marketing programs by posing opportunities or threats [292]

external failures Reducible costs incurred after defective products have left a plant [215]

external recruiting Attracting persons outside the organization to apply for jobs [232]

extranet Internet allowing outsiders access to a firm's internal information system [364]

factors of production Resources used in the production of goods and services—labor, capital, entrepreneurs, physical resources, and information resources [6]

factory outlet Bargain retailer owned by the manufacturer whose products it sells [336]

feature Tangible quality that a company builds into a product [302]

Federal Deposit Insurance Corporation (FDIC) Federal agency that guarantees the safety of all deposits up to $100,000 in the financial institutions that it insures [430]

Federal Reserve System (the Fed) Central bank of the United States, which acts as the government's bank, serves member commercial banks, and controls the nation's money supply [431]

finance (or corporate finance) Activities concerned with determining a firm's long-term investments, obtaining the funds to pay for them, conducting the firm's everyday, financial activities, and managing the firm's risks [481]

finance company Nondeposit institution that specializes in making loans to businesses and consumers [427]

financial accounting system Field of accounting concerned with external users of a company's financial information [387]

financial manager Manager responsible for planning and

controlling the acquisition and dispersal of a firm's financial resources [481]

financial plan A firm's strategies for reaching some future financial position [482]

financial statement Any of several types of reports summarizing a company's financial status and measuring its financial health [394]

firewall Software and hardware system that prevents outsiders from accessing a company's internal network [364]

first-line manager Manager responsible for supervising the work of employees [148]

fiscal policies Economic policies that determine how the government collects and spends its revenue [24]

fixed asset Asset with long-term use or value, such as land, buildings, and equipment [396]

fixed cost Cost unaffected by the quantity of a product produced or sold [327]

flat organizational structure Characteristic of decentralized companies with relatively few layers of management and relatively wide spans of control [175]

flextime programs Method of increasing job satisfaction by allowing workers to adjust work schedules on a daily or weekly basis [274]

float Total amount of checks written but not yet cleared through the Federal Reserve [433]

follow-up Production control activity for ensuring that production decisions are being implemented [209]

foreign currency exchange rate Value of a nation's currency as determined by market forces [406]

foreign direct investment (FDI) Arrangement in which a firm buys or establishes tangible assets in another country [119]

franchise Arrangement in which a buyer (*franchisee*) purchases the right to sell the good or service of the seller (*franchiser*) [79]

free-rein style Managerial style in which managers typically serve as advisers to subordinates who are allowed to make decisions [279]

functional departmentalization Departmentalization according to groups' functions or activities [171]

functional organization Form of business organization in which authority is determined by the relationships between group functions and activities [179]

functional strategy Strategy by which managers in specific areas decide how best to achieve corporate goals through productivity [137]

gainsharing plan Incentive plan that rewards groups for productivity improvements [237]

Gantt chart Production schedule diagramming the steps in a project and specifying the time required for each [207]

General Agreement on Tariffs and Trade (GATT) International trade agreement to encourage the multilateral reduction or elimination of trade barriers [103, 505]

general (or active) partner Partner who actively manages a firm and who has unlimited liability for its debts [87]

general partnership Business with two or more owners who share in both the operation of the firm and the financial responsibility for its debts [86]

generally accepted accounting principles (GAAP) Accepted rules and procedures governing the content and form of financial reports [388]

geographic departmentalization Departmentalization according to areas served by a business [170]

geographic variables Geographical units that may be considered in developing a segmentation strategy [297]

globalization Process by which the world economy is becoming a single interdependent system [102]

goal Objective that a business hopes and plans to achieve [136]

goods production Activities producing tangible products, such as radios, newspapers, buses, and textbooks [194]

goodwill Amount paid for an existing business above the value of its other assets [396]

government bond Bond issued by the federal government [460]

grapevine Informal communication network that runs through an organization [186]

graphical user interface (GUI) Software that provides a visual display to help users select applications [374]

gross domestic product (GDP) Total value of all goods and services produced within a given period by a national economy through domestic factors of production [19]

gross profit (or gross margin) Revenues obtained from goods sold minus cost of goods sold [397]

group life insurance Insurance underwritten for a group as a whole rather than for each individual in it [492]

groupware Software that connects members of a group for shared e-mail distribution, electronic meetings, appointments, and group writing [360]

hardware Physical components of a computer system [373]

Hawthorne effect Tendency for productivity to increase when workers believe they are receiving special attention from management [264]

health insurance Insurance covering losses resulting from medical and hospital expenses as well as income lost from injury or disease [492]

health maintenance organization (HMO) Organized health care system providing comprehensive care in return for fixed membership fees [493]

hierarchy of human needs model Theory of motivation describing five levels of human needs and arguing that basic needs must be fulfilled before people work to satisfy higher-level needs [265]

high-contact system   Level of customer contact in which the customer is part of the system during service delivery [198]

hostile work environment   Form of sexual harassment deriving from off-color jokes, lewd comments, and so forth [240]

human relations skills   Skills in understanding and getting along with people [150]

human resource management (HRM)   Set of organizational activities directed at attracting, developing, and maintaining an effective workforce [217]

icon   Small image in a GUI that enables users to select applications or functions [374]

implied authority   Agent's authority, derived from business custom, to bind a principal to a certain course of action [502]

implied warranty   Warranty, dictated by law, based on the principle that products should fulfill advertised promises and serve the purposes for which they are manufactured and sold [503]

import   Product made or grown abroad but sold domestically [102]

importer   Firm that buys products in foreign markets and then imports them for resale in its home country [118]

incentive program   Special compensation program designed to motivate high performance [236]

income statement (or profit-and-loss statement)   Financial statement listing a firm's annual revenues and expenses so that a bottom line shows annual profit or loss [396]

independent agent   Foreign individual or organization that agrees to represent an exporter's interests [118]

individual retirement account (IRA)   Tax-deferred pension fund with which wage earners supplement other retirement funds [428]

industrial (business) distribution   Network of channel members involved in the flow of manufactured goods to industrial customers [331]

industrial goods   Products purchased by companies to produce other products [291]

industrial market   Organizational market consisting of firms that buy goods that are either converted into products or used during production [301]

inflation   Occurrence of widespread price increases throughout an economic system [22]

informal organization   Network, unrelated to the firm's formal authority structure, of everyday social interactions among company employees [185]

information   Meaningful, useful interpretation of data [359]

information management   Internal operations for arranging a firm's information resources to support business performance and outcomes [358]

information manager   Manager responsible for designing and implementing systems to gather, organize, and distribute information [347]

information resources   Data and other information used by business [7]

information system (IS)   System for transforming raw data into information that can be used in decision making [358]

input market   Market in which firms buy resources from supplier households [9]

insider trading   Illegal practice of using special knowledge about a firm for profit or gain [57, 472]

institutional investor   Large investor, such as a mutual fund or a pension fund, that purchases large blocks of corporate stock [92]

institutional market   Organizational market consisting of such nongovernmental buyers of goods and services as hospitals, churches, museums, and charitable organizations [302]

insurance company   Nondeposit institution that invests funds collected as premiums charged for insurance coverage [427]

intangible asset   Nonphysical asset, such as a patent or trademark, that has economic value in the form of expected benefit [396]

intangible personal property   Property that cannot be seen but that exists by virtue of written documentation [501]

intellectual property   Property created through a person's creative activities [501]

intentional tort   Tort resulting from the deliberate actions of a party [499]

interactive marketing   Nonstore retailing that uses a Web site to provide real-time sales and customer service [338]

intermediary   Individual or firm that helps to distribute a product [330]

intermediate goal   Goal set for a period of one to five years into the future [138]

internal failures   Reducible costs incurred during production and before bad products leave a plant [214]

internal recruiting   Considering present employees as candidates for openings [231]

international competition   Competitive marketing of domestic products against foreign products [294]

international firm   Firm that conducts a significant portion of its business in foreign countries [118]

international law   Set of cooperative agreements and guidelines established by countries to govern actions of individuals, businesses, and nations [504]

International Monetary Fund (IMF)   United Nations agency consisting of about 150 nations that have combined resources to promote stable exchange rates, provide temporary short-term loans, and serve other purposes [440]

international organizational structures Approaches to organizational structure developed in response to the need to manufacture, purchase, and sell in global markets [181]

Internet Global data communication network serving millions of computers with information on a wide array of topics and providing communication flows among certain private networks [361]

Internet service provider (ISP) Commercial firm that maintains a permanent connection to the Net and sells temporary connections to subscribers [361]

intranet Private network of internal Web sites and other sources of information available to a company's employees [364]

intrapreneuring Process of creating and maintaining the innovation and flexibility of a small-business environment within the confines of a large organization [186]

inventory Materials and goods that are held by a company but that will be sold within the year [483]

inventory control In materials management, receiving, storing, handling, and counting of all raw materials, partly finished goods, and finished goods [210]

inventory turnover ratio Activity ratio measuring the average number of times that inventory is sold and restocked during the year [405]

investment bank Financial institution engaged in issuing and reselling new securities [450]

involuntary bankruptcy Bankruptcy proceedings initiated by the creditors of an indebted individual or organization [503]

ISO 9000 Program certifying that a factory, laboratory, or office has met the quality management standards of the International Organization for Standardization [215]

job analysis Systematic analysis of jobs within an organization [228]

job description Outline of the duties of a job, working conditions, and the tools, materials, and equipment used to perform it [229]

job enrichment Method of increasing job satisfaction by adding one or more motivating factors to job activities [272]

job redesign Method of increasing job satisfaction by designing a more satisfactory fit between workers and their jobs [273]

job satisfaction Degree of enjoyment that people derive from performing their jobs [251]

job specialization The process of identifying the specific jobs that need to be done and designating the people who will perform them [168]

job specification Description of the skills, abilities, and other credentials required by a job [229]

joint venture Strategic alliance in which the collaboration involves joint ownership of the new venture [92]

just-in-time (JIT) production Production method that brings together all materials and parts needed at each production stage at the precise moment they are required [210]

key person insurance Special form of business insurance designed to offset expenses entailed by the loss of key employees [493]

knowledge worker Employee who uses information and knowledge as raw materials and who relies on information technology to design new products or business systems [242, 367]

labor (or human resources) The physical and mental capabilities of people as they contribute to economic production [6]

labor relations Process of dealing with employees who are represented by a union [245]

labor union Group of individuals working together to achieve shared job-related goals, such as higher pay, shorter working hours, more job security, greater benefits, or better working conditions [244]

law of demand Principle that buyers will purchase (demand) more of a product as its price drops and less as its price increases [12]

law of supply Principle that producers will offer (supply) more of a product for sale as its price rises and less as its price drops [12]

laws Codified rules of behavior enforced by a society [495]

leadership Process of motivating others to work to meet specific objectives [275]

lean system Production system designed for smooth production flows that avoid inefficiencies, eliminate unnecessary inventories, and continuously improve production processes [210]

letter of credit Bank promise, issued for a buyer, to pay a designated firm a certain amount of money if specified conditions are met [429]

leverage Ability to finance an investment through borrowed funds [404]

liability Debt owed by a firm to an outside organization or individual [393]

liability insurance Insurance covering losses resulting from damage to people or property when the insured is judged responsible [491]

licensed brand Brand-name product for whose name the seller has purchased the right from an organization or individual [311]

licensing arrangement Arrangement in which firms choose foreign individuals or organizations to manufacture or market their products in another country [119]

life insurance Insurance paying benefits to the policyholder's survivors [492]

limit order Order authorizing the purchase of a stock only if its price is equal to or less than a specified amount [469]

limited liability Legal principle holding investors liable for a firm's debts only to the limits of their personal investments in it [88]

limited liability corporation (LLC) Hybrid of a publicly held corporation and a partnership in which owners are taxed as partners but enjoy the benefits of limited liability [89]

limited partner   Partner who does not share in a firm's management and is liable for its debts only to the limits of said partner's investment [87]

limited partnership   Type of partnership consisting of limited partners and an active or managing partner [87]

line authority   Organizational structure in which authority flows in a direct chain of command from the top of the company to the bottom [177]

line department   Department directly linked to the production and sales of a specific product [177]

line of credit   Standing arrangement in which a lender agrees to make available a specified amount of funds upon the borrower's request [484]

liquidity   Ease with which an asset can be converted into cash [395]

liquidity ratio   Solvency ratio measuring a firm's ability to pay its immediate debts [103]

load fund   Mutual fund in which investors are charged sales commissions when they buy in or sell out [462]

local area network (LAN)   Network of computers and workstations, usually within a company, that are linked together by cable [376]

local content law   Law requiring that products sold in a particular country be at least partly made there [123]

lockout   Management tactic whereby workers are denied access to the employer's workplace [251]

long-term goal   Goal set for an extended time, typically five years or more into the future [138]

long-term liability   Debt that is not due for more than one year [396]

low-contact system   Level of customer contact in which the customer need not be a part of the system to receive the service [199]

M-1   Measure of the money supply that includes only the most liquid (spendable) forms of money [420]

M-2   Measure of the money supply that includes all the components of M-1 plus the forms of money that can be easily converted into spendable form [422]

mail order (or catalog marketing)   Form of nonstore retailing in which customers place orders for catalog merchandise received through the mail [337]

management   Process of planning, organizing, directing, and controlling an organization's resources to achieve its goals [144]

management advisory services   Specialized accounting services to help managers resolve a variety of business problems [388]

management by objectives (MBO)   Set of procedures involving both managers and subordinates in setting goals and evaluating progress [269]

management information system (MIS)   System used for transforming data into information for use in decision making [371]

managerial (or management) accounting system   Field of accounting that serves internal users of a company's financial information [387]

managerial ethics   Standards of behavior that guide individual managers in their work [38]

managerial style   Pattern of behavior that a manager exhibits in dealing with subordinates [277]

margin   Percentage of the total sales price that a buyer must put up to place an order for stock of futures contracts [470]

market   Mechanism for exchange between buyers and sellers of a particular good or service [9]

market economy   Economy in which individuals control production and allocation decisions through supply and demand [8]

market index   Summary of price trends in a specific industry and/or the stock market as a whole [467]

market order   Order to buy or sell a security at the market price prevailing at the time the order is placed [469]

market price (or equilibrium price)   Profit-maximizing price at which the quantity of goods demanded and the quantity of goods supplied are equal [12]

market segmentation   Process of dividing a market into categories of customer types [297]

market share   As a percentage, total of market sales for a specific company or product [325]

market value   Current price of a share of stock in the stock market [451]

marketing   The process of planning and executing the conception, pricing, promotion, and distribution of ideas, goods, and services to create exchanges that satisfy individual and organizational objectives [279]

marketing manager   Manager who plans and implements the marketing activities that result in the transfer of products from producer to consumer [294]

marketing mix   The combination of product, pricing, promotion, and distribution strategies used to market products [294]

marketing plan   Detailed strategy for focusing marketing efforts on consumer needs and wants [294]

markup   Amount added to an item's cost to sell it at a profit [326]

mass-customization   Flexible production process that generates customized products in high volumes at low cost [364]

master production schedule   Schedule showing which products will be produced, when production will take place, and what resources will be used [207]

material requirements planning (MRP)   Production method in which a bill of materials is used to ensure that the right amounts of materials are delivered to the right place at the right time [211]

materials management   Planning, organizing, and controlling the flow of materials from design through distribution of finished goods [209]

matrix structure Organizational structure in which teams are formed and team members report to two or more managers [180]

media mix Combination of advertising media chosen to carry message about a product [343]

mediation Method of resolving a labor dispute in which a third party suggests, but does not impose, a settlement [251]

merchandise inventory Cost of merchandise that has been acquired for sale to customers and is still on hand [395]

merchant wholesaler Independent wholesaler who takes legal possession of goods produced by a variety of manufacturers and then resells them to other businesses [332]

merger The union of two corporations to form a new corporation [92]

merit salary system Individual incentive linking compensation to performance in nonsales jobs [236]

middle manager Manager responsible for implementing the strategies, policies, and decisions made by top managers [148]

mission statement Organization's statement of how it will achieve its purpose in the environment in which it conducts its business [138]

missionary selling Personal selling tasks in which salespeople promote their firms and products rather than try to close sales [345]

mixed market economy Economic system featuring characteristics of both planned and market economies [9]

monetary policies Policies by which the Federal Reserve manages interest rates and the size of the nation's money supply [433]

money Any object that is portable, divisible, durable, and stable and serves as a medium of exchange, a store of value, and a unit of account [408]

money market mutual fund Fund of short-term, low-risk financial securities purchased with the assets of investor-owners pooled by a nonbank institution [422]

monopolistic competition Market or industry characterized by numerous buyers and relatively numerous sellers trying to differentiate their products from those of competitors [17]

monopoly Market or industry in which there is only one producer, which can therefore set the prices of its products [18]

morale Overall attitude that employees have toward their workplace [260]

motivation The set of forces that cause people to behave in certain ways [262]

multimedia communication system Connected network of communication appliances (such as faxes or TVs) that may be linked to other forms of mass media (such as print publications or TV programming) [374]

multinational firm Firm that designs, produces, and markets products in many nations [118]

multinational or **transnational corporation** Form of corporation spanning national boundaries [90]

municipal bond Bond issued by a state or local government [460]

mutual fund Company that pools investments from individuals and organizations to purchase a portfolio of stocks, bonds, and other securities [462]

mutual savings bank Financial institution whose depositors are owners sharing in its profits [427]

Nasdaq Composite Index Value-weighted market index that includes all Nasdaq-listed companies, both domestic and foreign [468]

National Association of Securities Dealers Automated Quotation (Nasdaq) system Organization of securities dealers who own, buy, and sell their own securities over a network of electronic communications [458]

national brand Brand-name product produced by, widely distributed by, and carrying the name of a manufacturer [309]

national competitive advantage International competitive advantage stemming from a combination of factor conditions, demand conditions, related and supporting industries, and firm strategies, structures, and rivalries [110]

national debt Amount of money that a government owes its creditors [21]

natural monopoly Industry in which one company can most efficiently supply all needed goods or services [18]

negligence Conduct falling below legal standards for protecting others against unreasonable risk [500]

net income (or net profit or net earnings) Gross profit minus operating expenses and income taxes [398]

no-load fund Mutual fund in which investors pay no sales commissions when they buy in or sell out [462]

nominal GDP GDP measured in current dollars or with all components valued at current prices [19]

North American Free Trade Agreement (NAFTA) Agreement to gradually eliminate tariffs and other trade barriers among the United States, Canada and Mexico [103, 505]

obstructionist stance Approach to social responsibility that involves doing as little as possible and may involve attempts to deny or cover up violations [59]

Occupational Safety and Health Act of 1970 (OSHA) Federal law setting and enforcing guidelines for protecting workers from unsafe conditions and potential health hazards in the workplace [239]

odd lot Purchase or sale of stock in fractions of round lots [469]

odd-even pricing Psychological pricing tactic based on the premise that customers prefer prices not stated in even dollar amounts [329]

off-the-job training   Training conducted in a controlled environment away from the work site [234]

oligopoly   Market or industry characterized by a handful of (generally large) sellers with the power to influence the prices of their products [17]

on-the-job training   Training, sometimes informal, conducted while an employee is at work [232]

open-book credit   Form of trade credit in which sellers ship merchandise on faith that payment will be forthcoming [484]

open-market operations   The Federal Reserve's sales and purchases of securities in the open market [435]

operating expenses   Costs, other than the cost of goods sold, incurred in producing a good or service [397]

operating income   Gross profit minus operating expenses [398]

operational plan   Plan setting short-term targets for daily, weekly, or monthly performance [142]

operations control   Process of monitoring production performance by comparing results with plans [209]

operations (or production) management   Systematic direction and control of the processes that transform resources into finished products that create value and provide benefits to customers [197]

operations (or production) managers   Managers responsible for production, inventory, and quality control [197]

operations process   Set of methods used in the production of a good or service [197]

order fulfillment   All activities involved in completing a sales transaction, beginning with making the sale and ending with on-time delivery to the customer [339]

order processing   Personal selling task in which salespeople receive orders and see to their handling and delivery [345]

organization chart   Diagram depicting a company's structure and showing employees where they fit into its operations [167]

organizational analysis   Process of analyzing a firm's strengths and weaknesses [140]

organizational stakeholders   Those groups, individuals, and organizations that are directly affected by the practices of an organization and who therefore have a stake in its performance [45]

organizational structure   Specification of the jobs to be done within an organization and the ways in which they relate to one another [166]

organizing   Management process of determining how best to arrange an organization's resources and activities into a coherent structure [145]

output market   Market in which firms supply goods and services in response to demand on the part of households [9]

outsourcing   Strategy of paying suppliers and distributors to perform certain business processes or to provide needed materials or resources [216]

over-the-counter (OTC) market   Organization of securities dealers formed to trade stock outside the formal institutional setting of the organized stock exchanges [458]

owners' equity   Amount of money that owners would receive if they sold all of a firm's assets and paid all of its liabilities [393]

packaging   Physical container in which a product is sold, advertised, or protected [311]

paid-in capital   Additional money, above proceeds from stock sale, paid directly to a firm by its owners [396]

par value   Face value of a share of stock, set by the issuing company's board of directors [451]

participative management and empowerment   Method of increasing job satisfaction by giving employees a voice in the manage-

ment of their jobs and the company [271]

patent   Exclusive legal right to use and license a manufactured item or substance, manufacturing process, or object design [501]

pay for performance (or variable pay)   Individual incentive that rewards a manager for especially productive output [236]

pay-for-knowledge plan   Incentive plan to encourage employees to learn new skills or become proficient at different jobs [237]

penetration pricing   Setting an initially low price to establish a new product in the market [329]

pension fund   Nondeposit pool of funds managed to provide retirement income for its members [425]

perfect competition   Market or industry characterized by numerous small firms producing an identical product [16]

performance appraisal   Evaluation of an employee's job performance in order to determine the degree to which the employee is performing effectively [234]

performance quality   The performance features offered by a product [212]

personal selling   Promotional tool in which a salesperson communicates one-on-one with potential customers [344]

PERT chart   Production schedule specifying the sequence and critical path for performing the steps in a project [207]

physical distribution   Activities needed to move a product efficiently from manufacturer to consumer [339]

physical resources   Tangible things organizations use in the conduct of their business [7]

picketing   Labor action in which workers publicize their grievances at the entrance to an employer's facility [251]

planned economy   Economy that relies on a centralized government to control all or most factors of production and to make all or most production and allocation decisions [8]

planning Management process of determining what an organization needs to do and how best to get it done [144]

pledging accounts receivable Using accounts receivable as loan collateral [484]

point-of-purchase (POP) display Sales promotion technique in which product displays are located in certain areas to stimulate purchase [347]

point-of-sale (POS) terminal Electronic device that allows customers to pay for retail purchases with debit cards [437]

positioning Process of establishing an identifiable product image in the minds of consumers [341]

preferred provider organization (PPO) Arrangement whereby selected professional providers offer services at reduced rates and permit thorough review of their service recommendations [493]

preferred stock Stock that offers its holders fixed dividends and priority claims over assets but no corporate voting rights [90]

premium Fee paid by a policyholder for insurance coverage [491]

premium Sales promotion technique in which offers of free or reduced-price items are used to stimulate purchases [347]

prepaid expense Expense, such as prepaid rent, that is paid before the upcoming period in which it is due [395]

presentation graphics software Applications that enable users to create visual presentations that can include animation and sound [374]

price lining Setting a limited number of prices for certain categories of products [329]

price skimming Setting an initially high price to cover new product costs and generate a profit [327]

price-earnings ratio Current price of a stock divided by the firm's current annual earnings per share [465]

pricing Process of determining what a company will receive in exchange for its products [311]

pricing objectives Goals that producers hope to attain in pricing products for sale [325]

primary securities market Market in which new stocks and bonds are bought and sold [450]

prime rate Interest rate available to a bank's most creditworthy customers [426]

principal Individual or organization authorizing an agent to act on its behalf [502]

private accountant Salaried accountant hired by a business to carry out its day-to-day financial activities [388]

private brand (or private label) Brand-name product that a wholesaler or retailer has commissioned from a manufacturer [311]

private enterprise Economic system that allows individuals to pursue their own interests without undue governmental restriction [16]

private warehouse Warehouse owned by and providing storage for a single company [339]

privatization Process of converting government enterprises into privately owned companies [10]

proactive stance Approach to social responsibility by which a company actively seeks opportunities to contribute to the well-being of groups and individuals in its social environment [59]

process departmentalization Departmentalization according to production processes used to create a good or service [170]

process layout Spatial arrangement of production activities that groups equipment and people according to function [203]

product Good, service, or idea that is marketed to fill consumer needs and wants [294]

product departmentalization Departmentalization according to specific products being created [170]

product differentiation Creation of a product or product image that differs enough from existing products to attract consumers [294]

product layout Spatial arrangement of production activities designed to move resources through a smooth, fixed sequence of steps [204]

product liability tort Tort in which a company is responsible for injuries caused by its products [500]

product life cycle (PLC) Series of stages in a product's profit-producing life [308]

product line Group of similar products intended for a similar group of buyers who will use them in similar ways [306]

product mix Group of products that a firm makes available for sale [305]

productivity Measure of economic growth that compares how much a system produces with the resources needed to produce it [20]

professional corporation Form of ownership allowing professionals to take advantage of corporate benefits while granting them limited business liability and unlimited professional liability [89]

profit center Separate company unit responsible for its own costs and profits [169]

profitability ratio Financial ratio for measuring a firm's potential earnings [403]

profits The difference between a business's revenues and its expenses [4]

profit-sharing plan Incentive plan for distributing bonuses to employees when company profits rise above a certain level [237]

program trading Large purchase or sale of a group of stocks, often triggered by computerized trading programs that can be launched without human supervision or control [471]

promotion Aspect of the marketing mix concerned with the most effective techniques for selling a product [340]

promotional mix Combination of tools used to promote a product [342]

property Anything of value to which a person or business has sole right of ownership [500]

property insurance Insurance covering losses resulting from physical damage to or loss of the insured's real estate or personal property [492]

prospectus Registration statement filed with the SEC before the issuance of a new security [472]

protected class Set of individuals who by nature of one or more common characteristics are protected under the law from discrimination on the basis of that characteristic [238]

protectionism Practice of protecting domestic business against foreign competition [123]

psychographic variables Consumer characteristics, such as lifestyles, opinions, interests, and attitudes, that may be considered in developing a segmentation strategy [298]

psychological contract Set of expectations held by an employee concerning what he or she will contribute to an organization (referred to as contributions) and what the organization will in return provide the employee (referred to as inducements) [261]

psychological pricing Pricing tactic that takes advantage of the fact that consumers do not always respond rationally to stated prices [329]

public relations Company-influenced publicity directed at building goodwill with the public or dealing with unfavorable events [347]

public warehouse Independently owned and operated warehouse that stores goods for many firms [339]

publicity Promotional tool in which information about a company or product is transmitted by general mass media [347]

publicly held (or public) corporation Corporation whose stock is widely held and available for sale to the general public [89]

punitive damages Fines imposed over and above any actual losses suffered by a plaintiff [500]

purchasing Acquisition of the raw materials and services that a firm needs to produce its products [210]

pure risk Risk involving only the possibility of loss or no loss [489]

quality A product's fitness for use; its success in offering features that consumers want [211]

quality control Management of the production process designed to manufacture goods or supply services that meet specific quality standards [211]

quality/cost study Method of improving quality by identifying current costs and areas with the greatest cost-saving potential [214]

quality ownership Principle of total quality management that holds that quality belongs to each person who creates it while performing a job [212]

quality reliability Consistency of a product's quality from unit to unit [212]

quid pro quo harassment Form of sexual harassment in which sexual favors are requested in return for job-related benefits [240]

quota Restriction on the number of products of a certain type that can be imported into a country [122]

rational motives Reasons for purchasing a product that are based on a logical evaluation of product attributes [300]

real GDP GDP calculated to account for changes in currency values and price changes [19]

recession Period during which aggregate output, as measured by real GDP, declines [24]

recruiting Process of attracting qualified persons to apply for jobs an organization is seeking to fill [231]

registered bond Bond bearing the name of the holder and registered with the issuing company [461]

regulatory (or administrative) law Law made by the authority of administrative agencies [496]

reinforcement Theory that behavior can be encouraged or discouraged by means of rewards or punishments [268]

relationship marketing Marketing strategy that emphasizes lasting relationships with customers and suppliers [291]

replacement chart List of each management position, who occupies it, how long that person will likely stay in the job, and who is qualified as a replacement [229]

reseller market Organizational market consisting of intermediaries that buy and resell finished goods [302]

reserve requirement Percentage of its deposits that a bank must hold in cash or on deposit with the Federal Reserve [434]

responsibility Duty to perform an assigned task [173]

retailer Intermediary who sells products directly to consumers [330]

retained earnings Earnings retained by a firm for its use rather than paid as dividends [396, 486]

return on equity Profitability ratio measuring income earned for each dollar invested [405]

revenues Funds that flow into a business from the sale of goods or services [396]

revolving credit agreement Arrangement in which a lender agrees to make funds available on demand and on a continuing basis [484]

risk Uncertainty about future events [489]

risk avoidance Practice of avoiding risk by declining or ceasing to participate in an activity [490]

risk control Practice of minimizing the frequency or severity of losses from risky activities [490]

risk management Process of conserving the firm's earning power and assets by reducing the threat of losses due to uncontrollable events [489]

risk retention Practice of covering a firm's losses with its own funds [490]

risk transfer Practice of transferring a firm's risk to another firm [490]

risk-return relationship Principle that, whereas safer investments tend to offer lower returns, riskier investments tend to offer higher returns [487]

robotics Combination of computers and industrial robots for use in manufacturing operations [372]

round lot Purchase or sale of stock in units of 100 shares [469]

S corporation Hybrid of a closely held corporation and a partnership, organized and operated like a corporation but treated as a partnership for tax purposes [89]

salary Compensation in the form of money paid for discharging the responsibilities of a job [236]

sales agent/broker Independent intermediary who usually represents many manufacturers and sells to wholesalers or retailers [329]

sales promotion Short-term promotional activity designed to stimulate consumer buying or cooperation from distributors and sales agents [345]

savings and loan association (S&L) Financial institution accepting deposits and making loans primarily for home mortgages [427]

search engine Tool that searches Web pages containing the user's search terms and then displays pages that match [363]

secondary securities market Market in which stocks and bonds are traded [451]

secured bond Bond backed by pledges of assets to the bondholders [461]

secured loan Loan for which the borrower must provide collateral [484]

securities Stocks and bonds representing secured, or asset-based, claims by investors against issuers [450]

Securities and Exchange Commission (SEC) Federal agency that administers U.S. securities laws to protect the investing public and maintain smoothly functioning markets [450]

securities investment dealer (broker) Nondeposit institution that buys and sells stocks and bonds both for investors and for its own accounts [427]

selective credit controls Federal Reserve authority to set both margin requirements for consumer stock purchases and credit rules for other consumer purchases [435]

service operations Activities producing tangible and intangible products, such as entertainment, transportation, and education [194]

services Intangible products, such as time, expertise, or an activity that can be purchased [291]

sexual harassment Practice or instance of making unwelcome sexual advances in the workplace [240]

shopping agent (or e-agent) E-intermediary (middleman) in the Internet distribution channel that assists users in finding products and prices but that does not take possession of products [335]

shopping good/service Moderately expensive, infrequently purchased product [305]

short sale Stock sale in which an investor borrows securities from a broker to be sold and then replaced at a specified future date [471]

shortage Situation in which quantity demanded exceeds quantity supplied [15]

short-term goal Goal set for the very near future, typically less than one year [138]

slowdown Labor action in which workers perform jobs at a slower than normal pace [251]

small business Independently owned and managed business that does not dominate its market [70]

Small Business Administration (SBA) Federal agency charged with assisting small businesses [70]

Small Business Development Center (SBDC) SBA program designed to consolidate information from various disciplines and make it available to small businesses [78]

small-business investment company (SBIC) Government-regulated investment company that borrows money from the SBA to invest in or lend to a small business [77]

smart card Credit-card-size plastic card with an embedded computer chip that can be programmed with electronic money [437]

social audit Systematic analysis of a firm's success in using funds earmarked for meeting its social responsibility goals [61]

social responsibility The attempt of a bussiness to balance its commitments to groups and individuals in its environment, including customers, other businesses, employees, investors, and local communities. [45]

socialism Planned economic system in which the government owns and operates only selected major sources of production [11]

software Programs that instruct a computer in what to do [373]

sole proprietorship Business owned and usually operated by one person who is responsible for all of its debts [86]

solvency ratio Financial ratio, either short or long term, for estimating the risk in investing in a firm [399]

span of control Number of people supervised by one manager [175]

specialty good/service Expensive, rarely purchased product [305]

specialty store Small retail store carrying one product line or category of related products [336]

speculative risk Risk involving the possibility of gain or loss [489]

speed to market Strategy of introducing new products to respond quickly to customer or market changes [306]

spin-off Strategy of setting up one or more corporate units as new, independent corporations [92]

stability Condition in an economic system in which the amount of money available and the quantity of goods and services produced are growing at about the same rate [21]

stabilization policy Government policy, embracing both fiscal and monetary policies, whose goal is to smooth out fluctuations in output and unemployment and to stabilize prices [25]

staff authority Authority based on expertise that usually involves advising line managers [178]

staff members Advisers and counselors who aid line departments in making decisions but do not have the authority to make final decisions [178]

Standard & Poor's Composite Index Market index based on the performance of 400 industrial firms, 40 utilities, 40 financial institutions, and 20 transportation companies [468]

standard of living Total quantity and quality of goods and services that a country's citizens can purchase with the currency used in their economic system [19]

standardization Use of standard and uniform components in the production process [209]

statement of cash flows Financial statement describing a firm's yearly cash receipts and cash payments [398]

statistical process control (SPC) Methods for gathering data to analyze variations in production activities to see when adjustments are needed [213]

statutory law Law created by constitutions or by federal, state, or local legislative acts [495]

stock Share of ownership in a corporation [90]

stock exchange Organization of individuals formed to provide an institutional setting in which stock can be traded [454]

stockholder (or shareholder) Owner of shares of stock in a corporation [90]

stop order Order authorizing the sale of a stock if its price falls to or below a specified level [469]

strategic alliance (or joint venture) Arrangement in which a company finds a foreign partner to contribute approximately half of the resources needed to establish and operate a new business in the partner's country [119]

strategic alliance Strategy in which two or more organizations collaborate on a project for mutual gain [92]

strategic goal Long-term goal derived directly from a firm's mission statement [139]

strategic plan Plan reflecting decisions about resource allocations, company priorities, and steps needed to meet strategic goals [141]

strategy Broad set of organizational plans for implementing the decisions made for achieving organizational goals [136]

strategy formulation Creation of a broad program for defining and meeting an organization's goals [139]

strict product liability Principle that liability can result not from a producer's negligence but from a defect in the product itself [500]

strike Labor action in which employees temporarily walk off the job and refuse to work [249]

strikebreaker Worker hired as permanent or temporary replacement for a striking employee [251]

subsidy Government payment to help a domestic business compete with foreign firms [122]

substitute product Product that is dissimilar to those of competitors but that can fulfill the same need [292]

supermarket Large product line retailer offering a variety of food and food-related items in specialized departments [336]

supplier selection Process of finding and selecting suppliers from whom to buy [210]

supply The willingness and ability of producers to offer a good or service for sale [12]

supply chain Flow of information, materials, and services that starts with raw-materials suppliers and continues through other stages in the operations process until the product reaches the end customer [216]

supply chain management (SCM) Principle of looking at the supply chain as a whole in order to improve the overall flow through the system [216]

supply curve Graph showing how many units of a product will be supplied (offered for sale) at different prices [12]

surplus Situation in which quantity supplied exceeds quantity demanded [13]

SWOT analysis Identification and analysis of organizational strengths and weaknesses and environmental opportunities and threats as part of strategy formulation [139]

sympathy strike (or secondary strike) Strike in which one union strikes to support action initiated by another [250]

syndicated selling E-commerce practice whereby a Web site offers other Web sites commissions for referring customers [335]

synthetic process Production process in which resources are combined to create finished products [198]

system operations personnel Information-systems employees who run a company's computer equipment [368]

system program Software that tells the computer what resources to use and how to use them [373]

tactical plan Generally short-range plan concerned with implementing specific aspects of a company's strategic plans [142]

tall organizational structure Characteristic of centralized companies with multiple layers of management and relatively narrow spans of control [175]

tangible personal property Any movable item that can be owned, bought, sold, or leased [501]

tangible real property Land and anything attached to it [500]

target market Group of people that has similar wants and needs and that can be expected to show interest in the same products [295]

tariff Tax levied on imported products [122]

technical skills Skills needed to perform specialized tasks [150]

telecommuting Form of flextime that allows people to perform some or all of a job away from standard office settings [274]

telemarketing Nonstore retailing in which the telephone is used to sell directly to consumers [337]

tender offer Offer to buy shares made by a prospective buyer directly to a target corporation's shareholders, who then make individual decisions about whether to sell [89]

Theory X Theory of motivation holding that people are naturally irresponsible and uncooperative [265]

Theory Y Theory of motivation holding that people are naturally responsible, growth oriented, self-motivated, and interested in being productive [265]

time deposit Bank funds that cannot be withdrawn without notice or transferred by check [422]

time management skills Skills associated with the productive use of time [152]

top manager Manager responsible to the board of directors and stockholders for a firm's overall performance and effectiveness [147]

tort Civil injury to people, property, or reputation for which compensation must be paid [499]

total quality management (TQM) (or quality assurance) The sum of all activities involved in getting high-quality products into the marketplace [212]

trade credit Granting of credit by one firm to another [484]

trade deficit Situation in which a country's imports exceed its exports, creating a negative balance of trade [111]

trade show Sales promotion technique in which various members of an industry gather to display, demonstrate, and sell products [347]

trade surplus Situation in which a country's exports exceed its imports, creating a positive balance of trade [111]

trademark Exclusive legal right to use a brand name or symbol [501]

trial court General court that hears cases not specifically assigned to another court [497]

trust services Bank management of an individual's investments, payments, or estate [428]

turnover Annual percentage of an organization's workforce that leaves and must be replaced [261]

two-factor theory Theory of motivation holding that job satisfaction depends on two types of factors, hygiene and motivation [265]

unemployment Level of joblessness among people actively seeking work in an economic system [23]

unethical behavior Behavior that does not conform to generally accepted social norms concerning beneficial and harmful actions [37]

Uniform Commercial Code (UCC) Body of standardized laws governing the rights of buyers and sellers in transactions [503]

unlimited liability Legal principle holding owners responsible for paying off all debts of a business [86]

unsecured loan Loan for which collateral is not required [484]

utility Ability of a product to satisfy a human want or need [196, 291]

validation Process of determining the predictive value of a selection technique [232]

value Relative comparison of a product's benefits with its costs [290]

value package Product marketed as a bundle of value-adding attributes, including reasonable cost [304]

variable cost Cost that changes with the quantity of a product produced or sold [327]

venture capital Outside equity financing provided in return for part ownership of the borrowing firm [488]

venture capital company Group of small investors who invest money in companies with rapid growth potential [77]

vestibule training Off-the-job training conducted in a simulated environment [234]

video marketing Nonstore retailing to consumers via standard and cable television [338]

voluntary arbitration Method of resolving a labor dispute in which both parties agree to submit to the judgment of a neutral party [251]

voluntary bankruptcy Bankruptcy proceedings initiated by an indebted individual or organization [504]

wage reopener clause Clause allowing wage rates to be renegotiated during the life of a labor contract [249]

wages Compensation in the form of money paid for time worked [237]

warehouse club (or wholesale club) Bargain retailer offering large discounts on brand-name merchandise to customers who have paid annual membership fees [337]

warehousing Physical distribution operation concerned with the storage of goods [339]

warranty Seller's promise to stand by its products or services if a problem occurs after the sale [503]

Web server Dedicated workstation customized for managing, maintaining, and supporting Web sites [362]

whistle-blower Employee who detects and tries to put an end to a company's unethical, illegal, or socially irresponsible actions by publicizing them [56]

wholesaler Intermediary who sells products to other businesses for resale to final consumers [330]

wide area network (WAN) Network of computers and workstations located far from one another and linked by telephone wires or by satellite [375]

wildcat strike Strike that is unauthorized by the strikers' union [251]

word-processing program Applications program that allows computers to store, edit, and print letters and numbers for documents created by users [373]

work sharing (or job sharing) Method of increasing job satisfaction by allowing two or more people to share a single full-time job [273]

workers' compensation coverage Coverage provided by a firm to employees for medical expenses, loss of wages, and rehabilitation costs resulting from job-related injuries or disease [492]

workers' compensation insurance Legally required insurance for compensating workers injured on the job [237]

workforce diversity Range of workers' attitudes, values, and behaviors that differ by gender, race, and ethnicity [241]

working capital Difference between a firm's current assets and current liabilities [404]

working capital Liquid current assets out of which a firm can pay current debts [483]

World Bank United Nations agency that provides a limited scope of financial services, such as funding national improvements in undeveloped countries [440]

World Trade Organization (WTO) Organization through which member nations negotiate trading agreements and resolve disputes about trade policies and practices [105, 505]

World Wide Web Subsystem of computers providing access to the Internet and offering multimedia and linking capabilities [361]

INDEX

■ SUBJECT INDEX